Complete
BRITISH
RAILWAYS
MAPS
and
GAZETTEER

From 1830~1981

by

C. J. Wignall

Oxford Publishing Co. Oxford

To three ladies in my life
Joyce, my wife, Julie and Karen, my daughters,
who never failed to sustain me in my quest
to turn a dream into a reality
"a fully comprehensive Rail Atlas and Gazetteer."
As for accomplishment — only history can record.

Publishers Note:
As this is the first edition of a very important reference
work, we have endeavoured to achieve complete accuracy.
However, if there are any omissions or errors, please
inform us so that we may incorporate them in further
editions.

Maps drawn from author's originals by
Derek West

Printed by
Eastbourne Printers Ltd., Eastbourne, Sussex.

Published by
Oxford Railway Publishing Co. Ltd.
Link House,
West Street,
Poole, Dorset.

CONTENTS

INTRODUCTION

The ignition switch for the beginnings of this atlas was fired several years ago. At Christmas, an aunt knowing I was a railway enthusiast presented me with a book token. I tried to no avail to purchase a comprehensive map of the railway system. On checking with my local library, I found that the main source of information was contained in the very fine *British Railways Pre-Grouping Atlas*, by W. Philip Conolly.

After studying the publication it crossed my mind that it might be a good idea to take the concept a stage further and compile an atlas to locate all stations and rails built since the beginnings of Stockton and Darlington in 1825, as well as including information from 1923 to the present day. My feelings are that very few new lines and stations will be built in the future unless the government of the day determines a different transport policy to the one in use at present; therefore this atlas may not require much updating in the foreseeable future.

Whilst working on this project, another atlas was published in 1977, compiled by Stuart K. Baker, and this has also proved valuable in double checking current rails and stations. For the younger generation of enthusiast, emphasis has been placed on the use of three main colours. *Red* for current lines and stations, *green* for lines and stations closed in or after the Beeching Era (1-1-63), and *black* for closures prior to the Beeching Era. Older and more knowledgeable railmen will probably mourn the fact that the pre-grouping names of companies are omitted from the maps. However, this information, along with other facts, may be found by checking the station index. In addition to passenger stations, many goods stations have been included and for much of this information a vote of thanks must be recorded to C.R. Clinker for his excellent books on the matter.

Finally, may I thank the staff of Burnley Public Library, my colleagues from North West Gas (East Lancashire Branch), my wife Joyce for her patience in attempting to keep tidy the living room (which at times a visitor might mistake for British Rail Archives) and to my children Julie and Karen who coined the phrase at weekends, "Are we going out today or are you drawing your maps, Dad?"

In conclusion, I should like to thank the staff of the National Railway Museum, York, for supplying many of the more difficult station locations.

Clifford J. Wignall

Burnley, Lancashire
June 1982

KEY TO ATLAS

Lines still open to passengers

Lines closed in or after the Beeching Era, (1-1-63)

Lines closed prior to the Beeching Era

Preserved lines

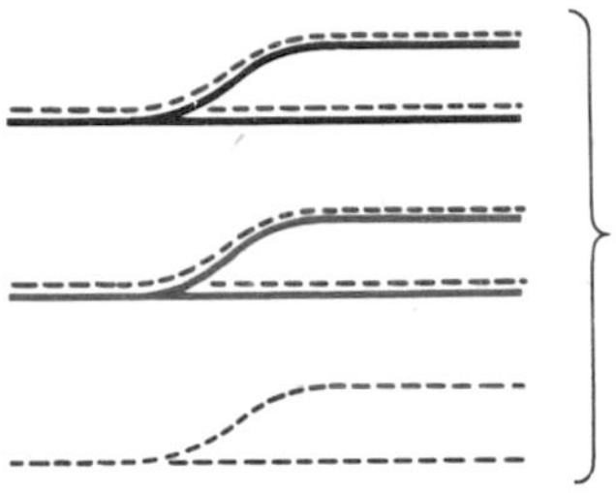

Freight lines only and still in use

Station Name

Burnley ———————— Station still open to passengers

Station Name

Burnley ———————— Station closed in or since the Beeching Era (1-1-63)

Station Name

Burnley ———————— Station closed prior to the Beeching Era

Station Name

Burnley*
or Burnley* } ———————— Station still used for unadvertised or excursion trains

⟶ U   Rails run underground at this point

(Gds) or (Goods)   Station has only ever been used for goods

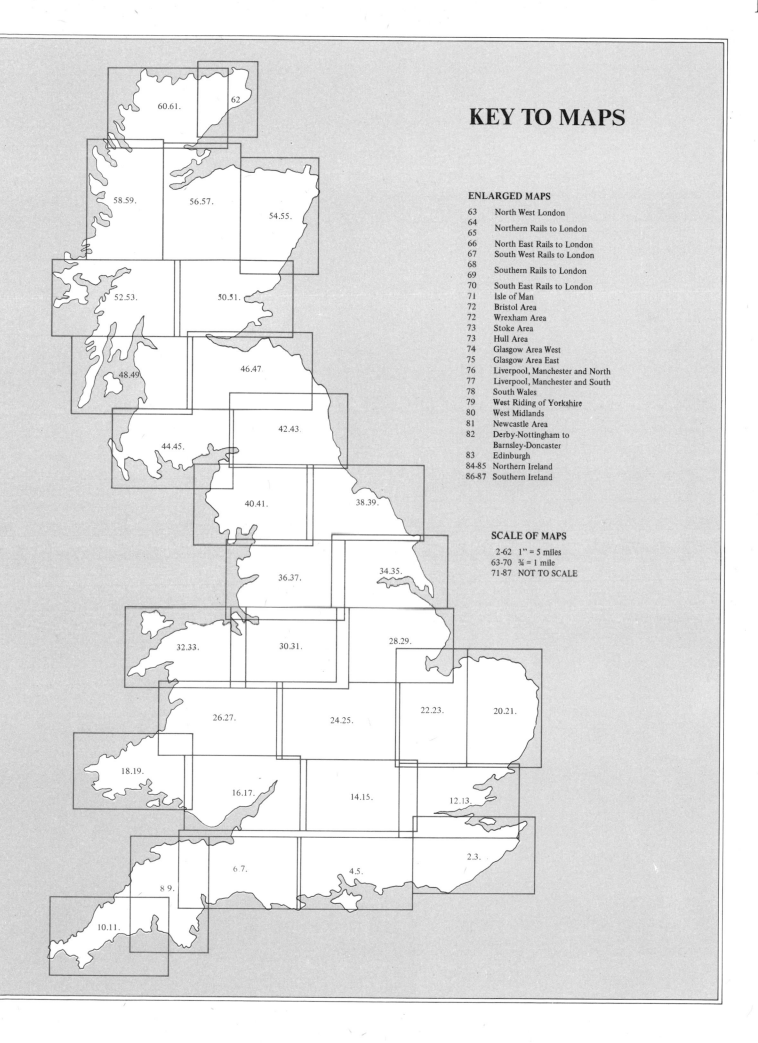

KEY TO MAPS

ENLARGED MAPS

63	North West London
64	Northern Rails to London
65	
66	North East Rails to London
67	South West Rails to London
68	Southern Rails to London
69	
70	South East Rails to London
71	Isle of Man
72	Bristol Area
72	Wrexham Area
73	Stoke Area
73	Hull Area
74	Glasgow Area West
75	Glasgow Area East
76	Liverpool, Manchester and North
77	Liverpool, Manchester and South
78	South Wales
79	West Riding of Yorkshire
80	West Midlands
81	Newcastle Area
82	Derby-Nottingham to Barnsley-Doncaster
83	Edinburgh
84-85	Northern Ireland
86-87	Southern Ireland

SCALE OF MAPS

2-62	1" = 5 miles
63-70	¾ = 1 mile
71-87	NOT TO SCALE

2

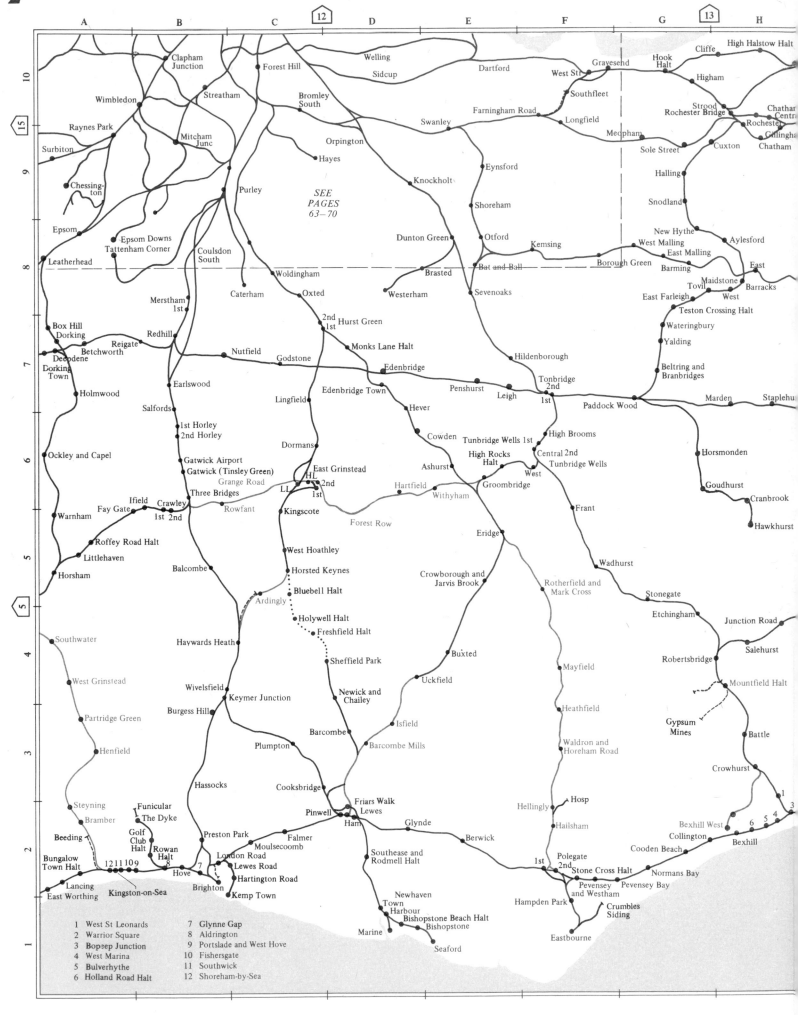

SEE PAGES 63–70

1 West St Leonards
2 Warrior Square
3 Bopeep Junction
4 West Marina
5 Bulverhythe
6 Holland Road Halt
7 Glynne Gap
8 Aldrington
9 Portslade and West Hove
10 Fishersgate
11 Southwick
12 Shoreham-by-Sea

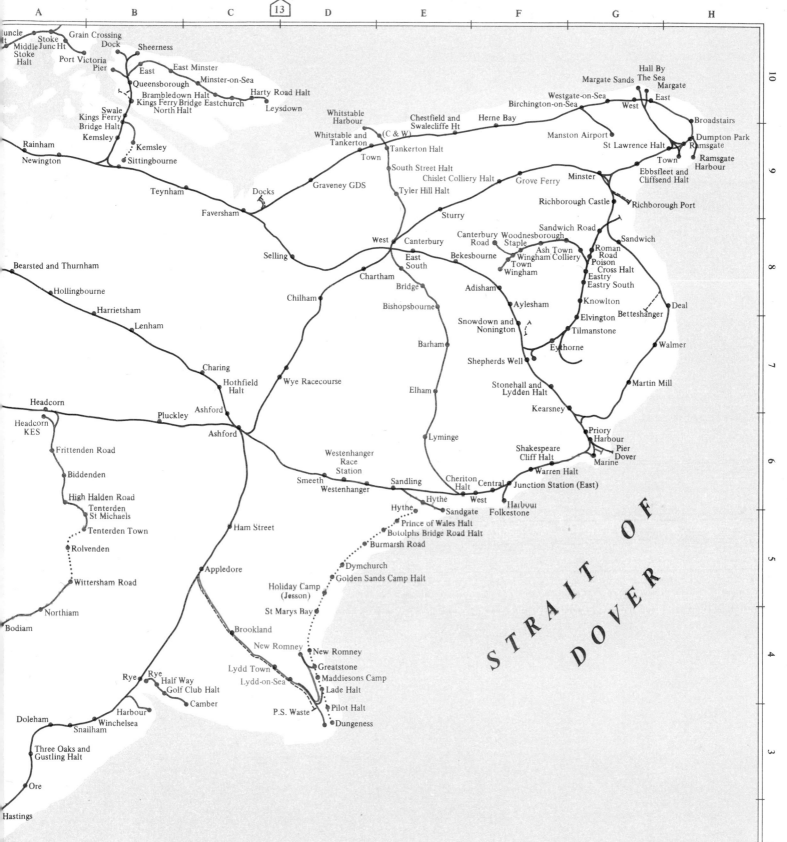

A B C 13 D E F G H

10

Uncle
Middle Stoke Junc Ht
Stoke Halt
Grain Crossing Dock
Sheerness
Port Victoria Pier
East Minster
East Queensborough
Minster-on-Sea
Brambledown Halt
Harty Road Halt
Kings Ferry Bridge North Halt
Eastchurch
Leysdown
Swale
Kings Ferry Bridge Halt
Kemsley North Halt
Rainham
Kemsley
Sittingbourne
Newington
Teynham
Faversham
Docks

Whitstable Harbour
Chestfield and Swalecliffe Ht
Herne Bay
Whitstable and Tankerton (C & W)
Tankerton Halt
Town
South Street Halt
Graveney GDS
Chislet Colliery Halt
Grove Ferry
Tyler Hill Halt
Sturry
Minster

Margate Sands
Hall By The Sea
Margate
Westgate-on-Sea
Birchington-on-Sea
West
East
Broadstairs
Manston Airport
Dumpton Park
St Lawrence Halt
Ramsgate
Town
Ramsgate Harbour
Ebbsfleet and Cliffsend Halt

9

Selling
West Canterbury
East South
Chartham
Bridge
Chilham
Bishopsbourne
Bekesbourne
Canterbury Road
Woodnesborough
Staple
Sandwich Road
Richborough Castle
Richborough Port
Ash Town
Wingham Colliery
Town
Wingham
Roman Road
Poison Cross Halt
Eastry
Eastry South
Sandwich

8

Bearsted and Thurnham
Hollingbourne
Harrietsham
Lenham
Barham
Adisham
Aylesham
Snowdown and Nonington
Knowlton
Elvington
Tilmanstone
Betteshanger
Deal
Eythorne

7

Charing
Hothfield Halt
Wye Racecourse
Elham
Shepherds Well
Walmer
Martin Mill
Ashford
Pluckley
Headcorn
Stonehall and Lydden Halt
Kearsney

6

Headcorn KES
Ashford
Lyminge
Priory
Harbour
Pier
Dover
Marine
Frittenden Road
Westenhanger Race Station
Shakespeare Cliff Halt
Biddenden
Smeeth
Sandling
Cheriton Halt
Central
Warren Halt
Junction Station (East)
Westenhanger
High Halden Road
Tenterden St Michaels
Ham Street
Hythe
West
Hythe
Sandgate
Harbour
Folkestone
Tenterden Town
Prince of Wales Halt
Rolvenden
Botolphs Bridge Road Halt
Burmarsh Road
Wittersham Road
Appledore
Dymchurch
Golden Sands Camp Halt
Northiam
Holiday Camp (Jesson)
Bodiam
St Marys Bay

5

Brookland
New Romney
New Romney
Greatstone
Rye
Rye Half Way
Golf Club Halt
Lydd Town
Maddiesons Camp
Lydd-on-Sea
Lade Halt
Camber
Doleham
Harbour
P.S. Waste
Pilot Halt
Winchelsea
Snailham
Dungeness
Three Oaks and Gustling Halt
Ore
Hastings

4

3

STRAIT OF DOVER

2

ENGLISH CHANNEL

1

4

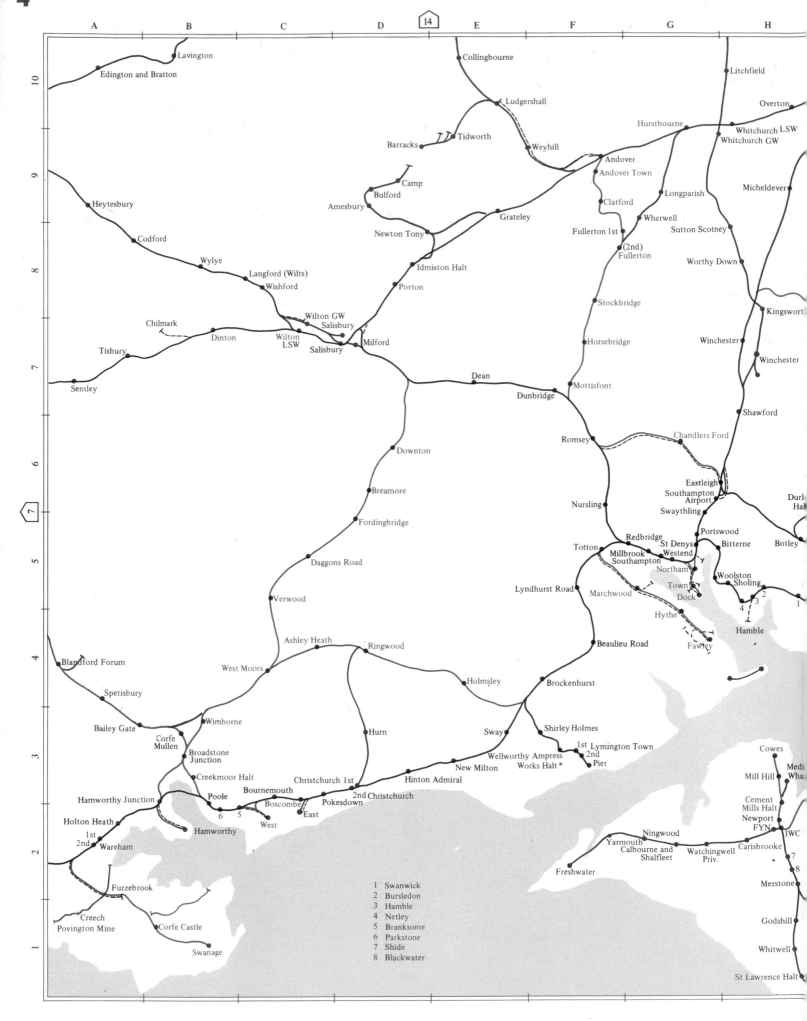

14

7

A	B	C	D	E	F	G	H

Lavington

Edington and Bratton

Collingbourne

Litchfield

Ludgershall

Overton

Tidworth

Hurstbourne

Whitchurch LSW
Whitchurch GW

Barracks

Weyhill

Heytesbury

Camp

Andover

Andover Town

Micheldever

Bulford

Amesbury

Grateley

Clatford

Longparish

Codford

Newton Tony

Wherwell

Sutton Scotney

Wylye

Fullerton 1st

Langford (Wilts)

Idmiston Halt

(2nd)
Fullerton

Worthy Down

Wishford

Porton

Chilmark

Wilton GW
Salisbury

Stockbridge

Kingswort

Dinton

Wilton
LSW

Milford

Horsebridge

Winchester

Tisbury

Salisbury

Winchester

Semley

Dean

Mottisfont

Shawford

Dunbridge

Downton

Romsey

Chandlers Ford

Breamore

Eastleigh
Southampton
Airport

Durl
Hal

Fordingbridge

Nursling

Swaythling

Daggons Road

Redbridge

Portswood

Westend

Bitterne

Botley

Verwood

Totton

Millbrook

St Denys

Woolston
Sholing

Southampton

Northam

Lyndhurst Road

Town

2
3

1

Ashley Heath

Ringwood

Marchwood

Dock

4

Blandford Forum

West Moors

Hythe

Hamble

Beaulieu Road

Fawley

Spetisbury

Holmsley

Brockenhurst

Cowes

Bailey Gate

Wimborne

Hurn

Sway

Shirley Holmes

Mill Hill

Medi
Wha

Corfe
Mullen

Broadstone
Junction

1st Lymington Town
2nd
Pier

Creekmoor Halt

Wellworthy Ampress
Works Halt *

Cement
Mills Halt

Christchurch 1st

New Milton

Newport

Hinton Admiral

FYN

Hamworthy Junction

Poole

Bournemouth

Pokesdown

2nd Christchurch

Ningwood

IWC

Holton Heath

Boscombe

East

Yarmouth

Calbourne and
Shalfleet

Watchingwell
Priv.

Carisbrooke

1st
2nd
Wareham

6
5
West

Merstone

Hamworthy

Freshwater

8

Furzebrook

Godshill

Creech
Povington Mine

Corfe Castle

Whitwell

Swanage

1 Swanick
2 Bursledon
3 Hamble
4 Netley
5 Branksome
6 Parkstone
7 Shide
8 Blackwater

St Lawrence Halt

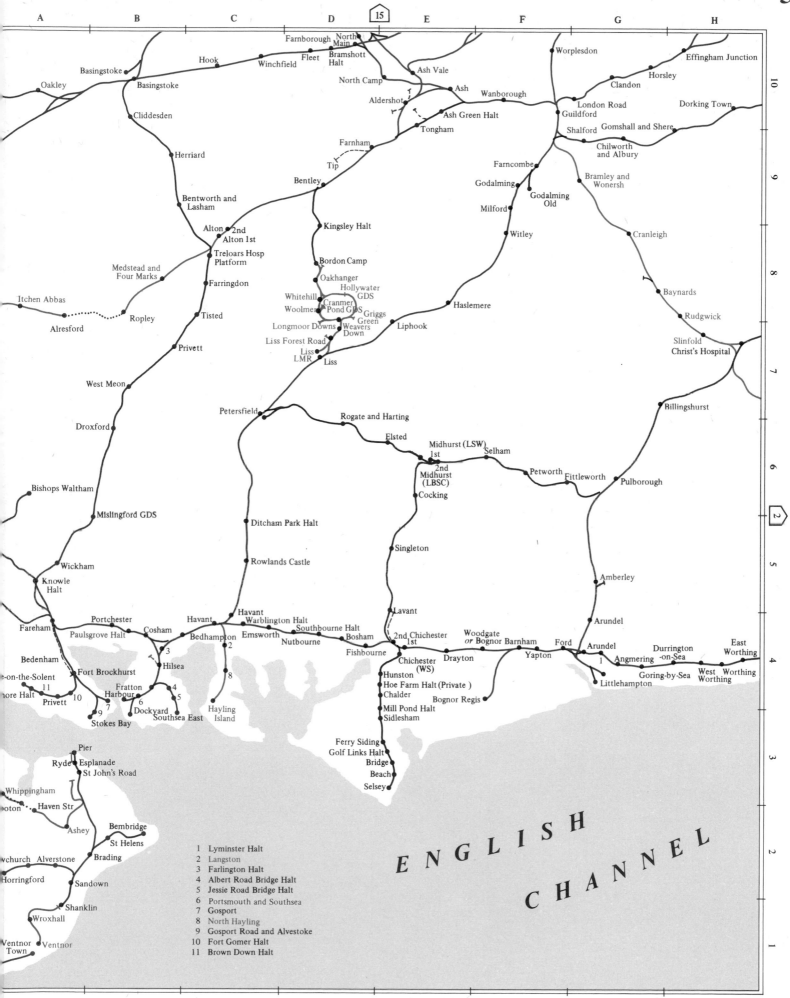

A B C D 15 E F G H

10
9
8
7
2
6
5
4
3
2
1

Oakley
Basingstoke
Basingstoke
Hook
Winchfield
Fleet
Farnborough North Main
Bramshott Halt
North Camp
Ash Vale
Ash
Wanborough
Worplesdon
Clandon
Horsley
Effingham Junction
Cliddesden
Aldershot
Ash Green Halt
Tongham
London Road
Guildford
Shalford
Dorking Town
Herriard
Farnham
Tip
Bentley
Godalming
Farncombe
Godalming Old
Gomshall and Shere
Chilworth and Albury
Bramley and Wonersh
Bentworth and Lasham
Alton 2nd
Alton 1st
Treloars Hosp Platform
Kingsley Halt
Milford
Witley
Cranleigh
Medstead and Four Marks
Farringdon
Bordon Camp
Oakhanger
Hollywater GDS
Baynards
Itchen Abbas
Tisted
Whitehill
Woolmer
Cranmer Pond GDS
Griggs Green
Haslemere
Rudgwick
Alresford
Ropley
Longmoor Downs
Weavers Down
Liss Forest Road
Liss LMR
Liss
Liphook
Slinfold
Christ's Hospital
Privett
West Meon
Petersfield
Rogate and Harting
Elsted
Midhurst (LSW) 1st
Selham
Billingshurst
Droxford
Midhurst (LBSC) 2nd
Petworth
Fittleworth
Pulborough
Bishops Waltham
Cocking
Mislingford GDS
Ditcham Park Halt
Singleton
Amberley
Wickham
Rowlands Castle
Lavant
Arundel
Knowle Halt
Portchester
Havant
Warblington Halt
Southbourne Halt
2nd Chichester 1st
Woodgate or Bognor
Barnham
Ford
Arundel
Durrington-on-Sea
East Worthing
Fareham
Paulsgrove Halt
Cosham
Bedhampton
Emsworth
Nutbourne
Bosham
Fishbourne
Chichester (WS)
Drayton
Yapton
1
Angmering
West Worthing
Worthing
Bedenham
3
Hilsea
2
Hunston
Hoe Farm Halt (Private)
Bognor Regis
Littlehampton
Goring-by-Sea
on-the-Solent
Fort Brockhurst
Fratton
Harbour
6
4
Dockyard
5
Southsea East
8
Hayling Island
Chalder
Mill Pond Halt
Sidlesham
ore Halt
Privett
11
10
7
9
Stokes Bay
Ferry Siding
Golf Links Halt
Bridge
Beach
Selsey

Pier
Ryde Esplanade
St John's Road
Whippingham
ooton
Haven Str
Ashey
Bembridge
St Helens
Brading
wchurch Alverstone
Horringford
Sandown
Shanklin
Wroxhall
Ventnor Town
Ventnor

1 Lyminster Halt
2 Langston
3 Farlington Halt
4 Albert Road Bridge Halt
5 Jessie Road Bridge Halt
6 Portsmouth and Southsea
7 Gosport
8 North Hayling
9 Gosport Road and Alverstoke
10 Fort Gomer Halt
11 Brown Down Halt

E N G L I S H
C H A N N E L

6

Brean Road Halt

Brent Knoll

Burnham-on-Sea

S

Highbridge

Dunball

S & D Bridgwater   GW

Durston

Ly

Creech St Michael

Thornfalcon

Hatch

Minehead

Dunster

Blue Anchor   Watchet

Washford   Washford   Williton

Roadwater

Stogumber

Gupworthy Mine   Combe Row

Crowcombe

South Radworthy

South Molton

Bishops Nympton and Molland

East Anstey

Yeo Mill Halt

Dulverton

Morebath Junction Halt

Morebath

Venn Cross

Bishops Lydeard

Wiveliscombe

Milverton

Taunton

Norton Fitzwarren

Bampton

Cove Halt

Bolham Halt

1st

Tiverton 2nd

Halberton

Tiverton Junction

West Exe Halt

Cadeleigh

Burn Halt

Up Exe

Thorverton

Bramford Speke

Wellington

Beam Bridge

Burlescombe

Sampford Peverell

Whitehall Halt

Uffculme

Culmstock

Hemyock

Coldharbour Halt

Cullompton

Hele and Bradninch

Silverton

Lapford

Morchard Road

Copplestone

Bow

Yeoford

Crediton

Newton St Cyres

1st
2nd   Stoke Canon

Honiton

Feniton

Whimple

Broad Clyst

Pinhoe

1   2

Ottery St Mary

Axmins

Seaton

Colyton

Colyford

Combpyne

Axmouth
Seaton

Exeter St Davids

St James Park

Central
City Basin

St Thomas

Longdown   Ide

Alphinton Halt

Dunsford Halt

Christow

Ashton

Trusham

Moreton Hamstead

Lustleigh

Hawkmoor Halt

Pullabrook

Bovey

Chudleigh

Exminster

Starcross

Dawlish Warren   2nd
1st

Dawlish

Polsloe Bridge

Clyst St Mary

Topsham

Exton

Lympstone Commando

Lympstone

Littleham

Exmouth

Newton Poppleford

East Budleigh

Budleigh Salterton

Tipton St Johns

Sidmouth

1 Mount Pleasant Road Halt
2 Whipton Bridge Halt

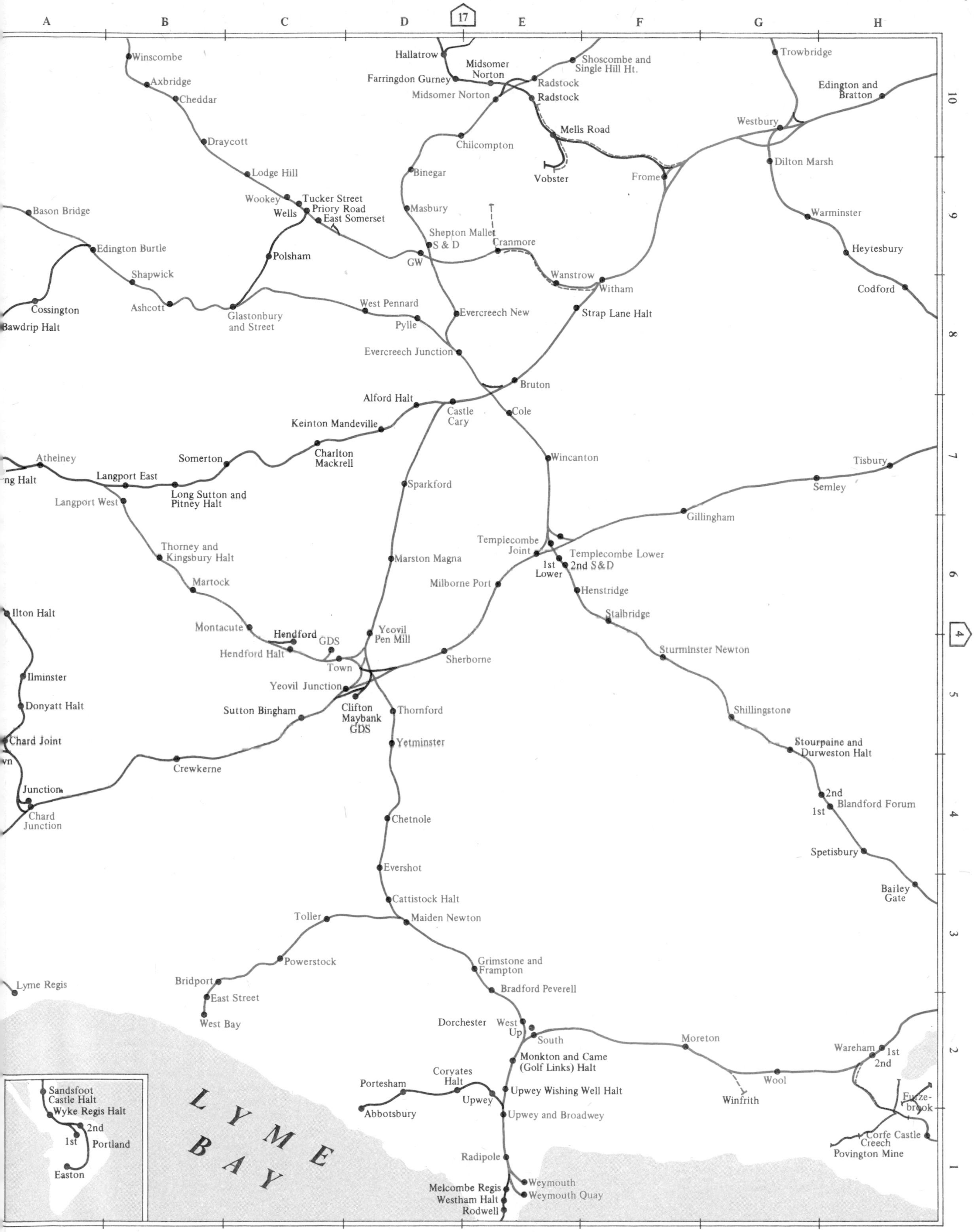

A B C D 17 E F G H

Winscombe
Axbridge
Cheddar
Draycott
Lodge Hill
Bason Bridge
Wookey
Tucker Street
Priory Road
Wells
East Somerset
Edington Burtle
Shapwick
Polsham
Ashcott
Cossington
Bawdrip Halt
Glastonbury and Street

Hallatrow
Farringdon Gurney
Midsomer Norton
Midsomer Norton
Shoscombe and Single Hill Ht.
Radstock
Radstock
Mells Road
Chilcompton
Vobster
Frome
Binegar
Masbury
Shepton Mallet S & D
Cranmore
GW
Wanstrow
Witham
West Pennard
Evercreech New
Strap Lane Halt
Pylle
Evercreech Junction
Bruton
Alford Halt
Castle Cary
Cole
Keinton Mandeville
Charlton Mackrell
Wincanton
Somerton
Sparkford
Langport East
Athelney
ng Halt
Long Sutton and Pitney Halt
Langport West
Thorney and Kingsbury Halt
Martock
Montacute
Hendford
GDS
Yeovil Pen Mill
Hendford Halt
Town
Sherborne
Yeovil Junction
Sutton Bingham
Clifton Maybank GDS
Thornford
Ilton Halt
Ilminster
Donyatt Halt
Chard Joint
Yetminster
wn
Junction
Crewkerne
Chard Junction
Chetnole
Evershot
Cattistock Halt
Toller
Maiden Newton
Powerstock
Bridport
East Street
West Bay
Grimstone and Frampton
Bradford Peverell
Lyme Regis
Dorchester
West Up
South
Moreton
Wareham
1st
2nd
Monkton and Came (Golf Links) Halt
Corvates Halt
Wool
Winfrith
Furze-brook
Portesham
Upwey Wishing Well Halt
Upwey
Abbotsbury
Upwey and Broadway
Corfe Castle
Creech
Povington Mine
Radipole
Melcombe Regis
Weymouth
Westham Halt
Weymouth Quay
Rodwell

Sandsfoot Castle Halt
Wyke Regis Halt
2nd
1st
Portland
Easton

Trowbridge
Edington and Bratton
Westbury
Dilton Marsh
Warminster
Heytesbury
Codford
Tisbury
Semley
Gillingham
Templecombe Joint
Templecombe Lower
1st Lower
2nd S & D
Milborne Port
Henstridge
Stalbridge
Sturminster Newton
Shillingstone
Stourpaine and Durweston Halt
2nd
1st
Blandford Forum
Spetisbury
Bailey Gate

L Y M E   B A Y

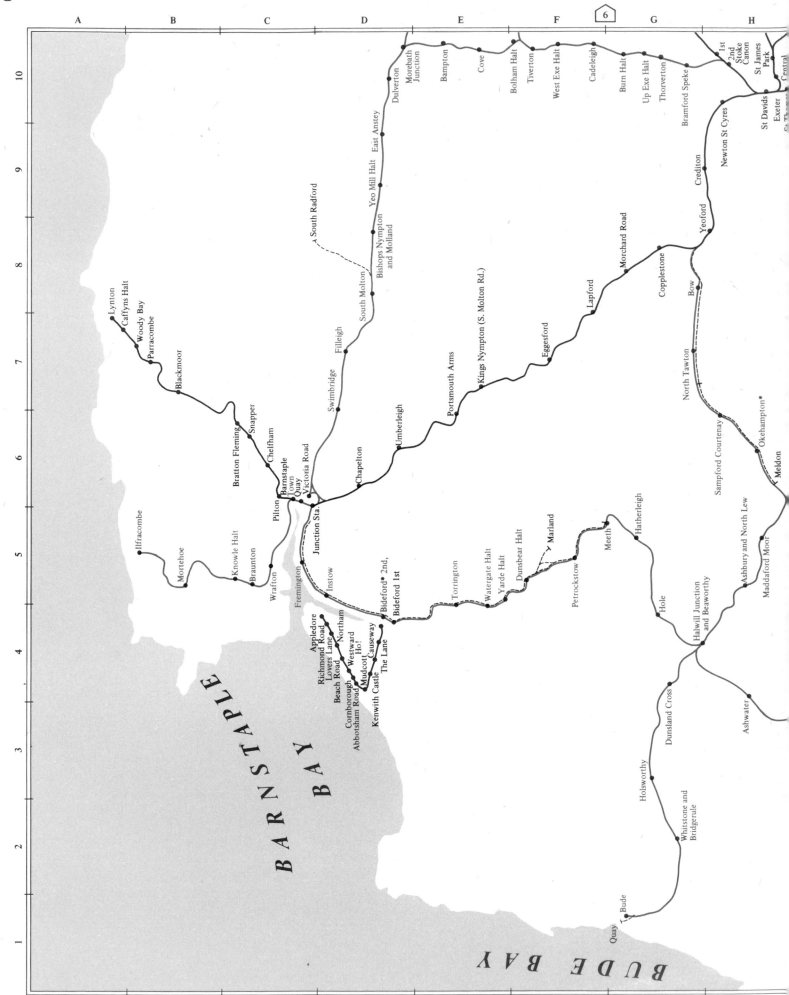

BARNSTAPLE BAY

BUDE BAY

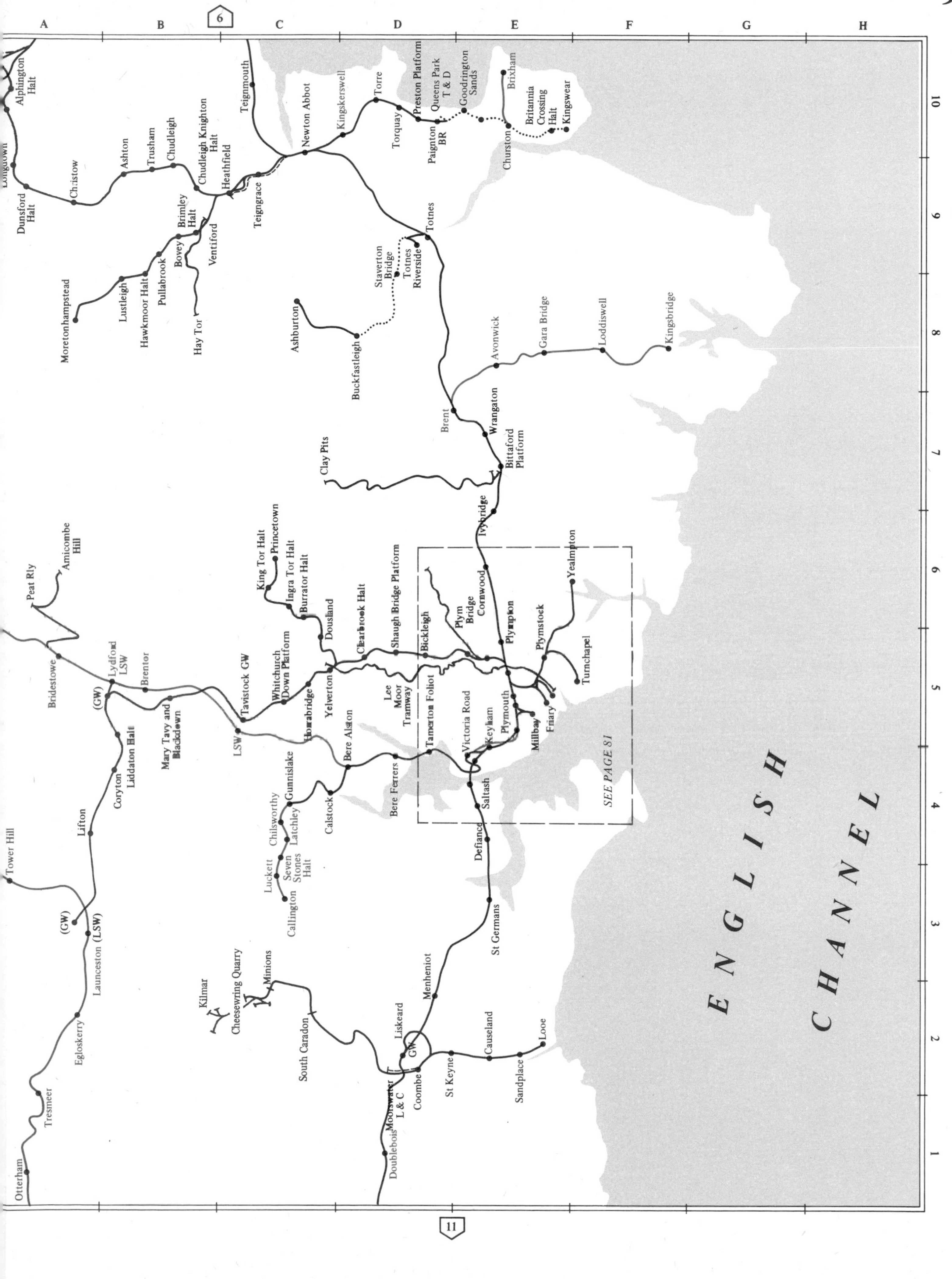

A B 6 C D E F G H

10 9 8 7 6 5 4 3 2 1

ENGLISH CHANNEL

Longdown
Alphington Halt
Dunsford Halt
Christow
Ashton
Trusham
Chudleigh
Chudleigh Knighton Halt
Heathfield
Teigngrace
Teignmouth
Newton Abbot
Kingskerswell
Torre
Torquay
Preston Platform
Queens Park T & D
Paignton BR
Goodrington Sands
Churston
Brixham
Britannia Crossing Halt
Kingswear

Moretonhampstead
Lustleigh
Hawkmoor Halt
Pullabrook
Bovey
Brimley Halt
Hay Tor
Ventiford

Staverton Bridge
Totnes Riverside
Totnes

Ashburton
Buckfastleigh
Brent
Wrangaton
Avonwick
Gara Bridge
Loddiswell
Kingsbridge

Bittaford Platform
Ivybridge
Clay Pits

Peat Rly
Amicombe Hill
Tower Hill
Tresmeer
Otterham

King Tor Halt
Princetown
Ingra Tor Halt
Burrator Halt
Dousland
Clearbrook Halt
Shaugh Bridge Platform
Bickleigh
Plym Bridge
Cornwood
Plympton
Plymstock
Yealmpton
Turnchapel

Lydford LSW
Brentor
(GW)
Bridestowe
Mary Tavy and Blackdown
Liddaton Halt
Coryton
Lifton
Launceston (LSW)
(GW)
Egloskerry

Tavistock GW
Whitchurch Down Platform
Horrabridge
Yelverton
Lee Moor Tramway
Tamerton Foliot
Victoria Road
Keyham
Plymouth
Millbay
Friary
LSW

Bere Alston
Calstock
Bere Ferrers
Saltash
Defiance

Chilsworthy
Gunnislake
Latchley
Luckett
Seven Stones Halt
Callington

Kilmar
Cheesewring Quarry
Minions
South Caradon
Liskeard
Menheniot
St Germans
Doublebois
Moorswater
L & C
Coombe
GW
St Keyne
Causeland
Sandplace
Looe

SEE PAGE 81

11

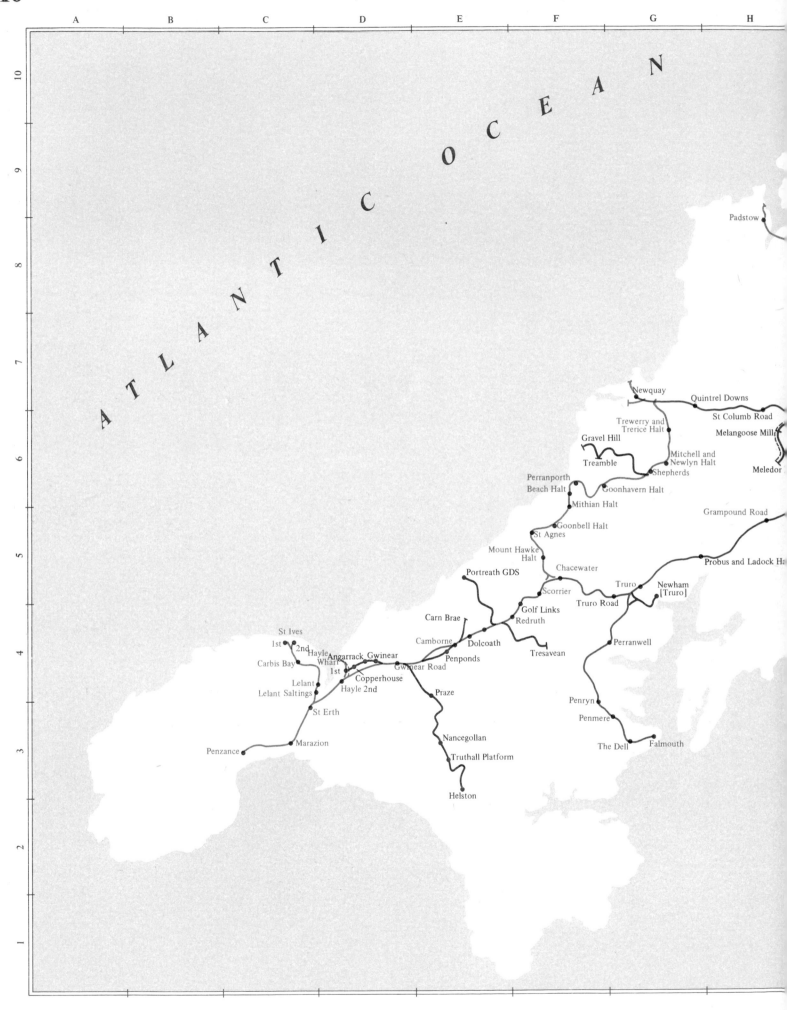

ATLANTIC OCEAN

Padstow

Newquay
Quintrel Downs
St Columb Road
Trewerry and
Trerice Halt
Melangoose Mill
Gravel Hill
Mitchell and
Newlyn Halt
Treamble
Meledor
Shepherds
Perranporth
Beach Halt
Goonhavern Halt
Mithian Halt
Grampound Road
Goonbell Halt
St Agnes
Mount Hawke
Halt
Probus and Ladock Halt
Portreath GDS
Chacewater
Truro
Scorrier
Newham
[Truro]
Truro Road
Golf Links
Carn Brae
Redruth
Camborne
Dolcoath
St Ives
Penponds
Tresavean
Perranwell
1st 2nd
Hayle
Angarrack Gwinear
Wharf
Carbis Bay
1st
Copperhouse
Gwinear Road
Lelant
Hayle 2nd
Praze
Penryn
Lelant Saltings
Penmere
St Erth
Nancegollan
The Dell
Falmouth
Penzance
Marazion
Truthall Platform
Helston

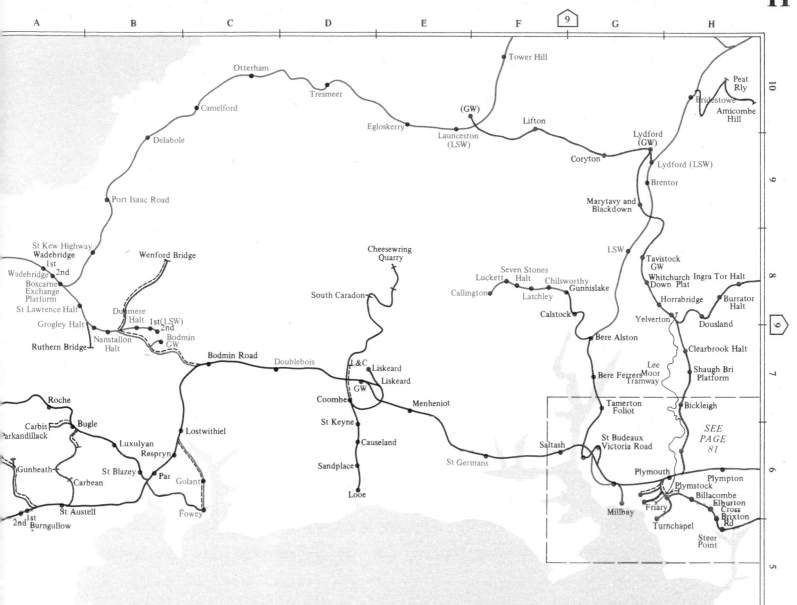

A B C D E F 9 G H

Tower Hill

Peat
Rly

Otterham

Bridestowe

Camelford

Tresmeer

Amicombe
Hill

Delabole

(GW)

Lifton

Egloskerry

Launceston
(LSW)

Lydford
(GW)

Coryton

Lydford (LSW)

Port Isaac Road

Brentor

Marytavy and
Blackdown

LSW

Tavistock
GW

St Kew Highway

Wadebridge
1st

Wenford Bridge

Cheesewring
Quarry

Whitchurch Ingra Tor Halt
Down Plat

Wadebridge
2nd

Seven Stones
Halt

Horrabridge

Burrator
Halt

Boscarne
Exchange
Platform

Luckett

Chilsworthy

Gunnislake

Dousland

St Lawrence Halt

Callington

Latchley

Yelverton

South Caradon

Grogley Halt

Dunmere
Halt

1st(LSW)

Calstock

Clearbrook Halt

2nd

Bodmin
GW

Shaugh Bri
Platform

Ruthern Bridge

Nanstallon
Halt

Bodmin Road

Bere Alston

Doublebois

Lee
Moor
Tramway

L&C

Liskeard

Bere Ferrers

Bickleigh

Liskeard

Coombe

GW

Tamerton
Foliot

Roche

Menheniot

SEE
PAGE
81

Carbis

Bugle

St Keyne

Parkandillack

Lostwithiel

St Budeaux
Victoria Road

Luxulyan

Causeland

Saltash

Respryn

St Germans

Plymouth

Plympton

Gunheath

St Blazey

Par

Sandplace

Plymstock

Golant

Billacombe

Carbean

Elburton
Cross

Millbay

Friary

Brixton
Rd

St Austell

1st

Looe

Turnchapel

2nd
Burngullow

Fowey

Steer
Point

E N G L I S H   C H A N N E L

12

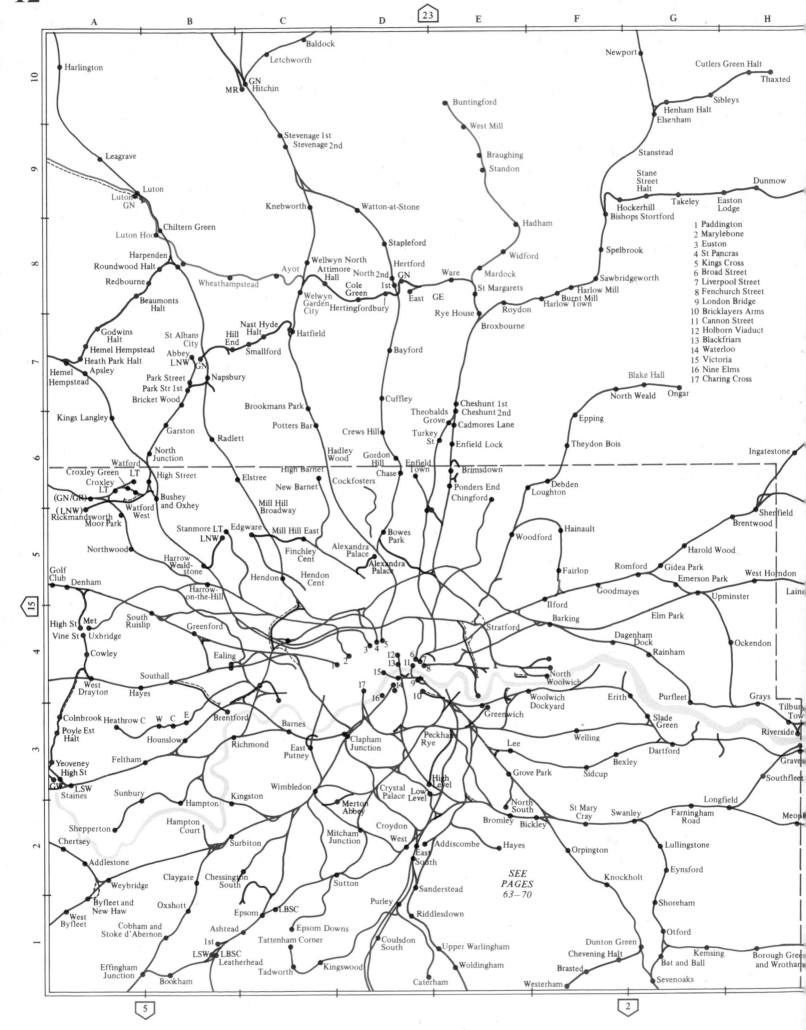

23

| | A | B | C | D | E | F | G | H |

Harlington

Baldock
Letchworth

Newport
Cutlers Green Halt
Thaxted

10

GN
MR   Hitchin

Sibleys
Henham Halt
Elsenham

Leagrave

Stevenage 1st
Stevenage 2nd

Buntingford
West Mill

Stanstead

9

Luton

Braughing
Standon

Stane
Street
Halt

Dunmow

Luton
GN

Knebworth

Watton-at-Stone

Hadham

Takeley
Hockerhill
Bishops Stortford

Easton
Lodge

Luton Hoo
Chiltern Green

Widford

Spelbrook

8

Harpenden
Roundwood Halt

Ayot

Wellwyn North
Attimore
Hall
North 2nd

Stapleford

Hertford
GN

Ware
Mardock

Sawbridgeworth

1 Paddington
2 Marylebone

Redbourne

Wheathampstead

Cole
Green
1st

St Margarets

Burnt Mill
Harlow Mill
Harlow Town

3 Euston
4 St Pancras

Beaumonts
Halt

Welwyn
Garden
City

East   GE

Roydon

5 Kings Cross
6 Broad Street

Hertingfordbury

Rye House

Broxbourne

7 Liverpool Street
8 Fenchurch Street

7

Godwins
Halt
Hemel Hempstead
Heath Park Halt

St Albans
City

Nast Hyde
Halt
Hill
End

Hatfield

Bayford

9 London Bridge
10 Bricklayers Arms

Smallford

11 Cannon Street
12 Holborn Viaduct

Abbey
LNW   GN

13 Blackfriars
14 Waterloo

Hemel
Hempstead
Apsley

Park Street
Park Str 1st

Napsbury

Cuffley

Blake Hall
North Weald
Ongar

15 Victoria
16 Nine Elms

Bricket Wood

Brookmans Park

Theobalds
Grove

Cheshunt 1st
Cheshunt 2nd
Cadmores Lane

17 Charing Cross

6

Kings Langley

Garston

Radlett

Potters Bar

Crews Hill

Turkey
St

Epping

Enfield Lock

Theydon Bois

Ingatestone

North
Junction
Watford

High Street

Elstree

Hadley
Wood

Gordon
Hill

Enfield
Town

Brimsdown

Debden
Loughton

Croxley Green LT
Croxley
LT

New Barnet

Cockfosters

Chase

Ponders End
Chingford

Shenfield
Brentwood

(GN/GR)

Bushey
and Oxhey

Mill Hill
Broadway

Bowes
Park

Woodford

Hainault

Harold Wood

5

(LNW)
Rickmansworth
Moor Park

Watford
West

Stanmore LT
LNW

Edgware
Mill Hill East

Finchley
Cent

Alexandra
Palace

Romford

Fairlop

Gidea Park
Emerson Park

West Horndon

Northwood

Harrow
Weald-
stone

Hendon

Hendon
Cent

Alexandra
Palace

Ilford

Barking

Goodmayes

Upminster

15

Golf
Club
Denham

Harrow-
on-the-Hill

Stratford

Elm Park

Laind

High St   Met
Vine St   Uxbridge

South
Ruislip

Greenford

3 4 5
2   12
13 11
6 7
8

North
Woolwich

Dagenham
Dock

Ockendon

4

Cowley

Ealing

15

9

Woolwich
Dockyard

Rainham

Southall

14

Erith

Purfleet

Grays

West
Drayton

Hayes

17
16

10

Woolwich
Greenwich

Welling

Slade
Green

Tilbury
Town

Colnbrook
Heathrow C
W C E
Brentford

Barnes

Peckham
Rye

Lee

Dartford

Riverside

3

Poyle Est
Halt

Hounslow

Richmond

East
Putney

Clapham
Junction

Greenwich

Bexley

Graves

Yeoveney
High St

Feltham

Grove Park

Sidcup

Southfleet

GW
LSW
Staines

Sunbury

Hampton

Kingston

Wimbledon

Crystal
Palace

High
Level
Low
Level

North
South

St Mary
Cray

Swanley

Longfield

Meop

2

Shepperton

Hampton
Court

Merton
Abbey

Croydon
West

Bromley
Bickley

Farningham
Road

Chertsey

Mitcham
Junction

East
South

Addiscombe

Hayes

Orpington

Lullingstone

Eynsford

Addlestone

Surbiton

Sutton

Sanderstead

Knockholt

Claygate
Chessington
South

SEE
PAGES
63–70

Weybridge

Purley

Shoreham

Byfleet and
New Haw

Oxshott

Sanderstead

Riddlesdown

Otford

1

West
Byfleet

Cobham and
Stoke d'Abernon

Ashtead

Epsom

LBSC

Coulsdon
South

Dunton Green
Chevening Halt

Kemsing
Bat and Ball

Borough Green
and Wrotham

Effingham
Junction

1st
LSW   LBSC
Leatherhead

Tattenham Corner
Epsom Downs

Kingswood

Upper Warlingham
Woldingham

Brasted

Sevenoaks

Bookham

Tadworth

Caterham

Westerham

5   2

A   23   B   C   D   E   F   21   G   H

Sible and Castle
Hedingham
Bures
Halstead
Earls Colne
White Colne
Chappel and Wakes Colne
Colchester

Manningtree
Mistley   Bradfield   Priory Halt
(Private)
Wrabness
Parkstone
Quay
Parkstone
Quay West
Harwich Town
Dovercourt

Rayne   Braintree
Bannister Green
Halt
Cressing
White Notley
Kelvedon (HL)
Feering Halt
Kelvedon Low Level
Inworth
Tiptree
Witham
Hatfield Peverel
Wickham Bishops
Tolleshunt Knights
Langford and Ulting
Maldon East
Maldon West
Barons Lane
Halt
Cold Norton
Chelmsford 1st
2nd

Marks Tey
St Botolphs   Hythe
Wivenhoe   Alresford   Great Bentley   Thorpe-le-Soken
Thorington   Weeley   Kirby Cross
Brightlingsea
Clacton-on-Sea
Walton-on-Naze
Frinton-on-Sea

Tolleshunt d'Arcy
Tollesbury
Tollesbury Pier

Margaretting Halt

Stow St Mary Halt
Fambridge   Althorne
Southminster
Woodham Ferrers
Battlesbridge
Burnham-on-Crouch
Billericay
Wickford
Hockley
Rayleigh
Rochford
Prittlewell
Basildon
Pitsea
Benfleet
1st
Leigh-on-Sea
Westcliff-
on-Sea
Southend
Victoria
Pigs Bay
2nd
Benfleet
Chalkwell   Central   East   Thorpe
Bay
Shoeburyness

Stanford-
le-Hope   Corringham   Coryton
Thames Haven

Low Street
East Tilbury
Allhallows-on-Sea
Uralite
Milton   Halt
Range
Cliffe
High
Halstow   Halt
Middle
Stoke
Grain Crossing Halt
Dock   Sheerness-on-Sea
Grain
Port Victoria
Beluncle
Sharnal
Street
Pier
East
Higham
Queenborough
East Minster
Kemsley
Hoo
Higham
Strood
Rochester Bridge
Gillingham
Kings Ferry
Bridge   North
Swale   Halt
Minster
Brambledown Halt
Eastchurch
Leysdown
Harty Rd Ht
Rochester   Chatham
Rainham
Kemsley
Cuxton
Halling
Newington
Sittingbourne
Teynham
Snodland
New Hythe
Aylesford
West Malling
Malling
Maidstone
East
Barracks
West
Bearsted and
Thurnham

Selling
Chilham   Chartham
Faversham
Whitstable
Tankerton
Harbour
Chestfield
and Swalecliffe
Herne Bay
South St
Halt
Blean and
Tyler Hill Halt
Sturry
West
C & W
Canterbury
East
South
Canterbury
Road
Bekesbourne
Adisham
Westgate-on-Sea
Birchington-on-Sea
Coll
Grove Ferry
Ash
Town
Wingham
Coll   Staple
Wingham Town
Woodnesboro
Coll
Poison Cross
Eastry
Eastry South

N O R T H

S E A

10

9

8

7

6

5

4

3

2

1

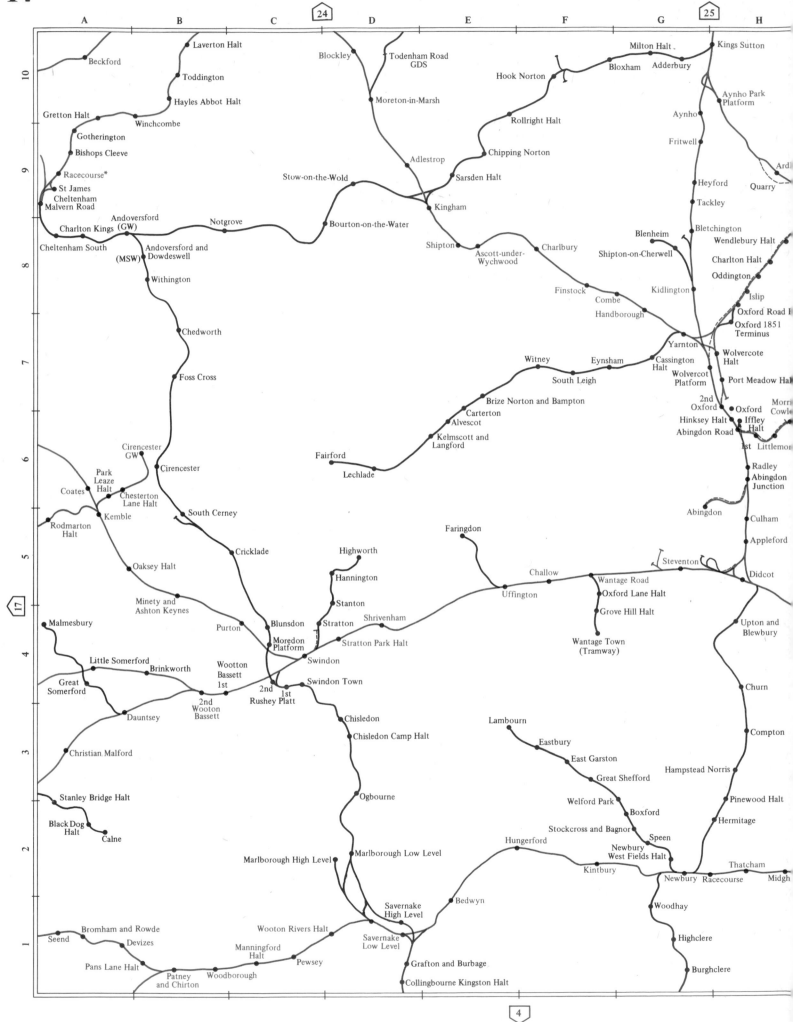

14

24
25
17
4

A   B   C   D   E   F   G   H

Beckford
Laverton Halt
Toddington
Hayles Abbot Halt
Gretton Halt
Winchcombe
Gotherington
Bishops Cleeve
Racecourse*
St James
Cheltenham
Malvern Road
Charlton Kings
Andoversford (GW)
Notgrove
Cheltenham South
Andoversford and
(MSW)
Dowdeswell
Withington
Chedworth
Foss Cross
Cirencester GW
Cirencester
Park Leaze Halt
Coates
Chesterton Lane Halt
Kemble
South Cerney
Rodmarton Halt
Cricklade
Oaksey Halt
Minety and Ashton Keynes
Malmesbury
Purton
Blunsdon
Highworth
Hannington
Stanton
Shrivenham
Stratton
Moredon Platform
Stratton Park Halt
Little Somerford
Brinkworth
Wootton Bassett 1st
Swindon
Great Somerford
2nd Wooton Bassett
2nd
1st
Rushey Platt
Swindon Town
Dauntsey
Chiseldon
Christian Malford
Chiseldon Camp Halt
Stanley Bridge Halt
Ogbourne
Black Dog Halt
Calne
Marlborough High Level
Marlborough Low Level
Seend
Bromham and Rowde
Devizes
Wooton Rivers Halt
Savernake High Level
Pans Lane Halt
Manningford Halt
Pewsey
Savernake Low Level
Patney and Chirton
Woodborough
Grafton and Burbage
Collingbourne Kingston Halt

Blockley
Todenham Road GDS
Moreton-in-Marsh
Hook Norton
Rollright Halt
Chipping Norton
Stow-on-the-Wold
Adlestrop
Sarsden Halt
Bourton-on-the-Water
Kingham
Shipton
Ascott-under-Wychwood
Charlbury
Witney
Eynsham
South Leigh
Brize Norton and Bampton
Carterton
Alvescot
Kelmscott and Langford
Fairford
Lechlade
Faringdon
Challow
Uffington
Wantage Road
Oxford Lane Halt
Grove Hill Halt
Wantage Town (Tramway)
Lambourn
Eastbury
East Garston
Great Shefford
Welford Park
Boxford
Stockcross and Bagnor
Speen
Newbury West Fields Halt
Hungerford
Kintbury
Newbury Racecourse
Bedwyn

Milton Halt
Kings Sutton
Bloxham
Adderbury
Aynho Park Platform
Aynho
Fritwell
Aynho Park
Ardl
Heyford
Quarry
Tackley
Blenheim
Bletchington
Wendlebury Halt
Shipton-on-Cherwell
Charlton Halt
Oddington
Finstock
Combe
Handborough
Kidlington
Islip
Oxford Road
Oxford 1851 Terminus
Yarnton
Cassington Halt
Wolvercote Halt
Wolvercot Platform
2nd Oxford
Morri
Oxford
Cowle
Hinksey Halt
Iffley Halt
Abingdon Road
1st Littlemor
Radley
Abingdon Junction
Abingdon
Culham
Appleford
Didcot
Upton and Blewbury
Steventon
Churn
Compton
Hampstead Norris
Pinewood Halt
Hermitage
Thatcham
Midgh
Woodhay
Highclere
Burghclere

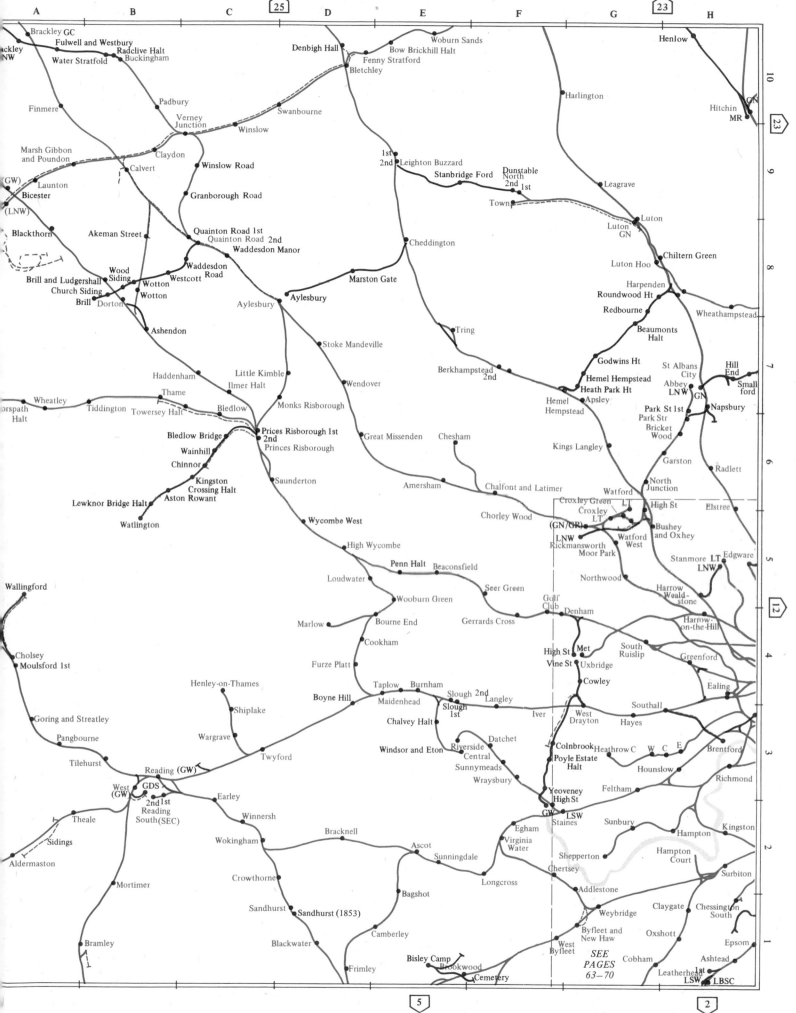

15

A   B   C   D   E   F   G   H

Brackley GC
Fulwell and Westbury
Brackley NW
Radclive Halt
Water Stratfold
Buckingham
Denbigh Hall
Woburn Sands
Bow Brickhill Halt
Fenny Stratford
Bletchley
Henlow
Padbury
Swanbourne
Harlington
Hitchin
GN
MR
Finmere
Verney Junction
Winslow
Marsh Gibbon and Poundon
Claydon
Calvert
Winslow Road
1st
2nd Leighton Buzzard
Stanbridge Ford
Dunstable North
2nd 1st
Leagrave
(GW)
Launton
Bicester
Granborough Road
Town
Luton
Luton GN
(LNW)
Akeman Street
Quinton Road 1st
Quinton Road 2nd
Waddesdon Manor
Cheddington
Chiltern Green
Blackthorn
Waddesdon Road
Marston Gate
Luton Hoo
Wood Siding
Westcott
Harpenden
Roundwood Ht
Brill and Ludgershall
Wotton
Aylesbury
Redbourne
Church Siding
Wotton
Beaumonts Halt
Brill Dorton
Stoke Mandeville
Tring
Godwins Ht
St Albans City
Hill End
Ashendon
Little Kimble
Ilmer Halt
Wendover
Berkhampstead 2nd
Hemel Hempstead
Heath Park Ht
Abbey LNW GN
Smallford
Haddenham
Thame
Monks Risborough
Hemel Hempstead
Apsley
Park St 1st
Napsbury
Wheatley
Tiddington
Towersey Halt
Bledlow
Prices Risborough 1st
2nd
Great Missenden
Chesham
Kings Langley
Park Str
Bricket Wood
orspath Halt
Bledlow Bridge
Wainhill
Princes Risborough
Saunderton
Amersham
Chalfont and Latimer
Garston
North Junction
Radlett
Chinnor
Watford
Elstree
Kingston Crossing Halt
Aston Rowant
Croxley Green
Croxley LT
High St
Lewknor Bridge Halt
Wycombe West
Chorley Wood
(GN/GR)
LNW
LT
Bushey and Oxhey
Watlington
High Wycombe
Rickmansworth
Moor Park
Watford West
Stanmore LT
Edgware
LNW
Penn Halt
Beaconsfield
Seer Green
Northwood
Harrow Weald-stone
Wallingford
Loudwater
Golf Club
Denham
Harrow-on-the-Hill
Wooburn Green
Gerrards Cross
Marlow
Bourne End
South Ruislip
Greenford
Cholsey
Moulsford 1st
Cookham
High St Met
Vine St Uxbridge
Cowley
Ealing
Furze Platt
Henley-on-Thames
Taplow Burnham
Slough 2nd
Langley
Southall
Goring and Streatley
Shiplake
Boyne Hill
Maidenhead
Slough 1st
Iver
West Drayton
Hayes
Pangbourne
Wargrave
Chalvey Halt
Datchet
Colnbrook
Heathrow C
W C E
Brentford
Tilehurst
Twyford
Windsor and Eton
Riverside
Central
Poyle Estate Halt
Hounslow
Richmond
Reading (GW)
Earley
Sunnymeads
Wraysbury
Yeoveney
High St
Feltham
West (GW)
GDS
2nd 1st
Reading South (SEC)
Winnersh
Egham
GW LSW
Staines
Sunbury
Kingston
Theale
Bracknell
Ascot
Virginia Water
Shepperton
Hampton
Hampton Court
Sidings
Wokingham
Sunningdale
Chertsey
Addlestone
Surbiton
Aldermaston
Crowthorne
Bagshot
Longcross
Weybridge
Claygate
Chessington South
Oxshott
Mortimer
Sandhurst
Sandhurst (1853)
Camberley
West Byfleet
Byfleet and New Haw
Cobham
Epsom
Bramley
Blackwater
Frimley
Bisley Camp
Brookwood
Cemetery
SEE PAGES 63–70
Leatherhead
1st
LSW LBSC
Ashtead

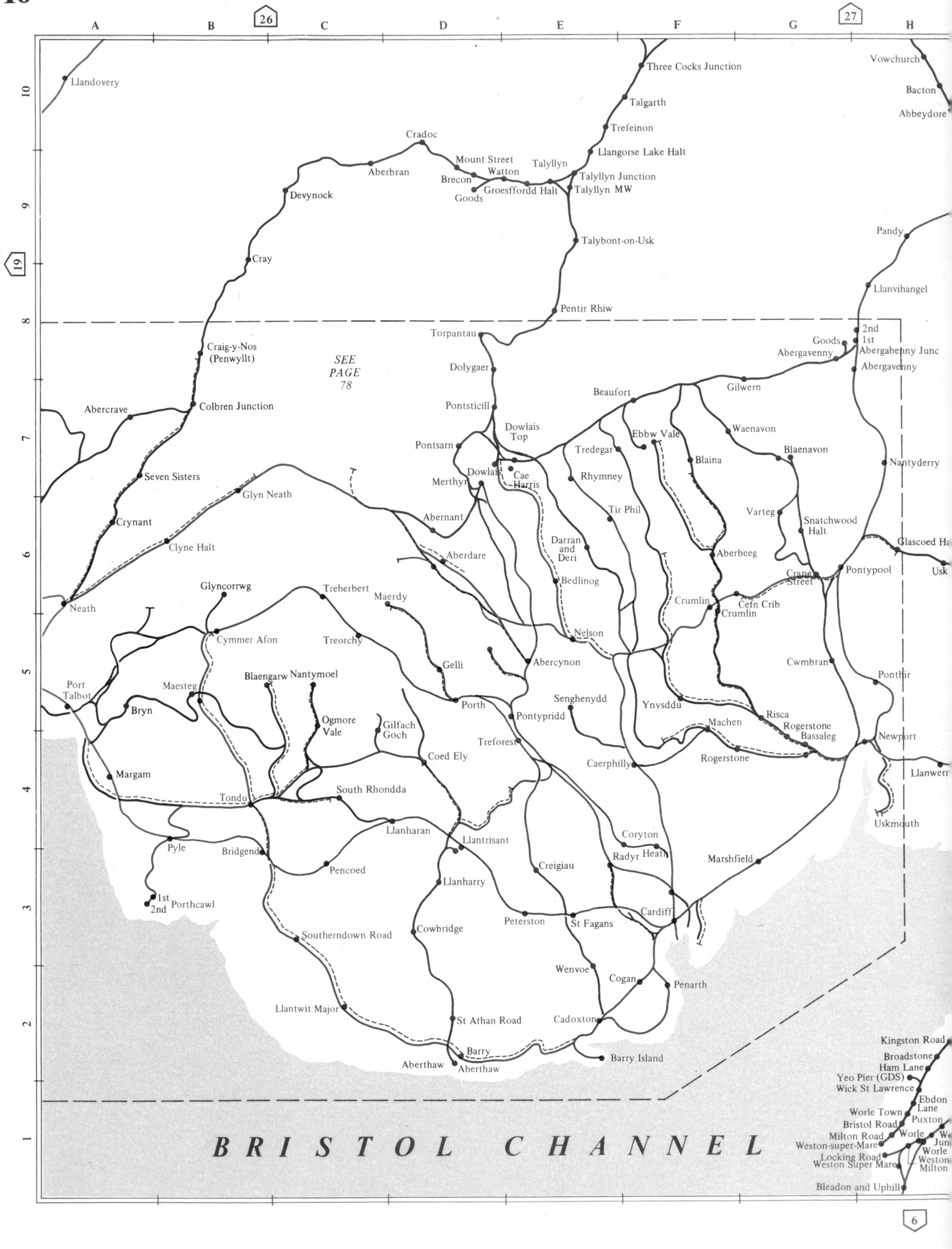

26

27

A B C D E F G H

19

Llandovery

Vowchurch

Three Cocks Junction

Bacton

Abbeydore

Talgarth

Trefeinon

Cradoc

Llangorse Lake Halt

Mount Street
Watton

Talyllyn

Aberbran

Brecon

Talyllyn Junction

Devynock

Groesffordd Halt

Talyllyn MW

Goods

Pandy

Cray

Talybont-on-Usk

Llanvihangel

Pentir Rhiw

Torpantau

Craig-y-Nos
(Penwyllt)

SEE
PAGE
78

Dolygaer

2nd
1st

Goods

Abergavenny

Abergavenny Junc

Beaufort

Gilwern

Abergavenny

Abercrave

Colbren Junction

Pontsticill

Dowlais
Top

Waenavon

Ebbw Vale

Tredegar

Blaina

Blaenavon

Nantyderry

Seven Sisters

Pontsarn

Rhymney

Glyn Neath

Merthyr

Dowlais

Cae
Harris

Tir Phil

Varteg

Snatchwood
Halt

Crynant

Abernant

Glascoed Ha

Clyne Halt

Darran
and
Deri

Aberbeeg

Crane
Street

Pontypool

Usk

Aberdare

Bedlinog

Glyncorrwg

Treherbert

Crumlin

Neath

Maerdy

Cefn Crib

Cymmer Afon

Treorchy

Nelson

Crumlin

Gelli

Abercynon

Cwmbran

Blaengarw Nantymoel

Maesteg

Porth

Senghenydd

Ynysddu

Machen

Risca

Ponthir

Port
Talbot

Ogmore
Vale

Gilfach
Goch

Pontypridd

Rogerstone

Bassaleg

Bryn

Treforest

Caerphilly

Rogerstone

Newport

Coed Ely

Margam

Llanwern

Tondu

South Rhondda

Coryton

Marshfield

Uskmouth

Pyle

Bridgend

Llanharan

Llantrisant

Radyr Heath

Pencoed

Creigiau

Llanharry

1st
2nd Porthcawl

Cowbridge

Peterston

St Fagans

Cardiff

Southerndown Road

Wenvoe

Cogan

Penarth

Llantwit Major

St Athan Road

Cadoxton

Kingston Road

Broadstone

Ham Lane

Barry

Yeo Pier (GDS)

Aberthaw

Barry Island

Wick St Lawrence

Aberthaw

Ebdon
Lane

Worle Town

Puxton

Bristol Road

Worle

W

Milton Road

Worle

Weston-super-Mare

Weston

Locking Road

Milton

Weston Super Mare

Bleadon and Uphill

B R I S T O L   C H A N N E L

6

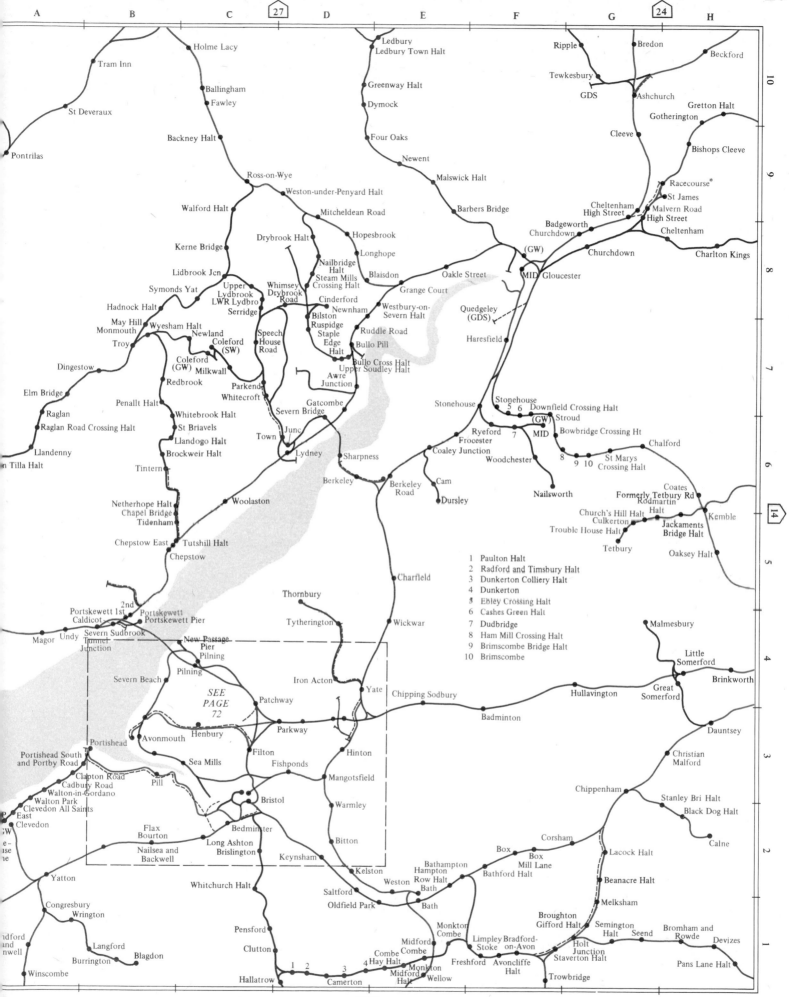

Tram Inn
Holme Lacy
Ripple
Bredon
Beckford
St Deveraux
Ballingham
Fawley
Tewkesbury
GDS
Ashchurch
Gretton Halt
Gotherington
Pontrilas
Backney Halt
Cleeve
Bishops Cleeve
Ross-on-Wye
Ledbury
Ledbury Town Halt
Greenway Halt
Dymock
Four Oaks
Newent
Malswick Halt
Racecourse*
St James
Weston-under-Penyard Halt
Cheltenham High Street
Malvern Road
High Street
Walford Halt
Mitcheldean Road
Barbers Bridge
Badgeworth
Churchdown
Cheltenham
Kerne Bridge
Drybrook Halt
Hopesbrook
Longhope
Oakle Street
(GW)
Churchdown
Charlton Kings
Lidbrook Jcn
Nailbridge Halt
Steam Mills
Crossing Halt
Blaisdon
Grange Court
MID Gloucester
Symonds Yat
Upper Lydbrook
LWR Lydbro
Serridge
Whimsey
Drybrook Road
Cinderford
Newnham
Westbury-on-Severn Halt
Quedgeley (GDS)
Hadnock Halt
Bilston
Ruspidge
Staple Edge Halt
Haresfield
May Hill
Monmouth
Wyesham Halt
Newland
Coleford (SW)
Speech House Road
Ruddle Road
Bullo Pill
Troy
Coleford (GW)
Milkwall
Parkend
Whitecroft
Upper Soudley Halt
Bullo Cross Halt
Awre Junction
Dingestow
Redbrook
Gatcombe
Stonehouse
Stonehouse
5 6 Downfield Crossing Halt
(GW)
Stroud
Elm Bridge
Penallt Halt
Whitebrook Halt
Severn Bridge
Ryeford
Frocester
7 MID
Bowbridge Crossing Ht
Raglan
St Briavels
Town
Junc
Coaley Junction
Woodchester
8 9 10 St Marys Crossing Halt
Chalford
Raglan Road Crossing Halt
Llandogo Halt
Lydney
Sharpness
Nailsworth
Llandenny
Brockweir Halt
Berkeley
Coates
Rodmartin
Formerly Tetbury Rd
Tilla Halt
Tintern
Berkeley Road
Cam
Dursley
Church's Hill Halt
Culkerton
Jackaments Bridge Halt
Kemble
Netherhope Halt
Chapel Bridge
Tidenham
Woolaston
Trouble House Halt
Tetbury
Oaksey Halt
Chepstow East
Tutshill Halt
Chepstow
Charfield
Malmesbury
Thornbury
Portskewett 2nd
Caldicot
Portskewett 1st
Portskewett Pier
Tytherington
Wickwar
Little Somerford
Magor
Undy
Severn
Tunnel
Junction
Sudbrook
New Passage Pier
Pilning
Iron Acton
Yate
Chipping Sodbury
Hullavington
Great Somerford
Brinkworth
Severn Beach
Pilning
Patchway
Badminton
Dauntsey
SEE PAGE 72
Parkway
Portishead
Avonmouth
Henbury
Hinton
Christian Malford
Portishead South
and Portby Road
Sea Mills
Filton
Fishponds
Chippenham
Clapton Road
Cadbury Road
Walton-in-Gordano
Walton Park
Clevedon All Saints
East
Clevedon
Pill
Mangotsfield
Stanley Bri Halt
Black Dog Halt
Bristol
Warmley
Corsham
Flax Bourton
Bedminster
Long Ashton
Brislington
Keynsham
Bitton
Box
Box Mill Lane
Lacock Halt
Calne
Nailsea and Backwell
Kelston
Bathampton
Bathford Halt
Beanacre Halt
Yatton
Whitchurch Halt
Saltford
Weston
Hampton Row Halt
Bath
Melksham
Congresbury
Wrington
Oldfield Park
Bath
Broughton Gifford Halt
Semington Halt
Seend
Bromham and Rowde
Langford
Pensford
Monkton Combe
Limpley Stoke
Bradford-on-Avon
Holt Junction
Staverton Halt
Devizes
Burrington
Blagdon
Clutton
1 2 3 4 Hay Halt
Combe
Midford
Monkton
Combe
Midford Halt
Wellow
Freshford
Avoncliffe Halt
Trowbridge
Pans Lane Halt
Winscombe
Hallatrow
Camerton

1 Paulton Halt
2 Radford and Timsbury Halt
3 Dunkerton Colliery Halt
4 Dunkerton
5 Ebley Crossing Halt
6 Cashes Green Halt
7 Dudbridge
8 Ham Mill Crossing Halt
9 Brimscombe Bridge Halt
10 Brimscombe

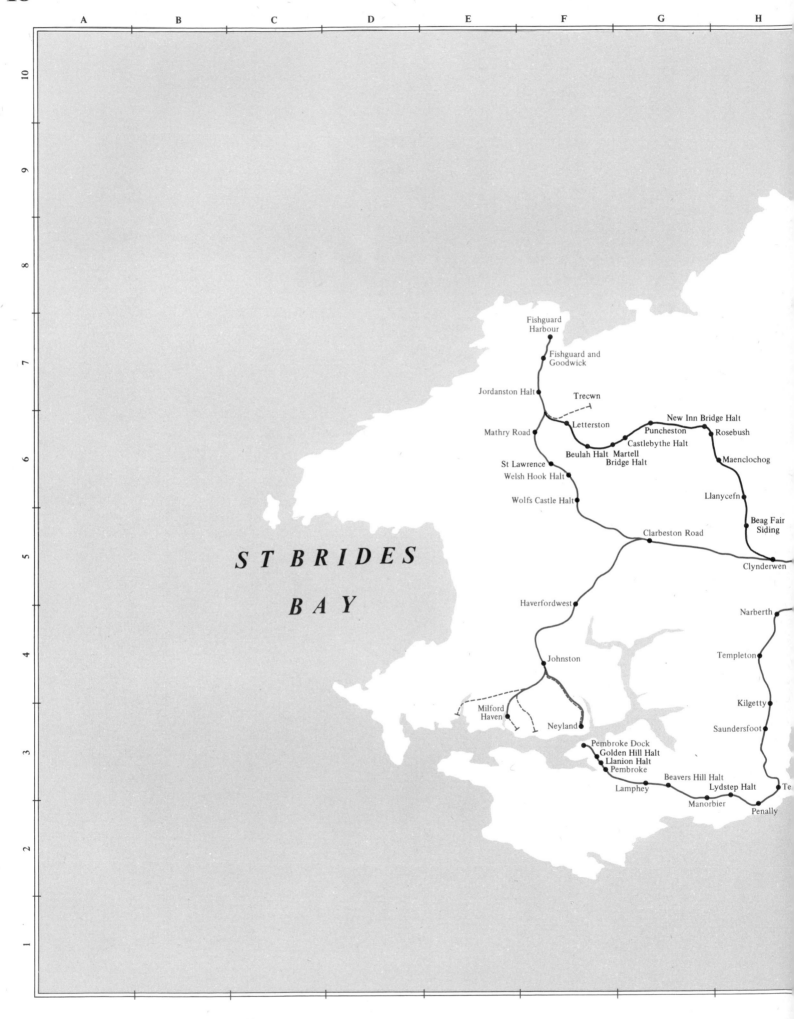

A B C D E F G H

ST BRIDES

BAY

Fishguard
Harbour

Fishguard and
Goodwick

Jordanston Halt

Trecwn

Letterston

New Inn Bridge Halt

Mathry Road

Puncheston
Rosebush

Castlebythe Halt

Beulah Halt Martell
Bridge Halt

Maenclochog

St Lawrence

Welsh Hook Halt

Wolfs Castle Halt

Llanycefn

Beag Fair
Siding

Clarbeston Road

Clynderwen

Haverfordwest

Narberth

Templeton

Johnston

Kilgetty

Milford
Haven

Saundersfoot

Neyland

Pembroke Dock

Golden Hill Halt

Llanion Halt

Pembroke

Beavers Hill Halt

Lamphey

Lydstep Halt

Te

Manorbier

Penally

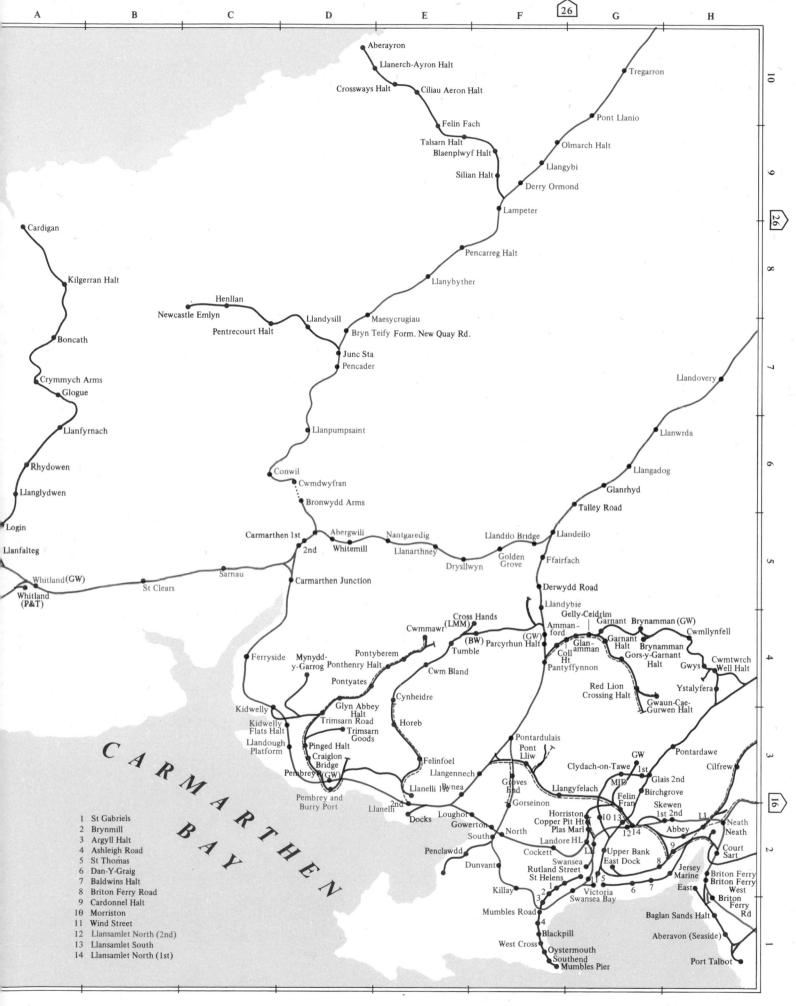

26

26

26

16

Aberayron
Llanerch-Ayron Halt
Crossways Halt
Ciliau Aeron Halt
Tregarron
Felin Fach
Talsarn Halt
Blaenplwyf Halt
Silian Halt
Pont Llanio
Olmarch Halt
Llangybi
Derry Ormond
Lampeter
Pencarreg Halt
Llanybyther
Cardigan
Kilgerran Halt
Henllan
Newcastle Emlyn
Llandysill
Pentrecourt Halt
Maesycrugiau
Bryn Teify Form. New Quay Rd.
Boncath
Junc Sta
Pencader
Llandovery
Crymmych Arms
Glogue
Llanwrda
Llanpumpsaint
Llanfyrnach
Llangadog
Rhydowen
Conwil
Glanrhyd
Cwmdwyfran
Llanglydwen
Bronwydd Arms
Talley Road
Login
Abergwili
Nantgaredig
Llandilo Bridge
Llandeilo
Llanfalteg
Carmarthen 1st
Whitemill
Llanarthney
Ffairfach
Llanfalteg
2nd
Dryslwyn
Golden Grove
Whitland (GW)
Sarnau
Carmarthen Junction
Whitland (P&T)
St Clears
Derwydd Road
Llandybie
Gelly-Ceidrim
Garnant
Brynamman (GW)
Cross Hands (LMM)
Amman-ford
Cwmmawr
(GW)
Garnant Halt
Cwmllynfell
(BW)
Parcyrhun Halt
Glan-amman
Brynamman
Ferryside
Mynydd-y-Garrog
Pontyberem
Coll Ht
Gors-y-Garnant Halt
Ponthenry Halt
Tumble
Pantyffynnon
Gwys
Cwmtwrch Well Halt
Cwm Bland
Red Lion Crossing Halt
Pontyates
Cynheidre
Gwaun-Cae-Gurwen Halt
Ystalyfera
Kidwelly
Glyn Abbey Halt
Horeb
Kidwelly Flats Halt
Trimsarn Road
Trimsarn Goods
Llandough Platform
Pinged Halt
Pontardulais
Craiglon Bridge
Pont Lliw
GW
Pontardawe
Pembrey (GW)
Felinfoel
Clydach-on-Tawe
1st
Glais 2nd
Cilfrew
Pembrey and Burry Port
Llangennech
Bynea
Groves End
Llangyfelach
MID
Birchgrove
Felin Fran
Skewen
Llanelli 1st
Gorseinon
Horriston
10 13
1st 2nd
LL
2nd
Docks
Loughor
North
Copper Pit Ht
Plas Marl
12 14
Abbey
Neath
Llanelli
Gowerton
South
Landore HL
9
Neath
Penclawdd
Cockett
LL
Upper Bank East Dock
8
Court Sart
Dunvant
Swansea
Rutland Street
11 5
7
Jersey Marine
Briton Ferry West
St Helens
1
Victoria
6
Briton Ferry East
Killay
2
Swansea Bay
3
Baglan Sands Halt
Briton Ferry Rd
Mumbles Road
4
Aberavon (Seaside)
West Cross
Blackpill
Oystermouth
Southend
Port Talbot
Mumbles Pier

CARMARTHEN BAY

1 St Gabriels
2 Brynmill
3 Argyll Halt
4 Ashleigh Road
5 St Thomas
6 Dan-Y-Graig
7 Baldwins Halt
8 Briton Ferry Road
9 Cardonnel Halt
10 Morriston
11 Wind Street
12 Llansamlet North (2nd)
13 Llansamlet South
14 Llansamlet North (1st)

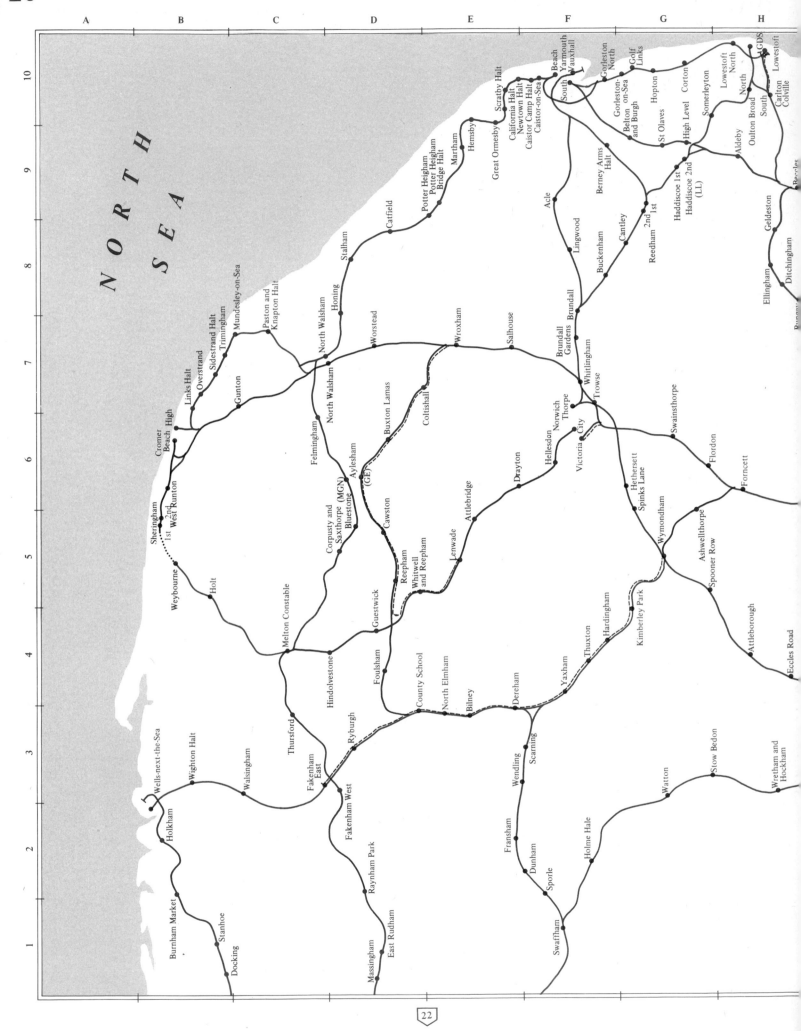

A   B   C   D   E   F   G   H

N O R T H

S E A

GDS

Lowestoft

Gorleston North
Beach
Yarmouth Vauxhall
Golf Links
Lowestoft North
South

Scratby Halt
California Halt
Newtown Halt
Caistor Camp Halt
Caistor-on-Sea
Gorleston-on-Sea
Belton on-Sea and Burgh
Hopton
High Level
Corton
Somerleyton
Lowestoft North
Carlton Colville

Great Ormesby
Potter Heigham
Potter Heigham Bridge Halt
Martham
Hemsby
Acle
Berney Arms Halt
St Olaves
Haddiscoe 1st
Haddiscoe 2nd (LL)
Aldeby
Oulton Broad South
Beccles

Catfield
Lingwood
Buckenham
Cantley
Reedham 2nd
1st
Ellingham
Geldeston
Ditchingham

Stalham
Honing
Salhouse
Brundall Gardens
Brundall
Whitlingham

North Walsham
Worstead
Wroxham
Swainsthorpe

Mundesley-on-Sea
Paston and Knapton Halt
Buxton Lamas
Coltishall
Hellesdon
Norwich Thorpe
Trowse

Sidestrand Halt
Trimingham
North Walsham
Aylsham (GE)
Victoria City

Links Halt
Overstrand
Gunton
Felmingham
Bluestone
Corpusty and Saxthorpe (MGN)
Flordon
Forncett

Cromer Beach High
Cawston
Reepham
Whitwell and Reepham
Lenwade
Attlebridge
Drayton
Hethersett
Spinks Lane
Wymondham
Ashwellthorpe
Spooner Row

Sheringham
1st 2nd West Runton
Guestwick
Hardingham
Kimberley Park
Attleborough
Eccles Road

Weybourne
Holt
Melton Constable
Foulsham
County School
North Elmham
Bilney
Dereham
Yaxham
Thuxton
Watton
Stow Bedon
Wretham and Hockham

Hindolvestone
Thursford
Ryburgh
Fransham
Wendling
Scarning
Holme Hale

Wighton Halt
Walsingham
Fakenham East
Fakenham West
Dunham
Sporle

Wells-next-the-Sea
Holkham
Raynham Park
Swaffham

Burnham Market
Stanhoe
Massingham
East Rudham

Docking

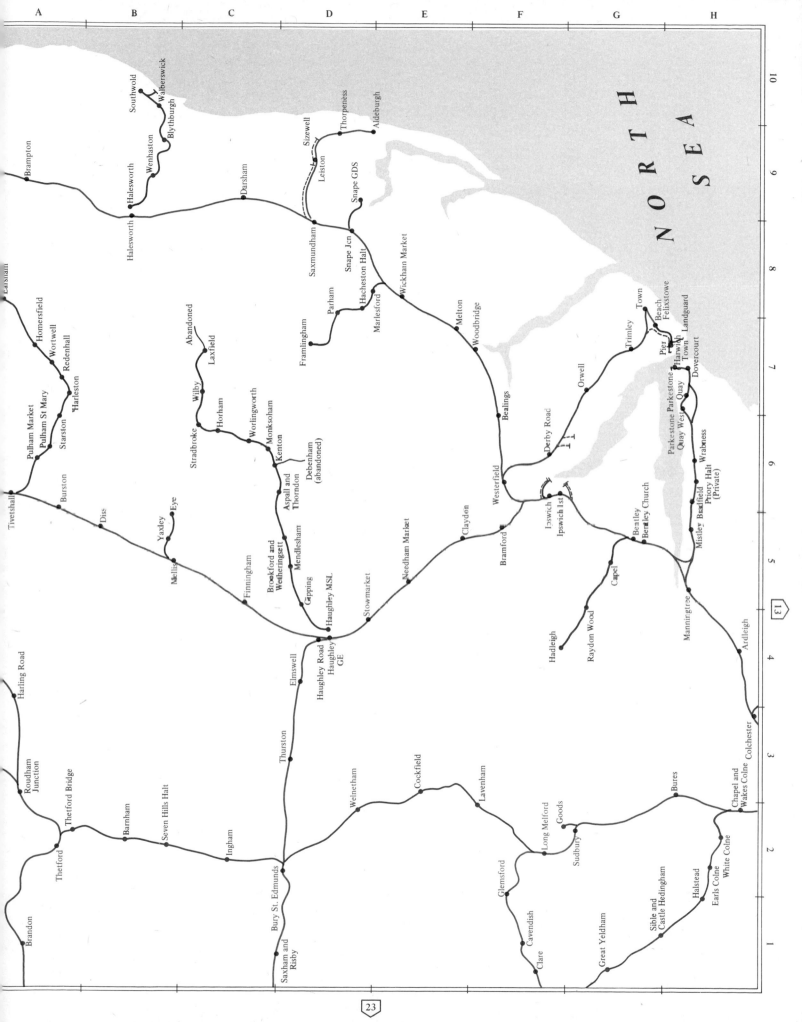

A   B   C   D   E   F   G   H

10

N O R T H

N O R S E A

Brampton

Southwold
Walberswick
Blythburgh
Wenhaston
Halesworth
Halesworth

Darsham

Sizewell
Leiston
Snape GDS
Thorpeness
Aldeburgh

Saxmundham
Snape Jcn
Hacheston Halt
Wickham Market

Leisham

Homersfield
Wortwell
Redenhall
Harleston
Pulham Market
Pulham St Mary
Starston
Harleston

Abandoned
Laxfield
Wilby
Stradbroke
Horham
Worlingworth
Monksoham
Kenton
Debenham
(abandoned)
Aspall and
Thorndon

Framlingham
Parham
Marlesford

Melton
Woodbridge

Orwell

Trimley
Town
Beach
Felixstowe
Landguard

Pier
Harwich
Town
Dovercourt
Quay West
Parkstone Parkestone Quay
Mistley Bradfield
Wrabness
Priory Halt
(Private)

Bealings

Derby Road

Westerfield
Ipswich 1st
Ipswich

Bramford

Claydon

Needham Market

Tivetshall
Burston
Dise
Yaxley
Eye
Mellis
Finningham
Brookford and
Wetheringsett
Mendlesham
Gipping
Haughley MSL
Haughley Road
GE
Elmswell
Stowmarket

Harling Road

Thurston

Beatley
Bentley Church

Capel

Hadleigh
Raydon Wood

Manningtree

Ardleigh

13

Roudham
Junction
Thetford Bridge
Barnham
Seven Hills Halt
Ingham

Cockfield

Lavenham

Bures

Chapel and
Wakes Colne Colchester

Brandon

Thetford

Bury St. Edmunds

Saxham and
Risby

Welnetham

Long Melford
Goods

Glemsford
Cavendish
Clare

Sudbury

Great Yeldham

Sible and
Castle Hedingham

Halstead
Earls Colne
White Colne

23

1   2   3   4   5   6   7   8   9

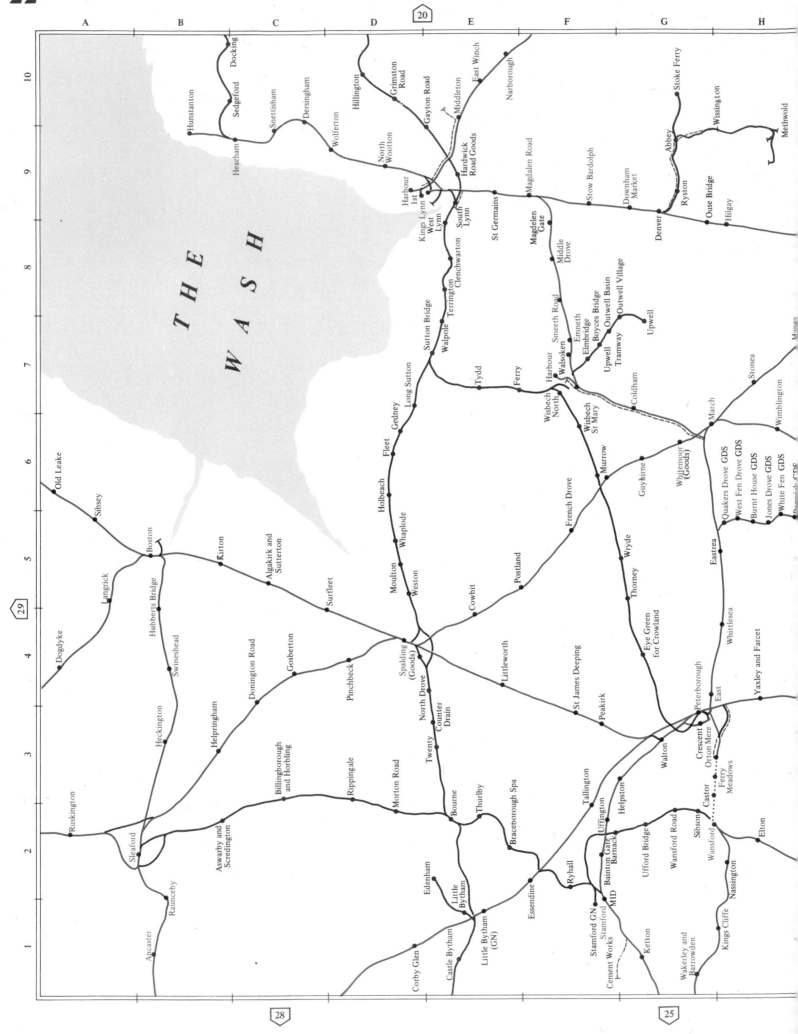

A B C D E F G H

THE
WASH

Hunstanton
Docking
Sedgeford
Snettisham
Heacham
Dersingham
Wolferton
Hillington
North Wootton
Grimston Road
Gayton Road
Middleton
East Winch
Narborough
Stoke Ferry
Abbey
Wissington
Methwold

Hardwick Road Goods
Magdalen Road
Stow Bardolph
Downham Market
Ryston
Ouse Bridge
Hilgay

Harbour 1st
Kings Lynn
West Lynn
South Lynn
St Germains
Magdelen Gate
Denver

Clenchwarton
Terrington
Middle Drove
Walpole
Sutton Bridge
Smeeth Road
Emneth
Elmbridge
Boyces Bridge
Outwell Basin
Outwell Village
Upwell Tramway
Upwell

Long Sutton
Tydd
Ferry
Wisbech Harbour
Walsoken
Coldham
Stonea

Gedney
Wisbech North
Wisbech St Mary
Whittlesea
Wimblington
March

Fleet
Holbeach
Whaplode
Murrow
Guyhirne
Whitemoor (Goods)
Quakers Drove GDS
West Fen Drove GDS
Burnt House GDS
Jones Drove GDS
White Fen GDS

Old Leake
Sibsey
Boston
Kirton
Algakirk and Sutterton
Surfleet
Moulton
Weston
French Drove
Thorney
Wryde
Eastrea

Langrick
Hubberts Bridge
Swineshead
Donington Road
Gosberton
Pinchbeck
Spalding (Goods)
Cowbit
Postland
Littleworth
Eye Green for Crowland
Whittlesea
Peterborough
East
Yaxley and Farcet

Dogdyke
Heckington
Helpringham
North Drove
Counter Drain
Twenty
St James Deeping
Peakirk
Walton
Crescent
Orton Mere
Ferry Meadows

Ruskington
Sleaford
Aswarby and Scredington
Billingborough and Horbling
Rippingale
Morton Road
Bourne
Thurlby
Braceborough Spa
Tallington
Uffington
Helpston
Castor
Sibson
Wansford
Elton

Ancaster
Rauceby
Corby Glen
Edenham
Little Bytham
Essendine
Ryhall
Bainton Gate
Barnack
Ufford Bridge
Wansford Road
Nassington

Castle Bytham
Little Bytham (GN)
Stamford GN
Stamford MID
Stamford Cement Works
Ketton
Wakerley and Barrowden
Kings Cliffe

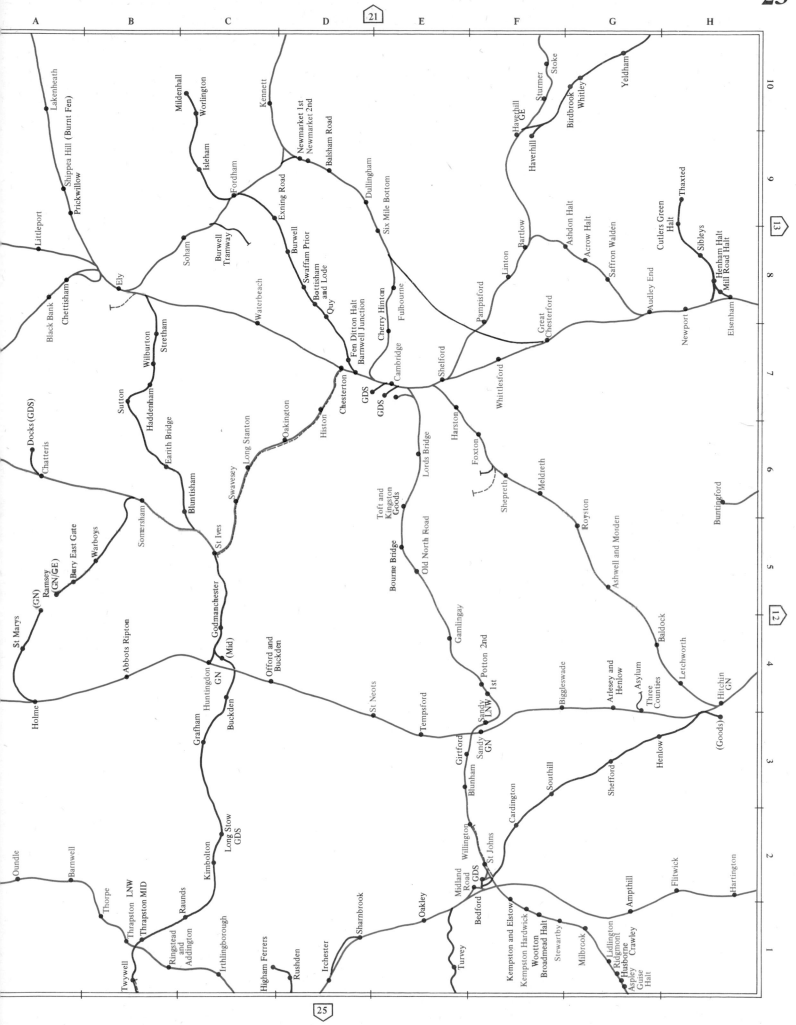

21
13
12
25

A   B   C   D   E   F   G   H

10   9   8   7   6   5   4   3   2   1

Lakenheath
Shippea Hill (Burnt Fen)
Prickwillow
Littleport
Black Bank
Chettisham
Ely
Docks (GDS)
Chatteris
St Marys (GN)
Ramsey (GN/GE)
Bury East Gate
Warboys
Somersham
Holme
Abbots Ripton
Grafham
Huntingdon GN
Godmanchester (Mid)
Buckden
Offord and Buckden
Kimbolton
Long Stow GDS
Oundle
Barnwell
Thorpe
Thrapston LNW
Thrapston MID
Ringstead and Addington
Raunds
Irthlingborough
Higham Ferrers
Rushden
Irchester
Sharnbrook
St Neots
Oakley
Turvey
Midland Road
Bedford
St Johns GDS
Willington
Blunham
Girtford
Sandy GN
Sandy LNW
Tempsford
Cardington
Southill
Shefford
Henlow
Hitchin GN
(Goods)
Letchworth
Baldock
Ashwell and Morden
Royston
Buntingford
Meldreth
Shepreth
Foxton
Harston
Lords Bridge
Old North Road
Toft and Kingston Goods
Bourne Bridge
Gamlingay
Potton 2nd
1st
Biggleswade
Arlesey and Henlow
Asylum
Three Counties
Flitwick
Hartington
Ampthill
Lidlington
Ridgmont
Husborne Crawley
Aspley Guise Halt
Millbrook
Stewartby
Wootton Broadmead Halt
Kempston Hardwick
Kempston and Elstow
Histon
Oakington
Long Stanton
Swavesey
St Ives
Bluntisham
Earith Bridge
Sutton
Haddenham
Wilburton
Stretham
Soham
Mildenhall
Worlington
Isleham
Fordham
Kennett
Newmarket 1st
Newmarket 2nd
Balsham Road
Exning Road
Burwell Tramway
Burwell
Swaffam Prior
Bottisham and Lode
Quy
Waterbeach
Fen Ditton Halt
Barnwell Junction
Cherry Hinton
Fulbourne
Dullingham
Six Mile Bottom
Chesterton GDS
GDS
Cambridge
Shelford
Whittlesford
Pampisford
Linton
Bartlow
Great Chesterford
Audley End
Newport
Elsenham
Saffron Walden
Acrow Halt
Ashdon Halt
Bardbrook
Whitley
Yeldham
Sturmer
Stoke
Haverhill GE
Haverhill
Cutlers Green Halt
Thaxted
Sibleys
Henham Halt
Mill Road Halt

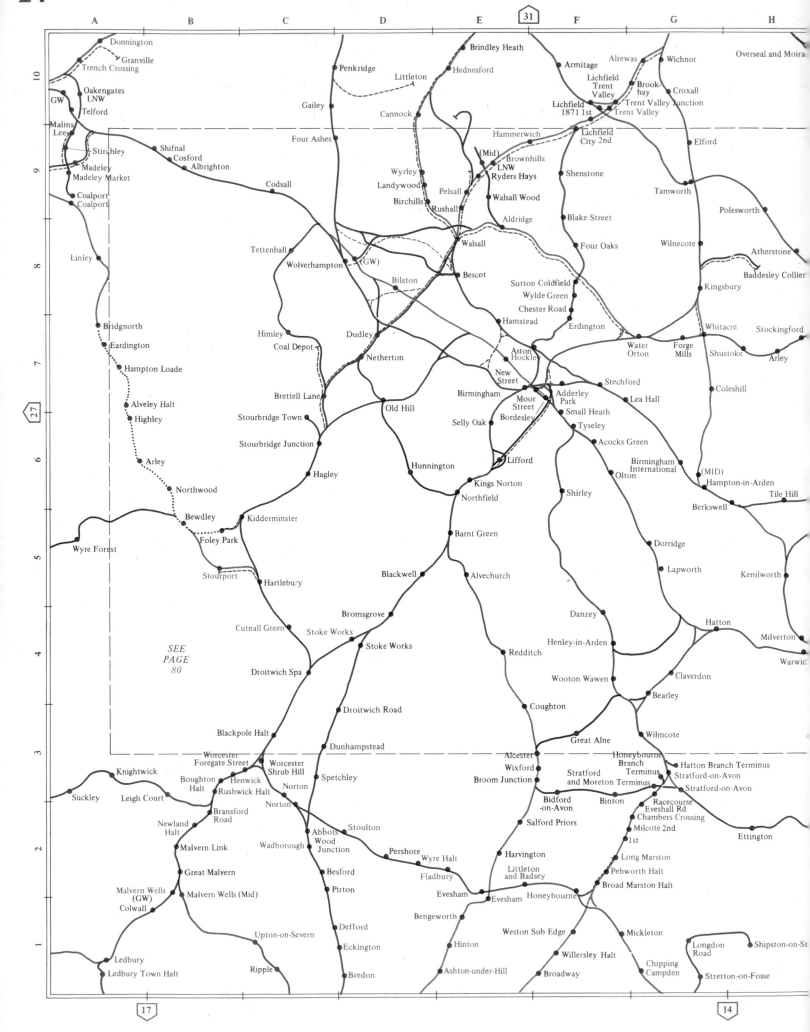

A · B · C · D · E · 31 · F · G · H

Donnington
Granville
Trench Crossing
Oakengates
LNW
GW
Telford
Malins
Lee
Stirchley
Shifnal
Cosford
Madeley
Madeley Market
Albrighton
Coalport
Coalport
Codsall

Penkridge
Littleton
Gailey
Cannock
Four Ashes

Brindley Heath
Hednesford
Armitage
Alrewas
Wichnor
Overseal and Moira
Lichfield
Trent Valley
Brook-
hay
Croxall
Lichfield
1871 1st
Trent Valley Junction
Trent Valley
Hammerwich
Lichfield
City 2nd
Elford

Linley
Bridgnorth
Eardington
Hampton Loade
Alveley Halt
Highley
Arley
Northwood
Bewdley
Foley Park
Wyre Forest
Stourport
Hartlebury

Tettenhall
Wolverhampton
(GW)
Himley
Coal Depot
Dudley
Netherton
Brettell Lane
Stourbridge Town
Stourbridge Junction
Hagley
Kidderminster

Wyrley
Landywood
Birchills
(Mid)
Pelsall
Rushall
Aldridge
Walsall
Bescot
Bilston

Brownhills
LNW
Ryders Hays
Walsall Wood
Shenstone
Blake Street
Four Oaks
Sutton Coldfield
Wylde Green
Chester Road
Hamstead
Erdington
Aston
Hockley
New
Street
Birmingham
Moor
Street
Bordesley
Selly Oak
Lifford

Tamworth
Polesworth
Wilnecote
Atherstone
Baddesley Collier
Kingsbury
Whitacre
Stockingford
Water
Orton
Forge
Mills
Shustoke
Arley
Stechford
Adderley
Park
Small Heath
Lea Hall
Coleshill
Tyseley
Acocks Green
Birmingham
International
Olton
(MID)
Hampton-in-Arden
Tile Hill
Berkswell

Hunnington
Kings Norton
Northfield
Barnt Green
Blackwell
Alvechurch
Bromsgrove
Cutnall Green
Stoke Works
Stoke Works
Droitwich Spa

Shirley
Dorridge
Lapworth
Kenilworth
Danzey
Henley-in-Arden
Redditch
Wooton Wawen
Claverdon
Bearley
Hatton
Milverton
Warwic

SEE
PAGE
80

Droitwich Road
Blackpole Halt
Worcester
Foregate Street
Knightwick
Boughton
Halt
Henwick
Rushwick Halt
Bransford
Road
Newland
Halt
Malvern Link
Great Malvern
Malvern Wells
(GW)
Malvern Wells (Mid)
Colwall
Ledbury
Ledbury Town Halt

Dunhampstead
Worcester
Shrub Hill
Spetchley
Norton
Norton
Wadborough
Abbots
Wood
Junction
Stoulton
Besford
Pirton
Ripple
Upton-on-Severn
Defford
Eckington
Bredon

Coughton
Great Alne
Alcester
Wixford
Broom Junction
Bidford
-on-Avon
Salford Priors
Pershore
Wyre Halt
Fladbury
Evesham
Bengeworth
Hinton
Ashton-under-Hill
Harvington
Littleton
and Badsey
Evesham
Honeybourne
Weston Sub Edge
Willersley Halt
Broadway

Wilmcote
Honeybourne
Branch
Terminus
Stratford
and Moreton Terminus
Binton
Hatton Branch Terminus
Stratford-on-Avon
Stratford-on-Avon
Racecourse
Eveshall Rd
Chambers Crossing
Milcote 2nd
1st
Long Marston
Pebworth Halt
Broad Marston Halt
Ettington
Mickleton
Chipping
Campden
Longdon
Road
Shipston-on-St
Stretton-on-Fosse

Suckley
Leigh Court

27

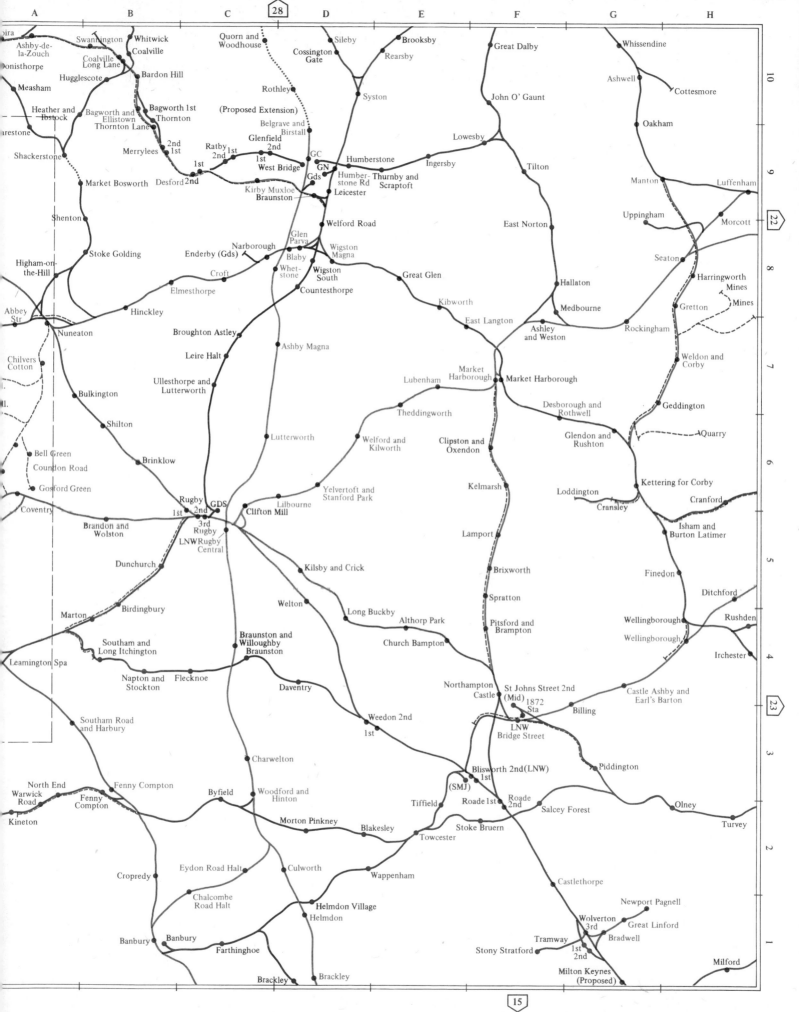

A   B   C   D   E   F   G   H

28

Moira
Ashby-de-la-Zouch
Donisthorpe
Measham
Swannington
Whitwick
Coalville
Long Lane
Coalville
Bardon Hill
Hugglescote
Bagworth 1st
Heather and Ibstock
Bagworth and Ellistown
Thornton Lane
Thornton
Moreston
Quorn and Woodhouse
Sileby
Brooksby
Great Dalby
Whissendine
Ashwell
Cottesmore
Rothley
Cossington Gate
Rearsby
(Proposed Extension)
Belgrave and Birstall
John O' Gaunt
Oakham
Shackerstone
Merrylees
2nd 1st
Ratby 1st
2nd
Glenfield 2nd
1st
West Bridge
GC
Humberstone
Syston
Lowesby
Tilton
Manton
Luffenham
Market Bosworth
Desford 2nd
Kirby Muxloe
Braunston
GN
Gds
Humber-stone Rd
Thurnby and Scraptoft
Leicester
Ingersby
East Norton
Uppingham
Morcott
22
Shenton
Welford Road
Seaton
Higham-on-the-Hill
Stoke Golding
Narborough
Enderby (Gds)
Glen Parva
Blaby
Whet-stone
Wigston Magna
Wigston South
Great Glen
Hallaton
Medbourne
Harringworth Mines
Mines
Abbey Str
Croft
Countesthorpe
Kibworth
Rockingham
Gretton
Nuneaton
Hinckley
Elmesthorpe
East Langton
Ashley and Weston
Weldon and Corby
Chilvers Cotton
Broughton Astley
Ashby Magna
Market Harborough
Market Harborough
Glendon and Rushton
Geddington
Leire Halt
Lubenham
Desborough and Rothwell
Quarry
Bulkington
Ullesthorpe and Lutterworth
Theddingworth
Kettering for Corby
Shilton
Lutterworth
Welford and Kilworth
Clipston and Oxendon
Glendon and Rushton
Bell Green
Coundon Road
Brinklow
Yelvertoft and Stanford Park
Kelmarsh
Loddington
Cransley
Cranford
Gosford Green
Rugby
1st 2nd
GDS
Lilbourne
Clifton Mill
Isham and Burton Latimer
Coventry
Brandon and Wolston
3rd Rugby
LNW Rugby Central
Kilsby and Crick
Lamport
Brixworth
Finedon
Ditchford
Dunchurch
Welton
Long Buckby
Althorp Park
Spratton
Wellingborough
Rushden
Marton
Birdingbury
Braunston and Willoughby
Braunston
Church Bampton
Pitsford and Brampton
Wellingborough
Leamington Spa
Southam and Long Itchington
Napton and Stockton
Flecknoe
Daventry
Northampton Castle
St Johns Street 2nd (Mid)
1872 Sta
Castle Ashby and Earl's Barton
Irchester
23
Southam Road and Harbury
Weedon 2nd
1st
Billing
LNW Bridge Street
Charwelton
Blisworth 2nd (LNW)
1st
(SMJ)
Piddington
North End Warwick Road
Fenny Compton
Byfield
Woodford and Hinton
Tiffield
Roade 1st
Roade 2nd
Salcey Forest
Olney
Kineton
Fenny Compton
Morton Pinkney
Blakesley
Stoke Bruern
Towcester
Turvey
Cropredy
Eydon Road Halt
Culworth
Wappenham
Castlethorpe
Chalcombe Road Halt
Helmdon Village
Newport Pagnell
Wolverton 3rd
Great Linford
Banbury
Banbury
Helmdon
Tramway
1st 2nd
Bradwell
Stony Stratford
Farthinghoe
Milton Keynes (Proposed)
Milford
Brackley
Brackley

15

A 32 B C D E F 33 G H

Llanaber
Barmouth Penmaenpool Dolgelly
Penryn Point
Golf Club Halt Arthog
Beach Halt Morfa Mawddach
Fairbourne
Fairbourne
Llwyngwril
Nant Gwernol
Quarry
Aberllefeni
Llangelynin Garneddwen
Halt Abergynolwyn Corris
Quarry Siding Quarry Esgairgeiliog
Tonfanau Brynglas Dolgoch Falls Lliwdy
Cynfal Tynyllwyn Dolwyddelen Llwyngwern
Rhydyronen Ffridd Gate
Fach Goch
Hendre Halt Machynlleth
Pendre (Corris)
Tywyn Wharf Machynlleth
Gogarth (CAM)
Abertafol Dovey Junction
2nd Penhelig
Aberdovey Glandyfi
Aberdovey GDS 1st

Dinas Mawddwy
Mallwyd
Aberangell
Cemmaes
Cemmaes Road
Cemmaes Llanbrynmair
Road Comins Coch
Halt
Talerddig
Carno
Pontdolgoch
Caersws Scafell
Trewythan GDS Moat Lane
Red House Junction
Trefeglwys
Van Garth Road Cerist Llandinam
Dolwen
Llanidloes
Tylwch
Glan-yr-Afon Halt
Pantydwr
St Harmons Halt
Marteg Halt
Rhayader
Doldowlod
Llandrindod Wells

Heniar
Halt
Dolrhr
Llanfair Mill
Caereinion

Ynys-Las
Borth
Pontgeifr Mines
Talybont (Pen Rhiw)
Llandre
Bow Street
Aberystwyth Glanrafon
Aberystwyth Lovesgrove Halt
2nd 1st Llanbadarn Rheidol Falls
Capel Bangor Rhiwfron
Nantyronen Aberffrwd
Llanrhystyd Road Devils Bridge
Llanilar
Felindyffryn Halt
Trawscoed
Caradog Falls Halt
Strata Florida
Alltddu Halt
Tregarron
Ciliau Aeron Halt Pont Llanio
Felin Fach
19 Blaenplwyf Halt Olmarch Halt
Talsarn Halt
Silian Halt Llangybi
Derry Ormond
Lampeter

Newbridge-on-Wye
Builth Road
Builth Road
Builth Wells
Cilmery
Llanfaredd Halt
Garth
Aberedw
Llangammarch Wells
Llanwrtyd Wells
Sugar Loaf Summit Halt
(Unadvertised)
Cynghordy Erwood

Llanybyther

CARDIGAN BAY

19 16

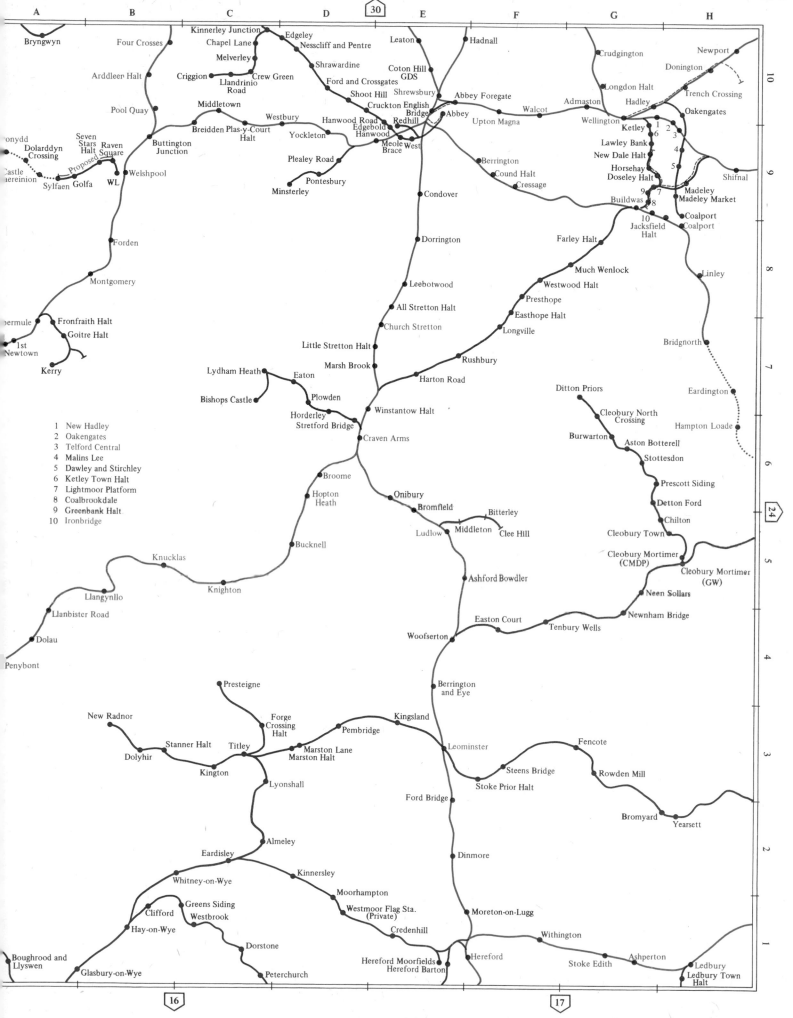

30

A B C D E F G H

Bryngwyn
Four Crosses
Kinnerley Junction
Chapel Lane
Edgeley
Nesscliff and Pentre
Leaton
Hadnall
Newport
Crudgington
Donington
Melverley
Arddleen Halt
Criggion
Crew Green
Shrawardine
Longdon Halt
Trench Crossing
Llandrinio
Road
Ford and Crossgates
Coton Hill
GDS
Admaston
Hadley
Oakengates
Middletown
Shoot Hill
Shrewsbury
Abbey Foregate
Wellington
Ketley
Shifnal
Pool Quay
Breidden Plas-y-Court
Halt
Westbury
Cruckton English
Bridge
Abbey
Walcot
Lawley Bank
New Dale Halt
Buttington
Junction
Yockleton
Hanwood Road
Edgebold
Redhill
Upton Magna
Horsehay
Doseley Halt
onydd
Dolarddyn
Crossing
Seven
Stars
Halt
Raven
Square
Hanwood
Meole
West
Brace
Berrington
Cound Halt
Cressage
Madeley
Madeley Market
Castle
Caereinion
Sylfaen
Proposed
Golfa
WL
Welshpool
Pontesbury
Plealey Road
Condover
Buildwas
Jacksfield
Halt
Coalport
Coalport
Minsterley
Forden
Dorrington
Farley Halt
Linley
Montgomery
Leebotwood
Much Wenlock
ermule
Fronfraith Halt
Goitre Halt
All Stretton Halt
Westwood Halt
Bridgnorth
1st
Newtown
Church Stretton
Presthope
Easthope Halt
Eardington
Kerry
Little Stretton Halt
Longville
Hampton Loade
Lydham Heath
Eaton
Marsh Brook
Rushbury
Ditton Priors
Bishops Castle
Plowden
Harton Road
Cleobury North
Crossing
Horderley
Stretford Bridge
Winstantow Halt
Burwarton
Aston Botterell
1 New Hadley
2 Oakengates
3 Telford Central
4 Malins Lee
5 Dawley and Stirchley
6 Ketley Town Halt
7 Lightmoor Platform
8 Coalbrookdale
9 Greenbank Halt
10 Ironbridge
Craven Arms
Stottesdon
Broome
Onibury
Prescott Siding
Hopton
Heath
Bromfield
Bitterley
Detton Ford
Ludlow
Middleton
Clee Hill
Chilton
Bucknell
Cleobury Town
Knucklas
Ashford Bowdler
Cleobury Mortimer
(CMDP)
Cleobury Mortimer
(GW)
Llangynllo
Knighton
Neen Sollars
Llanbister Road
Easton Court
Newnham Bridge
Dolau
Woofserton
Tenbury Wells
Penybont
Presteigne
Berrington
and Eye
Kingsland
New Radnor
Forge
Crossing
Halt
Pembridge
Fencote
Stanner Halt
Titley
Leominster
Rowden Mill
Dolyhir
Marston Lane
Marston Halt
Steens Bridge
Kington
Stoke Prior Halt
Bromyard
Yearsett
Lyonshall
Ford Bridge
Almeley
Dinmore
Eardisley
Kinnersley
Whitney-on-Wye
Moorhampton
Greens Siding
Westbrook
Westmoor Flag Sta.
(Private)
Moreton-on-Lugg
Clifford
Credenhill
Withington
Hay-on-Wye
Ashperton
Boughrood and
Llyswen
Dorstone
Hereford Moorfields
Hereford Barton
Hereford
Stoke Edith
Ledbury
Glasbury-on-Wye
Peterchurch
Ledbury Town
Halt

16 17

24

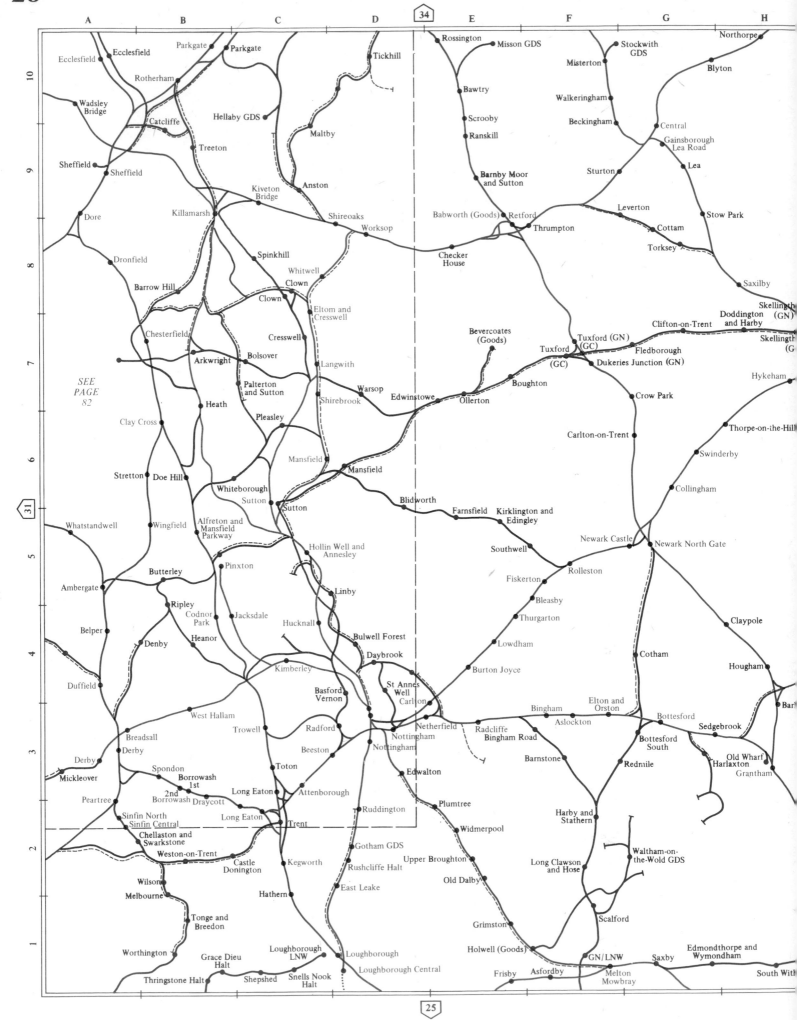

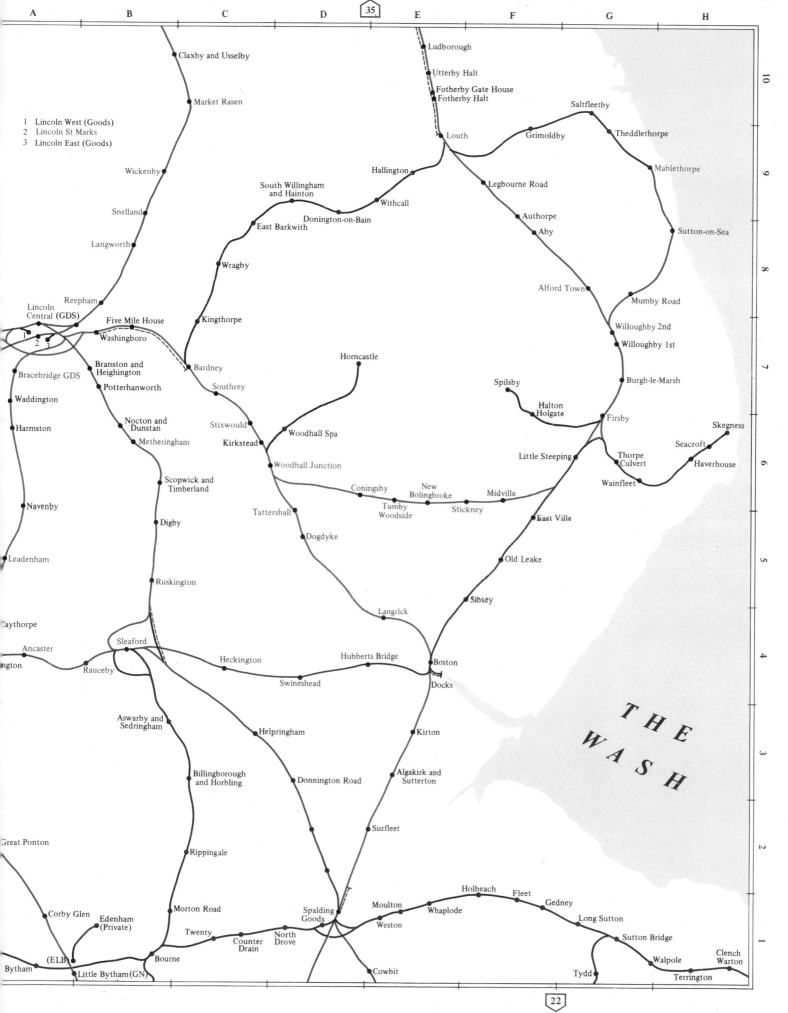

A B C D 35 E F G H

Claxby and Usselby

Ludborough

Market Rasen

Utterby Halt

Fotherby Gate House
Fotherby Halt

Saltfleetby

1 Lincoln West (Goods)
2 Lincoln St Marks
3 Lincoln East (Goods)

Louth

Grimoldby

Theddlethorpe

Wickenby

Mablethorpe

Snelland

South Willingham
and Hainton

Hallington

Legbourne Road

Withcall

Sutton-on-Sea

Langworth

Donington-on-Bain

Authorpe

East Barkwith

Aby

Reepham

Wragby

Alford Town

Mumby Road

Lincoln
Central (GDS)

Five Mile House

Kingthorpe

Washingboro

Willoughby 2nd

Willoughby 1st

Branston and
Heighington

Bardney

Horncastle

Bracebridge GDS

Southrey

Spilsby

Burgh-le-Marsh

Potterhanworth

Waddington

Halton
Holgate

Firsby

Skegness

Harmston

Nocton and
Dunstan

Stixwould

Woodhall Spa

Seacroft

Metheringham

Kirkstead

Little Steeping

Thorpe
Culvert

Haverhouse

Navenby

Scopwick and
Timberland

Woodhall Junction

Coningsby

New
Bolingbroke

Midville

Wainfleet

Digby

Tattershall

Tumby
Woodside

Stickney

Leadenham

Dogdyke

East Ville

Ruskington

Old Leake

Langrick

Sibsey

Caythorpe

Sleaford

ington

Ancaster

Raceby

Heckington

Hubberts Bridge

Boston

Docks

Swineshead

Aswarby and
Sedringham

Helpringham

Kirton

Billingborough
and Horbling

Donnington Road

Algakirk and
Sutterton

Great Ponton

Surfleet

Rippingale

Holbeach

Fleet

Corby Glen

Morton Road

Gedney

Edenham
(Private)

Spalding
Goods

Moulton

Whaplode

Long Sutton

Twenty

Weston

Counter
Drain

North
Drove

Sutton Bridge

Bourne

Clench
Warton

(ELB)

Walpole

Bytham

Little Bytham (GN)

Cowbit

Tydd

Terrington

THE
WASH

22

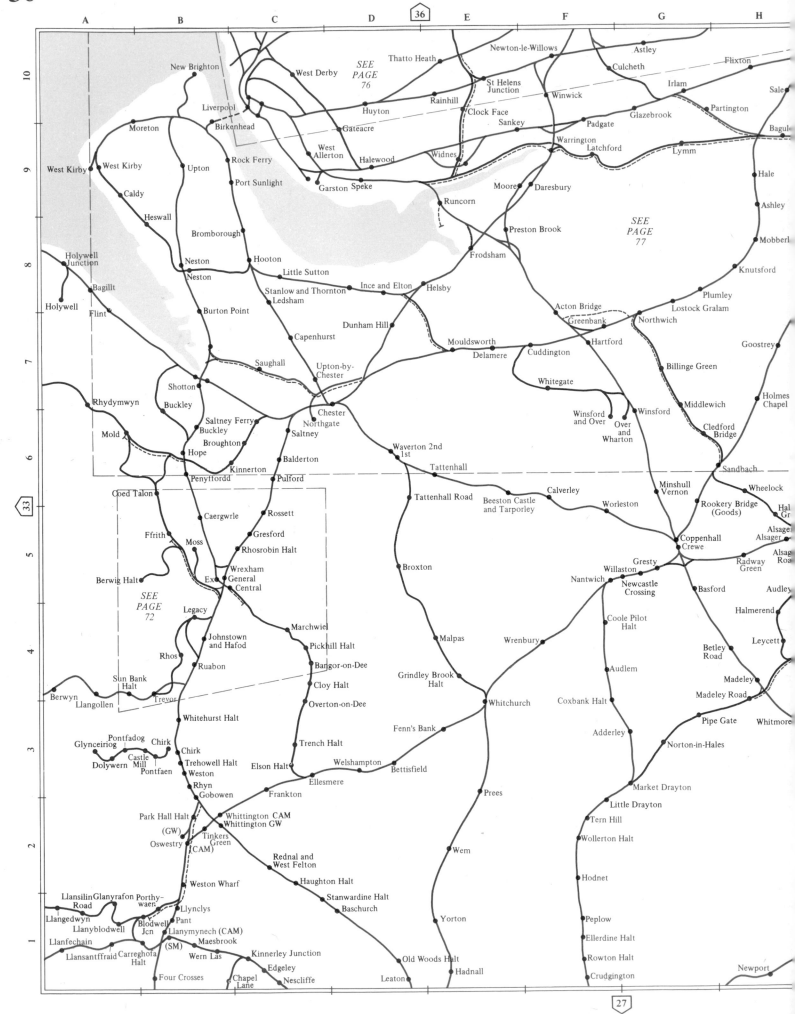

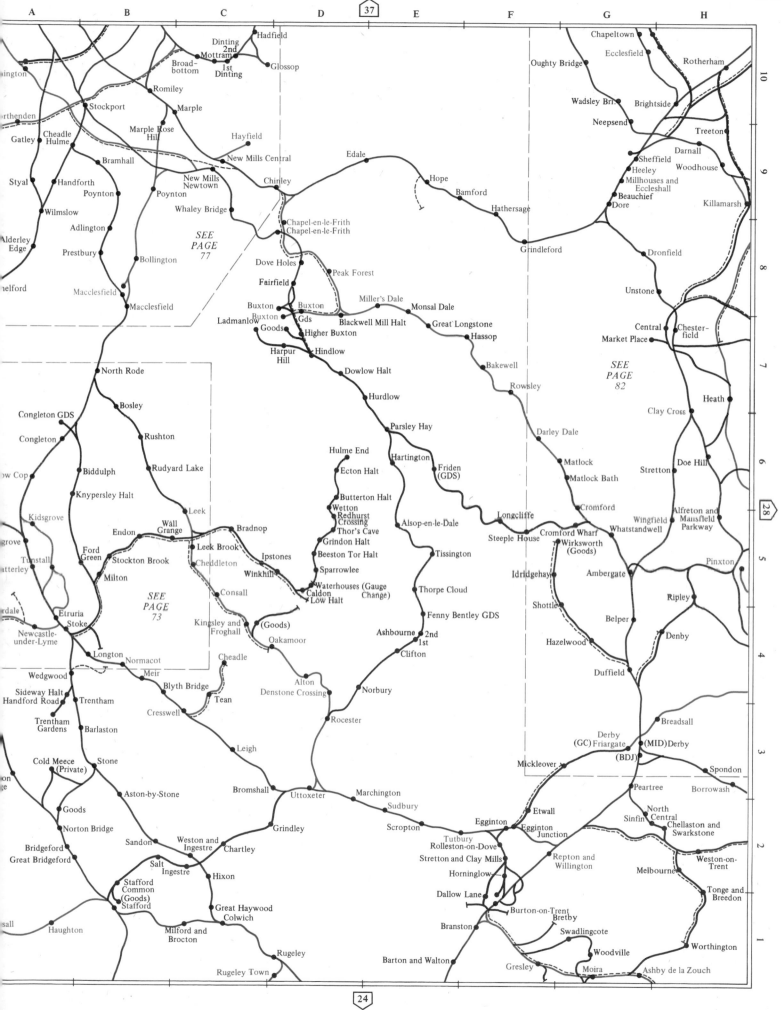

37

A B C D E F G H

Chapeltown
Ecclesfield
Oughty Bridge
Rotherham
Wadsley Bri.
Brightside
Neepsend
Treeton
Darnall
Sheffield
Woodhouse
Heeley
Millhouses and
Ecclesall
Beauchief
Dore
Killamarsh

Dinting
2nd
Mottram
Hadfield
Broad-
bottom
1st
Dinting
Glossop
Romiley
Marple
Stockport
Marple Rose
Hill
Hayfield
Cheadle
Hulme
Gatley
New Mills Central
Edale
Hope
Bramhall
Styal
Handforth
New Mills
Newtown
Chinley
Bamford
Poynton
Poynton
Hathersage
Wilmslow
Whaley Bridge
Adlington
Alderley
Edge
Prestbury
Bollington
Chapel-en-le-Frith
Chapel-en-le-Frith
Grindleford
Dronfield
SEE
PAGE
77
Dove Holes
helford
Macclesfield
Macclesfield
Fairfield
Peak Forest
Unstone
Buxton
Buxton
Miller's Dale
Monsal Dale
Central
Chester-
field
Buxton
Gds
Ladmanlow
Goods
Blackwell Mill Halt
Great Longstone
Market Place
Higher Buxton
Hassop
North Rode
Harpur
Hill
Hindlow
Bakewell
SEE
PAGE
82
Bosley
Dowlow Halt
Rowsley
Heath
Rushton
Hurdlow
Clay Cross
Congleton GDS
Darley Dale
Congleton
Rudyard Lake
Parsley Hay
Matlock
Doe Hill
ow Cop
Biddulph
Hulme End
Stretton
Knypersley Halt
Hartington
Matlock Bath
Ecton Halt
Friden
(GDS)
Kidsgrove
Leek
Cromford
Alfreton and
Mansfield
Parkway
Butterton Halt
Longcliffe
Wingfield
Endon
Wall
Grange
Bradnop
Wetton
Redhurst
Crossing
Alsop-en-le-Dale
Steeple House
Whatstandwell
grove
Ford
Green
Leek Brook
Thor's Cave
Cromford Wharf
Cheddleton
Ipstones
Grindon Halt
Wirksworth
(Goods)
Pinxton
Tunstall
atterley
Stockton Brook
Beeston Tor Halt
Tissington
Idridgehay
Ambergate
Milton
Winkhill
Sparrowlee
Thorpe Cloud
rdale
Consall
Waterhouses (Gauge
Change)
Shottle
Ripley
Etruria
Stoke
SEE
PAGE
73
Caldon
Low Halt
Thorpe Cloud
Belper
Denby
Kingsley and
Froghall
Fenny Bentley GDS
Hazelwood
Newcastle-
under-Lyme
(Goods)
Ashbourne
2nd
Longton
Oakamoor
1st
Duffield
Wedgwood
Normacot
Cheadle
Clifton
Meir
Sideway Halt
Handford Road
Blyth Bridge
Alton
Denstone Crossing
Norbury
Breadsall
Trentham
Tean
Derby
(GC) Friargate
(MID) Derby
Trentham
Gardens
Cresswell
Rocester
Mickleover
(BDJ)
Barlaston
Spondon
Leigh
Peartree
Borrowash
Cold Meece
(Private)
Stone
North
Central
Aston-by-Stone
Bromshall
Uttoxeter
Marchington
Sinfin
Chellaston and
Swarkstone
Goods
Sudbury
Etwall
Norton Bridge
Grindley
Scropton
Egginton
Melbourne
Sandon
Weston and
Ingestre
Chartley
Egginton
Junction
Repton and
Willington
Bridgeford
Great Bridgeford
Salt
Hixon
Tutbury
Rolleston-on-Dove
Weston-on-
Trent
Ingestre
Stretton and Clay Mills
Stafford
Common
(Goods)
Stafford
Horninglow
Tonge and
Breedon
Great Haywood
Colwich
Dallow Lane
Burton-on-Trent
Bretby
sall
Haughton
Milford and
Brocton
Branston
Swadlingcote
Worthington
Rugeley
Woodville
Rugeley Town
Barton and Walton
Gresley
Moira
Ashby de la Zouch

10

9

8

7

6

5

4

3

2

1

28

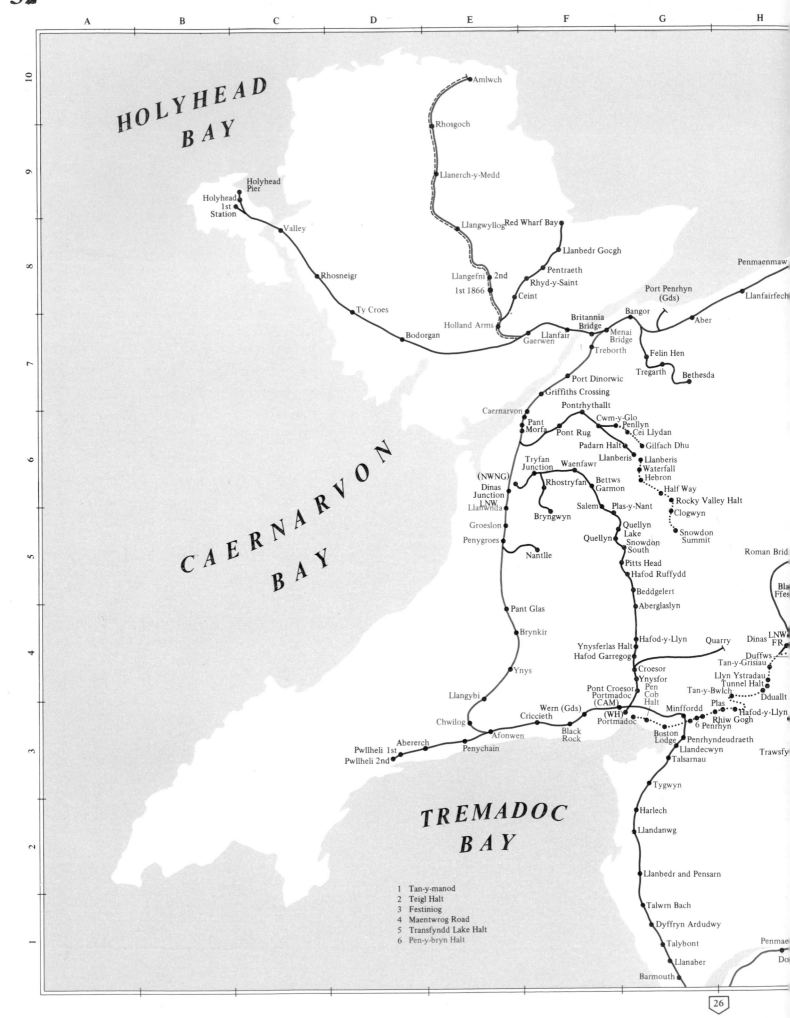

HOLYHEAD
BAY

Amlwch

Rhosgoch

Llanerch-y-Medd

Llangwyllog · Red Wharf Bay

Holyhead
Pier
Holyhead
1st
Station

Valley

Llanbedr Gocgh

Pentraeth

Rhosneigr

Rhyd-y-Saint

Llangefni 2nd
1st 1866

Ceint

Ty Croes

Holland Arms

Britannia
Bridge

Bangor

Port Penrhyn
(Gds)

Penmaenmaw

Llanfairfech

Bodorgan

Llanfair

Gaerwen

Menai
Bridge

Treborth

Aber

Felin Hen

Tregarth

Bethesda

CAERNARVON

BAY

Port Dinorwic

Griffiths Crossing

Pontrhythallt

Caernarvon

Cwm-y-Glo

Penllyn

Pant
Morfa

Cei Llydan

Pont Rug

Gilfach Dhu

Padarn Halt

Tryfan
Junction

Waenfawr

Llanberis

Llanberis

Waterfall

Hebron

Bettws
Garmon

(NWNG)
Dinas
Junction
LNW

Rhostryfan

Half Way

Rocky Valley Halt

Llanwnda

Salem

Plas-y-Nant

Clogwyn

Groeslon

Bryngwyn

Snowdon
Summit

Penygroes

Quellyn

Quellyn
Lake
Snowdon
South

Roman Brid

Nantlle

Pitts Head

Bla
Ffes

Hafod Ruffydd

Beddgelert

Pant Glas

Aberglaslyn

Brynkir

Hafod-y-Llyn

Quarry

Dinas

LNW
FR

Ynysferlas Halt

Ynys

Hafod Garregog

Duffws
Tan-y-Grisiau

Croesor
Ynysfor

Llyn Ystradau
Tunnel Halt

Llangybi

Pont Croesor
Portmadoc
(CAM)

Pen
Cob
Halt

Tan-y-Bwlch

Plas

Dduallt

Hafod-y-Llyn

Wern (Gds)

Minffordd

Chwilog

Criccieth

(WH)
Portmadoc

Rhiw Gogh

6 Penrhyn

Abererch

Afonwen

Black
Rock

Boston
Lodge

Penrhyndeudraeth

Pwllheli 1st
Pwllheli 2nd

Penychain

Llandecwyn

Trawsfy

Talsarnau

TREMADOC
BAY

Tygwyn

Harlech

Llandanwg

Llanbedr and Pensarn

1 Tan-y-manod
2 Teigl Halt
3 Festiniog
4 Maentwrog Road
5 Transfyndd Lake Halt
6 Pen-y-bryn Halt

Talwrn Bach

Dyffryn Ardudwy

Talybont

Penmae

Do

Llanaber

Barmouth

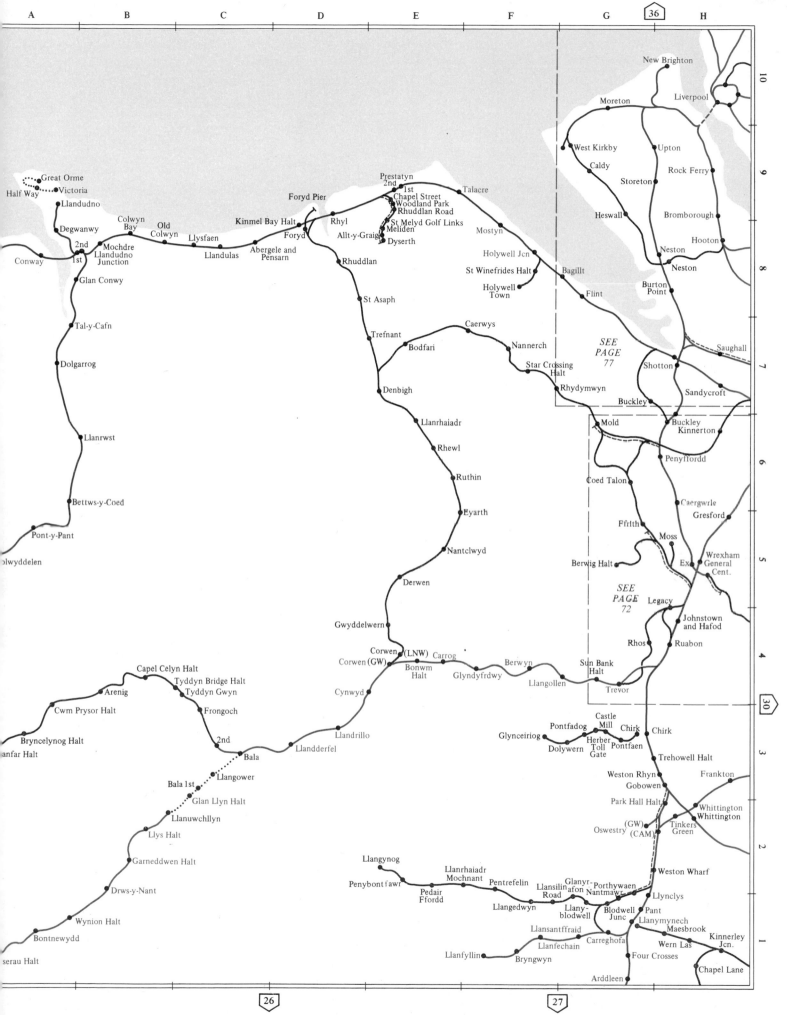

A   B   C   D   E   F   G   36   H

New Brighton
Moreton
Liverpool
West Kirkby
Caldy
Upton
Rock Ferry
Storeton
Heswall
Bromborough
Great Orme
Victoria
Half Way
Llandudno
Prestatyn
2nd
1st
Chapel Street
Woodland Park
Rhuddlan Road
St Melyd Golf Links
Meliden
Allt-y-Graig
Dyserth
Talacre
Hooton
Colwyn
Bay
Old
Colwyn
Llysfaen
Foryd Pier
Kinmel Bay Halt
Foryd
Rhyl
Mostyn
Degwanwy
Neston
Neston
Mochdre
2nd
Llandudno
Junction
Llandulas
Abergele and
Pensarn
Holywell Jcn
Bagillt
Burton
Point
Conway
1st
Glan Conwy
Rhuddlan
St Winefrides Halt
Holywell
Town
Flint
Tal-y-Cafn
St Asaph
Caerwys
SEE
PAGE
77
Saughall
Dolgarrog
Trefnant
Bodfari
Nannerch
Star Crossing
Halt
Rhydymwyn
Shotton
Llanrwst
Denbigh
Buckley
Sandycroft
Bettws-y-Coed
Llanrhaiadr
Mold
Buckley
Kinnerton
Pont-y-Pant
Rhewl
Coed Talon
Penyffordd
olwyddelen
Ruthin
Caergwrle
Gresford
Eyarth
Ffrlth
Berwig Halt
Moss
Wrexham
General
Cent.
Nantclwyd
Ex
SEE
PAGE
72
Derwen
Legacy
Gwyddelwern
Rhos
Johnstown
and Hafod
Ruabon
Capel Celyn Halt
Corwen (LNW)
Corwen (GW)
Carrog
Berwyn
Sun Bank
Halt
Tyddyn Bridge Halt
Tyddyn Gwyn
Bonwm
Halt
Glyndyfrdwy
Llangollen
Trevor
30
Arenig
Frongoch
Cynwyd
Castle
Mill
Chirk
Cwm Prysor Halt
2nd
Llandrillo
Pontfadog
Herber
Toll
Gate
Chirk
Bryncelynog Halt
Bala
Llandderfel
Glynceiriog
Pontfaen
anfar Halt
Bala 1st
Llangower
Dolywern
Trehowell Halt
Glan Llyn Halt
Weston Rhyn
Frankton
Llanuwchllyn
Gobowen
Llys Halt
Park Hall Halt
Whittington
Whittington
Garneddwen Halt
(GW)
Oswestry
(CAM)
Tinkers
Green
Llangynog
Weston Wharf
Drws-y-Nant
Llanrhaiadr
Mochnant
Pentrefelin
Glanyr-
afon
Porthywaen
Nantmawr
Llynclys
Wynion Halt
Penybontfawr
Pedair
Ffordd
Llansilin
Road
Llany-
blodwell
Blodwell
Junc
Pant
Bontnewydd
Llangedwyn
Llanymynech
Maesbrook
serau Halt
Llansantffraid
Carreghofa
Wern Las
Kinnerley
Jcn.
Llanfyllin
Llanfechain
Four Crosses
Bryngwyn
Chapel Lane
Arddleen
26   27

10
9
8
7
6
5
4
3
2
1

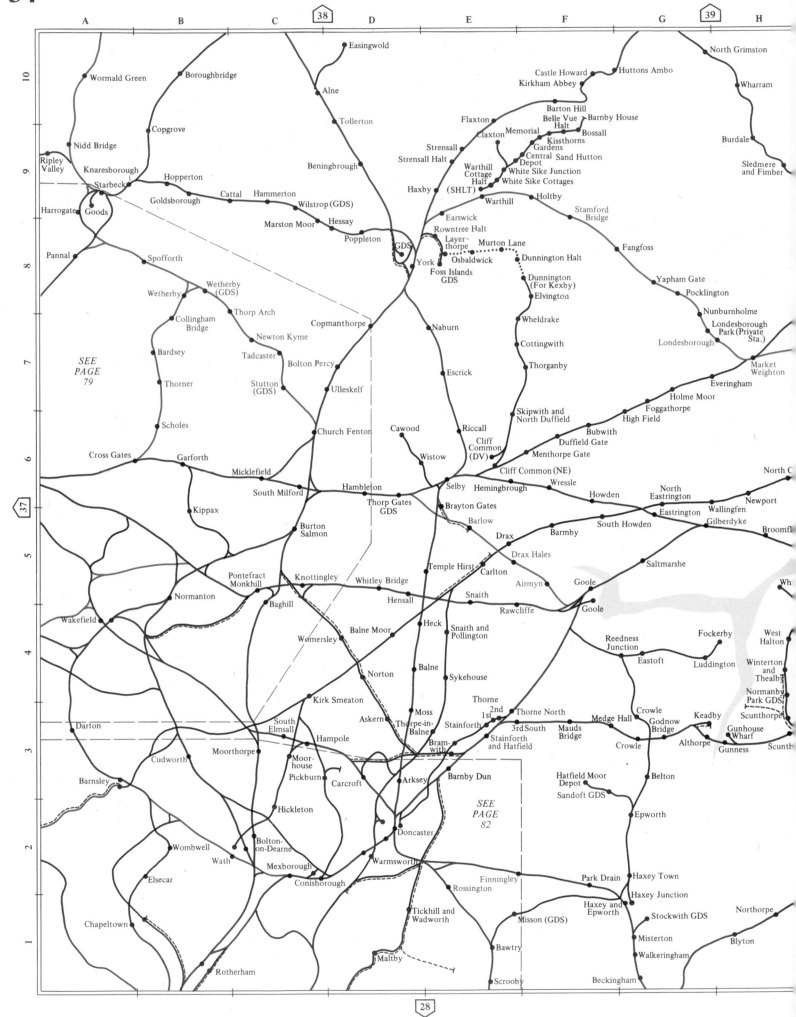

A   B   38   C   D   E   F   G   39   H

North Grimston
Wormald Green   Boroughbridge   Easingwold   Castle Howard   Huttons Ambo
Kirkham Abbey   Wharram
Copgrove   Alne   Barton Hill   Barnby House   Burdale
Nidd Bridge   Tollerton   Flaxton   Belle Vue Halt   Bossall
Memorial   Kissthorns   Sledmere and Fimber
Ripley Valley   Beningbrough   Claxton   Gardens   Central Sand Hutton
Knaresborough   Hopperton   Strensall   Depot
Starbeck   Cattal   Hammerton   Strensall Halt   White Sike Junction
Goldsborough   Wilstrop (GDS)   Warthill Cottage Halt   White Sike Cottages
Harrogate   Goods   Haxby   (SHLT)
Marston Moor   Hessay   Warthill   Holtby
Pannal   Poppleton   Earswick   Stamford Bridge   Fangfoss
Spofforth   GDS   Rowntree Halt   Murton Lane   Yapham Gate
Layer-thorpe   Osbaldwick   Dunnington Halt   Pocklington
Wetherby (GDS)   York   Dunnington (For Kexby)   Nunburnholme
Wetherby   Foss Islands GDS   Elvington   Londesborough Park (Private Sta.)
Thorp Arch   Copmanthorpe   Naburn   Wheldrake   Londesborough
Collingham Bridge   Newton Kyme   Cottingwith
SEE PAGE 79   Bardsey   Tadcaster   Escrick   Thorganby   Market Weighton
Thorner   Bolton Percy   Everingham
Stutton (GDS)   Ulleskelf   Skipwith and North Duffield   Holme Moor
Scholes   Riccall   Foggathorpe   High Field
Cross Gates   Garforth   Church Fenton   Cawood   Cliff Common (DV)   Bubwith   Duffield Gate
Wistow   Menthorpe Gate
Micklefield   Cliff Common (NE)   North C
South Milford   Hambleton   Selby   Wressle   Howden   North Eastrington   Newport
Kippax   Thorp Gates GDS   Hemingbrough   Eastrington   Wallingfen   Gilberdyke
Brayton Gates   Barlow   South Howden   Broomf
Wakefield   Burton Salmon   Drax   Barmby
Normanton   Drax Hales   Saltmarshe
Pontefract Monkhill   Knottingley   Whitley Bridge   Temple Hirst   Carlton   Airmyn   Goole
Baghill   Hensall   Snaith   Goole
Womersley   Balne Moor   Heck   Snaith and Pollington   Rawcliffe   Reedness Junction   Fockerby   West Halt
Darton   Norton   Balne   Sykehouse   Eastoft   Luddington   Winterton and Thealby
Kirk Smeaton   Thorne 2nd   Thorne North   Crowle   Normanby Park GDS
Cudworth   South Elmsall   Askern   Moss   Thorpe-in-Balne   Stainforth 1st   Medge Hall   Godnow Bridge   Keadby   Gunhouse Wharf   Scunthorpe
Hampole   Bramwith   3rd South   Mauds Bridge   Gunness   Scunth
Moorthorpe   Stainforth and Hatfield   Crowle   Althorpe
Moorhouse   Carcroft   Arksey   Barnby Dun   Hatfield Moor Depot   Belton
Barnsley   Pickburn   SEE PAGE 82   Sandoft GDS
Hickleton   Epworth
Wombwell   Bolton-on-Dearne   Doncaster   Park Drain   Haxey Town
Wath   Mexborough   Warmsworth   Finningley   Haxey Junction
Elsecar   Conisborough   Rossington   Haxey and Epworth   Stockwith GDS   Northorpe
Tickhill and Wadworth   Misson (GDS)   Misterton   Blyton
Chapeltown   Bawtry   Walkeringham
Maltby   Beckingham
Rotherham   Scrooby

28

Flamborough

Bridlington

Wilsthorpe Crossing Halt

Carnaby

Lowthorpe

Wetwang

Garton

Nafferton

Driffield

Southburn

Hutton Cranswick

Bainton

Kenwick Gate (GDS)

Middleton-on-the-Wolds

Lockington

Enthorpe

Arram

Hornsea Town

Kipling Cotes

Hornsea Bridge

Cherry Burton

Wassand

Sigglesthorne

Whitedale

Beverley

Ellerby

Ellerby

Form. Burton Constable

Skirlaugh

Swine

Little Weighton

Stoneferry GDS

South Cave

Cottingham

Sutton-on-Hull

SEE PAGE 73

Willerby and Kirk Ella

Marfleet

Hedon

Hedon Racecourse

Hedon Speedway Halt

Ryhill

Brough

Hull   Hull

Ferriby   Hessle

Keyingham

Withernsea

Ottringham

Hollym Gate

New Holland Pier

Winestead

Patrington

New Holland Town

New Holland (new stn.)

nteringham

Barrow Haven

Barton-on-Humber

Goxhill

East Halton Halt

Killingholme Halt

Thornton Abbey

Thornton Curtis

Immingham Dock

Appleby

Ulceby

Town

No 5 Passing Place

Brocklesby

Habrough

6

Marsh Road Level Crossing

5   4

Cleveland Bridge

Stallingborough

Healing   3

Corporation Bridge   Pier

Elsham

Great Coates   1 2

Docks   New Clee

Barnetby

Pyewipe Road

Grimsby Town

Cleethorpes

Brigg

Bigby Road Bridge

Howsham

Scawby and Hibaldstow

North Kelsey

Weelsby Road Halt and Hainton Street

Kirton Lindsey

Moortown

Waltham

Holton Village Halt

Holton-le-Clay

Grainsby Halt

Holton-le-Moor

North Thoresby

Ludborough

Utterby Halt

Claxby and Usselby

Fotherby Halt

Saltfleetby

1 Yarboro Street
2 Stortford Street
3 Jackson Street
4 Boulevard Recreation Ground
5 Cleveland Street
6 Kiln Lane Crossing

NORTH SEA

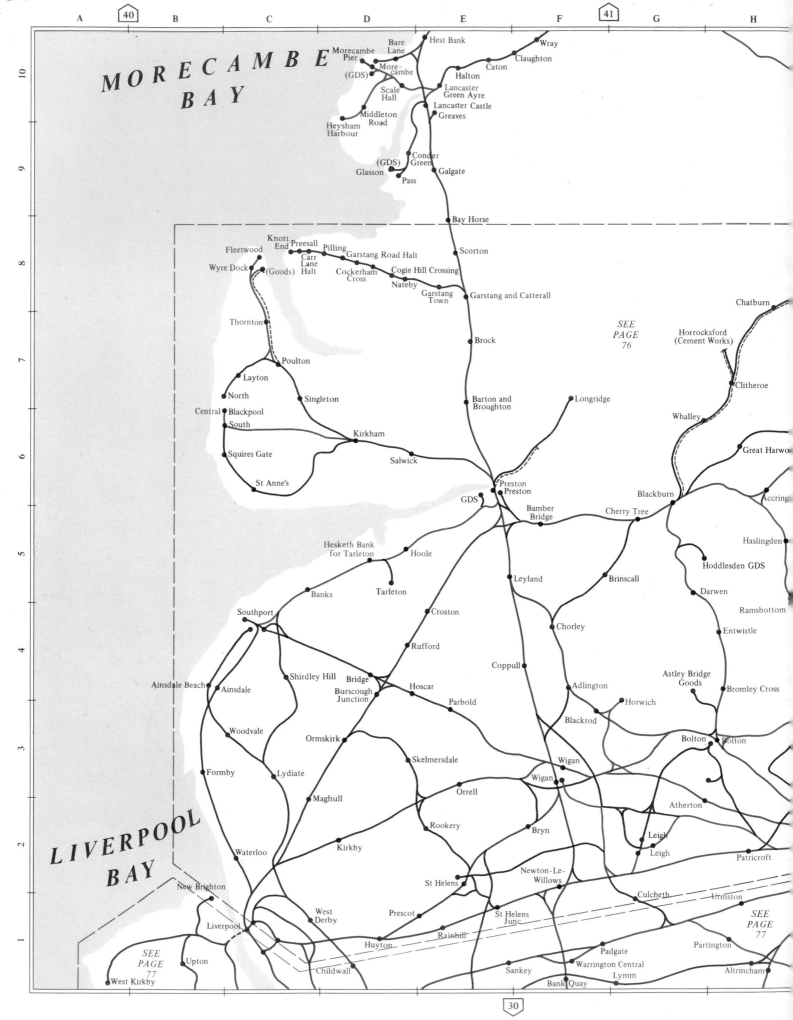

A | 40 | B | C | D | E | F | 41 | G | H

MORECAMBE BAY

LIVERPOOL BAY

Hest Bank
Wray
Bare Lane
Morecambe Pier
Claughton
Morecambe
Caton
(GDS)
Halton
Scale Hall
Lancaster Green Ayre
Lancaster Castle
Middleton Road
Greaves
Heysham Harbour
(GDS)
Conder Green
Glasson
Galgate
Pass
Bay Horse
Knott End
Preesall
Pilling
Fleetwood
Carr Lane Halt
Garstang Road Halt
Wyre Dock
(Goods)
Cockerham Cross
Cogie Hill Crossing
Scorton
Nateby
Thornton
Garstang Town
Garstang and Catterall
Poulton
Layton
Brock
North
Singleton
SEE PAGE 76
Chatburn
Horrocksford (Cement Works)
Central Blackpool
South
Kirkham
Barton and Broughton
Longridge
Clitheroe
Whalley
Squires Gate
Salwick
Great Harwo
St Anne's
Preston
Preston
GDS
Bamber Bridge
Cherry Tree
Blackburn
Accring
Hesketh Bank for Tarleton
Hoole
Haslingden
Banks
Tarleton
Leyland
Brinscall
Hoddlesden GDS
Darwen
Southport
Croston
Chorley
Ramsbottom
Rufford
Coppull
Adlington
Astley Bridge Goods
Entwistle
Shirdley Hill
Bridge
Hoscar
Bromley Cross
Ainsdale Beach
Ainsdale
Burscough Junction
Parbold
Horwich
Woodvale
Ormskirk
Skelmersdale
Blackrod
Bolton
Bolton
Formby
Lydiate
Wigan
Atherton
Maghull
Orrell
Wigan
Leigh
Rookery
Bryn
Leigh
Waterloo
Kirkby
Patricroft
New Brighton
St Helens
Newton-Le-Willows
Culcheth
Urmston
West Derby
Prescot
St Helens Junc
SEE PAGE 77
Upton
Rainhill
Padgate
Partington
Childwall
Liverpool
Huyton
Sankey
Warrington Central
Lymm
Altrincham
West Kirkby
Bank Quay
SEE PAGE 77

30

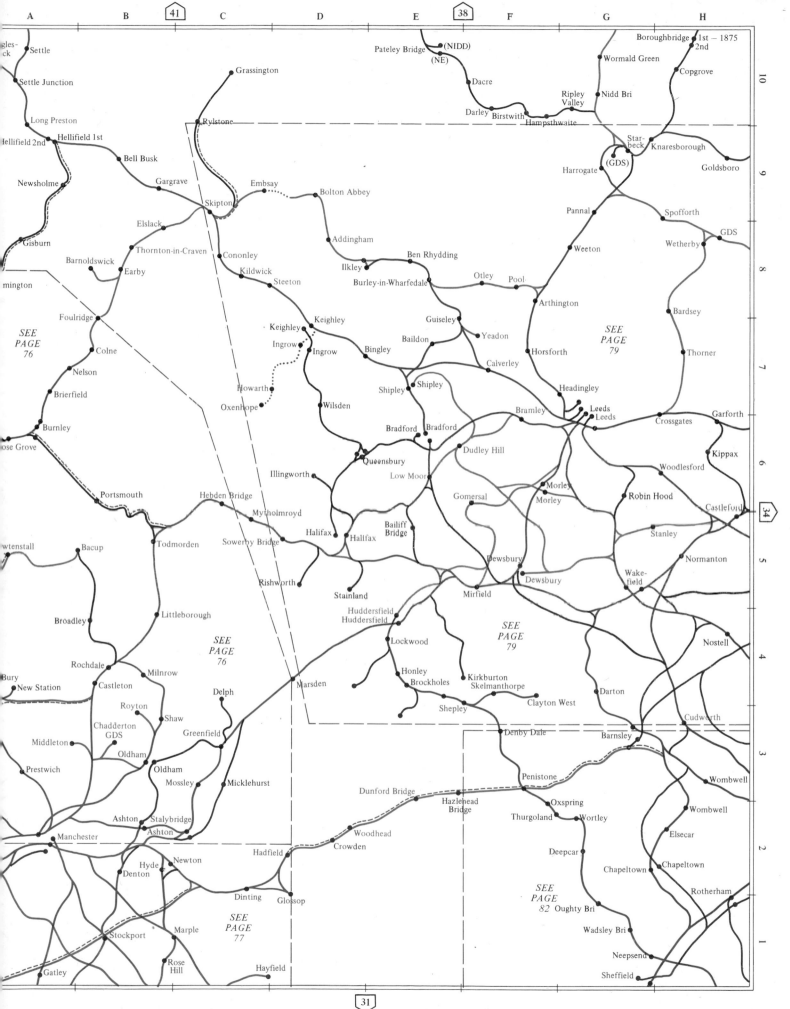

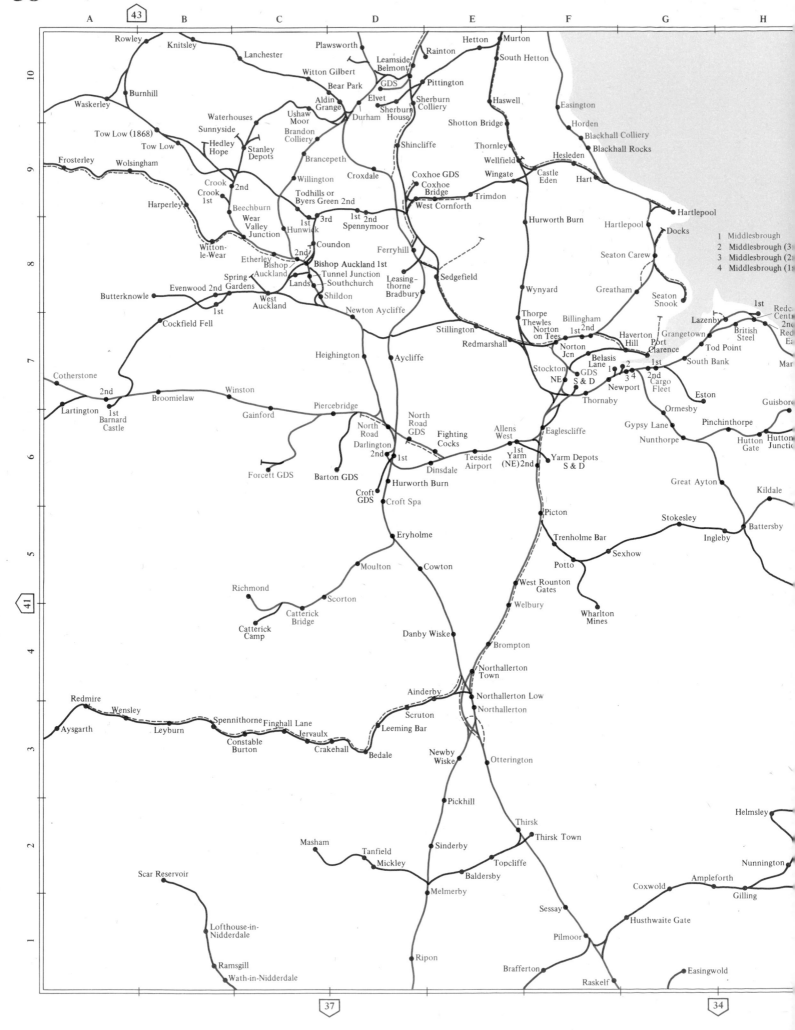

43

A   B   C   D   E   F   G   H

10

Rowley
Knitsley
Lanchester
Plawsworth
Hetton
Murton
Burnhill
Witton Gilbert
Leamside
Belmont
South Hetton
Rainton
Waskerley
Bear Park
GDS
Pittington
Aldin Grange
Elvet
Sherburn
Sherburn Colliery
Haswell
Easington
Durham
Sherburn House
Horden
Waterhouses
Ushaw Moor
Shotton Bridge
Blackhall Colliery
Tow Low (1868)
Sunnyside
Brandon Colliery
Blackhall Rocks
Hedley Hope
Thornley
Hesleden
Tow Low
Stanley Depots
Brancepeth
Wellfield
Frosterley
Willington
Croxdale
Coxhoe GDS
Wingate
Castle Eden
Hart
Hartlepool

9

Wolsingham
Crook 2nd
Crook 1st
Todhills or Byers Green 2nd
Coxhoe Bridge
Trimdon
Hartlepool
Harperley
Beechburn
West Cornforth
Hurworth Burn
Docks
Wear Valley Junction
1st   3rd
1st   2nd
Hunwick   Spennymoor
Seaton Carew

1 Middlesbrough
2 Middlesbrough (3
3 Middlesbrough (2
4 Middlesbrough (1

8

Witton-le-Wear
2nd
Coundon
Ferryhill
Wynyard
Greatham
Seaton Snook
Etherley
Bishop Auckland 1st
Leasing-thorne
Sedgefield
Spring Gardens
Tunnel Junction
Bradbury
Lazenby
1st
Evenwood 2nd
Bishop Auckland
Southchurch
Thorpe Thewles
Billingham
Redc Centr
2nd
Butterknowle
Lands
Shildon
Norton on Tees
1st 2nd
British Steel
Redc Ea
Cockfield Fell
West Auckland
Newton Aycliffe
Stillington
Redmarshall
Norton Jcn
Haverton Hill
Port Clarence
Grangetown
Tod Point
1st
Cotherstone
2nd
Winston
Heighington
Aycliffe
Stockton NE
Belasis Lane
GDS S & D
2nd
1st
Cargo Fleet
South Bank
Ma

7

Lartington
1st Barnard Castle
Broomielaw
Gainford
Piercebridge
North Road GDS
Fighting Cocks
Allens West
3 4
Newport
Thornaby
Ormesby
Eston
Guisbor

6

Forcett GDS
Barton GDS
North Road Darlington 2nd
1st
Dinsdale
1st Yarm (NE) 2nd
Yarm Depots S & D
Eaglescliffe
Gypsy Lane
Nunthorpe
Pinchinthorpe
Hutton Gate
Hutton Junctio
Croft GDS
Hurworth Burn
Teeside Airport
Picton
Great Ayton
Kildale

5

Croft Spa
Eryholme
Moulton
Cowton
Trenholme Bar
Sexhow
Potto
Stokesley
Ingleby
Battersby
Richmond
Scorton
West Rounton Gates

41

Catterick Bridge
Welbury
Wharlton Mines

4

Catterick Camp
Danby Wiske
Brompton
Redmire
Wensley
Spennithorne
Finghall Lane
Northallerton Town
Aysgarth
Leyburn
Constable Burton
Jervaulx
Crakehall
Leeming Bar
Ainderby
Northallerton Low
Scruton
Northallerton
Bedale
Newby Wiske
Otterington

3

2

Pickhill
Helmsley
Masham
Tanfield Mickley
Sinderby
Thirsk
Thirsk Town
Nunnington
Topcliffe
Scar Reservoir
Baldersby
Ampleforth
Coxwold
Gilling
Husthwaite Gate

1

Lofthouse-in-Nidderdale
Melmerby
Sessay
Ramsgill
Ripon
Pilmoor
Easingwold
Wath-in-Nidderdale
Brafferton
Raskelf

37   34

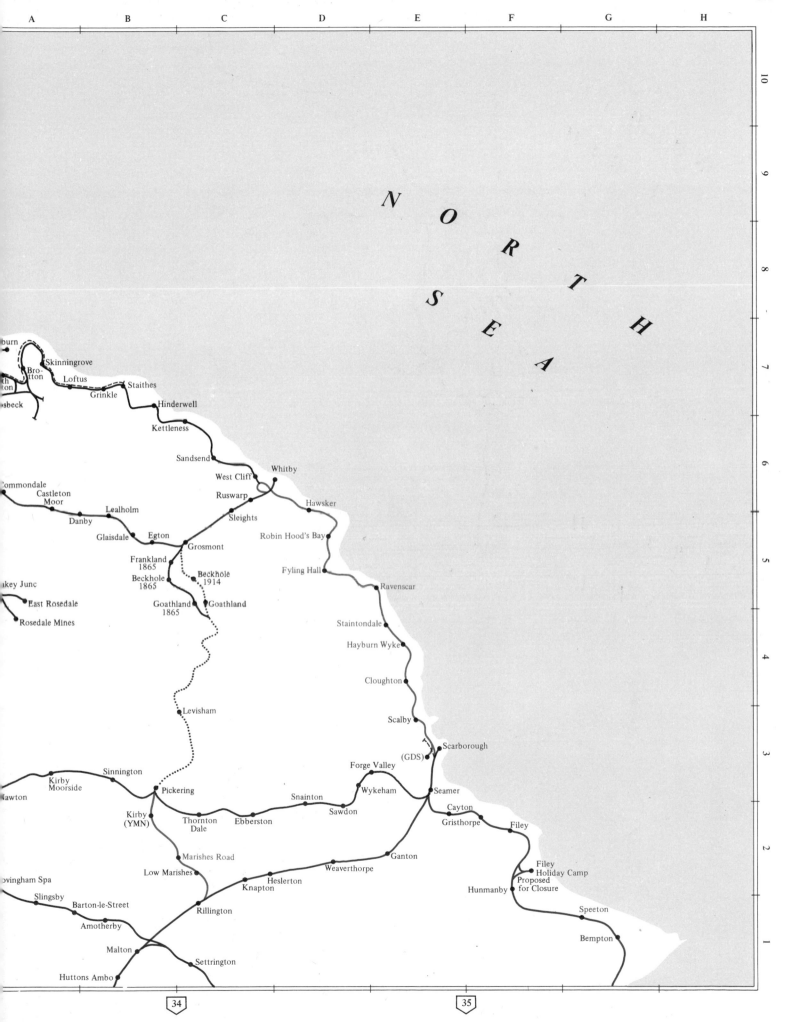

A   B   C   D   E   F   G   H

N O R T H

S E A

...burn
Skinningrove
Bro-
tton
Loftus
...th
...ton
Grinkle
Staithes
...sbeck
Hinderwell

Kettleness

Sandsend
West Cliff
Whitby
Commondale
Castleton
Moor
Ruswarp
Lealholm
Hawsker
Danby
Sleights
Glaisdale
Egton
Robin Hood's Bay
Grosmont
Frankland
1865
Beckhole
1914
Fyling Hall
...key Junc
Beckhole
1865
Ravenscar
East Rosedale
Goathland
1865
Goathland
Staintondale
Rosedale Mines
Hayburn Wyke

Cloughton

Levisham

Scalby

Scarborough
(GDS)

Sinnington
Forge Valley
Kirby
Moorside
Pickering
Wykeham
Seamer
...awton
Snainton
Cayton
Kirby
(YMN)
Thornton
Dale
Ebberston
Sawdon
Gristhorpe
Filey

Marishes Road
Ganton
Filey
Holiday Camp
Proposed
for Closure
...ovingham Spa
Low Marishes
Weaverthorpe
Heslerton
Slingsby
Knapton
Hunmanby
Barton-le-Street
Speeton
Amotherby
Rillington
Malton
Bempton
Settrington
Huttons Ambo

10
9
8
7
6
5
4
3
2
1

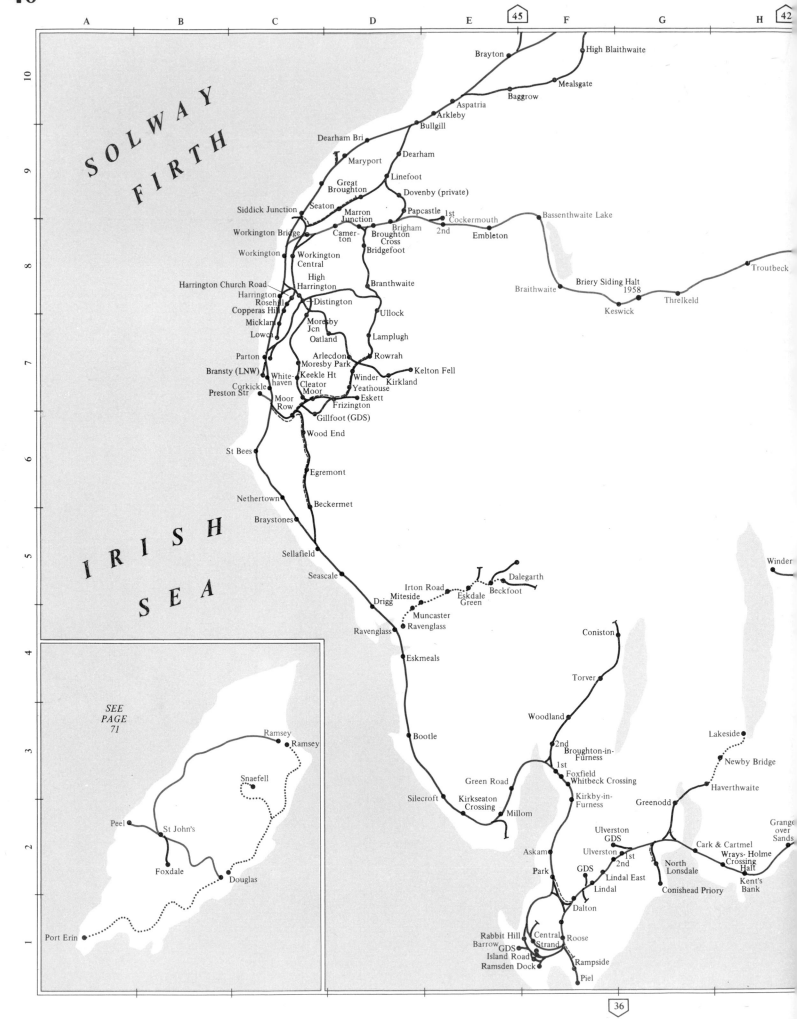

SOLWAY FIRTH

IRISH SEA

Brayton
High Blaithwaite
Mealsgate
Baggrow
Aspatria
Arkleby
Bullgill
Dearham Bri
Dearham
Maryport
Linefoot
Great Broughton
Dovenby (private)
Seaton
Marron Junction
Papcastle
Siddick Junction
1st
Cockermouth
2nd
Bassenthwaite Lake
Brigham
Workington Bridge
Camer-ton
Broughton Cross
Embleton
Bridgefoot
Workington
Workington Central
Branthwaite
Troutbeck
High Harrington
Harrington Church Road
Briery Siding Halt
1958
Braithwaite
Harrington
Distington
Ullock
Rosehill
Keswick
Threlkeld
Copperas Hill
Moresby Jcn
Micklam
Lamplugh
Oatland
Lowca
Arlecdon
Rowrah
Parton
Moresby Park
Kelton Fell
Bransty (LNW)
Keekle Ht
Winder
Kirkland
White-haven
Cleator
Corkickle
Moor
Yeathouse
Preston Str
Moor Row
Eskett
Frizington
Gillfoot (GDS)
Wood End
St Bees
Egremont
Nethertown
Beckermet
Braystones
Sellafield
Seascale
Winder
Irton Road
Dalegarth
Miteside
Beckfoot
Drigg
Eskdale Green
Muncaster
Ravenglass
Ravenglass
Coniston
Eskmeals
Torver
Woodland
Lakeside
Bootle
2nd
Broughton-in-Furness
Newby Bridge
1st
Foxfield
Whitbeck Crossing
Haverthwaite
Green Road
Kirkby-in-Furness
Greenodd
Silecroft
Kirkseaton Crossing
Grange over Sands
Millom
Ulverston GDS
Cark & Cartmel
Wrays- Holme Crossing Halt
Askam
Ulverston
North Lonsdale
1st
2nd
Kent's Bank
Park
GDS
Lindal East
Conishead Priory
Lindal
Dalton
Rabbit Hill
Central Strand
Roose
Barrow
GDS
Rampside
Island Road
Ramsden Dock
Piel

SEE PAGE 71

Ramsey
Ramsey
Snaefell
Peel
St John's
Foxdale
Douglas
Port Erin

45
42
36

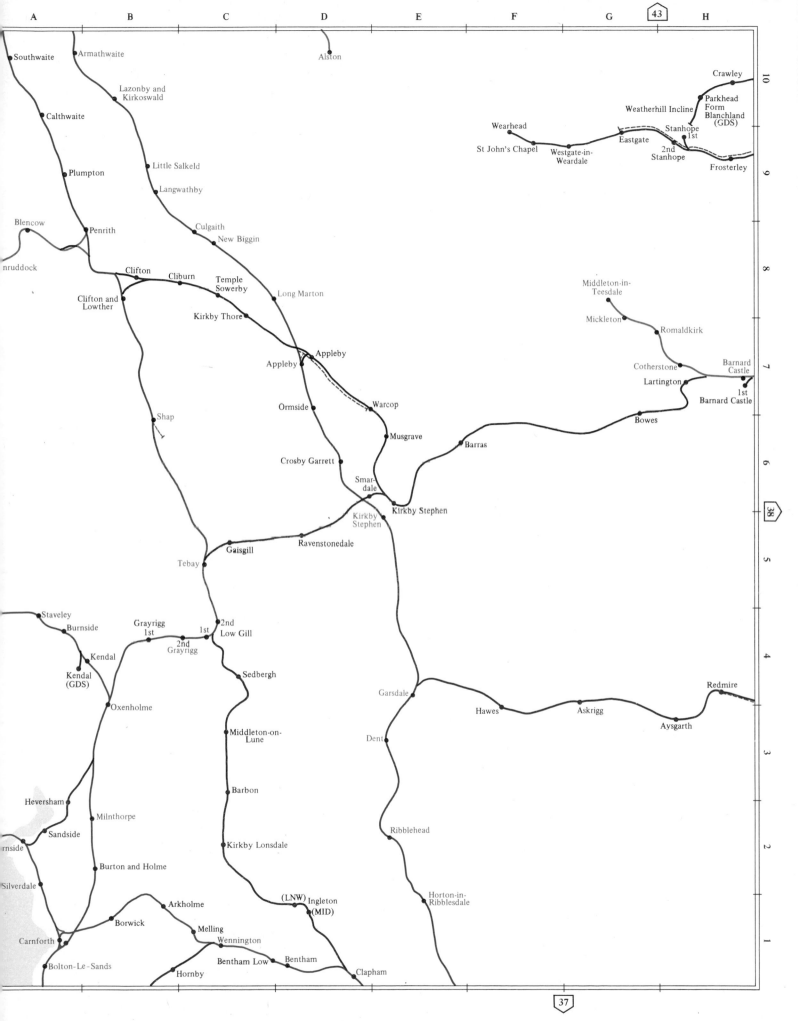

A B C D E F G 43 H

Southwaite
Armathwaite
Lazonby and Kirkoswald
Alston
Crawley
Parkhead Form Blanchland (GDS)
Weatherhill Incline
Calthwaite
Wearhead
Stanhope 1st
Little Salkeld
St John's Chapel
Westgate-in-Weardale
Eastgate
2nd Stanhope
Plumpton
Frosterley
Langwathby
Blencow
Culgaith
New Biggin
Penrith
nruddock
Clifton
Cliburn
Temple Sowerby
Middleton-in-Teesdale
Clifton and Lowther
Long Marton
Mickleton
Romaldkirk
Kirkby Thore
Appleby
Cotherstone
Barnard Castle
Appleby
Lartington
1st Barnard Castle
Ormside
Warcop
Bowes
Shap
Musgrave
Barras
Crosby Garrett
Smardale
Kirkby Stephen
Kirkby Stephen
38
Ravenstonedale
Gaisgill
Tebay
Staveley
Burnside
Grayrigg 1st
1st
2nd Low Gill
2nd Grayrigg
Kendal
Sedbergh
Garsdale
Redmire
Kendal (GDS)
Hawes
Askrigg
Aysgarth
Oxenholme
Middleton-on-Lune
Dent
Heversham
Milnthorpe
Barbon
Sandside
Ribblehead
rnside
Kirkby Lonsdale
Silverdale
Burton and Holme
(LNW) Ingleton
Arkholme
Horton-in-Ribblesdale
Borwick
(MID)
Melling
Carnforth
Wennington
Bolton-Le-Sands
Bentham Low
Bentham
Hornby
Clapham
37

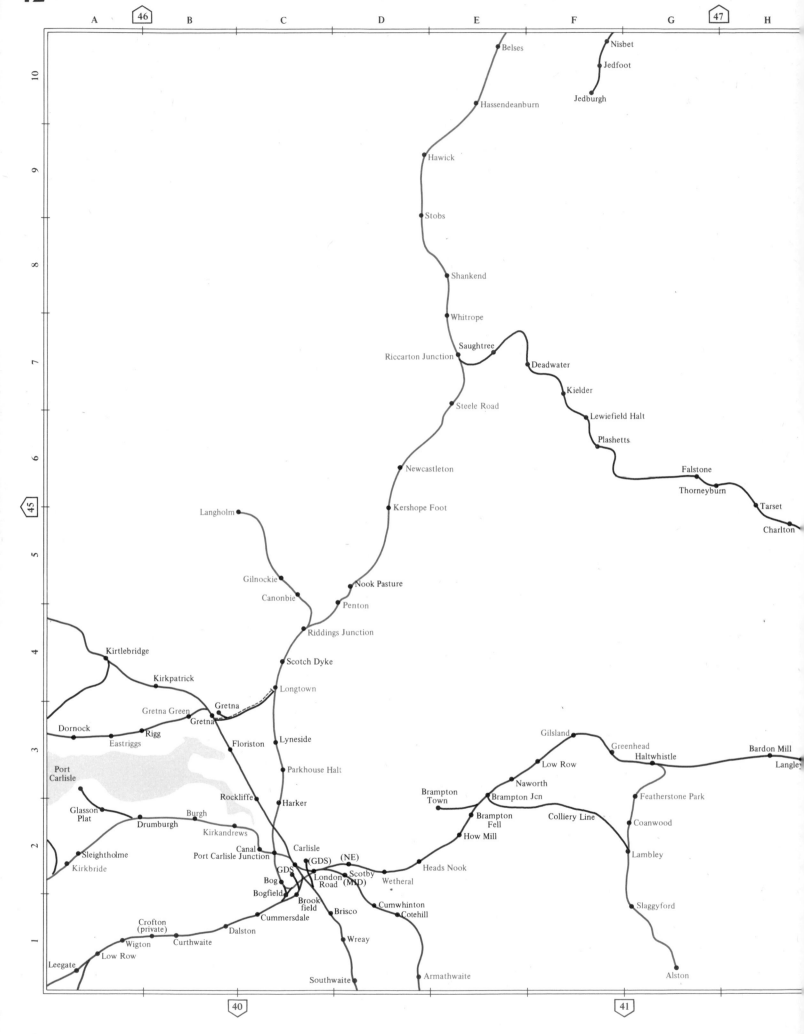

A 46 B C D E F 47 G H

Belses
Nisbet
Jedfoot
Hassendeanburn
Jedburgh

Hawick

Stobs

Shankend

Whitrope
Saughtree
Deadwater
Riccarton Junction
Kielder
Lewiefield Halt
Steele Road
Plashetts

Newcastleton
Falstone
Thorneyburn
Kershope Foot
Tarset
Charlton

45

Langholm

Gilnockie
Nook Pasture
Canonbie
Penton
Riddings Junction

Scotch Dyke

Kirtlebridge
Longtown
Kirkpatrick
Gilsland
Greenhead
Gretna
Bardon Mill
Gretna Green
Low Row
Haltwhistle
Dornock
Gretna
Langley
Rigg
Eastriggs
Floriston
Lyneside
Brampton
Town
Naworth
Featherstone Park
Parkhouse Halt
Brampton Jcn
Port
Carlisle
Rockliffe
Harker
Brampton
Fell
Colliery Line
Coanwood
Glasson
Plat
Burgh
How Mill
Drumburgh
Kirkandrews
Lambley
Sleightholme
Canal
Carlisle
(NE)
Heads Nook
Port Carlisle Junction
Kirkbride
GDS
(GDS)
Slaggyford
Bog
London
Scotby
Wetheral
Bogfield
Road
(MID)
Brook-
field
Cumwhinton
Crofton
(private)
Brisco
Cotehill
Cummersdale
Leegate
Wigton
Dalston
Wreay
Low Row
Curthwaite
Alston
Southwaite
Armathwaite

40 41

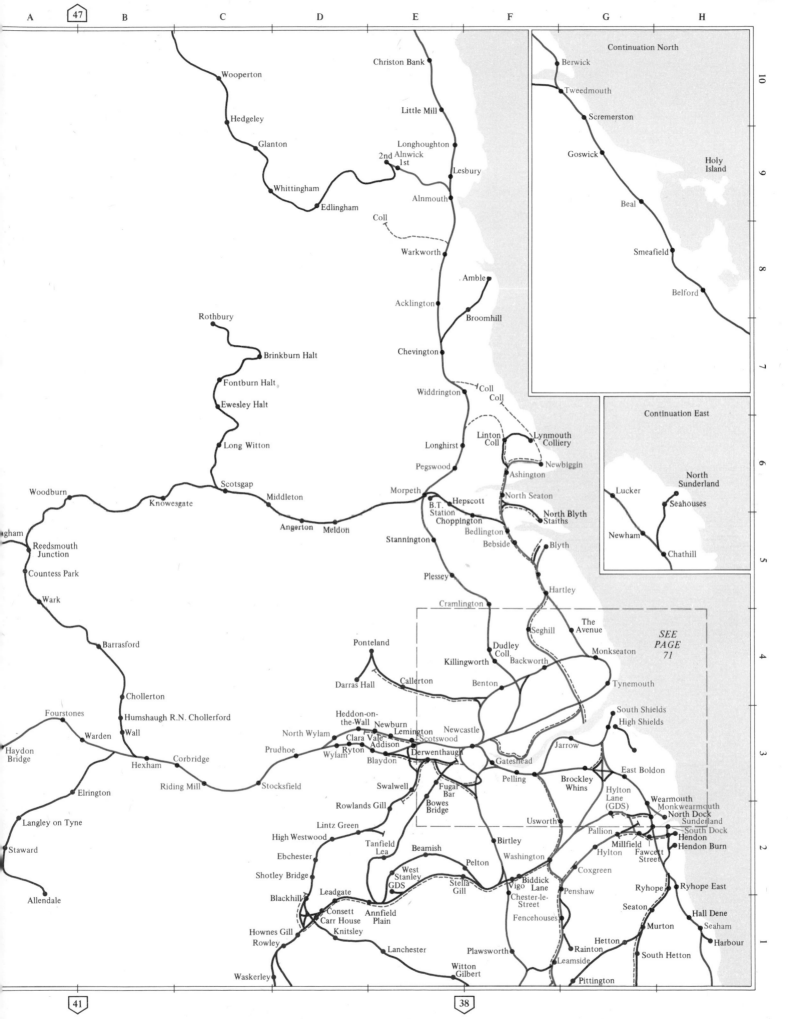

A   B   C   D   E   F   G   H

10

9

8

7

6

5

4

3

2

1

Continuation North

Berwick
Tweedmouth
Scremerston
Goswick
Holy Island
Beal
Smeafield
Belford

Continuation East

North Sunderland
Lucker
Seahouses
Newham
Chathill

SEE PAGE 71

Wooperton
Hedgeley
Glanton
Whittingham
Edlingham
Coll

Christon Bank
Little Mill
Longhoughton
2nd Alnwick 1st
Lesbury
Alnmouth
Warkworth
Amble

Rothbury
Brinkburn Halt
Fontburn Halt
Ewesley Halt
Long Witton
Scotsgap
Acklington
Broomhill
Chevington
Widdrington
Coll
Coll

Woodburn
Knowesgate
Middleton
Angerton   Meldon
Longhirst
Pegswood
Morpeth
B.T. Station
Hepscott
Choppington
Bedlington
Linton Coll
Lynmouth Colliery
Newbiggin
Ashington
North Seaton
North Blyth Staiths

gham
Reedsmouth Junction
Countess Park
Wark
Stannington
Bebside
Blyth
Plessey
Hartley
Cramlington

Barrasford
Seghill
The Avenue
Dudley Coll.
Killingworth
Backworth
Monkseaton

Chollerton
Humshaugh R.N. Chollerford
Ponteland
Darras Hall
Callerton
Benton
Tynemouth

Fourstones
Warden   Wall
Haydon Bridge
Corbridge
Hexham
Riding Mill
Stocksfield
Prudhoe
Wylam
Ryton
Blaydon
North Wylam
Clara Vale
Addison
Heddon-on-the-Wall
Newburn
Lemington
Scotswood
Derwenthaugh
Newcastle
Gateshead
Jarrow
South Shields
High Shields
East Boldon

Elrington
Langley on Tyne
Staward
Swalwell
Fugar Bar
Bowes Bridge
Rowlands Gill
Pelling
Brockley Whins
Hylton Lane (GDS)
Wearmouth
Monkwearmouth
North Dock
Sunderland
South Dock

Allendale
Lintz Green
High Westwood
Tanfield Lea
Beamish
Birtley
Usworth
Washington
Coxgreen
Pallion
Millfield
Hylton
Fawcett Street
Hendon
Hendon Burn

Ebchester
West Stanley GDS
Pelton
Vigo
Biddick Lane
Penshaw
Ryhope
Ryhope East

Shotley Bridge
Stella Gill
Chester-le-Street
Seaton
Hall Dene

Blackhill
Leadgate
Annfield Plain
Fencehouses
Murton
Seaham Harbour

Consett
Carr House
Knitsley
Hetton
South Hetton

Hownes Gill
Rowley
Lanchester
Plawsworth
Leamside
Rainton

Waskerley
Witton Gilbert
Pittington

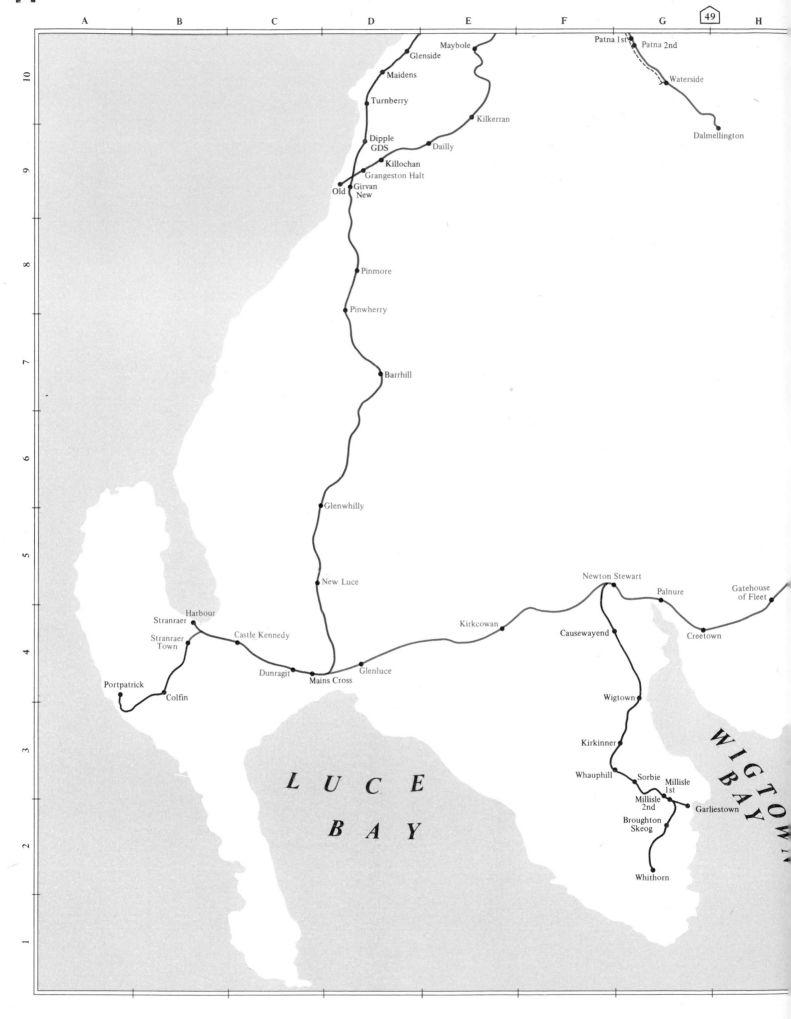

Patna 1st   Patna 2nd

Maybole

Glenside

Waterside

Maidens

Turnberry

Kilkerran

Dalmellington

Dipple
GDS   Dailly

Killochan

Grangeston Halt

Old   Girvan
New

Pinmore

Pinwherry

Barrhill

Glenwhilly

New Luce

Newton Stewart

Palnure   Gatehouse
of Fleet

Kirkcowan

Harbour   Causewayend   Creetown

Stranraer   Castle Kennedy

Stranraer
Town

Dunragit   Glenluce

Portpatrick   Mains Cross   Wigtown

Colfin

Kirkinner

W I G T O W N

Whauphill   Sorbie
Millisle
1st

L U C E   Millisle
2nd   Garliestown

Broughton
Skeog

B A Y   *B A Y*

Whithorn

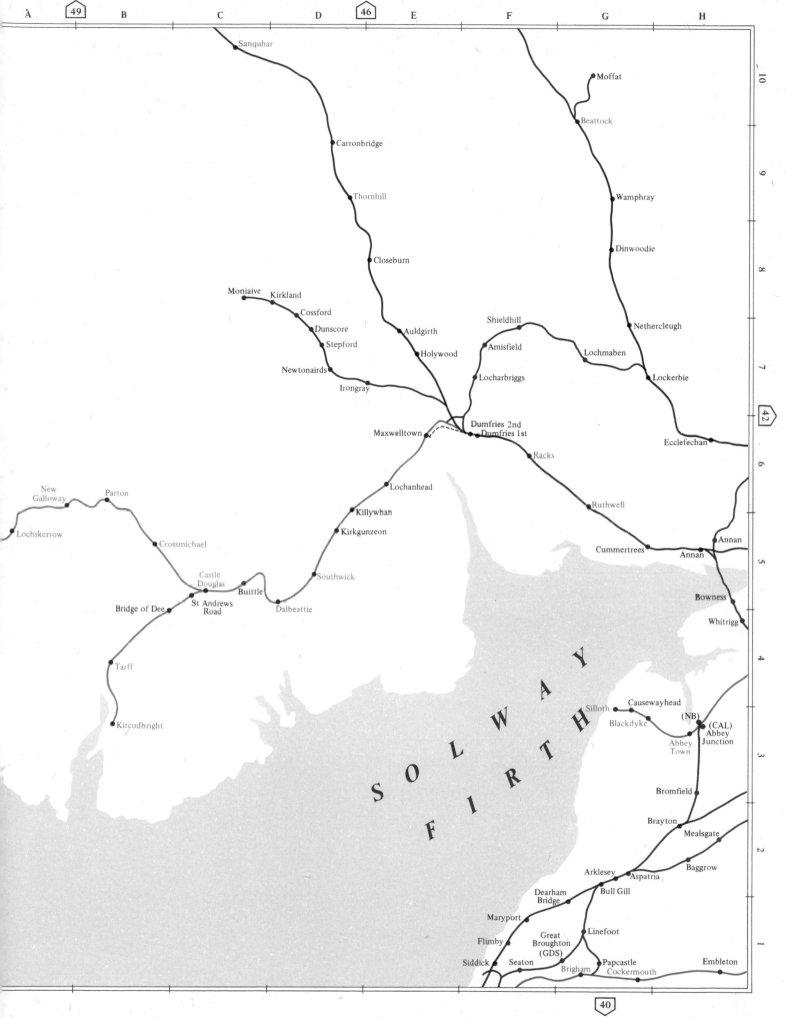

Sanquhar

Carronbridge

Thornhill

Closeburn

Moffat

Beattock

Wamphray

Dinwoodie

Nethercleugh

Moniaive
Kirkland
Cossford
Dunscore
Stepford
Newtonairds
Irongray
Auldgirth
Holywood

Shieldhill
Amisfield
Locharbriggs
Lochmaben
Lockerbie

Maxwelltown
Dumfries 2nd
Dumfries 1st
Racks
Ecclefechan

New
Galloway
Parton
Lochskerrow
Crossmichael
Lochanhead
Killywhan
Kirkgunzeon
Ruthwell

Castle
Douglas
Buittle
St Andrews
Road
Southwick
Bridge of Dee
Dalbeattie
Cummertrees
Annan
Annan

Bowness

Whitrigg

Tarff

Kircudbright

S O L W A Y
F I R T H

Silloth
Causewayhead
(NB)
Blackdyke
(CAL)
Abbey
Junction
Abbey
Town

Bromfield

Brayton
Mealsgate

Arklesey
Aspatria
Baggrow
Dearham
Bridge
Bull Gill
Maryport
Linefoot
Flimby
Great
Broughton
(GDS)
Siddick
Seaton
Brigham
Papcastle
Cockermouth
Embleton

49

46

42

40

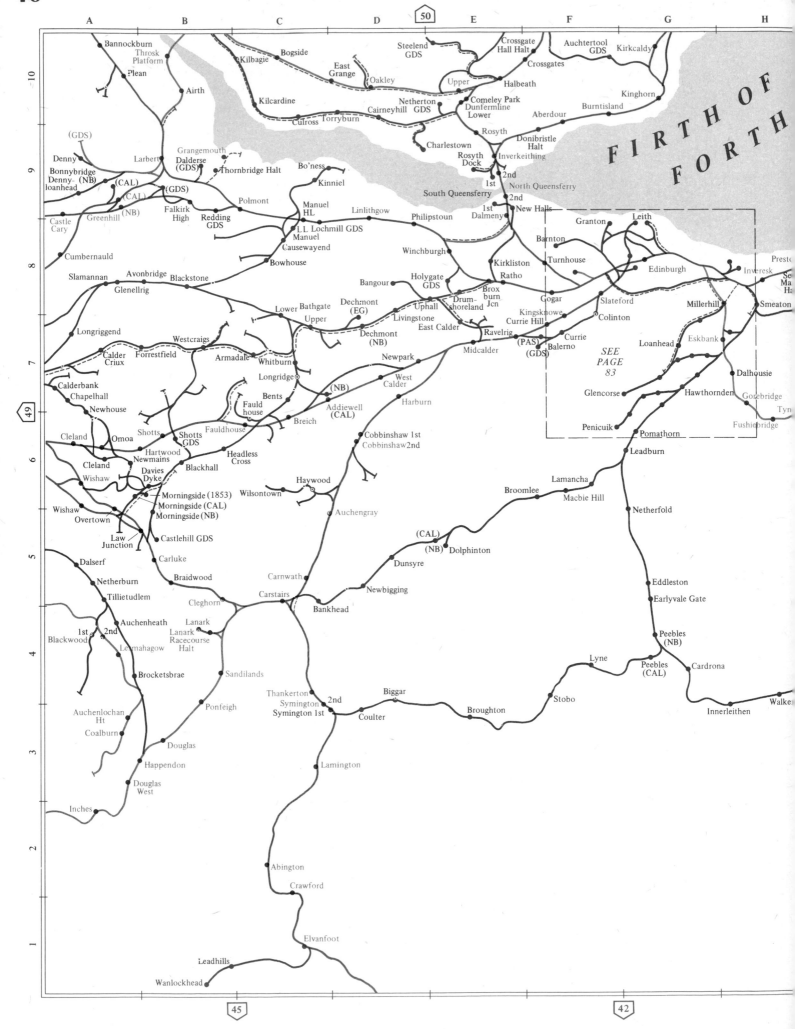

FIRTH OF FORTH

SEE PAGE 83

Bannockburn
Throsk Platform
Plean
Airth
Denny
Bonnybridge
Denny-loanhead
(NB)
(CAL)
(CAL)
(NB)
(GDS)
Larbert
Castle Cary
Greenhill
Cumbernauld
Slamannan
Glenellrig
Longriggend
Calder Criux
Forrestfield
Calderbank
Chapelhall
Newhouse
Cleland
Omoa
Cleland
Wishaw
Overtown
Wishaw
Law Junction
Dalserf
Netherburn
Tillietudlem
Auchenheath
Lanark
Lesmahagow
1st 2nd
Blackwood
Brocketsbrae
Auchenlochan Ht
Coalburn
Douglas
Happendon
Douglas West
Inches
Leadhills
Wanlockhead

Kilbagie
Bogside
East Grange
Oakley
Kilcardine
Culross Torryburn
Bo'ness
Kinniel
Polmont
Manuel HL
LL Lochmill GDS
Manuel
Causewayend
Bowhouse
Avonbridge
Blackstone
Westcraigs
Armadale
Whitburn
Longridge
Bents
Fauldhouse
Breich
Shotts
Shotts GDS
Fauldhouse
Hartwood
Newmains
Davies Dyke
Blackhall
Headless Cross
Morningside (1853)
Morningside (CAL)
Morningside (NB)
Castlehill GDS
Carluke
Braidwood
Carnwath
Carstairs
Cleghorn
Bankhead
Lanark Racecourse Halt
Sandilands
Ponfeigh
Thankerton
Symington 2nd
Symington 1st
Lamington
Abington
Crawford
Elvanfoot

Steelend GDS
Netherton
Cairneyhill
Torryburn
Charlestown
South Queensferry
Philipstoun
Linlithgow
Bangour
Dechmont (EG)
Upper
Dechmont (NB)
Lower Bathgate
Upper
Newpark
West Calder
(NB)
Addiewell (CAL)
Harburn
Cobbinshaw 1st
Cobbinshaw 2nd
Haywood
Wilsontown
Auchengray
Dunsyre
Newbigging
Coulter
Biggar
Broughton

Crossgate Hall Halt
Crossgates
Halbeath
Upper
Comeley Park
Dunfermline Lower
Rosyth
Rosyth Dock
Inverkeithing
1st 2nd
2nd
North Queensferry
New Halls
1st Dalmeny
Winchburgh
Holygate GDS
Uphall
Livingstone
East Calder
Drumshoreland
Brox burn Jcn
Ravelrig
Midcalder
(PAS)
(GDS)
Balerno
Currie Hill
Kingsknowe
Currie
Gogar
Slateford
Colinton
Barnton
Turnhouse
Kirkliston
Ratho
Edinburgh
Granton
Leith
Auchtertool GDS
Kirkcaldy
Kinghorn
Aberdour
Burntisland
Donibristle Halt

Millerhill
Smeaton
Inveresk
Preston
Sea Mar Ha
Loanhead
Eskbank
Dalhousie
Hawthornden
Gorebridge
Tyn
Fushiebridge
Glencorse
Penicuik
Pomathorn
Leadburn
Lamancha
Macbie Hill
Broomlee
Netherfold
Eddleston
Earlyvale Gate
Peebles (NB)
Peebles (CAL)
Cardrona
Lyne
Stobo
Innerleithen
Walke

Dolphinton (CAL) (NB)

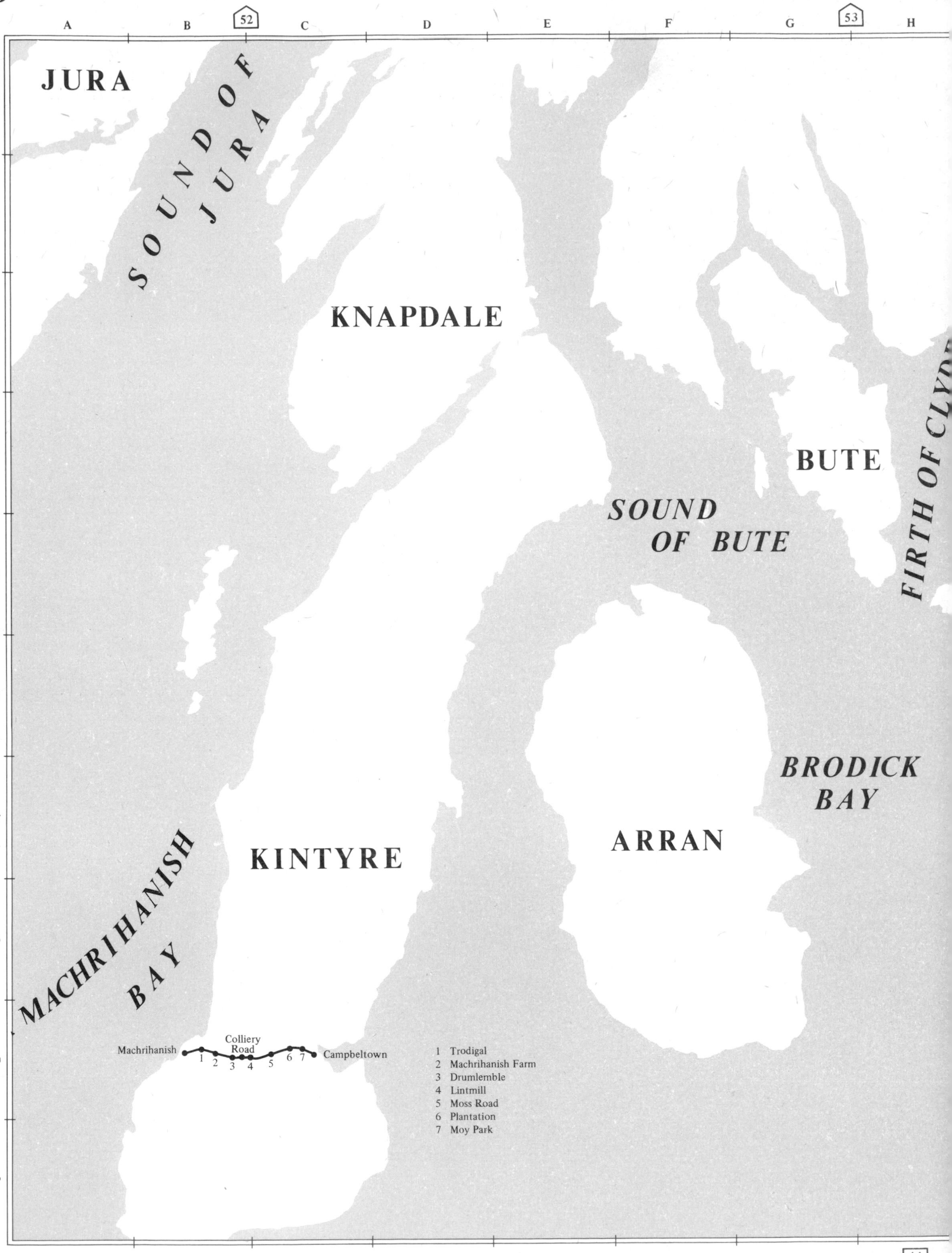

A　　　B　52　　C　　　D　　　E　　　F　　　G　53　H

JURA

S O U N D   O F   J U R A

KNAPDALE

BUTE

FIRTH OF CLYDE

SOUND

OF   BUTE

BRODICK
BAY

ARRAN

MACHRIHANISH

KINTYRE

B A Y

Colliery
Road
Machrihanish ●—●—●—●—●—●—● Campbeltown
　　　　　　1　2　3　4　5　6　7

1　Trodigal
2　Machrihanish Farm
3　Drumlemble
4　Lintmill
5　Moss Road
6　Plantation
7　Moy Park

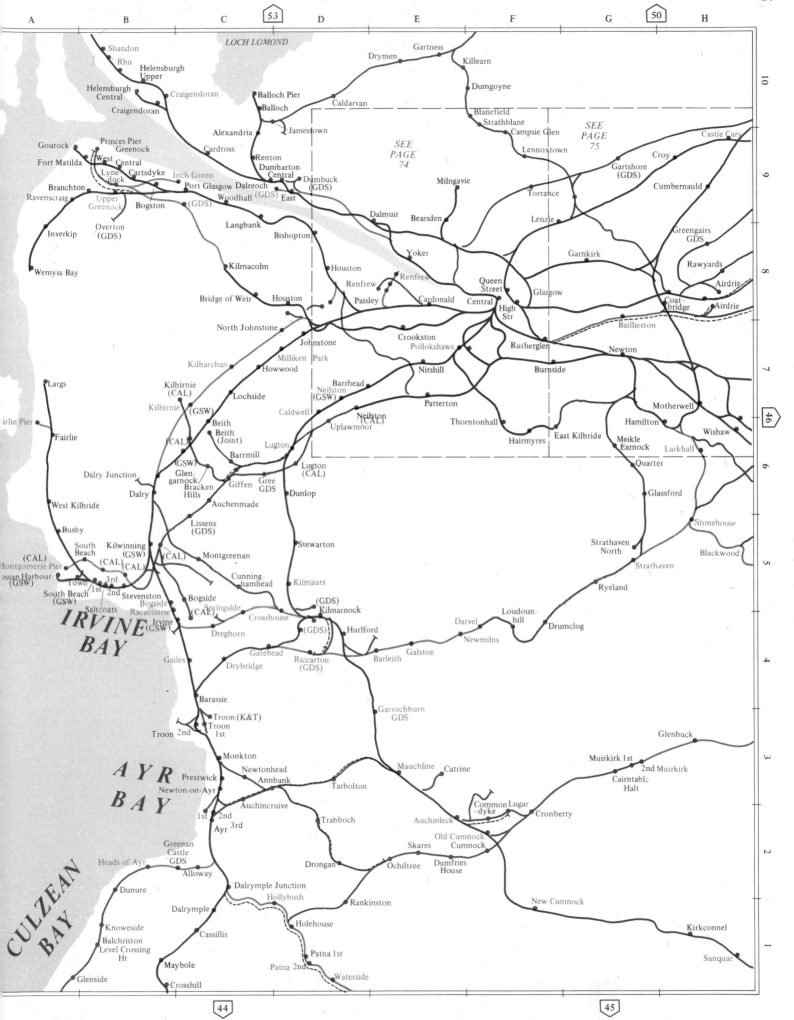

SEE PAGE 74

SEE PAGE 75

53

A B C D 55 E F G H

Lauriston
Marykirk
St Cyrus
Strathcathro
Craigo
Hillside
North Water Bridge
Broomfield Road Junction
Dubton
Careston
Brechin
Bridge of Dun
(NB) Montrose
Tannadice
Justinhaugh
Farnell Road
Kirriemuir
Forfar 2nd
1st
Clocksbriggs
Lunan Bay
Kirriemuir Junction
Auldbar Road
Guthrie Junction
Glasterlaw
Glamis
Kingsmuir
Leysmill
Inverkeilor
Alyth
Pitcrocknie
Jordanstone
Leason Hill
Colliston
Cauldcots
Meigle
Eassie
Gagie
Carmyllie
Letham Grange
emount
Washington
Kirkinch
Meigle Junction
Kirkbuddo
Denhead
Cuthlie
Arbroath (1848)
Alyth Junction
Newtyle 1st
Arbirlot
Arbroath
Ardler
2nd
Harbour GDS
Woodside and Burrelton
Coupar Angus
Auchterhouse
Balbeuchly Top
Monikie
Elliot
Elliot Jcn.
Dronley
Balbeuchly Foot
Baldragon
Kingennie
Easthaven
Rosemill GDS
Baldovan
Carnoustie 1st
Carnoustie 2nd
Inchture Village
Lochee West
Liff
Stannergate
Barnhill
West Broughty Ferry
Buddon
Golf Street Halt
Barry Links
Lochee
West Ferry
Ninewells Junction
Invergowrie
East 2
Camperdown
3 1
Monifieth
Balmossie
Longforgan
Magdalen Green
Esplanade
Dundee GDS
Broughty Ferry Pier
Tayport
Inchture
East Newport
West
Errol
Inchcoonans GDS
Wormit GDS
St Fort
N O R T H
Glencarse
Kilmany
Leuchars Old
Leuchars
Milton Junction
Guard Bridge
S E A
Newburgh
2nd
1st
Lindores
Glenbirnie
Luthrie
Dairsie
St Andrews
Cupar
Springfield
Stravithie
Boarhills
Mount Melville
Auchtermuchty
Collessie
Kingsbarns
Strathmiglo
Ladybank
Lochty
Crail
Kingskettle
Largoward GDS
Falkland Road
Montrave GDS
2nd
Anstruther
Auchmuty Mills (GDS)
Kennoway GDS
Lundin Links
Largo
Kilconquhar
1st
Pittenweem
Leslie
Markinch
Cameron Bridge
Leven
Elie
St Monans
Coll
Thornton Junction
Methil
Buckhaven
Wemyss Castle
Coll
West Wemyss
ochgelly
Cardenden
Sinclairtown
Dysart
Auchtertool (GDS)
Kirkcaldy

1 Dundee–Roodyards
2 Dundee–Back of Law
3 Dundee–Ward Street

F I R T H O F

F O R T H

Kinghorn

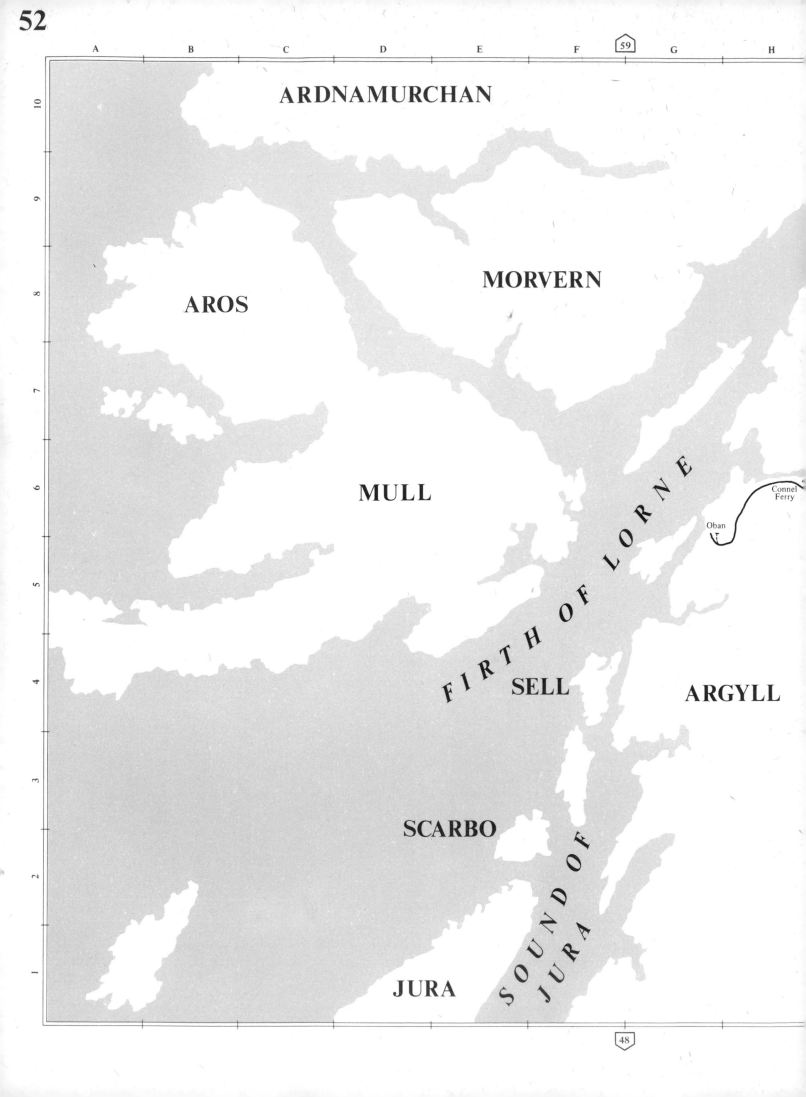

ARDNAMURCHAN

MORVERN

AROS

MULL

FIRTH OF LORNE

Connel
Ferry

Oban

SELL

ARGYLL

SCARBO

SOUND OF
JURA

JURA

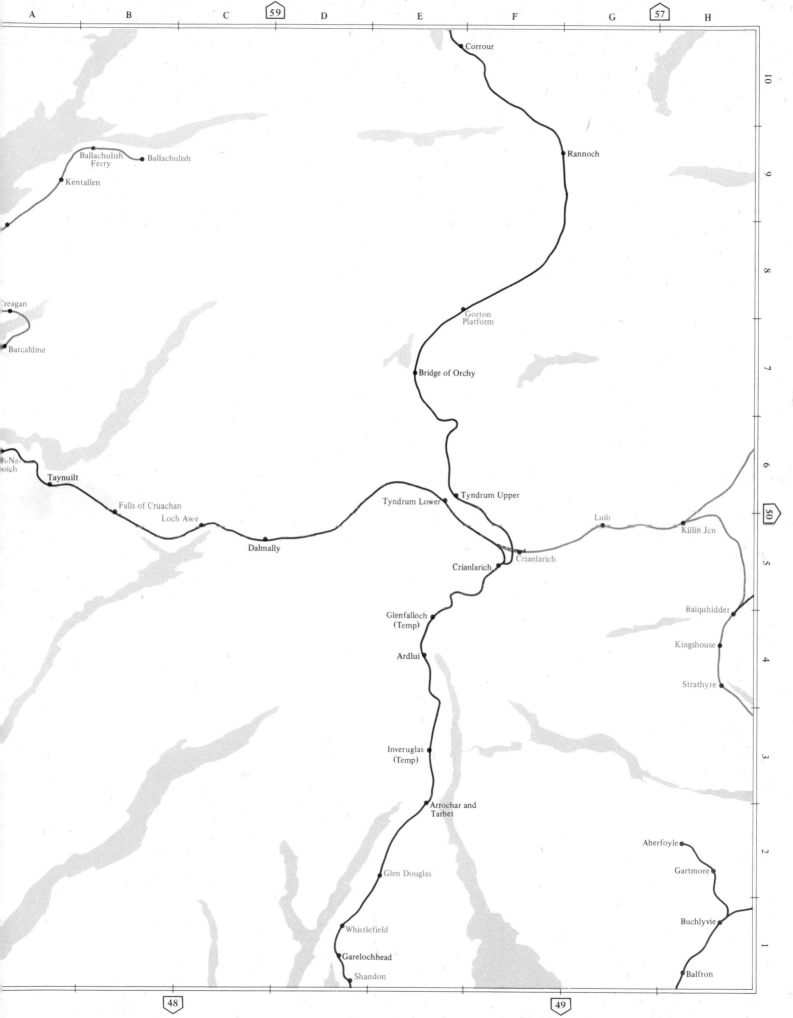

A　B　C　59　D　E　F　G　57　H

Corrour

Ballachulish
Ferry
Ballachulish
Kentallen

Rannoch

Creagan

Barcaldine

Gorton
Platform

Bridge of Orchy

h-Na-
oich
Taynuilt
Falls of Cruachan
Loch Awe
Tyndrum Lower
Tyndrum Upper
Luib
Killin Jcn

Dalmally
Crianlarich
Crianlarich

Crianlarich

Balquhidder

Glenfalloch
(Temp)
Kingshouse

Ardlui
Strathyre

Inveruglas
(Temp)

Arrochar and
Tarbet

Aberfoyle
Gartmore

Glen Douglas

Buchlyvie

Whistlefield

Garelochhead
Shandon
Balfron

48　49

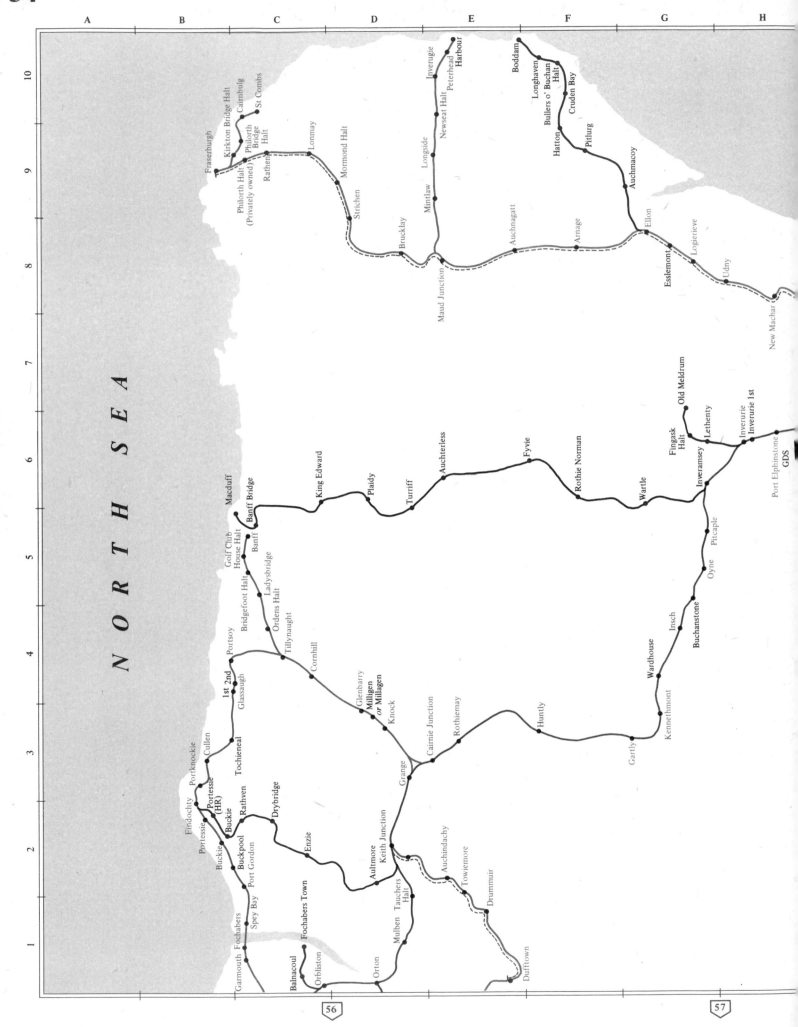

NORTH SEA

A B C D E F G H

Fraserburgh
Kirkton Bridge Halt
Cairnbulg
Philorth Halt
Philorth Bridge Halt
(Privately owned)
Rathen
Lonmay
Mormond Halt
Strichen
Brucklay
Maud Junction
Inverugie
Newseat Halt
Peterhead
Harbour
Longside
Mintlaw
Auchnagatt
Boddam
Longhaven
Bullers o' Buchan Halt
Hatton
Cruden Bay
Pitlurg
Auchmacoy
Arnage
Ellon
Logierieve
Esslemont
Udny
New Machar

Old Meldrum
Fingask Halt
Lethenty
Inverurie
Inverurie 1st
Port Elphinstone GDS
Inveramsey

Macduff
Banff Bridge
Golf Club House Halt
Banff
King Edward
Plaidy
Turriff
Auchterless
Fyvie
Rothie Norman
Wartle

Ladysbridge
Ordens Halt
Tillynaught
Cornhill
Bridgefoot Halt
Portsoy
1st 2nd
Glassaugh
Glenbarry
Milligen or Millagen
Knock
Cairnie Junction
Rothiemay
Huntly
Gartly
Kennethmont
Insch
Buchanstone
Wardhouse
Oyne
Pitcaple

Cullen
Portknockie
Findochty
Portessie
Portessie (HR)
Buckie
Rathven
Drybridge
Buckie
Buckpool
Port Gordon
Enzie
Aultmore
Keith Junction
Auchindachy
Towiemore
Drummuir
Grange
Mulben
Tauchers Halt

Garmouth
Fochabers
Spey Bay
Balnacoul
Orbliston
Fochabers Town
Orton
Dufftown

56 57

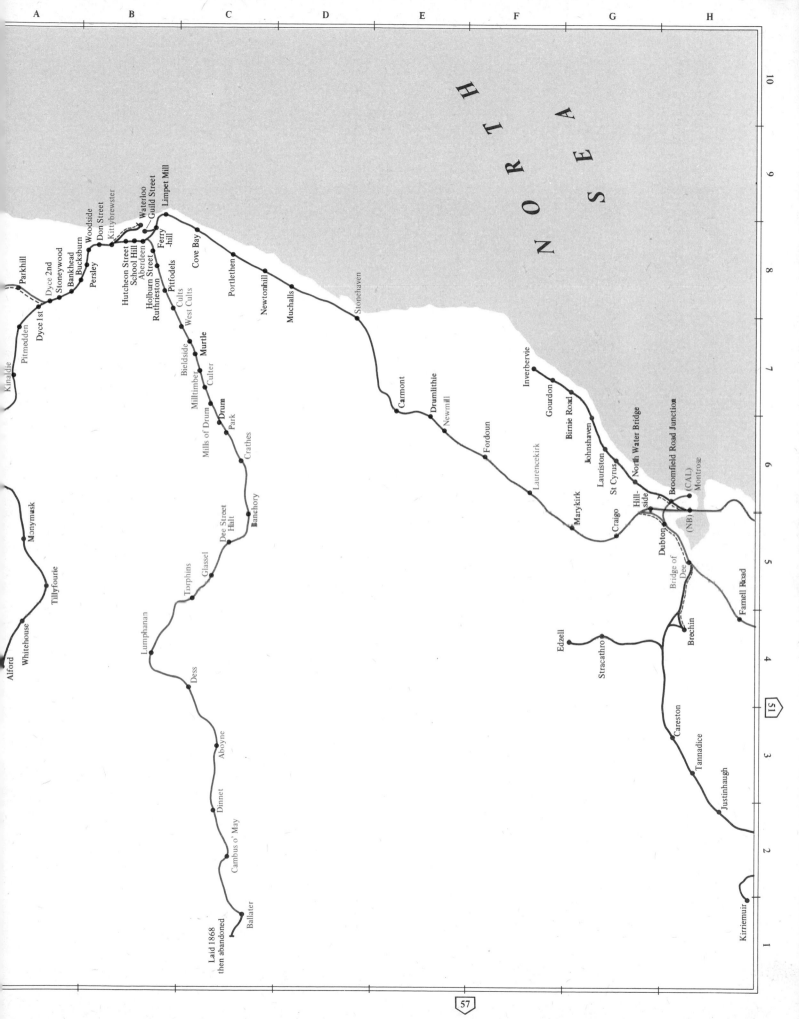

NORTH SEA

A B C D E F G H

10
9
8
7
6
5
4
3
2
1

Kinaldie
Parkhill
Pitmedden
Dyce 2nd
Stoneywood
Bankhead
Bucksburn
Dyce 1st
Persley
Woodside
Don Street
Kittybrewster
Waterloo
Guild Street
Limpet Mill
Hutcheon Street
School Hill
Aberdeen
Holburn Street
Ruthrieston
Ferry
-hill
Cove Bay
Pitfodels
Cults
West Cults
Bieldside
Milltimber
Murtle
Culter
Mills of Drum
Drum
Park
Crathes
Portlethen
Newtonhill
Muchalls
Stonehaven
Carmont
Drumlithie
Newmill
Fordoun
Banchory
Dee Street
Halt
Glassel
Torphins
Lumphanan
Dess
Aboyne
Dinnet
Cambus o' May
Ballater
Laid 1868
then abandoned

Monymusk
Tillyfourie
Whitehouse
Alford

Inverbervie
Gourdon
Birnie Road
Johnshaven
Lauriston
St Cyrus
North Water Bridge
Broomfield Road Junction
Laurencekirk
Marykirk
Craigo
Hill-
side
(NB)
(CAL)
Montrose
Dubton
Bridge of
Dee
Edzell
Stracathro
Brechin
Careston
Tannadice
Justinhaugh
Kirriemuir
Farnell Road

51

57

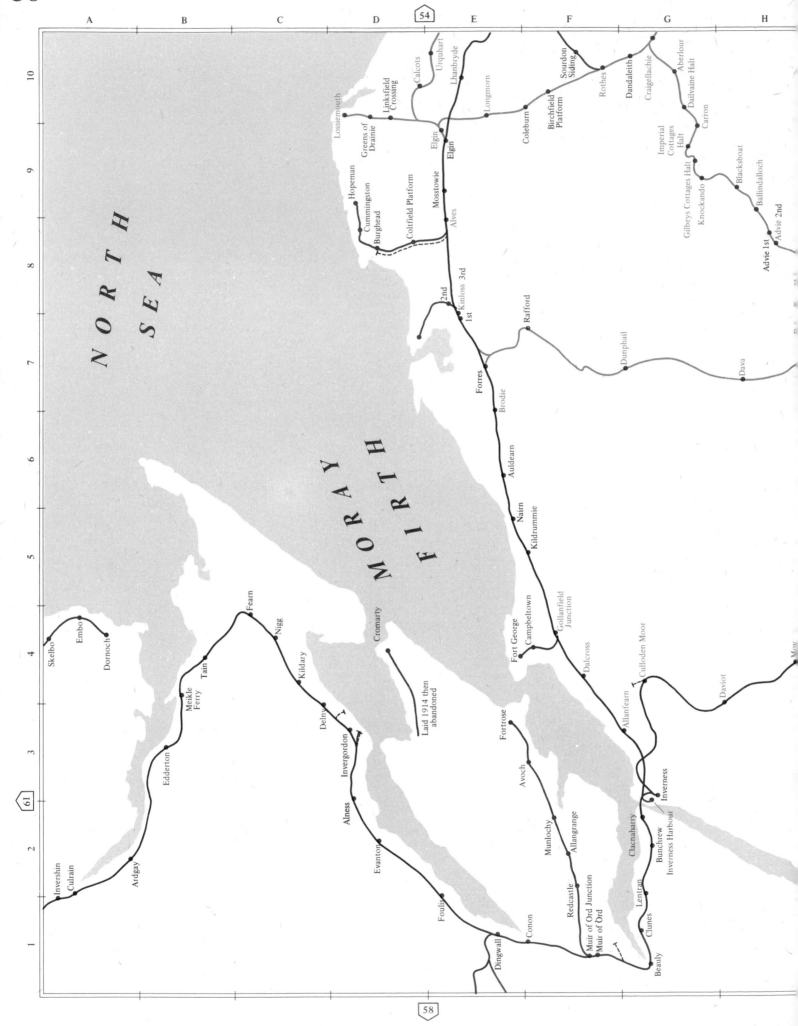

NORTH SEA

MORAY FIRTH

Skelbo
Embo
Dornoch
Inveoshin
Culrain
Ardgay
Edderton
Meikle Ferry
Tain
Fearn
Nigg
Kildary
Delny
Invergordon
Alness
Evanton
Foulis
Dingwall
Conon
Redcastle
Muir of Ord Junction
Muir of Ord
Clunes
Beauly
Lentran
Clachnaharry
Bunchrew
Inverness Harbour
Inverness
Allangrange
Munlochy
Avoch
Fortrose
Cromarty
Laid 1914 then abandoned
Fort George
Campbeltown
Gollanfield Junction
Dalcross
Allanfearn
Culloden Moor
Daviot
Moy
Nairn
Kildrummie
Auldearn
Brodie
Forres
Rafford
Dunphail
Dava
Kinloss 1st
2nd
3rd
Alves
Mosstowie
Coltfield Platform
Burghead
Cummingston
Hopeman
Greens of Drainie
Lossiemouth
Linksfield Crossing
Calcots
Urquhart
Lhanbryde
Elgin
Longmorn
Coleburn
Birchfield Platform
Sourdon Siding
Rothes
Dandaleith
Craigellachie
Aberlour
Dailvaine Halt
Carron
Imperial Cottages Halt
Gilbeys Cottages Halt
Knockando
Blacksboat
Ballindalloch
Advie 1st
Advie 2nd

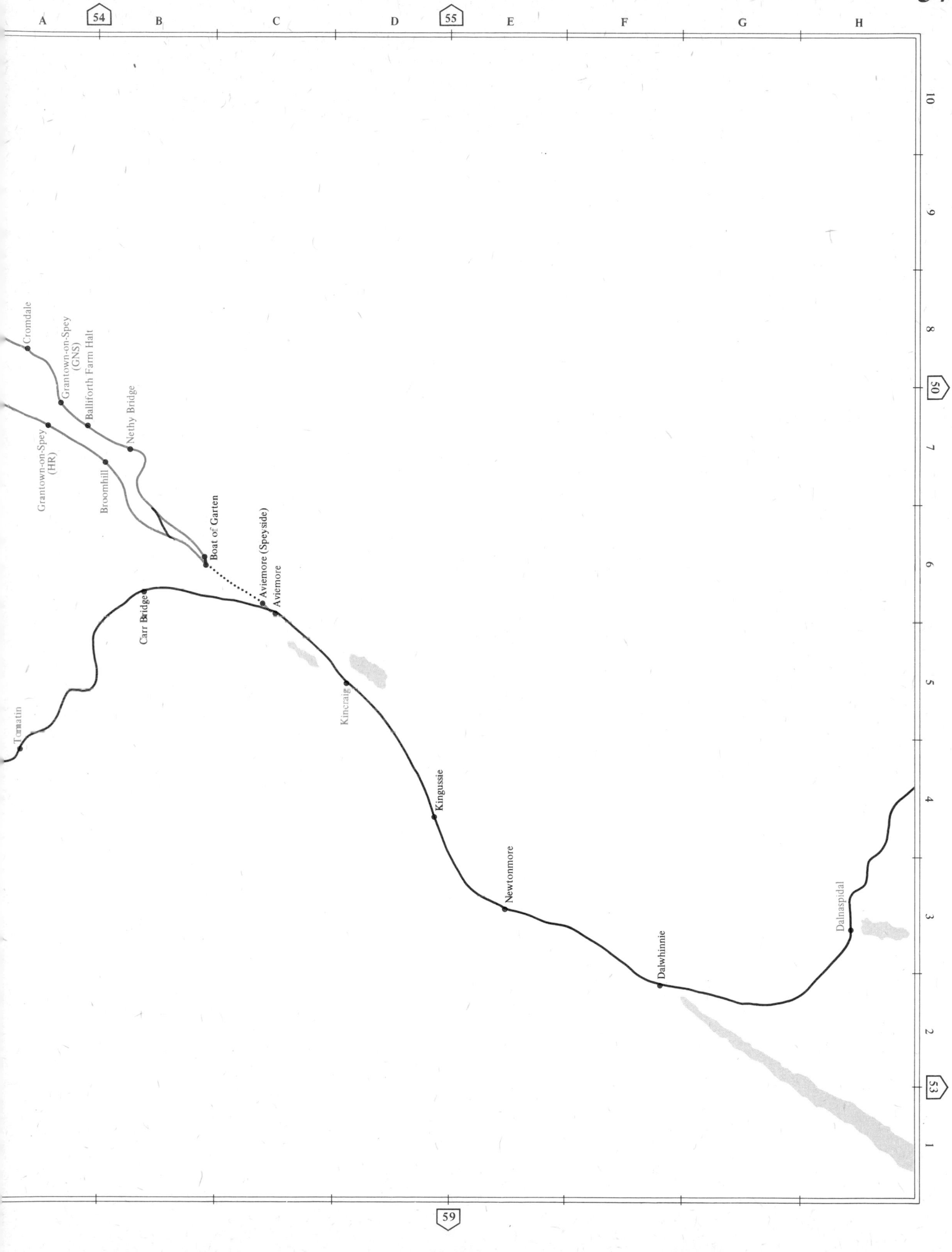

A 54 B C D 55 E F G H

10 9 50 8 7 6 5 4 3 53 2 1

Cromdale

Grantown-on-Spey (GNS)

Balliforth Farm Halt

Nethy Bridge

Grantown-on-Spey (HR)

Broomhill

Boat of Garten

Aviemore (Speyside)

Aviemore

Carr Bridge

Tomatin

Kincraig

Kingussie

Newtonmore

Dalwhinnie

Dalnaspidal

59

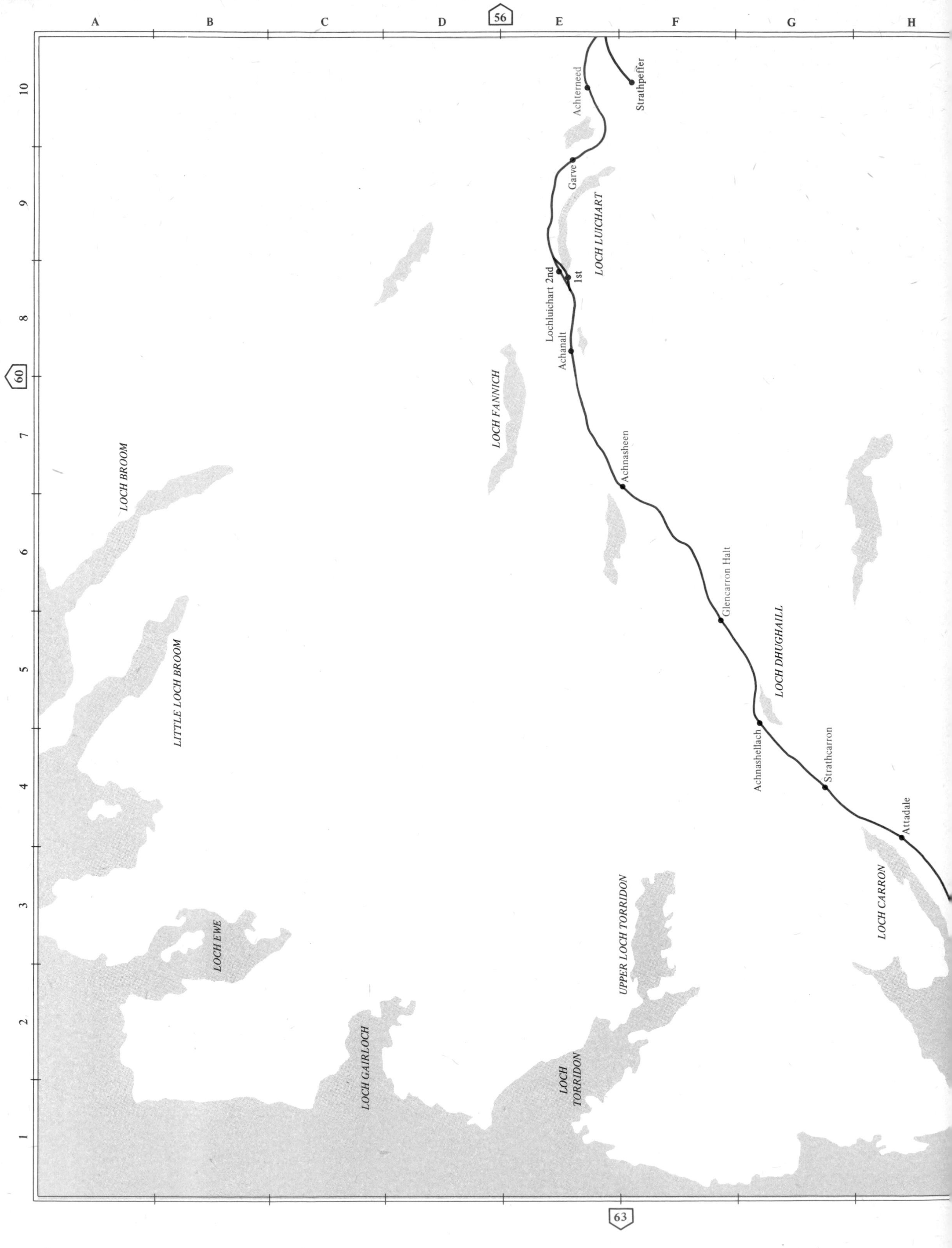

A   B   C   D   56   E   F   G   H

10

9

8

7

60

6

5

4

3

2

1

63

LOCH BROOM

LITTLE LOCH BROOM

LOCH EWE

LOCH GAIRLOCH

LOCH FANNICH

UPPER LOCH TORRIDON

LOCH TORRIDON

LOCH CARRON

LOCH LUICHART

LOCH DHUGHAILL

Strathpeffer

Achterneed

Garve

Lochluichart 2nd

1st

Achanalt

Achnasheen

Glencarron Halt

Achnashellach

Strathcarron

Attadale

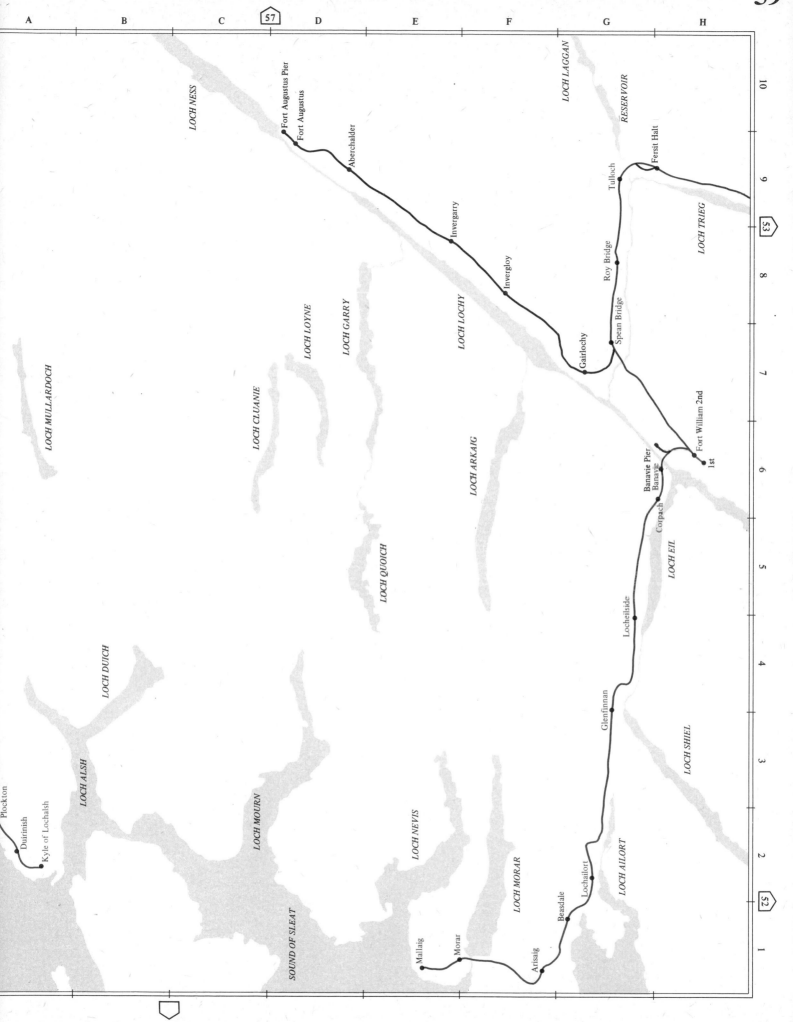

A   B   C   57   D   E   F   G   H

10   9   53   8   7   6   5   4   3   52   2   1

LOCH NESS

LOCH LAGGAN

RESERVOIR

Fort Augustus Pier

Fort Augustus

Aberchalder

Fersit Halt

Tulloch

LOCH TRIEG

Invergarry

Invergloy

Roy Bridge

Spean Bridge

LOCH LOYNE

LOCH GARRY

LOCH LOCHY

Gairlochy

LOCH CLUANIE

LOCH ARKAIG

Fort William 2nd

LOCH QUOICH

Banavie Pier
Banavie

1st

Corpach

LOCH EIL

LOCH MULLARDOCH

Locheilside

LOCH DUICH

Glenfinnan

LOCH SHIEL

Plockton

LOCH ALSH

Duirinish

Kyle of Lochalsh

LOCH MOURN

LOCH NEVIS

LOCH MORAR

LOCH AILORT

Lochailort

Beasdale

Mallaig

Morar

Arisaig

SOUND OF SLEAT

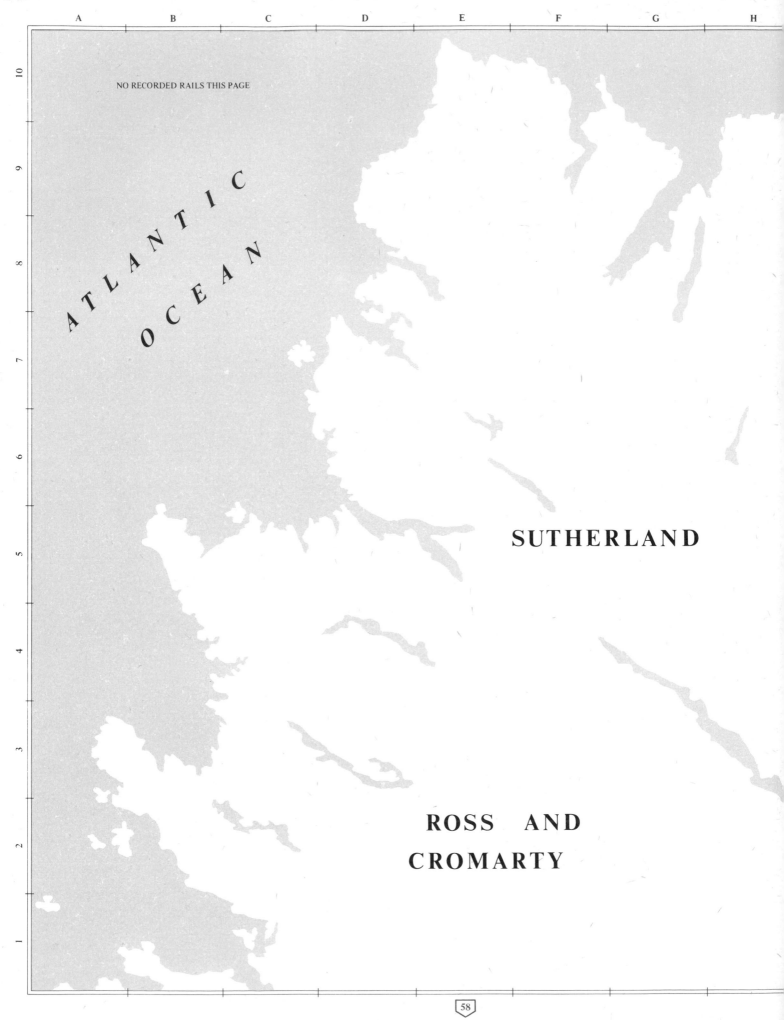

60

A   B   C   D   E   F   G   H

10

NO RECORDED RAILS THIS PAGE

9

A T L A N T I C

O C E A N

8

7

6

SUTHERLAND

5

4

3

ROSS   AND

2

CROMARTY

1

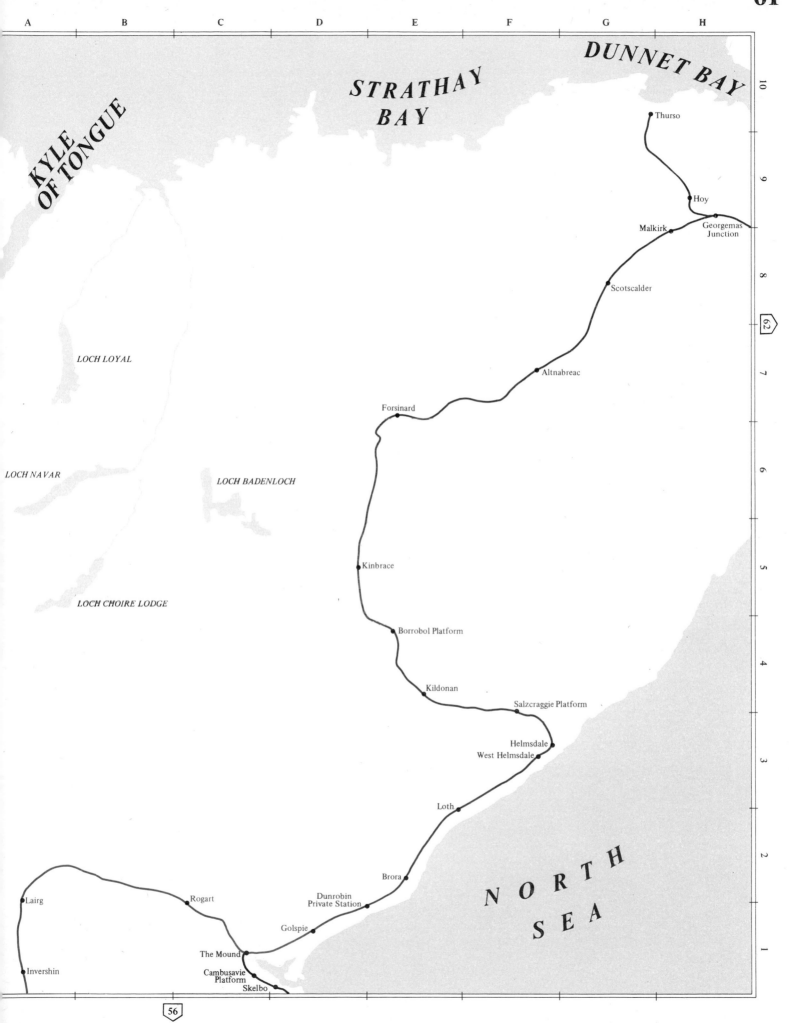

KYLE OF TONGUE

STRATHAY BAY

DUNNET BAY

Thurso

Hoy

Malkirk

Georgemas Junction

Scotscalder

LOCH LOYAL

Altnabreac

Forsinard

LOCH NAVAR

LOCH BADENLOCH

Kinbrace

LOCH CHOIRE LODGE

Borrobol Platform

Kildonan

Salzcraggie Platform

Helmsdale
West Helmsdale

Loth

NORTH SEA

Brora

Lairg

Rogart

Dunrobin Private Station

Golspie

The Mound

Invershin

Cambusavie Platform

Skelbo

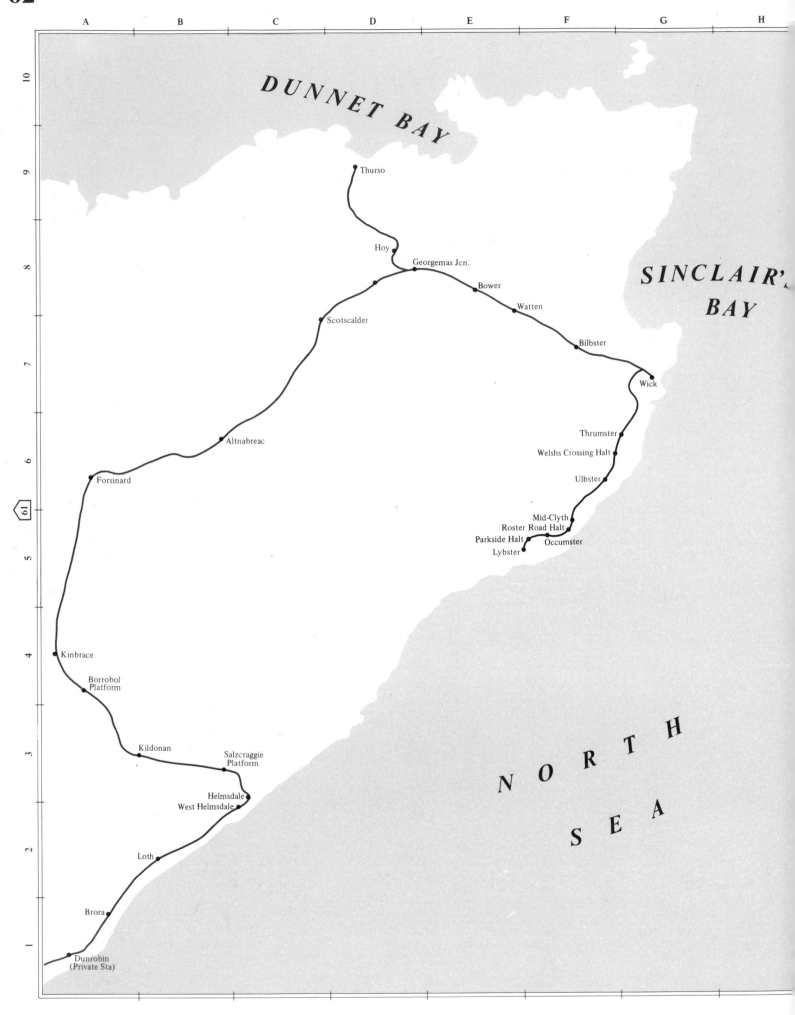

DUNNET BAY

SINCLAIR'S
BAY

Thurso

Hoy

Georgemas Jcn.

Bower

Watten

Scotscalder

Bilbster

Wick

Altnabreac

Thrumster

Welshs Crossing Halt

Ulbster

Forsinard

Mid-Clyth

Roster Road Halt

Parkside Halt

Occumster

Lybster

Kinbrace

Borrobol
Platform

Kildonan

Salzcraggie
Platform

Helmsdale

West Helmsdale

Loth

N O R T H

Brora

S E A

Dunrobin
(Private Sta)

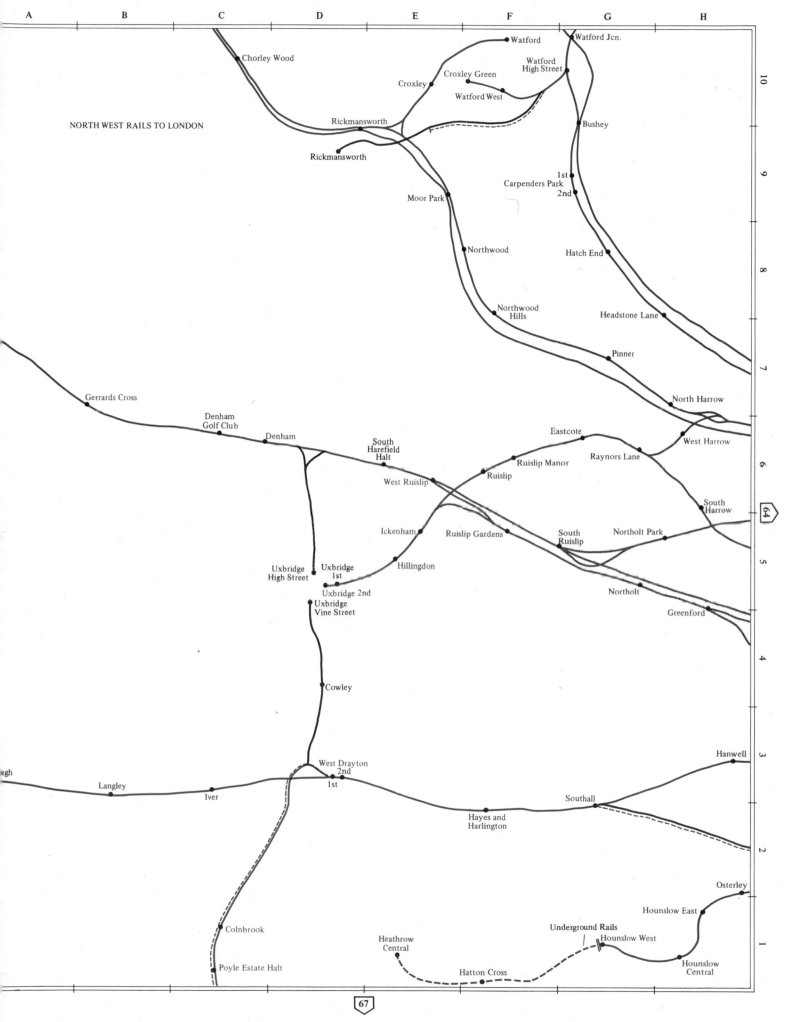

A   B   C   D   E   F   G   H

Watford
Watford Jcn.
Watford
High Street
Chorley Wood
Croxley Green
Croxley
Watford West

NORTH WEST RAILS TO LONDON

Rickmansworth
Bushey

Rickmansworth

1st
Carpenders Park
2nd

Moor Park

Northwood
Hatch End

Northwood
Hills
Headstone Lane

Pinner

North Harrow

Gerrards Cross

Denham
Golf Club
Eastcote
West Harrow
South
Harefield
Halt
Raynors Lane
Denham
Ruislip Manor

Ruislip
West Ruislip
South
Harrow

Ickenham
Ruislip Gardens
Northolt Park

Uxbridge
High Street
Uxbridge
1st
Hillingdon
South
Ruislip

Uxbridge 2nd
Northolt
Uxbridge
Vine Street
Greenford

Cowley

Hanwell

West Drayton
2nd
Langley
1st
Southall
Iver
Hayes and
Harlington

Osterley

Hounslow East

Colnbrook
Underground Rails
Hounslow West
Heathrow
Central
Poyle Estate Halt
Hatton Cross
Hounslow
Central

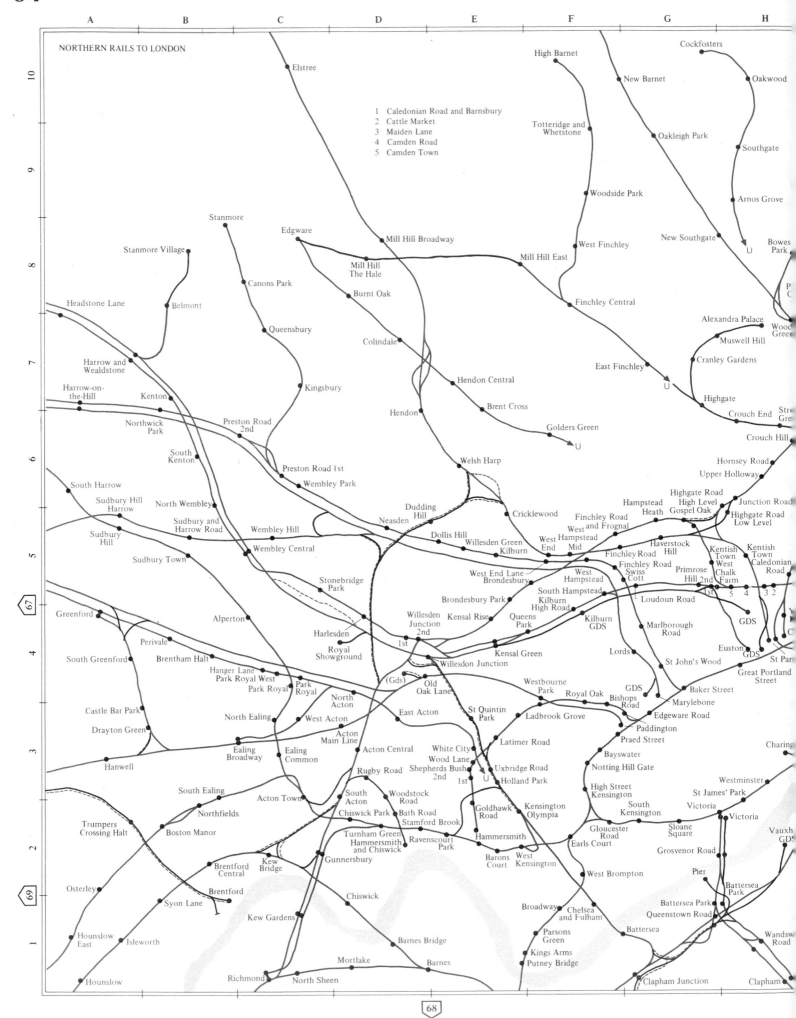

NORTHERN RAILS TO LONDON

1 Caledonian Road and Barnsbury
2 Cattle Market
3 Maiden Lane
4 Camden Road
5 Camden Town

High Barnet
New Barnet
Cockfosters
Oakwood
Totteridge and Whetstone
Oakleigh Park
Southgate
Elstree
Woodside Park
Arnos Grove
Mill Hill Broadway
Mill Hill East
New Southgate
U
Stanmore
Edgware
West Finchley
Bowes
Park
Mill Hill
The Hale
P
C
Canons Park
Finchley Central
Stanmore Village
Burnt Oak
Alexandra Palace
Wood
Green
Headstone Lane
Belmont
Queensbury
Muswell Hill
Colindale
Cranley Gardens
Harrow and
Wealdstone
Kingsbury
Hendon Central
East Finchley
U
Highgate
Harrow-on-
the-Hill
Kenton
Preston Road
2nd
Hendon
Brent Cross
Crouch End
Stro
Gre
Northwick
Park
South
Kenton
Golders Green
U
Crouch Hill
Welsh Harp
Hornsey Road
Preston Road 1st
Upper Holloway
South Harrow
Wembley Park
Highgate Road
High Level
Junction Road
Sudbury Hill
Harrow
North Wembley
Dudding
Hill
Cricklewood
Hampstead
Heath
Gospel Oak
Highgate Road
Low Level
Sudbury and
Harrow Road
Wembley Hill
Neasden
Dollis Hill
Finchley Road
and Frognal
West
End
Haverstock
Hill
Sudbury
Hill
Wembley Central
Willesden Green
Kilburn
West Hampstead
Mid
Kentish
Town
West
Kentish
Town
Sudbury Town
West End Lane
Brondesbury
Finchley Road
Swiss
Cott
West
Hampstead
Primrose
Hill 2nd
Chalk
Farm
Caledonian
Road
Stonebridge
Park
Brondesbury Park
South Hampstead
Loudoun Road
1st
5 4 3 2
Greenford
Alperton
Willesden
Junction
2nd
Kensal Rise
Queens
Park
Kilburn
High Road
Kilburn
GDS
GDS
Perivale
Harlesden
1st
Marlborough
Road
Euston
GDS
South Greenford
Royal
Showground
Kensal Green
Lords
St John's Wood
St Par
Brentham Halt
Willesden Junction
St John's Wood
Great Portland
Street
Hanger Lane
Park Royal West
(Gds)
GDS
Baker Street
Castle Bar Park
Park Royal
Old
Oak Lane
Westbourne
Park
Royal Oak
Bishops
Road
Marylebone
Park Royal
North
Acton
East Acton
St Quintin
Park
Paddington
Edgware Road
Drayton Green
North Ealing
West Acton
Ladbrook Grove
Praed Street
Ealing
Broadway
Ealing
Common
Acton
Main Line
White City
Wood Lane
Latimer Road
Bayswater
Charing
Acton Central
Shepherds Bush
2nd
Uxbridge Road
Notting Hill Gate
Hanwell
Rugby Road
1st
U
Holland Park
High Street
Kensington
Westminster
South Ealing
Woodstock
Road
Goldhawk
Road
Kensington
Olympia
St James' Park
Northfields
Acton Town
South
Acton
Bath Road
Stamford Brook
South
Kensington
Victoria
Trumpers
Crossing Halt
Boston Manor
Chiswick Park
Hammersmith
Gloucester
Road
Sloane
Square
Victoria
Turnham Green
Hammersmith
and Chiswick
Ravenscourt
Park
Grosvenor Road
Vauxh
GDS
Brentford
Central
Kew
Bridge
Gunnersbury
Barons
Court
West
Kensington
West Brompton
Pier
Battersea
Park
Osterley
Brentford
Chiswick
Broadway
Chelsea
and Fulham
Battersea Park
Queenstown Road
Syon Lane
Battersea
Hounslow
East
Isleworth
Kew Gardens
Parsons
Green
Wandsw
Road
Hounslow
Kings Arms
Putney Bridge
Richmond
North Sheen
Barnes Bridge
Mortlake
Barnes
Clapham Junction
Clapham

67
69
68

NORTHERN RAILS TO LONDON

Enfield Town
Turkey Street
Forty Hill
Brimsdown Power Station
Ordnance Factory
Carterhatch Lane Halt
Churchbury
Bush Hill Park
Southbury
Ponders End
field Chase
Grange Park
Winchmore Hill
Debden
Loughton
Chingford 2nd
Chingford 1st
Buckhurst Hill
Lower Edmonton
Lower Edmonton Low Level
Angel Road
Highams Park
Roding Valley
Chigwell
Grange Hill
Woodford
Silver St
almers Green
Hainault
White Hart Lane
Northumberland Park
South Woodford
Fairlop
Bruce Grove
Noel Park
Tottenham Hale
Barkingside
West Green
Blackhorse Road
Wood Street
Snaresbrook
Newbury Park
Seven Sisters
St James Street
Central Walthamstowe
Queens Road
Gants Hill
Chadwell Heath
nsey
Harringay
South Tottenham
Wanstead
Redbridge
Goodmayes
St Ann's Road
Harringay Stadium
Stamford Hill
Leyton Midland Road
Seven Kings
Finsbury Park
Lea Bridge
Leytonstone
Ilford
Stoke Newington
(GDS)
Leytonstone High Road
Rectory Road
Clapton
Leyton
Wanstead Park
Forest Gate (GDS)
Manor Park
Mildmay Park
Kingsland
Hackney Downs
Hackney Wick
U
Forest Gate
Woodgrange Park
Canonbury
Hackney Central
Victoria Park
Maryland (GDS)
East Ham
Barking
Upney
Becontree
Highbury and Islington
Dalston Junction
Stratford Lower
U
London Fields
(GDS)
West Ham (GDS)
West Ham
Plaistow
Upton Park
Haggerston
Old Ford
Cambridge Heath
Coborn Road
Bow Bromley
Farringdon
Globe Road
Bow Road
Bow Road
1st 2nd Bromley
Canning Town
Beckton Gas Works
Barbican
Broad Street
Shoreditch
Mile End
Devons Road
(GDS)
Beckton
Moorgate
Bishops-gate
Stepney Green
East India Tidal Basin
Liverpool Str
8
Poplar
Manor Way
Hill
1
2
3
4
St Marys
7
Stepney East
West India Docks
Central
Gallions
Mansion House
Cannon Street
6
5
9
Poplar
Blackwall
Custom House
Victoria Dock
Connaught Road
North Woolwich
Tower Hill
Shadwell
Limehouse
Silvertown
Black friars
Mark Lane
Wapping
Millwall Junction
(GDS)
erloo
Monument
London Bridge
South Dock
Angerstein Wharf
Woolwich Arsenal
Abbey Wood
nction
Blackfriars Road
Spa Road
Rotherhithe
Millwall Docks
Woolwich Dockyard
Plumstead
Church Manor Way Halt
Necro-polis
Borough Road
Willow Walk
Southwark Park
Surrey Docks
North Greenwich
Charlton
ephant d Castle
Bricklayers Arms
GDS
South Bermond-sey
Commercial Docks
Maze Hill
Westcombe Park
orth Road
Old Kent Road
Deptford
Greenwich
Greenwich Park
Blackheath Hill
Welling
mberwell
Queen's Road
New Cross Gate
10
New Cross
St Johns
Falconwood
orough nction
Denmark Hill
Peckham Rye
South Bermondsey
East London Sta
Brockley Lane
Lewisham Road
Blackheath
Kidbrooke
East Brixton
Nunhead
Brockley
Lewisham

1 Aldersgate
2 Moorgate Street
3 Liverpool Street (LT)
4 Aldgate
5 Fenchurch Street
6 Aldgate East
7 Whitechapel
8 Whitechapel
9 Shadwell (GE)
10 Deptford Road

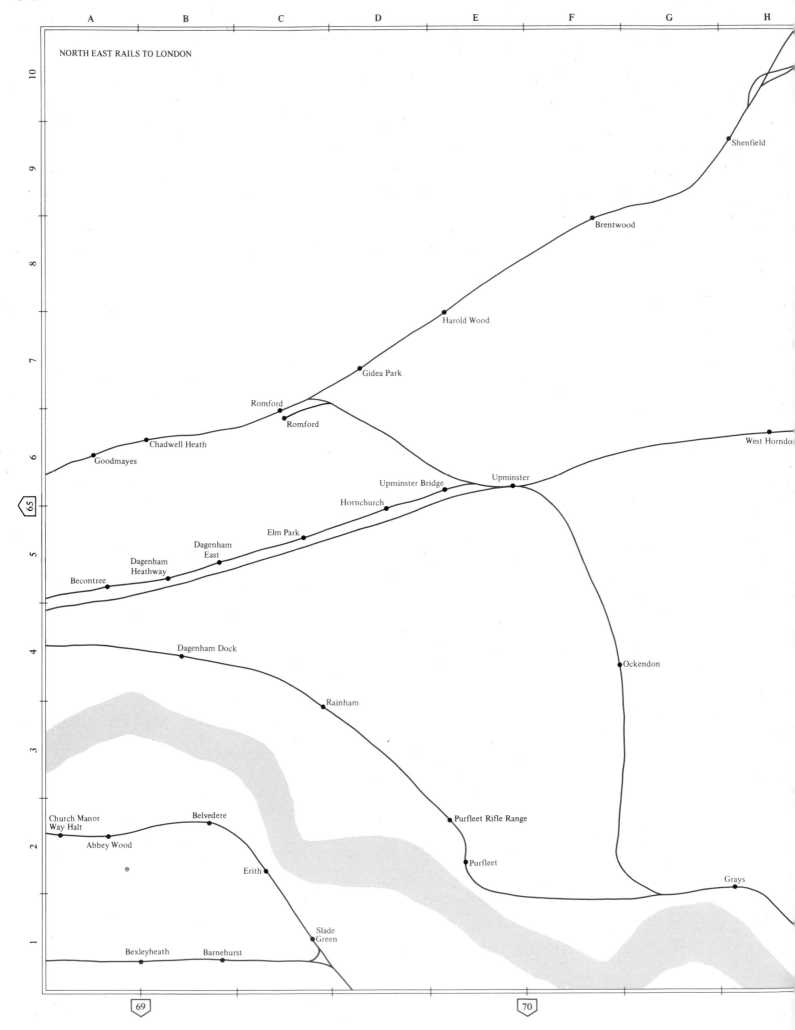

NORTH EAST RAILS TO LONDON

Shenfield

Brentwood

Harold Wood

Gidea Park

Romford

Romford

Chadwell Heath

Goodmayes

West Horndon

Upminster Bridge

Upminster

Hornchurch

Elm Park

Dagenham
East

Dagenham
Heathway

Becontree

Ockendon

Dagenham Dock

Rainham

Purfleet Rifle Range

Church Manor
Way Halt

Belvedere

Abbey Wood

Purfleet

Erith

Grays

Slade
Green

Bexleyheath

Barnehurst

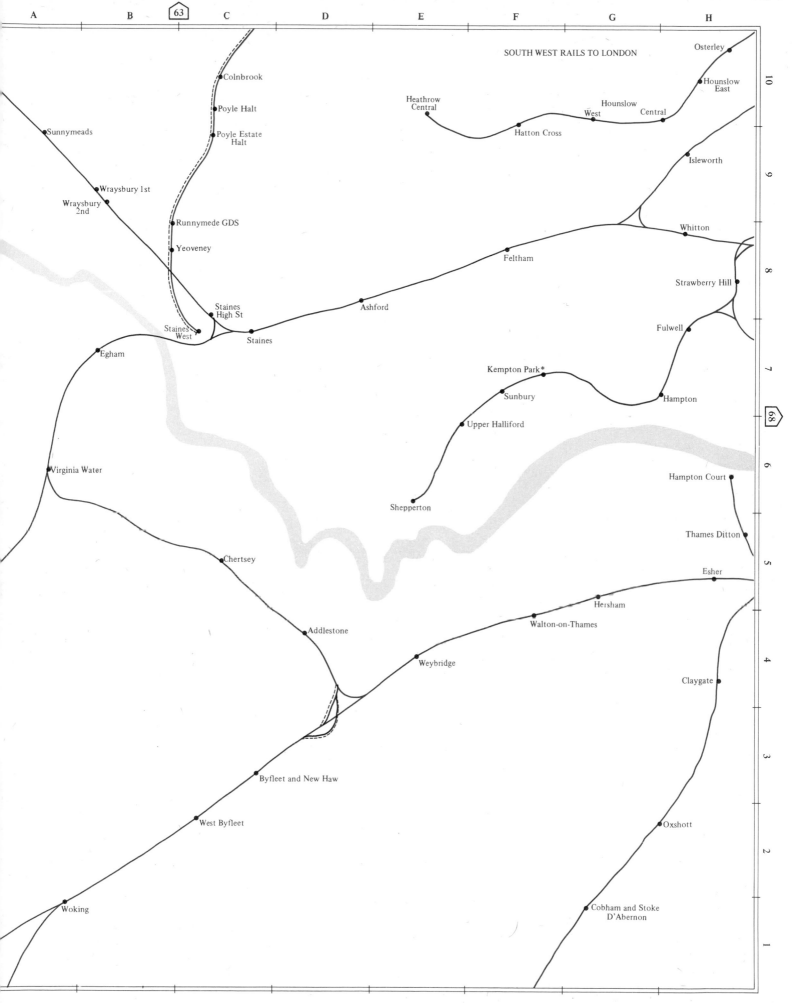

A   B   63   C   D   E   F   G   H

SOUTH WEST RAILS TO LONDON

Osterley

Colnbrook

Hounslow East

Poyle Halt

Heathrow Central

Hounslow West   Central

Poyle Estate Halt

Sunnymeads

Hatton Cross

Isleworth

Wraysbury 1st

Wraysbury 2nd

Runnymede GDS

Whitton

Yeoveney

Feltham

Strawberry Hill

Staines High St

Ashford

Staines West

Fulwell

Staines

Kempton Park*

Egham

Hampton

Sunbury

Upper Halliford

68

Virginia Water

Hampton Court

Shepperton

Thames Ditton

Chertsey

Esher

Hersham

Walton-on-Thames

Addlestone

Weybridge

Claygate

Byfleet and New Haw

West Byfleet

Oxshott

Woking

Cobham and Stoke D'Abernon

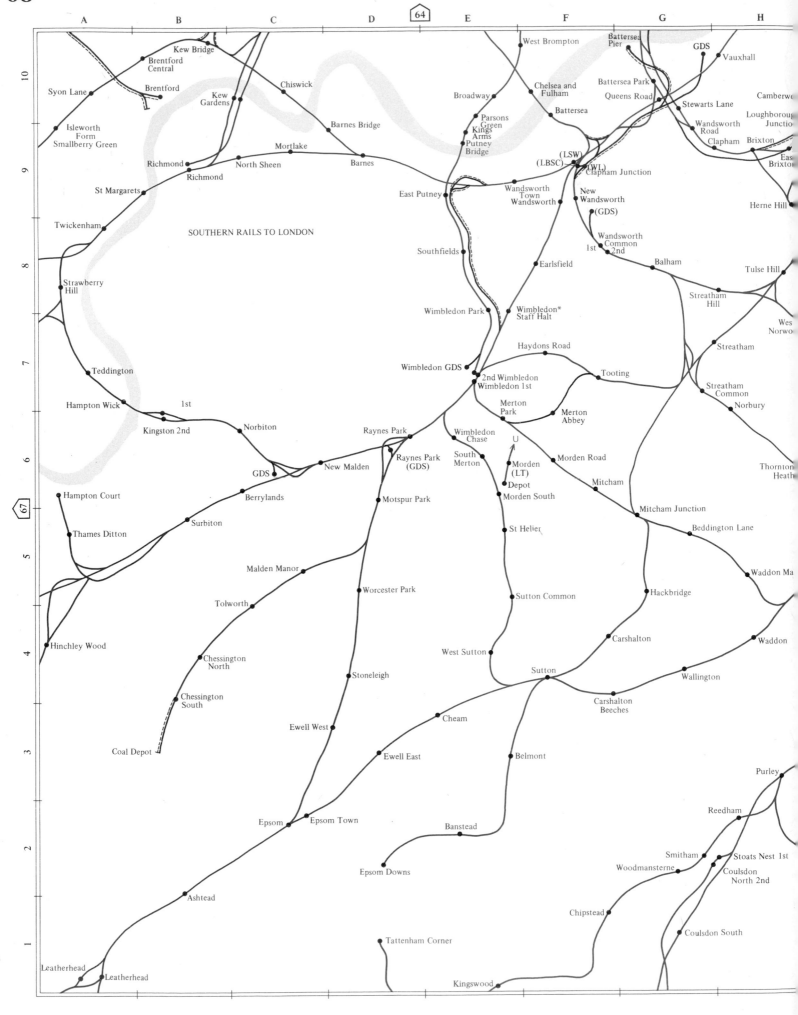

SOUTHERN RAILS TO LONDON

A B C D 64 E F G H

Syon Lane
Kew Bridge
Brentford Central
Brentford
Chiswick
Isleworth Form Smallberry Green
Kew Gardens
Barnes Bridge
West Brompton
Battersea Pier
GDS
Vauxhall
Broadway
Chelsea and Fulham
Battersea Park
Queens Road
Stewarts Lane
Battersea
Camberwell
Loughborough Junction
Mortlake
Parsons Green
Kings Arms Putney Bridge
Wandsworth Road
Clapham
Brixton
Richmond
Richmond
North Sheen
Barnes
(LSW)
(LBSC)
(WL)
Clapham Junction
East Brixton
St Margarets
East Putney
Wandsworth Town
Wandsworth
New Wandsworth (GDS)
Herne Hill
Twickenham
Southfields
Wandsworth Common 1st 2nd
Balham
Tulse Hill
Strawberry Hill
Earlsfield
Wimbledon Park
Wimbledon* Staff Halt
Streatham Hill
Wes Norwo
Teddington
Haydons Road
Streatham
Hampton Wick
1st
Wimbledon GDS
2nd Wimbledon Wimbledon 1st
Tooting
Streatham Common
Norbury
Kingston 2nd
Norbiton
Raynes Park
Merton Park
Merton Abbey
Hampton Court
GDS
New Malden
Raynes Park (GDS)
Wimbledon Chase
South Merton
Morden (LT)
Morden Road
Mitcham
Thornton Heath
Berrylands
Motspur Park
Depot
Morden South
Mitcham Junction
Thames Ditton
Surbiton
Beddington Lane
Malden Manor
St Helier
Hackbridge
Waddon Ma
Hinchley Wood
Tolworth
Worcester Park
Sutton Common
Carshalton
Waddon
Chessington North
Stoneleigh
West Sutton
Sutton
Wallington
Chessington South
Ewell West
Cheam
Carshalton Beeches
Coal Depot
Ewell East
Belmont
Purley
Reedham
Epsom
Epsom Town
Banstead
Smitham
Stoats Nest 1st
Woodmansterne
Coulsdon North 2nd
Ashtead
Epsom Downs
Chipstead
Tattenham Corner
Coulsdon South
Leatherhead
Leatherhead
Kingswood

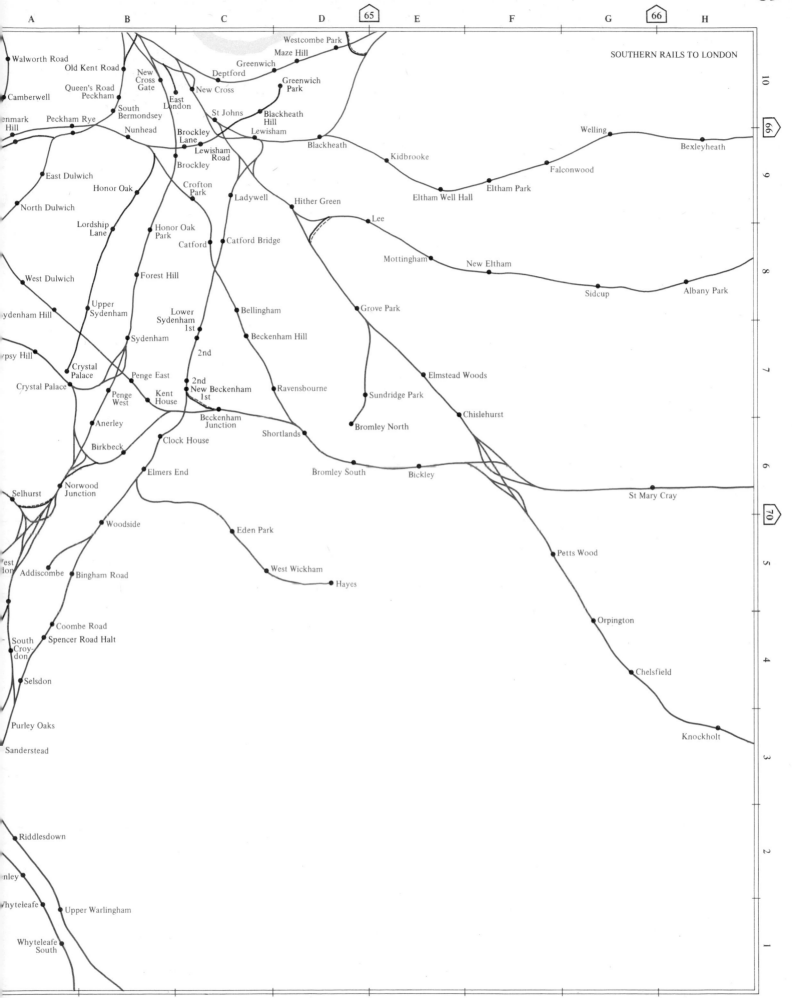

SOUTHERN RAILS TO LONDON

A · B · C · D · 65 · E · F · G · 66 · H

Walworth Road
Old Kent Road
New Cross Gate
Greenwich
Deptford
Westcombe Park
Maze Hill
Camberwell
Queen's Road Peckham
East London
New Cross
Greenwich Park
enmark Hill
Peckham Rye
South Bermondsey
St Johns
Blackheath Hill
Welling
Bexleyheath
Nunhead
Brockley Lane
Lewisham
East Dulwich
Brockley
Lewisham Road
Blackheath
Kidbrooke
Falconwood
North Dulwich
Honor Oak
Crofton Park
Ladywell
Hither Green
Eltham Well Hall
Eltham Park
Lordship Lane
Honor Oak Park
Catford
Catford Bridge
Lee
Mottingham
New Eltham
West Dulwich
Forest Hill
Bellingham
Grove Park
Sidcup
Albany Park
ydenham Hill
Upper Sydenham
Lower Sydenham 1st
Beckenham Hill
Upper Sydenham
Sydenham
2nd
psy Hill
Crystal Palace
Penge East
2nd
New Beckenham 1st
Ravensbourne
Elmstead Woods
Crystal Palace
Penge West
Kent House
Sundridge Park
Chislehurst
Anerley
Beckenham Junction
Shortlands
Bromley North
Birkbeck
Clock House
Selhurst
Norwood Junction
Elmers End
Bromley South
Bickley
St Mary Cray
Woodside
Eden Park
Petts Wood
West lon
Addiscombe
Bingham Road
West Wickham
Hayes
Coombe Road
Orpington
South Croy-don
Spencer Road Halt
Selsdon
Chelsfield
Purley Oaks
Sanderstead
Knockholt
Riddlesdown
nley
Whyteleafe
Upper Warlingham
Whyteleafe South

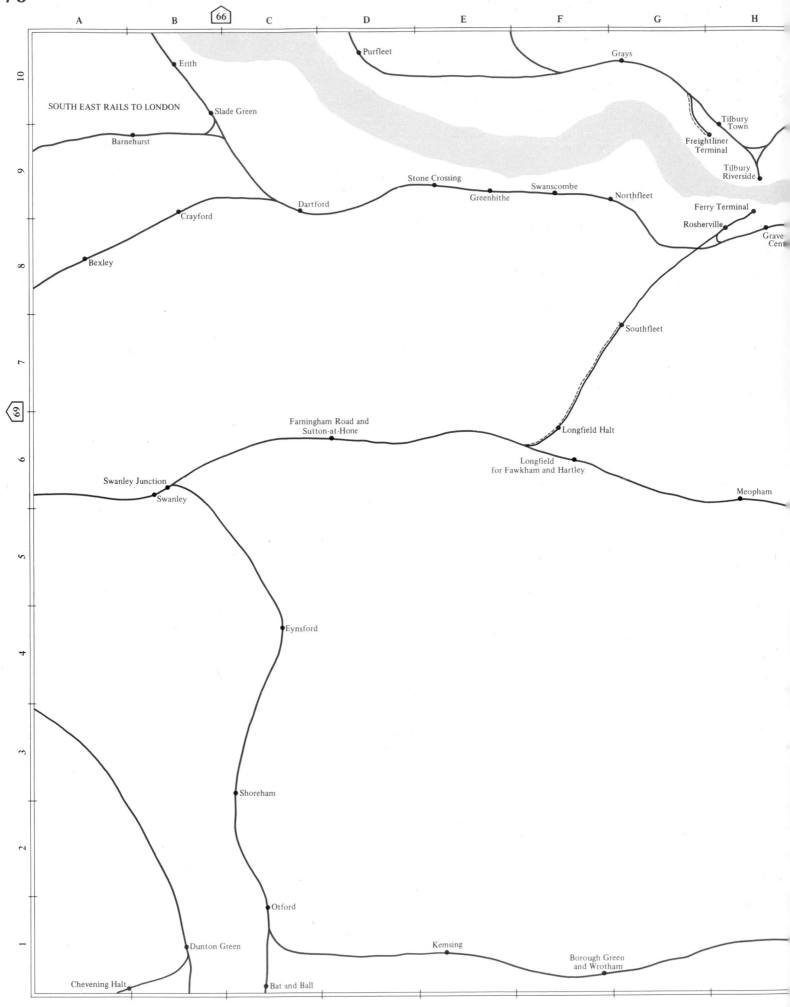

SOUTH EAST RAILS TO LONDON

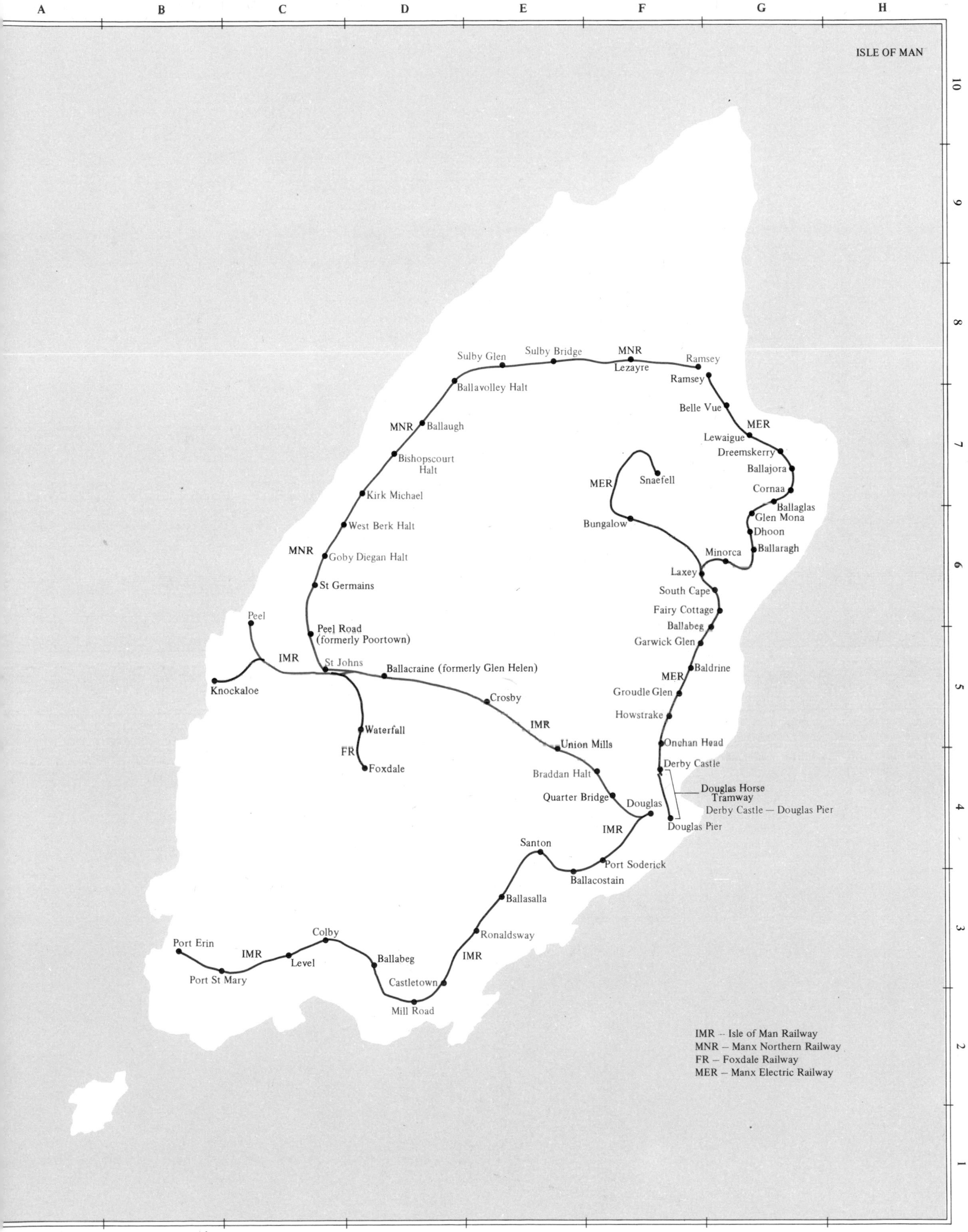

ISLE OF MAN

Sulby Glen   Sulby Bridge   **MNR**   Ramsey
                             Lezayre   Ramsey
Ballavolley Halt   Belle Vue
                                                MER
MNR Ballaugh   Lewaigue
                                        Dreemskerry
Bishopscourt   Ballajora
Halt   **MER** Snaefell   Cornaa
Kirk Michael   Ballaglas
                                                 Glen Mona
West Berk Halt   Bungalow   Dhoon
MNR Goby Diegan Halt   Ballaragh
                                        Minorca
St Germains   Laxey
                                        South Cape
Peel   Fairy Cottage
          Peel Road   Ballabeg
          (formerly Poortown)   Garwick Glen
IMR St Johns   Baldrine
         Ballacraine (formerly Glen Helen) **MER**
Knockaloe   Groudle Glen
                            Crosby   Howstrake
          Waterfall
FR   **IMR**   Onchan Head
          Foxdale   Union Mills Derby Castle

                           Braddan Halt
                                        Douglas Horse
          Quarter Bridge   Douglas   Tramway
                                        Derby Castle — Douglas Pier
                           IMR
                                        Douglas Pier
                    Santon
                            Port Soderick
                    Ballacostain
               Ballasalla
Port Erin   Colby   Ronaldsway
IMR   Ballabeg **IMR**
Port St Mary Level
                 Castletown
               Mill Road

IMR – Isle of Man Railway
MNR – Manx Northern Railway
FR – Foxdale Railway
MER – Manx Electric Railway

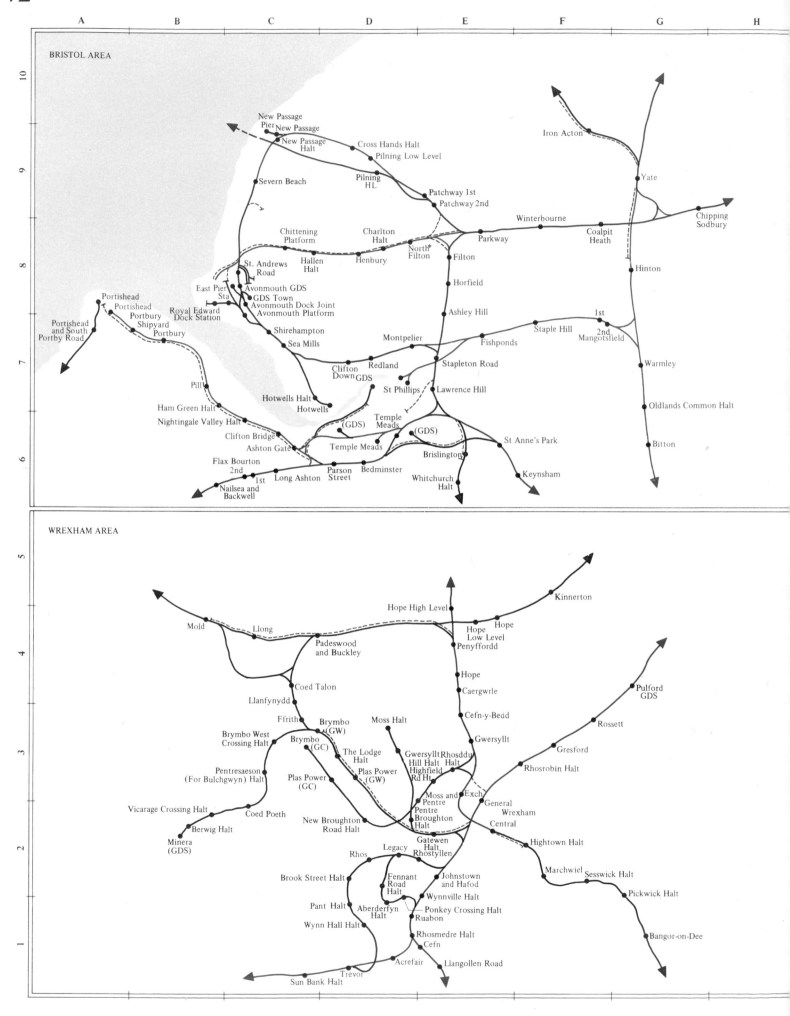

BRISTOL AREA

	A	B	C	D	E	F	G	H

New Passage Pier
New Passage
New Passage Halt
Cross Hands Halt
Pilning Low Level
Severn Beach
Pilning HL
Patchway 1st
Patchway 2nd
Iron Acton
Yate
Chipping Sodbury
Winterbourne
Coalpit Heath
Chittening Platform
Charlton Halt
Parkway
Hinton
North Filton
Filton
Henbury
Hallen Halt
St. Andrews Road
Horfield
East Pier Sta
Avonmouth GDS
GDS Town
Royal Edward Dock Station
Avonmouth Dock Joint
Avonmouth Platform
Ashley Hill
1st
Portishead
Portishead
Portbury Shipyard
Portishead and South Portby Road
Portbury
Shirehampton
Sea Mills
Montpelier
Staple Hill
2nd
Mangotsfield
Fishponds
Warmley
Pill
Clifton Down
Redland
GDS
Stapleton Road
Ham Green Halt
Hotwells Halt
St Phillips
Lawrence Hill
Oldlands Common Halt
Nightingale Valley Halt
Hotwells
Clifton Bridge
(GDS)
Temple Meads
(GDS)
St Anne's Park
Bitton
Ashton Gate
Temple Meads
Flax Bourton
2nd
Long Ashton
Parson Street
Bedminster
Brislington
Keynsham
1st
Whitchurch Halt
Nailsea and Backwell

WREXHAM AREA

	A	B	C	D	E	F	G	H

Hope High Level
Kinnerton
Mold
Llong
Hope
Hope Low Level
Penyffordd
Padeswood and Buckley
Hope
Pulford GDS
Coed Talon
Caergwrle
Llanfynydd
Cefn-y-Bedd
Rossett
Ffrith
Brymbo (GW)
Moss Halt
Gwersyllt
Gresford
Brymbo West Crossing Halt
Brymbo (GC)
The Lodge Halt
Gwersyllt Hill Halt
Rhosddu Halt
Rhosrobin Halt
Pentresaeson (For Bulchgwyn) Halt
Plas Power (GW)
Highfield Rd Ht
Plas Power (GC)
Moss and Pentre
Exch
Vicarage Crossing Halt
Coed Poeth
New Broughton Road Halt
Pentre Broughton Halt
General Wrexham
Berwig Halt
Central
Hightown Halt
Minera (GDS)
Gatewen Halt
Legacy
Rhostyllen
Rhos
Marchwiel
Sesswick Halt
Brook Street Halt
Fennant Road Halt
Johnstown and Hafod
Pickwick Halt
Wynnville Halt
Pant Halt
Aberderfyn Halt
Ponkey Crossing Halt
Wynn Hall Halt
Ruabon
Bangor-on-Dee
Rhosmedre Halt
Cefn
Acrefair
Llangollen Road
Trevor
Sun Bank Halt

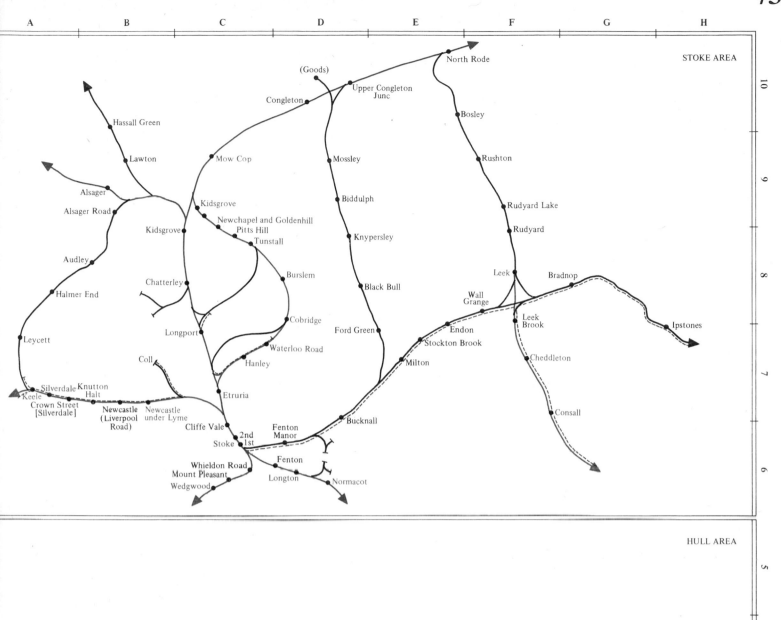

A B C D E F G H

10
9
8
7
6

North Rode

(Goods)

Upper Congleton Junc

Congleton

Bosley

Hassall Green

Lawton

Mow Cop

Rushton

Alsager

Alsager Road

Kidsgrove

Mossley

Rudyard Lake

Rudyard

Kidsgrove

Newchapel and Goldenhill
Pitts Hill
Tunstall

Biddulph

Knypersley

Audley

Chatterley

Burslem

Black Bull

Leek

Bradnop

Halmer End

Wall
Grange

Cobridge

Longport

Ford Green

Endon

Leek
Brook

Ipstones

Leycett

Waterloo Road

Hanley

Stockton Brook

Cheddleton

Coll

Etruria

Milton

Silverdale
Keele
Crown Street
[Silverdale]

Knutton
Halt

Newcastle
(Liverpool
Road)

Newcastle
under Lyme

Bucknall

Consall

Cliffe Vale

2nd
Stoke 1st

Fenton
Manor

Whieldon Road
Mount Pleasant

Fenton

Wedgwood

Longton

Normacot

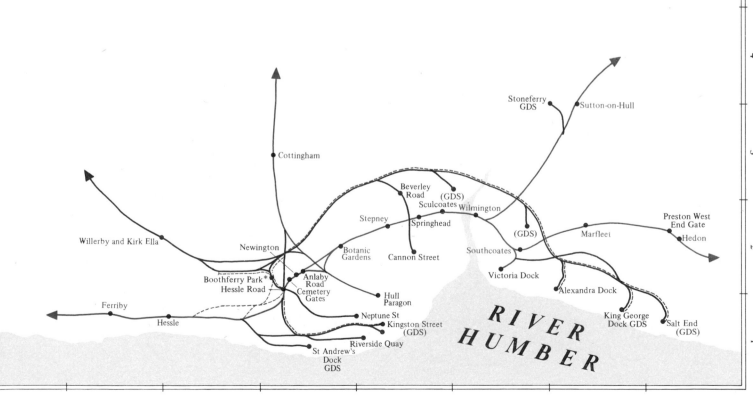

5
4
3
2
1

Stoneferry
GDS

Sutton-on-Hull

Cottingham

Beverley
Road

(GDS)

Sculcoates

Wilmington

Preston West
End Gate

Stepney

Springhead

(GDS)

Marfleet

Hedon

Willerby and Kirk Ella

Newington

Botanic
Gardens

Cannon Street

Southcoates

Boothferry Park
Hessle Road

Anlaby
Road
Cemetery
Gates

Hull
Paragon

Victoria Dock

Alexandra Dock

Ferriby

Hessle

Neptune St

Kingston Street
(GDS)

Riverside Quay

St Andrew's
Dock
GDS

King George
Dock GDS

Salt End
(GDS)

RIVER
HUMBER

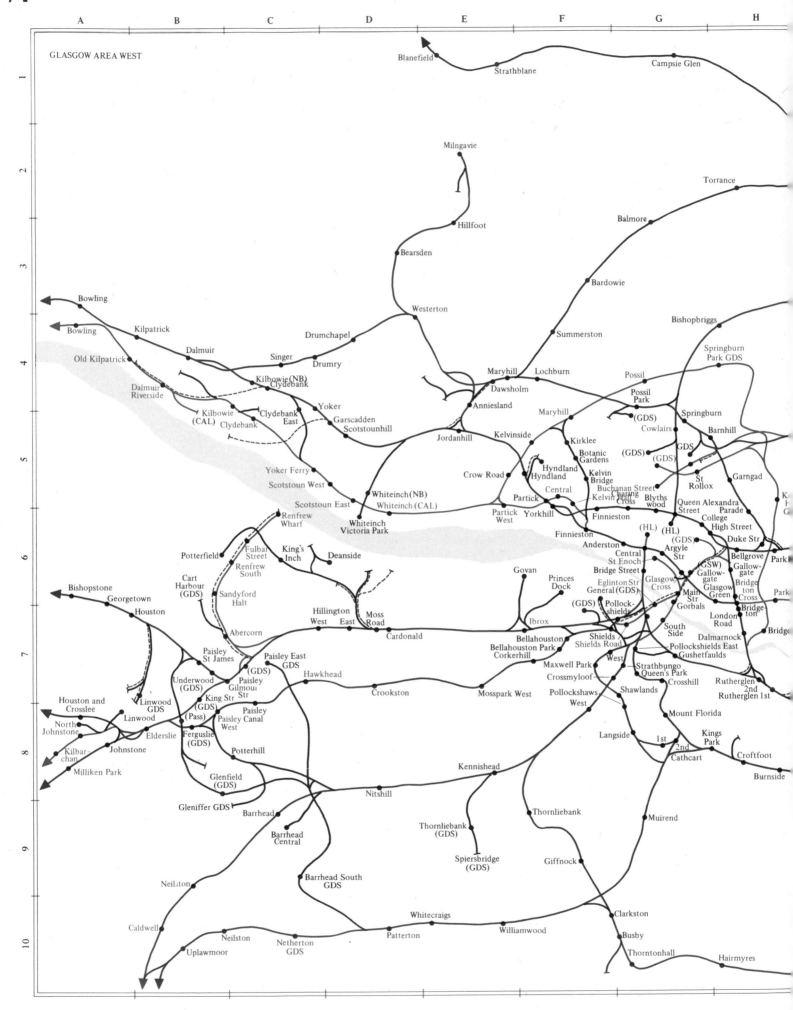

GLASGOW AREA WEST

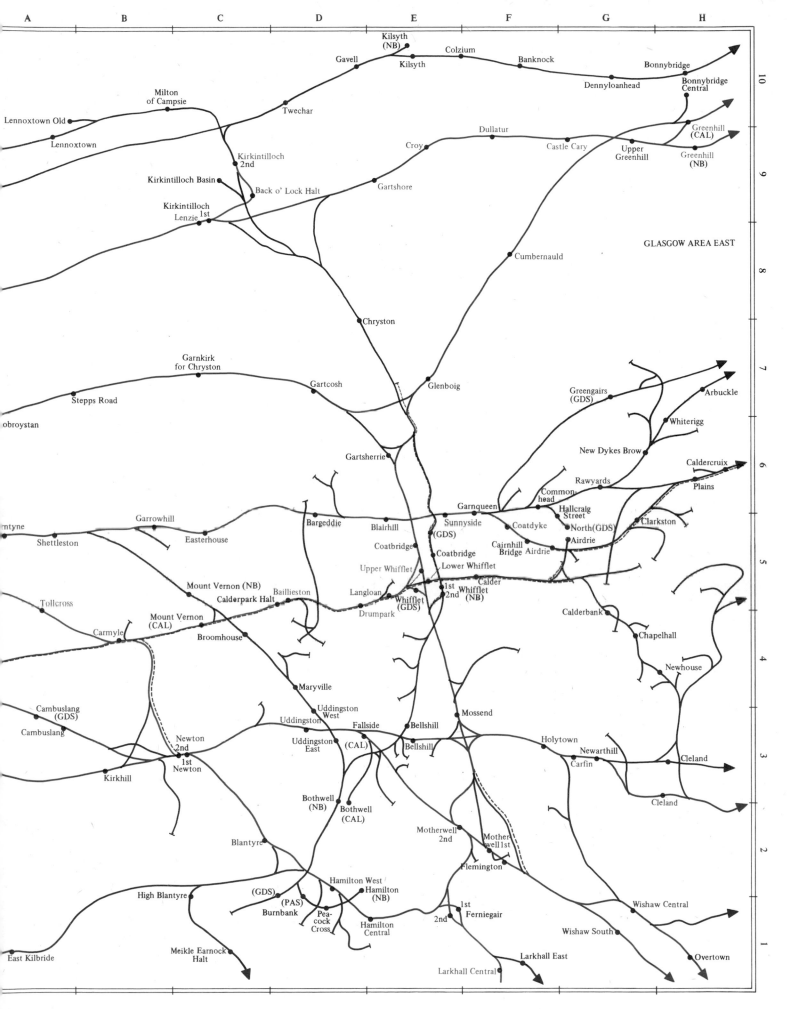

GLASGOW AREA EAST

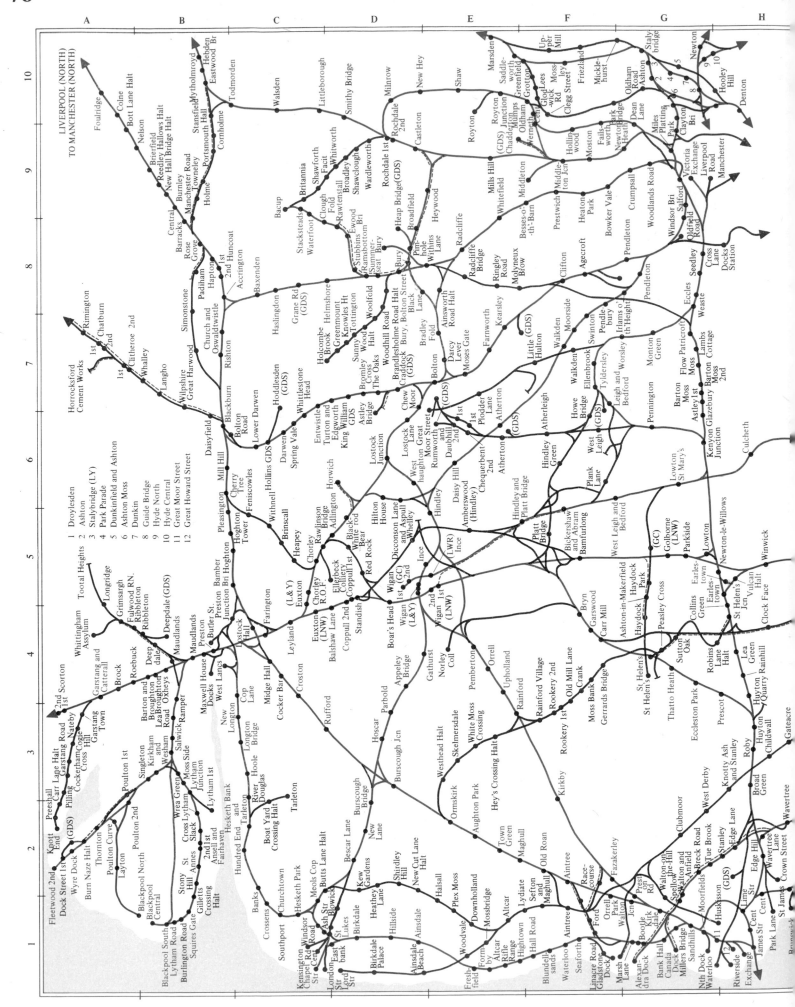

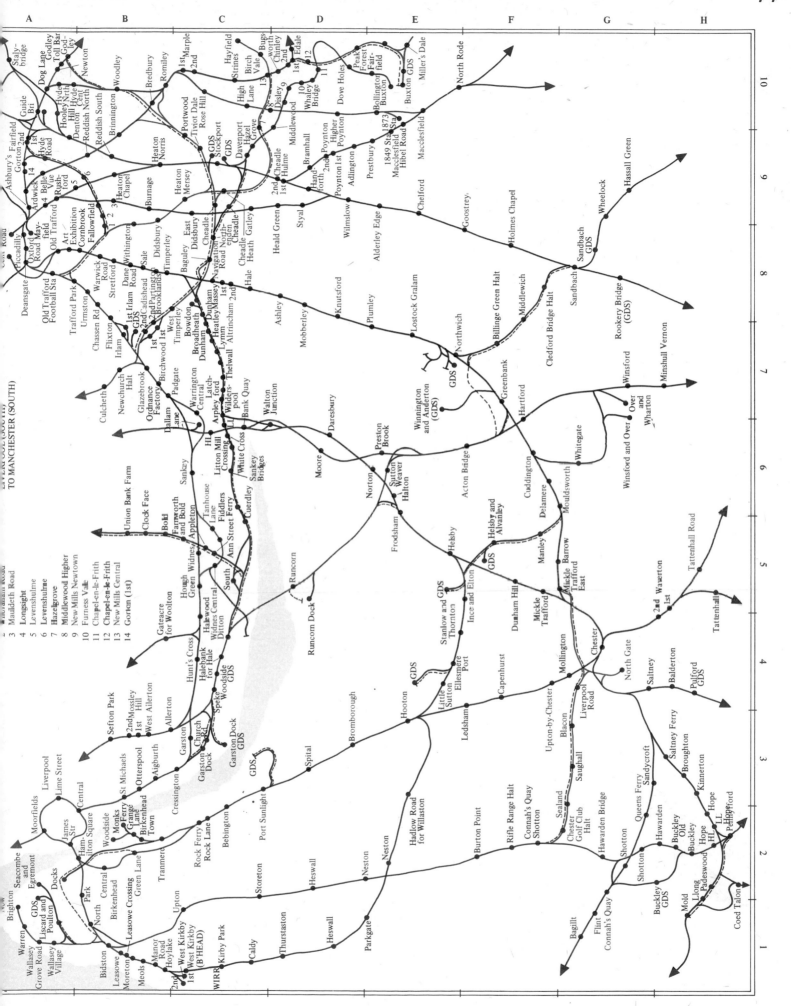

SOUTH WALES

	A	B	C	D	E	F	G	H

1 Commercial Street Platform
2 Abercwmboi
3 Aberaman
4 Nantgarw Halt Low Level
5 Nantgarw Halt High Level
6 Cardiff Riverside
7 Cardiff Clarence Road
8 Cardiff General
9 Cardiff Roath
10 Duffryn Crossing Halt

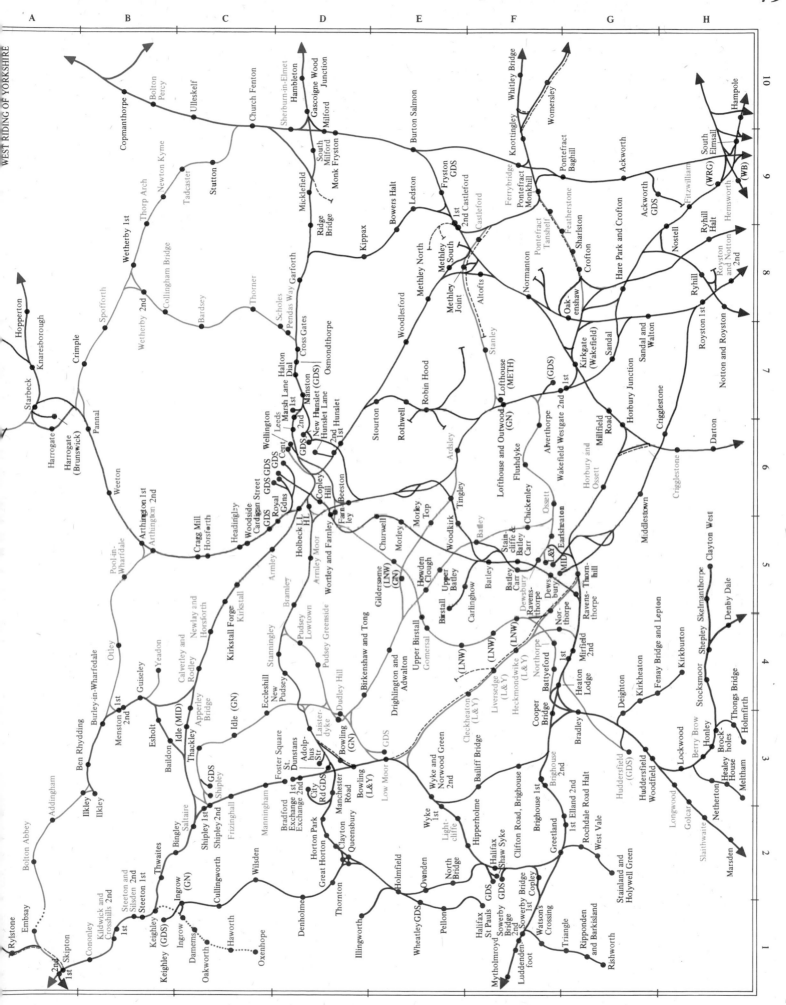

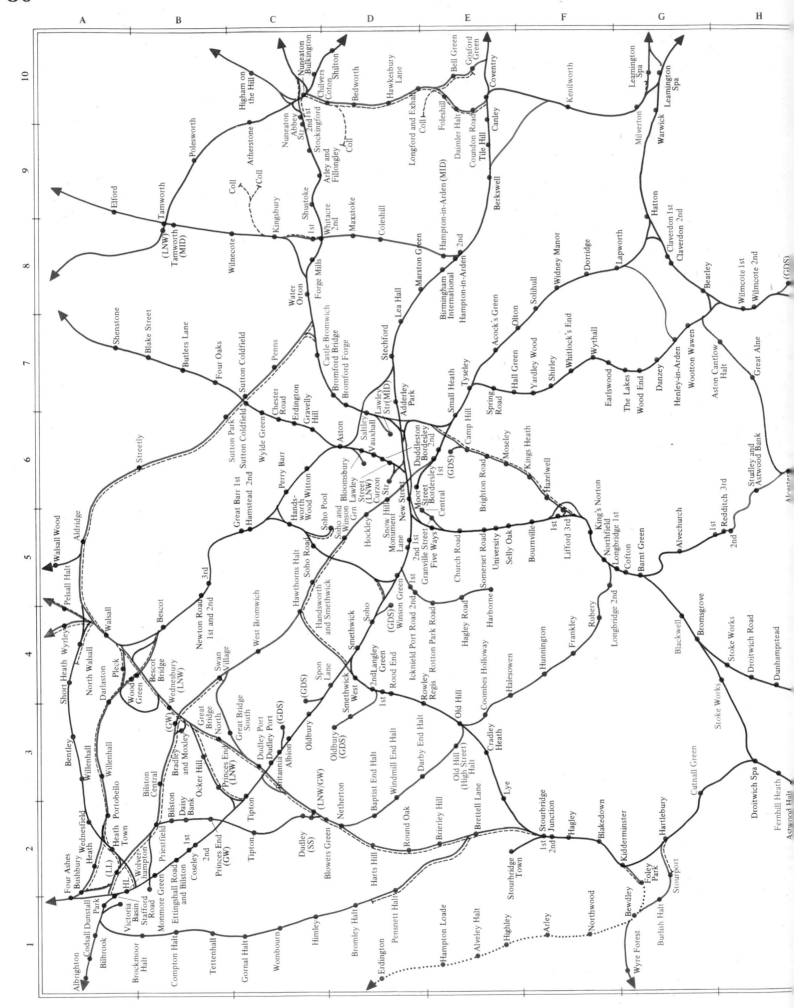

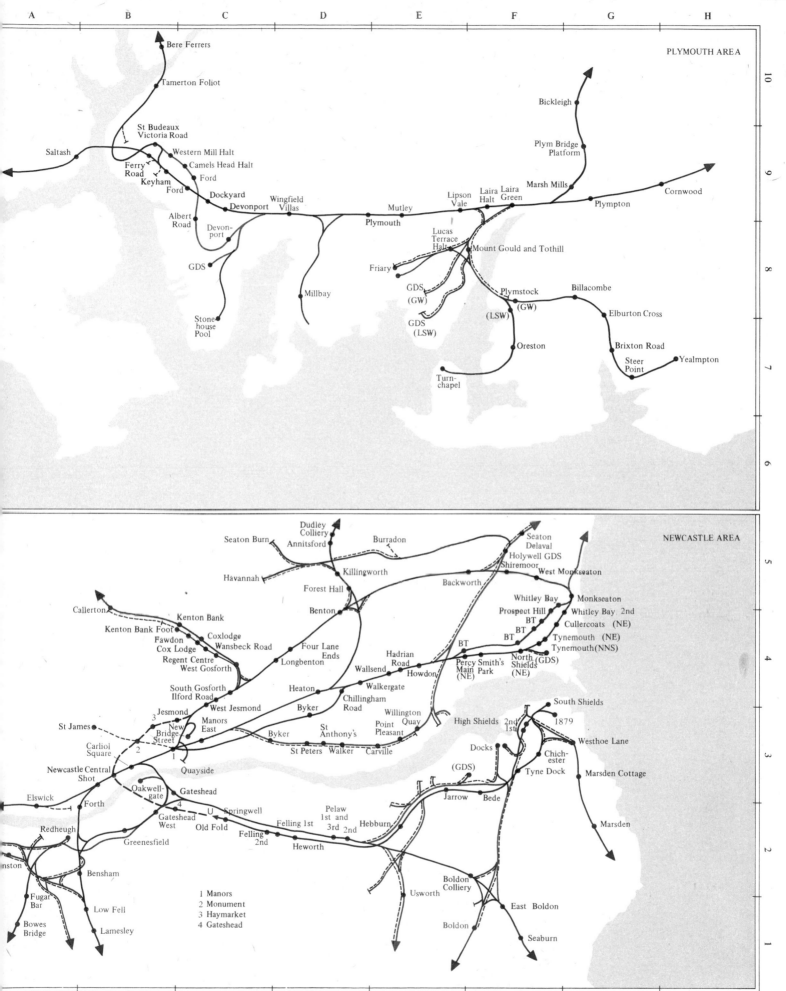

Bere Ferrers

Tamerton Foliot

St Budeaux
Victoria Road

Western Mill Halt

Saltash

Camels Head Halt

Ferry
Road

Keyham

Ford

Ford

Dockyard

Albert
Road

Devonport

Devon-
port

Wingfield
Villas

Mutley

Plymouth

Lipson
Vale

Laira
Halt

Laira
Green

Marsh Mills

Bickleigh

Plym Bridge
Platform

Plympton

Cornwood

GDS

Friary

Lucas
Terrace
Halt

Mount Gould and Tothill

Millbay

GDS
(GW)

Plymstock

Billacombe

Stone
house
Pool

GDS
(LSW)

(GW)

(LSW)

Elburton Cross

Oreston

Brixton Road

Steer
Point

Yealmpton

Turn-
chapel

Dudley
Colliery

Seaton Burn

Annitsford

Burradon

Seaton
Delaval

Holywell GDS

Shiremoor

West Monkseaton

Havannah

Killingworth

Forest Hall

Backworth

Whitley Bay

Monkseaton

Whitley Bay 2nd

Callerton

Kenton Bank

Benton

Prospect Hill

BT

Cullercoats (NE)

Kenton Bank Foot

Fawdon
Cox Lodge

Coxlodge

Wansbeck Road

Four Lane
Ends

BT

BT

Tynemouth (NE)

Tynemouth (NNS)

Regent Centre

Longbenton

Hadrian
Road

BT

North (GDS)
Shields
(NE)

West Gosforth

Wallsend

Howdon

Percy
Main

Smith's
Park
(NE)

South Gosforth
Ilford Road

Heaton

Walkergate

South Shields

St James

3

Jesmond

West Jesmond

Byker

Chillingham
Road

Willington
Quay

High Shields

2nd
1st

1879

Carliol
Square

2

New
Bridge
Street

Manors
East

Byker

St Peters

St
Anthony's

Point
Pleasant

Westhoe Lane

Newcastle Central

1

Walker

Carville

Docks

Chich-
ester

Elswick

Shot

Quayside

(GDS)

Tyne Dock

Marsden Cottage

Oakwell-
gate

Gateshead

Forth

4

U

Springwell

Jarrow

Bede

Redheugh

Gateshead
West

Old Fold

Pelaw
1st and
3rd 2nd

Hebburn

Marsden

Greenesfield

Felling 1st

Heworth

Felling
2nd

Bensham

Usworth

Boldon
Colliery

Fugar
Bar

Low Fell

1 Manors
2 Monument
3 Haymarket
4 Gateshead

East Boldon

Bowes
Bridge

Lamesley

Boldon

Seaburn

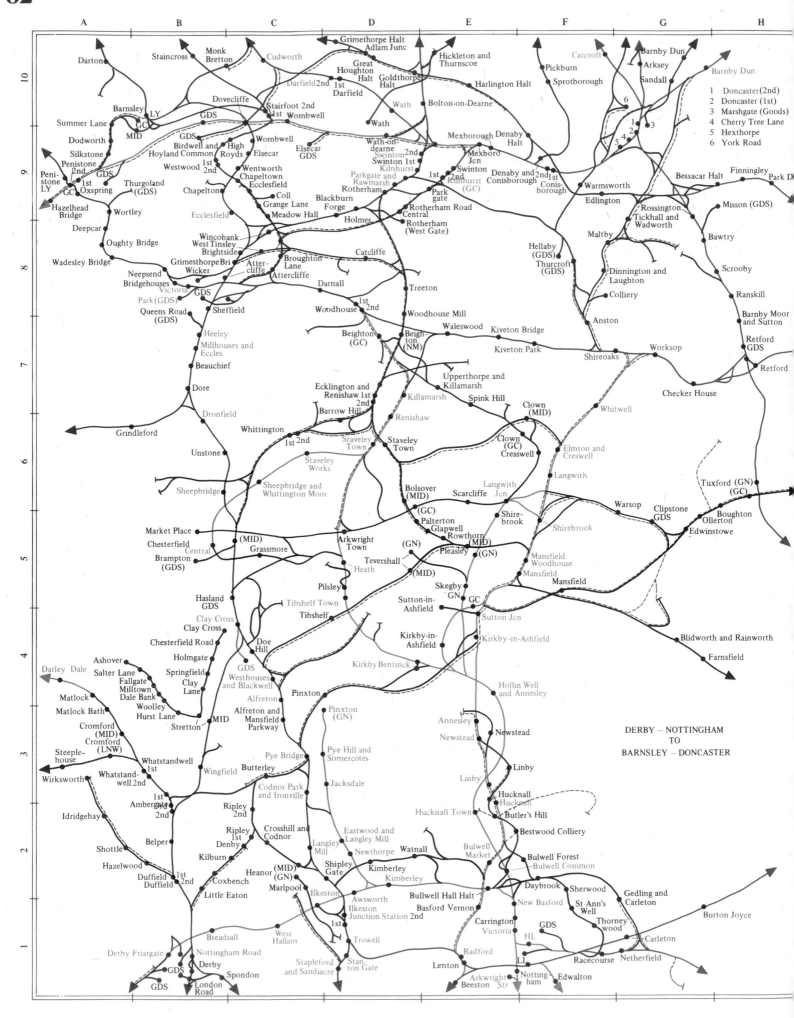

DERBY — NOTTINGHAM
TO
BARNSLEY — DONCASTER

1 Doncaster (2nd)
2 Doncaster (1st)
3 Marshgate (Goods)
4 Cherry Tree Lane
5 Hexthorpe
6 York Road

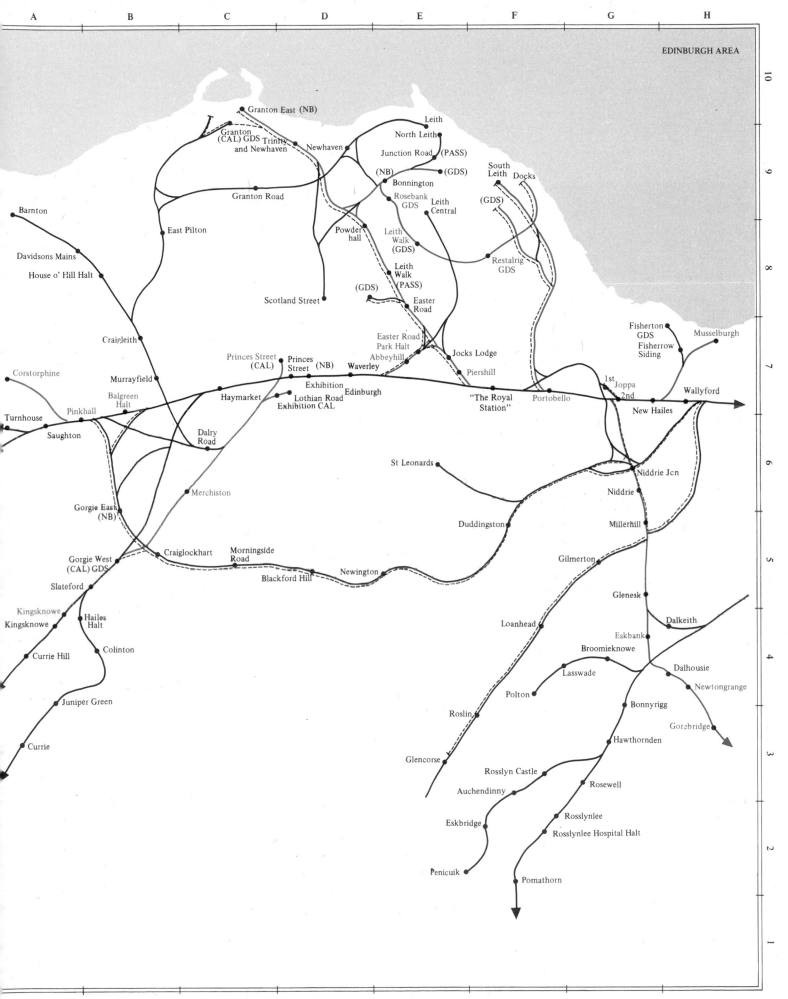

EDINBURGH AREA

Granton East (NB)

Granton (CAL) GDS Trinity and Newhaven

Newhaven

Leith

North Leith

Junction Road (PASS)

(NB) (GDS)

South Leith Docks

Bonnington

Rosebank GDS

Leith Central

(GDS)

Granton Road

Barnton

East Pilton

Powderhall

Leith Walk (GDS)

Restalrig GDS

Davidsons Mains

House o' Hill Halt

Leith Walk (PASS)

Scotland Street

(GDS)

Easter Road

Craigleith

Easter Road Park Halt
Abbeyhill

Jocks Lodge

Fisherton GDS

Musselburgh

Corstorphine

Princes Street (CAL)

Princes Street (NB)

Waverley

Fisherrow Siding

Murrayfield

Exhibition Edinburgh

Piershill

Balgreen Halt

Haymarket

"The Royal Station"

1st Joppa 2nd

Wallyford

Turnhouse

Pinkhall

Exhibition CAL

Lothian Road

Portobello

New Hailes

Saughton

Dalry Road

St Leonards

Merchiston

Niddrie Jcn

Gorgie East (NB)

Niddrie

Gorgie West (CAL) GDS

Craiglockhart

Morningside Road

Duddingston

Millerhill

Slateford

Blackford Hill

Newington

Gilmerton

Kingsknowe

Hailes Halt

Glenesk

Kingsknowe

Loanhead

Dalkeith

Currie Hill

Colinton

Eskbank

Broomieknowe

Juniper Green

Lasswade

Dalhousie

Newtongrange

Polton

Bonnyrigg

Gorebridge

Currie

Roslin

Hawthornden

Glencorse

Rosslyn Castle

Rosewell

Auchendinny

Rosslynlee

Eskbridge

Rosslynlee Hospital Halt

Penicuik

Pomathorn

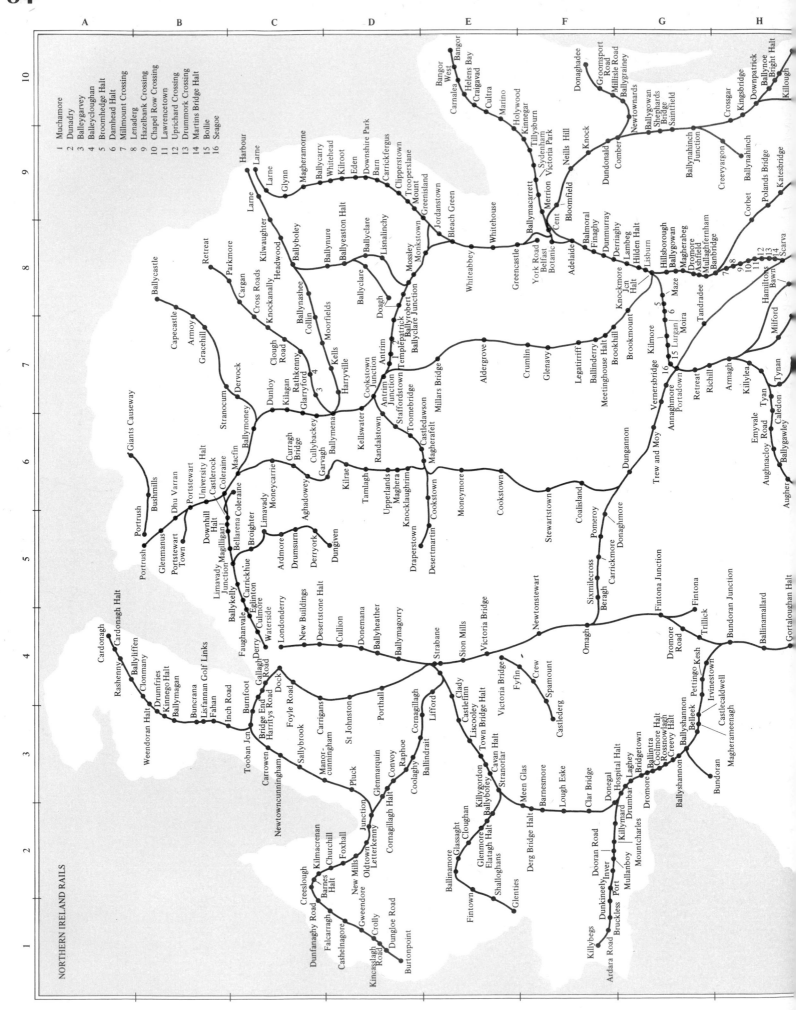

NORTHERN IRELAND RAILS

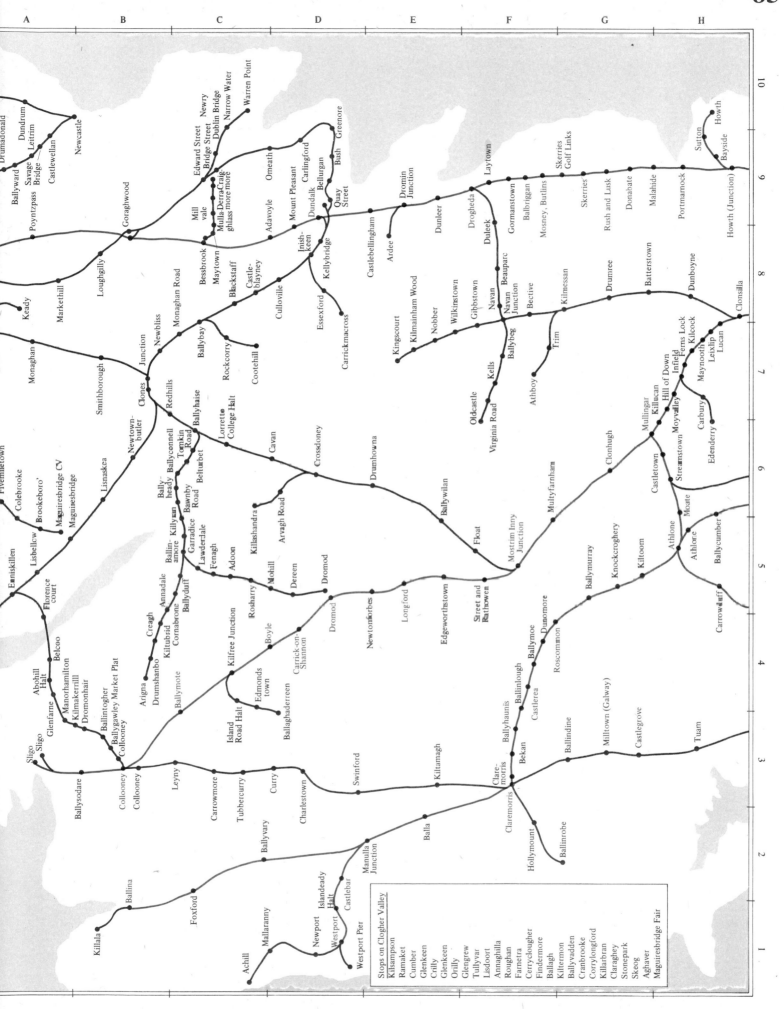

Drumadonald
Dundrum
Ballyward
Leitrim
Savage
Bridge
Castlewellan
Newcastle
Poyntzpass
Edward Street Newry
Bridge Street
Dublin Bridge
Narrow Water
Warren Point
Goraghwood
Mill vale
Maytown
Mulla Derra Craig
ghlass more more
Omeath
Adavoyle
Mount Pleasant
Carlingford
Bush
Greenore
Keady
Markethill
Loughgilly
Bessbrook
Blacksraff
Castle-
blayney
Culloville
Inish-
keen
Dundalk
Bellurgan
Quay
Street
Laytown
Skerries
Golf Links
Howth
Sutton
Bayside
Monaghan
Smithborough
Clones
Junction
Newbliss
Monaghan Road
Ballybay
Rockcorry
Cootehill
Carrickmacross
Essexford
Kellybridge
Castlebellingham
Ardee
Dromin
Junction
Dunleer
Drogheda
Duleek
Gormanstown
Balbriggan
Mosney, Butlins
Skerries
Rush and Lusk
Donabate
Malahide
Portmarnock
Howth (Junction)
Fivemiletown
Colebrooke
Brookeboro'
Maguiresbridge CV
Maguiresbridge
Enniskillen
Lisbellcw
Florence
court
Newtown-
butler
Lisnaskea
Redhills
Ballyhaise
Lorette
College Halt
Cavan
Crossdoney
Drumhowna
Kingscourt
Kilmainham Wood
Nobber
Wilkinstown
Gibbstown
Navan
Beauparc
Junction
Bective
Kilmessan
Drumree
Batterstown
Dunboyne
Clonsilla
Mullingar
Killucan
Hill of Down
Infield
Ferns Lock
Kilcock
Maynooth
Leixlip
Lucan
Carbury
Edenderry
Aboill
Halt
Glenfarne
Manorhamilton
Kilmakerrill
Dromonhair
Ballintogher
Ballygawley Market Plat
Collooney
Arigna
Drumshanbo
Kiltubrid
Cornabrone
Ballyduff
Kilfree Junction
Boyle
Carrick-on-
Shannon
Dromod
Newtonforbes
Longford
Edgeworthstown
Street and
Rathowen
Multyfarnham
Clonhugh
Castletown
Streamstown
Moyvalley
Mostrim Inny
Junction
Float
Ballywilan
Oldcastle
Virginia Road
Kells
Ballybeg
Athboy
Trim
Athlone
Moate
Ballycumber
Athlore
Carrowkuff
Sligo
Sligo
Ballysodare
Collooney
Collooney
Leyny
Carrowmore
Tubbercurry
Curry
Charlestown
Swinford
Kiltamagh
Clare-
morris
Ballyhaunis
Bekan
Castlerea
Ballindine
Ballinlough
Ballymoe
Ballymurray
Knockcroghery
Kiltoom
Milltown (Galway)
Castlegrove
Tuam
Killala
Ballina
Foxford
Achill
Mallaranny
Newport
Islandeady
Halt
Westport
Castlebar
Westport Pier
Manulla
Junction
Balla
Hollymount
Ballinrobe
Claremorris
Roscommon
Ballymoe
Dunamore
Ballinlough
Ballindine
Belcoo
Belturbet
Ballyconnell
Tomkin
Road
Ballinamore
Garradice
Bawnby
Road
Killyran
Fenagh
Lawderdale
Adoon
Killashandra
Arvagh Road
Mohill
Dromod
Rosharry
Dereen
Edmonds
town
Island
Road Halt
Ballaghaderreen
Ballymote
Creagh
Annadale
Ballyvary

A B C D E F G H
10 9 8 7 6 5 4 3 2 1

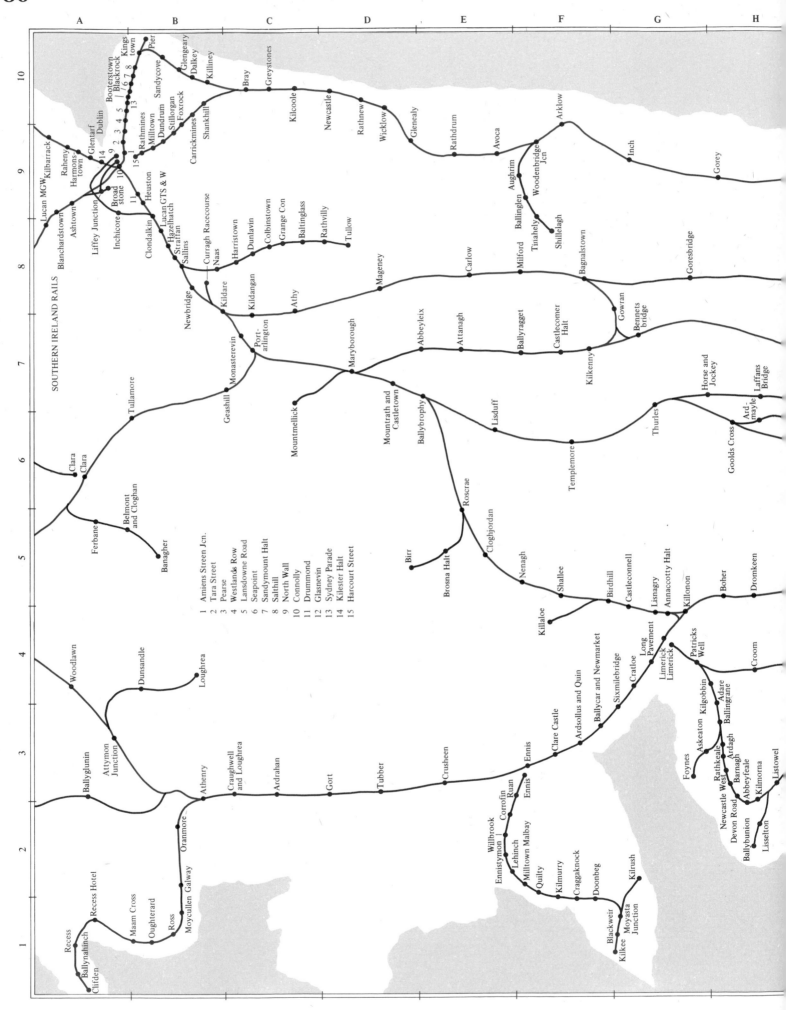

A   B   C   D   E   F   G   H

10

Camolin

Ferns

Enniscorthy

Edermine Ferry

Macmine Junction

Killurin

Rosslare Harbour Mainline

Borris

Chapel

Palace East

Rathgarogue

Ballywilliam

Wexford

Wexford South

Rosslare Strand

Rosslare Harbour

Thomastown

Ballyhale

New Ross

Glenmore and Aylwardstown

Wellington Bridge

Bridgetown

Kilrane

Duncormick

Kilrane

Ballycullane

Campile

9

8

Farranalleen

Fethard

Clonmel

Kilsheelan

Carrick-on-Suir

Fiddown

Mullinavat

Kilmacow

Grange

Waterford Adelphi Wharf

Waterford (WDL)

Waterford (W&T)

7

Dundrum

Limerick Jen

Tipperary

Bansha

Caher

Mitchelstown

Ballindangan

Glanworth

Fermoy

Clondulane

Ballyduff

Tallow Road

Lismore

Cappoquin

Cappagh

Dungarvan

Durrow

Kilmacthomas

Carrolls Cross

Kilmeaden

Tramore

6

Oola

Emly

Knocklong

Kilmallock

Castletownroche

Ballyhooly

Rathduff

Blarney

Mourne Abbey

Summerhill

Tivoli

Dunkettle

St Patricks Bridge

Little Island

Queenstown Junc

Fota

Carrigtohill

Midleton

Mogeely

Killeagh

Youghal

Carrigaloe

Rushbrooke

Queerstown

5

Bruee

Charleville

Buttevant and Doneraile

Mallow

Healys Bridge

Carrigrohane

Victoria

Western Road

Albert Street

Blackrock

Rochestown

Passage

Glenbrook

Monkstown

Raffeen

Carrigaline

Crosshaven

1 Cork – Glanmire Road
2 Cork – Capwell
3 Cork – Albert Quay

4

Abbeydorney

Ardfert

Tralee

Gortatlea

Castleisland

Farranfore

Newmarket (K&T)

Kanturk (K&T)

Kanturk

Banteer

Lombards-town

Blarney

St Annes

Tower Bridge

Coachford Junction

Gaol Cross

Gurth

Leemount

Kilrea

Kilumney

Ballincollig

Waterfall

Upton

Crossbarry

Ballinhassig

Kinsale Junction

Kinsale

Clonakilty Junction

Bandon

Ballymartle

Farrangalway

Ballinascarthy Junction

Ballinascarthy

Skeaf

Courtmacsherry

3

Fenit

Spa

Tralee Basin

Blennerville

Curragheen

Castlegregory Junction

Glenmore Junction

Castleisland

Ballybrack

Killarney

Headford Junction

Rathmore

Millstreet

Rathcool

Loo Bridge

Morleys Bridge

Kilgarvan

Firmount

Knockane

Foxs Bridge

Burnt Mill

Coachford

Peake

Dripsey

Kilmurry

Gurteen

Cloghroe

Dooniskey

Crookstown Road

Clonakilty

Ballineen

Desert

Dunmanway

Madore

Skibbereen

Timoleague

2

Kilfenora

Castlegregory

Aughacasla

Deelis

Brit

Castlegregory

Ballinorare

Garrynadur

Molahiffe

Castlemaine

Milltown (Kerry)

Killorglin

Caragh Lake

Docks

Glenbeigh

Mountain Stage

Kells

Kenmare

Donoughmore

Macroom

Knuckbue

Drimoleague Junction

Ballydehob

Church Cross

Newcourt

Hollyhill

Kilcoe

Creagh

1

Oola

Anascaul

Lispole

Ballinasteenig

Puck Island

Dingle

Cahersiveen

Valencia Harbour

Bantry

Aughaville Halt

Durrus Road

Woodlands

Schull

Baltimore

GAZETTEER TO MAPS

KEY

Abbey Wood _____ Station still open to passengers

Aberaman _____ Station closed to passengers since the Beeching Era (1.1.63)

Abercarn _____ Station closed to passengers prior to the Beeching Era

Armathwaite* _____ * Still open for private excursions

Hall Dene (Private) _____ Private station

Bebington and New Ferry _____ All black words since dropped from station name

Gilnockie for Claygate _____ All black words since dropped from station name

[Aberdare] _____ [ ] Town or city with more than two stations

2nd, 1st – 1851 _____ 2nd station, 1st station closed 1851

3rd, 1st – 1853, 2nd – 1936 _____ 3rd station, 1st station closed 1852, 2nd station closed 1936

CL.	– Closed or closure	LT	– London Transport
Form.	– Formerly	Plat.	– Platform
FR.	– From	PR.	– Private
GDS	– Goods	Rep.	– Replaced on site of
H.L.	– High Level	R.N.	– Re-named
Ht.	– Halt	R.O.	– Re-opened
Jcn.	– Junction	Sta.	– Station
Junc.	– Junction	Str.	– Street
L.L.	– Low Level	T.O.	– Taken over (privately)

Station	Page	Block	Comp	Year of CL
Abbey -- see [Shrewsbury]				
Abbey and West Dereham	22	G9	GE	1930
Abbey Dale -- see [Sheffield] Beauchief				
Abbeydore	16	H10	GW/Gold V	1941
Abbey Foregate -- see [Shrewsbury]				
Abbeyhill -- see [Edinburgh]				
Abbey Junction (Cumbria)	45	H3	CAL	1921
Abbey Junction (Cumbria)	45	H3	NB	1921
Abbey Town (Cumbria)	45	H3	NB	1964
Abbey Wood (Kent)	65	H2	SEC	
	66	A2		
Abbotsbury	7	D1	GW	1952
Abbotsford Ferry	47	B3	NB	1931
Abbots Langley -- see Kings Langley				
Abbotsham Road	8	D4	BWA	1917
Abbots Ripton	23	B4	GN	1958
Abbots Wood Junction	24	C2	MID	1855
Aber	32	G7	LNW	1960
Aber Junction Halt Form -- Beddau Halt	78	E6	RHY	
Aberaman 2nd, 1st -- 1856	78	C3	TV	1964
Aberangell	26	E9	HAW/CAM	1931
Aberavon (Seaside)	78	E1	RSB	1962
Aberavon Town	78	E1	RSB	1962
Aberavon -- see also Port Talbot				
Aberayron	19	D10	GW	1951
Aberbargoed	78	C7	BM	1962
Aberbeeg	78	C8	GW	1962
Aberbran Halt	16	C9	N & B	1962
Abercairny	50	E5	CAL	1951
Abercanaid -- see [Merthyr]				
Abercanaid -- see also Pentrebach				
Abercarn	78	D8	GW	1962
Aberchalder	59	D9	High/NB	1933
Abercorn -- see [Paisley]				
Abercrave	78	A1	N & B	1932
Abercwmboi Halt Form -- Duffryn				
Crossing Plat.	78	C4	TV	1956
Abercynon	16	E5	TV	
	78	E4		
Abercynon Upper -- see Travellers Rest				
[Aberdare]				
Black Lion Crossing Ht	78	C3	GW	1924
Commercial Street Plat.	78	C3	TV	1912
High Level	78	C3	GW	1964
Low Level*	78	C3	TV	1964
Mill Street Platform	78	C3	TV	1912
Trecynon Halt	78	C3	GW	1964
[Aberdeen]				
Aberdeen	55	B8	CAL/GNS	
Don Street	55	B8	GNS	1937
Ferryhill	55	B8	ABER	1854
Guild Street	55	B8	CAL	1867
Holburn Street	55	B8	GNS	1937
Hutcheon Street	55	B8	GNS	1937
Kittybrewster	55	B8	GNS	1968
Persley Halt	55	A8	GNS	1937
Pitfodels Halt	55	B8	GNS	1937
Ruthrieston	55	B8	GNS	1937
Schoolhill	55	B8	GNS	1937
Waterloo	55	B8	GNS	1867
Woodside	55	B8	GNS	1937
Aberderfyn Halt	72	D2	GW	1915
Aberdour	46	F9	NB	
Aberdovey 2nd, 1st -- 1967	26	B8	CAM	
Aberdovey Harbour GDS	26	B8	CAM	1964
Aberdylais Halt	78	C1	GW	1964
Aberedw	26	H2	CAM	1962
Abererch	32	D3	CAM	
Aberfan -- see [Merthyr]				
Aberfeldy	50	D8	HIGH	1965
Aberffrwd	26	C5	FEST	
Aberfoyle	53	H2	NB	1951
[Abergavenny]				
Abergavenny	16	H7	GW	
	78	A10		
Abergavenny Junction 2nd, 1st -- 1870	16	H8	GW	1958
	78	A10		
Brecon Road	78	A10	LNW	1958
Abergele and Pensarn	33	C8	LNW	
Aberglaslyn (Nantmor)	32	G4	WH	1936
Abergwili	19	D5	LNW	1963
Abergwynfi	78	D2	GW	1960
Abergynolwyn T.O. PR.	26	C9	TAL	
Aberlady	47	A9	NB	1932
Aberllefeni	26	D9	CORRIS	1931
Aberlour	56	G10	GNS	1965
Abermule	27	A8	CAM	1965
Abernant	78	B3	GW	1962
Abernethy	50	H4	NB	1955

Station	Page	Block	Comp	Year of CL
Abernethy Road	50	H4	EN	1848
Abersychan and Talywain	78	B9	LNW/GW	1941
Abersychan, Low Level	78	B9	GW	1962
Abertafol Halt	26	C8	CAM	
Aberthaw	78	H4	BARRY	1964
Aberthaw, Low Level	78	H4	TV	1930
Aberthin Halt	78	G3	TV	1920
Abertillery 2nd 1st -- 1893	78	B8	GW	1962
Abertridwr	78	E6	RHY	1964
Abertysswg	78	B6	BM	1930
Aberystwyth	26	B8	GW	
Aberystwyth (Rheidol) 2nd, 1st -- 1925	26	B8	GW	1968
Aberystwyth Harbour GDS	26	B8	GW	1909
Abingdon	14	H5	GW	1963
Abingdon Junction	14	H5	GW	1873
Abingdon Road Halt -- see [Oxford]				
Abington	46	C2	CAL	1965
Aboyne	55	C3	GNS	1966
Abram -- see Bickershaw				
Aby for Claythorpe	29	F8	GN	1961
Accrington	36	H5	EL	
	76	C8		
Achanalt	58	E7	HIGH	
Ach-Na-Cloich	53	A6	CAL	1965
Achnasheen	58	F6	HIGH	
Achnashellach	58	F5	HIGH	
Achterneed	58	E10	HIGH	1964
Acklington	43	E8	NE	
Ackworth	79	H9	SK JT	1951
Acle	20	F9	GE	
Acocks Green and South Yardley	80	F7	GW	
Acrefair	72	C1	GW	1965
Acrefair Low Level GDS	33	G4	GW	1960
	72	C1		
Acton -- see [London]				
Acton Bridge	30	F7	LNW	
	77	E6		
Adam Street -- see [Cardiff]				
Adderbury	14	G10	GW	1951
Adderley	30	F3	GW	1963
Adderley Park	80	E7	LNW	
Addiewell	46	D7	NB	
Addingham	37	D8	MID	1965
	79	A2		
Addington -- see Ringstead				
Addiscombe	69	A5	SEC	
Addison	43	E3	NE	1954
Addison Road -- see [London] Kensington Olympia				
Addlestone	15	F2	LSW	
	67	C4		
Adisham for Wingham	3	F8	SEC	
Adlestrop	14	D9	GW	1966
Adlington (Cheshire)	31	B8	LNW	
	77	D9		
Adlington (Lancashire)	76	D5	BP/LY	
Adlington (Lancashire) -- see also White Bear				
Admaston Halt	27	G10	S.WTN	1964
Admiralty Pier -- see [Dover]				
Admiralty Pier -- see Holyhead (Anglesey)				
Advie 2nd, 1st -- 1868	56	H8	GNS	1965
Adwalton -- see Drighlington				
Adwick-le-Street -- see Carcroft				
Aerodrome Halt -- see Cosford				
Afonwen	32	E2	CAM	1964
Agecroft	76	F8	LY	1861
Aigburth, Mersey Rd and -- see [Liverpool]				
Ainderby	38	E3	NE	1954
Ainsdale Beach -- see [Southport]				
Ainsdale (Seaside)	36	B4	LY	
	76	E1		
Ainsworth Road Halt	76	E8	LY	1953
Aintree Central -- see [Bootle]				
Aintree, Sefton Arms -- see [Bootle]				
[Airdrie]				
Airdrie	75	F6	CAL	1943
Airdrie North (Commonhead)	75	F6	NB	1930
Airdrie South	47	H8	NB	
	75	F6		
Hallcraig Street	75	F6	NB	1870
Airmyn	34	F5	NE	1964
Airth	46	B10	CAL	1954
	50	D1		
Akeld	47	H3	NE	1930
Akeman Street	15	B8	GC	1930
Albany Park	69	H8	SEC	
Alberta Place Halt	78	H6	TV	1968
Albert Park -- see [Manchester] Withington				

Station	Page	Block	Comp	Year of CL
Albert Road — see [Plymouth] Devonport				
Albert Road Bridge Halt — see [Portsmouth]				
Albert Road Halt — see [Plymouth]				
Albion — see [West Midlands]				
Albury — see Chilworth				
Albrighton	24	B9	GW	
	80	B2		
Alcester	24	E3	MID	1962
	80	H6		
Aldeburgh	21	E9	GE	1966
Aldeby	20	H9	GE	1959
Alderley Edge	31	A8	LNW	
	77	E8		
Aldermaston	15	A2	GW	
Aldershot Town	5	E10	LSW	
Aldin Grange for Bear Park	38	D10	NE	1939
Aldrington Form. Dyke JCN	2	B2	LBSC	
Aldwarke — see Parkgate				
Alexandra Dock — see [Bootle]				
Alexandra Palace — see [London]				
Alexandra Parade	74	H6	NB	
Alexandra Park — see [Manchester]				
Alexandra Parks — see [London]				
Alexandria and Bonhill	49	C10	DB JT	
Alford — Grampian	55	A4	GNS	1950
Alford Halt (Somerset)	7	D7	GW	1962
Alford Town (Lincs)	29	G8	GN	1970
Alfreton and Mansfield Parkway	82	C4	MID	
Alfreton and South Normanton	82	C4	MID	1967
Algakirk and Sutterton	22	C5	GN	1961
	29	E3		
Allanfearn	56	F3	HIGH	1965
Allangrange	56	F2	HIGH	1951
Allendale	43	A2	NE	1930
Allens West Halt	38	F6	NE	
Allerton	77	C3	CLC	
Allerton West for Garston	77	C3	LNW	
Allhallows-on-Sea	13	C3	SR	1961
[Alloa]				
Alloa	50	D1	NB	1968
Alloa Dock GDS	50	D1	NB	1961
Alloa Ferry	50	D1	ST & D	1852
Alloa Junction	50	D1	CAL	1865
Alloa North	50	D1	CAL	1885
Alloa South	50	D1	CAL	1885
Alloway	49	B2	GSW	1930
All Saints — see Clevedon				
All Stretton Halt	27	E8	SH JT	1958
Alltddu Halt	26	C4	GW	1965
Allt-y-Graig	33	E8	LMS	1930
Almeley	27	C2	GW	1940
Almondbank	50	F5	CAL	1951
Alne (Junction for Easingwold)	34	C10	NE	1958
Alness 2nd, 1st — 1960	56	C3	BR	
Alnmouth Form. Bilton R.N. 1892	43	E9	NE	
Alnwick 2nd, 1st — 1887	43	E9	NE	1968
Alphinton Halt — see [Exeter]				
Alresford (Essex)	13	F9	GE	
Alresford (Hants) R.O. PR. FR. 1973 CL.	5	A8	LSW	
Alrewas	24	G10	LNW	1965
Alsager	30	H5	NS	
	73	A9		
Alsager Road	73	B9	NS	1931
Alsop-en-le-Dale	31	E5	LNW	1954
Alston	41	D10	NE	1976
	42	H1		
Altcar and Hillhouse	76	E1	CLC	1952
Altcar Rifle Range	76	E6	LY	1921
Althorne	13	C6	GE	
Althorpe 2nd, 1st — 1916 for Keadby, Gunness & Burringham	34	H3	GC	
Althorp Park	25	E4	LNW	1960
Altnabreac	61	F7	HIGH	
	62	B6		
Altofts and Whitwood	34	B5	MID	
	79	F7		
Alton (Hants) 2nd, 1st — 1865	5	C8	LSW	
Alton Towers (Staffs)	31	D4	NS	1965
Altrincham	77	C8	MSJA	1881
Altrincham and Bowdon	30	H9	MSJA	
	77	C8		
Altrincham — see also Broadheath				
Alva	50	E2	NB	1954
Alvanley — see Helsby				
Alvechurch	80	G4	MID	
Alverstoke — see Gosport Road				
Alverstone (Isle of Wight)	5	A2	IWC	1956
Alverthorpe — see [Wakefield]				
Alves	56	E8	HIGH	1965
Alvescot	14	E6	GW	1962
Alyth Town	51	A8	CAL	1951
Alyth Junction Station	51	A8	CAL	1967
Ambergate 3rd, 1st — 1863, 2nd — 1876	28	A5	MID	
	82	B4		
Amberley	5	G5	LBSC	
Amberswood (Hindley)	76	E5	LNW	1872
Amble	43	F8	NE	1930
Amersham and Chesham Bois	15	E6	MET/GC	
Amesbury	4	D9	LSW	1952
Amisfield	45	E7	CAL	1952
Amlwch	32	E10	LNW	1964
Ammanford	19	G4	GW	1958
Ammanford and Tirydail	19	F4	GW	
Ammanford Colliery Halt	19	G4	GW	1958
Amotherby	39	B1	NE	1931
Ampleforth	38	G1	NE	1950
Ampthill	23	G1	MID	1959
Ancaster	22	B1	GN	
	28	A4		
Anderson Cross — see [Glasgow]				
Andover Junction	4	F9	LSW	
Andover Town	4	F9	LSW	1964
Andoversford	14	B8	GW	1962
Andoversford and Dowdeswell	14	B8	MSWJ	1927
Anerley	69	B7	LBSC	
Anfield — see [Liverpool] Walton				
Angarrack 2nd, 1st — 1852	10	D4	WC	1853
Angel Road	12	D5	GE	
	65	C8		
Angerton	43	D5	NB	1952
Angmering	5	G4	LBSC	
Anlaby Road — see [Hull]				
Annan	45	H5	GSW	
Annan (Shawhill)	45	H5	CAL	1931
Annbank	49	C3	GSW	1951
Annesley	82	E4	MID	1953
Annfield Plain	43	E1	NE	1955
Anniesland for Knightswood	74	D8	NB	
Annitsford	81	D5	NE	1958
Ann Street	77	C5	LNW	1951
Ansdell and Fairhaven 2nd, 1st — 1903	76	B2	PW JT	
Anston	25	C9	GC/MID	1929
	82	F8		
Anstruther 2nd, 1st — 1883 for Cellardyke	51	E3	NB	1965
Apperley Bridge and Rawdon	79	C3	MID	1965
Appin	52	H	CAL	1966
Appleby (Cumbria)	41	D7	MID	
Appleby East (Cumbria)	41	D7	NE	1962
Appleby (Lincs)	35	A3	GC	1967
Appledore (Devon)	8	D4	BWA	1917
Appledore (Kent)	33	C5	SEC	
Appleford	14	H5	GW	1849
Appleford Halt	14	H5	GW	
Appleton	77	C5	LNW	1951
Appley Bridge	76	E4	LY	
Apsley	12	A7	LNW	
	15	F6		
Arbirlot	51	F8	DA JT	1929
[Arbroath]				
Arbroath	51	F7	DA JT	
Arbroath Harbour GDS	51	F7	CAL	1963
Arbroath Station	51	F7	ABER/DA	1848
Arbuckle	75	H7	MONK/NB	1862
Arddleen Halt	33	G1	CAM	1965
Ardgay	56	A2	HR	
Ardingly	2	C4	LBSC	1963
Ardleigh	21	H4	GE	1967
Ardler	51	A7	CAL	1956
Ardwick-le-Street — see Carcroft				
Ardley	14	H9	GW	1963
Ardlui for Head of Loch Lomond	53	E4	NB	
[Ardrossan]				
Harbour	49	A5	GSW/CAL	
Montgomerie Pier	49	A5	CAL	1968
North	49	A5	CAL	1932
South Beach	49	A5	GSW/CAL	
Town	49	A5	GSW	1968
Ardsley	79	F6	GN	1964
Ardwick	77	A8	GC	
Arenig	33	B3	GW	1960
Argoed Halt	78	C7	LNW	1960
Argyle Halt — see [Swansea]				
Arisaig	59	F1	NB	
Arkholme for Kirkby Lonsdale	41	B1	FM JT	1960
Arkleby	40	E9	MC	1852
Arksey	34	D3	GN	1952
	82	F10		

Station	Page	Block	Comp	Year of CL
Arkwright Street — see [Nottingham]				
Arkwright Town	82	D6	GC	1951
Arlecdon	40	D7	CW JT	1917
Arlesey and Henlow	23	G4	GN	1959
Arley (Worcs)	80	F1	GW	1963
Arley re-opened priv. from clos. above	80	F1	SVR	
Arley and Fillongley (Warwicks)	24	A6	MID	1960
	80	C9		
Armadale	46	C7	NB	1956
Armathwaite*	41	B10	MID	1970
	42	D1		
Armitage	24	F10	LNW	1960
Armley — see [Leeds]				
Arnage	54	F8	GNS	1965
Arnside	41	A2	FUR	
Arram	35	B7	NE	
Arrochar and Tarbet	53	E2	NB	
Arthington 2nd, 1st — 1865	37	G7	NE	1965
	79	B5		
Arthog	26	C10	CAM	1965
Arundel	5	G4	LBSC	
Arundel and Littlehampton	5	G4	LBSC	1863
Ascot and Sunninghill	15	E2	LSW	
Ascott-under-Wychwood	14	E8	GW	
Asfordby	28	F1	MID	1951
Ash	5	E10	SEC	
Ashbourne 2nd, 1st — 1899	31	E4	LNW/NS	1954
Ashburton	9	C8	GW	1958
Ashbury and North Lew	8	H5	LSW	1966
Ashbury's (for Belle Vue)	77	A9	GC	
Ashby-de-la-Zouch	25	A1	MID	1964
	31	G1		
Ashby Magna	25	C8	GC	1969
Ashchurch	17	G10	MID	1971
Ashcombe Road — see [Weston-super-Mare]				
Ashcott	7	B8	SD JT	1966
Ashdon Halt	23	F8	GE	1964
Ashey (Isle of Wight)	5	A2	IWC	1966
Ashford (Kent) 2nd, 1st Alfred Town — 1899	3	C6	SEC	
Ashford (Surrey)	67	D8	LSW	
Ashford Bowdler (Worcs)	27	E5	SH	1855
Ash Green Halt	5	E10	LSW	1937
Ashington	43	F6	NE	1964
Ashleigh Road — see [Swansea]				
Ashley for Rostherne (Cheshire)	30	H9	CLC	
	77	D8		
Ashley and Weston (Northants)	25	F8	LNW	1951
Ashley Heath Halt (Hants)	4	C4	SR	1964
Ashley Hill — see [Bristol]				
Ashover (Butts)	82	B5	ASH	1936
Ashperton	27	G1	GW	1965
Ash Street — see [Southport]				
Ashtead	68	B2	LBSC/LSW	
Ashton	6	B2	GW	1958
Ashton — see [Bristol]				
Ashton Gate Halt* — see [Bristol]				
Ashton-in-Makerfield*	76	G4	GC	1952
Ashton Keynes — see Minety				
Ashton Keynes — see also South Cerney				
Ashton-on-Mersey — see Sale				
Ashton-under-Hill	24	D1	MID	1963
[Ashton-under-Lyme]				
Ashton Moss	76	G10	OAGB	1862
Ashton-under-Lyme (Charlestown)	37	B2	LY	
	76	G10		
Oldham Road	76	G10	OAGB	1959
Park Parade	76	G10	GC	1956
Ash Town	5	E10	EK	1948
Ashurst	2	E5	LBSC	
Ash Vale	5	F10	LSW	
Ashwater	8	H3	LSW	1966
Ashwell (Leics)	25	G10	MID	1966
Ashwell and Morden (Cambs)	23	G5	GN	
Ashwellthorpe	20	G6	GE	1939
Askam	40	F2	FUR	
Askern*	34	D3	LY	1947
Askrigg	41	G4	NE	1954
Aslockton	28	F3	GN	
Aspall and Thorndon	21	D6	MSL	1952
Aspatria	40	E10	MC	
	45	G1		
Aspley Guise Halt	23	G1	LNW	
Aspull — see Dicconson Lane				
Astley	76	G6	LNW	1956
Astley Bridge — see [Bolton]				
Aston	80	C6	LNW	
Aston Botterell Halt	27	G6	CMDP	1938
Aston-by-Stone	31	B3	NS	1947
Aston Cantlow Halt	80	H7	GW	1939
Aston Rowant	15	C5	GW	1957
Astwood Bank — see Studley				
Astwood Halt	80	H2	GW	1939
Aswarby and Scredington	22	B2	GN	1930
	29	B3		
Athelney	7	A7	GW	1964
Atherleigh	76	F6	LMS	1954
Atherstone	24	H8	LNW	
	80	C9		
Atherton, Bag Lane	76	F6	LNW	1954
Atherton Central	76	F6	LY	
Attadale	58	H3	HIGH	
Attenborough	28	C2	MID	
Attercliffe	37	G1	MID	
	82	C9		
Attercliffe	82	C9	GC	1927
Attleborough	20	H4	GE	
Attlebridge	20	E5	MGN	1959
Attimore Hall Halt	12	C8	GN	1905
Auchendinny	83	E2	NB	1951
Auchengray	46	D5	CAL	1966
Auchenheath	46	A4	CAL	1951
Auchenmade	49	C6	CAL	1932
Auchincruive	49	C3	GSW	1951
Auchindachy	54	E2	GNS	1968
Auchinleck	49	E2	GSW	1965
Auchmacoy	54	F9	GNS	1932
Auchnagatt	54	E8	GNS	1965
Auchterarder	50	E3	CAL	1956
	51	A1		
Auchterhouse 2nd, 1st — 1860	51	B7	CAL	1955
Auchterless	54	E6	GNS	1951
Auchtermuchty	51	A4	NB	1950
Auchtertool GDS	46	F10	NB	1960
Audenshaw	76	G10	LNW	1905
Audlem	30	F4	GW	1963
Audley and Bignall End (Staffs)	30	H4	NS	1931
	73	A8		
Audley End (Essex)	23	G8	GE	
Aughton Park Halt	76	E2	LY	
Auldbar Road	51	E8	CAL	1956
Auldearn	56	E6	HIGH	1960
Auldgirth	45	E7	GSW	1952
Aultmore	54	C2	HIGH	1915
Authorpe	29	E9	GN	1961
Aviemore	57	C5	HR	
Avoch	56	F3	HIGH	1951
Avonbridge	46	A8	NB	1930
Avoncliffe	17	F1	GW	
Avonmouth — see [Bristol]				
Avonwick	9	E8	GW	1963
Awre Junction	16	D7	GW	1959
Awsworth	82	D2	GN	1964
Axbridge	7	B10	GW	1963
Axminster	6	H3	LSW	
Aycliffe	38	D7	NE	1953
Aylesbury	15	C8	MET & GC/GW	
Aylesbury 2nd, 1st — 1889	15	C8	LNW	1953
Aylesford	2	H8	SEC	
Aylesham Halt (Kent)	3	F7	SEC	
Aylesham North (Norfolk)	20	D6	MGN	1959
Aylesham South (Norfolk)	20	D6	GE	1952
Aynho for Deddington	14	H9	GW	1964
Aynho Park Platform	14	H9	GW	1963
Ayot	12	C8	GN	1949
[Ayr]				
Ayr 3rd, 1st — 1857, 2nd — 1886	49	C2	GSW	
Newtonhead	49	C2	GSW	1868
Aysgarth	38	A3	NE	1954
	41	H3		
Ayton	47	G7	NB	1962
Babbacombe — see Torre				
Backney Halt	17	C9	GW	1962
Back of Law — see Dundee				
Back o' Lock Halt	75	C9	LNE	1964
Backwell — see Nailsea				
Backworth R.N. Holywell GDS	43	F4	BT/NE	1864
	81	F5		
Backworth	43	F4	NE	1977
	81	D4		
Bacton	16	H10	GW	1941
Bacup	37	A5	EL	1966
	76	B9		
Badgeworth	17	G8	MID	1846
Badminton	17	F4	GW	1968
Badsey — see Littleton				
Baggrow	40	E10	MC	1930
	45	H2	MC	1930

Station	Page	Block	Comp	Year of CL
Bagillt	30	A8	LNW	1966
	77	G1		
Bag Lane — see Atherton				
Baglan Sands Halt	78	E1	GW	1939
Bagnor — see Stockcross				
Bagshot	15	E1	LSW	
Baguley — see [Manchester]				
Bagworth and Ellistown 2nd, 1st — 1848	25	B10	MID	1964
Baildon R.O. 1973 FR. 1957 CL.	37	E7	MID	
	79	C3		
Baildon	37	E7	MID	1957
	79	C3		
Bailey Gate	4	A3	SD JT	1966
Bailieston — see Easterhouse				
Bailieston	75	C5	CAL	1964
Bailiff Bridge	79	F2	LY	1917
Bainton (Yorks)	35	A9	NE	1954
Bainton Gate (Cambs)	22	G2	MID	1856
Bakewell	31	F7	MID	1967
[Bala]				
Bala 2nd, 1st — 1882	33	C3	GW	1965
Bala Junction	33	C3	GW	1965
Bala R.O. Priv. from CL. above	33	C3	BLR	
Bala Lake Halt (Flag Sta.) — see Glan Llyn Ht.				
Balado	50	G2	NB	1964
Balbeuchly Foot	51	B7	DPA	1855
Balbeuchly Top	51	B7	DPA	1860
Balchriston Level Crossing Ht	49	A1	GSW	1930
Balcombe	2	B5	LBSC	
Baldersby	38	E2	NE	1959
Balderton	30	C6	GW	1952
	77	H3		
Baldock	23	G4	GN	
Baldovan and Downfield — see [Dundee]				
Baldragon	51	C7	CAL	1955
Baldwins Halt — see [Swansea]				
Balerno	46	F7	CAL	1943
Balfron	53	H1	NB	1951
Balgowan	50	F5	CAL	1951
Balgreen Halt — see [Edinburgh]				
Balham and Upper Tooting	68	G8	LBSC	
Ballachulish (Glencoe)	53	B9	CAL	1966
Ballachulish Ferry	53	B9	CAL	1966
Ballater	55	C1	GNS	1966
Ballathie	50	H7	CAL	1868
Ballencrieff	47	A9	NB	1847
Ballifurth Farm Halt	57	A7	BR	1965
Ballindalloch	56	H9	GNS	1965
Ballingham	17	C10	GW	1964
Ballinluig	50	F8	HIGH	1965
Bailliol Road — see [Bootle]				
Balloch Central	49	C10	DB JT	
Balloch Pier	49	C10	DB JT	
Balmore	74	H9	NB	1951
Balmossie Halt	51	D6	DA JT	
Balnacoul Halt	54	C1	HIGH	1931
Balnaguard	50	E8	LMS	1965
Balne	34	E4	NE	1958
Balquhidder 2nd, 1st — 1905	50	A5	CAL	1965
	53	H4		
Balsall Common — see Berkswell				
Balsham Road	23	D9	NT	1851
Balshaw Lane and Euxton	76	D4	LNW	1969
Bamber Bridge	76	B4	EL	
Bamford	31	E9	MID	
Bamfurlong	76	F5	LNW	1950
Bampton (Oxon) — see Brize Norton				
Bampton (Devon)	6	F7	GW	1963
Banavie	59	H6	NB	
Banavie Pier	59	H6	NB	1939
Banbury	25	B1	GW	
Banbury, Merton Street	25	B1	LNW	1961
Banchory 2nd, 1st — 1859	55	C5	GNS	1966
Bandon Halt	68	G4	LBSC	1914
Banff	54	B5	GNS	1964
Banff Bridge	54	C6	GNS	1951
Bangor for Beaumaris	32	G7	LNW	
Bangor-on-Dee	30	C4	CAM	1962
	72	F2		
Bangour	46	D8	NB	1921
Bank (City)	65	A4	LT	
Bankfoot	50	G6	CAL	1931
Bank Hall	76	G1	LY	
Bankhead (Strathclyde)	46	C4	CAL	1945
Bankhead (Aberdeen)	55	A8	GNS	1937
Banknock	75	F10	KB	1935
Bank Quay — see [Warrington]				
Banks	76	C2	LY	1964

Station	Page	Block	Comp	Year of CL
Bank Top — see Burnley Central				
Bank Top — see [Darlington] Darlington				
Bannister Green Halt	13	A9	GE	1952
Bannockburn	46	A10	CAL	1950
	50	D1		
Banstead and Burgh Heath	68	E2	LBSC	
Banstead Downs — see Chipstead				
Banwell — see Sandford				
Baptist End Halt — see [West Midlands]				
Barassie	49	B4	GSW	
Barbers Bridge	17	E9	GW	1959
Barbon	41	C2	LNW	1954
Barcaldine Halt	53	A7	LMS	1966
Barcombe	2	D3	LBSC	1955
Barcombe Mills	2	D3	LBSC	1969
Bardney	29	C7	GN	1970
Bardon Hill	25	B10	MID	1952
Bardon Mill	42	H3	NE	
Bardowie	74	G9	NB	1931
Bardsey	79	C7	NE	1964
Bare Lane	36	D10	LNW	
Bargeddie	75	D6	NB	1927
Bargoed Junction	78	C6	RHY	
Barham	3	E7	SEC	1940
Barking	65	G5	MID	
Barkingside	65	G7	GE	1966
Barkingside R.O. FR. CL. above	65	G7	LTS	
Barkisland — see Ripponden				
Barkston	28	H3	GN	1955
Barlaston and Tittensor	31	B3	NS	
Barlborough — see Clowne				
Barleith	49	D4	LMS	1964
Barlow	34	E6	NE	1964
Barmby	34	F5	HB	1932
Barming	2	G8	SEC	
Barmouth	26	B10	CAM	
	32	G1		
Barmouth Junction — see Morfa Mawddach				
Barnack	22	F2	GN	1929
Barnack — see also Uffington				
Barnard Castle 2nd, 1st — 1861	38	A7	NE	1964
Barnby Dun 2nd, 1st — 1866	34	E3	GC	1967
	82	G10		
Barnby Moor and Sutton	28	E8	GN	1949
	82	H8		
Barnehurst	66	B1	SEC	
	70	A10		
Barnes	64	D1	LSW	
	68	D9		
Barnes Bridge	64	D1	LSW	
	68	D9		
Barnetby	35	B3	GC	
Barnham (Norfolk)	21	B2	GE	1953
Barnham Junction (Sussex)	5	F4	LBSC	
	3	E7		
Barnhill	74	H6	NB	
Barnhill — see [Dundee]				
Barnhill — see [Perth]				
Barnoldswick	37	B8	MID	1965
Barnsbury — see [London] Caledonian Road				
[Barnsley]				
Central GDS	82	B10	GC	1967
Court House	82	B10	MID	1960
Exchange, Barnsley	37	G3	LY	
	82	B10		
Stairfoot 2nd, 1st — 1871	82	C10	GC	1957
Summer Lane	82	B10	MS & L/GC	1959
Barnsley Road — see Penistone				
[Barnstaple]				
Barnstaple Junction Sta.	8	D5	LSW	
Pilton Halt	8	C6	LB	1935
Town (L.B. Platform)	8	D5	LB	1935
Town 2nd, 1st — 1898	8	D5	LSW	1970
Victoria Road	8	D5	GW	1960
Barnston — see Storeton				
Barnstone	28	F3	GN/LNW	1953
Barnt Green	80	G4	MID	
Barnton — see [Edinburgh]				
Barnwell	23	A2	LNW	1964
Barnwell Junction Station	23	D7	GE	1962
Baron's Lane Halt	13	B7	GE	1939
Barras	41	E6	NE	1962
Barrasford	43	B4	NE	1956
Barrhead Joint	49	D7	GBK JT	
	74	C2		
Barrhead Central	74	C2	GSW	1917
Barrhead South GDS	74	C2	CAL	1963
Barrhill	44	D7	GSW	
Barrmill	49	C6	GBK JT	1962

Station	Page	Block	Comp	Year of CL
Barrmill GDS	49	C6	CAL	1932
Barrowden — see Wakerley				
Barrow for Tarvin	30	D7	CLC	1953
	77	G4		
Barrow Haven	35	B5	GC	
Barrow Hill and Staveley Works	82	D7	MID	1954
Barrow-on-Soar and Quorn	28	D1	MID	1968
[Barrow-in-Furness]				
Barrow-in-Furness	40	F1	FUR	
Barrow-in-Furness GDS	40	F1	FUR	1970
Barrow (Rabbit Hill)	40	F1	FUR	1862
Barrow (Strand)	40	F1	FUR	1882
Furness Abbey	40	F1	FUR	1950
Park GDS	40	F1	FUR	1962
Piel	40	F1	FUR	1936
Rampside	40	F1	FUR	1936
Ramsden Dock	40	F1	FUR	1915
Roose	40	F1	FUR	
[Barry]				
Barry	16	E1	BARRY	
	78	H5		
Barry Docks	16	E1	BARRY	
	78	H5		
Barry Island	16	E1	BARRY	
	78	H5		
Barry Links	51	E6	DA JT	
Barthomley — see Radway Green				
Bartlow	23	F8	GE	1967
Barton — see [Hereford]				
Barton GDS	38	D6	NE	1950
Barton and Broughton (Lancs) 2nd, 1st — 1840	36	E6	LNW	1939
	76	B4		
Barton and Walton	31	E1	MID	1958
Barton Hill	34	F10	NE	1930
Barton-le-Street	39	A1	NE	1931
Barton Moss 2nd, 1st — 1862	76	G7	LNW	1929
Barton-on-Humber	35	B5	GC	
Baschurch	30	D1	GW	1960
Basford	30	E4	LNW	1875
Basford — see [Stoke-on-Trent] Hartshill				
Basford North — see [Nottingham]				
Basford Vernon — see [Nottingham]				
Basildon	13	A5	MID	
Basingstoke	5	B10	LSW	
Basingstoke	5	B10	GW	1932
Bason Bridge	7	A9	SD JT	1966
Bassaleg	78	F9	BM	1962
Bassaleg Junction	78	F9	GW	1962
Bassenthwaite Lake	40	F8	CKP	1966
Bat and Ball	2	E8	SEC	
	70	B1		
[Bath]				
Bathampton	17	E2	GW	1966
Bathford Halt	17	E2	GW	1965
Green Park 2nd, 1st — 1870	17	E1	MID	1966
Hampton Row Halt	17	E1	GW	1917
Spa (Bath)	17	E1	GW	
Twerton-on-Avon	17	E1	GW	1917
Weston	17	E2	MID	1953
Bathampton — see [Bath]				
Bathford Halt — see [Bath]				
Bathgate Lower	46	C8	NB	1930
Bathgate Upper	46	C8	NB	1956
Bath Road Halt — see [London]				
Batley	37	F5	LNW	
	79	G5		
Batley Carr	37	F5	GN	1966
	79	G5		
Batley Carr — see also [Dewsbury]				
Batley Carr — see also Staincliffe				
Battersby	38	H5	NE	
Battersea — see [London]				
Battersea Park	64	H1	LBSC	
	68	G10		
Battersea Park Road — see [London]				
Battle	2	H3	SEC	
Battlesbridge	13	B5	GE	
Battyeford and Mirfield	79	G4	LNW	1953
Bawdrip Halt	7	A8	SD JT	1952
Bawtry	34	E1	GN	1958
	82	G9		
Baxenden	76	D8	EL	1951
Bayford	12	D7	GN	
Bay Horse	36	E9	LNW	1960
Baynards	5	H8	LBSC	1965
Beach Halt (Gwynedd)	26	B10	FAIRB.	1939
Beach Road Halt (Devon)	8	D4	BWA	1917
Beaconsfield for Penn	15	F5	GW/GC	
Beag Fair Siding	18	H5	NRM/GW	1883
Beal	43	G9	NE	1968
Bealings	21	F7	GE	1956
Beam Bridge	6	F6	BE	1844
Beamish	43	E2	NE	1953
Beanacre Halt	17	G2	GW	1955
Bearley	80	H7	GW	
Bear Park — see Aldin Grange				
Bearsden	49	E9	NB	
	74	D9		
Bearsted and Thurnham	3	A8	SEC	
Beasdale	59	G1	NB	
Beattock	45	G9	CAL	1972
Beauchief — see [Sheffield]				
Beaufort	78	A7	LNW	1958
Beaulieu Road 2nd, 1st — 1860	4	F4	LSW	
Beauly	56	F1	HIGH	1960
Beaumaris — see Bangor				
Beaumonts Halt	12	A8	MID	1947
	15	G7		
Beaver's Hill Halt	18	G2	GW	1964
Bebington and New Ferry	77	C2	BHEAD	
Bebside	43	F5	NE	1964
Beccles	20	H9	GE	
Beckenham Hill	69	C7	GE	
Beckenham Junction	69	C6	SEC	
Beckermet	40	C5	WCE JT	1947
Beckfoot	40	E4	ESK	
Beckford	17	H10	MID	1963
Beckhole	39	B5	NE	1865
Beck Holes	39	B5	NE	1865
Beckingham	34	G1	GN/GE	1959
	28	G9		
Beckley — see Northiam				
Beckton — see [London]				
Becontree — see [London]				
Bedale	38	D3	NE	1954
Beddau Halt	78	F5	TV	1952
Beddgelert	32	F4	WH	1936
Beddington Lane Halt	68	G5	LBSC	
Bedford, Midland Rd 2nd, 1st — 1978	23	F2	MID	
Bedford, St Johns	23	F2	LNW	
Bedhampton Halt	5	C4	LBSC	
Bedlington	43	F5	NE	1964
Bedlinog	78	C5	TB JT	1964
Bedminster	17	C2	GW	
	72	C6		
Bedwas	78	E7	BM	1962
Bedwelty Pits Halt	78	B7	LNW	1960
Bedworth	80	D10	LNW	1965
Bedwyn	14	E1	GW	
Beechburn	38	C9	NE	1965
Beeches — see Carshalton				
Beeston (Notts)	28	C3	MID	
Beeston (Yorks) — see [Leeds]				
Beeston Castle and Tarporley (Cheshire)	30	E6	LNW	1966
Beeston Tor Halt (Staffs)	31	D5	NS	1934
Beighton	82	D8	MSL/GC	1954
Beighton	82	D8	NM	1843
Beith North	49	C6	GSW	1951
Beith Town	49	C6	GBK JT	1962
Bekesbourne	3	E3	SEC	
Belasis Lane — see [Teeside]				
Belford	43	H8	NE	1968
Belgrave and Birstall — see [Leicester]				
Belgrave Road — see [Leicester]				
Bellahouston — see [Glasgow]				
Bellahouston Park Halt — see [Glasgow]				
Bell Busk for Malham	37	B9	MID	1959
Belle Vue (Yorks)	34	F9	SHLT	1930
Belle Vue (Lancs)	77	A9	GC/MID	
Bellgrove	74	H6	NB	
Bellingham	43	A5	NB	1956
Bellingham (Kent)	69	C8	SEC	
Bellshill	75	E4	CAL	
Bellshill	75	E4	NB	1951
Belmont (Durham)	38	D10	NE	1857
Belmont (Surrey)	68	E3	LBSC	
Belmont — see also [London]				
Belper 2nd, 1st — 1878	28	A4	MID	
	82	B3		
Belses	42	E10	NB	1969
Belton (Lincs)	34	G3	AX JT	1933
Belton and Burgh (Norfolk)	20	G9	GE	1959
Beltring and Branbridges Halt	2	G7	SEC	
Beluncle Halt	3	A10	SEC	1961
	13	B3		
Belverdere	66	B2	SEC	
Bembridge (Isle of Wight)	5	B2	IOW	1953
Bempton	39	G1	NE	

Station	Page	Block	Comp	Year of CL
Benderloch	52	H	CAL	1966
Benfleet (for Canvey Island) 2nd, 1st – 1911	13	B5	MID	
Bengeworth	24	E2	MID	1953
Beningbrough	34	D9	NE	1958
Benllech – see Red Wharf Bay				
Ben Rhydding	37	E8	MID	
	79	B2		
Bensham – see [Gateshead]				
Bentham	41	C1	MID	
Bentham Low	41	C1	NW/MID	1853
Bentley (Hants)	5	D9	LSW	
Bentley (Suffolk)	21	G5	GE	1966
Bentley – see [West Midlands]				
Bentley Church	21	G5	EU	1853
Benton 2nd, 1st – 1871	43	F4	NE	
	81	C4		
Benton Square – see [Newcastle]				
Bents	46	C7	NB	1930
Bentworth and Lasham	5	B9	LSW	1932
Benwick GDS	22	H5	GE	1966
Bere Alston	9	C5	LSW	
	11	G7		
Bere Ferrers	9	C5	LSW	
	11	G7		
Berkeley	17	E6	SW JT	1964
Berkeley Road	17	E6	MID	1965
Berkhampstead 2nd, 1st – 1874	15	F7	LNW	
Berkswell and Balsall Common	80	E8	LNW	
Bermondsey – see [London] Spa Road				
Berney Arms Halt	20	G9	GE	
Berrington	27	F9	GW	1963
Berrington and Eye	27	E4	SH JT	1958
Berry Brow – see [Huddersfield]				
Berrylands	68	B6	LSW	
Bervie – see Inverbervie				
Berwick	2	E2	LBSC	
Berwick-upon-Tweed	43	F10	NE/NB	
	47	H6		
Berwig Halt	30	B5	GW	1931
	33	G5		
Berw Road Halt Form – Beaconsfield Golf Links Ht.	78	E5	TV	1932
Berwyn Halt	33	F4	GW	1964
Bescar Lane	76	D2	LY	
Bescot Junction Station	80	B5	LNW	
Bescot Bridge – see [West Midlands]				
Besford	24	C2	MID	1846
Besses o' th' Barn	76	F8	LY	
Bestwood Colliery	82	E3	GN	1931
Betchworth	2	A7	SEC	
Bethesda	32	G7	LNW	1951
Bethnal Green	65	B4	GE	
Betley Road	30	H4	LNW	1945
Bettisfield	30	D3	CAM	1965
Bettws Garmon	32	F5	NWING/WW	1936
Bettws (Llangeinor)	78	E2	PT	1932
Bettws-y-Coed	33	A5	LNW	
Beulah Halt	18	F6	GW	1937
Beverley	35	B7	NE	
Beverley Road – see [Hull]				
Bewdley	24	B5	GW	1970
	80	F2		
Bewdley R.O. PR. FR. CL. above	24	B5	SVR	
	80	F2		
Bexhill Central	2	H2	LBSC	
Bexhill West	2	H2	SEC	1964
Bexley	70	A8	SEC	
Bexleyheath	66	A1	SEC	
	69	H10		
Bicester, London Road	15	A9	LNW	1968
Bicester North	15	A9	GW	
Bickershaw and Abram	76	F5	GC	1964
Bickleigh	9	D5	GW	1962
Bickley	69	E6	SEC	
Biddenden	3	A6	KES	1954
Biddick Lane	43	F2	NE	1869
Biddulph	31	B6	NS	1927
	73	C9		
[Bideford]				
Bideford* 2nd, 1st – 1872	8	D4	LSW	1965
Bideford Quay	8	D4	BWA	1917
Bideford (Strand Road) Halt	8	D4	BWA	1917
Bidford-on-Avon	24	E3	SMJ	1949
Bidston	77	B1	WIRRAL	
Bieldside	55	B7	GNS	1937
Bigby Road Bridge	35	B2	MS & L	1882
Biggar	46	D3	CAL	1950
Biggleswade	23	F4	GN	
Bignall End – see Audley				
Bilbrook, Birches and	80	B2	GW	
Bilbster	62	F7	HIGH	1960
Billacombe	9	E5	GW	1947
	11	H5		
Billericay	13	A5	GE	
Billing	25	F4	LNW	1952
Billingborough and Horbling	22	C2	GN	1930
	29	B3		
Billinge Green Halt	77	F7	LNW	1942
Billingham-on-Tees	38	F7	NE	
Billingshurst	5	H7	LBSC	
Bilney	20	E3	GE	1866
Bilston – see [West Midlands] Ettingshall Rd				
Bilston Central – see [West Midlands]				
Bilston Halt	17	D7	GN	1920
Bilston Street – see [West Midlands] Willenhall				
Bilston West – see [West Midlands]				
Binegar	7	D10	SD JT	1966
Bingham (Notts)	28	E3	GN	
Bingham Road (Notts)	28	E3	GN/LNW	1951
Bingham Road Halt (Surrey)	69	A5	SEC	
Bingley 2nd, 1st – 1872	79	D2	MID	
Binton	24	F3	SMJ	1949
Birches – see Bilbrook				
Birchfield Halt	56	E10	GNS	1956
Birchgrove	78	F6	GW	
Birchgrove – see also [Swansea]				
Birchills – see [West Midlands]				
Birchington-on-Sea	3	G10	SEC	
Birch Vale	31	C9	GC/MID	1970
	77	C10		
Birdbrook	23	F10	CVH	1962
Birdingbury	25	B5	LNW	1959
Birdwell and Hoyland Common	82	C10	GC	1953
Birkbeck	69	B6	LBSC	
Birkdale	76	D1	LY	
Birkdale Palace – see [Southport]				
[Birkenhead]				
Bidston	77	B1	WIRRAL	
Bidston GDS	77	B1	GC	1968
Docks	77	B1	HOY/WIRRAL	1878
Grange Lane	77	B1	CB	1844
Green Lane	77	C2	MERSEY	
Central	77	B1	CLC	
Hamilton Square	77	B1	CLC	
Monk's Ferry	77	B1	BHEAD	1878
North	77	B1	WIRRAL/GC	
Park	77	B1	WIRRAL/CLC	
Rock Lane	77	B1	BHEAD	1862
Town	77	B1	BHEAD	1945
Tranmere	77	B1	BLCJ	1857
Woodside	77	B1	BHEAD	1967
Birkenshaw and Tong – see [Bradford]				
Birmingham – see [West Midlands]				
Birnham – see Dunkeld				
Birnie Road Siding	55	G7	NB	1951
Birstall Lower (Yorks)	79	F4	LNW	1917
Birstall Town Form. Upper (Yorks)	79	F4	LNW	1951
Birstall – see [Leicester] Belgrave				
Birstwith	37	F10	NE	1951
Birtley	43	F2	NE	1955
Bishop Auckland 2nd, 1st – 1867	38	C8	NE	
Bishopbriggs	49	F8	NB	
	74	H8		
Bishopgate – see [London]				
Bishopsbourne	3	E7	SEC	1940
Bishop's Castle	14	A9	BC	1935
	27	C7		
Bishop's Cleeve	17	H9	GW	1960
Bishop's Lydeard	6	E7	GW	1971
Bishop's Lydeard R.O. Priv. from CL above	6	E7	WSR	
Bishop's Nympton and Molland	6	B7	GW	1966
	8	D9		
Bishops Road – see [London]				
Bishopstoke – see Eastleigh				
Bishopstone	2	D1	LBSC	
Bishopstone Beach Halt	2	D1	LBSC	1942
Bishops Stortford	12	F9	GE	
Bishops Waltham	5	A5	LSW	1933
Bishopton	74	B6	CAL	
Bispham – see Layton				
Bittaford Platform	9	E7	GW	1959
Bitterne	4	H5	LSW	
Bitton	17	D2	MID	1966
	72	F6		
Blaby	25	D8	LNW	1968

Station	Page	Block	Comp	Year of CL
Blackbank	23	A8	GE	1963
Black Bull	73	C8	NS	1927
[Blackburn]				
Blackburn 2nd, 1st — 1888	36	G5	LY	
	76	C6		
Bolton Road	76	C6	EL	1859
Daisyfield	76	B6	LY	1958
Lower Darwen	76	C6	LY	1958
Blackburn Forge	82	D8	S & R	Pre 1856
Black Dog Halt	17	H2	GW	1965
Blackdown — see Mary Tavy				
Blackdyke Halt	45	G3	NB	1964
Blackford	50	E3	CAL	1956
Blackford Hill — see [Edinburgh]				
Blackfriars — see [London]				
Blackgrange	50	D1	ST & D	1852
Blackhall (Strathclyde)	46	B6	NB	1893
Blackhall Colliery (Cleveland)	38	F9	NE	1964
Blackhall Rocks (Cleveland)	38	F9	NE	1960
Blackheath	65	D1	SEC	
	69	D10		
Blackheath — see [West Midlands]				
Rowley Regis				
Blackheath Hill — see [London]				
Blackhill	43	D1	NE	1955
Blackhorse Road	65	LTS/MID		
Black Lane — see Radcliffe				
Black Lion Crossing Halt — see Aberdare				
Blackmill	78	E3	GW	1958
Blackmoor	8	B7	LB	1935
Blackpill — see [Swansea]				
[Blackpool]				
Burlington Road	76	B1	PW JT	1949
Central	76	B1	PW JT	1964
North Form — Talbot Road	36	B6	PW JT	
	76	B1		
South Form — Waterloo Road	36	B6	PW JT	
	76	B1		
South Shore (Lytham Road)	76	B1	PW JT	1916
Black Rock Halt	32	F3	GW	1977
Blackrod	36	F3	LY	
	76	E5		
Blacksboat	56	H9	GNS	1965
Blackston Junction	46	B8	NB	1930
Blackthorn	15	A9	GW	1953
Blackwall — see [London]				
Blackwater (Isle of Wight)	4	H2	IWC	1956
Blackwater and York Town (Hants)	15	D1	SEC	
Blackwell	80	G4	MID	1966
Blackwell — see also Westhouses				
Blackwood (Strathclyde) 2nd, 1st — 1905	46	A4	CAL	1965
	49	H5		
Blackwood (Gwent)	78	C7	LNW	1960
Blacon — see [Chester]				
[Blaenau Festiniog]				
Blaenau Festiniog 2nd, 1st — 1881	32	H5	LNW	
Central	32	H4	GW	1960
Duffws	32	H4	FEST	1931
Station	32	H4	FEST	1939
Blaenavon	78	B9	LNW	1941
Blaenavon, Low Level	78	B9	GW	1962
Blaendare Road Halt — see [Pontypool]				
Blaengarw	78	D2	GW	1953
Blaengwynfi	78	D2	RSB	1968
Blaenplwyf Halt	19	F9	GW	1951
	26	B2		
Blaenrhondda	78	C2	RSB	1968
Blagdon	17	A2	GW	1931
Blaina	78	B8	GW	1962
Blairadam	50	H2	NB	1930
Blair Atholl	50	E2	HIGH	
Blairgowrie	50	H8	CAL	1955
Blairhill and Gartsherrie	75	D6	NB	
Blaisdon Halt	17	D8	GW	1964
Blakedown, Churchill and	80	F2	GW	
Blake Hall	12	G7	GE	1966
Blake Hall R.O. FR. CL. above	12	G7	LTS	
Blakesley	25	D2	SMJ	1952
Blake Street	80	B7	LNW	
Blandford Forum 2nd, 1st — 1863	4	A4	SD JT	1966
	7	H4		
Blanefield	49	E10	NB	1951
Blankney and Metheringham	29	B6	GN/GC	1961
Blantyre	75	C3	CAL	
Blaydon	43	E3	NE	
	81	G2		
Bleadon and Uphill	16	H1	GW	1964
Blean and Tyler Hill Halt	13	F1	SEC	1931
Bleasby	28	E4	MID	

Station	Page	Block	Comp	Year of CL
Bledlow	15	C6	GW	1963
Bledlow Bridge Halt	15	C6	GW	1957
Blencow	41	A8	CKP	1972
Blenheim and Woodstock	14	G8	GW	1954
Bletchington	14	G8	GW	1964
Bletchley	15	D10	LNW	
Blidworth and Rainworth	82	G5	MID	1929
Blisworth 2nd, 1st — 1853	25	E3	LNW	1960
Blisworth	25	E3	SMJ	1952
Blockley	14	D10	GW	1966
Blodwell Junction Station	30	B1	PSNW/CAM	1951
	33	G1		
Bloomsbury and Nechals — see [West Midlands]				
Blowick — see [Southport]				
Bloxham	14	F10	GW	1951
Bloxwich	80	A5	LNW	1965
Blue Anchor	6	E9	GW	1971
Blue Anchor R.O. PR. FR. CL. above	6	E9	WSR	
Bluestone	20	C5	MGN	1916
Blundellsands and Crosby	76	F1	LY	
Blunham	23	E3	LNW	1968
Blunsdon	14	C4	MSWJ	1924
Bluntisham	23	B5	GE	1931
Blyth North (Northumberland)	43	F5	NE	1964
Blythburgh for Wangford	21	B10	SWOLD	1929
Blyth Bridge (Staffs)	31	B4	NS	
Blyton for Corringham	28	H10	GC	1959
	34	H1		
Boarhills	51	E4	NB	1930
Boars Head	76	E4	LY/LU	1949
Boat of Garten	57	B6	HIGH	1965
Boat of Garten R.O. PR. FR. CL.	57	B6	HIGH	
Boat of Insh — see Kincraig				
Boat Yard Crossing Halt	76	C2	LY	1913
Bocking — see Braintree				
Boddam	54	E10	GNS	1932
Bodfari	33	E7	LNW	1962
Bodiam	3	A4	KES	1954
Bodmin 2nd, 1st — 1886	11	C7	LSW	1967
Bodmin General	11	C7	GW	1967
Bodmin Road	11	C7	GW	
Bodorgan	32	D7	LNW	
Bogfield — see [Carlisle]				
Bognor Regis	5	F7	LBSC	
Bogside (Strathclyde)	49	B5	GSW	1967
Bogside (Fife)	46	C10	NB	1958
	50	F1		
Bogside Moor Halt	49	B5	CAL	1930
Bogston	49	B9	CAL	
Bold	77	C4	ST H	1858
Bold — see also Farnworth				
Boldon	81	F1	YNB/NE	1853
Boldon Colliery Station	43	C3	NE	
	81	E2		
Bolham Halt	6	D5	GW	1963
Bollington	31	B8	GC/NS	1970
	77	D10		
Bolsover	82	D6	MID	1930
Bolsover South	82	D6	GC	1951
[Bolton] (Lancs)				
Astley Bridge	76	E6	LY	1879
Bolton	36	H3	LY	
	76	E7		
Chew Moor	76	E6	LY	1852
Darcy Lever	76	E7	LY	1951
Great Moor Str. 2nd, 1st — 1875	76	E6	LNW	1954
Lostock Junction Station	76	E6	LY	1966
Lostock Lane	76	E6	LY	1879
Rumworth and Daubhill 2nd, 1st — 1885	76	E6	LY	1952
Bolton (Yorkshire) — see Wath North				
Bolton Abbey	37	D9	MID	1965
	79	A1		
Bolton-le-Sands	41	A1	LNW	1969
Bolton-on-Dearne	34	C2	SK JT	
	82	D10		
Bolton Percy	34	D7	NE	1965
	79	B10		
Bolton Street — see [Bury] Bury				
Bolton Road — see [Blackburn]				
Bonar Bridge — see Ardgay				
Boncath	19	A7	GW	1962
Bo'ness	46	D9	NB	1956
Bonnington — see [Edinburgh]				
[Bonnybridge]				
Bonnybridge	46	B9	CAL	1930
Bonnybridge Central	46	B9	KB JT	1935
Bonnybridge High	46	B9	NB	1967
Bonnyrigg	46	H7	NB	1962

Station	Page	Block	Comp	Year of CL
Bonnyrigg	83	G3		
Bontnewydd 2nd, 1st — 1865	33	A1	GW	1965
Bonwm Halt	33	H5	GW	1964
Bookham	12	B1	LSW	
Boosbeck	39	A7	NE	1960
Boot	40	E5	ESK	1960
Boothferry Park* — see [Hull]				
Bootle (Cumbria)	40	D3	FUR	
[Bootle] (Merseyside)				
Aintree, Sefton Arms	36	C2	LY	
	76	F1		
Aintree Central	76	F2	CLC	1960
Aintree, Cinder Road	76	F2	LY	1951
Aintree Racecourse	76	F2	LY	1951
Alexandra Dock	76	G1	LNW	1948
Bootle Balliol Road	76	G1	LNW	1948
Bootle Oriel Road	36	B2	LY	
	76	G1		
Bootle New Strand Form. Marsh Lane	76	G1	LY	
Ford	76	G1	LY	1951
Gladstone Dock	76	F1	LY	1924
Old Roan Halt	76	F2	LY	1909
Bordesley	80	E6	GW	
Bordon	5	D8	LSW	1957
Borehamwood — see Elstree				
Boroughbridge 2nd, 1st — 1875	34	B10	NE	1950
	37	H10		
Borough Green and Wrotham	2	F8	SEC	
	70	F1		
Borrobel Platform	61	E4	HIGH	1965
	62	A4		
Borrowash 2nd, 1st — 1871	28	B3	MID	1966
	31	H3		
Borth	26	B7	CAM	
Borwick	41	B1	FM JT	1960
Boscarne Exchange Platform	11	A8	BR	1967
Boscombe — see [Bournemouth]				
Bosham	5	D4	LBSC	
Bosley	31	B6	NS	1960
	73	D10		
Bossall	34	F9	SH LT	1930
Boston (Lincs)	22	F8	GN	
	29	E4		
Boston Lodge Halt (Gwynedd)	32	G3	FEST	
Botanic Gardens — see [Glasgow]				
Botanic Gardens — see [Hull]				
Bothwell	75	D3	CAL	1950
Bothwell	75	D3	NB	1955
Botley	4	H5	LSW	
Botolphs Bridge Road Halt	3	E5	RHD	1947
Bottesford	28	G3	GN	
Bottesford South	28	G3	LNW	1882
Bottisham and Lode	23	D8	GE	1962
Bott Lane Halt	76	A9	LY	1956
Boughrood and Llyswen	27	A1	CAM	1962
Boughton	82	H6	GC	1955
Boughton Halt — see [Worcester]				
Bourne (Lincs)	22	E2	GN	1959
	29	B1		
Bourne Bridge	23	E5	NT	1851
Bourne End	15	D5	GW	
[Bournemouth]				
Boscombe	4	C2	LSW	1965
Bournemouth Central	4	C2	LSW	
East Replaced by Central	4	C2	LSW	1885
Meyrick Park Halt	4	C2	LSW	1917
West	4	C2	LSW	1965
Bournville Form. Stirchley Street	80	F5	MID	
Bournville (Mon) Halt Form. Tylers Arms Plat.	78	B8	GW	1962
Bourton-on-the-Water	14	C8	GW	1962
Bovey for Islington	6	B1	GW	1959
	9	B9		
Bow — see [London]				
Bow Brickhill Halt	15	E10	LNW	
Bowbridge Crossing Halt	17	F6	GW	1964
Bow (Devon)	6	A3	LSW	1972
	8	H8		
Bowdon	77	C7	MSJA	1881
Bowdon — see also Altrincham				
Bower	62	E8	HIGH	1960
Bowers Halt	79	E8	LNE	1951
Bowes	41	G7	NE	1962
Bowes Bridge	43	E3	BJ/NE	1844
	81	A1		
Bowes Park	64	H8	GN	
Bowhouse	46	C8	NB	1930
Bowker Vale	76	F9	LY	
Bowland	47	A4	NB	1953
Bowling (Strathclyde)	74	A8	CAL	1951
Bowling 2nd, 1st — 1858	74	A8	NB	
Bowling (Yorks) — see [Bradford]				
Bowling Junction — see [Bradford]				
Bowness	45	H4	CAL	1921
Bow Road — see [London]				
Bow Street	26	B6	CAM	1965
Box	17	F2	GW	1965
Box, Mill Lane Halt	17	F2	GW	1965
Boxford	14	G2	GW	1960
Box Hill R.N. Deepdene	2	A8	SEC	
Box Hill and Westhumble Form. Box Hill and Burford Bri.	2	A8	LBSC	
Boxmoor — see Hemel Hempstead				
Boyce's Bridge	22	F7	GE	1928
Braceborough Spa Halt	22	E2	GN	1951
Bracebridge GDS	29	A7	GN	1964
Brackenhills	49	B6	CAL	1930
Brackley Central	15	A10	GC	1966
	25	D1		
Brackley Town	15	A10	LNW	1961
	25	D1		
Bracknell	15	D2	LSW	
Bradbury	38	D8	NE	1950
Bradfield	13	G10	GE	1956
[Bradford]				
Adolphus Street Rep. by Exchange	79	E3	GN	1867
Birkenshaw and Tong	79	F4	GN	1953
Bowling	79	E3	GN	1895
Bowling Junction	79	E3	LY	1951
Bradford Exchange 2nd, 1st — 1973	37	E6	MID	
	79	E3		
Bradford, Foster Square	37	E6	MID	
	79	E3		
Clayton	79	E2	GN	1955
Dudley Hill 2nd, 1st — 1875	79	E4	GN	1952
Eccleshill	79	D3	GN	1931
Frizinghall	79	D3	MID	1965
Great Horton for Lidget Green	79	E2	GN	1955
Horton Park	79	E3	GN	1952
Idle	79	D3	GN	1931
Idle	79	D3	MID	1846
Laisterdyke	79	D3	GN	1966
Low Moor	79	F3	LY	1965
Manchester Road	79	E3	GN	1915
Manningham	79	D3	MID	1965
Market Street Rep. by Forster Sq.	79	E3	MID	1890
Queensbury	79	E2	GN	1955
St. Dunstan's	79	E3	GN	1952
Wyke and Norwood Green 1st — 1896	79	F3	LY	1953
Bradford-on-Avon	17	F1	GW	
Bradford Peverell and Stratton Halt	7	E2	GW	1966
Brading (Isle of Wight)	5	B2	IOW	
Bradley Fold for Little Lever	76	E7	LY	1970
Bradnop	31	C5	NS	1935
Bradwell	25	G1	LNW	1964
Brafferton	38	F1	NE	1950
Braidwood	46	B5	CAL	1962
Braintree and Bocking 2nd, 1st — 1869	13	A9	GE	
Braithwaite	40	F7	CKP	1966
Bramber	2	A2	LBSC	1966
Brambledown Halt	3	C10	SEC	1950
Bramford	21	F5	GE	1955
Bramhall	31	B9	LNW	
	77	D9		
Bramley (Hants) for Silchester	15	A1	GW	
Bramley — see [Leeds]				
Bramley and Wonersh (Surrey)	5	G5	LBSC	1965
Brampford Speke Halt	8	G10	GW	1963
Brampton (Cumbria) Junction	42	E2	NE	
Brampton (Suffolk)	21	A9	GE	
Brampton Fell	42	E2	NC	Pre 1850
Brampton Town	42	E2	BRAMP/NE	1923
Bramshot Halt	5	E7	LSW	1946
Bramwith	34	E3	MSL	1866
Bramwith GDS	34	E3	WRG	1961
Branbridges — see Beltring				
Brancepeth	38	C9	NE	1964
Brandlesham Road Halt — see [Bury]				
Brandon (Norfolk)	21	A1	GE	
Brandon and Wolston (Warwicks)	25	A6	LNW	1960
Brandon Colliery Station (Durham)	38	C9	NE	1964
Branksome	4	C2	LSW	
Bransford Road	24	B3	GW	1965
Branston (Staffs)	31	F1	MID	1930
Branston and Heighington (Lincs)	29	A7	GN/GE	1958
Bransty — see [Whitehaven] Whitehaven				
Branthwaite	40	D8	WCE JT	1931

Station	Page	Block	Comp	Year of CL
Brasted Halt	2	D8	SEC	1961
Bratton — see Edington				
Bratton Fleming	8	C7	LB	1935
Braughing	12	E9	GE	1964
Braunston — see [Leicester]				
Braunston, London Road	25	C4	LNW	1958
Braunston and Willoughby	25	C4	GC	1957
Braunton	8	C5	LSW	1970
Braystones	40	C5	FUR	
Brayton	40	E10	MC	1950
	45	H2		
Brayton Gates — see Selby				
Breadsall	31	G3	GN	1953
	82	B2		
Breamore	4	D6	LSW	1964
Brean Road Halt	6	H10	GW	1955
Breaston — see Draycott				
Brechin	51	F10	CAL	1952
	55	G4		
[Brecon]				
Ely Place GDS	16	D9	N & B	1955
Free Street	16	D9	BM	1962
Mount Street	16	D9	N & B	1874
Watton	16	D9	BM	1871
Brecon Road — see [Abergavenny]				
Breck Road — see [Liverpool]				
Bredbury	77	B10	GC/MID	
Bredon	17	G10	MID	1965
	21	C1		
Breedon — see Tong				
Breidden — see Middletown				
Brent (Devon)	9	D7	GW	1964
Brentford Central	64	B2	LSW	
	68	B10		
Brentford — see also [London]				
Brent Knoll	6	H10	GW	1971
Brentor	9	B5	LSW	1968
Brentwood and Warley	12	H5	GW	
	66	F8		
Brettell Lane — see [West Midlands]				
Bretton — see Broughton				
Bricket Wood	12	B6	LNW	
	15	G6		
Bridestowe	9	A5	LSW	1968
	11	H10		
Bridge	3	E8	SEC	1940
Bridgefoot (Cumbria)	40	D8	WCE JT	1931
Bridgefoot Halt (Grampian)	54	C5	GNS	1964
Bridgeford	31	A2	GJ	1840
[Bridgend]				
Bridgend	78	F2	L & OG	1873
Bridgend	16	C3	GW	
	78	F2		
Coity Road GDS	78	F2	BARRY	1965
Bridgehouses — see [Sheffield]				
Bridge of Allan	50	D2	CAL	1965
Bridge of Dee	45	B4	GSW	1949
Bridge of Dun	51	F9	CAL	1967
	55	H5		
Bridge of Earn 2nd, 1st — 1892	50	H4	NB	1964
Bridge of Orchy	53	E7	NB	
Bridge of Weir 2nd, 1st — 1868	49	C4	GSW	
Bridgeton — see also [Glasgow]	74	H5	CAL	
Bridgnorth	24	A8	GW	1963
	27	H7		
Bridgnorth R.O. PR. FR. CL. above	24	A8	SVR	
	27	H7		
Bridgerule — see Whitstone				
Bridge Street — see [Glasgow]				
Bridge Street — see [Greenock]				
Bridgeton Cross — see [Glasgow]				
Bridgwater	6	H8	GW	
Bridgwater North	6	H8	SD JT	1952
Bridlington	35	D10	NE	
[Bridport]				
Bridport, East Street	7	B2	GW	1930
Bridport for Lyme Regis	7	B2	GW	1975
Bridport, West Bay	7	B2	GW	1930
Briech	46	C5	CAL	
Brierfield Form. Marsden	37	A6	EL	
	76	B9		
Brierley Hill — see [West Midlands]				
Brigg	35	A2	GC	
Brigham	40	D8	LNW	1966
	45	F1		
Brighouse 2nd, 1st — 1893	79	G3	LY	1970
Brighouse — see also Clifton Road				
Brightlingsea	13	F8	GE	1964

Station	Page	Block	Comp	Year of CL
[Brighton]				
Brighton 2nd, 1st Falmer — 1865	2	B2	LBSC	
Hartington Road Halt	2	B2	LBSC	1911
Kemp Town	2	B2	LBSC	1933
Lewes Road Halt	2	B2	LBSC	1933
London Road	2	B2	LBSC	
Preston Park	2	B2	LBSC	
Brighton Road — see [West Midlands]				
Brightside	31	H1	MID	
	82	C9		
Brill	15	B8	MET/GC	1935
Brill and Ludgershall	15	B8	GW	1963
Brimington, Sheepbridge and	82	C6	GC	1956
Brimley Halt	6	B1	GW	1959
	9	B9		
Brimscombe	17	G6	GW	1964
Brimscombe Bridge Halt	17	G6	GW	1964
Brimsdown for Enfield Highway	12	E6	GE	
	65	C10		
Brindley Heath	24	E10	LMS	1959
Brinkburn Halt	43	C7	NB	1952
Brinklow and Stretton-under-Fosse	25	B6	LNW	1957
Brinkworth	14	B4	GW	1961
	17	H4		
Brinscall	76	C5	LY/LU	1960
Brisco	42	C1	LC	1852
Brislington — see [Bristol]				
[Bristol and Avonmouth]				
Ashley Hill	72	D7	GW	1964
Ashton — site of Long Ashton Plat.	72	B6	BE	1856
Ashton Gate Halt*	72	B6	GW	1964
Avonmouth	17	C3	CE	1903
	72	B7		
Avonmouth	17	C3	GW/CE	
	72	B7		
Avonmouth Docks	72	B7	GW	1915
Avonmouth Town GDS	72	B7	GW	1966
Bedminster	17	C2	GW	
	72	C6		
Brislington	17	C2	GW	1959
Brislington	72	D6		
Charlton Halt	72	D8	GW	1915
Chittening Platform	17	C3	GW	1964
	72	B8		
Clifton Bridge Halt	17	B2	GW	1964
	72	B6		
Clifton Down	17	C2	CE	
	72	C7		
Filton Junction 2nd, 1st — 1886	17	C3	GW	
	72	D8		
Filton Halt R.O. 1926 as North Filton Platform*				
Fishponds	72	E7	MID	1966
Hallen Halt	72	C8	GW	1915
Henbury	17	C3	GW	1964
	72	C8		
Horfield Platform	72	D8	GW	1964
Hotwells	72	C7	CE	1921
Hotwells Halt	72	C7	CE	1922
Keynsham and Somerdale	17	D2	GW	
	72	E6		
Lawrence Hill	17	C2	GW	
	72	D7		
Long Ashton Platform	72	C6	GW	1941
Montpelier	17	C2	CE	
	72	C7		
Nailsea and Backwell	17	B2	GW	
	72	B6		
North Filton Platform*	72	D8	GW	1964
Parkway	17	D2	BR	
	72	E8		
Parson Street	72	C6	GW	
Patchway 2nd, 1st — 1885	17	C4	GW	
	72	D8		
Pilning, High Level	17	C4	GW	
	72	D8		
Redland	72	C7	GW	
St. Andrews Road	17	E3	GW	
	72	B8		
St Anne's Park	72	E6	GW	1970
St. Phillip's	72	D7	MID	1953
Sea Mills	72	C7	GW	
Severn Beach	17	B4	GW	
	72	B9		
Shirehampton	17	B3	CE	
	72	B7		
Staple Hill	72	F7	MID	1966
Stapleton Road	17		GW	
	72	D7		

Station	Page	Block	Comp	Year of CL
Temple Meads	17	C2	GW	
	72	C6		
Temple Meads Old	17	C2	GW/MID	1965
	72	C6		
Bristol Road	16	H1	WCP	1940
Britannia (Lancs)	76	B9	LY	1917
Britannia Road	80	C3	LNW	1858
Brithdir	78	B6	RHY	
British Rhondda Halt	78	B2	GW	1911
[Briton Ferry]				
Briton Ferry	19	H2	GW	1964
Briton Ferry East	19	H2	RSB	1935
	78	E1		
Briton Ferry Road	19	H2	GW	1936
Briton Ferry West	19	H2	GW	1935
	78	E1		
Brixham — see Torbay				
Brixton and South Stockwell	65	A1	SEC	
	68	H9		
Brixton Road	9	E5	GW	1947
	11	H5		
Brixworth	25	F5	LNW	1960
Brize Norton and Bampton	14	E6	GW	1962
Broadbottom, Mottram and	31	C10	GC	
Broad Clyst	6	D3	LSW	1966
Broadfield	76	E8	LY	1970
Broad Green	76	H2	LNW	
Broadheath (Altrincham)	77	C8	LNW	1962
Broadley	76	C9	LY	1947
Broad Marston Halt	24	F2	GW	1916
Broadstairs	3	H10	SEC	
Broadstone (Dorset)	4	B3	LSW	1966
Broadstone (Avon)	16	H2	WCP	1940
Broad Street — see [London]				
Broadway (Worcs)	24	E1	GW	1960
Broadway — see [London]				
Broadway (Dorset) — see Upwey				
Brock	36	E7	LNW	1939
	76	A4		
Brockenhurst	4	F4	LSW	
Brocketsbrae	46	A4	CAL	1951
Brockford and Wetheringsett	21	D5	MSLT	1952
Brockholes	37	E4	LY	
	79	H3		
Brocklesby	35	C3	GC	
Brockley	65	C1	LBSC	
	69	C9		
Brockley Lane — see [London]				
Brockley Whins — Rep. by Boldon				
Colliery	81	E2	NE	
Brockmoor Halt — see [West Midlands]				
Brockton — see Milford				
Brockweir Halt	17	B6	GW	1959
Brodie	56	E7	HIGH	1965
Bromborough	77	D2	B HEAD	
Bromfield (Cumbria)	45	H2	CAL	1921
Bromfield (Salop)	27	E5	SH JT	1958
Bromford Forge — see [West Midlands]				
Bromford Lane — see [West Midlands]				
Oldbury				
Bromham and Rowde Halt	14	A1	GW	1966
	17	H1		
Bromley — see [London]				
Bromley Cross (Lancs)	36	H3	LY	
	76	D7		
Bromley Halt — see [West Midlands]				
Bromley North (Kent)	69	D6	SEC	
Bromley South (Kent)	69	D6	SEC	
Brompton	38	E4	NE	1965
Bromsgrove	24	C4	MID	
	80	G4		
Bromshall	31	C3	NS	1866
Bromyard	27	H2	GW	1964
Brondesbury	64	E4	LNW	
Brondesbury Park	64	E4	LNW	
Bronwydd Arms*	19	D6	GW	1965
Brookfield	42	C2	MC	1845
Brookhay	24	G10	SS	1849
Brookland Halt	3	C4	SEC	1967
Brooklands	77	B8	MSJA	
Brookmans Park	12	C7	GN	
Brooksby	25	E10	MID	1961
Brook Street Halt	72	C2	GW	1915
Brookwood Necropolis for Bisley Camp	15	E1	LSW	
Broome	27	D6	LNW	
Broomfield Road Junction	51	G10	CAL	1877
Broomfleet	34	H5	NE	
Broomhill (Inverness)	57	B7	HIGH	1965
Broomhill (Northumberland)	43	F8	NE	1930

Station	Page	Block	Comp	Year of CL
Broomhouse	75	B5	NB	1927
Broomieknowe	83	G3	NB	1951
Broomielaw	38	B7	NE	1964
Broom Junction Station	24	E2	MID	1962
Broomlee for West Linton	46	E5	NB	1933
Brora	61	E2	HR	
	62	A1		
Broseley — see Ironbridge				
Brotton	39	A7	NE	1960
Brough	35	A5	NE	
Broughton (Borders)	46	E3	CAL	1950
Broughton (Lancs) — see Barton				
Broughton and Bretton	30	C6	LNW	1962
Broughton Astley	25	C8	MID	1962
Broughton Cross	40	D8	LNW	1942
Broughton Gifford Halt	17	G1	GW	1955
Broughton-in-Furness 2nd, 1st — 1859	40	F3	FUR	1958
Broughton Lane — see [Sheffield]				
Broughton Skeog	44	G2	PPW JT	1885
Broughty Ferry (Dundee)	51	D6	DA JT	
Broughty — see also [Dundee]				
Browndown Halt	5	A4	LSW	1930
Brownhills	80	A6	LNW	1965
Brownhills, Watling Street	80	A6	MID	1930
Broxbourne and Hoddesdon	12	E7	GE	
Broxburn Junction	46	E8	EG/NB	1849
Broxton	30	D5	LNW	1957
Bruce Grove	65	B8	GE	
Brucklay	54	D8	GNS	1965
Brundall	20	F8	GE	
Brundall Gardens Halt	20	F8	GE	
Bruton	7	E8	GW	
Bruton — see also Cole				
Brunswick — see [Liverpool]				
[Brymbo]				
Brymbo	30	B5	GC	1917
	72	C4		
Brymbo	33	G5	GW	1950
	72	C4		
Brymbo West Crossing Halt	33	G5	GW	1931
	72	C4	GW	1931
Bryn (West Glam.)	78	E1	PT	1933
Bryn (Lancs) for Ashton-in-Makerfield	36	E2	LNW	
	76	F4		
Brynamman East	19	G4	MID	1950
Brynamman West	19	G4	GW	1958
Bryncelynog Halt	33	A3	GW	1960
Brynglas T.O. PR.	26	B9	TAL	
Bryngwyn Halt	33	F1	CAM	1965
Bryngwyn	32	E5	NWNG	1914
Brynkir	32	E4	LNW	1964
Brynmawr	78	A8	LNW	1962
Brynmenyn	78	F2	GW	1958
Brynmill — see [Swansea]				
Brynteg — see Dillwyn				
Bryn Teify Form. New Quay Rd.	19	D7	GW	1965
Bubwith	34	F6	NE	1954
Buchanan Street — see [Glasgow]				
Buchanstone	54	G5	GNS	1868
Buchlyvie	50	A1	NB	1951
	53	H1		
Buckden	23	C4	MID	1959
Buckenham	20	F8	GE	
Buckfastleigh	9	D8	GW	1952
Buckfastleigh R.O. PR. FR. CL. above	9	D8	DVR	
Buckhaven	51	B2	NB	1955
Buckhurst Hill	65	F9	GE	1966
Buckhurst Hill R.O. PR. FR. CL. above	65	F9	LTS	
Buckie	54	B2	GNS	1968
Buckie	54	B2	HIGH	1915
Buckingham	15	B10	LNW	1964
Buckingham — see also Finmere				
Buckley	77	G1	WMC/GC	1895
Buckley Junction Station	77	H2	GC	
Buckley — see also Padeswood				
Bucknall and Northwood — see [Stoke-on-Trent]				
Bucknell	27	D5	LNW	
Buckpool	54	B2	GNS	1960
Bucksburn	55	A8	GNS	1956
Buddon	51	D6	DA JT	1914
Bude	8	G1	LSW	1966
Budleigh Salterton	6	E1	LSW	1967
Bugle	11	A6	GW	
Buildwas	27	G9	GW	1963
[Builth Wells]				
Builth Road High Level	26	G2	LNW	
Builth Road Low Level	26	G2	CAM	1962
Builth Wells	26	G2	CAM	1962

Station	Page	Block	Comp	Year of CL
Buittle	45	C5	GSW	1894
Bulford (Wilts)	4	D9	LSW	1952
Bulford (Essex) — see Cressing				
Bulkington	80	D10	LNW	1931
Bullers o' Buchan Halt	54	F10	GNS	1932
Bullgill	40	D9	MC	1960
	45	G1		
Bullo Cross Halt	17	D7	GW	1958
Bullo Pill	17	D7	GW	1963
Bulwell Common — see [Nottingham]				
Bulwell Forest — see [Nottingham]				
Bulwell Hall Halt — see [Nottingham]				
Bulwell Market — see [Nottingham]				
Bunchrew	56	G2	HIGH	1960
Bungalow Town Halt	2	A1	LBSC	1940
Bungay	20	H8	GE	1953
Buntingford	12	D10	GE	1964
	23	H6		
Burbage — see Grafton				
Burdale	34	H9	NE	1950
Burdett Road — see [London]				
Bures	13	B10	GE	
Burgess Hill	2	B3	LBSC	
Burford — see Shipton				
Burford Bridge — see Box Hill and Westhumble				
Burgh — see Belton				
Burgh-by-Sands	42	B2	NB	1964
Burghclere	14	G1	GW	1960
Burghead 2nd, 1st — 1892	56	D8	HIGH	1931
Burgh Heath — see Banstead				
Burgh-le-Marsh	29	G7	GN	1970
Burlescombe	6	E5	GW	1964
Burley-in-Wharfedale	37	E8	O & I	
	79	B3		
Burlington Road — see [Blackpool]				
Burlish Halt	80	G1	GW	1970
Burmarsh Road	3	D5	RHD	1947
Burnage	77	C9	LNW	
Burnage — see also Levenshulme				
Burnbank	75	D2	NB	1952
Burneside	41	A4	LNW	
Burngullow 2nd, 1st — 1901	11	A5	GW	1931
Burn Halt	6	D4	GW	1963
	8	F10		
Burnham Beeches (Berks)	15	E4	GW	
Burnham Market (Norfolk)	20	B1	GE	1952
Burnham-on-Crouch (Essex)	13	D6	GE	
Burnham-on-Sea (Somerset)	6	H10	SD JT	1951
Burnhill	38	A10	NE	1939
[Burnley]				
Burnley Barracks	37	A6	EL	
	78	B8		
Burnley Central Form. Bank Top	37	A6	BR	
	78	B8		
Manchester Road	78	B8	LY	1961
New Hall Bridge Halt	78	B8	LY	1948
Reedley Hallows Halt	78	B8	LY	1956
Rose Grove 2nd, 1st — 1897	78	B8	LY	
Thorneybank 1st, 2nd Manch. Road	78	B9	LY	1866
Towneley	78	B9	LY	1952
Burnmouth	47	H7	NB	1962
Burn Naze Halt	76	A1	PW JT	1970
Burnside	74	H3	CAL	
Burnt Ash — see Lee				
Burnt House GDS	22	H5	GE	1964
Burntisland	46	F10	NB	
Burnt Mill	12	E7	GE	1960
Burrator Halt	9	C6	GW	1956
	11	H8		
Burrelton — see Woodside				
Burringham — see Gunness				
Burrington	17	A2	GW	1931
Burrows Lodge — see [Swansea] Wind Street				
Burry Port	19	D2	BPGV	1953
Burry Port — see also Pembrey				
Burscough Bridge	36	D4	LY	
	76	E2		
Burscough Junction Station	36	D4	LY	
	76	E2		
Bursledon	4	H4	LSW	
Burslem — see [Stoke-on-Trent]				
Burston	21	A6	GE	1966
Burstwick — see Ryehill				
Burton Agnes	35	C10	NE	1970
Burton and Holme	41	A2	LNW	1950
Burton Constable — see Ellerby				
Burton Joyce	28	E4	MID	

Station	Page	Block	Comp	Year of CL
Burton Joyce	82	H2		
Burton Latimer — see Isham				
[Burton-on-Trent]				
Burton-on-Trent	31	F1	MID	
Dallow Lane Wharf GDS	31	F1	LNW	1964
Hawkins Lane GDS	31	F1	GN	1966
Horninglow	31	F1	NS	1949
Burton Point	77	F1	GC	1955
Burton Salmon	79	G9	NE	1959
Burwarton Halt	27	G6	CMDP	1938
Burwell	23	C9	GE	1962
[Bury] (Lancs)				
Brandlesholme Road Halt	76	E8	LY	1952
Bury, Bolton Street	37	A4	EL	1980
	76	E8		
Bury	76	E8	BR	
Bury, Knowsley Street	76	E8	LY	1970
Woodhill Road Halt	76	E8	LY	1952
Woolfold	76	E8	LY	1952
Bury East Gate (Cambs)	23	A5	GE	1909
Bury Lane — see Glazebury				
Bury St. Edmunds	21	C2	GE	
Busby (Lanarks.)	74	G1	CAL	
Busby (Ayrshire)	49	A5	GSW	1850
Bushey and Oxhey	63	F10	LNW	
Bushey Park — see Teddington				
Bush Hill Park	65	B10	GE	
Bute Road — see [Cardiff]				
Butler's Hill	82	E3	GN	1931
Butlers Lane	80	B7	LNW	
Butterknowle	38	B8	S & D/NE	1859
Butterley for Ripley and Swanwick	82	C4	MID	1947
Butterton Halt	31	D6	NS	1934
Buttington	27	B9	CAM	1960
Butt's Lane Halt — see [Southport]				
Buxted	2	E4	LBSC	
[Buxton]				
Central GDS	31	D8	MID	1967
	77	D10		
Buxton	31	D8	LNW	
	77	D10		
Buxton	31	D8	MID	1967
	77	D10		
Higher Buxton	31	D8	LNW	1951
	77	D10		
Buxton Lamas	20	D6	GE	1952
Buxworth	77	D10	MID	1958
Byers Green 3rd, 1st — 1867, 2nd — 1885	38	C8	NE	1939
Byfield	25	C3	EWJ/SMJ	1952
Byfleet and New Haw Form. Byfleet and Woodham	67	C2	LSW	
Byker — see [Newcastle]				
Bynea	19	F2	GW	
Cadbury Road	17	A3	WCP	1940
Cadeleigh	6	C4	GW	1963
	8	F10		
Cadishead 2nd, 1st — 1893	77	B8	CLC	1964
Cadmore's Lane — see Cheshunt				
Cadoxton	78	H5	BARRY	
Cadoxton Terrace Halt	78	C1	GW	1962
Caerau	78	D2	GW	1970
Caergwrle Castle and Wells	30	B6	GC	
	72	D4		
Caerleon	78	E10	GW	1962
[Caernarfon] Form. spelt von				
Caernarfon	32	F6	LNW	1970
Caernarfon, Castle	32	F6	NANT	1865
Caernarfon, Morfa	32	F6	LNW	1870
Caernarfon, Pant	32	F6	LNW	1870
Caerphilly 2nd, 1st — 1871	16	F4	RHY	
	78	E6		
Caersws	26	G7	LNW	
Caersws	26	G7	VAN/CAM	1879
Caerwys	33	E7	LNW	1962
Caffyns Halt	8	B8	LB	1935
Cairnbulg	54	B10	GN	1965
Cairneyhill	46	D9	NB	1930
Cairnhill Bridge	75	F5	MONK	1894
Cairnie Junction, Exchange Platform	54	D3	GNS	1968
Cairntable Halt	49	G3	LMS	1950
Caistor Camp Halt	20	F10	MGN	1959
Caistor-on-Sea	20	F10	MGN	1959
Calbourne and Shalfleet (Isle of Wight)	4	G1	FYN	1953
Calcots	56	D10	GNS	1968
Caldarvan	49	D10	NB	1934
Calder	75	E5	CAL	1943
Calderbank	46	A7	CAL	1930
Caldercruix	75	H7	NB	1956
Calderpark Halt	75	C5	BR	1955

Station	Page	Block	Comp	Year of CL
Caldicot Halt	17	B4	GW	
Caldon Low Halt	31	D5	NS	1935
Caldwell	74	A1	GBK JT	1966
Caldy	77	C1	B HEAD	1954
Caledonian Road — see [London] Holloway				
Caledonian Road and Barnsbury	64	H5	LNW	
California Halt	20	E10	MGN	1959
Callander 2nd, 1st — 1870	50	B3	CAL	1965
Callerton	81	B5	NE	1929
Callington for Stoke Climsland	9	C3	PDSW	1966
	11	F8		
Calne	14	A2	GW	1965
	17	H2		
Calstock	9	C4	PDSW	
	11	G8		
Calthwaite	41	A10	LNW	1952
Calverley (Cheshire)	30	F6	LNW	1960
Calverley and Rodley (Yorkshire)	79	C4	MID	1965
Calvert	15	B9	GC	1963
Cam	17	E6	MID	1962
Camberley and York Town	15	D1	LSW	
Camber Sands	3	C3	RC	1939
Camberwell — see [London]				
Camborne	10	E4	WC/GW	
Cambridge	23	D7	GE	
Cambridge Heath (London)	65	C4	GE	
Cambus for Tullibody	50	D1	NB	1968
Cambusavie Halt	61	C1	HIGH	1960
Cambuslang	75	A4	CAL	
Cambusnethan	75	H2	CAL	1917
Cambus o' May Halt	55	C2	GNS	1966
Camden Road	64	H5	LNW	
Camden Town — see [London]				
Camelford	11	B10	LSW	1966
Camelon — see [Falkirk]				
Camel's Head Halt — see [Plymouth]				
Cameron Bridge	51	B2	NB	1969
Camerton (Cumbria)	40	D8	LNW	1952
Camerton (Somerset)	17	D1	GW	1925
Campbeltown	48		CM	1931
Campden — see Chipping Campden				
Camperdown Junction — see [Dundee]				
Camp Hill — see [West Midlands]				
Campsie Glen	74	H10	NB	1951
Canada Dock — see [Liverpool]				
Canal — see Carlisle				
Canal — see [Paisley] Paisley				
Canal Road — see [Leeds] Armley				
Cane Hill — see Coulsdon South				
Canley	24	H5	LNW	
	80	E9		
Canning Town	65	E4	GE	
Cannock	24	D10	LNW	1965
Cannon Street — see [Hull]				
Cannon Street — see [London]				
Canonbie	42	C4	NB	1964
Canonbury	65	A5	NL	
[Canterbury]				
Canterbury	3	E8	SE	1846
Canterbury East	3	E8	SEC	
Canterbury South	3	E8	SEC	1940
Canterbury West	3	E8	SEC	
Cantley	20	G8	GE	
Canvey Island — see Benfleet				
Capel (Suffolk)	21	G5	GE	1932
Capel (Surrey) — see Ockley				
Capel Bangour	26	C5	CAM	
Capel Celyn Halt	33	B4	GW	1960
Capenhurst	77	F3	B HEAD	
Caradog Falls Halt	26	C4	GW	1964
Carbean GDS	11	A6	GW	1965
Carbis GDS	11	A6	GW	
Carbis Bay	10	C4	GW	
Carcroft and Adwick-le-Street	33	D3	WRG JT	1967
	82	F10		
Cardenden for Bowhill	51	A2	NB	
[Cardiff]				
Adam Street	78	H6	RHY	1871
Bute Road	16	F2	TV	
	78	H6		
Cathys (Woodville Road) Halt	78	G6	TV	1958
Central	16	F2	GW	
	78	H6		
Clarence Road	78	H6	GW	1964
Docks	78	H6	TV	1958
Ely	78	G6	GW	1962
General	78	H6	GW	1964
Maindy (North Road) Halt	78	G7	TV	1958
Ninian Park*	78	G6	WR	
Queen Street	16	F2	TV	
	78	H6		
Riverside	78	H6	GW	1964
Roath	78	H7	GW	1917
Cardiff Road — see Mountain Ash				
Cardigan	19	A8	GW	1962
Cardington	23	F2	MID	1962
Cardonald	74	F4	GP JT	
Cardonnel Halt	19	H2	GW	1936
Cardrona	46	G3	NB	1962
Cardross	49	C9	NB	
Careston	51	E10	CAL	1952
	55	H3		
Carfin Halt	75	G3	CAL	
Cargill	50	H7	CAL	1956
Cargo Fleet 2nd, 1st Cleveland Port — 1885	38	G7	NE	
Carham	46	E3	NE	1955
Carisbrooke Halt (Isle of Wight)	4	H1	FYN	1953
Cark and Cartmel	40	G2	FUR	
Carlinghow	79	F4	LNW	1917
Carliol Square — see [Newcastle]				
[Carlisle]				
Bog GDS	42	B2	NE	1969
Bogfield	42	B2	MC	1844
Canal	42	B2	NB	1864
Carlisle	42	C2	JOINT	1849
Crown Street	42	C2	MC	1849
London Road	42	C2	NB	1864
Port Carlisle Junction	42	C2	NB	1864
Viaduct GDS	42	C2	CAL	1965
Carlton and Netherfield	82	G2	MID	
Carlton and Netherfield GDS	82	G2	MID	1965
Carlton Colville — see Oulton Broad South				
Carlton-on-Trent	28	G6	GN	1953
Carlton Towers	34	E5	HB	1932
Carluke	46	A5	CAL	
Carmarthen 2nd, 1st — 1902	19	C5	GW	
Carmarthen Junction	19	D5	GW	1926
Carmont	55	E7	CAL	1956
Carmyle	75	A5	CAL	1964
Carmyllie	51	E8	DA JT	1929
Carnaby	35	C10	NE	1970
Carn Brae	10	E4	WC/GW	1961
Carnforth	41	A1	LNW/FUR	
Carnforth	41	A1	FM JT	1880
Carno	26	G7	CAM	1965
Carnoustie 2nd, 1st — 1900	51	E6	DA JT	
Carntyne for Westmuir and Tolcross	75	A6	NB	
Carnwath	46	C5	CAL	1966
Carpenders Park for Oxhey Golf Club 2nd, 1st — 1952	63	F9	GE	
Carr Bridge	57	B5	HIGH	
Carreghofa Halt	30	A1	GW	1965
Carr House	38	G8	NE	1868
Carrington — see [Nottingham]				
Carr Lane	76	A2	KE	1930
Carr Mill	76	G4	LNW	1917
Carrog	33	E4	GW	1964
Carron	56	G10	GNS	1965
Carronbridge	45	D10	GSW	1953
Carshalton	68	F4	LBSC	
Carshalton Beeches	68	F4	LBSC	
Carstairs	46	C4	CAL	
Cartmell — see Cark				
Cartsdyke	49	B9	CAL	
Carterton	14	E6	GW	1962
Carville	81	D8	NE	1960
Cashes Green Halt	17	F7	GW	1964
Cassillis	49	B1	GSW	1954
Cassington Halt	14	G7	GW	1962
Castle Ashby and Earls Barton	25	G4	LNW	1964
Castle Bar Park Halt	64	A4	GW	
Castle Bromwich — see [West Midlands]				
Castle Bytham	22	E1	MID	1959
	29	A1		
Castlebythe Halt	18	G6	GW	1937
Castle Caereinion	27	A9	CAM	1931
Castle Caereinion R.O. PR. FR. CL. above	27	A9	W & L	
Castlecary (Strathclyde)	49	A9	NB	1967
	75	G10		
Castle Cary (Somerset)	7	D7	GW	
Castle Donnington and Shardlow	31	B2	MID	1930
Castle Douglas	45	C5	GSW	1965
Castle Douglas, St Andrew Street	45	C5	GSW	1867
Castle Eden	38	E9	NE	1952
Castleford 2nd, 1st — 1871	34	B5	NE	
	79	F8		

Station	Page	Block	Comp	Year of CL
Castleford, Cutsyke	34	B5	LY	1968
	79	F8		
Castle Hedingham — see Sible				
Castlehill (Carluke) GDS	46	A6	NB	1949
Castle Howard	34	F10	NE	1930
Castle Kennedy	44	B4	PPW JT	1965
Castle Mill	30	B3	GVT	1933
	33	G3		
Castlethorpe	25	F2	LNW	1964
Castleton (Gt. Manchester)	76	E9	LY	
Castleton Moor (Yorkshire)	39	A6	NE	
Castor	22	G2	LNW	1957
Catcliffe	82	D9	GC	1939
Caterham 2nd, 1st — 1900	2	C8	SEC	
Catfield	20	D8	MGN	1959
Catford	69	C8	SEC	
Catford Bridge	69	C8	SEC	
Cathcart 2nd, 1st — 1894 (Bridge St.)	74	G3	CAL	
Cathys (Woodville Rd.) Halt — see [Cardiff]				
Caton	36	E10	MID	1961
Catrine	49	E3	GSW	1943
Cattal	34	C9	NE	
Catterall — see Garstang				
Catterick Bridge	38	C5	NE	1969
Cattistock Halt	7	D3	GW	1966
Cauldcots	51	F8	NB	1930
Causeland	9	D9	LL	
	11	E2		
Causeway Halt	8	D4	BWA	1917
Causewayend (Central Scotland)	46	C8	NB	1930
Causewayend (Galloway)	44	F4	PPW JT	1885
Causeway Head (Cumbria)	45	G3	CS	1859
Causewayhead (Stirling)	50	D2	NB	1955
Cavendish	21	F1	GE	1967
Cawood	34	E6	NE	1930
Cawston	20	D5	GE	1952
Caythorpe	29	A4	GN	1962
Cayton	39	E2	NE	1952
Cefn	30	B4	GW	1960
	72	D1		
Cefn Coed	78	A4	BN/LNW	1961
Cefn Coed Colliery Halt	78	C1	GW	1962
Cefn Crib	78	D8	WM	1860
Cefn On Halt	78	F7	RHY	
Cefn Tilla Halt	17	A6	BR	1955
Cefn-y-Bedd	30	B5	GC	
	72	D4		
Cei Llydan	32	F6	LNW	1930
Cei Llydan R.O. PR. FR. CL. above	32	F6	LL	
Ceint	32	F7	LNW	1930
Celtic Park — see [Glasgow] Parkhead				
Celynen North Halt	78	D8	GW	1962
Celynen South Halt	78	D8	GW	1962
[Cemmaes]				
Cemmaes	26	E9	MAW/CAM	1931
Cemmaes Road	26	E9	MAW/CAM	1931
Cemmaes Road	26	E9	CAM	1965
Cerist	26	F6	CAM	1879
Cerney and Ashton Keynes — see South Cerney				
Chacewater	10	F4	GW	1964
Chadderton GDS	76	F9	LY	1970
Chadwell Heath for Becontree	65	H6	GE	
	66	A6		
Chailey — see Newick				
Chalcombe Road Halt	25	B2	GC	1956
Chalder	5	E3	WS	1935
Chalfont and Latimer	15	F6	MET/GC	
Chalford	17	G6	GW	1964
Chalk Farm — see [London]				
Chalkwell	13	C5	MID	
Challow	14	F4	GW	1964
Chalvey Halt	15	E3	GW	1930
Chambers Crossing Halt	24	G2	GW	1916
Chandlers Ford	4	G6	LSW	1969
Chapel Bridge	17	B6	MON	1876
Chapel-en-le-Frith Central	31	D8	MID	1967
	77	D10		
Chapel-en-le-Frith South	31	D8	LNW	
	77	D10		
Chapelhall	46	A7	CAL	1930
	75	G5		
Chapel Lane	27	C10	SM	1933
	33	H1		
Chapel Street, Prestatyn	33	E9	LNW	1930
Chapel Street — see [Southport] Southport				
Chapelton	8	D6	LSW	
Chapeltown South	34	B1	MID	
Chapeltown South	82	C9		
Chapeltown and Thorncliffe	82	C9	GC	1953
Chappel and Wakes Colne	13	C10	GE	
	21	H2		
[Chard]				
Central (Joint)	7	A5	GW/LSW	1962
Chard Junction	7	A5	LSW	1966
Chard Junction (Central Branch Sta.)	7	A5	LSW	1962
Town	7	A5	LSW	1917
Charfield for Wotton-under-Edge	17	D5	MID	1965
Charing	3	C7	SEC	
Charing Cross — see [Glasgow]				
Charing Cross — see [London]				
Charlbury	14	F8	GW	
Charlestown	46	D9	NB	1926
Charlestown — see Ashton-under-Lyne				
Charlton (Kent)	65	E2	SEC	
Charlton (Northumberland)	42	H5	NB	1862
Charlton Halt (Oxon)	15	H8	LNW	1926
Charlton Halt — see [Bristol]				
Charlton Kings	14	A8	GW	1962
	17	H8		
Charlton Mackrell	7	C7	GW	1962
Charlton Marshall Halt	14	H8	SD JT	1956
Charlton Road — see Shepton Mallet				
Chartham	3	D8	SEC	
Chartley	31	C2	GN	1939
Charwelton	25	C3	GC	1963
Chassen Road	77	B7	CLC	
Chatburn 2nd Sta., 1st — 1876	36	H7	LY	1962
	76	A6		
Chatham	2	H9	SEC	
Chatham Central	2	H9	SEC	1911
Chathill	43	G5	NE	
Chatteris	23	A6	GN/GE	1967
Chatteris Dock GDS	23	A6	GN/GE	1955
Chatterley — see [Stoke-on-Trent]				
Cheadle (Cheshire)	77	C8	LNW	1917
Cheadle (Staffs)	31	C4	NS	1963
Cheadle Heath — see [Stockport]				
Cheadle Hulme 2nd, 1st — 1856	77	C9	LNW	
Cheadle North	77	C9	CLC	1964
Cheam	68	E3	LBSC	
Checker House	28	E8	GC	1931
	82	G8		
Cheddar	7	B10	GW	1963
Cheddington	15	E8	LNW	
Cheddleton	31	C5	NS	1965
	73	E8		
Cheeswring Quarry GDS	11	E9	GW	
Chedworth Halt	14	B7	MSWJ	1961
Chelfham	8	C6	LB	1935
Chelford for Knutsford	77	E8	LNW	
Chellaston and Swarkstone	28	A2	MID	1930
	31	A8		
Chelmsford 2nd, 1st — 1856	13	A7	GE	
Chelsea and Fulham — see [London]				
Chelsfield	69	G4	SEC	
[Cheltenham Spa]				
Cheltenham Spa	14	A8	MID	
	17	G9		
High Street	17	G9	MID	1910
High Street Halt	17	G9	GW	1917
Leckhampton, Cheltenham South	14	A8	GW	1962
	17	G9		
Malvern Road	14	A9	GW	1966
	17	G9		
Racecourse*	17	G9	BR	
St James	14	A9	GW	1966
	17	G9		
Chepstow	17	B5	GW	
Chepstow East	17	B5	SW	1852
Chequerbent for Hulton Park 2nd, 1st — 1885	76	F6	LNW	1952
Cheriton Halt	3	E6	SEC	1947
Cherry Burton	35	A7	NE	1959
Cherry Hinton	23	D7	EC/GE	1854
Cherry Lane — see [Doncaster]				
Cherry Tree	76	C5	EL	
Chertsey 2nd, 1st — 1886	15	F2	LSW	
	67	C5		
Chesham	15	E6	MET/GC	
Chesham Bois — see Amersham				
Cheshunt 2nd, 1st — 1891	12	E6	GE	
Cheshunt, Cadmores Lane	12	E6	N & E	1842
Cheslyn Hay — see Wyrley				
Chessington North	68	B4	LSW	
Chessington South for Zoo	68	B4	LSW	
[Chester]				

Station	Page	Block	Comp	Year of CL
Blacon	77	G3	GC	1968
General	30	D7	JOINT	
	77	G4		
Liverpool Road	77	G3	GC	1951
Northgate	77	G3	CLC	1969
Saltney	77	G3	GW	1960
Station	77	G3	BLCJ	1848
[Chesterfield]				
Brampton GDS	82	B6	MID	1964
Central	82	B6	GC	1963
Chesterfield 2nd, 1st — 1870	31	H7	MID/GC	
	82	B6		
Market Place	31	H7	GC	1951
	82	D6		
Chesterfield Road	82	B5	ASH	1936
Chester-le-Street	43	F1	NE	1869
Chester-le-Street	43	F1	NE	
Chester Road	80	C7	LNW	
Chesterton (Cambs)	23	D8	EC	1860
Chesterton Lane Halt (Glos)	14	A6	BR	1964
Chestfield and Swalecliffe Ht	3	E10	SEC	
Chettisham	23	A8	GE	1960
Chetnole Halt	7	D3	GW	
Chevening Halt	70	A1	SEC	1961
Chevington	43	E7	NE	1958
Chew Moor — see [Bolton]				
Chichester 2nd, 1st — 1935	5	E4	LBSC	
Chickenley Heath	79	G5	GN	1909
Chiddingfold — see Witley				
Chigwell	65	G9	GE	1966
Chigwell R.O. by LTS FR. CL. above	65	G9	LTS	
Chigwell Lane — see Debden				
Chilcompton for Downside	7	D10	SD JT	1966
Childwall — see [Liverpool]				
Chilham	3	D8	SEC	
Chilsworthy	9	C4	PDSW	1966
	11	G8		
Chiltern Green	12	B8	MID	1952
	15	G8		
Chilton Halt	27	H5	CMDP	1917
Chilvers Coton	25	A7	LNW	1965
	80	C10		
Chilworth and Albury	5	G9	SEC	
Chingford 2nd, 1st — 1878	65	D9	GE	
Chinley 2nd, 1st — 1902	77	D10	MID	
Chinnor	15	C6	GW	1957
Chippenham	17	G2	GW	
Chipping Campden	24	G1	GW	1966
Chipping Norton 3rd, 1st — 1887, 2nd — 1962	14	E9	GW	
Chipping Ongar — see Ongar				
Chipping Sodbury	17	E4	GW	1961
	72	H8		
Chipstead and Banstead Downs	68	F1	SEC	
Chirk	30	B3	GW	
	33	H3		
Chirk	30	B3	GVT	1933
	33	H3		
Chirnside	47	F6	NB	1951
Chirton — see Patney				
Chiseldon	14	C3	MSWJ	1961
Chiseldon Camp Halt	14	C3	GW	1961
Chislehurst 2nd, 1st — 1868	69	F6	SEC	
Chislet Colliery Halt	3	F9	SEC	1971
Chiswick and Grove Park	64	C1	LSW	
	68	C10		
Chiswick — see also [London] Hammersmith				
Chittening Platform — see [Bristol]				
Chollerford R.N. Humshaugh 1919	43	B3	NB	1956
Chollerton	43	B3	NB	1956
Cholsey and Moulsford	15	A4	GW	
Choppington	43	F5	NE	1950
Chorley	36	F4	LY	
	76	D5		
Chorley Wood and Chenies	63	C10	MET/GC	
Chorlton-cum-Hardy — see [Manchester]				
Christchurch for Southbourne-on-Sea 2nd, 1st — 1886	4	D2	LSW	
	14	A3	GW	1965
Christian Malford Halt	17	H3		
Christon Bank	43	E10	NE	1958
Christow	9	A9	GW	1958
Christ's Hospital (West Horsham)	5	H7	LBSC	
Chryston	75	D8	MONK	1851
Chryston — see also Garnkirk				
Chudleigh	6	B1	GW	1958
	9	B9		
Chudleigh Knighton Halt	6	B1	GW	1958
Chudleigh Knighton Halt	9	B9		
Church Bampton	25	E4	LNW	1931
Church Bridge — see Wyrley and Cheslyn Hay				
Churchbury	65	B10	GE	1919
Churchdown	16	D9	GW/MID	1964
Church Fenton	34	C6	NE	
	79	C10		
Church and Oswaldtwistle	76	C7	LY	
Churchill — see Blakedown				
Church Road — see Harrington Halt				
Church Road — see [Liverpool]				
Church Road — see [West Midlands]				
Church's Hill Halt	17	G5	BR	1964
Church Siding	15	B8	WOTTON	1894
Church Street — see [Dunstable] North				
Church Stretton 2nd, 1st — 1914	27	E8	SH JT	
Churchtown — see [Southport]				
Church Village Halt	78	E5	TV	1952
Churn Halt	14	H3	GW	1962
Churston	9	E10	GW	1963
Churston R.O. PR. FR. CL. above	9	E10	T & D	
Churwell	79	E5	LNW	1940
Chwilog	32	E3	LNW	1964
Cilfrew	78	B1	N & B	1962
Cilfrew Platform	78	B1	N & B	1895
Cilfynydd	78	E5	TV	1932
Ciliau Aeron	19	E10	GW	1951
	26	A3		
Cilmery Halt	26	G2	LNW	
Cinderford 2nd, 1st — 1900	17	D8	SW JT	1958
Cirencester Town	14	B6	GW	1964
Cirencester Watermoor	14	B6	MSWJ	1961
Clacnaharry	56	F3	HIGH	1913
Clackmannan and Kennet	50	E1	NB	1930
Clackmannan Road	50	E1	NB	1921
Clacton-on-Sea and Southcliffe	13	G8	GE	
Clandon and Ripley	5	G10	LSW	
Clapham (Yorkshire)	41	D1	MID	
Clapham and North Stockwell (London)	64	H1	SEC	
Clapham Common — see [London]				
Clapham Junction	64	G1	LBSC	
	68	F9		
Clapton	65	B6	GE	
Clapton Road	17	B3	WCP	1940
Clara Vale Colliery GDS	43	E3	NE	
Clarbeston Road	18	F5	GW	
Clare	21	F1	GE	1967
Claremont — see Esher				
Clarence Street — see [Pontypool]				
Clarence Road — see [Cardiff]				
Clarks Lane — see [West Midlands] Small Heath				
Clarkston	75	G6	NB	1956
Clarkston and Stamperland Form. Clarkston for Eaglesham	74	F1	CAL	
Clatford	4	F9	LSW	1964
Claughton	36	F10	NW	1853
Claverdon 2nd, 1st — 1939	80	G8	GW	
Claxby and Usselby	29	B10	GC	1960
[Clay Cross]	35	B1		
Clay Cross	31	H7	MID	1967
Clay Cross and Egstow	31	H7	ASH	1936
Clay Cross Town	31	H7	MID	1963
Claydon (Bucks)	15	B9	LNW	1968
Claydon (Suffolk)	21	E5	GE	1963
Claygate (Dumfries) — see Gilnockie				
Claygate and Claremont	67	H4	LSW	
Clay Lane	82	B5	ASH	1936
Claypole	28	H4	GN	1957
Claythorpe — see Aby				
Clayton — see [Bradford]				
Clayton Bridge — see [Manchester]				
Clayton West (Yorks)	37	F3	LY	
	79	H5		
Clearbrook Halt	9	C5	GW	1962
	11	H7		
Cleator Moor East	40	C6	WCE JT	1931
Cleator Moor West	40	C6	CW JT	1931
Cleckheaton	79	F3	LY	1965
Cleckheaton Spen	79	F3	LNW	1953
Cledford Bridge	30	G6	LNW	1942
	77	F7		
Clee Hill GDS	27	F5	SH JT	1960
Cleethorpes	35	F3	GC	
Cleeve	17	G9	MID	1950
Cleghorn	46	B4	CAL	1965
Clegg Street — see [Oldham]				

Station	Page	Block	Comp	Year of CL
Cleland	75	H3	CAL	1930
Cleland Form. Omoa	75	H3	CAL	
Clenchwarton	22	E8	MGN	1959
	29	H1		
[Cleobury Mortimer]				
Cleobury Mortimer	27	H5	GW	1962
Cleobury North	27	H5	CHDP	1938
Cleobury Town	27	H5	CMDP	1938
[Clevedon]				
Clevedon	17	A2	GW	1966
Clevedon	17	A2	WCP	1940
Clevedon All Saints	17	A2	WCP	1940
Clevedon East	17	A2	WCP	1940
Cleveland Bridge — see [Grimsby]				
Cleveleys — see Thornton				
Cliburn	41	C8	NE	1956
Cliddesden	5	B10	LSW	1932
Cliff Common	34	E6	DV	1926
Cliff Common	34	E6	NE	1954
Cliffe	2	H10	SEC	1961
	13	A3		
Cliffe Park Halt	31	B6	NS	1960
Cliffe Vale	73	C6	NS	1865
Clifford	27	B1	GOLD V/GW	1941
Clifton Bridge Halt — see [Bristol]				
Clifton Junction Station	76	F8	EL	
Clifton and Lowther	41	B8	LNW	1938
Clifton Down	17	C2	CE	
	72	C7		
Clifton Mayfield	31	E4	NS	1954
Clifton Mill	25	C6	LNW	1953
Clifton Moor	41	B8	NE	1962
Clifton-on-Trent	28	G7	GC	1955
Clifton Road, Brighouse	79	G3	LY	1931
Clipston and Oxendon	25	F6	LNW	1960
Clipstone GDS	82	G6	GC	
Clitheroe* 2nd, 1st — 1893	36	H7	LY	1962
	76	A6		
Clock Face	76	H4	LNW	1951
	77	C5		
Clock House	69	C6	SEC	
Clocksbriggs	51	D9	CAL	1955
Clogwyn	32	G5	NWNG	
Closeburn	45	D8	GSW	1961
Clough Fold	76	F8	LY	1966
Cloughton	39	E4	NE	1965
Clovenfords	47	A3	NE	1962
Clowne and Barlborough	82	E7	MID	1954
Clowne South	82	E7	GC	1939
Cloy Halt	30	C4	GW	1962
Clunes	56	G1	HIGH	1960
Clutton	17	C1	GW	1959
Clydach	78	A8	LNW	1958
Clydach Court Halt	78	A8	TV	1952
Clydach-on-Tawe North GDS	19	G3	GW	1965
Clydach-on-Tawe South	19	G3	MID	1950
[Clydebank]				
Clydebank Central	74	C8	NB	
Clydebank East	74	C8	NB	1959
Clydebank Riverside	74	C8	CAL	1964
Clynderwen	18	H5	GW	
Clyne Halt	78	C1	GW	1964
Clyst St Mary and Digby Halt	6	D2	LSW	1948
Coalbrookdale	27	G9	GW	1962
Coalburn	46	A3	CAL	1965
Coaley Junction Station	17	E6	MID	1965
Coalpit Heath	72	F8	GW	1961
Coalport	24	A9	GW	1963
	27	H8		
Coalport East	24	A9	LNW	1952
	27	H8		
Coanwood	42	G2	NE	1976
[Coalville]				
Coalville	25	B10	MID	
Coalville East	25	B10	LNW	1931
Coalville Town	25	B10	MID	1964
[Coatbridge]				
Coatbridge Central	49	H7	NB	1951
	75	E6		
Coatbridge Central	49	H7	CAL	
	75	E6		
Coatbridge Sunnyside	49	H7	NB	
	75	E6		
Coatdyke	75	F6	NB	
Coates	17	H6	GW	1964
	14	A5		
Cobbinshaw 2nd, 1st — 1875	46	D5	CAL	1966
Cobham and Stoke d'Abernon	67	G1	LSW	
Coborn Road — see [London]				
Cobridge — see [Stoke-on-Trent]				
Cockburnspath	47	E8	NB	1951
Cocker Bar	76	C3	LY	1859
Cockerham Cross	36	D8	GKE/KE	1930
	76	A3		
Cockermouth for Buttermere 2nd, 1st — 1865	40	E8	CKP/LNW	1966
	45	G1		
Cockett — see [Swansea]				
Cockfield (Suffolk)	21	E3	GE	1961
Cockfield Fell (Durham)	38	B7	NE	1958
Cocking	5	E6	LBSC	1935
Codford	4	A8	GW	1955
Codnor — see Crosshill				
Codnor Park and Ironville	82	C3	MID	1967
Codnor Park and Selston — see Jacksdale				
Codsall	24	C9	GW	
	80	B2		
Coed Ely	78	E4	GW	1958
Coedpenmaen	78	E5	TV	1915
Coed Porth	30	B5	GW	1931
	72	G3		
Coed Talon	33	G6	LNW	1950
	72	C5		
Cofton	80	G5	BG	1842
Cogan	78	H6	BARRY	
Cogie Hill Crossing	36	D8	GKE/KE	1930
	76	A3		
Colbren Junction Station	16	B7	N & B	1962
	78	A3		
Colchester, Hythe	13	E10	GE	
	21	H3		
Colchester North GDS	13	E10	GE	1966
	21	H3		
Coldham for Pear Tree Hill	22	G7	GE	1966
Coldharbour Halt	6	E5	GW	1963
Cold Meece Secret wartime sta.	31	A3	LNW	1940
Cold Norton	13	B6	GE	1939
Coldstream	47	G4	NE	1964
Cole for Bruton	7	E8	SD JT	1966
Coleburn	56	E10	GNS	1867
Coleford	17	C7	GW	1917
Coleford	17	C7	SW JT	1929
Cole Green	12	C7	GN	1951
Colehouse Lane	17	A2	WCP	1940
Coleshill	80	D8	MID	1968
Colfin	44	B4	PPW JT	1950
Colinton — see [Edinburgh]				
Collessie	51	B4	NB	1955
Colliery Road	48	C2	CM	1927
Collingbourne	4	E10	MSWJ	1961
Collingbourne Kingston Halt	4	E10	GW	1961
	14	D1		
Collingham (Notts)	28	G6	MID	
Collingham Bridge (Yorks)	34	B8	NE	1964
	79	B8		
Collington Wood Halt	2	H2	LBSC	
Collins Green	76	H4	LNW	1951
Colliston	51	F8	CAL	1955
Collyweston — see Ketton				
Colnbrook	63	C2	GW	1965
	67	C10		
Colnbrook Estate Halt	63	C2	BR	1965
	67	C10		
Colne	37	B10	MID/LY	
	76	A9		
Coltfield Platform	56	D8	HIGH	1931
Coltishall	20	D7	GE	1952
Colwall	24	A1	GW	
Colwich	31	C1	LNW	1958
Colwyn Bay	33	B8	LNW	
Colyford	6	H2	LSW	1966
Colyton	6	H2	LSW	1966
Colzium	75	E10		1917
Combe Halt	14	G7	GW	
Combe Hay Halt	17	D1	GW	1925
Combe Row	6	E8	WSM	1898
Combpyne	6	H2	LSW	1965
Comins Coch Halt	26	E8	GW	1965
Commercial Street Platform — see [Aberdare]				
Commondale	39	A6	NE	
Commondyke	49	E2	GSW	1950
Commonhead (Airdrie North)	75	F6	NB	1930
Compton	14	H3	GW	1962
Compton Halt — see [West Midlands]				
Comrie	50	C5	CAL	1964
Condor Green	36	D9	LNW	1930
Condover	27	E9	SD JT	1958

Station	Page	Block	Comp	Year of CL
Congleton	31	A6	NS	
	73	D10		
Congleton, Upper Junction	73	D10	NS	1864
Congresbury	17	A1	GW	1963
Coningsby	29	D6	GN	1970
Conisborough 2nd, 1st – 1890	34	D1	GC	
	82	E10		
Conisborough – see also Denaby				
Conishead Priory	40	G2	FUR	1916
Coniston	40	F4	FUR	1958
Connah's Quay	77	G2	LNW	1966
Connah's Quay and Shotton	77	G2	GC	1955
Connaught Road – see [London]				
Connel Ferry	52	H	CAL	
Conon	56	E	HIGH	1960
Cononley	37	C8	MID	1965
	79	B1		
Consall	31	C4	NS	1965
	73	E7		
Consett	43	D1	NE	1955
Constable Burton	38	C3	NE	1954
Conway	33	A8	LNW	1966
Conwil	19	C6	CC/GW	1965
Cooden Beach	2	G2	LBSC	
Cookham	15	D4	GW	
Cooksbridge	2	C2	LBSC	
Coole Pilate Halt	30	F4	GW	1963
Coombe and Malden – see New Malden				
Coombe Road	69	A4	SEC	
Coombe Junction Halt	9	D2	GW	
Coombes Holloway Halt	80	E3	GW	1927
Cooper Bridge	79	G4	LY	1950
Copgrove	34	B9	NE	1950
Cop Lane Halt – see Penwortham				
Copley – see [Halifax]				
Copmanthorpe	79	A10	NE	1959
Coppenhall – see [Crewe]				
Copperas Hill	40	C8	CW JT	1921
Copperhouse	10	C4	WC	1852
Copperhouse Halt	10	C4	GW	1908
Copper Pit Platform – see [Swansea]				
Copplestone	6	A4	LSW	
	8	G4		
Coppull 2nd, 1st – 1895	76	D4	LNW	1969
Corbridge	43	C3	NE	
Corby	22	D1	GN	1959
	29	A2		
Corby, Weldon and	25	H7	MID	1966
Corfe Castle	7	H1	LSW	1972
Corfe Mullen Halt (East End)	4	B3	SD JT	1956
Corkerhill	74	G4	GSW	
Corkickle	40	C6	FUR	
Cornborough	8	D4	BWA	1917
Cornbrook – see [Manchester]				
Cornhill	54	C4	GNS	1968
Cornholme	76	G10	LY	1938
Cornwood	9	E6	GW	1959
Corpach	59	G5	NB	
Corporation Bridge – see [Grimsby]				
Corporation Pier – see [Hull]				
Corpusty and Saxthorpe	20	C5	MGN	1959
Corringham	13	A4	CORR	1952
Corris	26	D9	CORRIS	1931
Corrour	53	F10	NB	
Corsham	17	G2	GW	1965
Corstophine – see [Edinburgh]				
Corton	20	G10	NS JT	1970
Corwen	33	E4	GW	1964
Corwen	33	E4	LNW	1865
Coryates Halt	7	D1	GW	1952
Coryton (Devon)	9	A4	GW	1962
Coryton (Essex)	13	A4	CORR	1952
Coryton Halt (South Glamorgan)	16	E4	CARD	
	78	F6		
Coseley, Deepfields and	80	D3	LNW	
Cosford, Aerodrome Halt	24	B9	GW	
Cosham	5	B4	LSW/LBSC	
Cossall – see Ilkeston Junction				
Cossington (Somerset)	7	A8	SD JT	1952
Cossington Gate (Leics)	25	D10	MID	1873
Cotehill	42	D1	MID	1952
Cotham	28	G4	GN	1939
Cotherstone	41	H7	NE	1964
Coton Hill GDS	27	E10	GW	1965
Cottam	28	G8	GC	1959
Cottesmore GDS	25	H10	MID	1964
Cottingham	35	B6	NE	
	73	C4		
Cottingwith	34	F17	DV	1926

Station	Page	Block	Comp	Year of CL
Coughton	24	E3	MID	1952
Coulsdon North 2nd, 1st – (Stoats Nest) 1856	68	G2	LBSC	
Coulsdon South and Cane Hill	2	B8	SEC	
	68	G2		
Coulter	46	D3	CAL	1950
Cound Halt	27	F9	GW	1963
Coundon	38	C8	NE	1939
Coundon Road – see [Coventry]				
Counter Drain	22	E3	ME/MGN	1959
	29	C1		
Countess Park	43	A5	NB	1861
Countesthorpe	25	D8	MID	1962
County School	20	D3	GE	1964
Coupar Angus	51	A7	SCMS/CAL	1967
Court House – see [Barnsley]				
Court Sart	78	D1	RSB	1935
Courty Bella – see [Newport]				
Cove Bay	55	B8	CAL	1956
Cove Halt	6	D6	GW	1963
[Coventry]				
Bell Green	80	E10	LNW	1965
Canley	24	H5	LNW	
	80	E9		
Coundon Road	80	E10	LNW	1965
Coventry	80	E10	LNW	
Daimler Halt	80	E10	LNW	1965
Foleshill	80	E10	LNW	1965
Gosford Green GDS	80	E10	LNW	1965
Longford and Exhall	80	E10	LNW	1949
Tile Hill	24	H5	LNW	
	80	E9		
Coventry Road – see [Warwick] Warwick				
Cowbit	22	E4	GN/GE	1961
	29	D1		
Cowbridge 2nd, 1st – 1892	78	E4	TV	1951
Cowbridge – see Hertford North				
Cowden	2	E6	LBSC	
Cowdenbeath	50	H1	NB	
Cowdenbeath Old	50	H1	NB	1919
Cowes (Isle of Wight)	4	H3	IWC	1966
Cowgate – see [Peterborough]				
Cowlairs – see [Glasgow]				
Cowley – see [London]				
Cowton	38	D5	NE	1958
Coxbank Halt	31	F3	GW	1963
Coxbench	82	B2	MID	1930
Coxgreen	43	G2	NE	1964
Coxhoe	38	D9	CLAR/NE	1902
Coxhoe Bridge	38	D9	NE	1952
Coxwold	38	G1	NE	1953
Cradley	24	D6	GW	
	80	E3		
Cradoc	16	D9	N & B	1962
Cragg Mill	79	C5	NE	1877
Craigellachie	56	G10	GNS	1968
Craigendoran	49	B10	NB	
Craigie – see [Dundee]				
Craigleith – see [Edinburgh]				
Craiglochart – see [Edinburgh]				
Craiglon Bridge Halt	19	D3	GW	1953
Craigmiller – see [Edinburgh] Duddingston				
Craigo	51	G10	CAL	1956
	55	G5		
Craig-y-Nos (Penwyllt)	16	B8	N & B	1962
	78	A1		
Crail	51	E3	NB	1965
Crakehall	38	D3	NE	1954
Cramlington	43	F4	NE	
Cranbrook	2	H5	SEC	1961
Crane Street – see [Pontypool]				
Cranford	25	H6	MID	1956
Crank Halt	76	G3	LNW	1951
Cranleigh for Ewhurst	5	G8	LBSC	1965
Cranley Gardens – see [London]				
Cranmore	7	E9	GW	1963
Cransley GDS	25	G6	MID	
Crathes	55	C6	GNS	1966
Craven Arms and Stokesay	27	E6	SH JT	
Crawford	46	C2	CAL	1965
Crawley (Sussex) 2nd, 1st – 1968	2	B5	LBSC	
Crawley (Durham)	41	H10	S & D	1846
Cray	16	B9	N & B	1962
Crayford	70	B9	SEC	
Creagan	53	A7	CAL	1966
Credenhill	27	E1	MID	1962
Crediton 2nd, 1st – 1854	6	B3	LSW	
	8	H9		

Station	Page	Block	Comp	Year of CL
Creech St Michael Halt	6	H6	GW	1964
Creekmoor Halt	4	B3	SR	1966
Creetown	44	G4	PPW JT	1965
Creigiau	78	F5	BARRY	1962
Crescent — see [Peterborough]				
Cressage	27	F9	GW	1963
Cressing Form. Bulford	13	B9	GE	
Cressington and Grassendale	77	D2	CLC	1972
Cressington R.O. by B.R. FR. CL. above	77	D2	BR	
Cresswell (Staffs)	31	C3	NS	1966
Cresswell — see also Elmton				
Cresswell and Welbeck (Derbys)	82	E7	GC	1939
Crewe	30	G5	LNW	
Crewe — Coppenhall	30	G5	GJ	1840
Crew Green	27	C10	PSNW/SM	1932
Crewkerne	7	B4	LSW	
Crews Hill	12	D6	GN	
Crianlarich Upper	53	F5	NB	
Crianlarich Lower	53	F5	CAL	1965
Criccieth	32	F3	CAM	
Crick — see Kilsby				
Cricklade	14	C5	MSWJ	1961
Cricklewood	64	E5	MID	
Crieff 2nd, 1st — 1893	50	E2	CAL	1964
Criggion	27	C10	PSNW/SM	1932
Crigglestone	79	H5	LY	1965
Crigglestone	79	H5	MID	1960
Crimple	79	A7	NE	1869
Croesor Junction	32	F4	WH	1936
Croft	25	C8	LNW	1968
Croftfoot	74	H3	CAL	
Crofthead — see Fauldhouse				
Crofton	79	H7	LY	1931
Crofton — see also Hare Park				
Crofton Park	69	C9	SEC	
Croft Spa	38	D6	NE	1969
Cromdale	57	A8	GNS	1965
[Cromer]				
Cromer, Beach	20	B6	MGN	
Cromer High	20	B6	GE	1954
Cromer Links Halt	20	B6	NS JT	1953
Cromford	82	A4	LNW	1877
Cromford	31	G5	MID	
	82	A4		
Cronberry	49	F2	GSW	1951
Crook 2nd, 1st — 1845	38	B9	NE	1965
Crook of Devon for Fossoway	50	G2	NB	1964
Crookston	74	F3	GSW	
Cropredy	25	B2	GW	1956
Crosby — see Blundelsands				
Crosby Garrett	41	D6	MID	1952
Crossens — see [Southport]				
Crossford	45	D8	GSW	1943
Crossgate Hall Halt (Fife)	46	F10	NB	1930
Crossgates (Fife)	46	E10	NB	1949
	50	H1		
Cross Gates (Yorks)	34	B6	YNM/NE	
	79	D7		
Crossgates (Salop) — see Ford				
Cross Hands GDS	19	F4	LMM	1963
Cross Hands (for Penygroes) GDS	19	F4	GW	1950
Cross Hands Halt (Glos)	72	D9	GW	1964
Crosshill (Ayr)	49	B1	GSW	1862
Crosshill (Strathclyde)	74	G3	CAL	
Crosshill and Codnor (Notts)	82	C3	MID	1926
Crosshills — see Kildwick				
Crosshouse	49	C4	GSW	1966
Cross Inn	78	F4	TV	1952
Cross Keys	78	E8	GW	1962
Cross Lane — see [Manchester]				
Crosslee — see Houston				
Crossmichael	45	B5	PPW JT	1965
Crossmyloof	74	G3	GBK JT	
Cross Slack	76	B2	PW JT	1873
Crossways Halt	19	E10	GW	1951
Croston	36	D4	LY	
	76	C3		
Crouch End — see [Glasgow]				
Crouch Hill	64	H6	LTS	
Crowborough and Jarvis Brook	2	E5	LBSC	
Crowcombe	6	E8	GW	1971
Crowcombe R.O. PR. FR. CL. above	6	E8	WSR	
Crowden	37	D2	GC	1957
Crowhurst	2	H2	SEC	
Crowland — see Eye Green				
Crowle	34	G3	AX JT	1933
Crowle Central	28	G6	GC	
	34	G3		
Crown Street — see [Cardiff]				

Station	Page	Block	Comp	Year of CL
Crown Street — see [Liverpool]				
Crown Street — see [Silverdale]				
Crow Park for Sutton-on-Trent	82	H6	GN	1958
Crow Road — see [Glasgow]				
Crowthorne Form. Wellington College	15	C2	SEC	
Croxall	24	G10	MID	1928
Croxdale	38	D9	NE	1938
Croxley	63	E10	LTS	
Croxley Green	15	F3	LNW	
	63	E10		
Croy	49	H9	NB	
	75	E9		
Croydon — see [London] East, South and West Croydon				
Cruckton	27	D9	SM	1933
Cruden Bay	54	F10	GNS	1932
Crudgington	27	G10	GW	1963
	30	F1		
[Crumlin]				
Crumlin	78	C8	NAH	1857
Crumlin, High Level	78	C8	GW	1964
Crumlin, Low Level	78	C8	GW	1962
Crumpsall	76	F9	LY	
Crymmych Arms	19	A7	GW	1962
Crynant	78	B1	N & B	1962
Crynant New Colliery Halt	78	B1	N & B	1962
Crystal Palace	69	B7	LBSC	
Crystal Palace — see also [London]				
Cuddington	30	F7	CLC	
	77	F6		
Cudworth	34	B3	HB	1907
	79	H7		
Cudworth	79	H7	MID	1968
	82	C10		
Cuerdley	77	D5	ST H	1858
Cuffley and Goffs Oak	12	D7	GN	
Culcheth	76	H6	GC	1964
	77	B7		
Culgaith	41	C9	MID	1970
Culham	14	H5	GW	
Culkerton	17	G5	GW	1964
Cullen	54	B3	GNS	1968
Cullercoates 2nd, 1st — 1882	81	F4	NE	
Cullingworth	79	D2	GN	1955
Culloden Moor	56	F4	HIGH	1965
Cullompton	6	E4	GW	1964
Culmstock Halt	6	F5	GW	1963
Culrain	56	A1	HIGH	
Culross	46	C10	NB	1930
Culter	55	C7	GNS	1966
Cults 2nd, 1st — 1885	55	B8	GNS	1966
Culworth	25	C2	GC	1958
Cumberland Street — see [Glasgow]				
Cumbernauld	49	H9	CAL	
	75	F8		
Cumberworth — see Denby Dale				
Cummersdale	42	C1	MC	1951
Cummertrees	45	G5	GSW	1955
Cummingston	56	D8	HIGH	1904
Cumnock	49	E2	GSW	1965
Cumnock Old	49	E2	GSW	1951
Cumwhinton	42	D1	MID	1956
Cunninghamhead	49	C5	GSW	1951
Cupar	51	C4	NB	
Currie	46	F7	CAL	1943
	83	A3		
Currie Hill	83	A4	CAL	1951
Curthwaite	42	B1	MC	1950
Curzon Street — see [West Midlands] Birmingham				
Custom House Victoria Dock	65	F3	GE	
Cuthlie	51	F8	DA JT	1929
Cutler's Green Halt	12	H10	GE	1952
	23	H9		
Cutnall Green	24	C4	GW	1965
	80	G3		
Cuxton	2	H9	SEC	
Cwm	78	B8	GW	1962
[Cwmaman]				
Cwmaman GDS	78	C3	GW	1936
Cwmaman Colliery Halt	78	C3	GW	1924
Cwmaman Crossing Halt	78	C3	GW	1924
Cwmavon	78	E1	RSB	1962
Cwmavon Halt	78	B9	GW	1962
Cwmbach Halt	78	C3	GW	1964
Cwm Bargoed — see [Merthyr]				
Cwmblawd GDS	19	E4	LMM	1959
Cwmbran 2nd, 1st — 1880	78	D10	GW	1962
Cwmcarn	78	D8	GW	1962

Station	Page	Block	Comp	Year of CL
[Derby]				
Derby	31	G3	MID	
	82	B1		
Friargate	82	B1	GN	1964
Nottingham Road	82	B1	MID	1967
Pear Tree and			MID	1968
Normanton 1st				
Pear Tree 2nd Sta.	31	G3	MID	
Station (London Road)	31	G3	BDJ	1840
Station (Derwent Bridge)	31	G3	MID C	1840
Derby Road, Ipswich	21	B6	GE	
Dereham	20	E3	GE	1969
Deri — see Darren				
Derry Ormond	19	F9	GW	1965
	26	B2		
Dersingham	22	C9	GE	1969
Derwenthaugh	43	F3	NC	1868
Derwentwater — see Keswick				
Derwydd Road	19	F5	GW	1954
Desborough and Rothwell	25	G7	MID	1968
Desford 2nd, 1st — 1848	25	C9	MID	1964
Dess	55	C4	GNS	1966
Detton Ford Halt	27	H6	CMDP	1938
Devils Bridge	26	D5	CAM	
Devizes	14	A1	GW	1966
Devonport — see [Plymouth]				
Devonshire Street — see [London]				
Globe Road				
Devons Road — see [London]				
Devynock and Sennybridge	16	C9	N & B	1962
[Dewsbury]				
Batley Carr	79	G5	GN	1950
Central	79	G5	GN	1964
Dewsbury	79	G5	MID	1960
Dewsbury, Wellington Road	37	F5	LNW	
	79	G5		
Earlsheaton	79	G5	GN	1953
Market Place	79	G5	LY	1930
Ravensthorpe and Thornhill	37	F5	LNW	
	79	H4		
Ravensthorpe Lower	79	G5	LY	1952
Staincliffe and Batley Carr	79	G5	LNW	1952
Thornhill	79	H5	LY	1962
Dicconson Lane and Aspull	76	E5	LY	1954
Didcot	14	H4	GW	
Didsbury — see [Manchester]				
Digby	29	B5	GN/GE	1961
Diggle	76	F10	LNW	1968
Dillwyn and Brynteg Halt	78	B1	N & B	1962
Dilton Marsh Halt	7	G10	GW	
Dinas	32	H4	FEST	1870
Dinas	32	H4	LNW	1951
Dinas Junction	32	E6	NWNG/WH	1936
Dinas Mawddwy	26	E10	MAW/CAM	1931
Dinas Powis	78	H6	BARRY	
Dinas Rhondda	78	E4	TV	
Dingestow	17	B7	GW	1955
Dingle Road Platform	78	H6	GW	
Dingwall	56	E1	HR	
Dinmore	27	E2	SH JT	1958
Dinnet	55	C2	GNS	1966
Dinnington and Laughton	82	F9	SY JT	1929
Dinsdale	38	D6	NE	
Dinting 2nd, 1st — 1847	31	C10	GC	
Dinton	4	B7	LSW	1966
Dinwoodie	45	G8	CAL	1960
Dipple GDS	44	D9	GSW	1955
Dirleton	47	B9	NB	1954
Disley	31	B9	LNW	
	77	C10		
Diss	21	B5	GE	
Distington	40	C8	CW JT/WCE JT	1931
Ditchford	25	H5	LNW	1924
Ditchingham	20	H8	GE	1953
Ditton Junction 2nd, 1st — 1871	77	D4	LNW	
Ditton — see also Hough Green				
Ditton Priors	27	G7	CMDP	1938
Dixon Fold	76	F8	LY	1931
Dobcross	76	F10	LNW	1955
Dobcross — see also Saddleworth				
Docking	20	B	GE	1952
	22	B10		
Dock Street — see [Newport]				
Dockyard Halt, Devonport	9	E4	GW	
Dockyard — see Sheerness				
Doddington and Harby	28	H7	GC	1955
Dodworth	82	A10	GC	1959
Doe Hill	28	B6	MID	1960
	82	C5		

Station	Page	Block	Comp	Year of CL
Dogdyke	22	A4	GN	1963
	29	D5		
Dog Lane	77	A10	MS & L	1947
Dolarddyn Crossing	27	A9	CAM	1931
Dolau	27	A4	LNW	
Dolcoath Halt	10	E4	GW	1908
Doldowlod	26	G6	CAM	1962
Doleham Halt	3	A3	SEC	
Dolgarrog R.O. by BR FR. 1964 CL.	33	A7	LNW	
Dolgellau Form. spelt Dolgelly	26	C10	GW	1965
	32	H1		
Dolgoch Falls T.O. PR.	26	C8	TAL	
Dollar	50	E2	NB	1964
Dollis Hill — see [London]				
Dolphinton	46	D5	CAL	1945
Dolphinton	46	D5	NB	1933
Dolserau Halt	33	A1	GW	1951
Dolwen	26	G6	CAM	1962
Dolwyddelen	33	A5	LNW	
Dolygaer	78	A4	BM	1962
Dolyhir	27	B3	GW	1951
Dolywern	30	A3	GVT	1933
	33	F3		
[Doncaster]				
Cherry Lane	34	D2	SY	1852
	82	F10		
Doncaster 2nd, 1st — 1849	34	E2	GN	
	82	F10		
Hexthorpe	82	F10	SY	1855
York Road GDS	34	D2	MB/GC	1965
Donington	24	A10	LNW	1964
	27	H10		
Donington-on-Bain	29	D7	GN	1951
Donington Road	29	C3	GN/GE	1961
	22	C3		
Donisthorpe	25	H10	AN JT	1931
Donnington — see Speen				
Don Street — see [Aberdeen]				
Donyatt Halt	7	A5	GW	1962
Dorchester South	7	E2	LSW	
Dorchester West	7	E2	GW	
Dore and Totley	31	G2	MID	
	82	B7		
Dorking North	2	A7	LBSC	
Dorking Town	5	H10	SEC	
Dormans	2	C6	LBSC	
Dornoch	56	A4	HIGH	1960
Dornock	42	A3	GSW	1942
Dorridge, Knowle and	80	F8	GW	
Dorrington	27	E8	SH JT	1958
Dorstone	27	C1	GOLD V/GW	1941
Dorton Halt	15	B8	GW	1963
Doseley Halt	27	G9	GW	1962
Doublebois	9	D1	GW	1964
	11	D7		
Douglas	46	A3	CAL	1964
Douglas West	46	A3	CAL	1964
Doune	50	C2	CAL	1965
Dousland	9	C5	GW	1956
Dovecliffe for Worsborough	82	C10	GC	1953
Dove Holes	31	D8	LNW	
	77	D10		
[Dover]				
Admiralty Pier	3	G6	SEC	1914
Harbour 2nd, 1st — 1863	3	G6	SEC	1927
Marine	3	G6	SEC	
Priory	3	G6	SEC	
Town	3	G6	SEC	1914
Dovercourt Bay	13	H10	GE	
	21	H7		
Dovey Junction Station	26	C8	CAM	
Dowdeswell — see Andoversford				
Dowlais — see [Merthyr]				
Dowlow Halt	31	D7	LMS	1954
Downfield — see [Dundee] Baldovan				
Downfield Crossing Halt	17	F7	GW	1964
Downham Market	22	F9	GE	
Downholland	76	E1	LY	1938
Downton	4	D6	LSW	1964
Drax Abbey	34	E5	HB	1932
Drax Hales	34	E5	NE	1964
Draycott (Somerset)	7	B10	GW	1963
Draycott and Breaston (Derbys)	28	B2	MID	1966
Drayton (Sussex)	5	E4	LBSC	1930
Drayton for Costessey (Norfolk)	20	E6	MGN	1959
Drayton Green Halt (Middx)	64	A3	GW	
Drayton Park (London)	65	A5	GN/LT	
Dreghorn	49	B4	GSW	1964
Drem	47	B9	NB	

Station	Page	Block	Comp	Year of CL
Driffield	35	B9	NE	
Drigg	40	D4	FUR	
Drighlington and Adwalton	79	E4	GN	1962
Droitwich Road	24	C3	MID	1855
	80	H3		
Droitwich Spa	24	C4	GW	
	80	H3		
Dromore — see Gatehouse of Fleet				
Dronfield	31	G8	MID	1967
	82	B7		
Drongan	49	D2	GSW	1951
Dronley	51	B7	CAL	1955
Droxford	5	B6	LSW	1955
Droylsden	76	G10	LNW/LY	1968
Drum	55	C7	GNS	1951
Drumburgh	42	A2	NB	1955
Drumchapel	74	C8	NB	
Drumclog	49	F4	CAL	1939
Drumlemble Halt	48		CM	1931
Drumlithie	55	E6	CAL	1956
Drummuir	54	E1	GNS	1968
Drumpark	75	D5	LMS	1964
Drumry	49	E9	NB	
	74	B8		
Drumshoreland	46	E8	NB	1951
Drws-y-Nant	33	B2	GW	1965
Drybridge (Ayr)	49	C4	GSW	1969
Drybridge Platform (Banff)	54	C2	HIGH	1915
Drybrook Halt	17	C8	GW	1930
Drybrook Road	17	C8	SW JT	1929
Drymen	49	E10	NB	1934
Drysllwyn	19	E5	LNW	1963
Dubton	51	G10	CAL	1952
	55	H5		
Ducie Bridge — see [Manchester]				
Dudbridge	17	F6	MID	1947
Duddeston, Vauxhall and	80	D6	LNW	
Duddeston — see also [West Midlands]				
Duddingston and Craigmillar — see [Edinburgh]				
Dudley — see [West Midlands]				
Dudley Colliery	43	F4	NE	1878
	81	D5		
Dudley Hill — see [Bradford]				
Dudley Port — see [West Midlands]				
Duffield 2nd, 1st — 1867	28	A4	MID	
	82	B2		
Duffield Gate	34	F6	NE	1890
Duffryn Crossing Halt	78	D2	GW	1917
Duffryn Rhondda GDS	78	D2	RSB	1965
Duffryn Rhondda Halt	78	D2	RSB	1962
Dufftown	54	E1	GNS	1968
Duffws — see [Blaenau Festiniog]				
Duirinish	59	A2	HIGH	
Dukeries Junction	28	F7	GC	1950
Dukeries Junction	28	F7	GN	1950
Duke Street — see [Glasgow]				
[Dukinfield]				
Dukinfield — rep. Dog Lane	77	A10	MS & L	1845
Dukinfield and Ashton	77	A10	LNW	1950
Dukinfield Central	76	G10	GC	1959
	77	A10		
Dullatur	75	F10	NB	1967
Dullingham	23	D9	GE	
Dulverton	6	D7	GW	1966
	8	D10		
Dulwich — see [London]				
Dumbarton Central	49	C9	DB JT	
Dumbarton East	49	C9	CAL	
Dumfries 3rd, 1st — 1849, 2nd — 1859	45	E6	GSW	
Dumfries House	49	E1	GSW	1949
Dumgoyne Form. Killearn Old	49	F10	NB	1951
Dumpton Park	3	H10	SEC	
Dunball Halt	6	H9	GW	1964
Dunbar	47	D9	NB	
Dunblane	50	C2	CAL	
Dunbridge	4	F7	LSW	
Dunchurch	25	B4	LNW	1959
Duncraig	59	A2	HIGH	1964
Duncraig R.O.	59	A2	BR	
[Dundee]				
Back of Law	51	C6	DPA	1855
Baldovan and Downfield	51	C6	CAL	1955
Balmossie	51	D6	BR	
Barnhill	51	D6	CAL	1955
Broughty Pier	51	D6	NB/DA JT	1887
Broughty Ferry	51	D6	DA JT	
Camperdown Junction	51	D6	DA JT	1880
Craigie Rep. by Roodyards	51	D6	DA	1839

Station	Page	Block	Comp	Year of CL
Dundee Tay Bridge	51	C6	NB	
East	51	C6	DA JT	1959
Esplanade	51	C6	NB	1939
Liff	51	B6	CAL	1955
Lochee	51	B6	CAL	1955
Lochee West	51	B6	CAL	1917
Maryfield GDS	51	B6	CAL	1967
Magdalen Green	51	C6	CAL	1956
Ninewells Junction	51	C6	CAL	1865
Roodyards	51	C6	DA	1840
Stannergate	51	D6	DA JT	1916
Tay Bridge — see Dundee				
Ward Street	51	C6	DPA	1861
West	51	C6	CAL	1965
[Dunfermline]				
Dunfermline, Comeley Park	46	E10	NB	1890
Dunfermline Lower	46	E10	NB	
	50	G1		
Dunfermline Upper	46	E10	NB	1968
	50	G1		
Dunford Bridge	37	E2	GC	1970
Dungeness	3	D3	SEC	1937
Dungeness (Lighthouse)	3	D3	RHD	
Dunham	20	E2	GE	1968
Dunham	77	C8	W & S	1855
Dunham Hill	77	F4	B HEAD	1952
Dunham Massey	77	C8	LNW	1962
Dunhampstead	24	C3	MID	1855
Dunkeld and Birnham	50	G7	HIGH	
Dunkerton	17	D1	GW	1925
Dunkerton Colliery Halt	17	D1	GW	1925
Dunlop	49	C6	GBK JT	1967
Dunmere Halt	11	B7	LSW	1967
Dunmow	12	H9	GE	1952
Dunning	50	F4	CAL	1956
Dunnington for Kexby	34	F8	DV	1926
Dunnington Halt	34	F8	DV	1926
Dunphail	56	F7	HIGH	1965
Dunragit	44	C4	PPW JT	1965
Dunrobin Private Station	61	D1	HIGH	1965
	62	A1		
Duns	47	E6	NB	1951
Dunsbear	8	E5	SR	1965
Dunscore	45	D7	GSW	1943
Dunsford Halt	6	B2	GW	1958
	9	A9		
Dunsland Cross	8	G4	LSW	1966
Dunstable North 2nd, 1st — 1866	15	F9	LNW	1965
Dunstable Town Form. London Road	15	F9	GN	1965
Dunstall Park — see [West Midlands]				
Dunster	6	G9	GW	1971
Dunster R.O. PR. FR. CL. above	6	G9	WSR	
Dunston — see Nocton				
Dunston-on-Tyne	81	A2	NE	1926
Dunsyre	46	D5	CAL	1945
Dunton Green	2	E8	SEC	
	70	A1		
Dunure	49	A2	GSW	1930
Dunvant — see [Swansea]				
[Durham]				
Durham	38	D10	NE	
Elvet	38	D10	NE	1931
Gilesgate	38	D10	NE	1857
Durley Halt	5	A5	LSW	1933
Duror	53	A8	CAL	1966
Durrington-on-Sea	5	H4	LBSC	
Dursley	17	E6	MID	1962
Durston	6	H7	GW	1964
Durweston — see Stourpaine				
Dyce 2nd, 1st — 1861	55	A8	GNS	1968
Dyffryn Ardudwy	32	G1	CAM	
Dyke Junction Halt — see Aldrington				
Dymchurch	3	D5	RHD	
Dymock	17	D10	GW	1959
Dynea Halt	78	E5	ASNW	1956
Dysart	51	B1	NB	1969
Dyserth	33	E8	LNW	1930
Eaglescliffe Form. Preston Junction	38	F7	NE	
Eaglesham — see [Glasgow] Clarkston				
Ealing Broadway	64	B3	GW/MET	
Ealing — see also [London]				
Ealing West	64	B3	GW	
Earby	37	B8	MID	1970
Eardington Halt	24	A7	GW	1963
	80	D1		
Eardington R.O. PR. FR. CL. above	24	A7	SVR	
	80	D1		
Eardisley	27	C2	MID	1962
Earith Bridge	23	B6	GE	1931

Station	Page	Block	Comp	Year of CL
Earlestown	76	G5	LNW	1965
Earlestown Junction	76	G5	LNW	
Earley	15	C3	SEC	
Earls Barton — see Castle Ashby				
Earls Colne	13	C10	CVH	1962
	21	H2		
Earls Court	64	F2	DIST	
Earlsfield and Summers Town	68	F8	LSW	
Earlsheaton — see [Dewsbury]				
Earlston	47	C4	NB	1948
Earlswood (Surrey)	2	B7	LBSC	
Earlswood Lakes (West Midlands)	80	G7	GW	
Earlyvale Gate	46	G4	PEEB	1857
Earsham	21	A8	GE	1953
Easingthorne GDS	38	D8	NE	
Easington	38	F10	NE	1964
	43	H1		
Easingwold	34	D10	EAS	1948
	38	G1		
Eassie	51	B8	CAL	1956
East Anstey	6	C7	GW	1966
	8	D10		
Eastbank Street — see [Southport]				
East Barkwith	29	C8	GN	1951
East Boldon	43	G3	NE	
	81	F4		
Eastbourne 2nd, 1st — 1866	2	F1	LBSC	
East Brixton — see [London]				
East Budleigh	6	E2	LSW	1967
Eastbury Halt	14	F3	GW	1960
East Calder GDS	46	E7	NB	1959
Eastcote Halt — see [London]				
East Croydon	69	A5	LBSC	
Eastchurch	3	C10	SEC	1950
Easterhouse for Baillieston	75	C6	NB	
East Didsbury and Parrs Wood	77	C9	LNW	
East Dock — see [Swansea]				
Easter Road — see [Edinburgh]				
East Farleigh	2	H8	SEC	
East Finchley — see [London]				
East Fortune	47	C9	NB	1964
East Garston	14	F3	GW	1960
Eastgate	41	G10	NE	1953
East Gate — see Bury				
East Grange	46	C10	NB	1958
	50	F1		
East Grinstead 3rd, 1st — 1866, 2nd — 1883	2	C6	LBS	
East Halton Halt	35	C4	GC	1963
East Ham — see [London]				
Easthaven	51	E7	DA JT	1967
Easthope Halt	27	F8	GW	1951
East Horndon — see [London]				
East India Road — see [London] Poplar				
East Kilbride	49	F6	CAL	
	75	A1		
East Langton	25	E8	MID	1968
East Leake	28	D2	GC	1969
Eastleigh and Bishopstoke	4	H5	LSW	
East Linton	47	C9	NB	1964
East Malling Halt	2	G8	SEC	
East Minster-on-Sea	3	B10	SEC	1950
East Newport — see Newport-on-Tay East				
East Norton	25	F9	GN/LNW	1953
Eastoft	34	G4	AX JT	1933
Easton	7	A1	GW/LNW	1952
Easton Court for Little Hereford	27	F4	TEN JT	1961
Easton Lodge Halt	12	H9	GE	1952
East Pilton — see [Edinburgh]				
East Putney — see [London]				
Eastrea	22	G5	GE	1866
Eastriggs	42	A3	GSW	1965
Eastrington	34	G6	NE	
East Rudham	20	D1	MGN	1959
Eastry	3	G8	EK	1948
Eastry South	3	G8	EK	1948
East Sheen — see Mortlake				
East Somerset — see Wells				
East Southsea — see [Portsmouth]				
East Street — see Bridport				
East Tilbury	13	A4	MID	
East Ville	29	F5	GN	1961
East Winch	22	E10	GE	1968
Eastwood	76	B10	LY	1951
Eastwood and Langley Mill	82	D3	GN	1963
Eastwood — see also Langley Mill				
East Worthing Form. Ham Bri. Ht.	5	H4	LBSC	
Eaton	27	D7	BC	1935

Station	Page	Block	Comp	Year of CL
Ebberston	39	C2	NE	1950
Ebbsfleet and Cliffsend Halt	3	G9	SEC	1933
Ebbw Vale High Level	16	F7	LNW	1951
	78	A7		
Ebbw Vale Low Level	16	F7	GW	1962
	78	A7		
Ebchester	43	D2	NE	1953
Ebdon Lane	16	H1	WCP	1940
Ebley Crossing Halt	17	F7	GW	1964
Ecclefechan	45	H2	CAL	1960
Eccles	76	G8	LNW	
Ecclesall — see [Sheffield] Millhouses				
Ecclesfield 1st	82	C9	ST	1856
Ecclesfield East 2nd op. 1876	82	C9	GC	1953
Ecclesfield West	82	C9	MID	1967
Eccleshill — see [Bradford]				
Eccles Road	20	H4	GE	
Eccleston Park	76	G3	LNW	
Eckington	23	C1	MID	1965
Eckington and Renishaw 2nd, 1st — 1874	82	D7	MID	1951
Ecton Halt	31	D6	NS	1934
Edale	31	D9	MID	
	77	D10		
Edderton	56	B3	HIGH	1960
Eddleston	46	G5	NB	1962
Edenbridge	2	D7	SEC	
Edenbridge Town	2	D7	LBSC	
Edenham	22	D2	ELB	1871
Eden Park	69	C5	SEC	
Edgebold	27	E10	PSNW/SM	1933
Edge Hill — see [Liverpool]				
Edge Lane — see [Liverpool]				
Edgeley	27	C10	PSNW/SM	1933
	30	C1		
Edgeware — see [London]				
Edgeworth — see Turton				
[Edinburgh and Leith]				
Abbeyhill	83	E7	NB	1964
Balgreen Halt	83	B6	LNE	1968
Barnton	83	A9	CAL	1951
Blackford Hill	83	C5	NB	1962
Bonnington	83	E8	NB	1947
Colinton	83	B4	CAL	1943
Corstorphine	83	A6	NB	1968
Craigleith for Blackhall	83	B7	CAL	1962
Craiglockhart	83	C5	NB	1962
Dalry Road	83	C6	CAL	1962
Davidsons Mains	83	A9	CAL	1951
Duddingston and Craigmillar	83	F5	NB	1962
Easter Road	83	E7	NB	1947
East Pilton	83	C8	LMS	1962
Exhibition	83	D7	CAL	1890
Exhibition	83	D7	NB	1891
Exhibition	83	D7	NB	1908
Gilmerton	83	G4	NB	1933
Gorgie East	83	B5	NB	1962
Gorgie West GDS	83	B5	CAL	1959
Granton East	83	C10	NB	1925
Granton High GDS	83	C10	CAL	1968
Granton Road	83	C9	CAL	1962
Haymarket	83	D6	NB	
House o' Hill Halt	83	B8	LMS	1951
Jock's Lodge	83	E6	NB	1848
Joppa 2nd, 1st — 1859	83	G6	NB	1964
Junction Road	83	E9	NB	1947
Juniper Green	83	A3	CAL	1943
Kingsknowe	83	A4	CAL	1964
Kingsknowe	83	A4	BR	
Leith Central	83	E8	NB	1930
Leith North	83	E8	CAL	1962
Leith Rosebank GDS	83	E9	CAL	1965
Leith Walk	83	E8	NB	1930
Lothian Road	83	D6	CAL	1870
Merchiston	83	C6	CAL	1965
Morningside Road	83	C5	NB	1962
Murrayfield	83	B7	CAL	1962
New Hailes	83	G7	NB	1950
Newhaven	83	D9	CAL	1962
Newington	83	D5	NB	1962
North Leith	83	E9	NB	1947
Piershill	83	F7	NB	1964
Pinkhall	83	A6	NB	1968
Portobello	83	G6	NB	1964
Powderhall	83	D8	NB	1917
Princes Street	83	D6	CAL	1965
Princes Street	83	D6	NB	1868
Restalrig GDS	83	F8	NB	1968
St Leonards	83	E6	NB	1847
Saughton	83	A6	NB	1921

Station	Page	Block	Comp	Year of CL
Scotland Street	83	D8	NB	1868
Slateford	46	F8	CAL	
	83	B5		
South Leith	B3	E9	NB	1905
"The Royal Station"	83	F7	NB	
Trinity and Newhaven	83	D9	NB	1925
Turnhouse	83	A6	NB	1930
Waverley Edinburgh	46	F8	NB	
	83	D6		
Edingley — see Kirklington				
Edington and Bratton	4	A10	GW	1952
	7	G10		
Edington Burtle	7	A9	SD JT	1966
Edlingham	43	D9	NE	1930
Edlington	82	F10	DEARNE	1951
Edlington Street — see [Glasgow]				
Edmondthorpe and Wymondham	28	G1	MID	1959
Edrom	47	F6	NB	1951
Edwalton	82	F1	MID	1941
Edwinstowe	82	G6	GC	1956
Edzell	55	G4	CAL	1938
Efail Isaf	78	F5	BARRY	1962
Effingham Junction Station	5	H10	LSW	
	12	F1		
Eggesford	8	F7	LSW	
Egginton	31	F2	NS	1878
Egginton Junction Station	31	F2	GN/NS	1962
Egham for Englefield Green	15	F2	LSW	
	67	A8		
Egloskerry	9	A2	LSW	1966
	11	E10		
Eglwysbach — see Tal-y-Cafn				
Egremont (Cumbria)	40	C6	WCE JT	1947
Egremont — see [Wallasey] Seacombe				
Egstow — see Clay Cross				
Egton	39	C5	NE	
Elburton Cross	9	E5	GW	1947
	11	H5		
Elderslie	49	D7	GSW	1966
	74	B3		
Elephant and Castle	65	A3	SEC	
Elford	80	A9	MID	1952
Elgin	56	E9	GNS	
Elham	3	E7	SEC	1940
Elie	51	D2	NB	1965
Elland 2nd, 1st — 1865	79	G2	LY	1962
Ellaston — see Norbury				
Ellenbrook for Brookestown	76	G7	LNW	1961
Ellerbeck Colliery GDS	76	D4	LY	
Ellerby	35	D7	NE	1902
Ellerby Form. Burton Constable	35	D7	NE	1964
Ellerdine Halt	30	F1	GW	1963
Ellesmere	30	C3	CAM	1965
Ellesmere Port	77	E3	B HEAD	
Ellingham	20	H8	GE	1953
Elliott Junction Station	51	F7	DA JT	1967
Ellistown — see Bagworth				
Ellon	54	G9	GWS	1965
Elm Bridge	22	F7	GE	1928
Elmers End	69	B6	SEC	
Elmesthorpe for Barwell and Earls Shilton	25	B8	LNW	1968
Elmore Halt	5	A4	LSW	1930
Elm Park — see [London]				
Elms Bridge Halt	17	A7	GW	1955
Elmstead Woods	69	E7	SEC	
Elmswell	21	D3	GE	
Elmton and Creswell	82	F7	MID	1964
Elrington	43	A2	NE	1930
Elsecar and Hoyland	82	C10	MID	
	37	H2		
Elsecar East GDS	82	C10	GC	1963
Elsenham	12	G9	GE	
	23	H8		
Elsham	35	B3	GC	
Elslack	37	B9	MID	1952
Elson Halt	30	C3	GW	1962
Elsted	5	E6	LSW	1955
Elstree and Borehamwood	64	C10	MID	
Elswick — see [Newcastle]				
Eltham — see Mottingham				
Eltham Park, Shooters Hill and	69	F9	SEC	
Eltham Well Hall	69	E9	SEC	
Elthorne — see Hanwell				
Elton (Northants)	22	H2	LNW	1953
Elton and Orston (Notts)	28	F3	GN	
Elvanfoot	46	C1	CAL	1965
Elvet — see [Durham]				
Elvington (Yorkshire)	34	F8	DV	1926
Elvington (Kent)	3	G7	EK	1948

Station	Page	Block	Comp	Year of CL
Ely (Cambs)	23	B8	GE	
Ely — see [Cardiff]				
Embleton	40	E8	CKP	1958
	45	H1		
Embo	56	A4	HIGH	1960
Embsay* R.O. PR. FR. CL.	37	C9	MID	1965
	79	A1		
Emerson Park Halt	66	D6	LTS	
Emneth	22	F7	GE	1968
Emsworth	5	D4	LBSC	
Endon	31	B5	NS	1956
	73	D8		
[Enfield]				
Enfield Chase	12	D6	GN	
	65	A10		
Enfield Lock for Enfield Wash	12	D6	GE	
	65	A10		
Enfield Town	12	D6	GE	
	65	A10		
English Bridge — see [Shrewsbury]				
Enthorpe	35	A8	NE	1954
Entwistle Form. Chapeltown	76	C6	LY	
Enzie	54	C2	HIGH	1915
Epping	12	F7	GE	1966
Epping R.O. by LTS FR. CL. above	12	F7	LTS	
[Epsom]				
Epsom	68	C2	LSW	
Epsom Downs	68	D2	LBSC	
Epsom Town	68	D2	LBSC	1929
Epworth	34	G2	AX JT	1933
Epworth — see also Haxey				
Erdington	7	A9	LNW	
	80	C6		
Eridge	2	E5	LBSC	
Erith	66	B2	SEC	
	70	A10		
Errol	51	A6	CAL	
Erwood	26	H1	CAM	1962
Eryholme	38	D5	NE	1911
Escrick	34	E7	NE	1953
Escairgeiliog	26	D9	CORRIS	1931
Esher and Claremont	67	H5	LSW	
Esholt	37	E7	MID	1940
	79	C3		
Eskbank and Dalkeith	83	G4	NB	1969
Eskbridge	83	E1	NB	1930
Eskdale Green R.N. The Green	40	E5	ESK	
Eskett	40	D7	WCE JT	1874
Eskmeals	40	D4	FUR	1959
Esplanade				
Essendine	22	E2	GN	1959
Essex Road	65	A5	GN	
Esslemont	54	G8	GNS	1952
Eston — see [Teeside]				
Etchingham	2	G4	SEC	
Etherley	38	C8	NE	1965
Eton — see Windsor				
Etruria	31	A4	NS	
	73	C7		
Ettingshall Road and Bilston — see [West Midlands]				
Ettington	23	H2	EWJ/SMJ	1952
Etwall	31	F2	GN	1939
Euston — see [London]				
Euxton	76	C4	LNW	1895
Euxton	76	C4	LY	1917
Euxton — see also Balshaw Lane				
Evanton Form. Novar	56	D2	HIGH	1960
Evenwood 2nd, 1st — 1864	38	B8	NE	1957
Evercreech Junction Station	7	D8	SD JT	1966
Evercreech New	7	D8	SD JT	1966
Everingham	34	H7	NE	1954
Evershot	7	D4	GW	1966
Evesham	24	E2	MID	
Evesham	24	E2	GW	1963
Evesham Road Crossing — see [Stratford-on-Avon]				
Ewell East for Worcester Park	68	D3	LBSC	
Ewell West	68	D3	LSW	
Ewesley Halt	43	C7	NB	1952
Ewood Bridge and Edenfield	76	D8	EL	1972
Exchange — see [Barnsley] Barnsley				
Exchange — see [Liverpool]				
Exchange — see [Manchester]				
Exchange — see [Wrexham]				
Exchange Platform — see Boscarne				
Exchange Platform — see Cairnie Junction				
[Exeter]				
Alphinton Halt	6	C2	GW	1958

Station	Page	Block	Comp	Year of CL
Central Form. Queen Street	6	C2	LSW	1928
Lions Holt Halt	6	C2	LSW	1928
Mount Pleasant Road Halt	6	C2	LSW	1928
St Davids	6	C2	GW	
St James Park Ht. Form. Lions Holt Halt	6	C2	LSW	
St Thomas	6	C2	GW	
Whipton Bridge Halt	6	C2	LSW	1923
Exhall — see [Coventry] Longford				
Exhibition — see [Edinburgh]				
Exminster	6	D2	GW	1964
Exmouth	6	D1	LSW	
Exmouth Ferry	6	D1	LSW	
Exning Road Halt	23	C9	GE	1962
Exton Form. Woodbury Road	6	D2	LSW	
Eyarth	33	E6	LNW	1953
Eydon Road Halt	25	C2	GC	1956
Eye	21	B6	GE	1931
Eye — see Berrington				
Eye Green for Crowland	22	G4	MGN	1957
Eyemouth	47	C7	NB	1962
Eynsford	70	B6	SEC	
Eynsham	14	G7	GW	1962
Eythorne	3	F7	EK	1948
Fach Goch	26	B8	TAL	
Facit	76	C9	LY	1947
Failsworth	76	G10	LY	
Fairbourne	26	B10	CAM	
Fairbourne	26	B10	FR	
Fairfield for Droylsden 2nd, 1st — 1892	77	A10	GC	
Fairfield for Golf Links	77	D10	LNW	1939
Fairfields Siding	50	B2	NB	1866
Fairford	14	C6	GW	1962
Fairhaven — see Ansdell				
Fairlie High	49	A6	GSW	
Fairlie Pier	49	A6	GSW	1971
Fairlop	65	G7	GE	1966
Fairlop R.O. by LTS FR. CL. above	65	G7	LTS	
Fakenham East	20	D3	GE	1964
Fakenham West	20	D3	MGN	1959
Falahill	47	A6	NB	1960
Fair Mile — see Oxshott				
[Falkirk]				
Camelon 2nd, 1st — 1844	46	B9	NB	1967
Grahamston	46	B9	NB	
High	46	B9	NB	
Falkland Road	51	B3	NB	1958
Fallgate	82	B5	ASH	1936
Fallowfield — see [Manchester]				
Fallside	75	D4	CAL	1953
Falls of Cruachan Halt	53	B5	CAL	1965
Falmer 2nd, 1st — 1865	2	C2	LBSC	
Falmouth	10	G3	GW	
Falmouth, The Dell	10	G3	GW	
Falstone	42	G6	NB	1956
Fambridge	13	B6	GE	
Fangfoss	34	G8	NE	1959
Farset — see Yaxley				
Fareham	5	A4	LSW	
Faringdon	14	E5	GW	1951
Farington	76	C4	NU JT	1960
Farley Halt	27	G8	GW	1962
Farlington Halt — see [Portsmouth]				
Farnborough Main	5	E10	LSW	
Farnborough North	5	E10	SEC	
Farncombe	5	F9	LSW	
Farnell Road	51	F9	CAL	1956
	55	A4		
Farnham	5	D9	LSW	
Farnley — see [Leeds] Wortley				
Farningham Road and Sutton-at-Home	70	D6	SEC	
Farnsfield	28	D5	MID	1929
	82	H5		
Farnworth — see [Widnes] Widnes				
Farnworth and Bold	77	C5	LNW	1951
Farnworth and Halsall Moor	36	H3	LY	
	76	F7		
Farringdon	5	C8	LSW	1955
Farrington Gurney Halt	7	D10	GW	1969
Farrington Street — see [London]				
Farsley — see Stanningly				
Farthinghoe	25	C1	LNW	1952
Fauldhouse and Crofthead	46	B7	WMC/NB	1930
Fauldhouse North	46	B7	CAL	
Faversham	3	C9	SEC	
Fawcett Street — see [Sunderland]				
Fawkham — see Longfield				
Fawley (Hereford)	17	C9	GW	1964
Fawley (Hants)	4	H3	LSW	1966

Station	Page	Block	Comp	Year of CL
Fay Gate	2	A5	LBSC	
Fazakerley	76	G2	LY	
Fearn	56	C4	HR	
Featherstone (Yorks)	79	H8	LY	1967
Featherstone Park (Northumberland)	42	G3	NE	1976
Feering Halt	13	C9	LNE	1951
Felindyffryn Halt	26	B5	GW	1964
Felin Fach	19	E9	GW	1951
	26	A3		
Felinfoel GDS	19	E3	LMM	1963
Felin Fran Halt — see [Swansea]				
Felin Hen Halt	32	G7	LNW	1951
[Felixstowe]				
Beach	21	H7	GE	1967
Felixstowe Town	21	H7	GE	
Pier	21	H7	GE	1951
Felling 2nd, 1st — 1896	43	F2	NE	1979
	81	C2		
Felmingham	20	C6	MGN	1959
Felsted	12	A9	GE	1952
Feltham	67	E8	LSW	
Fenay Bridge and Lepton	79	H4	LNW	1930
Fencehouses	43	F1	NE	1964
Fenchurch Street — see [London]				
Fencote	27	G3	GW	1952
Fen Ditton Halt	23	D8	GE	1962
Feniscowles	76	C5	LY/LU	1960
Feniton Form. Sidmouth Junction	6	F3	LSW	
Fennant Road Halt	30	B4	GW	1915
	72	C2		
Fenns Bank	30	E3	CAM	1965
Fenny Bentley GDS	31	E4	LNW	1963
Fenny Compton	25	A3	GW	1964
Fenny Compton West	25	A3	EWJ/SMJ	1952
Fenny Stratford	15	D10	LNW	
Fenton — see [Stoke-on-Trent]				
Fenton Manor — see [Stoke-on-Trent]				
Ferndale	78	D3	TV	1964
Fernhill Heath	80	H2	GW	1965
Ferniegair 2nd, 1st — 1876	75	E1	CAL	1917
Ferriby	35	A5	NE	
	73	B2		
Ferry	22	E7	MGN	1959
Ferry Meadows	22	G3	WO	
Ferry Siding	5	E3	WS	1935
Ferrybridge	79	F9	SK JT	1965
Ferryhill (Durham)	38	D1	NE	1967
Ferryhill — see [Aberdeen]				
Ferryside	19	C4	GW	
Fersit Halt	59	H9	LNE	1934
Festiniog	32	H3	GW	1960
Ffairfach	19	F5	GW	
Ffrid Gate	26	D8	CORRIS	1931
Ffronfraith Halt	27	A7	CAM	1931
Fidler's Ferry and Penketh	77	D5	LNW	1950
Fighting Cocks	38	E6	NE	1887
Filey	39	F2	NE	
Filey Holiday Camp	39	F2	NE	
Filleigh	8	D7	GW	1966
Fillongley — see Arley				
Filton Halt — see [Bristol]				
Filton Junction — see [Bristol]				
Fimber — see Sledmere				
Finchley — see [London]				
Finchley Road — see [London]				
Finchley Road and Frognal	64	F5	LNW	
Findhorn	56	D8	HIGH	1869
Findochty	54	B3	GNS	1968
Finedon	25	H5	MID	1940
Fingask Halt	56	G6	GNS	1931
Finghall Lane	38	C3	NE	1954
Finmere for Buckingham	15	A10	GC	1963
Finningham	21	C4	GE	1966
Finningley	34	E2	GN/GE	1961
	82	G10		
Finnieston — see [Glasgow]				
Finsbury	65	A6	GN	
Finstock Halt	14	F7	GW	
Firsby	29	G6	GN	1970
Fishbourne	5	D4	LBSC	
Fishersgate Halt 2nd Halt	2	B2	BR	
Fisherrow Siding	83	G7	NB	1947
Fishguard and Goodwick	18	F7	GW	1964
Fishguard Harbour	18	F7	GW	
Fishponds — see [Bristol]				
Fiskerton	28	E5	MID	
Fittleworth	5	F6	LBSC	1955
Fitzwilliam	79	H8	LNE	1967

Station	Page	Block	Comp	Year of CL
Five Mile House	29	B7	GN	1958
Five Ways — see [West Midlands]				
Fladbury	23	D2	GW	1966
Flag Station — see Glan Llyn Halt				
Flamborough	35	D10	NE	1970
Flax Bourton 2nd, 1st — 1893	72	B6	GW	1963
Flaxton	34	E9	NE	1930
Flecknoe	25	C3	LNW	1952
Fledborough	28	F7	GC	1955
Fleet (Hampshire)	5	D10	LSW	
Fleet (Lincolnshire)	29	F1	MGN	1959
Fleetwood 2nd, 1st — (Dock St.) — 1883	36	C8	PW JT	1966
	76	A1		
Fleetwood Form. Wyre Dock R.N. in 1966	76	A1	PW JT	1970
Flemington	75	F2	CAL	1965
Fleur de Lis Halt, Pengam and	78	D6	GW	1962
Flimby	40	C9	LNW	
	45	F1		
Flint	33	G7	LNW	
	77	G1		
Flitwick	15	F10	MID	
	23	G2		
Flixton	77	B7	CLC	
Flordon	20	G6	GE	1966
Floriston	42	B3	CAL	1950
Flow Moss	76	G7	LM	1842
Flushdyke	79	G5	GN	1941
Fochabers	54	C1	GNS	1968
Fochabers Town	54	C1	HIGH	1931
Fochriw	80	B6	BM	1962
Fockerby	34	G4	AX JT	1933
Foggathorpe	34	G6	NE	1954
Foleshill — see [Coventry]				
Foley Park Halt	24	C5	GW	1970
	80	G2		
Foley Park R.O. PR. FR. CL. above	24	C5	SVR	
	80	G2		
[Folkestone]				
Folkestone	3	E5	SE	1843
Folkestone Central Form. Cheriton Arch or Radnor Park	3	E5	SEC	
Folkestone East	3	E5	SEC	1965
Folkestone Harbour 2nd, 1st — 1850	3	E5	SEC	
Folkstone Warren Halt*	3	F6	SEC	1939
Folkstone West 2nd, 1st — Shorncliffe Camp			SEC	
Shorncliffe Camp — see West			SE	1881
Fontburn Halt	43	C7	NB	1952
Forcett GDS	38	C6	NE	1964
Ford — see Bootle				
Ford (Devon) — see [Plymouth]				
Ford Junction (Sussex)	5	G4	LBSC	
Ford and Crossgates (Salop)	27	D10	PSNW/SM	1933
Ford Bridge	26	E3	SM JT	1954
Forden	27	B8	CAM	1965
Ford Green and Smallthorpe — see [Stoke-on-Trent]				
Ford Halt — see [Plymouth]				
Fordham	23	C9	GE	1965
Fordingbridge	4	C5	LSW	1964
Fordoun	55	F6	CAL	1956
Foregate Street — see [Worcester]				
Forest Gate for Upton	65	E5	GE	
Forest Hall	81	C7	BT	1871
Forest Hall	81	C7	NE	1958
Forest Hill	69	B8	LBSC	
Forest Hill — see also [London] Lordship Lane				
Forest Mill	50	E1	NB	1930
Forest Row for Ashdown Forest	2	D5	LBSC	1967
Forfar	51	D9	ABER	1848
Forfar	51	D9	CAL	1967
Forgandenny	50	G4	CAL	1956
Forge Crossing Halt	27	C4	GW	1951
Forge Mills — see [West Midlands]				
Forge Valley	39	D3	NE	1950
Formby	36	B3	LY	
	76	E1		
Forncett	20	H6	GE	1966
Forres 2nd, 1st — 1863	56	E7	BR	
Forrestfield	46	A7	NB	1930
Forsinard	61	E6	HIGH	
	62	A6		
Fort Augustus	59	D9	HIGH/NB	1933
Fort Augustus Pier	59	D9	HIGH/NB	1906
Fort Brockhurst	5	A4	LSW	1953
Forteviot	50	F4	CAL	1956
Fort George	56	E4	HIGH	1943
Fort Gomer Halt	5	A4	LSW	1930

Station	Page	Block	Comp	Year of CL
Forth — see [Newcastle]				
Fort Matilda	49	A9	CAL	
Fortrose	56	E4	HIGH	1951
Fort William 2nd, 1st — 1975	59	H6	NB	
Foryd	33	D8	LNW	1885
Foryd Pier	33	D8	LNW	1885
Foss Cross	14	B7	MSWJ	1961
Foss Island GDS	34	E8	NE	
Fotherby Gate House	29	E10	GN	1872
Fotherby Halt	29	E10	GN	1961
	35	E1		
Foulis	56	E2	HIGH	1960
Foulridge	37	B8	MID	1959
	76	A10		
Foulsham	20	B4	GE	1952
Fountain Bridge Halt	78	E7	BM	1956
Fountainhall Junction Station	47	A6	NB	1969
Four Ashes	80	A1	LNW	1959
Four Crosses	27	B10	CAM	1965
	30	B1		
Four Oaks	80	B7	LNW	
Four Oaks Halt	17	E9	GW	1959
Fourstones	43	A3	NE	1967
Fowey	11	C5	GW	1965
Fowlis	56	E1	HIGH	1960
Foxfield Junction Station	40	F3	FUR	
Foxton	23	E7	GE	
Framlingham	21	D7	GE	1952
Frampton — see Grimstone				
Frankland	39	C5	NE	1877
Frankton	30	C3	CAM	1965
Fransham	20	E3	GE	1968
Frant	2	F5	SEC	
Frazerburgh	54	B9	GNS	1965
Fratton and Southsea	5	B4	LSW/LBSC	
Free Street — see [Brecon]				
Fremington	8	C5	LSW	1965
French Drove and Gedney Hill	22	F5	GW/GE	1961
Freshfield (Merseyside)	76	E1	LY	
Freshfield Halt (Sussex)	2	C4	LBSC	1968
Freshfield R.O. PR. FR. CL. above	2	C4	BLU	
Freshford	17	F1	GW	
Freshwater (Isle of Wight)	4	F2	FYN	1953
Friargate — see [Derby]				
Friary — see [Plymouth]				
Frickley	82	D10	SK JT	1953
Friden	31	E6	LNW	1967
Friezland	76	G10	LNW	1917
Frimley	15	D1	LSW	
Frinton-on-Sea	13	H9	GE	
Friockheim	51	E8	CAL	1955
Frisby	28	E1	MID	1961
Frittenden Road	3	A6	KES	1954
Fritwell and Somerton	14	G9	GW	1964
Frizinghall — see [Bradford]				
Frizington	40	D6	WCE JT	1931
Frocester	17	F6	MID	1961
Frodingham and Scunthorpe	34	H3	GC	1928
Frodsham	77	E5	B HEAD	
Frogmore — see Park Street				
Frognal — see [London] Finchley Road				
Frome	7	F9	GW	
Frongoch	33	C3	GW	1960
Frosterley	38	A9	NE	1953
	41	H9		
Fryston GDS	79	E9	NE	1960
Fugar Bar	81	A1	BJ	Pre 1844
Fulbar Street — see [Renfrew]				
Fulbourne	23	E8	GE	1967
Fulham — see [London] Chelsea				
Fullerton Junction 2nd, 1st — 1885	4	G8	LSW	1964
Fulwell for Hampton Hill (Middx)	67	H7	LSW	
Fulwell and Westbury (Bucks)	15	A10	LNW	1961
Furness Abbey — see [Barrow-in-Furness]				
Furness Vale	31	C9	LNW	
	77	D10		
Furze Platt Halt	15	D4	GW	
Fushiebridge	46	H6	NB	1943
Fyling Hall	39	D5	NE	1965
Fyvie	54	F6	GNS	1951
Gaerwen	32	F7	LNW	1966
Gagie	51	D8	LMS	1955
Gailes	49	B4	GSW	1967
Gailey	24	C10	LNW	1951
Gainford	38	C6	NE	1964
Gainsborough Central	28	G9	GC/GN GE	
	34	G1		
Gainsborough Lea Road	28	G9	GN/GE	
	34	G1		

Station	Page	Block	Comp	Year of CL
Gairlochy	59	G7	HIGH/NB	1933
Gaisgill	41	C5	NE	1952
Galashiels	47	B4	NB	1969
Galgate	36	E9	LNW	1939
Gallions— see [London]				
Gallowgate — see [Glasgow]				
Galston	49	E4	GSW	1964
Gamlingay	23	E4	LNW	1968
Ganton	39	D2	NE	1930
Gara Bridge	9	E8	GW	1963
Garelochhead	53	D1	NB	
Garforth	34	B6	NE	
	79	D8		
Gargrave	37	B9	MID	
Gargunnock	50	C1	NB	1934
Garlieston — see Millisle				
Garliestown 2nd, 1st — R.N. Millisle	44	G2	PPW JT	1903
Garliestown Harbour GDS	44	G2	PPW JT	1964
Garmouth	54	B1	GNS	1968
Garnant	19	G4	GW	1958
Garnant Halt	19	G4	GW	1926
Garndiffaith	78	B9	LNW	1941
Garneddwen	26	D9	CORRIS	1931
Garneddwen Halt	33	B2	GW	1965
Garngad — see [Glasgow]				
Garnkirk for Chryston	75	C7	CAL	1960
Garnqueen	75	E6	MONK	1851
Garn-yr-Erw	78	B9	LNW	1941
Garrochburn GDS	49	D2	GSW	1965
Garrowhill Halt	75	B6	NB	
Garsgadden	74	C8	NB	
Garsdale*, Hawes Junction for	41	E4	MID	1970
Garsington Bridge Halt — see [Oxford] — Morris Cowley				
Garstang and Catterall	36	E7	LNW	1969
	76	A4		
Garstang Road Halt	36	E8	GKE/KE	1930
	76	A4		
Garstang Town	36	E8	GKE/KE	1930
	76	A4		
Garston	15	G6	LNW	
Garston (Merseyside) — see [Liverpool]				
Garston (Merseyside) — see also [Liverpool] Allerton West				
Garston (Merseyside) — see also [Liverpool] Church Road				
Garston Dock — see [Liverpool]				
Garswood	76	G4	LNW	
Gartcosh	75	D7	CAL	1962
Garth	78	D2	PT	1913
Garth	26	G2	LNW	
Garth and Van Road	26	F6	VAN/CAM	1879
Gartly for Lumsden and Strathdon	54	G3	GNS	1968
Gartmore	53	H2	NB	1950
Gartness	49	E10	NB	1934
Garton	35	B9	NE	1950
Gartsherrie 2nd, 1st — 1851	49	H8	CAL	1940
	75	E7		
Gartsherrie — see also Blairhill				
Gartshore	75	D9	NB	1964
Garve	58	E10	HIGH	
Gascoigne Wood Junction	79	D10	NE	1902
Gatcombe	17	D7	GW	1869
Gateacre — see [Liverpool]				
Gatehead	49	C4	GSW	1969
Gatehouse of Fleet Form. Dromore	44	H4	PPW JT	1965
[Gateshead]				
Bensham	81	B2	NE	1954
Gateshead East	43	F3	NE	
	81	B3		
Gateshead West	81	B3	NE	1965
Greenesfield	81	B3	YNB	1850
Low Fell	81	B1	NE	1952
Oakwellgate	81	B3	NDJ	1844
Redheugh	81	A2	NC	1853
Gateside	50	H3	NB	1950
Gatewen Halt	72	D3	GW	1931
Gathurst	36	E3	LY	
	76	E4		
Gatley	77	C8	LNW	
	31	A9		
Gatwick Airport (Tinsley Green)	2	B6	LBSC	1907
Gatwick Airport Form. Racecourse	2	B6	LBSC	
Gavell	75	D10	NB	1951
Gayton Road	22	E9	MGN	1959
Geddington	25	H7	MID	1948
Gedling and Carleton	82	G2	GN	1960
Gedney	22	D7	MGN	1959
	29	F1		

Station	Page	Block	Comp	Year of CL
Gedney Hill — see French Drove				
Gelderston	20	H9	GE	1953
Gelli Felen Halt	78	D3	LMS	1958
Gelli Platform	78	D4	TV	1912
Gelly-Ceidrim	19	G4	LLAN	1861
George Lane — see [London]				
Georgemas Junction	61	H9	HR	
	62	D8	HR	
Georgetown	74	C6	CAL	1959
Gerrards Bridge — see [St Helens]				
Gerrards Cross	15	F4	GW/GC	
	63	A7		
Gidea Park and Squirrels Heath	12	G7	GE	
	66	D7		
Giffen	49	C6	CAL	1932
Giffnock	74	F2	CAL	
Gifford	47	B8	NB	1933
Giggleswick	37	A10	MID	
Gilbey's Cottages Halt	56	G9	BR	1965
Gildersome East	79	E5	LNW	1921
Gildersome West	79	E5	GN	1955
Gilesgate — see [Durham]				
Gileston	78	H3	BARRY	1964
Gilfach Dhu (Llanberis) T.O. PR.	32	F6	GW	
Gilfach Fargoed Halt	78	C6	RHY	
Gilfach Goch	78	E3	GW	1930
Gillett's Crossing	76	B1	PW JT	1939
Gilling for Ampleforth College	38	H2	NE	1953
Gillingham (Dorset)	7	F7	LSW	
Gillingham (Kent) for New Brompton	2	H10	SEC	
Gilmerton — see [Edinburgh]				
Gilmour Street — see [Paisley]				
Gilnockie for Claygate	42	C5	NB	1964
Gilsland	42	F3	NE	1967
Gilwern Halt	78	A9	LNW	1958
Gipsy Hill	69	A7	LBSC	
Girtford Halt	23	E3	LMS	1940
Girvan New	44	D9	GSW	
Girvan Old	44	D9	GSW	1893
Gisburn	37	A8	LY	1962
Gladsmuir — see Macmerry				
Gladstone Dock — see [Bootle]				
Glais	19	H3	MID	1950
Glaisdale	39	B5	NE	
Glamis	51	C8	CAL/SLMJ	1956
Glanamman	19	G4	GW	1958
Glan Conway R.O. by BR FR. 1964 CL.	33	A8	LNW	
Glandyfi	26	C8	CAM	1965
Glan Llyn Ht Form. Bala Lake Flag Station	33	C3	GW	1965
Glanrafon	26	B5	CAM	
Glanrhyd	19	G6	VT JT	1955
Glanton	43	C9	NE	1930
Glanyllyn	78	F5	CDFF	1931
Glanyrafon	30	A1	CAM	1951
	33	G1		
Glan-yr-Afon Halt	26	G5	GW	1962
Glapwell	82	E6	MID	1930
Glasbury-on-Wye	27	A1	MID	1962
Glascoed Halt	16	H4	GW	1952
[Glasgow]				
Alexandra Parade	74	H6	NB	
Anderston	74	G6	BR	
Anderston Cross	74	G6	CAL	1959
Anniesland for Knightswood	74	E7	NB	
Argyle Street	74	G6	BR	
Barnhill	74	H6	NB	
Bellahouston	74	G4	GSW	1954
Bellahouston — see Ibrox	74	G4	GP JT	1845
Bellahouston Park Halt	74	G4	LMS	1939
Bellgrove for Cattle Market	74	H6	NB	
Blythswood	74	G6	BR	
Botanic Gardens	74	F7	CAL	1939
Bridge Street	74	G5	CAL	1905
Bridgeton	74	H5	CAL	1895
Bridgeton	74	H5	CAL	
Bridgeton Cross	74	H5	CAL	1964
Buchanan Street	74	H5	CAL	1966
Cambuslang	75	A4	CAL	
Carntyne for Westmuir & Tollcross	75	A6	NB	
Central High Level	49	F8	NB	
	74	G6		
Central Low Level	74	G6	CAL	1964
Charing Cross	74	G6	NB	
College	76	H6	NB	1917
Cowlairs	74	H7	NB	1964
Crosshill	74	G3	CAL	
Crossmyloof	74	G3	GBK JT	

Station	Page	Block	Comp	Year of CL
Crow Road	74	E7	CAL	1960
Cumberland Street	74	G5	GSW	1966
Dalmarnock	74	H5	CAL	1964
Dawsholm	74	E8	CAL	1908
Eglington Street	74	G4	CAL	1965
Finnieston	74	F6	NB	1917
Finnieston	74	F6	BR	
Gallowgate	74	H5	GSW	1902
Gallowgate Central	74	H5	NB	1917
Garngad	74	H6	NB	1910
Garscadden	74	C8	NB	
Glasgow Cross	74	H5	CAL	1964
Glasgow Green	74	H6	CAL	1953
Gorbals	74	H4	GBK JT	1928
Govan	74	G5	GP JT	1921
Great Western Road R.N. Hyndland				
Gushetfaulds — see also South Side	74	H4	CAL	1907
High Street	74	H6	NB	
Hyndland	74	E7	NB	
Ibrox on site of Bellahouston	74	G4	GP JT	1967
Jordanhill	74	D8	NB	
Kelvin Bridge	74	F7	CAL	1952
Kelvin Hall	74	F7	CAL	1964
Kelvinside	74	E7	CAL	1942
Kirklee	74	F7	CAL	1939
Lochburn	74	G8	NB	1917
London Road	74	H8	CAL	1898
Main Street	74	G5	GSW	1900
Maryhill Central	74	E8	CAL	1964
Maryhill Park	74	F8	NB	1961
Maxwell Park	74	G3	CAL	
Moss Road	74	D4	GP JT	1845
Newton	75	B4	CAL	
Parkhead for Celtic Park	74	H5	CAL	1965
Parkhead North	75	A6	NB	1955
Partick Central	74	E7	CAL	1964
Partick Hill	74	E7	NB	
Partick West	74	E7	CAL	1964
Pollockshaws East	74	G3	CAL	
Pollockshaws West	74	G3	CAL	
Pollockshields East	74	G4	CAL	
Pollockshields West	74	G4	CAL	
Possil	74	G7	CAL	1964
Possil Park	74	G7	NB	1917
Queens Park	74	G3	CAL	
Queen Street	74	H6	NB	
Robroyston	75	A7	CAL	1956
Rutherglen	74	H4	CAL	
St Enoch	74	H5	GSW	1966
St Rollox	74	H6	CAL	1849
St Rollox	74	H6	CAL	1962
Scotstoun East	74	D7	CAL	1964
Scotstounhill	74	D8	NB	
Scotstoun West	74	D7	CAL	1964
Shawlands	74	G3	CAL	
Shettleston	75	A7	NB	
Shields	74	G4	GSW	1954
Shields Road	74	G4	GSW	1966
South Side R.N. Gushetfaulds 1924	74	G4	CAL	1879
South Side	74	G4	GBK JT	1877
Spiersbridge	74	E2	GBK JT	1849
Springburn	74	H7	NB	
Springburn Park GDS	74	H7	CAL	1965
Stepps Road	75	A7	CAL	1962
Stobcross R.O. as Finnieston	74	F6	CAL	1959
Strathbungo	74	G4	GBK JT	1962
Summerston	74	F9	NB	1951
Tollcross	75	A5	CAL	1964
Whiteinch Riverside	74	D7	CAL	1964
Whiteinch Victoria Park	74	D7	NB	1951
Yoker	49	E8	NB	
	74	C8		
Yoker Ferry	74	C8	CAL	1964
Yorkhill	74	F7	NB	1921
Glasgow Cross — see [Glasgow]				
Glasgow Green — see [Glasgow]				
Glasgow Road — see [Perth]				
Glassaugh	54	B4	GNS	1953
Glassel	55	C5	GNS	1966
Glassford	49	G6	CAL	1945
Glasson	42	A2	NB	1932
Glasson Dock	36	D9	LNW	1930
Glasterlaw	51	E8	SCNE/CAL	1951
Glastonbury and Street	7	B8	SD JT	1966
Glazebrook	77	B7	CLC	
Glazebury and Bury Lane	76	H6	LNW	1958
Glemsford	20	F2	GE	1967
Glenbarry	54	D4	GNS	1968
Glenbirnie	51	A4	EN	1848

Station	Page	Block	Comp	Year of CL
Glenboig	75	E7	CAL	1956
Glenbuck	49	H3	CAL	1952
Glencarron Halt	58	F5	HIGH	1964
Glencarse	51	A5	CAL	1956
Glencorse	46	F6	NB	1933
	83	D2		
Glendon and Rushton	25	G6	MID	1960
Glen Douglas Halt	53	E2	NB	1964
Gleneagles	50	E3	CAL	
Glenellrig	46	A8	MONK	1850
Glenesk	83	G5	NB	1874
Glenfarg	50	H3	NB	1964
Glenfield 2nd, 1st — 1876	25	C9	MID	1928
Glenfinnan (Loch Shiel)	59	G3	NB	
Glenfoot	50	E2	ST & D	1851
Glengarnock	49	B6	GSW	
Glengarnock High	49	B6	CAL	1930
Gleniffer GDS	74	B2	GSW	1959
Glenluce	44	D4	PPW JT	1965
Glenochie — see Menstrie				
Glen Parva — see Wigtown				
Glenrothes — see Markinch				
Glenside	44	D10	GSW	1930
	49	A1		
Glenwhilly	44	D5	GSW	1965
Globe Road — see [London]				
Glodwick Road — see [Oldham]				
Glogue	19	A7	GW	1962
Glossop	31	D10	GC	
[Gloucester]				
Gloucester	17	E8	GW	
Gloucester Eastgate 2nd, 1st — 1896	17	E8	MID	1975
Station	17	E8	GW	1851
Gloucester Road — see [London]				
Glyn Abbey Halt Form. Pontnewynydd Ht	19	D3	BP/GW	1953
Glynceiriog	30	A3	GVT	1933
	33	F3		
Glyncorrwg	16	B6	SWM	1930
	78	C2		
Glyncorrwg — see also Cymmer Afan				
Glynde	2	D2	LBSC	
Glyndyfrdwy	33	F4	GW	1964
Glyne Gap Halt	2	H2	LBSC	1915
Glyn Neath	78	Bs	GW	1964
Glyntaff Halt	78	E4	ANSW	1930
Gnosall	31	A1	LNW	1964
Goathland 2nd, 1st — 1865	39	C5	NE	1965
Goathland R.O. PR. FR. CL. above	39	C5	NYM	
Gobowen	33	H3	GW	
Godalming	5	F9	LSW	
Godalming, Old	5	F9	LSW	1897
Goddall Road — see [London] Leyton				
Godley Junction Station	77	A10	CLC	
Godley Toll Bar	77	A10	SAM	1842
Godmanchester	23	C4	GN/GE	1959
Godnow Bridge	34	G3	GC	1917
Godreaman Halt 2nd, 1st — 1922	78	C3	GW	1924
Godshill Halt (Isle of Wight)	4	H1	IWC	1952
Godstone	2	C7	SEC	
Godwins Halt	12	A7	MID	1947
	15	G7		
Gogar	46	E8	NB	1930
Gogarth Halt	26	C8	CAM	
Goitre Halt	27	A7	CAM	1931
Golant Halt	11	C6	GW	1965
Golbourne North	76	G5	GC	1952
Golbourne South	76	G5	LNW	1961
Golden Grove	19	F5	LNW	1963
Goldenhill — see [Stoke-on-Trent] Newchapel				
Golden Hill Halt	18	F3	GW	1940
Golden Sands Camp Halt	3	D4	RHD	1947
Goldhawk Road — see [London]				
Goldsborough	34	B9	NE	1958
Goldthorpe and Thurnscoe Halt	82	E10	DEARN	1951
Golfa	27	B9	CAM	1931
Golf Club Halt	26	B10	FAIRB	1939
Golf Club House Halt	54	C5	GNS	1964
Golf Links	10	E4	RC	1939
Golf Street Halt	51	E6	DA JT	
Golgar	79	H2	LNW	1968
Gollanfield Junction	56	F4	HIGH	1965
Golspie	61	D1	HR	
Gomersal	37	E5	LNW	1953
	79	F4		
Gomshall and Shere	5	H9	SEC	
Goodleigh — see Snapper				
Goodmayes	65	H6	GE	
Goodrich Castle — see Kerne Bridge				

Station	Page	Block	Comp	Year of CL
Goodrington Sands	9	E10	GW	1963
Goodrington Sands T.O. PR. FR. CL. above	9	E10	T & D	
Goodwick — see Fishguard				
Goole	34	F5	LY	1879
Goole	34	F5	NE	
Goonbell Halt	10	F5	GW	1963
Goonhavern Halt	10	F5	GW	1963
Goostrey	77	F8	LNW	
Gorbals — see [Glasgow]				
Gordon	47	C4	NB	1948
Gordon Hill	12	D6	GN	
Gorebridge	46	H6	NB	1969
	83	G2		
Gorgie — see [Edinburgh]				
Goring and Streatley	15	A4	GW	
Goring-by-Sea	5	G4	LBSC	
Gorleston-on-Sea — see [Yarmouth]				
Gornal Halt — see [West Midlands]				
Gorseinon	19	F2	LNW	1964
Gors-y-Garnant Halt	19	G4	GW	1926
Gorton and Openshaw	77	A9	GC	
Gosberton	22	C4	GN/GE	1961
	29	C2		
Gospel Oak	64	G5	LNW	
Gosport	5	A4	LSW	1953
Gosport Road and Alverstoke	5	B3	LSW	1915
Goswick	43	G9	NE	1958
Gotham GDS	28	D2	GC	1964
Gotherington Halt	14	A10	GW	1955
Goudhurst	2	G5	SEC	1961
Gourdon	55	F7	NB	1951
Gourock	49	A9	CAL	
Govilon	78	A9	LNW	1958
Gowerton North	19	F2	GW	
Gowerton South	19	F2	LNW	1968
Goxhill	35	C4	GC	
Grace Dieu Halt	28	B1	LNW	1931
Grafham	23	C3	MID	1959
Grafton and Burbage	14	D1	MSWJ	1961
Graig — see [Pontypridd]				
Grahamstoun — see [Falkirk]				
Grain	13	C3	BR	1961
Grain Crossing Halt	3	A10	SEC	1951
	13	C3		
Grainsby Halt	35	E2	GN	1939
Grampound Road	10	H5	GW	1964
Granborough Road	15	B9	MET/GC	1936
Grandtully	50	E9	HIGH	1965
Grange	54	D3	GNS	1968
Grange Court	17	D8	BW	1964
Grange Hill	65	G8	GE	1966
Grange Hill R.O. by LTS FR. CL. above	65	G8	LTS	
Grange Lane	82	C9	GC	1953
Grange Lane — see [Birkenhead]				
Grangemouth	46	C9	CAL	1968
Grange over Sands	40	H2	FUR	
Grange Park	65	A10	GN	
Grange Road for Crawley Down and Turners Hill	2	C5	LBSC	1967
Grange Road GDS	76	D8	LY	1966
Grangeston Halt	44	D9	GSW	1965
Grangetown (South Glamorgan)	78	H6	TV	
Grangetown (Cleveland) Form. Eston Grange	38	H7	NE	
Grantham	28	H3	GN	
Grantham, Old Wharf	28	H3	GN	1852
Granton — see [Edinburgh]				
Granton Road — see [Edinburgh]				
Grantown-on-Spey East	57	A7	GNS	1965
Grantown-on-Spey West	57	A7	HIGH	1965
Grants House	47	F7	NB	1964
Granville Street — see [West Midlands] Birmingham				
Grasscroft	37	C3	LNW	1955
Grassendale — see Cressington				
Grassington and Threshfield	37	C10	MID	1930
Grassmoor	82	C6	GC	1940
Grateley	4	E8	SEC	
Gravel Hill GDS	10	F6	GW	1949
Gravelly Hill	80	C6	LNW	
Graveney GDS	3	D9	SEC	1962
[Gravesend]				
Gravesend	70	G8	SE	1849
Gravesend Central	70	G8	SEC	
Gravesend Town Pier R.N. Gravesend West Street				
Gravesend West Street	70	G8	SEC	1953
Grayrigg 2nd, 1st — 1849	41	C4	LNW	1954
Grays	66	H1	LTS	
Grays	70	F10		
Greasey — see Newthorpe and Shipley Gate				
Great Alne	24	F3	GW	1939
	80	H7		
Great Ayton	38	H6	NE	
Great Barr — see [West Midlands] Hampstead				
Great Bentley	13	F9	GE	
Great Bridgeford	31	A2	LNW	1949
Great Bridge — see [West Midlands]				
Great Broughton	40	D9	CW JT	1908
	45	F1		
Great Chesterford	23	F8	GE	
Great Coates	35	E3	GC	
Great Coates Level Crossing	35	E3	GC/GI	1961
Great Dalby	25	F10	GN/LNW	1953
Great Glen	25	E8	MID	1951
Greatham	38	G8	NE	
Great Harwood	36	H6	LY	1957
	76	B7		
Great Haywood Halt	31	C1	NS	1947
Great Horton — see [Bradford]				
Great Houghton Halt	82	D10	DEARNE	1951
Great Linford	25	G1	LNW	1964
Great Longstone for Ashford	31	F8	MID	1962
Great Malvern	24	B2	GW	
Great Missenden	15	D7	MET/GC	
Great Moor Street — see [Bolton]				
Great Orme	33	A9	GO	
Great Ormesby	20	E10	MGN	1959
Great Ponton	29	A2	GN	1958
Great Portland Street — see [London]				
Great Shefford	14	F2	GW	1960
Great Somerford	14	A4	GW	1933
	17	H4		
Greatstone	3	D4	RHD	
Greatstone-on-Sea Halt	3	D4	SR	1967
Great Western Road — see [Glasgow]				
Great Yarmouth — see [Yarmouth]				
Gree GDS	49	C6	CAL	1932
Greenan Castle GDS	49	B2	GSW	1959
Greenbank	30	G7	CLC	
	77	F6		
Greenbank — see also Hartford				
Green Bank Halt	27	G9	GW	1962
Greenfield	37	C3	LNW	
	76	F10		
Greenford	63	H4	GW	
	64	A4		
Greenford — see also [London]				
Greengairs GDS	75	G8	NB	1954
Greenhead	42	F3	NE	1967
Greenhill	46	A9	CAL	1966
	75	H10		
Greenhill	46	A9	NB	1967
	75	H10		
Greenhithe	70	E9	SEC	
Green Lane	77	C2	MERSEY	
Greenlaw	47	E6	NB	1948
Greenloaning for Braco	50	D3	CAL	1956
Greenmount	76	D7	LY	1952
[Greenock]				
Bridge Street — see Cathcart			CAL	1889
Greenock Central	49	B9	CAL	
Greenock West	49	B9	CAL	
Lynedoch Street	49	B9	GSW	1959
Princes Pier 2nd, 1st — 1894	49	B9	GSW	1959
Upper Greenock	49	B9	CAL	1967
Greenodd	40	G2	FUR	1946
Green Park — see [Bath]				
Green Road	40	E2	FUR	
Greenside — see Pudsey				
Greens of Drainie	56	D9	GNS	1859
Green's Siding	27	C1	GW	1941
Greenway Halt	17	D10	GW	1959
Greenwich	65	D2	SEC	
	69	D10		
Greenwich Park — see [London]				
Greetland	79	G2	LY	1962
Gresford (for Llay) Halt	30	C5	GW	1962
	72	E3		
Gresley	31	G1	MID	1964
Gresty	30	G5	LNW	1918
Gretna	42	B3	CAL	1951
Gretna	42	B3	NB	1915
Gretna Green	42	B3	GSW	1965
Gretton	25	H8	MID	1966
Gretton Halt	14	A10	GW	1960

Station	Page	Block	Comp	Year of CL
Gretton Halt	17	H10		
Griffith's Crossing Halt	32	F6	LNW	1937
Griffithstown — see Panteg				
Grimes Hill — see Wythall				
Grimesthorpe Bridge — see [Sheffield]				
Grimethorpe Halt	82	D10	DEARNE	1951
Grimoldby	29	F9	GN	1960
Grimsargh for Whittingham	76	B4	PL JT	1930
[Grimsby]				
Cleveland Bridge	35	E3	GC/GI	1961
Corporation Bridge	35	E3	GC/GI	1956
Docks	35	E3	GC	
Hainton Street Halt	35	E3	GN	1961
Pyewipe Halt	35	E3	GC	1912
Town	35	E3	GC	
Weelsby Road Halt	35	E3	GN	1940
Grimston (Leics)	27	E1	MID	1957
Grimston Road (Norfolk)	22	D10	MGN	1959
Grimstone and Frampton	7	E3	GW	1966
Grindleford	31	F8	MID	
	82	A7		
Grindley	31	D2	GN	1939
Grindley Brook Halt	30	E4	LMS	1957
Grindon Halt	31	D5	NS	1934
Grinkle	39	B7	NE	1939
Gristhorpe	39	E2	NE	1959
Groesffordd Halt	16	E9	GW	1962
Groeslon	32	E5	NANT/LNW	1964
Groeswen Halt	78	E5	ANSW	1956
Grogley Halt	10	B7	LSW	1967
Groombridge	2	E5	LBSC	
Grosmont	39	C5	NE	1965
Grosmont	39	C5	NYM	
Grosvenor Road — see [London]				
Grotton and Springhead	76	F10	LNW	1955
Grove Ferry and Upstreet	3	F9	SEC	1966
	13	H2		
Grove Hill Halt	14	F4	WT	1925
Grove Park	69	D8	SEC	
Grove Park — see also [London] Chiswick				
Grove Road — see [London] Hammersmith				
Grove Road — see [Wallasey] Wallasey				
Grovesend	19	F2	LNW	1932
Guard Bridge	51	D5	NB	1965
Guay	50	F8	HIGH	1959
Guestwick	20	D4	MGN	1959
Guide Bridge North	31	B10	GC	
	77	A10		
Guide Bridge South GDS	77	A10	LNW	1965
Guildford	5	F10	LSW	
Guildford — see also London Road				
Guild Street — see [Aberdeen]				
Guisborough	38	H6	NE	1964
Guiseley	37	E7	MID	
	79	C3		
Gullane	47	B9	NB	1932
Gunheath GDS	11	A6	GW	1965
Gunnersbury	64	C2	LSW	
Gunness and Burringham	34	H3	GC	1916
Gunness Wharf GDS	34	H3	GC	
Gunnislake	9	C4	PDSW	
	11	G8		
Gunton	20	B6	GE	
Gurnos Junction Station GDS	19	H4	MID	1965
Gushetfaulds — see [Glasgow]				
Guthrie Junction	51	E8	CAL	1955
Guyhirne	22	G6	GN/GE	1953
Gwaun-Cae-Gurwen Halt	19	H4	GW	1926
Gwernydomen Halt	78	E7	BM	1956
Gwersyllt and Wheatsheaf	30	B5	GC	
	72	E3		
Gwersyllt Hill Halt	30	B5	GW	1931
	72	D3		
Gwinear	10	D4	WC	1852
Gwinear Road	10	D4	GW	1964
Gwyddelwern	33	E4	LNW	1953
Gwys	19	H4	MID	1950
	78	A1		
Gyfeillon Platform	78	E4	TV	1918
Gypsy Lane	38	G6	BR	
Habrough	35	C3	GC	
Hacheston Halt	21	D8	GE	1952
Hackbridge	68	G5	LBSC	
Hackney — see [London]				
Hackney Downs	65	B5	GE	
Haddenham (Bucks)	15	C7	GW/GC	1963
Haddenham (Cambs)	23	B7	GE	1931
Haddington	47	B8	NB	1949
Haddiscoe 2nd, 1st — 1904	20	G9	GE	

Station	Page	Block	Comp	Year of CL
Haddiscoe High Level	20	G9	GE	1959
Hadfield for Hollingworth	31	D10	GC	
Hadham	12	E8	GE	1964
Hadleigh	21	G4	GE	1932
Hadley	27	G10	LNW	1964
Hadley Wood	12	C6	GN	
Hadlow Road for Willaston	77	E2	B HEAD	1956
Hadnall	27	E10	LNW	1960
	30	E1		
Hadnock Halt	17	B8	GW	1959
Hafod — see Johnstown				
Hafod Garregog	32	F4	WH	1936
Hafod-y-Llyn	32	F4	WH	1936
Hafod Ruffydd	32	F5	WH	1936
Hafod-y-Llyn Rep. by Tan-y-Grisiau	32	G3	FEST	1872
Hafodyrynys Platform	78	D9	GW	1964
Haggerston — see [London]				
Hagley	80	F3	GW	
Hagley Road — see [West Midlands]				
Haigh	79	H5	LY	1965
Hailes Halt	83	A4	LMS	1943
Hailsham	2	F2	LBSC	1968
Hainault	65	G8	GE	1966
Hainault R.O. by LTS FR. CL. above	65	G8	LTS	
Hainton — see South Willington				
Hainton Street Halt — see [Grimsby]				
Hairmyres	49	F6	CAL	
	74	H1		
Halbeath	46	E10	NB	1930
Halberton Halt	6	D5	GW	1964
Hale for Altrincham and Bowden	30	H9	CLC	
	77	C8		
Halebank for Hale	77	D4	LNW	1958
Hale End — see [London] Highams Park				
Halesowen	80	E4	GW	1927
Halesworth	21	B8	S WOLD	1929
Halesworth and Southwold	21	B8	GE	
Halewood	77	C3	CLC	1951
Half Way Station	32	G5	NWNG	1924
Half Way R.O. PR.FR. CL. above	32	G5	SMR	
Half Way	33	A8	GO	
[Halifax]				
Copley	79	G2	LY	1931
Halifax	37	D5	LY	
	79	F2		
Holmfield	79	F2	HO JT	1955
Illingworth GDS	79	E2	HO JT	1955
North Bridge	79	F2	HO JT	1955
Ovenden	79	F2	HO JT	1955
Pellon	79	F2	HHL	1917
St Pauls	79	F2	HHL	1917
Shaw Syke	79	F2	LY	1850
Wheatley GDS	79	F2	HHL	1965
Halkirk	61	H9	HIGH	1960
	62	D8		
Hallaton	25	F8	GN/LNW	1953
Hallatrow	7	D10	GW	1959
Hallcraig Street — see [Airdrie]				
Hallen Halt — see [Bristol]				
Hall Green	80	F6	GW	
Halling	2	G9	SEC	
Hallington	29	E9	GN	1951
Hall Road	76	F1	LY	
Halmerend	30	H4	NS	1931
Halsall Green	36	C3	LY	1938
	76	E2		
Halsall Moor — see Farnworth				
Halstead	13	B10	CVH	1962
Halton (Cheshire)	77	E5	B HEAD	1952
Halton (Lancs)	36	E10	MID	1966
Halton Dial — see [Leeds]				
Halton Holgate	29	F6	GN	1939
Haltwhistle	42	G2	NE	
Halwill Junction	8	H4	LSW	1966
Hamble Halt	4	H4	LSW	
Hambleton	34	D6	NE	1959
	79	D10		
Ham Bridge Halt — see East Worthing				
Ham Green Halt	72	B7	GW	1964
[Hamilton]				
Hamilton	75	D2	NB	1952
Hamilton Central	49	G6	CAL	
	75	D2		
Hamilton West	49	G6	CAL	
	75	D2		
Hamilton Square — see [Birkenhead]				
Ham Lane	16	H2	WCP	1940
Hammersmith — see [London]				
Hammerton	34	C9	NE	

Station	Page	Block	Comp	Year of CL
Hammerwich	24	E9	LNW	1965
Hammill Colliery GDS	3	G8	EK	1948
Ham Mill Crossing Halt	17	F6	GW	1964
Hampden Park for Willingdon	2	F1	LBSC	
Hampole	34	C3	WRG JT	1952
	79	H9		
Hampstead Heath	64	G5	LNW	
Hampstead South — see South Hampstead				
Hampstead West — see West Hampstead				
Hampstead Norris	14	H3	GW	1962
Hampsthwaite	37	F10	NE	1951
Hampton Court	67	G7	LSW	
Hampton-in-Arden	80	E8	MID	1917
Hampton-in-Arden 3rd, 1st — 1884, 2nd — 1966	80	E8	LNW	
Hampton Loade	27	H6	GW/SV	1963
	80	D1		
Hampton Loade R.O. PR. FR. CL. above	80	D1	SVR	
Hampton Row Halt — see [Bath]				
Hampton Wick	68	B7	LSW	
Hampstead 2nd, 1st (Gt. Barr) — 1899	80	C5	LNW	
Ham Street and Orlestone	3	C5	SEC	
Hamworthy	4	B2	LSW	1896
Hamworthy Junction Sta.	4	B2	LSW	
Handborough	14	G7	GW	
Handford Road Halt — see [Stoke-on-Trent]				
Handforth	31	A9	LNW	
	77	D9		
Handsworth — see Darnall				
Handsworth and Smethwick — see [West Midlands]				
Handsworth Wood — see [West Midlands]				
Hanley — see [Stoke-on-Trent]				
Hannington	14	C5	GW	1953
Hanwell and Elthorne	63	H3	GW	
	64	A3		
Hanwood	27	E9	S & WPL	1960
Hanwood Road	27	E9	PSNW/SM	1933
Happendon	46	A3	CAL	1964
Hapton	76	C8	LY	
Harbourne — see [West Midlands] Somerset Road				
Harburn	46	D6	CAL	1966
Harbury — see Southam and Long Itchington				
Harby — see Duddingston				
Harby and Strathern	28	F3	GN/LNW	1953
Hardingham	20	F6	GE	1969
Hardwick — see Rowthorn				
Harecastle — see Kidsgrove				
Harefield — see Denham				
Hare Park and Crofton	79	H7	WRG JT	1952
Haresfield	17	F7	MID	1965
Harker	42	C2	NB	1929
Harlaxton GDS	28	G3	GE	
Harlech	32	G2	CAM	
Harlesden — see [London]				
Harlesdon	64	D4	LNW	
Harleston	21	A7	GE	1953
Harling Road	21	A4	GE	
Harlington (Beds)	12	A10	MID	
	15	F10		
Harlington (Middlesex) — see Hayes				
Harlington Halt	82	E10	DEARNE	1951
Harlow Mill	12	E7	GE	
Harlow Town	12	E7	GE	
Harmston	29	A6	GN	1962
Harold Wood	66	D7	GE	
Harpenden Central	12	B8	MID	
Harpenden East	12	B8	GN	1965
Harperley	38	B9	NE	1953
Harrietsham	3	B7	SEC	
Harringay West	65	A7	GN	
Harringay Stadium	65	A7	MID	
Harrington	40	C8	LNW	
Harrington Church Road Halt	40	C8	CW JT	1926
Harringworth	25	H8	MID	1948
Harrogate	79	A6	NE	
Harrogate, Brunswick	79	A6	NE	1862
Harrow — see [London]				
Harrow and Wealdstone — see [London]				
Harrow-on-the-Hill — see [London]				
Harrow Road, Sudbury and — see [London]				
Harston	23	E7	GE	1963
Hart — see [Hartlepool]				
Hartfield	2	E5	LBSC	1967
Hartford	77	F6	LNW	

Station	Page	Block	Comp	Year of CL
Hartford — see also Greenbank				
Harting — see Rogate				
Hartington	31	E6	LNW	1954
Hartington Road Halt — see [Brighton]				
Hartlebury	80	G2	GW	
[Hartlepool]				
Hart	38	F9	NE	1953
Hartlepool	38	F9	NE	1947
West Hartlepool 2nd, 1st — 1880	38	F9	NE	
Hartley	43	G4	NE	1964
Hartley — see [Longfield]				
Harton Road	27	E7	GW	1951
Hartshill and Basford Halt — see [West Midlands]				
Harts Hill and Woodside — see [West Midlands]				
Harty Road Halt	3	C10	SEC	1950
	13	E2		
Hartwood	46	A6	CAL	
Harvington	24	E2	MID	1962
[Harwich]				
Harwich Parkeston Quay	13	H10	GE	
	21	H7		
Harwich Parkeston Quay West	13	H10	LNE	1972
	21	H7		
Harwich Town	13	H10	GE	
	21	H7		
Harwich — see also Dovercourt				
Hasland GDS	31	H7	MID	1965
	82	B5		
Haslemere	5	E6	LSW	
Haslingden	36	H5	EL	1960
	76	D8		
Hassendean	42	E10	NB	1969
	47	B2		
Hassocks	2	B3	LBSC	
Hassop	31	F8	MID	1942
[Hastings and St Leonards]				
Hastings	3	A2	SEC	
St Leonards Bulverhythe	2	H2	LBSC	1846
St Leonards Warrior Square	2	H2	SEC	
St Leonards West Marina 2nd, 1st — 1882	2	H2	LBSC	1967
West St Leonards	2	H2	SEC	
Haswell 2nd, 1st — 1877	38	E10	NE	1952
Hatch	6	H6	GW	1962
Hatcham — see [London] Old Kent Road				
Hatch End, Pinner and	63	G8	LNW	
[Hatfield]				
Hatfield	12	C7	EC	1849
Hatfield	12	C7	GN	
Hatfield Hyde Halt	12	C7	GN	1905
Hatfield Moor GDS	34	F2	AX JT	1963
Hatfield Peverel	13	B8	GE	
Hatherleigh	8	G5	SR	1965
Hathern	28	C1	MID	1960
Hathersage	31	F9	MID	
Hattersley	31	B10	BR	
Hatton (Warwicks)	80	G8	GW	
Hatton (Aberdeen)	54	F9	DPA	1865
Hatton (Aberdeen)	54	F9	GNS	1932
Hatton Branch Terminus — see [Stratford-on-Avon]				
[Haughley]				
Haughley	21	D4	GE	1967
Haughley	21	D4	MSL	1925
Haughley Road	21	D4	EU	1849
Haughton	31	A1	LNW	1949
Haughton Halt	30	C1	GW	1960
Havant	5	C4	LBSC	
Havant	5	C4	LSW	1859
Havenhouse	29	H6	GN	
Haven Street (Isle of Wight)	5	A2	IWC	1966
Haverfordwest	18	F4	GW	
Haverhill North	23	F10	GE	1967
Haverhill South	23	F10	CUH	1924
Haverstock Hill — see [London]				
Haverthwaite	40	G2	FUR	1946
Haverthwaite R.O. PR. FR. CL. above	40	G2	L & H	
Haverton Hill — see [London]				
Hawarden	33	H7	GC	
	77	G2		
Hawarden Bridge	33	H7	GC	
	77	G2		
Hawes	41	F4	MID/NE	1959
Hawes Junction — see Garsdale				
Hawick 2nd, 1st — 1862	42	D9	NB	1969
	74	B1	NB	1969
Hawkesbury Lane	80	D10	LNW	1965

Station	Page	Block	Comp	Year of CL
Hawkhead — see [Paisley]				
Hawkhurst	2	H5	SEC	1961
Hawkhurst — see also Junction Road				
Hawkmoor Halt	6	A1	GW	1959
	9	B9		
Haworth CL. 1962 T.O. PR. R.O. 1968	37	C7	MID/KWVR	
	79	D1		
Hawsker	39	D6	NE	1965
Hawthornden	83	F2	NB	1962
Haxby	34	E9	NE	1930
[Haxey]				
Haxey and Epworth	34	G2	GN/GE	1959
Haxey Junction	34	G2	AX JT	1933
Haxey Town	34	G2	AX JT	1933
Hayburn Wyke	39	E4	NE	1965
Haydock	76	G4	GC	1952
Haydock Park	76	G4	GC	1952
Haydon Bridge 2nd, 1st — 1838	43	A3	NE	
Haydons Road	68	F7	LBSC/LSW	
Hayes (Kent)	69	D5	SEC	
Hayes and Harlington (Middx)	63	E3	GW	
Hayfield	31	D9	GC/MID	1970
	77	C10		
Hayle	10	C3	GW	
Hayles Abbey Halt	14	B10	GW	1960
Hayle Wharves GDS 2nd, 1st — 1852	10	C3	GW	1964
Hayling Island	80	C3	LBSC	1963
Haymarket	83	D6	NB	
Hay-on-Wye	27	B1	MID	1962
Haywards Heath	2	B4	LBSC	
Haywood	46	C6	CAL	1951
Hazel Grove	77	C9	MID	1917
Hazel Grove	77	C9	LNW	
Hazelhead Bridge	38	E3	MS & L/GC	1950
	82	A9		
Hazelwell — see [West Midlands]				
Hazelwood	31	G4	MID	1947
	82	B2		
Heacham	22	B9	GE	1969
Headcorn	3	A6	SEC	
Headcorn Junction	3	A6	KES	1954
Headingley	37	F7	NE	
	79	D5		
Headless Cross	46	B6	WMC	1852
Heads Nook	42	D2	NE	1967
Heads of Ayr 2nd, 1st — 1930	49	B2	LMS	1968
Headstone Lane	63	G8	LNW	
Heald Green	77	C8	LNW	
Healey — see [Rochdale] Shawclough				
Healey House	79	H2	LY	1949
Healing	35	D3	GC	
Heanor	31	H4	GN	1939
	82	C3		
Heanor	82	C3	MID	1926
Heap Bridge GDS	76	E8	LY	1967
Heapey	76	C5	LY/LU	1960
Heath	28	B6	GC	1963
	82	C6		
Heath Town — see [West Midlands]				
Heather and Ibstock	25	A10	AN JT	1931
Heathey Lane Halt	76	D1	LY	1938
Heath High Level Halt	78	F6	GW	
Heath Low Level Halt	78	F6	GW	
Heathfield (Devon)	9	C9	GW	1959
Heathfield (Sussex)	2	F4	LBSC	1965
Heath Park Halt	12	A7	MID	1947
	15	F7		
Heatley and Warburton	77	C7	LNW	1962
Heaton	81	C3	NE	
Heaton Chapel and Heaton Moor	77	B9	LNW	
Heaton Lodge	79	G3	LNW	1864
Heaton Mersey — see [Stockport]				
Heaton Norris — see [Stockport]				
Heaton Park	77	F9	LY	
Hebburn	81	D2	NE	
Hebron	32	G5	NWNG	
Hebron T.O. PR. FR. CL. above	32	G5	SMR	
Hebden Bridge	37	C6	LY	
	79	F1		
Heck	34	E4	NE	1958
Heckington	22	B3	GN	
	29	C4		
Heckmondwike	79	G4	LY	1965
Heckmondwike Spen	79	G4	LNW	1953
Heddon-on-the-Wall	43	E3	NE	1958
Hedgeley	43	C9	NE	1930
Hedingham — see Sible				
Hednesford for Cannock Chase	24	E10	LNW	1965

Station	Page	Block	Comp	Year of CL
[Hedon]				
Hedon	35	D5	NE	1964
Hedon Racecourse	35	D5	LNE	not tabled
Hedon Speedway Halt	35	D5	LNE	not tabled
Heeley — see [Sheffield]				
Heighington (Durham)	38	D7	NE	
Heighington (Lincs) — see Branston				
Hele and Bradninch	6	D3	GW	1964
Helensburgh Central	49	B10	NB	
Helensburgh Upper	49	B10	NB	
Hellaby GDS	82	E9	GC/HB	1966
Hellesden — see [Norwich]				
Hellifield 2nd, 1st — 1880	37	A9	MID	
Hellingly	2	F2	LBSC	1965
Helmdon for Sulgrave	25	C2	GC	1963
Helmdon Village	25	C2	SMJ	1951
Helmsdale	61	F3	HR	
Helmshore	76	D8	EL	1966
Helmsley	38	H2	NE	1953
Helpringham	22	B3	GN/GE	1955
	29	C3		
Helpston for Market Deeping	22	F3	MID	1966
Helsby	77	E4	B HEAD	
Helsby and Alvanley	77	E4	CLC	1964
Helston	10	E2	GW	1962
Hemel Hempstead	12	A7	MID	1947
	15	F7		
Hemel Hempstead, Boxmoor and	12	A7	LNW	
	15	F7		
Hemingbrough	34	E6	NE	1967
Hemsby	20	E9	MGN	1959
Hemsworth	79	H9	WRG JT	1967
Hemsworth and South Kirkby	79	H9	HB	1932
Hemyock	6	F5	GW	1963
Henbury — see [Bristol]				
Hendford — see [Yeovil]				
Hendford Halt — see [Yeovil]				
Hendon (London)	64	D6	MID	
Hendon — see [Sunderland]				
Hendon Burn — see [Sunderland]				
Hendreforgan	78	F3	GW	1930
Hendy Form. Hendre Halt	26	B8	TAL	
Henfield	2	A3	LBSC	1966
Hengoed — see Maesycwmmer				
Hengoed High Level	78	C6	GW	1964
Hengoed Low Level	78	C6	RHY	
Henham Halt	12	G10	GE	1952
	23	H8		
Heniarth Gate Closed 1931 R.O. PR.	26	H9	W & L	
Henley-in-Arden 2nd, 1st	24	H4	GW	
	80	H7		
Henley-on-Thames	15	C4	GW	
Henllan	19	C8	GW	1952
Henlow — see Arlesey				
Henlow Camp	23	G3	MID	1962
Hensall	34	E4	LY	
Henstridge	7	E6	SD JT	1966
Henwick — see [Worcester]				
Heolgerrig Halt — see [Merthyr]				
Hepscott	43	E5	NE	1950
Herber Toll Gate	33	G3	GVT	1881
[Hereford]				
Barton	27	E1	GW	1893
Hereford	27	E1	MID	
Moorfields	27	E1	MID	1874
Heriot	47	A6	NB	1969
Hermitage	14	H2	GW	1962
Herne Bay	3	F10	SEC	
Herne Hill	68	H9	SEC	
Herriard	5	B9	LSW	1932
Hersham, Walton and	67	F5	LSW	
Hertford East 2nd, 1st — 1888	12	D8	GE	
Hertford North 2nd, 1st — 1924	12	D8	GN	
Hertingfordbury	12	D8	GN	1951
Hesketh Bank for Tarleton	76	C3	LY	1964
Hesketh Park — see [Southport]				
Heseleden	38	F9	NE	1952
Heslerton	39	C1	NE	1930
Hessay	34	D8	NE	1958
Hessle	35	B5	NE	
	73	C2		
Hessle Road — see [Hull]				
Hest Bank	36	D10	LNW	1969
Heswall	77	D1	B HEAD	1956
Heswall Hills	77	D1	GC	
Hethersett	20	F5	NOR/GE	1966
Hetton	38	E19	NE	1953
	43	G1		
Hever	2	D6	LBSC	

Station	Page	Block	Comp	Year of CL
Heversham	41	A3	FUR	1942
Hexham	43	B3	NE	
Hexthorpe — see [Doncaster]				
Heybridge — see Maldon East				
Heyford	14	G9	GW	
Heys Crossing Halt	76	F3	LY	1951
Heysham Harbour	36	D9	MID	1970
Heytesbury	4	A8	GW	1955
	7	H9		
Heywood 2nd, 1st — 1848	76	E9	LY	1970
Hibaldstow — see Scawby				
Hickleton and Thurnscoe	82	E10	HB	1929
Higham (Kent)	2	G10	SEC	
	13	A3		
Higham (Suffolk)	13	A3	GE	1967
Higham Ferrers and Irthlingboro	23	C1	MID	1959
Higham-on-the-Hill	25	A8	AN JT	1931
	80	C10		
Highams Park and Hale End	65	D8	GE	
High Barnet — see [London]				
High Blaithwaite	40	F10	HC	1921
High Blantyre	75	B2	CAL	1945
Highbridge East	6	H9	SD JT	1966
Highbridge West	6	H9	GW	
High Brooms	2	F6	SEC	
Highbury and Islington	65	A5	NL	
Highclere	14	G1	GW	1960
Higher Buxton — see [Buxton]				
Higher Poynton	77	D10	GC/NS	1970
High Field	34	F6	NE	1954
Highfield Road Halt	77	D3	GC	1917
Highgate — see [London]				
High Halden Road	3	A5	KES	1954
High Halstow Halt	2	H10	SEC	1961
	13	B3		
High Harrington	40	C8	CW JT	1931
Highlandman	50	E4	CAL	1964
High Lane	77	C10	GC/NS	1970
High Lane — see Middlewood				
Highley	24	A6	GW	1963
	80	E1		
Highley R.O. PR. FR. CL. above	24	A6	SVR	
	80	E1		
High Rocks Halt	2	E5	LBSC	1952
High Royds	82	B9	GC	1856
High Shields 2nd, 1st — 1879	43	G3	NE	1979
	81	F3		
High Street (Glasgow)	74	H6	NB	
High Street — see [Cheltenham]				
High Street — see [Lincoln] Lincoln				
High Street — see [London] Uxbridge				
High Street — see Shepton Mallet				
High Street — see [West Midlands] Old Hill				
High Street Halt — see [Cheltenham]				
Hightown (Lancs)	76	F1	LY	
Hightown Halt	72	F2	GW	1962
High Westwood	43	D2	NE	1942
Highworth	14	D5	GW	1953
High Wycombe 2nd, 1st — 1864	15	D5	GW/GC	
Hildenborough	2	F7	SEC	
Hilgay	22	H9	GE	1963
Hill End	12	B7	GN	1951
Hillfoot	74	D9	NB	
Hillhouse — see Altcar				
Hillingdon — see [London]				
Hillington for Sandringham	22	D10	MGN	1959
Hillington East	74	E4	LMS	
Hillington West	74	E4	LMS	
Hillside	76	D1	LY	
Hillside	51	G9	NB	1927
	55	H5		
Hilsea	5	B4	LSW/LBSC	
Hilton House	76	E5	LY	1954
Himley — see [West Midlands]				
Hinchley Wood	68	A4	SR	
Hinckley	25	B8	LNW	
Hinderwell for Runswick Bay	39	B7	NE	1958
[Hindley]				
Hindley Green	76	F5	LNW	1961
Hindley North	76	E5	LY	
Hindley South and Platt Bridge	76	F5	GC	1964
Hindlow	31	D7	LNW	1954
Hindolvestone	20	C4	MGN	1959
Hinksey Halt — see [Oxford]				
Hinton (Glos)	17	D3	MID	1963
	72	F7	MID	1963
Hinton — see Woodford Halse				
Hinton Admiral	4	D2	LSW	
Hipperholme	79	F2	LY	1953
Hirwaun	78	B2	GW	1964
Histon	23	D7	GE	1970
Hitchin	12	B10	GN	
	23	H4		
Hither Green	69	D9	SEC	
Hixon Halt	31	C2	NS	1947
Hockerill Halt	12	G9	GE	1952
Hockham — see Wretham				
Hockley (Essex)	13	C5	GE	
Hockley — see [West Midlands]				
Hoddesdon — see Broxbourne				
Hoddlesdon GDS	76	C6	LY	1950
Hodnet	30	F2	GW	1963
Hoe Street — see [London] Walthamstone Central				
Hoghton	76	B4	LY	1960
Hoghton Tower	76	B4	EL	1848
Holbeach	22	D6	MGN	1959
	29	F1		
Holbeck — see [Leeds]				
Holborn Viaduct — see [London]				
Holborn Viaduct, Low Level — see [London]				
Holborn Street — see [Aberdeen]				
Holcombe Brook	76	D7	LY	1952
Hole	8	G3	LSW	1965
Holehouse Junction	49	C1	GSW	1950
Holiday Camp (Jesson)	3	D5	RHD	1940
Holkham	20	B2	GE	1952
Holland Arms	32	E7	LNW	1952
Holland Road Halt	2	B2	LBSC	1956
Hollingbourne	3	A8	SEC	
Hollingworth — see Hadfield				
Hollins GDS	76	C6	LY	1968
Hollin Well and Annesley	82	E4	GC	1963
Hollinwood	76	F10	LY	
Holloway — see [London]				
Hollybush (Ayr)	49	C2	GSW	1964
Holly Bush (Mid Glam)	78	B7	LNW	1960
Hollym Gate	35	E5	NE	1870
Holme 1st (Cambs)	23	A4	EA	1853
Holme 2nd (Cambs)	23	A4	GN	1959
Holme (Lancashire)	76	B9	LY	1930
Holme Hale	20	F2	GE	1964
Holme Lacy	17	C10	GW	1964
Holme Moor (Yorkshire)	34	G6	NE	1954
Holmes — see [Rotherham]				
Holmes Chapel	77	F8	LNW	
Holmfield — see [Halifax]				
Holmfirth	37	E3	LY	1959
	79	H3		
Holmgate	82	B5	ASH	1936
Holmsley	4	E4	LSW	1964
Holmwood	2	A7	LBSC	
Holsworthy 2nd, 1st — 1898	8	G3	LSW	1966
Holt (Norfolk)	20	B5	MGN	1964
Holtby	34	E9	NE	1939
Holton Heath	4	A2	LSW	
Holt Junction Station	17	G1	GW	1966
Holton-le-Clay	35	E2	GN	1952
Holton-le-Moor	35	B1	GC	1965
Holton Village Halt	35	E2	GN	1961
Holygate GDS	46	E8	NB	1965
Holyhead 3rd, 1st — 1851, 2nd — 1866	32	B8	LNW	
Holyhead, Admiralty Pier	32	B8	LNW	1925
Holytown	75	F4	LNW	
Holywell (Northumberland) GDS	81	E4	NE	1965
Holywell Green — see Stainland				
Holywell Junction Station	30	A8	LNW	1966
	33	F8		
Holywell Town	30	A8	LNW	1954
	33	F8		
Holywood	45	E7	GSW	1949
Homersfield	21	A7	GE	1953
Homerton — see [London]				
Honeybourne	24	F1	GW	1969
Honeybourne Branch Terminus — see [Stratford-on-Avon]				
Honing for Worstead	20	D8	MGN	1959
Honington	29	A4	GN	1962
Honiton	6	G3	LSW	
Honley	37	E4	LY	
	79	H3		
Honor Oak — see [London]				
Honor Oak Park	69	B8	LBSC	
Hook	5	C10	LSW	
Hook Norton	14	F10	GW	1951

Station	Page	Block	Comp	Year of CL
Hoole	76	C3	LY	1964
Hooley Hill, Guide Bridge	77	A10	LNW	1950
Hoo Staff Halt*	2	G10	SR	
Hooton	77	E3	LNW	
Hope (Derbyshire) for Castleton and Bradwell	31	E9	MID	
[Hope] Clwyd				
Hope and Penyffordd	30	B6	LNW	1962
	72	D5		
Hope High Level	30	B6	GC	1958
	72	D5		
Hope Low Level	30	B6	LNW	1958
	72	D5		
Hope Village	72	D4	GC	
Hopeman	56	D8	HIGH	1931
Hopesbrook	17	D8	GW	1855
Hopperton	34	B9	NE	1958
Hopton Heath	27	D6	LNW	
Hopton-on-Sea	20	G10	NSJT	1970
Hopton Top Wharf	31	F5	LNW	1877
Horbling — see Billingboro				
Horeham Road, Waldron and	2	F3	LBSC	1965
[Horbury]				
Horbury and Osset	79	H5	LY	1970
Horbury Junction	79	H5	LY	1927
Horbury Millfield Road	79	H5	LMS	1961
Horden	38	F9	NE	1964
Horderley	27	D7	BC	1935
Horeb GDS	19	E3	LMM	1959
Horfield — see [Bristol]				
Horham	21	C6	MSL	1952
Horley 2nd, 1st — 1905	2	B6	LBSC	
Hornby	41	B1	MID	1957
Horncastle	29	D7	GN	1954
Hornchurch — see [London]				
Horninglow — see [Burton-on-Trent]				
Hornsea Bridge	35	D8	NE	1964
Hornsea Town	35	D8	NE	1964
Hornsey	65	A7	GN	
Hornsey Road — see [London]				
Horrabridge	9	C5	GW	1962
Horringford (Isle of Wight)	5	A2	IWC	1956
Horsebridge	4	F2	LSW	1964
Horsehay and Dawley	27	G9	GW	1962
Horsforth	37	F7	NE	
	79	C5		
Horsforth — see also [Leeds] Newlay				
Horsham 2nd, 1st — 1859	2	A5	LBSC	
Horsley and Ockham and Ripley	5	G10	LSW	
Horsmonden	2	G6	SEC	1961
Horspath Halt 2nd, 1st — 1915	15	A7	GW	1963
Horsted Keynes	2	C4	LBSC	1958
Horsted Keynes R.P. PR. FR. CL. above	2	C4	BLUE	
Horton-in-Ribblesdale*	41	E2	MID	1970
Horton Park — see [Bradford]				
Horwich	36	G3	LY	1965
	76	D5		
Hoscar	76	E3	LY	
Hose — see Long Clawson				
Hothfield for Westwell	3	C7	SEC	1959
Hotwells — see [Bristol]				
Hotwells Halt — see [Bristol]				
Hougham	28	H4	GN	1957
Hough Green for Ditton	77	C4	CLC	
Hounslow — see [London]				
House o' Hill Halt — see [Edinburgh]				
Houston (Crosslee)	49	D8	GSW	
	74	A4		
Houston	74	A4	CAL	1959
Hove	2	B2	LBSC	
Hove R.N. Holland Road (GDS)	2	B2	LBSC	1880
Hovingham Spa	39	A1	NE	1931
Howden	34	F6	NE	
Howden Clough	79	F5	GN	1952
Howden-on-Tyne	81	D3	NE	
Howe Bridge Form. Chow Bent	76	G6	LNW	1959
Howick — see New Longton and Sutton				
How Mill	42	E2	NE	1959
Hownes Gill	43	D1	NE	1858
Howood	49	C7	GPKA	1840
Howsham	35	B2	GC	1965
Howwood	49	C7	GSW	1955
Hoy Halt	61	H9	HIGH	1965
	62	D8		
Hoylake	77	C1	WIRRAL	
Hoyland — see Elsecar				
Hoyland Common — see Birdwell				
Hoyland Common — see also Wentworth				
Hubberts Bridge	22	B4	GN	

Station	Page	Block	Comp	Year of CL
[Hucknall]				
Hucknall Byron	82	E3	MID	1964
Hucknall Central	82	E3	GC	1963
Hucknall Town	82	E3	GN	1931
[Huddersfield]				
Berry Brow	79	H3	LY	1966
Bradley 2nd, 1st — 1849	79	H3	LNW	1950
Deighton	79	H3	LNW	1930
Huddersfield	37	E4	LY/LNW	
	79	H3		
Kirkheaton	79	H4	LNW	1930
Lockwood	79	H3	LY	
Longwood and Milnsbridge	79	H3	LNW	1968
Newtown GDS	79	H3	MID	1968
Woodfield	79	H3	LY	1874
Hugglescote	25	B10	AN JT	1931
[Hull]				
Anlaby Road	73	D2	NE	1854
Alexandra Dock GDS	73	F3	HB	
Beverley Road	73	D3	HB	1924
Boothferry Park*	73	C1	LNE	
Botanic Gardens	73	D3	NE	1964
Cannon Street	73	F4	HB	1924
Hessle Road	73	D3	NE	1853
Hull	35	C5	NE	
	73	D3		
King George Dock GDS	73	G3	HB	
Marfleet	35	C5	NE	1964
	73	G3		
Riverside Quay	73	D2	NE	1938
Sculcoates	73	E3	NE	1912
Southcoates	73	F3	NE	1964
Stepney	73	D3	NE	1964
Stoneferry GDS	73	F4	NE	
Sutton-on-Hull	35	C6	NE	1964
	73	F4		
Victoria Dock	73	F3	NE	1864
Wilmington 2nd, 1st — 1912	73	E3	NE	1964
Hullavington	17	G4	GW	1961
Hulme End	31	D6	NS	1934
Hulton Park — see Chequerbent				
Humberstone — see [Leicester]				
Humberstone Park — see [Leicester]				
Humbie	47	B7	NB	1933
Humshaugh — see Chollerford				
Huncoat 2nd, 1st — unknown	76	C8	LY	
Hundred End	76	C2	LY	1962
Hungerford, 2nd, 1st — 1862	14	E2	GW	
Hunmanby	39	F2	NE	
Hunnington	80	F4	HAL JT	1919
Hunslet — see [Leeds]				
Hunslet Lane — see [Leeds]				
Hunstanton	22	B9	GE	1969
Hunston	5	E4	WS	1935
Huntingdon	23	C4	GN/GE	
Huntingdon East	23	C4	MID	1959
Huntly	54	E3	GNS	
Hunts Cross	77	C3	CLC	
Hunwick	38	C8	NE	1964
Hurdlow	31	D7	LNW	1949
Hurlford	49	D4	GSW	1955
Hurlingham — see [London] Putney Bridge				
Hurn	4	D3	LSW	1935
Hurstbourne	4	G9	LSW	1964
Hurst Green 2nd	2	D7	LBSC	
Hurst Green Halt 1st	2	D7	LBSC	1961
Hurst Lane	82	B5	ASH	1936
Hurworth Burn	38	D6	NE	1931
Husborne Crawley Halt	23	G1	LNW	1941
Huskisson — see [Liverpool]				
Hustwaite Gate	38	G1	NE	1953
Hutcheon Street — see [Aberdeen]				
Hutton — see New Longton				
Hutton — see Shenfield				
Hutton Cranswick	35	B8	NE	
Hutton Gate	38	H6	NE	1964
Hutton Junction	38	H6	NE	1891
Huttons Ambo	34	G10	NE	1930
	39	B1		
Huyton	36	D1	LNW	
	76	H3		
Huyton Quarry	76	H3	LNW	1958
[Hyde]				
Hyde Central 2nd, 1st — 1862	31	B10	GC/MID	
	77	A10		
Hyde North	77	A10	MID/GC	
Hyde, Newton for	77	A10	MID/GC	
Hyde Road — see [Manchester]				

Station	Page	Block	Comp	Year of CL
Hykeham	28	H6	MID	
Hylton — see [Sunderland]				
Hyndland Form. Gt. Western Road	74	E7	NB	
Hyndland, Old	74	E7	NB	1960
Hythe (Essex)	13	E9	GE	
Hythe (Essex) — see also Colchester				
Hythe (Hampshire)	4	G4	SR	1966
Hythe (Hampshire)	4	G4	SR	
Hythe (Kent) Private	3	E5	RHD	
Hythe (Kent)	3	E5	SEC	1951
Ibrox — see [Glasgow]				
Ibstock — see Heather				
Ickenham Halt — see [London]				
Ickenham — see also [London] West Ruislip				
Icknield Port Road — see [West Midlands]				
Ide	9	A10	GW	1958
Idle — see [Bradford]				
Idmiston Halt	4	D8	SR	1968
Idridgehay	31	F5	MID	1947
	82	A3		
Iffley Halt — see [Oxford]				
Ifield Halt	2	D5	LBSC	
Ilderton	47	H2	NE	1930
Ilford	65	F6	GE	
Ilfracombe	8	A5	LSW	1970
[Ilkeston]				
Ilkeston Junction and Cossall 2nd, 1st — 1870	82	C2	MID	1967
Ilkeston North	82	C2	GN	1964
Ilkeston Town	82	C2	MID	1947
Ilkley	79	B2	O & I	
Ilkley	79	B2	MID	
Ilmer Halt	15	C7	GW/GC	1963
Ilminster	7	A5	GW	1962
Ilton Halt	7	A6	GW	1962
[Immingham]				
Immingham Dock	35	D4	GC/GI	1961
Immingham Dock	35	D4	GC	1969
Immingham Road Halt	35	D4	GC	1912
Immingham Town	35	D4	GC/GI	1961
Imperial Cottages Halt	56	G9	BR	1965
Ince and Elton (Cheshire)	77	E4	B HEAD	
Inchbare — see Stracathro				
Inchcoonans GDS	51	A5	CAL	1964
Inches	46	A3	CAL	1964
Inch Green GDS	49	B9	GSW	1961
Inchture	51	A6	CAL	1956
Inchture Village	51	A6	CAL	1917
Incline Top	78	E4	TV	1857
Ingatestone	12	H6	GE	
Ingersby	25	E9	GN	1957
Ingestre	31	B2	GN	1939
Ingestre — see also Weston				
Ingham	21	C2	GE	1953
Ingleby	38	H5	NE	1954
Ingleton 2nd, 1st — 1861	41	D1	MID	1954
Ingleton	41	D1	LNW	1917
Ingra Tor Halt	9	C6	GW	1956
Ingrow CL. 1962 R.O. 1968 T.O. from BR Private	79	D1	KWVR	
Ingrow East	79	D1	GN	1955
Innerleithen	46	G3	NB	1962
Innerpeffray	50	E5	CAL	1951
Innerwick	47	E9	NB	1951
Insch	54	G4	GNS	
Instow	8	D4	LSW	1965
Inveramsey	54	G6	GNS	1951
Inverbervie Form. Bervie	55	F7	NB	1951
Inveresk	46	H7	NB	1964
Invergarry	59	E8	HIGH/NB	1933
Invergloy Platform	59	F8	HIGH/NB	1933
Invergordon	56	D3	HR	
Invergowrie	51	B6	CAL	
Inverkeilor	51	F8	DA JT	1930
Inverkeithing	46	E9	NB	
Inverkip	49	A9	CAL	
Inverness	56	C6	HR	
Inverness Harbour	56	C6	HIGH	1867
Invershin	61	A1	HIGH	
Inverugie	54	D10	GNS	1965
Inverurie 2nd, 1st — 1902	54	H6	GNS	
Inworth	13	C9	GE	1951
Ipstones	31	C5	NS	1935
Ipswich 2nd, 1st — 1902	21	F5	GE	
Irchester	23	D1	MID	1960
Irlam and Cadishead 2nd, 1st — 1893	77	B7	CLC	
Irlams o' th' Height	76	G8	LY	1956
Iron Acton	17	D4	MID	1944

Station	Page	Block	Comp	Year of CL
Iron Acton	72	F9		
Iron Bridge and Broseley	27	G8	GW	1963
Irongray	45	D7	GSW	1943
Irthlingborough	23	C1	LNW	1964
Irton Road T.O. Private	40	E5	R & E	
Irvine	49	B4	GSW	
Irvine, Bank Street	49	B4	CAL	1930
Isfield	2	D3	LBSC	1963
Isham and Burton Latimer	25	H5	MID	1950
Isleham	23	C9	GE	1962
Isleworth and Spring Grove	64	A1	LSW	
	67	H10		
Islington — see Bovey				
Islington — see [London] Highbury				
Islip	13	H7	LNW	1968
Itchin Abbas	5	A8	LSW	1973
Iver	63	C3	GW	
Ivybridge	9	E7	GW	1959
Jackaments Bridge Halt	17	H5	GW	1948
Jacksfield Halt 2nd, 1st — 1954	27	H9	GW	1963
Jacksdale Form. Codnor Pk & Selston	82	C3	GN	1963
James Bridge — see [West Midlands] Darlaston				
Jamestown	49	D10	NB	1934
James Street — see [Liverpool]				
Jarrow 2nd, 1st — 1872	43	G3	NE	
	81	E2		
Jarrow	81	E2	NE	1872
Jarvis Brook — see Crowborough				
Jedburgh	42	F10	NB	1948
	47	D2		
Jedfoot Bridge	42	F10	NB	1948
	74	D2		
Jersey Marine	19	H2	RSB	1933
Jervaulx	38	C3	NE	1954
Jesmond	81	B3	NE	
Jessie Road Bridge Halt — see [Portsmouth]				
Jesson — see Holiday Camp				
Jocks Lodge — see [Edinburgh]				
John o' Gaunt	25	F10	GN/LNW	1957
Johnshaven	55	G7	NB	1951
Johnston	18	C3	GW	
Johnstone	74	A3	GSW	
Johnstone North 2nd, 1st — 1905	74	A4	GSW	1955
Johnstown and Hafod	33	H4	GW	1960
	72	D3		
Jones Drove GDS	22	H5	GE	1964
Joppa — see [Edinburgh]				
Jordanhill	74	D8	NB	
Jordanston Halt	18	F6	GW	1964
Jordanstone	51	A8	CAL	1951
Junction Road — see [Edinburgh]				
Junction Road — see [London]				
Junction Road for Hawkhurst	2	H4	KES	1954
Juniper Green — see [Edinburgh]				
Justinhaugh	51	D9	CAL	1952
	55	H2		
Keadby	34	H3	MS & L	1874
Kearsley Form. Stoneclough	76	F7	LY	
Kearsney	3	G7	SEC	
Keele	30	H4	NS	1956
Kegworth	28	C2	MID	1968
Keighley	37	D7	MID	
	79	C1		
Keighley South GDS	79	C1	GN	1961
Keinton Mandeville	7	D7	GW	1962
Keith Junction Station	54	D2	GNS	
Keith Town	54	D2	GNS	1968
Kelmarsh	25	F6	LNW	1960
Kelmscott and Langford	14	E6	GW	1962
Kelso	47	E3	NB	1964
Kelston for Saltford	17	D1	MID	1949
Kelton Fell	40	D7	CWJC	1922
Kelty	50	H1	NB	1930
Kelvedon	13	C8	GE	
Kelvedon Low Level	13	C8	GE	1951
Kelvin Bridge — see [Glasgow]				
Kelvin Hall — see [Glasgow]				
Kelvinside — see [Glasgow]				
Kemble Junction	14	A5	GW	
	17	H5		
Kemney	55	A6	GNS	1950
Kempston and Elstow Halt	23	E2	LNW	1941
Kempston Hardwick Halt	23	F1	LNW	
Kempton Park*	67	F7	LSW	
Kemsing	70	E1	SEC	
Kemsley	3	B9	SEC	
Kemsley Down Form. Paper Mill T.O. Private	3	B9	S & K	

Station	Page	Block	Comp	Year of CL
Kendal	41	A4	LNW	
Kenfig Hill	78	F2	GW	1958
Kenilworth	24	H5	LNW	1965
	80	G10		
Kenley for Riddlesdown	69	A2	SEC	
Kennethmont	54	G6	GNS	1968
Kennett (Cambs)	23	C10	GE	
Kennett — see Clackmannan				
Kennishead	74	E2	GBK JT	
Kennoway GDS	51	C3	NB	1964
Kensal Green	64	E4	LNW	
Kensal Rise	64	E4	LNW	
Kensington Olympia	64	E2	WL	
Kensington — see also [London]				
Kentallen	53	A9	CAL	1966
Kent House (Beckenham)	69	B6	SEC	
Kentish Town	64	H5	LNW	
Kentish Town West	64	H5	MID	
Kenton (Suffolk)	21	D6	MSL	1952
Kenton (Middx)	64	B7	LNW	
Kenton Bank (Northumberland)	81	D5	NE	1929
Kenton South (Middx)	64	B6	LNW	
Kents Bank	40	H2	FUR	
Kenwith Castle Halt	8	D4	BWA	1917
Kenyon Junction	76	H6	LNW	1961
Kerne Bridge for Goodrich Castle	17	C8	GW	1959
Kerry	27	A7	CAM	1931
Kershope Foot	42	D5	NB	1969
Keswick for Derwentwater	40	G7	CKP	1972
Ketley	27	G10	GW	1962
Ketley Town Halt	27	G10	GW	1962
Kettering for Corby	25	G6	MID	
Kettleness	39	C6	NE	1958
Ketton and Collyweston	22	F1	LNW	1966
Kew — see [London]				
Kew Bridge	64	C2	LSW	
	68	B10		
Kew Bridge — see also [London]				
Kew Gardens (London)	64	C1	LSW	
Kew Gardens (Lancashire) — see [Southport]				
Kexby — see Dunnington				
Keyham	9	E4	GW	
Keyingham	35	E5	NE	1964
Keymer Junction — see Wivelsfield				
Keynsham and Somerdale	17	D2	GW	
	72	E6		
Kibworth	25	E8	MID	1968
Kidbrooke	65	E1	SEC	
	69	E9		
Kidderminster	80	G2	GW	
Kidlington	14	H8	GW	1964
[Kidsgrove]				
Kidsgrove Form. Harecastle	31	A5	NS	
	73	B9		
Kidsgrove, Liverpool Road	31	A5	NS	1964
	73	B9		
Kidsgrove, Market Street Halt	73	B9	NS	1950
Kidwelly	19	D3	GW	
Kielder Forest	42	F6	NB	1956
Kilbagie	46	B10	NB	1930
	50	E1		
Kilbarchan	49	C7	GSW	1966
	74	A3		
Kilbirnie	49	B6	GSW	1966
Kilbirnie South	49	B6	CAL	1930
Kilbowie	74	B8	CAL	1964
Kilbowie	74	B8	NB	1907
Kilburn (Derbyshire)	82	B3	MID	1930
Kilburn — see [London]				
Kilburn High Road Form. Kilburn and Maida Vale	64	F4	LNW	
Kilconquhar	51	D2	NB	1965
Kildale	38	H5	NE	
Kildary	56	C4	HIGH	1960
Kildonan	61	E4	HIGH	
	62	A3		
Kildrummie	56	E5	I & N	1858
Kildwick and Crosshills 2nd, 1st — 1889	79	C1	MID	1965
Kilgerran Halt	19	A8	GW	1962
Kilgetty	18	H3	GW	
Kilkerran	44	E10	GSW	1965
Killamarsh Central	28	B8	GC	1963
	82	D7		
Killamarsh West 2nd, 1st — 1843	82	D7	MID	1954
Killay	19	F1	LNW	1964
Killearn	49	E10	NB	1951
Killiecrankie Pass	50	E10	HIGH	1965
Killin	50	A7	CAL	1965

Station	Page	Block	Comp	Year of CL
	53	H5		
Killin Jcn. 2nd, 1st — 1886	50	A7	CAL	1965
Killingholme Halt	35	D4	GC	1963
Killingworth	81	D5	NE	1958
Killochan	44	D9	GSW	1951
Killywhan	45	D5	GSW	1959
Kilmacolm	49	C8	GSW	
Kilmany	51	C5	NB	1951
[Kilmarnock]				
Kilmarnock	49	D4	GSW	
Riccarton GDS	49	D4	GSW	1965
Station	49	D4	GPKA	1846
Kilmaurs	49	C5	GBK JT	1966
Kilnhurst Central 2nd, 1st — 1871	34	C2	GC	1968
	82	E9		
Kilnhurst West 2nd, 1st — 1851	34	C2	MID	1968
	82	E9		
Kiln Lane Crossing (Stallingboro)	35	D4	GC(GI)	1961
Kilpatrick	74	A8	NB	
Kilsby and Crick	25	D5	LNW	1960
Kilsyth New	75	E10	KB	1935
Kilsyth Old	75	E10	NB	1951
Kilwinning	49	B5	GSW/CAL	
Kilwinning East	49	B5	CAL	1932
Kimberley East (Notts)	28	C4	GN	1964
	82	D3		
Kimberley West (Notts)	28	C4	MID	1917
	82	D3		
Kimberley Park (Norfolk)	20	G6	GE	1969
Kimbolton	23	C2	MID	1959
Kinaldie	55	A7	GNS	1964
Kinbrace	61	E5	HIGH	
	62	A5		
Kinbuck	50	C3	CAL	1956
Kincardine	46	C10	NB	1930
	50	E1		
Kincraig Form. Boat of Insh	57	D5	HIGH	1965
Kineton	25	A2	EWJ/SHJ	1952
Kinfauns	50	H5	CAL	1950
King Edward	54	C6	GNS	1951
Kingennie	51	D7	CAL	1955
Kingham	14	D9	GW	
Kinghorn	46	G10	NB	
	50	A1		
Kingbarns	51	E4	NB	1930
Kingsbridge	9	F8	GW	1963
Kingsbury	24	G8	MID	1968
	80	C9		
Kings Cliffe	22	G1	LNW	1966
Kingscote	2	C5	LBSC	1955
King's Cross — see [London]				
King's Ferry Bridge Halt	3	B9	SR	1923
	13	B10		
Kings Heath — see [West Midlands]				
Kingshouse Platform	50	A4	CAL	1965
	53	H4		
Kings Inch — see [Renfrew]				
Kingskerswell	9	C10	GW	1964
Kingskettle	51	B3	NB	1967
Kingsknowe — see [Edinburgh]				
Kingsland (Hereford)	27	E3	GW	1955
Kingsland — see [London]				
King's Langley and Abbots Langley	15	G6	LNW	
Kingsley and Froghall	31	C4	NS	1965
Kingsley Halt	5	D8	LSW	1957
King's Lynn 2nd, 1st — 1871	22	E9	GE	
King's Lynn Harbour GDS	22	E9	GE	1968
Kingsmuir	51	D8	CAL	1955
Kings Norton	80	F5	MID	
King's Nympton Form. South Molton Rd	8	E7	LSW	
Kings Park	74	H3	CAL	
King's Sutton	14	H10	GW	
Kingston 2nd, 1st — 1934	68	B6	LSW	
Kingston Crossing Halt	15	C6	GW	1957
Kingston-on-Sea	2	A2	LBSC	1879
Kingston Road	16	H2	WCP	1940
Kingswear Ferry — see Dartmouth				
Kingswood and Burgh Heath	68	E1	SEC	
Kingsworthy	4	H7	GW	1960
Kingthorne	29	C7	GN	1951
Kington 2nd, 1st — 1875	27	C3	GW	1955
King Tor Halt	9	C6	GW	1956
Kingussie	57	D4	HIGH	
King William GDS	76	D6	LY	1939
Kinloch Rannoch — see Rannoch				
Kinloss 3rd, 1st — 1860, 2nd — 1904	56	E8	HIGH	1965
Kinmel Bay Halt	33	D9	LNW/LMS	1939
Kinnerley Junction Station	27	C10	PSNW/SM	1933
	33	H1		

Station	Page	Block	Comp	Year of CL
Kinnersley	27	C2	MID	1962
Kinnerton	72	E5	LNW	1962
	77	H2		
Kinniel	46	C9	NB	1930
Kinross on site of Loch Leven	50	G3	KIN	1860
Kinross Junction Station	50	G2	NB	1970
Kintbury	14	F2	GW	
Kintore	54	H7	GNS	1964
Kipling Cotes	35	A7	NE	1965
Kippax	79	E8	NE	1951
Kippen	50	B2	NB	1934
Kirby or Black Bull	39	B2	YNM	1847
Kirby Cross	13	G9	GE	
Kirby Moorside	39	B2	NE	1953
Kirby Muxloe	25	C9	MID	1964
Kirby Park	77	C1	B HEAD	1954
Kirkandrews	42	C2	NB	1964
Kirkbank	47	D3	NB	1948
Kirkbride	42	A2	NB	1964
Kirkbuddo	51	D8	CAL	1955
Kirkburton	37	E4	LNW	1930
	79	H4		
Kirkby	76	F2	LY	
Kirkby Bentinck and Pinxton	82	E4	GC	1963
Kirkby-in-Ashfield Central	82	E4	GC	1956
Kirkby-in-Ashfield East	82	E4	MID	1965
Kirkby-in-Furness	40	F3	FUR	
Kirkby Lonsdale	41	C2	LNW	1954
Kirkby Lonsdale — see also Arkholme				
Kirkby Stephen East	41	E6	NE	1962
Kirkby Stephen West* Form. Kirkby Stephen and Ravenstonedale	41	E6	MID	1970
Kirkby Thorpe	41	C7	NE	1953
Kirkcaldy	46	G10	NB	
	50	A1		
Kirkconnel	49	H1	GSW	
Kirkcowen	44	E4	PPW JT	1965
Kirkcudbright	45	B3	GSW	1965
Kirkdale	76	G1	LY	
Kirk Ella — see Willerby				
Kirkgate — see [Wakefield]				
Kirkgunzeon	45	D5	GSW	1950
Kirkham Abbey	34	F10	NE	1930
Kirkham and Wesham	36	D6	PW JT	
	76	B3		
Kirkheaton — see [Huddersfield]				
Kirkhill	75	A4	CAL	
Kirkinch	51	B8	SCMJ	1847
Kirkinner	44	G3	PPW JT	1950
Kirkintilloch 2nd, 1st — 1847	49	G9	NB	1964
	75	B9		
Kirkintilloch Basin	75	B9	MK	1846
Kirkland	45	D7	GSW	1943
Kirklee — see [Glasgow]				
Kirklington and Edingley	28	E5	MID	1929
Kirkliston	46	E8	NB	1930
Kirknewton	47	G3	NE	1930
Kirkoswald — see Lazonby				
Kirkpatrick	42	B4	CAL	1960
Kirkseaton Crossing	40	E2	WFJ	1857
Kirk Smeaton	34	D3	HB	1932
Kirkstall — see [Leeds]				
Kirkstall Forge — see [Leeds]				
Kirkstead — see Woodhall Junction				
Kirkton Bridge Halt	54	B9	GNS	1965
Kirriemuir	51	C9	CAL	1952
	55	H1		
Kirriemuir Junction	51	C9	SCNE	1864
Kirtlebridge	42	A4	CAL	1960
Kirton	22	C5	GN	1961
	29	E3		
Kirton Lindsey	35	A2	GC	
Kissthorns	34	F9	SHLT	1930
Kittybrewster — see [Aberdeen]				
Kiveton Bridge	82	E8	GC	
Kiveton Park	82	E8	GC	
Knapton	39	C1	NE	1930
Knaresborough	37	H9	YNM	1851
Knaresborough	37	H9	NE	
Knebworth	12	C9	GN	
Knighton	27	C5	LNW	
Knightwick	24	A3	GW	1964
Knitsley	38	B10	NE	1939
	43	E1		
Knock	54	D3	GNS	1968
Knockholt	69	H3	SEC	
Knockando	56	G9	GNS	1965
Knott End	76	A2	KE	1930
Knottingley for Ferrybridge	79	F10	LY/GN	
Knott Mill — see [Manchester] Deansgate				
Knott Mill and Deansgate — see [Manchester]				
Knotty Ash and Stanley — see [Liverpool]				
Knowesgate	43	B5	NB	1952
Knoweside	49	A1	GSW	1930
Knowle — see Dorridge				
Knowle Halt	8	C5	LSW	1964
Knowles Level Crossing Halt	76	D7	LY	1918
Knowlsley Street — see [Bury]				
Knowlton	3	G8	EK	1948
Knucklas	27	C5	LNW	
Knutsford	30	H8	CLC	
	77	E7		
Knutsford — see also Chelsford				
Knutton Halt	73	B7	NS	1926
Knypersley Halt	31	B6	NS	1927
	73	C8		
Kyle of Lochalsh	59	A2	HR	
Lacock Halt	17	G2	GW	1966
Ladbrook Grove — see [London]				
Lade Halt	3	D4	RHD	
Ladmanlow	31	D7	LNW	1877
Ladybank	51	B3	NB	
Ladylands Platform	50	B2	NB	1934
Ladysbridge	54	C4	GNS	1964
Ladywell	69	C8	SEC	
Laindon	12	H4	MID	
Laira Green — see [Plymouth]				
Laira Halt — see [Plymouth]				
Lairg	61	A2	SEC	
Laisterdyke — see [Bradford]				
Lakenheath	23	A10	GE	
Lakeside	40	H3	FUR	1946
Lakeside R.O. PR. FR. CL. above	40	H3	L & H	
Lakeside — see also Windermere				
Lamancha	46	F5	NB	1933
Lambley	42	G2	NE	1976
Lambourn	14	F3	GW	1960
Lamb's Cottage	76	G7	LM	1842
Lamesley	81	B1	NE	1945
Lamington	46	C3	CAL	1965
Lampeter	19	F8	GW	1956
	26	B2		
Lamphey	19	G2	GW	
Lamplugh	40	D7	WCE JT	1931
Lamport	25	F5	LNW	1960
Lanark	46	B4	CAL	
[Lancaster]				
Lancaster Castle	36	D9	LNW	
Greaves	36	D9	LPJ	1849
Green Ayre	36	D9	MID	1966
Lanchester	38	B10	NE	1939
Lancing	2	A1	LBSC	
Landore High Level — see [Swansea]				
Landore Low Level — see [Swansea]				
Lands	38	C8	NE	1872
Landywood Halt	24	D9	LNW	1916
Langbank	49	D9	CAL	
Langford (Wilts)	4	C8	GW	1857
Langford (Somerset)	17	A1	GW	1931
Langford and Ulting (Essex)	13	B7	GE	1964
Langho	76	B6	LY	1956
Langholm	42	C5	NB	1964
Langley (Northumberland)	42	H3	NE	1930
Langley (Bucks)	15	F3	GW	
	63	B3		
Langley Green and Rood End	80	D4	GW	
Langley Mill and Eastwood	82	C3	MID	1967
Langloan	75	E5	CAL	1964
Langport East	7	B7	GW	1962
Langport West	7	B7	GW	1964
Langrick	22	A5	GN	1963
	29	D4		
Langside and Newlands	74	G3	CAL	
Langston	5	C4	LBSC	1963
Langwathby*	41	B9	MID	1970
Langwith	82	F7	MID	1964
Langworth for Wragby	29	B7	GC	1965
Lapford	6	A4	LSW	
	8	F8		
Lapworth	80	G8	GW	
Larbert	46	B9	CAL	
Largo	51	D2	NB	1965
Largoward GDS	51	E3	NB	1964
Largs	49	A7	GSW	
Larkhall Central	46	A6	CAL	1965
	75	F1		
Larkhall East	46	A6	CAL	1951

Station	Page	Block	Comp	Year of CL
	75	F1		
Lartington	38	A7	NE	1962
	41	H7		
Lasham — see Bentworth				
Lasswade	83	F3	NB	1951
Latchford — see [Warrington]				
Latchley Halt	9	C4	PDSW	1966
	11	F8		
Latimer Road — see [London]				
Lauder	47	B5	NB	1932
Laughton — see Dinnington				
Launceston North	9	A3	GW	1952
	11	E10		
Launceston South	9	A3	LSW	1966
	11	E10		
Launton	15	A9	LNW	1968
Laurencekirk	55	F6	CAL	1967
Lauriston	51	H10	NB	1951
	55	G7		
Lavant	5	E5	LBSC	1935
Lavenham	21	F2	GE	1961
Lavernock	78	H6	TV	1968
Laverton Halt	14	B10	GW	1960
Lavington	4	B10	GW	1966
Law Junction Station	46	A5	CAL	1965
Lawley Bank	27	G9	GW	1962
Lawley Street — see [West Midlands] Birmingham				
Lawrence Hill	17	C2	GW	
	72	D7		
Lawton	73	B9	NS	1930
Laxfield	21	B7	MSL	1952
Layerthorpe* — see [York]				
Layton Form. Bispham	76	A1	PW JT	
Lazenby — see [Teeside]				
Lazonby and Kirkoswald*	41	B10	MID	1970
Lea	28	G9	GN/GE	1957
Lea Bridge	65	C6	GE	
Leadburn	46	F6	NB	1955
Leadenham	29	A5	GN	1965
Leadgate	43	E1	NE	1955
Leadhills	46	B1	CAL	1939
Leagrave	12	A9	MID	
Lea Green	76	H4	LNW	1955
Lea Hill	80	D7	LNW	
Lealholm	39	B6	NE	
Leamington Spa, Avenue	80	H10	LNW	1965
Leamington Spa, General	25	A4	GW	
	80	H10		
Leamside	38	D10	NE	
	43	G1		
Lea Road (Lancs)	76	B3	PW JT	1938
Lea Road — see Gainsborough				
Leasingthorne	38	D8	NE	1867
Leason Hill	51	B8	SCMJ	1847
Leasowe	77	B1	WIRRAL	
Leasowe Crossing — see [Wallasey]				
[Leatherhead]				
Leatherhead	68	A1	LSW/LBSC	1869
Leatherhead	68	A1	LSW	1927
Leatherhead	68	A1	LBSC	
Leaton	27	E10	GW	1960
Lechlade	14	D6	GW	1962
Leckhampton — see [Cheltenham]				
Ledbury	17	E10	GW	
	24	A1		
Ledbury Town Halt	17	E10	GW	1959
	24	A1		
Ledsham	77	E3	B HEAD	1959
Ledstone	79	F9	NE	1951
Lee for Burnt Ash	69	D9	SEC	
Leebotwood	27	E8	SH JT	1958
[Leeds]				
Armley Canal Road	79	D5	MID	1965
Armley Moor Form. Armley and Wortley	79	D5	GN	1966
Beeston	79	E5	GN	1953
Bramley	79	D5	GN	1966
Central	79	D6	JOINT	1967
Farnley and Wortley	79	D5	LNW	1952
Halton Dial	79	D7	NE	1864
Headingley	79	D5	NE	
Holbeck High Level	79	D6	GN	1958
Holbeck Low Level 2nd, 1st — 1862	79	D6	MID	1958
Hunslet 2nd, 1st — 1873	79	D6	MID	1960
Hunslet Lane	79	D6	MID	1851
Kirkstall	79	D5	MID	1965
Kirkstall Forge	79	C4	MID	1905

Station	Page	Block	Comp	Year of CL
Leeds City	79	D5		
Manston	79	D6	NE	1869
Marsh Lane 2nd, 1st — 1869	79	D6	NE	1958
Newlay and Horsforth	79	C4	MID	1965
Osmondthorpe Halt	79	D5	LNE	1960
Penda's Way	79	D8	LNE	1964
Royal Gardens	79	D5	NE	1857
Wellington	79	D6	MID	1850
Woodside	79	D5	LN/NE	1864
Wortley and Farnley	79	D5	LNW	1882
Leegate	42	A1	MC	1950
Leek	31	C5	NS	1965
Leek Brook Halt	31	C5	NS	1956
Leeming Bar	38	D3	NE	1954
Lee-on-the-Solent	5	A4	LSW	1931
Lees	76	F10	LNW	1955
Legacy	72	C2	GW	1931
Legbourne Road	29	E9	GN	1953
[Leicester]				
Belgrave and Birstall	25	D9	GC	1963
Belgrave Road	25	D9	GN	1957
Braunston	25	D9	MID	1859
Central	25	D9	GC	1969
Humberstone	25	D9	GN	1957
Humberstone Road	25	D9	MID	1968
Leicester	25	D9	MID	
Welford Road	25	D9	MID	1918
West Bridge 2nd, 1st — 1893	25	D9	MID	1928
Leigh (Kent)	2	E7	SEC	
Leigh (Staffs)	31	C3	NS	1966
Leigh and Bedford (Lancs)	36	G3	LNW	1963
	76	G6		
Leigh Court	24	A3	GW	1964
Leigh-on-Sea 2nd, 1st — 1934	13	C4	LMS	
Leighton Buzzard 2nd, 1st — 1859	15	E9	LNW	
Leire Halt	25	C7	LMS	1962
Leiston	21	D9	GE	1966
Leith — see [Edinburgh]				
Leith North — see [Edinburgh]				
Leith Walk — see [Edinburgh]				
Lelant	10	C3	GW	
Leman Street — see [London]				
Lemington	43	E3	NE	1958
Lemsford Road Halt	12	C8	GN	1951
Lenham	3	B7	SEC	
Lennoxtown	49	F9	NB	1951
	75	A10		
Lennoxtown Old	75	A10	NB	1881
Lenton — see [Nottingham]				
Lentran	56	F2	HIGH	1960
Lenwade	20	E5	MGN	1959
Lenzie Junction for Garngaber Junc.	49	F8	NB	
	75	B9		
Leominster	27	F3	SH JT	
Lepton — see Fenay Bridge				
Lesbury	43	E9	YNB	1851
Leslie	51	A3	NB	1932
Lesmahagow	46	A4	CAL	1965
Letchworth 2nd, 1st — 1913	23	H4	GN	
Letham Grange	51	F8	NB	1930
Lethenty	54	G6	GNS	1931
Letterston	18	F6	GW	1937
Leuchars Junction 2nd, 1st — 1878	51	D5	NB	
Leuchars Old	51	D5	NB	1921
Leven 2nd, 1st — 1857				
Levenshulme and Burbage	77	B9	LNW	
Levenshulme — see also [Manchester]				
Leverton	28	F8	GC	1959
Levisham	39	B4	NE	1965
Levisham R.O. PR. FR. CL. above	39	B4	NYM	
Lewiefield Halt	42	F6	LNE	1956
[Lewes]				
Ham Platform	2	C2	LBSC	1857
Lewes 3rd, 1st — 1857, 2nd — 1889	2	C2	LBSC	
Pinwell Platform	2	C2	LBSC	1857
Lewisham	65	D1	SEC	
	69	C9		
Lewisham Road — see [London]				
Lewis Road Halt — see [Brighton]				
Lewistown Halt	78	E3	GW	1951
Lewknor Bridge Halt	15	B5	GW	1957
Leyburn	38	B3	NE	1954
Leycett	30	H4	NS	1931
Leyland	36	E5	NU JT	
	76	C4		
Leysdown	3	C10	SEC	1950
Leysmill	51	F8	CAL	1955
Leyton, Goddall Road — see [London]				
Leyton, Midland Road	65	D7	MID	

Station	Page	Block	Comp	Year of CL
Leytonstone High Road	65	E6	MID	
Leytonstone — see also [London]				
Lhanbryde	56	E10	HIGH	1960
[Lichfield]				
Lichfield	80	A7	LNW	1871
Lichfield City 2nd, 1st — 1884	24	F9	LNW	
	80	A7		
Trent Valley Low Level	24	F9	LNW	
	80	A7		
Trent Valley High Level	80	A7	LNW	1965
Trent Valley Junction	80	A7	LNW	1871
Liddaton Halt	9	B5	GW	1962
Lidlington	23	G1	LNW	
Liff — see [Dundee]				
Lifford — see [West Midlands]				
Lifton	9	A4	GW	1962
	11	F10		
Lightcliffe	79	F2	LY	1965
Lightmoor	27	G9	GW	1864
Lightmoor Halt	27	G9	GW	1962
Lilbourne	25	C6	LNW	1966
Limehouse — see [London]				
Lime Street — see [Liverpool]				
Limpet Mill	55	B8	ABER	1850
Limpley Stoke	17	E1	GW	1966
Limpsfield — see [Oxford] Oxford				
Linacre Road	76	G1	LY	1951
Linby	28	C5	GN	1916
	82	E4		
Linby	82	E4	MID	1964
[Lincoln]				
Lincoln Central Form. High Street	29	A7	GN	
Lincoln East GDS	29	A7	GC	1965
Lincoln St Marks	29	A7	MID	
Lincoln West GDS	29	A7	GC	1965
Lindal	40	F2	FUR	1951
Lindean	47	B3	NB	1951
Lindores 2nd, 1st — 1847	51	A4	NB	1951
Linefoot	40	D9	CW JT	1908
	45	G1		
Lingfield	2	C7	LBSC	
Lingwood	20	F8	GE	
Linksfield Crossing	56	D10	GNS	1859
Linkley Halt	24	A8	GW	1963
	27	H8		
Linlithgow	46	C9	NB	
Lintmill Hall	48		CM	1931
Linton	23	F8	GE	1967
Lintz Green	43	E2	NE	1953
Linwood GDS	49	D8	CAL	1967
	74	B4		
Lions Holt Halt — see [Exeter]				
Liphook	5	D6	LSW	
Lipson Vale Halt — see [Plymouth]				
Liscard and Poulton — see [Wallasey]				
Liskeard	9	D2	GW/LL	
	11	D7		
Liskeard, Moorswater	9	D2	GW/LL	1901
	11	D7		
Liss	5	D6	LSW	
Litchfield	4	H10	GW	1960
Litherland — see Seaforth				
Littleborough	37	B4	LY	
	76	D10		
Little Bytham	22	E1	ELB	1871
	29	A1		
Little Bytham	22	E1	GN	1959
	29	A1		
Little Drayton Halt	30	F2	GW	1941
Little Eaton	31	G4	MID	1930
	82	B2		
Littleham	6	D1	LSW	1967
Littlehampton	5	G4	LBSC	
Littlehampton GDS	5	G4	LBSC	1970
Littlehaven Halt	2	A5	LBSC	
Little Hulton	76	G7	LNW	1954
Little Kimble	15	C7	GW/GC	
Little Mill	43	E10	NE	1958
Little Mill Junction	78	C10	WM/GC	1955
Littlemoor — see [Oxford]				
Littleport	23	A8	GE	
Little Salkeld	41	B9		1970
Little Somerford	14	A4	GW	1961
	17	H4		
Little Steeping	29	F6	GN	1961
Littleston-on-Sea — see New Romney				
Little Stretton Halt	27	E7	SH JT	1958
Little Sutton	77	E3	B HEAD	
Littleton and Badsey	24	E2	GW	1966

Station	Page	Block	Comp	Year of CL
Little Weighton	35	A6	HB	1955
Littleworth	22	E3	GN	1961
Litton Mill Crossing — see [Warrington] White Cross				
[Liverpool]				
Aigburth, Mersey Road and	77	C2	BR	
Allerton for Garston	77	C3	CLC	
Allerton West	77	C3	LNW	
Bank Hall	76	G1	LY	
Breck Road	76	H1	LNW	1948
Broad Green	76	H2	LNW	
Brunswick	76	H1	CLC	
Canada Dock	76	G1	LNW	1941
Central	76	H1	CLC/MER	
Central High Level	76	H1	CLC	1972
Childwall	76	H3	CLC	1931
Church Road, Garston	77	D2	LNW	1939
Clubmoor	76	G2	CLC	1960
Cressington and Grassendale	77	D2	CLC	1972
Cressington R.O. by BR FR. CL. above	77	D2	BR	
Crown Street	76	H1	LM	1836
Edge Hill	76	H2	LNW	
Edge Lane	76	H1	LNW	1948
Exchange	77	B1	LY	1977
Garston — see Allerton				
Garston	77	D3	CLC	1972
Garston R.O. by BR FR. CL. above	77	D3	BR	
Garston Dock Station	77	D2	LNW	1947
Gateacre	77	C3	CLC	1972
Great Howard Street	76	H1	LY/EL	1850
Hunts Cross	77	C3	CLC	
Huskisson	76	H1	CLC	1885
James Street	76	H1	CLC	
Kirkdale	76	G1	LY	
Knotty Ash and Stanley	76	H3	CLC	1960
Lime Street	76	H1	LNW	
Millers Bridge	76	G1	LY	1876
Mersey Road and Aigburth R.O. by BR as Aigburth	77	C2	CLC BR	1972
Moorfields	76	H1	LY	
Mossley Hill 2nd, 1st — 1891	77	C3	LNW	
North Docks GDS	76	H1	LY	1966
Otterspool	77	C2	CLC	1951
Park Lane GDS	77	H1	LNW	1965
Riverside	76	H1	MDHB	1971
St James	76	H1	CLC	1917
St Michael's	76	H1	CLC	1972
	77	C2		
St Michaels R.O. by BR FR. CL. above	77	C2	BR	
Sandhills for North Dock	76	G1	LY	
Sefton Park	77	C3	LNW	1960
Spellow	76	G1	LNW	1948
Stanley	76	H2	LNW	1948
Tue Brook	76	G2	LNW	1948
Walton and Anfield	76	G2	LNW	1948
Walton-on-the-Hill	76	G2	CLC	1918
Warbreck	76	G2	CLC	1960
Wavertree	76	H2	LNW	1858
Wavertree Lane	76	H2	LM	circa 1838
West Allerton — see Allerton West				
West Derby	76	G2	CLC	1960
Liverpool Road — see [Cheltenham]				
Liverpool Road — see [London]				
Liverpool Road — see [Manchester]				
Liverpool Road Halt — see [Kidsgrove]				
Liversedge	79	G4	LY	1965
Liversedge Spen	79	G4	LNW	1953
Livingstone	46	D7	NB	1948
Llafar Halt	33	A3	GW	1960
Llanaber Halt	26	B10	GW	
Llanarthney Halt	19	E5	LNW	1963
Llanbadarn	26	B6	CAM	
Llanbedr and Pensarn	32	G2	CAM	
Llanbedr Gogh	32	F8	LNW	1930
Llanberis	32	G6	LNW	1930
Llanberis Gilfach Ddu	32	G6	LL	
Llanberis	32	G6	SMR	
Llanberthy Platform	78	H4	TV	1920
Llanbister Road	27	A5	LNW	
Llanbradach	78	E6	RHY	
Llanbrynmair	26	F8	CAM	1965
Llancaiach — see Nelson				
Llandaff (for Whitchurch)	78	G6	TV	
Llandanwg Halt	32	G2	CAM	
Llandarcy Platform	78	E1	CW	1947
Llanderfel	33	C3	GW	1964
Llandecwyn Halt	32	G3	GW	
Llandenny	17	A6	GW	1955
Llandeilo	19	F5	GW	

Station	Page	Block	Comp	Year of CL
Llandilo Bridge	19	F5	LNW	1963
Llandinam	26	G7	CAM	1962
Llandogo Halt	17	B6	GW	1959
Llandogo — see also St Briavels				
Llandough Platform	78	H6	TV	1918
Llandovery	16	A10	LNW	
	19	H7		
Llandow Halt	78	H2	BARRY	1964
Llandow (Wick Road) Halt	78	H2	GW	1964
Llandre Form. Llanfihangel	26	B6	CAM	1965
Llandrillo	33	D3	GW	1964
Llandrindod Wells	26	H3	LNW	
Llandrinio Road	27	C10	PSNW/SM	1932
[Llandudno]				
Llandudno	33	A8	LNW	
Llandudno Junction	33	A8	LNW	
Llandudno Victoria	33	A8	GO	
Llandulas	33	C8	LNW	1952
Llandybie	19	F4	GW	
Llandysill	19	D8	LNW	1952
[Llanelli]				
Llanelli 2nd	19	E2	GW	
Llanelli 1st	19	E2	GW	1879
Llanelli Dock	19	E2		1879
Llanerch-Ayron Halt	19	D10	GW	1951
Llanerch-y-Medd	32	E9	LNW	1964
Llanfabon Road Halt	78	D5	TV	1932
Llanfair 2nd, 1st — 1966	26	H9	BR	
Llanfair Caereinion	26	H9	CAM	1931
Llanfair Caereinion R.O. PR. FR. CL. above	26	H9	W & L	
Llanfairfechan	32	H7	LNW	
Llanfairpwll	32	F7	LNW	
Llanfalteg	19	A5	GW	1962
Llanfaredd Halt	26	H2	GW	1962
Llanfechain	30	A1	CAM	1965
	33	F1		
Llanfihangel — see Llandre				
Llanfyllin	33	F1	CAM	1965
Llanfynydd	30	B6	WM JT	1950
	72	C4		
Llanfyrnach	19	A7	GW	1962
Llangadog	19	G6	VT JT	
Llangammarch Wells	26	F1	LNW	
Llangedwyn	30	A1	CAM	1951
	33	F1		
Llangefni	32	E6	LNW	1964
Llangeinor	78	E2	GW	1953
Llangeinor — see also Bettws				
Llangelynin Halt	26	B9	GW	
Llangennech	19	F2	GW	
Llanglydwen	19	A6	GW	1962
Llangollen	33	F4	GW	1965
Llangollen Road	72	D1	GW	1852
Llangonoyd — see Llangynyd				
Llangorse Lake Halt	16	E9	GW	1962
Llangower Halt	33	B3	GW	1965
Llangower R.O. PR. FR. CL. above	33	B5	BLR	
Llangunllo	27	B5	LNW	
Llangwyllog	32	E8	LNW	1964
Llangybi (Cardigan)	26	B2	GW	1965
Llangybi (Caernarvon)	32	E3	LNW	1964
Llangyfelach	19	G2	GW	1924
Llangynog	33	E2	CAM	1951
Llangynwyd Form. Llangonoyd	78	E2	GW	1970
Llanharan	78	F3	GW	1964
Llanharry	78	G4	TV	1951
Llanhilleth	78	C8	GW	1962
Llandiloes 2nd, 1st — 1862	26	G6	CAM	1962
Llanilar	26	B5	GW	1964
Llanion Halt	18	F3	GW	1908
Llanishen	78	F6	RHY	
Llanmorlais	19	E2	LNW	1931
Llanpumpsaint	19	D6	GW	1965
Llanrhaiadr	33	E6	LNW	1953
Llanrhaiadr Mochnant	33	F1	CAM	1951
Llanrhystyd Road	26	B5	GW	1964
Llanrwst and Trefriw 2nd, 1st — 1868	33	A6	LNW	
Llansantffraid	30	A1	CAM	1965
	33	F1		
Llansilin Road	30	A1	CAM	1951
	33	F1		
Llansimlet — see [Swansea]				
Llanstephen Crossing Halt	27	A1	GW	1925
Llanstephen Halt	27	A1	GW	1962
Llantarnam 2nd, 1st — 1880	78	E10	GW	1962
Llantrisant	78	F4	TV	1951
Llantrisant	78	F4	GW	1964
Llantwit Fadre	78	F4	TV	1952
Llantwit Major	78	H3	BARRY	1964
Llanuwchllyn	33	B2	GW	1965
Llanuwchllyn R.O. PR. FR. CL. above	33	B5	BLR	
Llanvihangel	16	H8	GW	1958
Llanwern	16	H4	GW	1960
Llanwnda	32	E6	NANT/LNW	1964
Llanwrda (Carmarthan)	19	G6	VT JT	
Llanwrtyd Wells	26	F1	LNW	
Llanyblodwell	30	A1	CAM	1931
	33	G1		
Llanybyther	19	E8	GW	1965
	26	A1		
Llanycefn	18	H5	NRM/GW	1937
Llanymynech	33	H1	CAM	1967
Llanymynech Junction Sta.	33	H1	PSNW/SM	1930
Llay — see Gresford				
Lletty Brongu	78	E2	PT	1932
Lliwdy	26	D9	CORRIS	1931
Llong	33	G6	LNW	1962
	72	C5		
Llwydcoed	78	B3	GW	1962
Llwyngwern	26	D9	CORRIS	1931
Llwyngwril	26	B9	CAM	
Llwynypia	78	D3	TV	
Llynclys	33	H1	CAM	1965
Llyn Ystradau	32	H5	FEST	
Llys Halt	33	B2	GW	1965
Llysfaen	33	C8	LNW	1931
Llyswen — see Boughrood				
Loanhead	46	G7	NB	1933
	83	F3		
Lochailort	59	G2	NB	
Lochanhead	45	D5	GSW	1939
Locharbriggs	45	E7	CAL	1952
Loch Awe	53	C5	CAL	1965
Lochburn — see [Glasgow]				
Lochearnhead	50	A5	CAL	1951
Lochee — see [Dundee]				
Lochee West — see [Dundee]				
Locheilside	59	G4	NB	
Lochgelly	50	H1	NB	
Loch Leven	50	G2	NB	1921
Lochluichart 2nd, 1st — 1954	58	E9	HIGH	
Lochmaben	45	B7	CAL	1952
Lochmill GDS	46	C8	NB	1965
Lochside	49	C7	GSW	
Lochskerrow Halt	45	A5	PPW JT	1963
Loch Tay	50	A7	CAL	1935
Lochty* GDS R.O. PR. FR. CL.	51	E3	NB	1964
Lochwinnoch	49	C7	GSW	1966
Lockerbie	45	G7	CAL	
Locking Road — see [Weston-super-Mare]				
Lockington	35	B8	NE	1960
Lockwood	79	H3	LY	
Loddington GDS	25	G6	MID	
Loddiswell Halt	9	F8	GW	1963
Lode — see Bottisham				
Lodge Hill	7	C9	GW	1963
Lofthouse and Outwood	79	F6	GN	1960
Lofthouse and Outwood	79	F6	METH	1957
Lofthouse-in-Nidderdale	38	B1	NIDD	1960
Loftus	39	A7	NE	1960
Logierieve	54	G8	GNS	1965
Login	19	A6	GW	1962
Londesborough	34	H7	NE	1965
Londesborough Park (Private Sta.)	34	H7	NE	1965
[London]				
Acton Central Form. Churchfield Road	64	D3	NSWJ	
Acton Main Line	64	D3	GW	
Acton South	64	D3	NSWJ	
Acton Town	64	D3	LT	
Aldersgate Street	65	A3	MET	1916
Aldgate East	65	B4	MET/DIST	1938
Alexandra Palace	64	H7	GN	1954
Alperton	64	C4	LT	
Angel Road	12	D5	GE	
	65	C8		
Arnos Grove	64	H9	LT	
Baker Street	64	G3	MET	
Balham	68	G8	LT	
Balham and Upper Tooting	68	G8	LBSC	
Barking	65	G5	LT/MID	
Barkingside	65	G7	LT	
Barnes	64	D1	LSW	
	68	D9		
Barnes Bridge	64	D1	LSW	
	68	D9		
Barons Court	64	E2	LT	
Bath Road Halt	64	C2	NSWJ	1917

Station	Page	Block	Comp	Year of CL
Battersea	64	G1	WLE	1940
	68	F10		
Battersea Park	64	G1	LBSC	1870
Battersea Park	64	H1	LBSC	
	68	G10		
Battersea Park Road	68	G10	SEC	1916
Bayswater	64	F3	LT/MET	
Becontree	66	A5	LT/LTS	
Beckton	65	G3	GE	1940
Beckton Gas Works	65	G3	GE	1940
Belmont	64	B8	LMS	1964
Bethnel Green	65	B4	LT/GE	
Bishopsgate	65	B4	GE	1875
Bishopsgate	65	B4	GE	1916
Bishops Road	64	F3	GW	1947
Blackfriars	65	A4	LT/DIST	
Blackfriars	65	A4	SE	1869
Blackfriars	65	A4	LCD/SEC	1885
Blackheath	65	D1	SEC	
	69	D10		
Blackheath Hill	65	D1	SEC	1917
	69	D10		
Blackhorse Road	65	C7	LTS/LT MID	
Blackwall	65	D3	GE	1926
Borough Road	65	A3	SEC	1907
Boston Manor	64	B2	LT	
Bow	65	C4	EC/BLACK	1851
Bow	65	C4	NL	1945
Bow Road 2nd, 1st — 1892	65	C4	GE	1949
Bow Road	65	C4	LT	
Bowes Park	64	H8	GN	
Brent Cross	64	E6	LT	
Brentford	64	B1	GW	1942
Brentford Central	64	B2	LSW	
	68	B10		
Brentham Halt	64	B4	GW	1947
Bricklayer's Arms	65	A2	SE	1852
Brixton and South Stockwell	68	H9	SEC	
Broad Street	65	A4	NL/LNW	
Broadway Fulham Form. Waltham Green	64	F1	LT	
Brockley	65	C1	LBSC	
	69	C9		
Brockley Lane	65	C1	SEC	1917
	69	C9		
Bromley	65	D4	GE	1926
Bromley 2nd, 1st — 1894	65	D4	LTS	
Brondesbury	64	E4	LNW	
Brondesbury Park	64	E4	LNW	
Bruce Grove	65	B8	GE	
Burdett Road	65	C4	GE	1941
Burnt Oak	64	C8	LT	
Caledonian Road	64	H5	NL	1870
Caledonian Road and Barnsbury	64	H5	NL	
Camberwell	65	A1	SEC	1916
Cambridge Heath	65	C4	GE	
Camden Road	64	H4	MID	1916
Camden Road 2nd, 1st — 1870	64	H4	LNW	
Camden Town	64	H4	NL	1917
Canning Town	65	E4	GE	
Cannons Park	64	B8	LT	
Cannon Street	65	A4	SEC	
Cannon Street	65	A4	MET/DIST	
Cannon Street Road	65	A4	BLACK	1848
Canonbury	65	A5	NL	
Carterhatch Lane Halt	65	B10	GE	1919
Castle Bar Park Halt	64	A4	GW	
Catford	69	C8	SEC	
Catford Bridge	69	C8	SEC	
Cattle Market	64	H4	NL	1866
Central	65	F3	PLA	1940
Chadwell Heath	65	H6	GE	
Chalk Farm 1st Sta.	64	H4	NL	1872
Chalk Farm 2nd, 1st — 1872	64	H4	LNW	1915
Charing Cross	64	H3	SEC	
Charing Cross	64	H3	MET	
Charlton	65	E2	SEC	
Chelsea and Fulham	64	F1	WLE	1940
	68	F10		
Chigwell	65	G9	GE	1966
Chigwell R.O. by L.T.	65	G9	LT	
Chiswick and Grove Park	64	C1	LSW	
	68	C10		
Chiswick Park	64	D2	LT	
Church Manor Way Halt	65	H2	SEC	1920
	66	A2		
Clapham and North Stockwell	64	H1	LBSC	
Clapham Common	68	G9	LSW	1863
Clapham Junction	64	G1	LBSC	
Clapham Junction	68	F9		
Clapham Junction Station	64	G1	LSW	
	68	F9		
Clapton	65	B6	GE	
Clapton GDS	65	B6	GE	1964
Coborn Road 2nd, 1st — 1883	65	C4	GE	1946
Cockfosters	64	G10	GE	1966
Cockfosters R.O. by LT	64	G10	LT	
Colindale	64	D7	LT	
Commercial Docks	65	C2	SE	1867
Connaught Road	65	E3	PLA	1940
Cowley	63	C4	GW	1962
Cranley Gardens	64	G7	GN	1954
Cricklewood	64	E5	MID	
Crofton Park	69	C9	SEC	
Crouch End	64	H6	GN	1954
Crouch Hill	64	H6	LTS	
Croydon Central	64	H6	LBSC	1890
Crystal Palace (HL) & Upper Norwood	69	B7	SEC	1954
Custom House (Victoria Dock)	65	F3	GE	
Dagenham Dock	65	B5	GE	
Dagenham East	67	B5	GE	
Dagenham Heathway	67	B5	GE	
Dalston Junction	65	B5	NL	
Denmark Hill	65	A1	SEC	
Deptford	65	C2	SEC	
	69	C10		
Deptford Road	65	C2	EL	1886
Devons Road GDS	65	D4	LNW	1964
Dollis Hill	64	D5	MET	
Drayton Green, Ealing	64	A3	GW	
Drayton Park	65	A5	GN	
Dudding Hill	64	D5	MID	1902
Ealing Broadway	64	B3	GW/MET	
Ealing Common	64	B3	MET	
Earls Court 2nd, 1st — 1878	64	F2	LT	
Earlsfield and Summerstown	68	F8	LSW	
East Acton	64	D3	LT	
East Brixton	65	A1	LBSC	1976
East Dulwich	69	A9	LDSC	
Eastcote Halt	63	F6	MET	
East Finchley	64	G7	GN	
East Ham	65	F5	GE	
East Ham GDS	65	F5	GE	
East Putney for West Hill	68	E9	LSW	1941
East Putney	68	E9	LT	
East Smithfield GDS	65	B3	GE	1966
Edgware	64	C8	GN	1939
Edgware	64	C8	LT	
Edgware Road	64	C8	MET	
Elephant and Castle 2nd, 1st = 1863	65	A2	SEC	
Elm Park	66	C5	GE	
Eltham Park, Shooters Hill and	69	F9	SEC	
Eltham Well Hall	69	E9	SEC	
Essex Road	65	A5	GN	
Euston 2nd, 1st —	64	H4	BR	
Euston Square	64	H4	MET	
Fairlop	65	G7	GE	1966
Fairlop R.O. by LT	65	G7	LT	
Falconwood	65	G1	SEC	
	69	F9		
Farringdon Street 1st			MET	1866
Farringdon Street 2nd	65	A4	MET	
Fenchurch Street	65	B3	GE	
Finchley Central	64	F7	GN	
Finchley Road 2nd, 1st — 1884	64	F5	MID	
Finchley Road and Frognal	64	F5	LNW	
Finsbury Park	65	A6	GN	
Forest Gate for Upton	65	E5	GE	
Forest Hill	69	B8	LBSC	
Gallions, Royal Albert Dock	65	G3	PLA	1940
George Lane — see South Woodford				
Globe Road and Devonshire Street	65	C4	GE	1916
Gloucester Road	64	F2	LT	
Golders Green	64	F6	LT	
Goldhawk Road	64	E2	MET/GW	
Goodmayes	65	H6	GE	
Gospel Oak	64	G5	GE	1926
Gospel Oak	64	G5	LNW	
Grange Hill	65	G9	LT/GE	
Great Portland Street	64	H4	MET	
Greenford	63	H4	GW	
	64	A4		
Greenford (G.W. Platforms)	64	A4	GW	1963
Greenwich	65	D2	SEC	
	69	D10		
Greenwich Park	65	D2	SEC	1917
	69	D10		

Station	Page	Block	Comp	Year of CL
Grosvenor Road	64	H2	LBSC	1907
Grosvenor Road	64	H2	SEC	1911
Gunnersbury	64	C2	LSW	
Hackney 2nd, 1st — 1870 R.O. as Hackney Central	65	C5	NL	1945
Hackney Downs	65	B5	GE	
Hackney Wick GDS	65	C5	NL	1967
Haggerston	65	B4	NL	1940
Haggerston GDS	65	B4	LNW	1950
Hainault	65	H8	GE	1966
Hainault R.O. by LT	65	H8	LT	
Hammersmith 2nd, 1st — 1868	64	D2	H & C	
Hammersmith	64	D2	MET/DIST	
Hammersmith and Chiswick	64	D2	NSWJ	1917
Hammersmith, Grove Road	64	D2	LSW	1916
Hampstead Heath	64	G5	LNW	
Hanwell and Elthorne	63	H3	GW	
	64	A3		
Harlesden	64	D4	MID	1902
Harlesden	64	D4	LNW	
Harringay West	65	A7	GN	
Harringay Stadium	65	A7	TH JT	
Harrow and Sudbury Hill	64	A5	GC	
Harrow and Wealdstone	64	A7	LNW	
Harrow-on-the-Hill	64	A7	MET/GC	
Hatch End, Pinner and	63	G8	LNW	
Hatton Cross	63	E1	LT	
	67	F10		
Haverstock Hill	64	G7	MID	1916
Hayes and Harlington	63	E3	GW	
Headstone Lane	63	G8	LNW	
Heathrow Central	63	E1	LT	
	67	E10		
Hendon	64	D6	MID	
Hendon Central	64	E7	LT	
Herne Hill	68	H9	SEC	
Highams Park and Hale End	65	D8	GE	
High Barnet	64	F10	GN/LT	
Highgate	64	H6	GN	1954
Highgate Road High Level	64	H5	TH JT	1915
Highgate Road Low Level	64	H5	MID	1918
High Street Kensington	64	F2	MET	
Hillingdon	63	D5	MET	
Hither Green	69	D9	SEC	
Holborn	65	A3	MET	
Holborn Viaduct	65	A4	SEC	
Holborn Viaduct Low Level	65	A4	SEC	1916
Holloway and Caledonian Rd	65	A6	GN	1915
Homerton R.O. Hackney Wick	65	C5	NL	1945
Honor Oak	69	B9	SEC	1954
Honor Oak Park	69	B8	LBSC	
Hornchurch	66	D5	GE	
Hornsey	65	A7	GN	
Hornsey Road	64	H6	TH JT	1943
Hounslow and Whitton	67	H9	LSW	
Hounslow Central	67	G10	LT	
Hounslow East	67	G10	LT	
Hounslow Smallberry Green	68	A10	LSW	1850
Hounslow West	67	G10	LT	
Ickenham Halt	63	D5	MET	
Ilford	65	F6	GE	
Isleworth and Spring Grove	64	A1	LSW	
Junction Road	64	G5	TH JT	1943
Kensal Rise 2nd, 1st — 1873	64	E4	LNW	
Kensington	64	E2	WL	1844
Kensington Olympia Form. Addison Road	64	E2	WL	
Kentish Town	64	H5	LNW	
Kentish Town West	64	H5	MID	
Kenton	64	B7	LNW	
Kenton South	64	B6	LNW	
Kew Bridge (NSWJ Platforms)	64	C2	LSW	1940
Kidbroke	65	E1	SEC	
	69	E9		
Kilburn GDS	64	F4	LNW	
Kilburn High Road	64	F4	LNW	
King's Cross	64	H4	MET	1940
King's Cross	64	H4	CSL	
King's Cross	64	H4	LT	
Kingsland	65	B5	NL	1865
Ladbrook Grove	63	E3	MET/GW	
Ladywell	69	C8	SEC	
Latimer Road	64	E3	MET/GW	
Lea Bridge	65	C6	GE	
Lee for Burnt Ash	69	D9	SEC	
Leman Street	65	B3	GE	1941
Lewisham	65	D1	SEC	
Lewisham	69	C9		
Lewisham Road	65	C1	SEC	1917
	69	D10		
Leyton Goddall Road	65	D7	GE	1966
Leyton, Goddall Road R.O. by LT	65	D7	LT	
Leyton Midland Road	65	D7	MID	
Leytonstone	65	E6	GE	1966
Leytonstone R.O. by LT	65	E6	LT	
Leytonstone High Road	65	E6	MID	
Limehouse	65	C3	GE	1926
Liverpool Street	65	B4	GE	
Liverpool Street	65	B4	MET	
London Bridge	64	G4	LBSC/SEC	
London Fields	65	B3	GE	
Lord's	64	G4	MET	1939
Lordship Lane, Forest Hill	69	B8	SEC	1954
Loudoun Road	64	F4	LNW	1917
Loughborough Junction	65	A1	SEC	
Loughborough Park R.N. Loughborough Junction				
Lower Edmonton	65	B9	GE	
Lower Edmonton Low Level	65	B9	GE	1939
Lower Sydenham	69	C7	SEC	
Ludgate Hill 2nd, 1st — 1865	65	A3	SEC	1929
Ludgate Hill	65	A3	MET	
Maiden Lane	64	H4	GN	1852
Maiden Lane	64	H4	NL	1917
Manor Park	65	F5	GE	
Manor Way	65	F3	PLA	1940
Mansion House	65	A3	MET/DIST	
Mark Lane R.N. Tower Hill	65	B3	MET/DIST	
Marlborough Road	64	F4	MET	1939
Maryland Point	65	D5	GE	
Marylebone	64	G4	GC	
Maze Hill for National Maritime Museum	65	D2	SEC	
	69	D10		
Merton Abbey	68	F6	LSW/LBSC	1929
Mildmay Park	65	A5	NL	1934
Mile End	65	C4	GE	1872
Mill Hill Broadway	64	D8	MID	
Mill Hill, The Hale	64	D8	GN	1939
Mill Hill East	64	E8	GN	
Millwall Docks	65	D2	GE	1926
Millwall Junction	65	C3	GE	1926
Minories	65	B3	BLACK	1853
Mitre Bridge GDS	64	E4	LNW	1967
Monument	65	A3	MET/DIST	
Moorgate	65	A3	MET	
Moorgate Street	65	A3	MET	1916
Mortlake and East Sheen	64	D1	LSW	
	68	C9		
Mottingham, Eltham and	69	E8	SEC	
Muswell Hill	64	G7	GN	1954
Neasden GDS	64	D5	MET	1968
Neasden — Kingsbury	64	D5	MET	
Newbury Park	65	G7	GE	1966
Newbury Park R.O. by LT	65	G7	LT	
New Cross	65	C1	E. LOND	1886
New Cross	65	C1	LBSC	
	69	C10		
New Cross Gate	65	C1	LBSC	
New Eltham and Pope Street	69	F8	SEC	
New Southgate and Friern Barnet	12	D5	GN	
	64	G8	GN	
New Wandsworth	68	F9	LBSC	1869
Nine Elms	69	H2	LSW	1848
Noel Park and Wood Green	65	A8	GE	1963
North Acton	64	D3	LT	
North Acton (Steam Platforms)	64	D3	GW	1947
North Acton Halt	64	D3	GW	1913
North Dulwich	69	A9	LBSC	
North Ealing	64	C3	LT	
Northfields	64	B2	LT	
North Greenwich	65	D2	GE	1926
North Harrow	63	G7	LT	
Northolt Halt for West End	65	G5	GW	
Northolt Park	65	G5	LT	
North Sheen	64	C1	LSW	
	68	B9		
Northumberland Park	65	C8	GE	
North Wembley	64	B6	LNW	
Northwick Park	64	B7	LT	
North Woolwich	65	F3	GE	
Norwood Junction 2nd, 1st — 1859	69	A6	LBSC	
Notting Hill Gate	64	E3	MET/GC	
Nunhead 2nd, 1st — 1925	65	C1	SR	
Oakwood	64	H10	LT	
Old Ford	65	C4	BLACK	1850

Station	Page	Block	Comp	Year of CL
Old Ford	65	C4	NL	1945
Old Kent Road and Hatcham	65	C2	LBSC	1917
	69	B10		
Old Oak Lane Halt	64	D3	GW	1947
Old Street	65	A4	GN	
Ordnance Factory	65	C10	GE	1886
Osterley and Spring Grove	64	A1	DIST	1934
Osterley	64	A1	LT	
Paddington 2nd, 1st — 1854	64	F3	GW	
Paddington GDS	64	F3	GW	
Palace Gates, Wood Green	64	H8	GE	1963
Palmers Green and Southgate	65	A9	GN	
Park Royal	64	C4	GW	1937
Park Royal and Twyford Abbey	64	C4	DI	1931
Park Royal R.O. by LT	64	C4	LT	
Park Royal West Halt	64	C4	GW	1947
Parsons Green	64	E1	LT	
Peckham Rye	65	B1	SEC	
Perivale	64	B4	LT	
Perivale Halt	64	B4	GW	1947
Pimlico	64	G2	LBSC	1860
Pinner	63	G7	MET/GC	
Plaistow	65	D4	GE	
Plaistow and West Ham GDS	65	D4	GE	1964
Plumstead	65	G2	SEC	
Poplar	65	C4	GE	1926
Poplar, East India Dock	65	C4	NL	1945
Praed Street R.N. Paddington (LT)	64	F3	DIST/MET	
Preston Road Halt 2nd, 1st — 1932	64	B6	MET	
Primrose Hill	64	G4	LNW	
Putney	68	E9	LSW	
Putney Bridge	68	E9	LT	
Putney Bridge and Hurlingham	68	E9	LSW	1941
Queensbury	64	C7	LT	
Queens Park	64	E4	LNW	
Queens Park (L.N.W. Platforms)	64	E4	LNW	1917
Queens Road Battersea	64	H1	LSW	
	68	G10		
Queens Road Peckham	65	C1	LBSC	
	69	B10		
Ravenscourt Park	64	D2	LT	
Ravenscourt Park (L.S.W. Platforms)	64	D2	LSW	1916
Rayners Lane Halt	63	G6	MET	
Rectory Road	65	B6	GE	
Richmond	68	B9	LT	
Richmond, Old 2nd, 1st — 1849	68	B9	LT	
Roding Valley	65	E8	GE	1966
Roding Valley R.O. by LT	65	E8	LT	
Rotherhithe	65	B3	LT/E LOND	
Royal Albert Dock — see Gallions				
Royal Oak	64	F3	GW	
Royal Showground	64	C4	LNW	1903
Royal Victoria Dock — see Custom House				
Rugby Road Halt	64	C3	NSWJ	1917
Ruislip	63	E6	LT	
Ruislip Gardens	63	E6	LT	
Ruislip Gardens (Steam Platforms)	63	E6	GW/GC	1958
Ruislip Manor	63	E6	LT	
St Ann's Road	65	A7	TH JT	1942
St Johns	65	D1	SEC	
	69	D10		
St James Park	64	H2	MET/DIST	
St Margarets	68	A9	LSW	
St Mary's Whitechapel	65	B3	MET/DIST	1938
St Pancras	64	H4	MID	
St Pauls	65	A4	LCD	1939
St Quintin Park and Wormwood Scrubs	64	E3	WL	1940
Seven Kings	65	C6	GE	
Seven Sisters	65	B7	GE	
Shadwell	65	B3	LT/EL	
Shadwell and St Georges East	65	B3	GE	1941
Shepherds Bush	64	E3	LSW	1916
Shepherds Bush (Uxbridge Rd)	64	E3	WL	1844
Shepherds Bush 2nd, 1st — 1914	64	E3	LT	
Shoreditch	65	B4	E. LOND	1940
Silver St, Tottenham	65	B8	GE	
Silvertown	65	F3	GE	
Sloane Square	64	G2	MET/DIST	
Snaresbrook	65	E7	GE	1966
Snaresbrook R.O. by LT	65	E7	LT	
Snow Hill	65	A4	LCD	1916
Southall	65	F2	GW	
South Bermondsey 2nd, 1st — 1928	65	B2	LBSC	
	69	B10		
South Bromley	65	C4	NL	1945
South Dock	65	D3	GE	1926
South Ealing	64	B2	LT	
Southfields	68	C8	LT/LSW	
Southgate	64	H0	GE	1966
Southgate	64	H9	LT	
South Greenford	64	A4	GW	
South Hampstead	64	F4	LNW	
South Harefield Halt	63	D6	GW	1931
South Kensington	64	G2	MET/DIST	
South Harrow 2nd, 1st — 1935	63	H5	MET	
South Ruislip Form. Northolt Jcn	63	F5	GW	
South Tottenham & Stamford Hill	65	B7	GE	
Southwark Park, Deptford Road	65	C2	SEC	1915
South Woodford	65	E8	GE	1966
South Woodford R.O. by LT	65	E8	LT	
Spa Road, Bermondsey	65	B3	SEC	1915
Stamford Brook	64	D2	LT	
Stamford Hill	65	B6	GE	
Stanmore	64	B8	MET	
Stanmore Village	64	B8	LNW	1952
Stepney East	63	C3	GE	
Stepney Green	65	C4	GE	1872
Stewarts Lane	68	G10	LCD	1867
Stewarts Lane	68	G10	LBSC	1858
Stoke Newington	65	B6	GE	
Stonebridge Park	64	C4	LNW	
Stratford Central	65	D5	GE	
Stratford Lower	65	D5	GE	1943
Stratford Market R.O. West Ham	65	D5	GE	1943
Stroud Green	64	H6	GN	1954
Strawberry Hill	67	H8	LSW	
	68	A8		
Streatham Hill	68	G7	LBSC	
Sudbury and Harrow Road	64	B5	GC	
Sudbury Hill, Harrow	64	A5	LT	
Sudbury Town	64	B5	LT	
Surrey Docks	65	C2	E LOND/LT	
Swiss Cottage	64	F5	MET	1940
Syon Lane	64	B1	LSW	
	68	A10		
Temple	65	A3	MET/DIST	
Tidal Basin	65	D3	GE	1943
Tottenham Hale	65	B7	GE	
Totteridge and Whetstone	64	F9	GN	
Tower Hill 2nd, 1st — 1967	65	B3	MET	
Tower of London	65	B3	MET	1884
Trumper's Crossing Halt	64	A2	GW	1926
Tulse Hill	68	H8	LBSC	
Turnham Green	64	D2	LT	
Turnham Green (L.S.W. Platforms)	64	D2	LSW	1916
Twickenham 2nd, 1st — 1954	68	A8	BR	
Twyford Abbey Halt	64	C4	GW	1911
Upminster Bridge	66	E5	LT/GE	
Upney	65	H5	LT/GE	
Upper Holloway	64	H6	LTS	
Upper Sydenham	69	B7	SEC	1954
Upton Park	65	E4	LT/GE	
Uxbridge 2nd, 1st — 1938	65	E3	LT	
Uxbridge High Street	63	D5	GW	1939
	15	F4		
Uxbridge Road	64	F3	WL	1940
Uxbridge Vine Street	63	D5	GW	1962
Vauxhall	64	H2	LSW	
	68	G10	LSW	
Victoria	64	H2	LBSC	
Victoria	64	H2	MET	
Victoria Park 2nd, 1st — 1866	65	C5	NL	1943
Victoria Park	65	C5	GE	1942
Victoria Dock — see Custom House				
Walthamstow Central Form. Hoe Street	65	D7	GE	
Walthamstow Queens Road	65	D7	GE	
Walthamstow, Sharnall Street	65	D7	GE	1873
Walthamstow, St James Street	65	D7	GE	
Walworth Road	65	A2	SEC	1916
Wandsworth Common 2nd, 1st — 1858	68	F8	LBSC	
Wandsworth Road	68	G9	SEC	
Wandsworth Town	68	E9	LSW	
Wanstead Park	65	E6	MID	
Wapping	65	B3	LT/E LOND	
Waterloo	65	A3	LSW	
Waterloo East Form. Junction	65	A3	LT	
Welsh Harp	64	E7	MID	1903
Wembley Central	64	B5	LNW	
Wembley GDS	64	B5	LNW	1965
Wembley Hill (Complex 1978)	64	C5	BR	
Wembley Park	64	C6	LT	
West Acton	64	C3	LT	
West Brompton	64	F2	WLE	1940
West Brompton	64	F2	LT	
Westbourne Park	64	F3	GW	
Westcombe Park	65	D2	SEC	

Page Forty Two

Station	Page	Block	Comp	Year of CL
West Drayton and Yiewsley 2nd, 1st — 1884	12	A4	GW	
	63	D2		
West Ealing	64	B3	GW	
West End for Kilburn 1st	64	E5	MID	1897
West End Lane R.N. West Ham	64	F5	LNW	
West Finchley	64	F8	GN	
West Green	65	A7	GE	1963
West Ham	65	E4	LTS	
West Hampstead	64	F5	MET	
West Hampstead, Midland 2nd, 1st — 1897 West End for Kilburn	64	F5	MID	
West Harrow	63	H6	LT	
West India Docks	65	C3	GE	1926
West Kensington	64	E2	LT	
West London Junction	64	D4	L & B	1844
Westminster	64	H2	MET/DIST	
West Ruislip Form. Ruislip and Ickenham	63	E6	GW/GC	
Whitechapel Combined	65	B3	LT/E LOND	
Whitechapel	65	B3	HC JT	
White City	64	E3	HC JT	1959
White City	64	E3	LT	
White Hart Lane	65	B8	GE	
Whitton	67	H8	LSW	
Willesden Green	64	E5	MET	
Willesden Junction (Main Line Platforms)	64	D4	LNW	1962
Willesden Junction 2nd, 1st — 1866	64	D4	LNW	
Willow Walk GDS	65	B2	LBSC	1932
Wimbledon Park	68	E7	LSW	
Woodford	65	E8	GE	1966
Woodford R.O. by LT	65	E8	LT	
Woodgrange Park	65	F5	MID	
Wood Green, Alexander Parks	64	H8	GN	
Wood Lane	64	E3	CL	1947
Woodside Park	64	F9	GN	
Woodstock Road	64	D2	NSWJ	1917
Wood Street, Walthamstow	65	D7	GE	
Woolwich Arsenal	65	F2	SEC	
Woolwich Dock	65	F2	SEC	
York Road	64	H4	MET/DIST	1932
London Bridge — see [London]				
London Fields — see [London]				
London Road — see Bicester				
London Road — see Braunston				
London Road — see [Brighton]				
London Road — see [Carlisle]				
London Road — see Dunstable Town				
London Road — see [Glasgow]				
London Road, Guildford	5	F10	LSW	
London Road, High Level — see [Nottingham]				
London Road, Low Level — see [Nottingham]				
London Street — see [Southport]				
Long Ashton — see [Bristol]				
Longbenton Halt	81	B4	NE	
Longbridge — see [West Midlands]				
Long Buckby	25	D4	LNW	
Long Clawson and Hose	28	F2	GN/LNW	1953
Longcross	15	E2	LSW	
Longdon Halt	27	G10	GW	1963
Longdon Road	24	G1	GW	1929
Longdown	6	B2	GW	1958
	9	A9		
[Long Eaton]				
Long Eaton Form. Sawley Jcn	82	D1	MID	
Long Eaton	28	B2	MID	1967
	82	D1		
Long Eaton Junction	28	B2	MID	1862
Longfield for Fawkham and Hartley	70	F6	SEC	
Longfield Halt	70	F6	SEC	1953
Longford and Exhall — see [Coventry]				
Longforgan	51	B6	CAL	1956
Longhaven	54	F10	GNS	1932
Longhirst	43	E6	NE	1951
Longhope	17	D8	GW	1964
Longhoughton	43	E9	NE	1962
Long Itchington — see Southam				
Long Lane	25	B10	MID	1848
Long Marston	24	F2	GW	1966
Long Marton	41	C8	MID	1970
Long Melford	21	F2	GE	1967
Longmoor Camp	5	D6	LONG	1957
Longmorn	56	D10	GNS	1968
Longniddry	47	A9	NB	
Longparish	4	G9	LSW	1931
Longport, Wool Station	31	A5	NS	
Longport, Wool Station	73	C7		
Long Preston	37	A10	MID	
Longridge	36	F6	PL JT	1930
	76	A4		
Longridge	46	C7	WMC/NB	1852
Longriggend	46	A8	NB	1930
Longsdon — see Wall Grange				
Longside	54	D9	GNS	1965
Longsight — see [Manchester]				
Long Stanton	23	C6	GE	1970
Longstow GDS	23	C2	MID	1953
Long Sutton (Lincolnshire)	22	D7	MGN	1959
	29	G1		
Long Sutton and Pitney Halt	7	B7	GW	1962
Longton	31	B4	NS	
	73	C6		
Longton Bridge	76	C3	LY	1964
Longtown	42	C3	NB	1969
Longville	27	F7	GW	1951
Longwitton	43	C6	NB	1952
Longwood — see [Huddersfield]				
Lonmay	54	C9	GNS	1965
Looe	9	E2	GW	
Lord's — see [London]				
Lord's Bridge	23	E6	LNW	1968
Lordship Lane — see [London]				
Lord Street — see [Southport]				
Loseby	25	E9	GN	1957
Lossiemouth	56	D10	GNS	1964
Lostock Gralam	30	G7	CLC	
	77	E7		
Lostock Hall	76	C4	LY	1969
Lostock Junction — see [Bolton]				
Lostock Lane — see [Bolton]				
Lostwithiel	11	B6	GW	
Loth	61	E2	HIGH	1960
	62	B2		
Lothian Road — see [Edinburgh]				
Loudounhill	49	F4	GSW	1939
Loudoun Road — see [London]				
Loudwater	15	D4	GW	1970
[Loughborough]				
Loughborough	28	C1	MID	
Loughborough Central R.O. PR.	28	C1	GC	1969
Loughborough, Derby Road	28	C1	LNW	1931
Loughborough Junction — see [London]				
Loughor	19	F2	GW	1960
Loughton 2nd, 1st — 1865	12	F6	GE	1966
Loughton R.O. by LT	12	F6	LT	
	65	F10		
Lough	29	E9	GN	1970
Lover's Lane Halt	8	D4	BWA	1917
Lovesgrove Halt (Temp. Halt RE Territorials)	26	B6	VR	circa 1918
Low Bentham GDS	41	C1	MID	1964
Lowca	40	C7	CW JC	1926
Lowdham	28	E4	MID	
Lower Darwen — see [Blackburn]				
Lower Edmonton — see [London]				
Lower Edmonton Low Level — see [London]				
Lower Ince	76	F5	GC	1964
Lower Lydbrook	17	C8	SW JT	1903
Lower Penarth Halt	78	H6	TV	1954
Lower Pontnewydd	78	D10	GW	1958
Lower Sydenham 2nd, 1st — 1906	69	C7	SEC	
Lowestoft	20	H10	GE	
Lowestoft North	20	H10	NS JT	1970
Low Fell — see [Gateshead]				
Low Gill 2nd, 1st — 1861	41	C4	LNW	1960
Low Moor — see [Bradford]				
Low Row	42	A1	MC	1845
Low Row	42	F2	NE	1959
Low Street	13	A4	MID	1967
Lowther — see Clifton				
Lowthorpe	35	C10	NE	1970
Lowton	76	G5	LNW	1949
Lowton St Mary's	76	G5	GC	1964
Lowtown — see Pudsey				
Lubenham	25	E7	LNW	1966
Lucas Terrace Halt — see [Plymouth]				
Lucker	43	G6	NE	1953
Luckett Form. Stoke Climsland	9	C3	PDSW	1966
	11	F8		
Ludborough	29	E10	GN	1961
	35	E1		
Luddendenfoot	79	F1	LY	1962
Luddington	34	G4	AX JT	1933
Ludgate Hill — see [London]				

Station	Page	Block	Comp	Year of CL
Ludgershall*	4	E10	MSWJ	1961
Ludgershall — see also Brill				
Ludlow	27	F5	SH JT	
Luffenham	25	H9	MID	1966
Lugar	49	F2	GSW	1950
Lugton	49	D6	GBK JT	1966
Lugton High	49	D6	CAL	1932
Luib	53	G5	CAL	1965
Lumphanan	55	B4	GNS	1966
Lumsden — see Gartley				
Lunan Bay	51	G9	NB	1930
Luncarty	50	G6	CAL	1951
Lundin Links	51	C3	NB	1965
Lustleigh	9	B9	GW	1959
Luthrie	51	B5	NB	1951
[Luton]				
Luton	12	A9	MID	
	15	G8		
Luton Bute Street	12	A9	GN	1965
	15	G8		
Luton Hoo for New Mill End	12	A9	GN	1965
	15	G8		
Lutterworth	25	C6	GC	1969
Luxulyan	11	B6	GW	
Lybster	62	F5	HIGH	1944
Lydbrook Junction Station	17	C6	GW	1959
Lydden — see Stonehall				
Lydd-on-Sea Halt	3	D4	SR	1967
Lydd Town	3	D4	SEC	1967
Lydford	9	B5	GW	1962
	11	H9		
Lydford	9	B5	LSW	1968
	11	H9		
Lydham Heath	27	C7	BC	1935
Lydiate	76	F1	CLC	1952
[Lydney]				
Lydney Junction	17	C6	GW	
Lydney Junction	17	C7	SW JT	1960
Lydney Town	17	C6	SW JT	1960
Lydstep Halt	18	H2	GW	1956
Lye	80	E3	GW	
Lyme Regis	7	A2	LSW	1965
Lyme Regis — see also Bridport				
Lyminge	3	E6	SEC	1947
Lymington Pier	4	F3	LSW	
Lymington Town 2nd, 1st — 1860	4	F3	LSW	
Lyminster Halt	5	G4	LBSC	1914
Lymm	77	C7	LNW	1962
Lympstone	6	D1	LSW	
Lympstone Commando	6	D1	BR/LSW	
Lyndhurst Road	4	F5	LSW	
Lyne	46	G3	CAL	1950
Lynedoch — see [Greenock]				
Lynemouth Colliery GDS	43	F6	NE	
Lyneside	42	C3	NB	1929
Lyng Halt	7	A7	GW	1964
Lynn — see King's Lynn				
Lynton Colliery GDS	43	F6	NE	
Lynton and Lynmouth	8	A8	LB	1935
Lyonshall	27	C	GW	1940
Lytham	36	C6	PW JT	
	76	B2		
Lytham Junction	76	B2	PW JT	1853
Lytham Road — see [Blackpool] South Shore				
Mablethorpe	29	G9	GN	1970
Macbie Hill	46	F6	NB	1933
[Macclesfield]				
Macclesfield	31	B8	NS	
	77	D10		
Macclesfield	77	D10	MB	1849
Macclesfield	77	D10	MS & L/NS	1873
Macclesfield, Hibel Road	77	D10	LNW	1960
Macduff	54	B5	GNS	1951
Macduff (Banff)	54	B5	GNS	1872
Machen	78	E7	BM	1962
Machynlleth	26	D8	CORRIS/CAM	
Machynlleth	26	D8	CORRIS	
Macrihanish	48		CM	1931
Macrihanish Farm Halt	48		CM	1931
Macmerry, Gladsmuir	47	A8	NB	1925
Maddaford Moor Halt	8	H5	SR	1966
Madderty	50	E5	CAL	1951
Maddiesons Camp	3	D4	RHD	
Madeley (Salop)	24	A9	GW	1925
	27	H9		
Madeley Market (Salop)	24	A9	LNW	1952
	27	H9		
Madeley (Staffs)	30	H3	LNW	1952

Station	Page	Block	Comp	Year of CL
Madeley Road (Staffs)	30	H3	NS	1931
Maenclochog	18	H6	NRM/GW	1937
Maentwrog Road	32	H3	GW	1960
Maerdy	78	C3	TV	1964
Maesbrook	30	B1	PSNW/SM	1933
	33	H1		
Maesteg	78	D2	GW	1970
Maesteg, Neath Road	78	D2	PT	1933
Maesycrugiau	19	D8	GW	1965
Maesycwmmer and Hengoed	78	C6	BM	1962
Magdalen Gate	22	F8	GE	1866
Magdalen Green — see [Dundee]				
Magdalen Road	22	E9	BR	
Magdalen Road	22	E9	GE	1968
Maghull	76	F2	LY	
Magor	17	A4	GW	1964
Maida Vale — see [London] Kilburn High Road				
Maidenhead	15	D3	GW	
Maidenhead, Boyne Hill	15	D3	GW	1871
Maiden Lane — see [London]				
Maiden Newton	7	D3	GW	
Maidens	44	D10	GSW	1930
[Maidstone]				
Barracks	2	H8	SEC	
East	2	H8	SEC	
West	2	H8	SEC	
Maindy North Road Halt — see [Cardiff]				
Main's Cross	44	C4	PPW JT	1885
Main Street — see [Glasgow]				
Maldon East and Heybridge	13	C7	GE	1964
Maldon Manor	68	C5	GE	
Maldon West	13	C7	GE	1939
Malham — see Bell Busk				
Malins Lee	24	A10	LNW	1952
	27	H9		
Mallaig	51	E1	NB	
Malling — see East Malling				
Malling — see also West Malling				
Mallwyd	26	E10	MAW/CAM	1931
Malmesbury	17	H4	GW	1951
Malpas	30	E4	LNW	1957
Malswick Halt	17	E9	GW	1959
Maltby	33	D1	SY JT	1929
	82	F9		
Malton	39	B1	NE	
Malvern — see Great Malvern				
Malvern, Hanley Road	24	B2	MID	1952
Malvern Link	24	B2	GW	
Malvern Road — see [Cheltenham]				
Malvern Wells	24	B2	WM/GW	1965
Malvern Wells	24	B2	MID	1961
[Manchester]				
Alexandra Park	77	B8	GC	1958
Ardwick	77	A8	LNW	1902
Ardwick	77	A8	GC	
Art Treasures Exhibition 1st, 2nd — Warwick Road	77	B9	MSJA	1887
Ashburys for Belle Vue	77	A9	GC	
Baguley	77	C8	CLC	1964
Belle Vue	77	A9	GC	
Brindle Heath GDS	76	G8	LY	
Chorlton-cum-Hardy	77	A8	CLC	1967
Clayton Bridge	76	G9	LY	1968
Cornbrook	77	B8	MSJA	1865
Cross Lane	76	G8	LNW	1959
Dean Lane, Newton Heath	76	G9	LY	
Deansgate, Knott Mill and	77	A8	MSJA	
Didsbury	77	B8	MID	1967
Ducie Bridge absorbed into Victoria			LY	1884
Fallowfield	77	B8	GC	1958
Gorton and Openshaw 2nd, 1st — 1906	77	A9	GC	
Hyde Road	77	A9	GC	1958
Knott Mill — see Deansgate				
Levenshulme and Burnage	77	B9	LNW	
Levenshulme South	77	B9	GC	1958
Liverpool Road R.O. Temp. for 1980 events	76	G9	LM	1844
London Road	77	A8	MSJA	1958
Longsight	77	A9	LNW	1958
Manchester Central 2nd, 1st — 1880	77	A8	CLC	1969
Manchester Exchange	76	G9	LNW	1969
Manchester Mayfield	77	A9	LNW	1960
Manchester United Football Club*	77	A9	CLC	
Mauldreth Road	77	B9	LNW	
Miles Platting	76	G9	LY	
Newton Heath	76	G9	LY	1966
Northenden for Wythenshaw	77	C8	CLC	1964
Oldfield Road	76	G9	LY	1872

Station	Page	Block	Comp	Year of CL
Oldham Road	76	G9	ML	1844
Old Trafford	77	A8	MSJA	
Ordsall Lane for Salford	76	G9	LNW	1957
Oxford Road	77	A9	CLC	
Park	76	G9	LY	
Pendleton	76	G8	LY	
Pendleton, Broad Street	76	G8	LY	1966
Piccadilly	77	A9	BR	
Rushford	77	A9	MB	1843
Salford	76	G9	LY	
Seedley	76	G8	LNW	1958
Trafford Park	77	B8	CLC	
Travis Street	77	A9	MB	1842
Victoria	76	G9	LY	
Warwick Road, Old Trafford	77	A8	MSJA	
Weaste	76	G8	LNW	1942
Wilbraham Road	77	B9	GC	1958
Windsor Bridge	76	G9	ML	1846
Withington and West Didsbury Form.				
Withington and Albert Park	77	B8	MID	1961
Manchester Road — see [Bradford]				
Manchester Road — see [Burnley]				
Manea	22	H8	GE	
Mangotsfield 2nd, 1st — 1869	17	D3	MID	1966
	72	F7		
Manley	77	F4	CLC	1875
Manningford Halt	14	C1	GW	1966
Manningham — see [Bradford]				
Manningtree	21	H5	GE	
Manod	32	H4	GW	1960
Manorbier	18	G2	GW	
Manor Park for Little Ilford	65	F5	GE	
Manor Road	77	C1	WIRRAL	
Manors East — see [Newcastle]				
Manors West — see [Newcastle]				
Manor Way — see [London]				
[Mansfield]				
Central	28	D6	GC	1956
	82	F6		
Town 2nd, 1st — 1872	82	F6	MID	1964
Woodhouse	82	F6	MID	1964
Mansfield — see also Alfreton				
Mansion House — see [London]				
Manston — see [Leeds]				
Manston Airport	3	G9	SEC	
Manton for Uppingham	25	H9	MID	1966
Manuel	46	C8	NB	1967
Manuel Low Level	46	C8	NB	1933
Marazion	10	C3	GW	1964
March	22	G7	GE	
Marchington	31	D2	NS	1958
Marchmont	47	E5	NB	1948
Marchwiel	30	C4	CAM	1962
	72	E2	CAM	1962
Marchwood	4	F4	SR	1966
Marden	2	H7	SEC	
Mardock	12	E8	GE	1964
Marfleet — see [Hull]				
Margam	78	F1	BR	1964
[Margate]				
Margate Form. West	3	G10	SEC	
Margate East	3	G10	SEC	1953
Margate Sands	3	G10	SEC	1926
Margate West Form. Buenos Aires	3	G10	SEC	1863
Marine — see [Dover]				
Marishes Road	39	B2	NE	1965
Market Bosworth* R.O. PR. FR. CL.	25	A9	AN JT	1931
Market Deeping — see Helpston				
Market Drayton	30	G3	MID	
Market Harborough	25	E7	MID	
Market Harborough 2nd, 1st — 1885	25	E7	LNW	1966
Market Place — see [Chesterfield]				
Market Place — see [Dewsbury]				
Market Rasen	29	B9	GC	
Market Weighton	34	H7	NE	1965
Markham Village Halt	78	C7	LNW	1960
Markinch for Glenrothes	51	B2	NB	
Mark Lane — see [London]				
Marks Tey	13	D9	GE	
Marlborough High Level	14	D2	GW	1933
Marlborough Low Level	14	D2	MSWJ	1961
Marlborough Road — see [London]				
Marlesford	21	D8	GE	1952
Marlow 2nd, 1st — 1967	15	D4	GW	
Marlpool for Shipley Hill	82	C2	GN	1928
Marple 2nd, 1st — 1865	31	G6	GC/MID	
	77	C10		
Marple Rose Hill	31	G6	GC/MID	
	77	C10		

Station	Page	Block	Comp	Year of CL
Marron Junction	40	D8	LNW	1897
Marsden (Yorkshire)	37	D4	LNW	
	79	H2		
Marsden (Durham)	81	G2	SSMWC	1953
Marsden Cottage Halt (Durham)	81	G2	SSMWC	1953
Marsh Brook	27	E7	SH JT	1958
Marshfield	78	G8	GW	1959
Marsh Gibbon and Poundon	15	A9	LNW	1968
Marsh Gate GDS	82	F9	GC	1971
Marsh Lane — see [Leeds]				
Marsh Lane and Strand Road — see [Bootle]				
Marsh Mills — see [Plymouth]				
Marsh Road Level Crossing	35	D4	GC/GI	1961
Marske	38	H7	NE	
Marston Gate	15	D8	LNW	1953
Marston Green	80	D8	LNW	
Marston Halt (Adj. to Marston Lane)	27	D3	GW	1955
Marston Lane	27	D3	GW	1864
Marston Magna	7		GW	1966
Marston Moor	34	D8	NE	1958
Marteg Halt	26	F4	GW	1962
Martell Bridge Halt	18	F6	GW	1937
Martham for Rollesby	20	E9	MGN	1959
Martin Mill for St Margarets Bay	3	G7	SEC	
Martock	7	B6	GW	1964
Marton	25	A4	LNW	1959
	80	H10		
Maryhill Central — see [Glasgow]				
Maryhill Park — see [Glasgow]				
Marykirk	51	G10	CAL	1956
	55	G5		
Maryland Point	65	D5	GE	
Marylebone — see [London]				
Maryport 2nd, 1st — 1860	40	D9	MC	
	45	F1		
Mary Tavy and Blackdown	9	B5	GW	1962
Maryville	75	D3	NB	1908
Masboro — see [Rotherham]				
Masbury Halt	7	D9	SD JT	1966
Masham	38	D2	NE	1931
Massingham	20	D1	MGN	1959
Mathry Road	18	E6	GW	1964
Matlock	31	G6	MID	
	82	A4		
Matlock Bath	31	G6	MID	1967
	82	A4		
Matlock Bath	31	G6	MID	
	82	A4		
Matthewstown Halt	78	D4	TV	1964
Mauchline	49	D3	GSW	1965
Maud Junction	54	D8	GNS	1965
Maudlands — see [Preston]				
Maudlands Bridge — see [Preston]				
Mauds Bridge	34	F3	GC	1866
Mauldreth Road	77	B9	LNW	
Mawcarse Junction	50	H3	NB	1964
Maxstoke	80	D8	MID	1917
Maxton	47	C3	NB	1964
Maxwell House — see [Preston]				
Maxwell Park	74	G3	CAL	
Maxwelltown	45	E6	GSW	1939
Maybole 2nd, 1st — 1860	44	E10	GSW	
	49	B1		
May Hill — see Monmouth				
Mayfield (Sussex)	2	F4	LBSC	1965
Mayfield — see [Manchester]				
Maze Hill, East Greenwich	65	D2	SEC	
	69	D10		
Meadow Hall — see [Rotherham]				
Meadow Hall — see [Sheffield] Wincobank				
Mealsgate	40	F10	MC	1930
	45	H2		
Measham	25	A10	AN JT	1931
Measurements Halt	37	C3	LMS	1955
Medbourne	25	F8	GN/LNW	1916
Medge Hall	34	F3	GC	1960
Medstead and Four Marks	5	B8	LSW	1973
Meeth Halt	8	G5	SR	1965
Meigle	51	B8	CAL	1951
Meigle Junction	51	B8	SCNE	1861
Meikle Earnock Halt	49	G6	CAL	1943
	75	C1		
Meikle Ferry	56	B3	HIGH	1869
Meir — see [Stoke-on-Trent]				
Melangoose Mill GDS	10	H6	GW	
Melbourne	28	B2	MID	1930
	31	H2		
Melbourn — see Meldreth				

Station	Page	Block	Comp	Year of CL
Melcombe Regis – see Weymouth				
Meldon	43	D5	NB	1952
Meldreth and Melbourn	23	F6	GN	
Meledor Mill GDS	10	H6	GW	
Meliden	33	E8	LNW	1930
Melksham	17	G1	GW	1966
Melling	41	C1	FM JT	1952
Mellis	21	B5	GE	1966
Mells Road Halt	7	E10	GW	1959
Melmerby	38	E2	NE	1967
Melrose	47	B3	NB	1969
Meltham	79	H2	LY	1949
Melton*	21	E7	GE	1955
Melton Constable	20	C4	MGN	1964
Melton Mowbray	28	F1	GN/LNW	1953
Melton Mowbray	28	F1	MID	
Melverley	27	C10	PSNW/SM	1933
	33	H1		
Melyncourt Halt	78	C1	GW	1964
Memorial	34	F9	SH LT	1930
Menai Bridge	32	F9	LNW	1966
Mendlesham	21	D5	MSL	1952
Menheniot	9	D2	GW	
Menston 2nd, 1st – 1876	37	E8	MID	
	79	B3		
Menstrie and Glenochil	50	D2	NB	1954
Menthorpe Gate	34	E6	NE	1953
Meole Brace	27	E10	SM	1933
Meols	77	C1	WIRRAL	
Meols Cop	76	D1	LY	
Meopham	2	G9	SEC	
	70	G6		
Merchiston – see [Edinburgh]				
Merrylees 2nd, 1st – 1848	25	B9	MID	1871
Mersey Road and Aigburgh – see [Liverpool]				
Merstham 2nd, 1st – 1845	2	B8	SEC	
Merstone Junction (Isle of Wight)	4	H1	IWC	1956
[Merthyr]				
Abercanaid	78	B4	GW/RHY	1951
Aberfan	78	C4	GW/RHY	1951
Cwm Bargoed	78	B4	TB JT	1964
Dowlais	78	A4	TV	1854
Dowlais Cae Harris	78	A4	TB JT	1964
Dowlais Central	78	B4	BM	1960
Dowlais High Street	78	B4	LNW	1958
Dowlais Junction	78	B4	TV	1854
Dowlais Top	78	A4	BM	1962
Dowlais Top	78	A4	LNW	1885
Heolgerrig Halt	78	B4	GW/LMS	1961
Merthyr	16	D6	TV	
	78	B4		
Merthyr Plymouth Street	78	A4	TV	1877
Merthyr Vale	16	D6	TV	
	78	C4		
Pant Junction	78	A4	BM	1962
Pantysgallog Halt, High Level	78	A4	BM	1960
Pantysgallog Halt, Low Level	78	A4	LNW	1958
Quakers Yard, High Level	78	D5	GW	1964
Quakers Yard, Low Level	78	D5	GW/TV	
Treharris	78	C4	GW	1964
Troedyrhiw Halt	78	C4	GW/RHY	1951
Merthyr Road	78	C4	VN	1853
Merton Abbey – see [London]				
Merton Park	68	E6	LBSC/LW	
Merton Street – see [Banbury]				
Metheringham	29	B6	GN/GE	
Metheringham – see also Blankney				
Methil	51	C2	NB	1955
[Methley]				
Methley Junction	79	F7	LY	1943
Methley North	79	F7	MID	1957
Methley South	79	F7	METH	1960
Methven	50	F5	CAL	1937
Methven Junction	50	F5	CAL	1951
Mexborough	34	C2	GC	
	82	E10		
Mexborough Junction	82	E10	MS & L	1871
Meyrick Park Halt – see [Bournemouth]				
Micheldever	4	H9	LSW	
Micklam	40	C7	CWJC	1926
Micklefield	34	C6	YNM/NE	
	79	D9		
Micklehurst	76	G10	LNW	1907
Mickleover for Radburn	31	G3	GN	1939
	82	A1		
Mickleton (Yorks)	41	G8	NE	1964
Mickleton Halt (Glos)	24	F1	GW	1941
Mickle Trafford	30	D7	B HEAD	1951

Station	Page	Block	Comp	Year of CL
Mickle Trafford	77	G4		
Mickle Trafford East	30	D7	CLC	1951
	77	G4		
Mickley	38	D2	NE	1915
Midcalder	46	E7	CAL	
Mid-Clyth	62	F6	HIGH	1944
Middle Drove	22	F8	GE	1968
Middlesbrough	38	F7	NE	
Middle Stoke Halt	3	A10	SEC	1961
	12	C3		
Middlestown	79	G6	MID	1960
Middleton Towers	22	E10	GE	1968
Middleton (Lancs)	37	B4	LY	1964
	76	F9		
Middleton-in-Teesdale	41	G8	NE	1964
Middleton Junction (Lancs)	76	F9	LY	1966
Middleton North	43	D5	NB	1952
Middleton-on-Lune	41	C3	LNW	1931
Middleton-on-the-Wolds	38	A8	NE	1954
Middleton Road Bridge Halt	36	D10	MID	1905
Middletown R.N. Breidden	27	C10	S & WPL	1960
Middlewich	30	G6	LNW	1960
	77	F7		
Middlewood for High Lane	31	B9	LNW/GC/NS	
	77	C10		
Middlewood Higher	77	C10	GC/NS	1960
Mid Fearn 1st, 2nd – Fearn	56	B4	HIGH	1865
Midford	17	E1	SD JT	1966
Midford Halt	17	E1	GW	1915
Midge Hall	76	C3	LY	1961
Midgham	14	H1	GW	
Midhurst	5	E6	LSW	1925
Midhurst 2nd, 1st – 1881	5	E6	LBSC	1955
Midland Road – see Bedford				
Midland Road – see [London] Leyton				
Midsomer Norton and Welton	7	E10	GW	1959
Midsomer Norton South	7	E10	SD JT	1966
Midville	29	F6	GN	1970
Milborne Port	7	E6	LSW	1966
Milcote for Weston-on-Avon and Welford-on-Avon 2nd, 1st – 1908	24	F2	GW	1966
Mildenhall	23	B10	GE	1962
Mildmay Park – see [London]				
Mile End – see [London]				
Miles Platting	76	G9	LY	
Milford (Yorks)	79	D10	NE	1904
Milford (Surrey)	5	F9	LSW	
Milford and Brocton	31	B1	LNW	1950
Milford Haven	18	C2	GW	
Milkwall	17	C7	SW JT	1929
Millbay – see [Plymouth]				
Millbrook	23	G1	LNW	
Millbrook (Hampshire)	4	G5	LSW	
Millers Bridge – see [Liverpool]				
Millerhill for Edmondstone	46	G8	NB	1955
	83	G5		
Miller's Dale	31	D7	MID	1967
	77	D10		
Millfield – see [Sunderland]				
Mill Hill (Isle of Wight)	4	H2	IWC	1966
Mill Hill (Lancs)	76	C6	LY	
Mill Hill Broadway – see [London]				
Mill Hill East – see [London]				
Mill Hill (The Hale) – see [London]				
Millhouses and Eccleshall – see [Sheffield]				
Milligen or Millagen	54	D3	GNS	1863
Milliken Park	49	D7	GSW	1966
	74	A3		
Mill Lane – see Box				
Millisle for Garlieston 2nd, 1st – 1903	44	G2	PPW JT	1950
Millom	40	E2	FUR	
Mill Pond Halt	5	E3	WS	1935
Mill Road Halt	23	H8	GE	1952
Mills Hill	76	E9	ML	1842
Mills of Drum	55	C7	DEE	1963
Mill Street – see [Newport]				
Mill Street Platform – see [Aberdare]				
Milltimber	55	C7	GNS	1937
Milltown	82	B5	ASH	1936
Millwall Docks – see [London]				
Millwall Junction – see [London]				
Milnathort	50	H3	NB	1964
Milngavie	49	E9	NB	
	74	E10		
Milnrow	37	B4	LY	
	76	D10		
Milnsbridge – see [Huddersfield] Longwood				
Milnthorpe	41	A3	LNW	1968

Station	Page	Block	Comp	Year of CL
Milton — see [Stoke-on-Trent]				
Milton Halt	14	G10	GW	1951
Milton Range Halt	13	A3	SEC	1932
Milton Regis — see Sittingbourne				
Milton Road	16	H1	WCP	1940
Milton Road Halt	13	A3	SEC	1915
Milton of Campsie	75	B10	NB	1951
Milverton (Somerset)	6	F7	GW	1966
Milverton (Leamington Spa) Warwicks	80	H10	LSW	1965
Mindrum	47	F3	NE	1930
Minehead	6	D9	GW	1971
Minehead R.O. PR. FR. CL. above	6	D9	WSR	
Minera	33	G5	GW	1971
	72	B3		
Minety and Ashton Keynes	14	B5	GW	1964
[Minffordd]				
Minffordd	32	G3	CAM	
Minffordd	32	G3	FEST	1939
Minffordd R.O. PR. FR. CL. above	32	C3	FR	
Minories — see [London]				
Minshull Vernon	77	G6	LNW	1942
Minster Junction (Thanet)	3	G9	SEC	
Minster-on-Sea	3	C10	SEC	1950
Minsterley	27	D9	S & WPL	1951
Mintlaw	54	D9	GNS	1965
Mirfield 2nd, 1st — 1866	79		LY	
Mislingford GDS	5	B5	LSW	1962
Misson GDS	28	E10	GN	1964
	34	E1		
Misterton	28	F10	GN/GE	1961
	34	G1		
Mistley	13	F10	GE	
	21	H5		
Mitcham	68	F5	LBSC	
Mitcham Junction Station	68	F5	LBSC	
Mitcheldean Road	17	D9	GW	1964
Mitchell and Newlyn Halt	10	G6	GW	1963
Mithian Halt	10	F5	GW	1963
Moat Lane Junction Station	26	H7	CAM	1962
Mobberley	30	H8	CLC	
	77	D7		
Mochdre and Pabo	33	A8	LNW	1931
Moffat	45	G10	CAL	1954
Moira	25	A10	MID	1964
	31	G1		
Moira — see also Overseal				
Mold	72	B5	LNW	1962
	77	H1		
Molland — see Bishop's Nympton				
Mollington	77	G3	B HEAD	1960
Molyneux Brow	76	F8	EL	1931
Moniaive	45	C8	GSW	1943
Monifieth	51	D6	DA JT	
Monikie	51	D7	CAL	1955
Monk Bretton	82	B10	MID	1937
Monk Fryston	79	E9	NE	1959
Monkseaton 2nd, 1st — 1915	43	G4	NE	
	81	F4		
Monks Ferry — see [Birkenhead]				
Monks Lane Halt	2	D7	LBSC	1939
Monks Risborough and Whiteleaf Halt	15	C7	GW/GC	
Monkton	49	B3	GSW	1940
Monkton and Came (Golf Links) Halt	7	E2	GW	1957
Monkton Combe	17	E1	GW	1925
Monkwearmouth — see [Sunderland]				
Monmore Green — see [West Midlands]				
Monmouth — May Hill	17	C8	GW	1959
Monmouth — Troy	17	C8	GW	1959
Monsal Dale	31	E7	MID	1959
Montacute	7	C6	GW	1964
Montgomerie Pier — see [Ardrossan]				
Montgomery	27	B8	CAM	1965
Montgreenan	49	C5	GSW	1955
Monton Green	76	G7	LNW	1969
Montpelier	17	C2	CE	
	72	C7		
Montrave GDS	51	C3	NB	1964
Montrose 3rd, 1st — 1849, 2nd — 1934	51	G9	CAL	
	55	H6		
Monument — see [London]				
Monymusk	55	A5	GNS	1950
Moor — see [Sunderland]				
Moore	77	D6	LNW	1943
Moor End GDS	82	B9	GC	1960
Moorfields — see [Liverpool]				
Moorgate	37	C3	LNW	1955
Moorgate — see [London]				
Moorgate Street — see [London]				
Moorhampton	27	D1	MID	1962

Station	Page	Block	Comp	Year of CL
Moorhouse and South Elmsall	34	C3	HB	1929
Moorpark — see Stevenston				
Moor Park and Sandy Lodge	63	E9	MET/GC	
Moor Row	40	C6	WCE JT	1947
Moorside and Wardley	36	H2	LY	
	76	G7		
Moor Street — see [West Midlands] Birmingham				
Moorswater — see Liskeard				
Moorthorpe and South Kirkby	34	C2	SK JT	
Moortown for Caistor	35	B2	GC	1965
Morar	59	E1	NB	
Morchard Road	6	A4	LSW	
	8	F8		
Morcott	25	H9	LNW	1966
Morden — see Ashwell				
Morden	68	F6	LT	
Morden Road Halt	68	F6	LBSC	
Morden South	68	F6	LBSC	
Morebath	6	D7	GW	1966
Moorbath Junction Halt	6	C7	GW	1966
[Morecambe]				
Euston Road	36	D10	LNW	1958
Harbour	36	D10	MID	1904
Pier	36	D10	MID	1857
Poulton Lane	36	D10	LNW	1886
Promenade, Morecambe 2nd, 1st — 1907	36	D10	MID	
Moresby Junction	40	C7	CWJC	1923
Moresby Parks	40	C7	CWJC	1931
Moreton (Merseyside)	77	B1	WIRRAL	
Moreton (Dorset)	7	F2	LSW	
Moretonhampstead	9	A8	GW	1959
Moreton-in-Marsh	14	D10	GW	
Moreton-on-Lugg	27	E1	SH JT	1958
Morfa — see [Caernarvon]				
Morfa Mawddach Form. Barmouth Jcn	26	B10	CAM	
Morley Low	79	E5	LNW	
Morley Top	79	E5	GN	1961
Mormond Halt	54	C9	GNS	1965
[Morningside]				
Morningside	46	A6	CAL	1853
Morningside	46	A6	CAL	1930
Morningside Road	46	A6	NB	1930
Morpeth	43	E5	NE	
Morpeth	43	E5	BT	1880
Morris Cowley — see [Oxford]				
Morriston — see [Swansea]				
Mortehoe and Woolacombe	8	B5	LSW	1970
Mortimer	15	B2	GW	
Mortlake and East Sheen	64	D1	LSW	
	68	C9		
Morton Pinkney for Sulgrave	25	D2	EWJ/SMJ	1952
Morton Road	22	D2	GN	1930
	29	B1		
Moseley — see [West Midlands]				
Moses Gate	76	E7	LY	
Moss (Yorks)	34	E3	NE	1953
Moss and Pentre (Clwyd)	72	D2	GC	1917
Moss Bank — see [St Helens]				
Mossbridge	76	E1	CLC	1917
Mossend	75	E4	CAL	1962
Mossley (Lancs)	37	C3	LNW	
	76	G10		
Mossley Halt (Staffs)	73	C9	NS	1925
Mossley Hill 2nd, 1st — 1891	77	C2	LNW	
Mosspark West	74	F3	GSW	
Moss Halt	72	D3	GW	1931
Moss Road — see [Glasgow]				
Moss Road Halt	48		CM	1931
Moss Side	76	B2	PW JT	1961
Mosstowie	56	E8	HIGH	1955
Moston	37	A3	LY	
	76	F9		
Mostyn	33	F8	LNW	1966
Motherwell 2nd, 1st — 1885	49	H7	CAL	
	75	E1		
Motspur Park	68	D6	LBSC	
Mottingham, Eltham and	69	E8	SEC	
Mottisfont	4	F7	LSW	1964
Mottram Staff Halt*	31	C10	GC	
Mouldsworth	30	E7	CLC	
	77	B5		
Moulsford 1st, 2nd R.N. Cholsey	15	A4	GW	1892
Moulton (Lincs)	22	D5	MGN	1959
	29	D1		
Moulton (Yorks)	38	D5	NE	1969
Mountain Ash, Cardiff Road	78	D4	GW	1964
Mountain Ash*, Oxford Street	78	D4	TV	1964

Station	Page	Block	Comp	Year of CL
Mountfield Halt	2	G3	SEC	1969
Mount Florida	74	C3	CAL	
Mount Gould and Tothill Halt — see [Plymouth]				
Mount Hawke Halt	10	F5	GW	1963
Mount Melville	51	D4	NB	1930
Mount Pleasant Halt — see [Stoke-on-Trent]				
Mount Pleasant Road Halt — see [Exeter]				
Mount Street — see [Brecon]				
Mount St Mary — see Spink Hill				
Mount Vernon North	78	B5	NB	1955
Mount Vernon South	78	B5	CAL	1943
Mow Cop and Scholar Green	31	A6	NS	1964
	73	B9		
Moxley — see [West Midlands] Bradley				
Moy	56	H3	HIGH	1965
Moy Park	48		CM	1912
Muchalls	55	D8	CAL	1950
Much Wenloch 2nd, 1st — 1884	27	G8	GN	1962
Mudcott	8	D4	BWA	1917
Muirend	74	G2	CAL	
Muirkirk 2nd, 1st — 1896	49	G3	GSW	1964
Muir of Ord	56	F1	HIGH	
Muir of Ord Junction	56	F1	HIGH	1960
Mulben	54	D1	HIGH	1964
Mumbles Pier — see [Swansea]				
Mumbles Road — see [Swansea]				
Mumby Road	29	G8	GN	1970
Mumps — see [Oldham]				
Muncaster Mill T.O. PR.	40	D4	ESK	
Mundesley-on-Sea	20	C7	NSJT	1964
Munlochy	56	F2	HIGH	1951
Murrayfield — see [Edinburgh]				
Murrow East	22	F6	MGN	1959
Murrow West	22	F6	GN/GE	1953
Murthly	50	G7	HIGH	1967
Murtle	55	C7	GNS	1937
Murton Junction	38	E10	NE	1953
	43	H1		
Murton Lane	34	F8	DV	1926
Musgrave	41	E7	NE	1952
Musselburgh	46	H8	NB	1964
	83	G7		
Muswell Hill — see [London]				
Mutford — see Oulton Broad North				
Muthill	50	E4	CAL	1964
Mytholmroyd	37	C5	LY	
	79	F1	LY	
	82	B10		
Naburn	34	E7	NE	1953
Nafferton	35	C9	NE	
Nailbridge Halt	17	D8	GW	1930
Nailsea and Backwell	17	B2	GW	
	72	B6		
Nailsworth	17	F6	MID	1947
Nairn	56	E6	HR	
Nancegollan	10	D3	GW	1962
Nanerch	33	F7	LNW	1962
Nanstallon Halt	11	B7	LSW	1967
Nantclwyd	33	E5	LNW	1953
Nantgaredig	19	E5	LNW	1963
Nantgarw Halt High Level	78	F5	ANSW	1956
Nantgarw Halt Low Level	78	F5	CDFF	1931
Nantlle	32	F5	NANT/LNW	1932
Nantmawr GDS	33	G1	CAM	1964
Nantmor	78	A7	LNW	1960
Nantwich	30	F5	LNW	
Nantybwch	78	A7	LNW	1960
Nantyderry	78	B10	GW	1958
Nantyffyllon	78	D2	GW	1970
Nantyglo	78	A8	GW	1962
Nantymoel	78	E3	GW	1958
Nantyronen	26	C5	CAM	
Napsbury	12	B7	MID	1959
	15	H6		
Napton and Stockton	25	B4	LNW	1958
Narberth	18	H4	GW	
Narborough (Leicestershire)	25	C8	LNW	
Narborough and Pentney (Norfolk)	22	F10	GE	1968
Nassington	22	G2	LNW	1957
Nast Hyde Halt	12	C7	GN	1951
Nateby Form. Winmarleigh	36	D8	GKE/KE	1930
	76	A4		
Navenby	29	A6	GN	1962
Navigation Road, Altrincham	77	C8	MSJA	
Naworth	42	E3	NE	1952
Nawton	39	A2	NE	1953
Neasden — see [London]				

Station	Page	Block	Comp	Year of CL
Neasden-Kingsbury — see [London]				
[Neath]				
Abbey	78	C1	GW	1936
Canal Side	78	C1	RSB	1935
Neath General	16	A5	GW	
	78	C1		
Riverside 2nd, 1st — 1892	78	C1	GW/N & B	1964
Nechals — see [West Midlands] Bloomsbury				
Necropolis — see Brookwood				
Needham	21	E5	GE	1967
Needham Market	21	E5	GE	
Neen Sollars	27	G5	GW	1962
Neepsend — see [Sheffield]				
Neilston	74	C1	GBK JT	1966
Neilston High	49	D7	CAL	
	74	B1		
Nelson (Lancs) for Barrowford 2nd, 1st — 1892	37	A7	LY	
	76	A9		
Nelson (Glamorgan)	78	D5	TV	1932
Nelson and Llancaiach 2nd, 1st — 1912	78	D5	GW	1964
Nesscliff and Pentre	27	D10	PSNW/SM	1933
	30	C1		
Neston North Form. Neston & Parkgate	77	E1	GC	
Neston South	77	E1	B HEAD	1956
Netherburn	46	A5	CAL	1951
Nethercleugh	45	G7	CAL	1960
Netherfield and Colwick	28	D3	GN	
Netherhope Halt	17	B6	GW	1959
Netherton GDS (Fife)	46	E10	NB	1959
Netherton GDS (Renfrew)	74	C1	CAL	1959
Netherton (Staffs) — see [West Midlands]				
Netherton (Yorks)	79	H3	LY	1959
Nethertown	40	C5	FUR	
Nethertown — see [West Midlands]				
Nethy Bridge	57	B7	GNS	1965
Nethy Bridge — see also Broomhill				
Netley	4	H4	LSW	
Newark Caste	28	G5	MID	
Newark North Gate	28	G5	GN	
Newarthill	75	G3	CAL	1880
New Barnet	64	F10	GN	
New Basford — see [Nottingham]				
New Beckenham 2nd, 1st — 1867	69	C7	SEC	
New Biggin	41	C8	MID	1970
Newbiggin-by-the-Sea	43	G6	NE	1964
Newbigging	46	D5	CAL	1945
New Bolingbroke	29	E6	GN	1970
Newbridge	78	D8	GW	1962
Newbridge-on-Wye	26	G3	CAM	1962
Newbridge Street — see [Newcastle]				
New Brighton	36	B1	WIRRAL	
	77	A1		
New Brompton — see Gillingham				
New Broughton Road Halt	72	D3	GC	1917
Newburgh	51	A5	NB	1955
Newburgh (Lancs) — see Parbold				
Newburn	43	E3	NE	1958
Newbury	14	G2	GN	
Newbury Park — see [London]				
Newbury Racecourse*	14	G2	GN	
Newbury West Fields Halt	14	E2	GW	1957
Newby Bridge	40	H3	FUR	1946
Newby Bridge R.O. PR. FR. CL. above	40	H3	L & H	
Newby Wiske	38	E3	NE	1939
[Newcastle]				
Benton Square R.N. Longbenton	81	C4	NE	
Byker	81	C3	NE	1954
Carliol Square	81	B3	YNB	1950
Coxlodge	81	B4	NE	1929
Elswick	81	A3	NE	1967
Forth	81	B3	NC	1951
Heaton	81	C3	NE	
Jesmond	81	B3	NE	
Manors West	81	B3	NE	
Manors East	81	B3	NE	1954
Newcastle Central	43	F3	NE	
	81	B3		
New Bridge Street	81	B3	NE	1909
St Anthony's	81	D3	NE	1960
St Peter's	81	C3	NE	1960
Scotswood	43	F3	NE	1967
Shot Tower	81	B3	NC	1847
South Gosforth	43	F3	NE	
	81	B4		
West Gosforth	81	B4	NE	1929
West Jesmond	81	B3	NE	
Newcastle (Brampton) Halt	73	B7	NS	1923

Station	Page	Block	Comp	Year of CL
Newcastle Crossing	30	F4	LNW	1918
Newcastle Emlyn	19	B8	GW	1952
Newcastle (Liverpool Road) Halt	81	B6	NS	1926
Newcastleton	42	D6	NB	1969
Newcastle-under-Lyme	31	A4	NS	1964
	73	B7		
Newchapel and Goldenhill — see [Stoke-on-Trent]				
Newchurch (Isle of Wight)	5	A2	IWC	1956
Newchurch (Lancs) — see Waterfoot				
Newchurch Halt	77	B7	LNE	1964
New Clee	35	E3	GC	
New Cross — see [London]				
New Cross Gate — see [London]				
New Cumnock	49	F2	GSW	1965
New Cut Lane Halt	76	E2	LY	1938
New Dale Halt	27	G9	GW	1962
New Dykes Brow	75	H6	NB	1866
New Eltham and Pope Street	69	F8	SEC	
Newent	17	E9	GW	1959
New Ferry — see Bebington				
New Galloway	45	A5	PPW JT	1965
New Hadley Halt	27	G10	GW	
New Hall Bridge Halt — see [Burnley]				
New Halls	46	E9	NB	1878
New Hailes — see [Edinburgh]				
Newham (Northumberland)	43	G5	NE	1950
Newham (Cornwall) — see Truro				
Newham GDS (Truro)	10	G4	GW	
Newhaven — see [Edinburgh]				
Newhaven Harbour	2	D1	LBSC	
Newhaven Town	2	D1	LBSC	
New Haw — see Byfleet				
New Hey	76	E10	LY	
New Holland Pier	35	B5	GC	
New Holland Town	35	B5	GC	
Newhouse	49	H8	CAL	1930
	75	H4		
New Hythe	2	H8	SEC	
Newick and Chailey	2	C3	LBSC	1958
Newington (Kent)	3	A9	SEC	
Newington — see [Edinburgh]				
New Inn Bridge Halt	18	G6	GW	1937
Newland	17	C7	GW	1917
Newland Halt	24	B2	GW	1965
Newlands — see Langside				
New Lane	76	D2	LY	
Newlay and Horsepath — see [Leeds]				
New Longton and Hutton Form. Howick	76	C3	LY	1964
New Luce	44	C4	GSW	1965
Newmachar	54	H8	GNS	1965
Newmains	46	A6	CAL	1930
New Malden Form. Coombe and Malden	68	C6	LSW	
Newmarket 2nd, 1st — 1902	23	D9	GE	
Newmill	55	E6	CAL	1967
New Mills Central	31	C9	GC/MID	
	77	C10		
New Mills Newtown	31	C9	LNW	
	77	C10		
Newmilns	49	F4	GSW	1964
New Milton for Milford-on-Sea	4	D2	LSW	
Newnham	17	D8	GW	1964
Newnham Bridge	27	G4	GW	1962
Newpark	46	D7	CAL	1959
[New Passage]				
New Passage	72	C10	GW	1886
New Passage Halt	17	C4	GW	1964
	72	C10		
New Passage Pier	17	C4	GW	1886
	72	C10		
Newport — see [Teeside]				
[Newport] (Isle of Wight)				
Newport	4	H2	FYN	1923
Newport	4	H2	IWC	1966
Pan Mill	4	H2	IOW/NJ	1879
Newport (Essex)	23	G8	GE	
Newport (Salop)	30	H1	LNW	1964
[Newport] (Gwent)				
Courtybella	78	F10	MON	1852
Dock Street	78	F10	GW	1880
Mill Street	78	F10	GW	1880
Newport High Street	16	F4	GW	
	78	F10		
Station (Marshes Turnpike Gate)	78	F10	MON	1853
Newport-on-Tay East	51	C6	NB	1969
Newport-on-Tay West	51	C6	NB	1969
Newport Pagnell	25	H1	LNW	1964
New Pudsey	79	E4	GN	

Station	Page	Block	Comp	Year of CL
Newquay	10	G7	GW	
New Quay Road — see Bryn Teify				
New Radnor	27	B3	GW	1951
New Road — see Ynysbwl Halt				
New Romney Private	3	D4	RHD	
New Romney and Littlestone-on-Sea	3	D4	SEC	1967
Newseat Halt	54	D10	GNS	1965
Newsham	43	F5	NE	1964
Newsholme	37	A9	LY	1957
New Southgate and Friern Barnet	64	G8	GN	
Newstead (Borders)	47	B3	NB	1852
Newstead (Notts)	82	E4	GN	1931
Newstead West (Notts)	82	E4	MID	1964
New Strand — see [Bootle]				
New Street — see [West Midlands] Birmingham				
Newthorpe, Greasley & Shipley Gate	82	D3	GN	1963
Newton (Lanarkshire) 2nd, 1st — 1873	75	B3	CAL	
Newton for Hyde (Cheshire)	37	C2	GC	
Newton Abbot	9	C10	GW	
Newtonairds	45	D7	GSW	1943
Newton Aycliffe	38	D7	NE	
Newtongrange	83	G3	NB	1969
Newtonhead	49	C3	GSW	1868
Newton Heath — see [Manchester]				
Newton Heath — see also [Manchester] Dean Lane				
Newtonhill	55	C8	CAL	1956
Newton Kyme	34	C7	NE	1964
	79	B9		
Newton-le-Willows	36	F1	LNW	
	76	G5		
Newtonmore	56	E3	HR	
Newton-on-Ayr	49	B3	GSW	
Newton Poppleford	6	E2	LSW	1967
Newton Road — see [West Midlands]				
Newton St Cyres	6	C3	LSW	
	8	H10		
Newton Stewart	44	F4	PPW JT	1965
Newton Tony	4	E8	LSW	1952
Newtown 2nd, 1st — 1861	27	A7	CAM	
Newtown (Cumbria) — see [Whitehaven]				
Newtown Halt (Norfolk) — see [Yarmouth]				
New Tredegar and Tir Phil	78	B6	BM	1962
New Tredegar — see also Tir Phil				
New Wandsworth — see [London]				
Newtyle 2nd, 1st — 1868	51	B7	CAL	1955
Neyland	18	F3	GW	1964
Nidd Bridge	34	A9	NE	1962
	37	G10		
Niddrie	83	G5	NB	1955
Niddrie Junction	83	G5	NB	1847
Nigg	56	C4	HIGH	1960
Nightingale Valley Halt	72	C6	GW	1929
Nine Elms — see [London]				
Nine Mile Point	78	E8	LNW	1959
Ninewells Junction — see [Dundee]				
Ningwood (Isle of Wight)	4	G1	FYN	1953
Ninian Park* — see [Cardiff]				
Nisbet	42	G10	NB	1948
	47	D2		
No 5 Passing Place	35	D4	GC/GI	1961
Nitshill	49	E7	GBK JT	
	74	D2		
Nocton and Dunstan	29	B6	GN/GE	1955
Noel Park and Wood Green — see [London]				
Nook Pasture	42	D5	NB	1874
Norbiton for Kingston Hill	68	C6	LSW	
Norbury (Surrey)	68	C6	LBSC	
Norbury and Ellaston (Derbys)	31	D4	NS	1954
Norham	47	G5	NE	1964
Normacot — see [Stoke-on-Trent]				
Normans Bay Halt	2	G2	LBSC	
Normanby Park GDS	34	H3	GC	1964
Normanton	38	E4	MID	
	79	F7		
Normanton — see also [Derby] Pear Tree				
North Acton - see [London]				
North Acton Halt — see [London]				
[Northallerton]				
Northallerton	38	E4	NE	
Northallerton Low	38	E4	NE	1901
Northallerton Town	38	E4	NE	1956
Northam (Devon)	8	D4	BWA	1917
Northam (Hants) — see [Southampton]				
[Northampton]				
Bridge Street	25	F3	LNW	1964

Station	Page	Block	Comp	Year of CL
Northampton Castle	25	F3	LNW	
St John's Street 2nd, 1st – 1872	25	F3	MID	1962
North Berwick	47	B10	NB	
North Bridge – see [Halifax]				
North Camp Form. Aldershot	5	E10	SEC	
North Cave	34	H6	HB	1955
North Connel	52	H	CAL	1966
North Docks – see [Liverpool] Sandhills				
North Drove	22	E4	ME/MGN	1958
	29	D1		
North Dulwich	69	A9	LBSC	
North Eastrington	34	G5	HB	1955
North Elmham	20	D3	GE	1964
North Elmsall – see Upton				
North End	25	A3	EWJ	1877
Northenden – see [Manchester]				
Northfield	80	F5	MID	
North Filton Platform* – see [Bristol]				
Northfleet	70	F9	SEC	
Northgate – see [Chester]				
North Greenwich – see [London]				
North Grimston	34	H10	NE	1950
North Hayling	5	C4	LBSC	1963
Northiam for Beckley and Sandhurst	3	A4	KES	1954
North Kelsey	35	B2	GC	1965
North Leith – see [Edinburgh]				
North Lew – see Ashbury				
North Lonsdale Crossing	40	G2	FUR	1916
Northolt Junction – see [London] South Ruislip				
Northolt Park – see [London]				
Northorpe (Lincs)	28	H10	GC	1955
	34	H1		
Northorpe Higher (Yorks)	79	G4	LNW	1953
Northorpe, North Road (Yorks)	79	G4	LY	1965
North Queensferry 2nd, 1st – 1890	46	E9	NB	
North Road	38	D7	NE	
North Rode	31	B7	NS	1962
	73	D10		
North Seaton	43	F6	NE	1964
North Sheen	64	C1	LSW	
	68	B9		
North Shields	81	E3	NE	
North Shields – see also [Tynemouth]				
North Skelton	39	A9	NE	1951
North Stockwell – see [London]				
North Sunderland	43	H6	N SUND	1951
North Tawton	8	H7	LSW	1972
North Thoresby	35	E2	GN	1970
Northumberland Park	65	C8	GE	
North Walsall – see [West Midlands]				
North Walsham	20	C7	GE	
North Walsham Town	20	C7	MGN	1959
North Water Bridge	51	G10	NB	1951
	55	G6		
North Weald	12	F6	GE	1966
North Weald R.O. by LT	12	F6	LT	
North Wembley	64	B6	LNW	
North Western – see [Wigan]				
Northwich	30	G7	CLC	
	77	F7		
Northwood	63	E8	MET/GC/LT	
Northwood Hills	63	E8	LT	
Northwood – see [Stoke-on-Trent] Bucknall				
Northwood Halt	80	F1	GW	1963
Northwood Halt R.O. PR. FR. CL. above	80	F1	SVR	
North Woolwich	65	F3	GE	
North Wootton	21	D9	GE	1969
North Wylam	43	E3	NE	1968
	81	F1		
Norton (Cheshire)	77	D5	B HEAD	1952
Norton (Worcs)	24	C2	MID	1846
Norton (Yorks)	34	D4	LY	1947
Norton Bridge 2nd, 1st – 1876	31	A2	LNW	
Norton Fitzwarren	6	C7	GW	1961
Norton Halt	24	C2	GW	1966
Norton-in-Hales	30	G2	NS	1956
Norton Junction (Teeside)	38	F7	NE	1870
Norton Road	19	F1	SIT	1960
[Norwich]				
City	20	F6	MGN	1959
Hellesdon	20	F6	MGN	1952
Thorpe Norwich 2nd, 1st – 1886	20	F6	GE	
Trowse 2nd, 1st – 1845	20	F6	GE	1939
Victoria	20	F6	GE	1916
Norwood Green – see [Bradford] Wyke				
Norwood Junction and South Norwood	69	A9	LBSC	
Nostell	79	H7	WRG JT	1951
Notgrove	14	C8	GW	1962
Nottage Halt	78	G1	GW	1963
[Nottingham]				
Arkwright Street	82	F1	GC	1969
Basford North	82	F2	GN	1964
Basford Vernon	82	F2	MID	1960
Bulwell Common	82	E3	GC	1963
Bulwell Forest	82	E3	GN	1929
Bulwell Halt	82	F2	GC	1930
Bulwell Market	82	E3	MID	1960
Carrington	82	F2	GC	1928
Daybrook for Arnold	82	F3	GN	1960
Lenton	82	E1	MID	1911
London Road, High Level	82	F1	GN	1967
London Road, Low Level	82	F1	LNW	1944
New Basford	82	F2	GC	1964
Nottingham 2nd, 1st – 1848	28	D3	MID	
	82	F1		
Radford	82	F1	MID	1964
St Ann's Well	82	F2	GN	1916
Sherwood	82	F2	GN	1916
Thorneywood	82	H2	GN	1916
Victoria	82	F2	GC/GN	1967
Nottingham Road – see [Derby]				
Notting Hill – see [London]				
Notting Hill Gate	64	E3	MET/GC	
Notton – see Royston				
Notton and Royston	79	H7	GC	1930
Novar – see Evanton				
Nunburnholme	34	H7	NE	1951
Nuneaton, Abbey Street 2nd, 1st – 1873	80	C10	MID	1968
Nuneaton, Trent Valley	25	A7	LNW	
	80	C10		
Nunhead	65	C1	SR	
Nunnington	38	H2	NE	1953
Nunthorpe	38	G6	NE	
Nursling	4	F5	LSW	1957
Nutbourne Halt	5	D4	LBSC	
Nutfield	2	B7	SEC	
Oakamoor	31	C4	NS	1965
Oakdale Halt	78	C7	GW	1932
Oakengates, Market Street	27	H10	LNW	1952
Oakengates West	27	H10	GW	
Oakenshaw	79	G7	MID	1870
Oakham	25	G10	MID	
Oakington	23	C6	GE	1970
Oakleigh Park for East Barnet	64	G10	GN	
Oakle Street	17	E8	GW	1964
Oakley (Beds)	23	E2	MID	1958
Oakley (Fife)	46	D10	NB	1968
	50	G1		
Oakley (Hants)	5	A10	LSW	1963
Oaks, The – see The Oaks				
Ouksey Halt	14	A5	GW	1964
	17	H5		
Oakwellgate – see [Gateshead]				
Oakworth CL. 1962 R.O. 1968 T.O.				
Private	79	D1	MID/KWVR	
Oatlands	40	D7	CWJC	1922
Oban	52	G	CAL	
Occumster	62	F5	HIGH	1944
Ochiltree	49	D2	GSW	1951
Ockendon	66	G4	MID	
Ocker Hill – see [West Midlands]				
Ockham – see Horsley				
Ockley and Capel	2	A6	LBSC	
Oddington Halt 1st Sta. 1851	14	H7	LNW	1926
Offord and Buckden	23	C4	GN	1959
Ogbourne	14	C2	MSWJ	1961
Ogilvie Village Halt	78	B6	GW	1962
Ogmore Vale	78	E3	GW	1958
Okehampton*	8	H5	LSW	1972
Old Bescot – see [West Midlands] Wood Street				
Oldbury and Bromford Lane	80	D4	GW	
Old Colwyn	33	C8	LNW	1952
Old Cumnock – see Cumnock				
Old Dalby	28	E2	MID	1966
Oldfield Park (Bath)	17	D1	GW	
Oldfield Road – see [Manchester]				
[Oldham]				
Central	76	F10	LY	1966
Clegg Street	76	F10	OAGB	1959
Glodwick Road	76	F10	LNW	1955
Mumps	76	F10	LY	
Mumps	76	F10	LNW	1862
Werneth	37	B3	LY	
	76	F10		
Oldham Road – see [Manchester]				

Station	Page	Block	Comp	Year of CL
Old Hill	83	E3	GW	
Old Hill (High Street) Halt — see [West Midlands]				
Old Kent Road — see [London]				
Old Kilpatrick	74	A8	CAL	1964
Oldlands Common Halt	72	F6	LMS	1966
Old Leake	22	A6	GN	1956
	29	F5		
Oldmeldrum	54	G7	GNS	1931
Old Mill Lane	76	F3	LNW	1951
Old North Road	23	E5	LNW	1968
Old Oak Lane Halt — see [London]				
Old Roan	76	F2	LY	
Old Roan — see also [Bootle]				
Old Street	65	A4	GN	
Old Trafford	77	A8	MSJA	
Oldwoods Halt	30	D1	GW	1960
Old Ynysybwl Halt	78	D4	TV	1952
Ollerton	28	D6	GC	1955
	82	H6		
Olmarch Halt	19	F9	GW	1965
	26	B3		
Olney	25	H3	MID	1962
Olton	80	F7	GW	
Omoa — see Cleland				
Ongar Form. Chipping Ongar	12	G6	GE	1966
Ongar R.O. by LT	12	G6	LT	
Onibury	27	E6	SH JT	1958
Onllwyn	78	B1	N & B	1962
Openshaw — see Gorton				
Orbliston	54	C1	HIGH	1964
Ordens Halt	54	C4	GNS	1964
Ordnance Factory — see [London]				
Ordsall Lane — see [Manchester]				
Ore	3	A2	SEC	
Oreston — see [Plymouth]				
Orleston — see Ham Street				
Oriel Road — see [Bootle]				
Ormesby	38	G6	NE	
Ormiston	47	A8	NB	1933
Ormside	41	D7	MID	1952
Ormskirk	76	E2	LY	
Orpington	2	D9	SEC	
	69	G5		
Orrell	76	F4	LY	
Orrell Park Halt	76	F4	LY	
Orston — see Elton				
Orton	54	D1	HIGH	1964
Orton Waterville	22	G3	LNW	1952
Orton Waterville R.O. PR. FR. CL. above			NVR	
Orwell	21	G7	GE	1959
Osbaldwick	34	E8	DV	1915
Osmondthorpe Halt — see [Leeds]				
Ossett	79	G5	GW	1964
Ossett — see also Horbury				
Osterley — see [London]				
Oswaldtwistle — see Church				
Oswestry	33	G2	CAM	1966
Oswestry 2nd, 1st — 1866	33	G2	GW	1924
Otford Junction	2	E6	SEC	
Otley	37	F8	O & I	1965
	79	B4		
Otterham	9	A1	LSW	1966
	11	C10		
Otterington	38	E3	NE	1958
Otterspool — see [Liverpool]				
Ottery St Mary	6	E3	LSW	1967
Otteringham	35	E5	NE	1964
Oughty Bridge	31	G10	GC	1959
	82	A9		
Oulton Broad North Form. Carleton Colville	20	H10	GE	
Oulton Broad South	20	H10	GE	
Oundle	23	A2	LNW	1964
Ouse Bridge	22	H8	GE	1864
Outwell Basin	22	F7	GE	1928
Outwell Village	22	G8	GE	1928
Outwood — see Lofthouse				
Outwood — see [Halifax]				
Over — see Winsford				
Over and Wharton	30	G6	LNW	1947
Overseal and Moira	24	H10	AN JT	1890
Overstrand	20	B7	NS JT	1953
Overton	4	H10	LSW	
Overton-on-Dee	30	C4	CAM	1962
Overtown 2nd, 1st — 1881	46	A6	CAL	1942
	75	H1		
Owen Street — see Tipton				
Oxenholme	41	A3	LNW	

Station	Page	Block	Comp	Year of CL
Oxenhope CL. 1962 R.O. 1968				
T.O. Private	37	C6	KWVR	
	79	E1		
[Oxford]				
Abingdon Road Halt	14	H6	GW	1915
Garsington Bridge Halt	14	H6	GW	1915
Hinksey Halt	14	H6	GW	1915
Iffley Halt	14	H6	GW	1915
Littlemoor	14	H6	GW	1963
Morris Cowley Opened 1928 on site of Garsington Bridge Halt	14	H6	GW	1963
Oxford, Limpsfield 2nd, 1st — 1852	14	H6	GW	
Oxford, Rewley Road	14	H6	LNW	1951
Oxford Road (Temp. Terminus)	14	H6	LNW	1851
Oxford Road Halt	14	H7	LNW	1926
Port Meadow Halt Form. Summertown	14	H6	LNW	1926
Wolvercot Platform	14	H6	GW	1916
Wolvercot	14	H6	LNW	1926
Yarnton	14	H6	GW	1962
Oxford Lane Halt	14	F4	WT	1925
Oxford Road — see [Manchester]				
Oxford Road Halt — see Oxford				
Oxford Street — see Mountain Ash				
Oxhey — see Bushey				
Oxheys — see [Preston]				
Oxshott for Fair Mile	67	H2	LSW	
Oxspring	37	F2	MS & L/GC	1847
	82	A9		
Oxted and Limpsfield	2	C7	CO JT	
Oxton	47	A6	NB	1932
Oyne	54	G5	GNS	1968
Oystermouth — see [Swansea]				
Pabo — see Mochdre				
Padbury	15	B10	LNW	1964
Paddington — see [London]				
Paddock Wood	2	G7	SEC	
Padeswood and Buckley	30	B6	LNW	1958
	72	C5		
Padgate	77	C6	CLC	
Padiham	76	B8	LY	1957
Padstow	10	H8	LSW	1967
Paignton	9	D10	GW	
Paignton, Queens Park Private	9	D10	T & D	
[Paisley]				
Abercorn 2nd, 1st — 1866	74	E4	GSW	1967
East GDS	74	C3	CAL	1958
Ferguslie GDS	74	C3	GSW	1959
Hawkhead	74	D3	GSW	1966
Paisley, Canal	49	D7	GSW	
	74	D3		
Paisley, Gilmour Street	49	D7	CAL/GSW	
	74	D3		
Potterhill	74	C3	GSW	1917
St James	49	D7	CAL	
	74	D3		
West	74	C3	GSW	1966
Palace Gates — see [London]				
Pallion — see [Sunderland]				
Palmers Green and Southgate	65	A9	GN	
Palnure	44	G4	PPW JT	1951
Palterton and Sutton	82	E6	MID	1930
Pampisford	23	F8	GE	1967
Pandy	16	H8	GW	1958
Pandy	78	D3	TV	1886
Pangbourne	15	A3	GW	
Pannal	37	G8	NE	
	79	A6		
Pans Lane Halt	17	H1	GW	1966
Pant	30	B1	CAM	1965
Pant — see [Caernarvon]				
Panteg and Griffithstown 2nd, 1st — 1880	78	D10	GW	1962
Pant Glas	32	E4	LNW	1957
Pant Halt	33	H1	GW	1915
	72	C2		
Pant Junction — see [Merthyr]				
Pantydwr	26	G5	CAM	1962
Pantyffordd Halt	78	B1	GW	1962
Pantyffynnon	19	F4	GW	
Pantysgalliog Halt — see [Merthyr]				
Pantywaun Halt	78	A5	GW	1962
Papcastle	40	D8	MC	1921
	45	G1		
Paper Mills T.O. R.N. Kemsley Down	3	B9	S & K	
Par	11	B6	GW	
Parbold for Newburgh	36	E4	LY	
	76	E3		
Parcyrhun Halt	19	G4	GW	1955
Parham	21	D8	GE	1952
Park (Grampian)	55	C7	GNS	1966

Station	Page	Block	Comp	Year of CL
Park (Lancs)	76	G9	LY	
Park Bridge	76	G10	OAGB	1959
Park Drain	34	F2	GN/GE	1955
	82	H10		
Parkend	17	C7	SW JT	1929
Parkgate 2nd, 1st — 1886	77	G1	B HEAD	1956
Parkgate — see also Neston				
Parkgate and Aldwarke	82	D9	GC	1951
Parkgate and Rawmarsh	82	D9	MID	1968
Park Hall Halt	30	B2	GW	1966
	33	H2		
Parkhead North — see [Glasgow]				
Parkhead for Celtic Park — see [Glasgow]				
Parkhill	55	A7	GNS	1950
Park Leaze Halt	14	A6	BR	1964
Park Royal — see [London]				
Parkside	76	G4	LNW	1878
Parkside Halt	62	F5	LMS	1944
Parkstone for Sandbanks	4	B2	LSW	
Parkestone Quay — see [Harwich]				
Park Street and Frogmore 2nd, 1st — 1890	12	B7	LNW	
Parkway — see [Bristol]				
Parracombe Halt	8	B7	LB	1935
Parrs Wood — see East Didsbury				
Parsley Hay 2nd, 1st — 1899	31	E6	LNW	1954
Parsons Green — see [London]				
Parsons Street Platform	72	C6	GW	
Partick Central — see [Glasgow]				
Partick Hill — see [Glasgow]				
Partick West — see [Glasgow]				
Partington 2nd, 1st — 1893	77	B8	CLC	1964
Parton (Cumbria)	40	C7	LNW	
Parton (Dumfries)	45	B5	PPW JT	1965
Partridge Green	2	A3	LBSC	1966
Paston and Knapton Halt	20	C7	NS JT	1964
Patchway 2nd, 1st — 1885	17	C4	GW	
	72	D8		
Pateley Bridge	37	E10	NE	1951
Pateley Bridge	37	E10	NIDD	1930
Patna 2nd, 1st — 1897	44	G10	GSW	1964
	49	D1		
Patney and Chirton	14	B1	GW	1966
Patricroft	36	H2	LNW	
	76	G7		
Patrington	35	E5	NE	1964
Patterton for Darnley Rifle Range	74	D1	CAL	
Paulton Halt	17	D1	GW	1925
Peacock Cross	75	D2	NB	1917
Peak Forest for Peak Dale	31	D8	MID	1967
Peakirk	22	F3	GN	1961
Peartree and Normanton	28	A2	MID	
	31	G3		
Peartree — see also [Derby]				
Pear Tree Hill — see Coldham				
Peasley Cross — see [St Helens]				
Pebworth Halt	24	F2	GW	1966
Peckham — see [London] Queens Road				
Peckham Rye	65	B1	LBSC	
Pedair Ffordd	33	E2	CAM	1951
Peebles West	46	G3	CAL	1950
Peebles East 2nd, 1st — 1864	46	G3	NB	1962
Pegswood	43	E6	NE	
Pelaw (3rd, 1st — 1857, 2nd — 1896) Jcn	43	G3	NE	1979
	81	D2		
Pellon — see [Halifax]				
Pelsall	80	A5	LNW	1965
Pelton 2nd, 1st — 1869	43	F2	NE	1953
Pemberton	76	F4	LY	
Pembrey and Burry Port	19	D2	GW	
Pembrey Halt	19	D3	BPGV	1953
Pembridge	27	D3	GW	1955
Pembroke	18	F2	GW	
Pembroke Dock	18	F2	GW	
Penallt Halt	17	B1	GW	1959
Penally	18	H2	GW	
Penally	18	H2	GW	1971
Penar Junction Halt	78	C7	GW	1917
Penarth Dock	78	H6	TV	1962
Penarth Town	78	H6	TV	
Pencader	19	D7	GW	1965
Pencader Junction	19	D7	MM	1880
Pencaitland	47	A8	NB	1933
Pencarreg Halt	19	E8	GW	1965
Penclawdd	19	E2	LNW	1931
Pen Cob Halt	32	G3	FEST	1965
Pencoed	78	G3	GW	1964
Pendas Way — see [Leeds]				
Pendleton	76	G8	LY	
Pendleton — see also [Manchester]				

Station	Page	Block	Comp	Year of CL
Pendlebury	76	G8	LY	1960
Pengam (Glam)	78	C6	RHY	
Pengam	78	C6	GW	1962
Pengam — see also Fleur de Lis				
Penge East	69	B6	SEC	
Penge West 2nd, 1st — 1841	69	B6	LBSC	
Penhelig Halt	26	C8	CAM	
Penicuik	46	G6	NB	1951
	83	D1		
Penistone 2nd, 1st — 1874	37	F3	GC/LY	
	82	A9		
Penistone, Barnsley Road	82	A9	LY	1916
Penketh — see Fiddlers Ferry				
Penketh — see also Sankey				
Penkridge	24	C10	LNW	
Penmaen Halt	78	C7	GW	1939
Penmaenmawr	32	H8	LNW	
Penmaenpool	26	C10	CAM	1965
	32	H1		
Penmere Platform	10	G3	GW	
Pen Mill — see Yeovil				
Penn Halt	15	E5	GW	1932
Pennington	76	G6	LNW	1954
Penns — see [West Midlands]				
Penpergwm	78	B10	GW	1958
Penponds	10	D4	WC	1852
Penrhiwceiber High Level	78	D4	GW	1964
Penrhiwceiber* Low Level	78	D4	TV	1964
Penrhyn	32	G3	FEST	1939
Penrhyn R.O. PR. FR. CL. above	32	G3	FR	
Penrhyndeudraeth	32	G3	CAM	
Penrith for Ullswater Lake	41	A8	LNW	
Penruddock	41	A8	CKP	1972
Penryn 2nd, 1st — 1923	10	G3	GW	
Penryn Point T.O. Priv.	26	B10	FAIR B	
Pensarn — see Llanbadr				
Pensarn — see also Abergele				
Penscynor Halt	78	C1	GW	1962
Pensford	17	C1	GW	1951
Penshaw	43	G2	NE	1964
Penshurst	2	E7	SEC	
Pensnett Halt — see [West Midlands]				
Pentir Rhiw	16	E8	BM	1962
Penton	42	D4	NB	1969
Pentraeth	32	F8	LNW	1930
Pentre — see Moss				
Pentrebach for Abercanaid	78	B4	TV	
Pentre Broughton Halt	72	D3	GW	1931
Pentrecourt Halt	19	C8	GW	1952
Pentrefelin	33	F1	CAM	1951
Pentrefelin Halt (Glam) — see [Swansea]				
Pentrepiod Halt	78	C9	GW	1941
Pentre Platform	78	D3	TV	1912
Pentresaeson Halt	72	C3	GW	1931
Penwyllt — see Craig-y-Nos				
Pentwyn Halt	78	C9	GW	1941
Pentwynmawr Halt	78	D7	GW	1964
Pentyrch	78	G6	TV	1863
Penwortham, Cop Lane	76	C3	LY	1964
Penybont	27	A4	LNW	
Penybontawr	33	E2	CAM	1951
Pen-y-Brin Halt	32	G3	FEST	1967
Penychain, for Pwllheli Camp	32	E3	CAM	
Penyffordd for Leeswood	33	H6	GC	
	77	H2		
Penyffordd — see also Hope				
Penygraig	78	E3	GW	1958
Penygroes 2nd, 1st — 1865	32	E5	LNW	1964
Penygroes — see Cross Hands				
Penyrheol	78	E6	RHY	1964
Penzance	10	B3	GW	
Peplon	30	F2	GW	1963
Percy Main 2nd, 1st — 1861	81	E3	NE	
Perivale Halt — see [London]				
Perranporth	10	F5	GW	1963
Perranporth Beach Halt	10	F5	GW	1963
Perranwell	10	G4	GW	
Perry Barr	80	C6	LNW	
Pershore	24	D2	GW	
Persley Halt — see [Aberdeen]				
[Perth]				
Barnhill	50	H5	DPA	1849
Central GDS	50	H5	NB	1970
Glasgow Road	50	H5	SCNE	1860
Perth	50	H5	CAL	
Princes Street	50	H5	CAL	1966
[Peterborough]				
Crescent	22	G3	MID	1866
East	22	G3	GE	1966

Station	Page	Block	Comp	Year of CL
Monkhill	34	C5	LY	
	79	G9		
Tanshelf	79	G7	LY	1967
Ponteland	43	E4	NE	1929
	81	B5		
Pontesbury	27	D9	S & WPL	1951
Pontfadog	30	A3	GVT	1933
	33	G3		
Pontfaen	30	A3	GVT	1933
	33	G3		
Ponthenry Halt	19	D4	BPGV	1953
Ponthir	78	E10	GW	1962
Pont Lawrence Halt	78	E8	LNW	1957
Pontllanfraith High Level	78	C7	LNW	1960
Pontllanfraith Low Level	78	C7	GW	1964
Pont Llanio	26	C3	GW	1965
Pont Lliw	19	F2	GW	1924
Pontlottyn	78	A6	RHY	
Pontnewynydd (Gwent)	78	D10	GW	1962
Pontnewynydd Halt (West Glam.) — see Glyn Abbey Halt				
Pontrhydyfen	78	E1	RSB	1962
Pontrhydyrun	78	C10	GW	1917
Pontrhydyrun Halt	78	D10	GW	1962
Pontrhythallt	32	F6	LNW	1930
Pontrilas	17	A9	GW	1958
Pont Rug	31	F6	LNW	1930
Pontsarn Halt for Vaynor	78	A4	BM/LNW	1961
Pontsticill Junction	16	D7	DM	1962
	78	A4		
Pontwalby Halt	78	C2	GW	1964
Pontyates	19	D3	BPGV	1953
Pontyberem	19	E4	BPGV	1953
Pontycymmer	78	E2	GW	1953
Pontygwaith Halt	78	C4	GW	1951
Pontygwaith Platform	78	C4	TV	1914
Pont-y-Pant	33	A5	LNW	
[Pontypool]				
Blaendare Road Halt	78	C10	GW	1962
Clarence Street	78	C10	GW	1964
Crane Street	78	C10	GW	1962
Pontypool Road 2nd, 1st — 1909	16	E4	GW	
	78	C10		
[Pontypridd]				
Graig	78	E4	BARRY	1930
Pontypridd	78	E4	TV	
Tram Road	78	E4	ANSW	1922
Pontyrhyll	78	E2	GW	1953
Poole for Longfleet	4	B2	LSW	
Pool-in-Wharfedale	37	F8	NE	1965
	79	B		
Pool Quay	27	B10	CAM	1965
Pope Street — see New Eltham				
Poplar — see [London]				
Poppleton	34	D8	NE	
Portbury	17	B3	GW	1962
	72	A7		
Portbury Shipyard	17	B3	GW	1923
	72	A7		
Portby Road — see Portishead				
Port Carlisle	42	A3	NB	1932
Port Carlisle Junction — see [Carlisle]				
Portchester	5	B4	LSW	
Port Clarence — see [Teeside]				
Port Dinorwic 2nd, 1st — 1873	32	F7	LNW	1960
Port Edgar	46	E9	NB	1890
Port Elphinstone GDS	54	H6	GNS	1964
Porterfield — see [Renfrew]				
Portesham	7	D1	GW	1952
Portessie	54	C2	GNS	1968
Portessie	54	C2	HIGH	1915
[Port Glasgow]				
Inchgreen	49	B9	GSW	1961
Port Glasgow	49	B9	CAL	
Port Glasgow Upper GDS	49	B9	GSW	1959
Portgordon	54	B2	GNS	1968
Porth 2nd, 1st — 1876	78	E4	TV	
Porthcawl 2nd, 1st — 1916	16	A3	GW	1963
	78	G2		
Porthywaen	30	B1	CAM	1951
	33	H1		
Port Isaac Road	11	B9	LSW	1966
[Portishead]				
Portishead 2nd, 1st — 1854	17	B3	GW	1964
	72	A7		
Portishead	17	B3	WCP	1940
	72	A7		
Portishead South and Portby Road	72	A7	WCP	1940
Portknockie	54	B3	GNS	1968

Station	Page	Block	Comp	Year of CL
Portland 2nd, 1st — 1905	7	A1	WP JT	1952
Portlethan	55	C8	CAL	1956
[Portmadoc]				
Portmadoc	32	F3	WH	1936
Portmadoc	32	F3	CAM	
Portmadoc	32	F3	FEST	1939
Portmadoc R.O. PR. FR. CL. above	32	F3	F & R	
Port Meadow Halt — see [Oxford]				
Portobello — see [Edinburgh]				
Portobello — see [West Midlands]				
Port of Mentieth	50	B2	NB	1934
Porton	4	D8	LSW	1968
Portpatrick	44	A4	PPW	1950
Portreath GDS	10	E5	GW	1936
Portskewett 2nd, 1st — 1863	17	B4	GW	1964
Portskewett Pier	17	B4	GW	1886
Portslade and West Hove	2	B2	LBSC	
[Portsmouth] (Hants)				
Albert Road Bridge Halt	5	B4	LSW/LBSC	1914
Cosham	5	B4	LSW	1970
East Southsea	5	B4	LSW/LBSC	1914
Farlington Halt	5	B4	LBSC	1937
Jessie Road Bridge Halt	5	B4	LSW/LBSC	1914
Portsmouth and Southsea	5	B4	LSW/LBSC	
Portsmouth Harbour	5	B4	LSW/LBSC	
Portsmouth (Yorks)	76	B9	LY	1958
Portsmouth Arms (Devon)	8	D7	LSW	
Portsoy 2nd, 1st — 1884	54	B4	GNS	1964
Port Sunlight	77	D2	BJ	
[Port Talbot]				
Central	78	E1	PT	1933
Docks	78	E1	RSB	1895
Port Talbot and Aberavon	16	A4	GW	
	78	E1	GW	
Port Talbot (Aberavon Town)	78	E1	RSB	1962
Port Victoria	3	A10	SEC	1951
	13	C3		
Portwood — see [Stockport]				
Possil — see [Glasgow]				
Possil Park — see [Glasgow]				
Postland for Crowland	22	E4	GN/GE	1961
Potterhanworth	29	B7	GN/GE	1955
Potter Heigham	20	E9	MGN	1959
Potter Heigham Bridge Halt	20	E9	MGN	1959
Potterhill — see [Paisley]				
Potters Bar and South Mimms	12	C6	GN	
Potto	38	F5	NE	1954
Potton 1st Sta.	23	F4	LNW	1861
Potton 2nd Sta.	23	F4	LNW	1968
Poulton — see [Wallasey] Liscard				
Poulton-le-Fylde 2nd, 1st — 1896	76	B2	PW JT	
Poulton Curve Halt	76	A1	PW JT	1952
Poundon — see Marsh Gibbon				
Powderhall — see [Edinburgh]				
Powerstock	7	C3	GW	1975
Poyle Halt for Stanwell Moor	67	B10	GW	1965
Poyle Estate Halt	67	B10	BR	1965
Poynton 2nd, 1st — 1887	77	D10	LNW	
Praed Street — see [London]				
Praze	10	D3	GW	1962
Prees	30	E3	LNW	
Preesall	36	C8	KE	1930
	76	A2		
Preesgweene — see Weston Rhyn				
Prescot	76	G3	LNW	
Prescott Siding	27	H6	CMDP	1938
Prestatyn 2nd, 1st — 1897	33	E9	LNW	
Prestatyn — see also Chapel Street				
Prestbury	31	B8	LNW	
	77	D9		
Presteigne	27	C4	GW	1951
Presthope	27	F8	GW	1951
[Preston]				
Deepdale	76	B4	PL JT	1930
Deepdale	76	B4	FPWR JT	1856
Fishergate Hill GDS	76	B3	LY	1965
Maudland Bridge	76	B4	LY/LNW	1885
Maudlands	76	B4	PW	1844
Maxwell House	76	B4	NU	1844
Oxheys	76	B4	LNW	1925
Preston	36	E6	LY/NU	
	76	B4		
Preston Junction R.N. Todd Lane Junction	76	B4	EL	1968
Ribbleton	76	B4	LY/LNW	1866
Ribbleton Form. Fulwood	76	B4	PL JT	1930
West Lancs (Fishergate)	76	B4	LY	1900
Preston Brook	77	E5	LNW	1948
Preston Junction — see [Preston]				

Station	Page	Block	Comp	Year of CL
Prestopans for Tranent	46	H8	NB	
Preston Park — see [Brighton]				
Preston Platform — see [Torbay]				
Preston Road	76	G2	LY	
Preston Road Halt — see [London]				
Preston West End Gate	73	H2	HH	1854
Prestwich	37	A3	LY	
	76	F9		
Prestwick	49	B3	GSW	
Prickwillow	23	A9	EC	1850
Priestfield — see [West Midlands]				
Primrose Hill	64	G4	LNW	
Prince of Wales Halt	3	E5	RHD	1947
Princes End — see [West Midlands]				
Princes Pier — see [Greenock]				
Princes Risborough 2nd, 1st — 1906	15	C6	GC/GW	
Princes Street — see [Edinburgh]				
Princes Street — see [Perth]				
Princetown	9	C6	GW	1956
Priory — see [Dover]				
Priory Road — see [Warrington]				
Prittlewell	13	C5	GE	
Privett	5	A4	LSW	1955
Probus and Ladock Halt	10	H4	GW	1957
Prospect Hill	81	F4	BT	1864
Prudhoe	43	D3	NE	
	81	F1		
Pudsey Greenside	79	E4	GN	1964
Pudsey Lowtown	79	E4	GN	1964
Pudsey New — see New Pudsey				
Pulborough	5	G6	LBSC	
Pultord	30	C6	GW	1855
	77	H3		
Pulham Market	20	A6	GE	1953
Pulham St Mary	20	A6	GE	1953
Pullabrook Halt	9	B9	GW	1959
Puncheston	18	G6	GW	1937
Purfleet	66	D2	MID	
	70	D10		
Purfleet Rifle Range Halt	66	D2	MID	1948
Purley	2	C9	LBSC	
	68	H3		
Purley Oaks	69	H3	LBSC	
Purton	14	C4	GW	1964
Putney	68	E9	LSW	
Putney Bridge — see also [London]				
Puxton and Worle	16	H1	GW	1964
Pwllheli for Nevin 2nd, 1st — 1909	32	D2	CAM	
Pwllheli Camp — see Penychain				
Pwll-y-Pant	78	E6	RHY	1893
Pye Bridge	82	C4	MID	1967
Pye Hill and Somercotes	82	C4	GN	1963
Pyewipe Road — see [Grimsby]				
Pyle 2nd, 1st — 1876	16	B4	GW	1964
	78	F1		
Pylle Halt	7	D8	SD JT	1966
Quainton Road 2nd, 1st — 1896	15	C8	MET/GC	1963
Quakers Drove	22	H5	GE	1964
Quakers Yard, High Level — see [Merthyr]				
Quakers Yard, Low Level — see [Merthyr]				
Quarry Siding	26	B9	TAL	
Quarter Road	49	G6	CAL	1945
Queensborough	3	B10	SEC	
Queensborough Pier	3	B10	SEC	1923
Queensbury — see [Bradford]				
Queens Ferry	77	G2	LNW	1966
Queens Park, Glasgow	74	G3	CAL	
Queens Park, London	64	E4	LNW	
Queenstown Rd., Battersea	64	H1	LSW	
	68	G10		
Queens Road, Peckham	65	C1	LBSC	
	69	B10		
Queens Road — see [London] Walthamstone				
Queen Street — see [Cardiff]				
Queen Street — see [Glasgow]				
Quellyn	32	F5	NWNG	1878
Quellyn Lake	32	F5	NWNG/WH	1936
Quintrel Downs	10	G6	GW	
Quorn and Woodhouse R.O. PR.	25	C10	GC	1963
Quorn — see also Barrow-on-Soar				
Quy	23	D8	GE	1962
Rabbit Hill — see [Barrow-in-Furness]				
Radburn — see Mickleover				
Racks	45	F4	GSW	1965
Radcliffe	78	F8	LY	
Radcliffe, Black Lane	78	E7	LY	1970
Radcliffe Bridge	78	E8	EL	1958
Radcliffe-on-Trent	28	E3	GN	

Station	Page	Block	Comp	Year of CL
Radclive Halt	15	B10	BR	1961
Radford — see [Nottingham]				
Radford and Timsbury Halt (Somerset)	17	D1	GW	1925
Radipole Halt	7	E1	GW	
Radlett	12	B6	MID	
Radley	14	H6	GW	
Radstock North	7	E10	SD JT	1966
Radstock West	7	E10	GW	1959
Radway Green and Barthomley	31	H5	NS	1966
Radyr	78	G6	TV	
Rafford	56	E7	HIGH	1865
Raglan	17	A6	GW	1955
Raglan Road	17	A7	GW	1876
Raglan Road Crossing Halt	17	A7	GW	1955
Rainford Jcn Sta. 2nd, 1st — Rainford 1858	76	F3	LY	
Rainford Village	76	F3	LNW	1951
Rainham (Essex)	66	C4	MID	
Rainham (Kent)	3	A10	SEC	
Rainhill	76	H3	LNW	1844
Rainton Meadows	38	D10	NDJ	1844
Ramper	76	B4	PW	1843
Ramsden Dock — see [Barrow-in-Furness]				
Rampside — see [Barrow-in-Furness]				
Ramsbottom	36	H4	EL	1972
	76	E8		
Ramsey East	23	A5	GN/GE	1930
Ramsey North	23	A5	GN	1947
Ramsgate Harbour	3	H9	SEC	1926
Ramsgate Town 2nd, 1st — 1926	3	H9	SEC	
Ramsgill	38	C1	NIDD	
Rankinston	49	D1	GSW	1950
Rannoch for Kinloch Rannoch	53	F9	NB	
Ranskill	28	E9	GN	1958
	82	G9		
Raskelf	38	F1	NE	1958
Ratby 2nd, 1st — 1876	25	C9	MID	1928
Rathen	54	C9	GNS	1965
Ratho	46	E8	NB	1951
Ratho Low Level	46	E8	NB	1930
Rathven	54	C2	HIGH	1915
Raunceby	22	B2	GN	
	29	B4		
Raunds	23	C2	MID	1959
Ravelrig Halt	46	E7	CAL	1920
Ravenglass for Eskdale	40	D2	FUR	
Ravenglass	40	D2	R & E	
Ravensbourne	69	D6	SEC	
Ravenscar	39	E5	NE	1965
Ravenscourt Park — see [London]				
Ravenscraig	49	A9	CAL	1944
Raven Square — see [Welshpool]				
Ravensthorpe and Thornhill	37	F5	LNW	
	79	H4		
Ravensthorpe — see also [Dewsbury]				
Ravenstonedale	41	D5	NE	1952
Ravenstonedale — see also Kirkby Stephen West				
Rawcliffe	34	F5	LY	
Rawdon — see Apperley Bridge				
Rawlinson Bridge	76	D5	BP	1841
Rawmarsh — see Parkgate				
Rawtenstall	37	A5	EL	1972
	76	C8		
Rawyards	75	F6	NB	1930
Raydon Wood	21	G4	GE	1932
Rayleigh	13	B5	GE	
Rayne	13	A9	GE	1952
Raynes Park	68	D6	LSW	
Raynham Park	20	D2	MGN	1959
Rayners Lane Halt	63	G6	LT	
[Reading]				
Reading 2nd, 1st — 1855	15	B3	SEC	1965
Reading	15	B3	GW	
Reading West	15	B3	GW	
Rearsby	25	E10	MID	1951
Rectory Road	65	B6	GE	
Redbourne	12	A8	MID	1947
	15	G8		
Redbridge (Hants)	4	G5	LSW	
	65	F7		
Redbrook-on-Wye	17	B7	GW	1959
[Redcar]				
Redcar, British Steel	38	H7	BR	
Redcar Central 2nd, 1st — 1861	38	H7	NE	
Redcar East	38	H7	NE	
Redcastle	56	F2	HIGH	1951
Redding GDS	46	B9	NB	1964
Reddish North	77	B9	GC/MID	
Reddish South	77	B9	LNW	

Station	Page	Block	Comp	Year of CL
Redditch 3rd, 1st — 1866, 2nd — 1973	80	G5	MID	
Redenhall	21	A7	GE	1866
Redheugh — see [Gateshead]				
Redhill Junction	2	B7	SEC	
Red Hill Form. Hookagate	27	E10	PSNW/SM	1933
Red House	26	G7	VAN/CAM	1879
Redhurst Crossing	31	D5	NS	1934
Redland	72	C7	GW	
Red Lion Crossing Halt	19	G4	GW	1926
Redmarshall	38	E7	NE	1952
Redmile	28	G3	GN/LNW	1953
Redmire	38	A3	NE	1954
Rednal and West Felton	30	C2	GW	1960
Red Rock	76	E5	LY/LU	1949
Redruth 2nd, 1st — 1852	10	E4	GW	
Red Wharf Bay and Benllech	32	F8	LNW	1930
Reedham (Norfolk) 2nd, 1st — 1904	20	G9	GE	
Reedham (Suffolk)	68	G2	SEC	
Reedness Junction Station	34	F4	AX JT	1933
Reedley Hallows Halt — see [Burnley]				
Reedsmouth	43	A5	NB	1956
Reepham (Lincs)	29	B7	GC	1965
Reepham (Norfolk)	20	D5	GE	1952
Reepham (Norfolk) — see also Whitwell				
Reigate LBSC & SEC combined to				
Redhill	2	A7	LBSC	1844
Reigate 2nd, 1st — 1844	2	A7	SEC	
[Renfrew]				
Deanside	74	E6	GP JT	1905
Fulbar Street	74	E6	GSW	1967
Kings Inch	74	E6	GP JT	1926
Porterfield	74	E6	GP JT	1926
South Renfrew	74	E6	GSW	1967
Wharf	74	E6	GSW	1967
Renishaw Central	82	D7	GC	1963
Renishaw — see also Eckington				
Renton	49	C9	DB JT	
Repton and Willington	31	F2	MID	1968
Resolven	78	B1	GW	1964
Respryn	11	B6	C WALL	1859
Restalrig — see [Edinburgh]				
Reston for St Abbs	47	G7	NB	1964
[Retford]				
Babworth GDS	28	E8	GN	1966
	82	H8		
Retford	28	E8	GN	
	82	H8		
Thrumpton	82	H8	MS & L/GC	1859
Rewley Road — see [Oxford]				
Rhayader	26	G4	CAM	1962
Rheidol — see [Aberystwyth]				
Rheidol Falls	26	C5	CAM	
Rhewl	33	E6	LNW	1962
Rhigos Halt	78	B2	GW	1964
Rhiwbina Halt	78	F6	CDFF	
Rhiwderin	78	F9	BM	1954
Rhiwfron	26	D5	CAM	
Rhiw Gogh	32	H3	FR	not known
Rhoose	78	H4	BARRY	1964
Rhos 2nd, 1st — 1855	33	G4	GW	1931
	72	C2		
Rhosddu Halt	72	D3	GC	1917
Rhosgogh	32	E10	LNW	1964
Rhosneigr	32	D8	LNW	
Rhosrobin Halt	30	C5	GW	1947
	72	E3		
Rhostryfan	32	E5	NWNG	1914
Rhostyllen	72	C2	GW	1931
Rhosymedre	72	D1	SC	1849
Rhosmedre Halt	72	D1	GW	1959
Rhu	49	B10	NB	1964
Rhuddlan	33	E8	LNW	1955
Rhuddlan Road	33	E9	LNW	1930
Rhydowen	19	A6	GW	1932
Rhydyfelin Halt, High Level 2nd, 1st — 1928	78	E5	CDFF	1931
Rhydyfelin Halt, Low Level	78	E5	GW	1953
Rhydymwyn	30	A7	LNW	1962
	33	F7		
Rhydyronen T.O. PR.	26	B9	TAL	
Rhyd-y-Saint	32	F8	LNW	1930
Rhyl	33	D8	LNW	
[Rhymney]				
Rhymney	16	E6	RHY	
	78	A6		
Rhymney Bridge	78	A6	NR JT	1958
Rhymney Lower and Pontlottyn	78	B6	BM	1930
Ribblehead *	41	E2	MID	1970
Ribbleton — see [Preston]				

Station	Page	Block	Comp	Year of CL
Ribchester — see Wilpshire				
Riccall	34	E6	NE	1958
Riccarton Junction Station	42	E7	NB	1969
Richborough Castle Halt	3	E9	SR	1939
Richmond New (Surrey)	68	B9	LT	
Richmond Old (Surrey)	68	B9	LSW	
Richmond (Yorks)	38	C5	NE	1969
Richmond Road Halt (Devon)	8	D4	BWA	1917
Rickmansworth Church Street	63	D9	LNW	1952
Rickmansworth High Street	15	G5	MET/GC	
	63	D10		
Riddings Junction Station	42	C4	NB	1964
Riddlesdown	69	A3	CO JT	
Riddlesdown — see also Kenley				
Ridge Bridge Form. Roman Rd. CL. 1834	79	D8	NE	1914
Ridgmont	23	G1	LNW	
Riding Mill	43	C3	NE	
Rifle Range Halt	80	G2	GW	1920
Rigg	42	A3	GSW	1942
Rillington	39	B1	NE	1930
Rimington	37	A8	LY	1958
	76	A7		
Ringley Road	76	F8	EL	1953
Ringstead and Addington	23	B1	LNW	1964
Ringwood	4	D4	LSW	1964
Ripley 2nd, 1st — 1889	28	B5	MID	1930
	82	C3		
Ripley — see Horsley				
Ripley Valley	34	A9	NE	1951
	37	G10		
Ripon	38	D1	NE	1967
Rippingale	22	D2	GN	1930
	29	B2		
Ripple	17	G10	MID	1961
	24	C1		
Ripponden and Barkisland	79	G1	LY	1929
Risby — see Saxham				
Risca	16	G4	GW	1962
	78	E9		
Rishton	76	C6	EL	
Rishworth	79	H1	LY	1929
River Douglas	76	C2	W LANCS	1887
Riverside — see [Cardiff]				
Riverside — see [Clydbank]				
Riverside — see Dalmuir				
Riverside — see [Liverpool]				
Riverside — see [Swansea]				
Riverside — see Totnes				
Riverside — see Windsor and Eton				
Riverside Quay — see [Hull]				
Roade 2nd, 1st — 1881	25	F3	LNW	1964
Roadwater	6	E8	WSM	1898
Roath — see [Cardiff]				
Robertsbridge	2	B4	SEC	
Robertstown Halt	78	E4	TV	1952
Robin Hood	79	E6	EWYU	1904
Robin Hood's Bay	39	D7	NE	1965
Robins Lane Halt	76	H4	LMS	1938
Robroyston — see [Glasgow]				
Roby	76	H3	LNW	
Rocester	31	D3	NS	1965
[Rochdale]				
Rochdale 2nd, 1st — 1889	76	D9	LY	
Shawclough and Healey	76	D9	LY	1947
Wardleworth	76	D9	LY	1947
Rochdale Road Halt	79	G2	LY	1929
Roche	11	A7	GW	
[Rochester]				
Rochester	2	H9	SE	
	13	A3	SE	
Rochester Bridge	13	A3	SEC	1917
Rochester Central	13	A3	SEC	1911
Rochford, for Southend Airport	13	C5	GE	
Rockliffe	42	C3	CAL	1950
Rock Ferry	36	B1	B HEAD	
	77	C2		
Rockingham	25	G8	LNW	1966
Rock Lane — see [Birkenhead]				
Rocky Valley Halt	32	G5	SMR	1924
Rode Heath — see Alsager				
Roding Valley — see [London]				
Rodley — see Calverley				
Rodmarton Platform	14	A5	GW	1964
	17	H6		
Rodwell — see [Weymouth]				
Roebuck	76	B3	LPJ	1849
Roffey Road Halt	2	A5	LBSC	1937
Rogart	61	B2	HIGH	
Rogate and Harting	5	D6	LSW	1955

Station	Page	Block	Comp	Year of CL
Rogerstone	78	F8	GW	1962
Rohallion — see Martham	50	G6	HIGH	1864
Rollesby — see Martham				
Rolleston Junction Station	28	F5	MID	
Rolleston-on-Dove	31	F2	NS	1949
Rollright Halt	14	E10	GW	1951
Rolvenden	3	A5	KES	1954
Rolvenden R.O. PR. FR. CL. above	3	A5	K & ES	
Romaldkirk	41	H7	NE	1964
Roman Bridge	32	H5	LNW	
Roman Road, Woodnesborough	3	G8	EK	1928
Romford	66	C6	GE	
Romiley	31	B10	GC/MID	
	77	C10		
Romsey	4	F6	LSW	
Rood End — see Langley Green				
Roodyards — see [Dundee]				
Rookery 2nd, 1st — 1862	76	F3	LNW	1951
Roose	40	F1	FUR	
Ropley R.O. PR. FR. 1973 CL.	5	B8	LSW	
Rosebush	18	G6	NRM/GW	1937
Rose Grove — see [Burnley]				
Rosehill (Archer Str.) Halt	40	C7	CW JC	1926
Rose Hill — see Marple				
Rosemill GDS	51	C7	CAL	1964
Rosemount Halt	51	A8	CAL	1955
Rosewell and Hawthornden	83	F2	NB	1962
Rosherville Halt	2	F10	SEC	1933
	70	G8		
Roskear GDS	10	E4	GW	
Roslin	83	F3	NB	1933
Rossett	30	C6	GW	1964
	72	E4		
Rossington	28	D10	GN	1958
	82	G10		
Roslyn Castle	46	G7	NB	1951
	83	F2		
Rosslynlee	83	F2	NB	1962
Rosslynlee Hospital Halt	83	F2	BR	1962
Ross-on-Wye	17	C9	GW	1964
Roster Road Halt	62	F5	LMS	1944
Rostherne — see Ashley				
Rosyth Halt	46	E10	NB	
Rothbury	43	C7	NB	1952
Rotherfield and Mark Cross	2	F5	LBSC	1965
[Rotherham]				
Central Form. Rotherham and Masborough	82	D9	GC	1966
Holmes	82	D9	MID	1955
Masborough	28	B10	MID	
	82	D9		
Meadow Hall	82	C9	GC	1953
Rotherham Road	82	C9	GC	1953
Westgate	82	D9	MID	1952
Rotherhithe — see [London]				
Rothes	56	F10	GNS	1968
Rothiemay	54	D3	GNS	1968
Rothie-Norman	54	F6	GNS	1951
Rothley R.O. PR. Rothley	25	C10	GC	1963
Rothwell (Yorks)	79	E6	EWYU	1904
Rothwell (Northants) — see Desborough				
Rotton Park Road — see [West Midlands]				
Roudham Junction	21	A3	GE	1932
Rouken Glen — see Whitecraigs				
Round Oak — see [West Midlands]				
Roundwood Halt	15	G8	LMS	1947
Row — see Rhu				
Rowan Halt	2	B2	SR	1939
Rowde — see Bromhall				
Rowden Mill	27	G3	GW	1952
Rowfant	2	B5	LBSC	1967
Rowlands Castle	5	C5	LSW	
Rowlands Gill	43	E2	NE	1954
	81	H2		
Rowley Form. Cold Rowley	38	A10	NE	1939
	43	D1		
Rowley Regis and Blackheath	80	E3	GW	
Rowntree Halt* — see [York]				
Rowrah	40	D7	WCE JT	1931
Rowsley 2nd, 1st — 1862	31	F7	MID	1967
Rowthorn and Hardwick	82	E6	MID	1930
Rowton Halt	30	F1	GW	1963
Roxburgh	47	D3	NB	1964
Royal Albert Docks — see [London] Gallions				
Royal Gardens — see [Leeds]				
Royal Oak — see [London]				
Royal Pier — see [Southampton]				
Royal Station — see [Edinburgh]				

Station	Page	Block	Comp	Year of CL
Royal Showground — see [London]				
Royal Victoria Docks — see [London] Custom House				
Roy Bridge	59	G8	NB	
Roydon	12	E7	GE	
Royston (Herts)	23	G6	GN	
Royston and Notton (Yorks) 2nd, 1st — 1900	79	H7	MID	1968
Royton	37	B3	LY	1966
	76	F10		
Royton Junction Station	76	F10	LY	
Ruabon	30	B4	GW	
	72	D1		
Rubery	80	F5	HAL JT	1919
Ruddington	28	D3	GC	1963
	82	F1		
Ruddle Road Halt	17	D8	GW	1917
Rudgwick	5	H7	LBSC	1965
Rudyard	31	C6	NS	1960
	73	E9		
Rudyard Lake	31	B6	NS	1960
	73	E9		
Rufford	76	D3	LY	
Rugby 3rd, 1st — 1840, 2nd — 1886	25	C5	LNW	
Rugby Central	25	C5	GC	1969
Rugby Road Halt — see [London]				
Rugeley Town	31	D1	LNW	1965
Rugeley, Trent Valley	31	D1	LNW	
Ruislip — see [London]				
Ruislip Manor — see [London]				
Rumbling Bridge 2nd, 1st — 1868	50	F2	NB	1964
Rumworth and Daubhill — see [Bolton]				
Runcorn	77	D4	LNW	
Runcorn Gap — see [Widnes]				
Runemede GDS	67	B9	GW	1966
Runnymede Range — see Yeoveney				
Runswick Bay — see Hinderwell				
Rushall	24	E9	LNW	1909
Rushbury	27	E7	GW	1951
Rushcliffe Halt	28	D2	GC	1963
Rushden	23	C1	MID	1959
	25	H4		
Rushey Platt 2nd, 1st — 1895	14	C4	MSWJ	1905
Rushford — see [Manchester]				
Rushwick Halt — see [Worcester]				
Rushton	31	B6	NS	1960
	73	D9		
Ruspidge Halt	17	D7	GW	1958
Ruswarp	39	C5	NE	
Rutherford	47	D3	NB	1968
Rutherglen 2nd, 1st — 1879	74	H4	CAL	
Ruthern Bridge GDS	11	B7	LSW	1934
Ruthin	33	E5	LNW	1962
Ruthrieston — see [Aberdeen]				
Ruthven Road Crossing	50	G5	CAL	1951
Rutland Street — see [Swansea]				
Ruthwell	45	G5	GSW	1965
Ryburgh	20	C3	GE	1964
[Ryde] Isle of Wight				
Esplanade	5	B3	LSW/LBSC	
Pier	5	B3	LSW/LBSC	
St John's Road	5	B3	IOW	
Ryder's Hays	24	E9	SS	1858
Rye	3	B3	R & C	1939
Rye	3	B3	SEC	
Rye Harbour GDS	3	B3	SEC	
Rye House	12	E7	GE	
Ryeford	17	F6	MID	1947
Ryeland	49	G4	CAL	1939
Ryhall and Belmisthorpe	22	F2	GN	1959
Ryhill — see Wintersett				
Ryhill Halt	79	H7	DEARNE	1951
Ryhope	43	H1	NE	1953
Ryhope East	43	H1	NE	1960
Rylstone	37	C10	MID	1930
Ryston	22	G9	GE	1930
Ryton	81	G1	NE	1954
St Agnes	10	F5	GW	1963
[St Albans]				
Abbey	12	B7	LNW	
City	12	B7	MID	
London Road	12	B7	GN	1951
St Andrews 2nd, 1st — 1867	51	D4	NB	1969
St Andrews Road	17	B3	GW	
	72	B8		
St Annes-on-Sea	76	B2	PW JT	
St Annes Park — see [Bristol]				
St Annes Road — see [London]				
St Annes Well — see [Nottingham]				

Station	Page	Block	Comp	Year of CL
St Asaph	33	D8	LNW	1955
St Athan Halt	78	H3	GW	1964
St Athan Road	78	G4	TV	1930
St Austell	11	A6	GW	
St Bees	40	C6	FUR	
St Blazey	11	B6	GW	1925
St Boswells	47	C3	NB	1969
St Botolphs	13	E9	GE	
St Briavels and Llandogo	17	B6	GW	1959
St Budeaux, Ferry Road	9	D4	GW	
St Budeaux, Victoria Road	9	D4	LSW	
St Clears	19	B5	GW	1964
St Columb Road	10	H6	GW	
St Combs	54	C10	GNS	1965
St Cyres — see Newton				
St Cyrus	51	H10	NB	1951
	55	G6		
St Davids — see [Exeter]				
St Denys 2nd, 1st — Portwood 1866	4	G5	LSW	
St Deveraux	17	A10	GW	1958
St Dunstans — see [Bradford]				
St Enoch — see [Glasgow]				
St Erth	10	C3	GW	
St Fagans	78	G5	GW	1962
St Fillans	50	B5	CAL	1951
St Fort	51	C5	NB	1965
St Gabriels — see [Swansea]				
St Georges East — see [London] Shadwell				
St Germain's	22	E9	EA	1850
St Germans	9	E3	GW	
St Harmons Halt	26	G5	CAM	1962
St Helens (Glam) — see [Swansea]				
St Helens (Isle of Wight)	5	B2	IOW	1953
[St Helens] (Lancs)				
Central	76	G3	GC	1952
Gerrards Bridge	76	H4	LNW	1905
Junction Station	36	E2	LNW	
	76	H4		
Moss Bank	76	G3	LNW	1951
Peasley Cross	76	G4	LNW	1951
Shaw Street 3rd, 1st — 1849, 2nd — 1858	76	H4	LNW	
Sutton Oak	76	G4	LNW	1951
St Helier (London)	68	E5	SR	
St Hilary Platform	78	G4	TV	1920
St Ives (Cornwall) 2nd, 1st — 1973	10	C4	BR	
St Ives	23	C5	GN/GE	1970
St James — see [Cheltenham]				
St James — see [Liverpool]				
St James — see [Paisley]				
St James Deeping	22	F3	GN	1961
St James Park — see [London]				
St James Street — see [London] Walthamstowe				
St Johns — see [Bedford] Bedford				
St Johns — see [London]				
St Johns — see [West Midlands] Tipton				
St Johns Chapel	41	F9	NE	1953
St Johns Road (Isle of Wight)	5	A3	JOINT	
St Kew Highway	10	B8	LSW	1966
St Keyne Halt	9	D2	LL	
St Lawrence Halt	11	B8	LSW	1967
St Lawrence Halt (Isle of Wight)	4	H1	IWC	1952
St Lawrence Pegwell Bay	3	H9	SEC	1916
St Lawrence Platform	18	F6	GW	1917
St Leonards — see [Hastings]				
St Lukes — see [Southport]				
St Margaret's (Herts) for Stanstead Abbots	12	E7	GE	
St Margarets (Middlesex)	68	A9	LSW	
St Margarets Bay — see Martin Mill				
St Mary — see [Wisbech]				
St Mary Church Road	78	G4	TV	1930
St Mary Cray	69	G6	SEC	
St Mary's	23	A4	GN	1947
St Mary's Bay	3	D5	RHD	
St Mary's Crossing Halt	17	G6	GW	1964
St Mary's Whitechapel — see [London]				
St Mawes — see Falmouth				
St Melyd Golf Links	33	D9	LNW	1930
St Michaels — see [Liverpool]				
St Monans	51	D3	NB	1965
St Neots	23	D4	GN	
St Olave's	20	G9	GE	1959
St Pancras — see [London]				
St Pauls — see [Halifax]				
St Pauls — see [London]				
St Peters — see [Newcastle]				
St Phillips — see [Bristol]				
St Quintin Park — see [London]				

Station	Page	Block	Comp	Year of CL
St Rollox — see [Glasgow]				
St Thomas — see [Exeter]				
St Thomas — see [Swansea]				
St Winefride's Halt	33	F8	LNW	1954
St Y-Nyll Halt	78	G5	BARRY	1905
Saddleworth for Dobcross	76	F10	LNW	1968
Saffron Walden	23	G8	GE	1964
Salcey Forest	25	F3	GWJ/SMJ	1893
Sale and Ashton-on-Mersey	77	B8	MSJA	
Salehurst Halt	2	H3	KES	1954
Salem	32	F5	WH	1936
Salford	76	G9	LY	
Salford — see also [Manchester] Ordsall Lane				
Salford Priors	24	E2	MID	1962
Salfords	2	B7	LBSC	
Salhouse	20	E7	GE	
[Salisbury]				
Salisbury	4	C7	LSW	
Salisbury	4	C7	GW	1932
Salisbury, Milford	4	C7	LSW	1859
Saltaire	37	D7	MID	1965
	79	D2		
Salt and Sandon	31	B2	GN	1939
Saltash	9	E4	GW	
Saltburn	39	A7	NE	
Saltcoats 3rd, 1st — 1858, 2nd — 1882	49	B5	GSW	
Saltcoats North	49	B5	CAL	1932
Salter Lane	82	B5	ASH	1936
Saltfleetby	29	G10	GN	1960
	35	G1		
Saltford	17	D2	GW	1970
Saltford — see also Kelston				
Saltley — see [West Midlands]				
Saltmarshe	34	G5	NE	
Saltney — see [Chester]				
Saltney Ferry (Mold Junction)	77	G3	LNW	1962
Saltoun	47	A7	NB	1933
Salvation Army Halt	15	F7	GN	1951
Salwick	76	B3	PW JT	
Salzcraggie Halt	61	F3	HIGH	1965
	62	B3		
Sampford Courtenay	8	H6	LSW	1972
Sampford Peverell Halt	6	E5	GW	1964
Sandal — see [Wakefield]				
Sandal and Walton — see [Wakefield]				
Sandal	82	G10	SY	1859
Sandbach	77	G8	LNW	
Sandbach — see also Wheelock				
Sanderstead	69	A3	CO JT	
Sandford and Banwell	17	A1	GW	1963
Sandgate	3	E5	SEC	1931
Sandhills for North Docks	76	G1	LY	
Sandholme	34	H5	HB	1955
Sandhurst Halt	15	C1	SEC	
Sandhurst	15	C1	SE	1853
[Sand Hutton]				
Central	34	F9	SH LT	1930
Depot	34	F9	SH LT	1930
Gardens	34	F9	SH LT	1930
Sandiacre — see Stapleford				
Sandilands	46	B4	CAL	1964
Sandling Junction for Hythe	3	E6	SEC	
Sandoff GDS	34	F2	AX JT	1963
Sandon	31	B2	NS	1947
Sandon — see also Salt				
Sandown Junction (Isle of Wight)	5	B2	IOW	
Sandplace Halt	9	E2	LL	
Sandsend	39	C6	NE	1958
Sandsfoot Castle Halt	7	A1	WP JT	1952
Sandside	41	A2	FUR	1942
Sandwich	3	G8	SEC	
Sandwich Road	3	G8	EK	1928
Sandy	23	E3	LNW	1968
Sandy	23	F4	GN	
Sandycroft	77	G2	LNW	1961
Sandyford Halt	74	E5	LMS	1967
Sankey Bridges	77	C6	LNW	1949
Sankey for Penketh	77	C5	CLC	
Sanquhar	45	C10	GSW	1965
	49	H1		
Sarnau	19	C5	GW	1964
Sarsden Halt	14	E9	GW	1962
Sauchie	50	E2	NB	1930
Saughall	77	G3	GC	1954
Saughton — see [Edinburgh]				
Saughtree	42	E7	NB	1956
Saundersfoot	18	H3	GW	
Saunderton	15	C6	GW/GC	

Station	Page	Block	Comp	Year of CL
Savernake Low Level	14	D1	GW	1966
Savernake High Level	14	D1	MSWJ	1958
Sawbridgeworth	12	F8	GE	
Sawdon	39	D2	NE	1950
Sawley	28	B2	MID	1930
Sawley Junction — see Long Eaton				
Saxby 2nd, 1st — 1892	28	G1	MID	1961
Saxham and Risby	21	C1	GE	1967
Saxilby	28	H8	GN/GE	
Saxmundham	21	D9	GE	
Saxthorpe — see Corpusty				
Scafell	26	H7	CAM	1955
Scalby	39	E3	NE	1953
Scale Hall	36	D10	BR	1966
Scalford	28	F1	GN/LNW	1953
Scarborough	39	E3	NE	
Scarborough, Londesborough Rd.	39	E3	NE	1963
Scarcliffe	82	E6	GC	1951
Scarning	20	E3	EA	1850
Scawby and Hibaldstow	35	A2	GC	1968
Scholar Green — see Mow Cop				
School Hill — see Aberdeen				
Scholes	34	B6	NE	1964
	79	D8		
Scopwick and Timberland	29	B6	GN/GE	1955
Scorrier	10	F5	GW	1964
Scorton (Lancs) 2nd, 1st — 1840	36	E8	LNW	1939
	76	A3		
Scorton (Yorks)	38	D5	NE	1969
Scotby	42	D2	MID	1942
Scotby	42	D2	NE	1959
Scotch Dyke	42	C4	NB	1949
Scotland Street — see [Edinburgh]				
Scotscalder	61	G8	HIGH	
	62	C7		
Scotsgap	43	C5	NB	1952
Scotstoun — see [Glasgow]				
Scotstounhill — see [Glasgow]				
Scotswood — see [Newcastle]				
Scraptoft — see Thurnby				
Scratby Halt	20	E10	MGN	1959
Scredington — see Aswarby				
Scremerston	43	G10	NE	1951
	47	H5		
Scrooby	28	E9	GN	1931
	82	G9		
Scropton	31	E2	NS	1866
Scruton	38	D3	NE	1954
Sculcoates — see [Hull]				
Scunthorpe	34	H3	GC	
Scunthorpe	34	H3	GC	1925
Scunthorpe — see also Froddingham				
Seaburn	43	G8	NE	
	81	F1		
Seacombe — see [Wallasey]				
Seacroft	29	H6	GN	1953
Seaford	2	E1	GN	1953
Seaforth and Litherland	76	G1	LY	
[Seaham]				
Seaham	43	H1	NE	
Seaham Colliery R.N. Seaham	43	H1	NE	1925
Seaham Harbour	43	H1	NE	1939
Seahouses	43	H6	N SUND	1951
Sealand	77	G2	GC	1968
Seamer	39	E2	NE	
Sea Mills	72	C7	GW	
Seascale	40	D5	FUR	
Seaside — see Aberavon				
Seaside — see [Southport] Ainsdale				
Seaton (Cumbria)	45	F1	GWJC	1922
Seaton (Leics)	25	H8	LNW	1966
Seaton (Devon)	6	H2	LSW	1966
Seaton (Durham)	40	D8	NE	1952
	43	H1		
Seaton Carew	38	G8	NE	
Seaton Delaval	81	E5	NE	1964
Seaton Junction Station	6	G3	LSW	1966
Seaton Snook GDS	38	G8	NE	1957
Sebastapol	78	D10	GW	1962
Sedbergh	41	C4	LNW	1954
Sedgebrook	28	H3	GN	1956
Sedgefield	38	D8	NE	1952
Sedgeford	21	B10	GE	1952
Seedley — see [Manchester]				
Seend	14	A1	GW	1966
	17	G1		
Seer Green and Jordans	15	F5	GW/GC	
Sefton and Maghull	76	F1	CLC	1952
Sefton Arms — see [Liverpool] Aintree				

Station	Page	Block	Comp	Year of CL
Sefton Park — see [Liverpool]				
Seghill	43	F4	NE	1964
	81	E5		
Selby 2nd, 1st — 1840	34	E6	NE	
Selby, Brayton Gates	34	E6	NE	1904
Selham	5	F6	LBSC	1955
Selhurst	69	A6	LBSC	
Selkirk	47	A3	NB	1951
Sellafield	40	D5	FUR	
Selling	3	D8	SEC	
Selly Oak	80	E5	MID	
Selsdon Road	69	A4	CO JT	
[Selsey]				
Beach	5	E3	WS	1904
Bridge	5	E3	WS	1935
Golf Links Halt	5	E3	WS	1914
Town	5	E3	WS	1935
Selston — see Pinxton				
Semington Halt	17	G1	GW	1966
Semley	4	A7	LSW	1966
	7	G7		
Senghenydd	78	D5	RHY	1964
Sennybridge — see Devynock				
Serridge Platform	17	C8	SW JT	1879
Sessay	38	F1	NE	1958
Sesswick Halt	30	C4	CAM	1962
	72	F2		
Seton Mains Halt	46	H8	NB	1930
Settle 2nd, 1st R.N. Giggleswick 1877	37	A10	MID	
Settle Junction	37	A10	MID	1877
Settrington	39	C1	NE	1950
Seven Hills Halt	21	C2	GE	1953
Seven Kings	65	C6	GE	
Sevenoaks, Tubs Hill	2	E8	SEC	
Seven Sisters (Glam)	78	B1	N & B	1962
Seven Sisters (Middlesex)	65	B7	GE	
Seven Stars — see [Welshpool]				
Seven Stones Halt	9	C4	PDSW	1917
	11	F8		
Severn Beach	17	B4	GW	
	72	B9		
Severn Bridge	17	D6	SW JT	1960
Severn Tunnel Junction	17	B4	GW	
Sexhow	38	F5	NE	1954
Shackerstone* R.O. PR. FR. CL.	25	A9	AN JT	1931
Shadwell — see [London]				
Shalfleet (I.O.W.) — see Calbourne (I.O.W.)				
Shalford	5	F9	SEC	
Shandon	49	B10	NB	1964
	53	D1		
Shankend	42	E8	NB	1969
Shanklin (Isle of Wight)	5	A1	IOW	
Shap	41	B7	LNW	1968
Shapwick	7	A9	SD JT	1966
Shardlow — see Castle Donnington				
Sharlston	79	H7	LY	1958
Sharnal Street	13	B3	SEC	1961
Sharnbrook	23	D1	MID	1960
Sharpness 2nd, 1st — 1879	17	D6	SW JT	1964
Shaugh Bridge Platform	9	D5	GW	1962
Shaw and Crompton	76	E10	LY	
Shawclough — see [Rochdale]				
Shawford and Twyford	4	H6	LSW	
Shawforth	76	C9	LY	1947
Shawlands	74	G3	CAL	
Shaw Syke — see [Halifax]				
Sheepbridge and Whittington Moor	82	C6	MID	1967
Sheepbridge — see also Brimington				
[Sheerness]				
Dockyard	3	B10	SEC	1922
East	3	B10	SEC	1950
Sheerness-on-Sea	3	B10	SEC	
[Sheffield]				
Attercliffe	82	C9	GC	1927
Attercliffe	31	G10	MID	
	82	B9		
Beauchief and Abbey Dale	31	G9	MID	1961
	82	B9		
Bridgehouses	82	B9	MS & L/GC	
Brightside	31	H1	MID	
	82	C9		
Broughton Lane	82	C9	GC	1956
Grimesthorpe Bridge	82	B9	S & R	1843
Heeley	31	G9	MID	1968
Millhouses and Eccleshall	31	G9	MID	1968
Neepsend	82	B9	GC	1940
Nunnery GDS	82	C8	LNW	1977
Park GDS	82	B9	GC	1963
Pond Street GDS	82	B8	MID	1960

Station	Page	Block	Comp	Year of CL
Sheffield	28	A9	GC	
	82	B9		
Tinsley	82	C9	GC	1951
Victoria	82	B9	GC	1970
Wadsley Bridge*	82	A9	GC	1959
West Tinsley	82	C9	GC	1939
Wicker	82	B9	MID	1870
Wincobank and Meadow Hall	82	C9	MID	1956
Sheffield Park	2	C4	LBSC	
Shefford	23	G3	MID	1962
Shefford Road — see Arlesey and Henlow				
Shelford	23	E7	GE	
Shelley — see Shipley				
Shenfield 1st	66	H9	EC	1850
Shenfield and Hutton Junc. 2nd	12	H7	GE	
	66	H9		
Shenstone	80	A7	LNW	
Shenton	25	A9	AN JT	1931
Shepherds	10	G6	GW	1963
Shepherds Bush — see [London]				
Shepherd's Well	3	F7	EK	1948
Shepherd's Well	3	F7	SEC	
Shepley and Shelley	37	E3	LY	
	79	H4		
Shepperton	67	E6	LSW	
Shepreth	23	F6	GN	
Shepshed	28	C1	LNW	1931
Shepton Mallet, Charlton Road	7	D9	SD JT	1966
Shepton Mallet, High Street	7	D9	GW	1963
Sherborne	7	D5	LSW	
Sherburn Colliery Station	38	D9	NE	1941
Sherburn House 2nd, 1st — 1893	38	D10	NE	1931
Sherburn-in-Elmet	79	D10	NE	1965
Shere — see Gomshall				
Sheringham 2nd, 1st — 1967	20	B5	BR	
Sheringham Private	20	B5	NNR	
Sherwood — see [Nottingham]				
Shettleston	75	A6	NB	
Shide	4	H1	IWC	1956
Shieldhill	74	F6	CAL	1952
Shield Row	43	E2	NE	1953
Shields — see [Glasgow]				
Shields Road — see [Glasgow]				
Shifnal	24	B9	GW	
	80	B1		
Shildon	38	D8	NE	
Shillingstone	7	G5	SD JT	1966
Shilton	80	D10	LNW	1957
Shincliffe 2nd	38	D9	NE	1941
Shincliffe Town 1st	38	D9	NE	1893
Shiplake	15	C4	GW	
Shipley, Station Road 2nd, 1st — 1875	37	E7	MID	
	79	C3		
Shipley and Windhill Form. Bridge Street	37	E7	GN	1931
Shipley Gate	82	D3	MID	1948
Shipley Gate — see also Newthorpe				
Shipley Hall — see Marlpool				
Shippea Hill	23	A9	GE	
Shipston-on-Stour 2nd, 1st — 1859	24	H1	GW	1929
Shipton for Burford	14	E8	GW	
Shipton-on-Cherwell Halt	14	G8	GW	1954
Shirdley Hill	76	D2	LY	1938
[Shirebrook]				
North	82	F6	GC	1955
South	82	F6	GN	1931
West	82	F6	MID	1964
Shirehampton	17	B3	CE	
	72	B7		
Shireoaks	28	C8	GC	
	82	F8		
Shirley	24	F5	GW	
	80	G6		
Shoeburyness	13	D4	LTS	
Sholing	4	H10	LSW	
Shoot Hill	27	D10	SM	1933
Shooters Hill — see Eltham Park				
Shoreditch — see [London]				
Shoreham (Kent)	70	B3	SEC	
Shoreham Airport (Bungalow Twn. Ht.)	2	A1	LBSC	1940
Shoreham-by-Sea (Sussex)	2	A1	LBSC	
Shorncliffe Camp — see [Folkstone] West				
Short Heath — see [West Midlands]				
Shortlands	69	D6	SEC	
Shoscombe and Single Hill Ht.	7	E10	SD JT	1966
Shotley Bridge	43	D2	NE	1953
Shottle	31	G5	MID	1947
	82	A3		
Shotton (Clwyd)	33	H7	LNW	
	77	G2		
Shotton, Low Level (Clwyd)	77	G2	LNW	1966
Shotton — see also Connah's Quay				
Shotton Bridge (Durham)	38	E9	NE	1952
Shot Tower — see [London]				
Shotts Central	46	B6	CAL	
Shotts East GDS	46	B6	NB	1963
Shrawardine	27	D10	PSNW/SM	1933
[Shrewsbury]				
Abbey	27	E10	PSNW/SM	1933
Abbey Foregate	27	E10	S & WTN	1912
English Bridge	27	E10	GW/LNW	1898
S.C. Station	27	E10	SC	1849
Shrewsbury	27	E10	SM	
West	27	E10	SM	1933
Shrivenham	14	D4	GW	1964
Shrub Hill — see [Worcester]				
Shustoke	80	C8	MID	1968
Sible and Castle Hedingham	13	B10	CVH	1962
	21	G1		
Sibleys	12	G10	GE	1952
	23	H8		
Sibsey	22	A6	GN	1961
	29	E4		
Sibson	22	G2	GN	1898
Sidcup	69	F8	SEC	
Siddick Junction	40	C8	LNW/CW JT	1934
	45	F1		
Sidestrand Halt	20	B7	NS JT	1953
Sideway Halt — see [Stoke-on-Trent]				
Sidlesham	5	E3	WS	1935
Sidley	2	H2	SEC	1964
Sidmouth	6	E2	LSW	1967
Sidmouth Junction R.O. 1971 Feniton	6	E3	LSW	1967
Sigglesthorne	35	D7	NE	1964
Sileby	25	D10	MID	1968
Silecroft	40	D2	FUR	
Silian Halt	19	F9	GW	1951
	26	B2		
Silkstone	82	A9	GC	1959
Silloth	45	G3	NB	1964
Silsden — see Steeton				
Silverdale (Lancs)	41	A2	FUR	
Silverdale (Staffs) 2nd, 1st — 1870	31	A4	NS	1964
	73	B7		
Silverdale (Crown Street) Halt	73	B7	NS	1949
Silver Street	65	B8	GE	
Silverton	6	D3	GW	1964
Silvertown	65	F3	GE	
Simonstone	76	B8	LY	1957
Sinclairtown	51	A2	NB	1969
Sinderby	38	E2	NE	1962
Sindlesham — see Winnersh				
Sinfin Central	28	A2	MID	
	31	G2		
Sinfin North	28	A2	MID	
	31	G2		
Singer	74	B8	NB	
Single Hill — see Shoscombe				
Singleton (Lancs)	76	B2	PW JT	1932
Singleton (Sussex)	5	E5	LBSC	1935
Sinnington	39	B2	NE	1953
Sirhowy	78	A7	LNW	1960
Sittingbourne and Milton Regis	3	B9	SEC	
Six Bells Halt	78	B8	GW	1962
Six Mile Bottom	23	E8	GE	1967
Skares	49	E2	GSW	1951
Skegby	82	E5	GN	1931
Skegness	29	H6	GN	
Skelbo	56	A4	HIGH	1960
	61	C1		
Skellingthorpe	28	H7	GC	1955
Skellingthorpe	28	H7	GN	1868
Skelmanthorpe	37	F4	LY	
	79	H4		
Skelmersdale Form. Blaguegate	36	D3	LY	1956
	76	F3		
Skewen 2nd, 1st — 1910	19	H2	GW	1964
Skinningrove	39	A8	NE	1952
Skipton 2nd, 1st — 1876	37	C9	MID	
	79	B1		
Skipwith and North Duffield	34	F7	DV	1926
Skirlaugh	35	C6	NE	1957
Slade Green	66	C1	SEC	
Slaggyford	42	G1	NE	1976
Slaithwaite	79	H2	LNW	1968
Slamannan	46	A8	NB	1930
Slateford	46	F8	CAL	
	83	B5		
Slate Wharf — see Towyn Wharf				

Station	Page	Block	Comp	Year of CL
Sleaford	22	B2	GN	
	29	B4		
Sledmere and Fimber	34	H9	NE	1950
Sleightholme	42	A2	CS	1857
Sleights	39	C5	NE	
Slinfold	5	H7	LBSC	1965
Slingsby	39	A1	NE	1931
Sloane Square — see [London]				
Slough 2nd, 1st — 1884	15	E4	GW	
Smallberry Green — see [London] Hounslow				
Smallford for Colney Heath	12	B7	GN	1951
Small Heath and Sparkbrook	80	E6	GW	
Smallthorpe — see [Stoke-on-Trent] Ford Green				
Smardale	41	E6	NE	1952
Smeafield	43	H8	NE	1930
Smeaton	46	H8	NB	1930
Smeeth	3	D6	SEC	1954
Smeeth Road	22	F8	GE	1968
Smethwick — see [West Midlands]				
Smitham	68	G2	SEC	
Smithy Bridge	76	D10	LY	1960
Snailham Halt	3	A3	SEC	1959
Snainton	39	D2	NE	1950
Snaith and Pollington	34	E4	LY	
Snape GDS	21	D9	GE	1960
Snapper (for Goodleigh) Halt	8	C7	LB	1935
Snaresbrook and Wanstead	65	E7	GE	1966
Snaresbrook R.O. by LT FR. CL. above	65	E7	LT	
Snarestone	25	A10	AN JT	1931
Snatchwood Halt	78	C10	GW	1953
Snelland	29	B8	GC	1965
Snells Nook Halt	28	C1	LNW	1931
Snettisham	22	C9	GE	1969
Snodland	2	H9	SEC	
Snowdon	32	F5	NWNG/WH	1936
Snowdon Summit	32	G5	SMR	
Snowdown and Nonington	3	F7	SEC	
Snow Hill — see [London]				
Snow Hill — see [West Midlands] Birmingham				
Soham	23	B8	GE	1965
Soho — see [West Midlands]				
Soho Road — see [West Midlands]				
Soho and Winson Green — see [West Midlands]				
Sole Street	2	G9	SEC	
Solihull	80	F7	GW	
Somercotes — see Pye Hill				
Somerdale — see [Bristol] Keynsham				
Somerleyton	20	H10	GE	
Somerset Road — see [West Midlands]				
Somersham	23	B6	GN/GE	1967
Somerton	7	B7	GW	1962
Sorbie	44	G3	PPW JT	1950
Sourdon Siding	56	F10	GNS	1866
South Acton — see [London]				
Southall	63	F2	GW	
Southam and Long Itchington	25	B4	LNW	1958
[Southampton]				
Airport	4	H5	BR	
Northam	4	H5	LSW	1966
Royal Pier	4	G5	LSW	1914
Southampton Central	4	H5	LSW	
Terminus PR. known as Town	4	G5	LSW	1966
West Form. Blechynden				
West End	4	G5	LSW	1895
Southam Road and Harbury	25	A3	GW	1964
South Aylesbury Halt	15	C7	GW/GC	1967
South Bank	38	G7	NE	
Southborough R.N. High Brooms	2	F6	SEC	
South Beach — see Ardrossan				
South Bermondsey — see [London]				
South Bromley — see [London]				
Southbourne Halt	5	D4	LBSC	
Southburn	35	A9	NE	1954
Southbury	65	B10	GE	
South Camp — see Aldershot				
South Caradon GDS	11	E8	LC	
South Cave	35	A6	HB	1955
South Cerney and Ashton Keynes	14	B5	MSWJ	1961
Southchurch	38	C8	S & D	1845
Southcliffe — see Clacton-on-Sea				
Southcotes — see [Hull]				
South Croydon	69	A4	LBSC	
South Dock — see [London]				
Southease and Rodmell Halt	2	D2	LBSC	
South Elmsall	34	C3	WRG JT	

Station	Page	Block	Comp	Year of CL
South Elmsall	79	H9		
[Southend]				
Airport — see Rochford				
Central	13	C4	GE	
East	13	C4	MID	
Rochford for Southend Airport	13	C5	GE	
Victoria	13	C4	GE	
Southend (Glam) — see [Swansea]				
Southerndown Road	78	G2	BARRY	1961
Southfields — see [London]				
Southfleet, Springhead	2	F10	SEC	1953
	70	F7		
Southgate — see [London] Palmers Green				
South Gosforth	43	F3	NE	
	81	B4		
South Greenford Halt	64	A4	GW	
South Hampstead	64	F4	LNW	
South Harefield Halt — see [London]				
South Harrow — see [London]				
South Hetton	38	E10	NE	1952
	43	H1		
South Howden	34	G5	HB	1955
Southill	23	F3	MID	1962
South Kensington — see [London]				
South Kenton — see Kenton South				
South Kirkby — see Moorthorpe				
South Kirkby — see also Hemsworth				
South Leigh	14	F7	GW	1962
South Leith — see [Edinburgh]				
South Lynn	22	E9	MGN	1959
South Merton	68	E6	LSW	
South Milford	34	C6	YNM/NE	
	79	D9		
South Mimms — see Potters Bar				
South Molton	8	D8	GW	1966
South Molton Road — see Kings Nympton				
South Normanton — see Alfreton				
South Norwood — see Woodside				
South Pit Halt R.N. North Rhondda Ht.	78	C2	SWM	1930
[Southport]				
Ainsdale	36	B4	LY	
	76	E1		
Ainsdale Beach	76	E1	CLC	1952
Ash Street	76	D1	WL	1902
Birkdale	76	D1	LY	
Birkdale Palace	76	D1	CLC	1952
Blowick Form. Cop End	76	D1	LY	1939
Butts Lane Halt	76	D1	LY	1938
Central	76	D1	LY	1901
Churchtown	76	C1	LY	1964
Crossens	76	C2	LY	1964
Eastbank Street	76	D1	LCS	1851
Hesketh Park	76	C1	LY	1964
Hillside	76	D1	LY	
Kew Gardens	76	D2	LY	1938
London Street	76	D1	EL	1857
Lord Street	76	D1	CLC	1952
Meols Cop	76	C1	LY	
St Lukes	76	D1	LY	1968
Southport, Chapel Street	36	C4	LY	
	76	D1		
Windsor Road	76	D1	WL	1902
Woodvale	76	E1	CLC	1952
South Queensferry	46	E9	NB	1929
South Queensferry — see also Dalmeny				
South Renfrew — see [Renfrew]				
Southrey	29	C7	GN	1970
South Rhondda GDS	78	F3	GW	1930
South Ruislip Form. Northolt Jcn.	63	F5	GW/GC	
Southsea East — see [Portsmouth]				
[South Shields]				
South Shields	81	F3	BJ	1842
South Shields	81	F3	NE	1879
South Shields	81	F3	PSS	1844
South Shields	43	G3	NE	
	81	F3		
Westoe Lane	81	F3	SSMWC	1953
South Shore — see [Blackpool]				
South Side — see [Glasgow]				
South Stockwell — see Brixham				
South Street Halt	3	E9	SEC	1931
	13	E2		
South Tottenham — see [London]				
Southwater	2	A4	LBSC	1966
Southwell	28	E5	MID	1959
Southwick (Dumfries)	45	D4	GSW	1965
Southwick (Sussex)	2	A1	LBSC	
South Willingham and Hainton	29	D9	GN	1951

Station	Page	Block	Comp	Year of CL
South Witham	28	H1	MID	1959
Southwold	21	B10	S WOLD	1929
South Woodford — see [London]				
South Woodford — see also [London] George Lane				
South Yardley — see [West Midlands] Acocks Green				
Sowerby Bridge 2nd, 1st — 1876	79	F2	LY	
Spalding	22	D4	GN	
	29	D1		
Sparkbrook — see [West Midlands] Small Heath				
Sparkford	7	D7	GW	1966
Spa Road — see [London]				
Sparrowlee Halt	31	D5	NS	1934
Spean Bridge	59	G7	NB	
Speech House Road	17	C7	SW JT	1929
Speen for Donnington	14	G2	GW	1960
Speeton	39	G1	NE	1970
Speke	77	D3	LNW	1930
Spelbrook	12	F8	N & E	1842
Spellow — see [Liverpool]				
Spencer Road Halt	69	A4	SEC/LBSC	1915
Spenithorne	38	B3	NE	1954
Spennymoor 2nd, 1st — 1878	38	D8	NE	1952
Spetchley	24	C3	MID	1855
Spetisbury Halt	4	A4	SD JT	1956
	7	H4		
Spey Bay	54	B1	GNS	1968
Spiersbridge — see [Glasgow]				
Spilsby	29	F6	GN	1939
Spink Hill for Mount St Mary	82	E7	GC	1939
Spink's Lane (Temporary Station)	20	G5	NOR	1845
Spital	77	D2	B HEAD	
Spofforth	37	H8	NE	1964
	79	A7		
Spondon	28	B3	MID	
	82	C1		
Spon Lane — see [West Midlands]				
Spooner Row	20	G5	EC/GE	
Sporle	20	E1	EA	1850
Spratton	25	F5	LNW	1949
Springburn	74	H7	NB	
Springfield (Fife)	51	B4	NB	
Springfield (Derbys)	82	B5	ASH	1936
Spring Grove — see [London] Isleworth				
Springhead — see Grotton				
Springhead — see Southfleet				
Springhead Halt	73	E3	LNE	1955
Spring Road Halt	80	F6	GW	
Springside	49	C4	GSW	1964
Spring Vale Form. Sough	76	C6	LY	1958
Springwell	81	B2	NE	1872
Sprotborough	82	E10	HB	1903
Sprouston	47	E3	NE	1955
Squires Gate	76	B1	LMS	
Stacksteads	76	C8	LY	1966
Staddlethorpe — see Gilberdyke				
Stafford	31	B1	LNW	
Stafford Common	31	B1	GN	1939
Stafford Road — see [West Midlands] Wolverhampton				
Stafford Street — see [West Midlands] Willenhall				
Staincliffe and Batley Carr — see [Dewsbury]				
Staincross	82	B10	GC	1930
[Staines]				
High Street	15	F3	LSW	1916
	67	C8		
Staines Junction	15	F3	LSW	
	67	C8		
West	15	F3	GW	1965
	67	C8		
Stainforth	34	E3	MS & L	1866
Stainforth and Hatfield	34	E3	GC	
Stainland and Holywell Green	79	H2	LY	1929
Staintondale	39	E4	NE	1965
Stairfoot — see [Barnsley]				
Staithes	39	B7	NE	1958
Stalbridge	7	F6	SD JT	1966
Staley and Millbrook	76	G10	LNW	1909
Stalham	20	D8	MGN	1959
Stallingborough	35	D3	GC	
Stallingborough — see also Kiln Lane Crossing				
Stalybridge	37	C2	GW/LNW	
	76	G10		
Stalybridge	76	G10	LY	1917
Stamford (Lincs) 2nd, 1st — 1848	22	G1	MID	
Stamford Bridge (Yorks)	34	F9	NE	1965
Stamford East Form. Water Str.	22	G1	GN	1957
Stamford Hill	65	B6	GE	
Stamford Park — see Yelvertoft				
Stamperland — see [Glasgow] Clarkston				
Stanbridge Ford	15	E9	LNW	1962
Standish	76	E4	LNW	1949
Standon	12	E9	GE	1964
Standon Bridge	31	A3	LNW	1952
Stane Street Halt	12	F9	GE	1952
Stanford-le-Hope	13	A4	LTS	
Stanhoe	20	B1	GE	1952
Stanhope 2nd, 1st — 1895	41	H9	NE	1953
Stanley Depots (Durham)	38	C9	NE	
Stanley (Lancs) — see [Liverpool]				
Stanley Junction	50	G6	CAL	1956
Stanley	79	F7	METH	1964
Stanley Bridge Halt	14	A3	GW	1965
	17	G2		
Stanlow and Thornton	77	E4	B HEAD	
Stanmore Village — see [London]				
Stanner Halt	27	B3	GW	1951
Stannergate — see [Dundee]				
Stanningley for Farsley	79	D4	GN	1968
Stannington	43	E5	NE	1958
Stansfield Hall	37	B5	LY	1944
	76	B10		
Stanstead	12	G8	GE	
Stanton	14	C4	GW	1953
Stanton Gate	82	E1	MID	1967
Stanwardine Halt	30	C1	GW	1960
Staple	3	F8	EK	1948
Staple Edge Halt	17	D7	GW	1958
Stapleford	12	D8	GN	1939
Stapleford and Sandiacre (Notts)	82	D1	MID	1967
Staple Hill — see [Bristol]				
Staplehurst	2	H7	SEC	
Stapleton Road	17	C3	GW	
	72	D7		
Starbeck	34	A9	NE	
Starcross for Exmouth	6	D1	GW	
Star Crossing	33	F7	LNW	1962
Starston	21	A7	GE	1866
Stathern — see Harby				
Station Road — see Shipley				
Staveley	41	A4	LNW	
[Staveley] (Derbyshire)				
Central	82	D7	GC	1963
Town 2nd, 1st — 1888	82	D7	MID	1952
Works	82	D7	GC	1963
Staverton	9	D9	GW	1958
Staverton Bridge R.O. PR. FR. CL. above	9	D9	DVR	
Staverton Halt	17	F1	GW	1966
Staward	43	A2	NE	1930
Steam Mills Crossing Halt	17	D8	GW	1930
Stechford	80	D7	LNW	
Steelend GDS	46	D10	NB	1941
Steele Road	42	E7	NB	1969
Steens Bridge	27	F3	GW	1952
Steeplehouse and Wirksworth	31	F5	LNW	1877
	82	A4		
Steer Point	9	E5	GW	1947
	11	H5		
Steeton and Silsden 2nd, 1st — 1892	37	C8	MID	1965
	79	C1		
Stella Gill GDS	43	F1	NE	
Stepford	45	D7	GSW	1943
Stepney (Yorks) — see [Hull]				
Stepney East — see [London]				
Stepney Green — see [London]				
Stepps — see [Glasgow]				
Stevenage 2nd, 1st — 1973	12	C9	GN	
Stevenston	49	B5	GSW	
Stevenston, Moorpark	49	B5	CAL	1932
Steventon	14	G4	GW	1964
Stewartby Form. Wooton Pillinge	23	G1	LNW	
Stewarton	49	C5	GBK JT	
Stewarts Lane — see [London]				
Steyning	2	A2	LBSC	1966
Stickney	29	E5	GN	1970
Stillington	38	E7	NE	1952
Stirchley — see Dawley				
Stirchley Street — see Bournville				
[Stirling]				
Stirling	50	C1	CAL	
Stirling Central	50	C2	CAL	1966
Stirling East	50	C1	NB	1966
Stixwould	29	C6	CN	1970

Station	Page	Block	Comp	Year of CL
Stoats Nest — see Coulsdon North				
Stobcross — see [Glasgow]				
Stobo	46	F3	CAL	1950
Stobs	42	E8	NB	1969
Stockbridge	4	F7	LSW	1964
Stockcross and Bagnor	14	G2	GW	1960
Stockingford	80	C9	MID	1968
[Stockport]				
Cheadle Heath	77	C9	MID	1967
Heaton Mersey	77	C9	MID	1961
Heaton Norris	77	C9	LNW	1959
Portwood	77	C9	CLC	1875
Stockport	31	B10	LNW	
	77	C9		
Tiviot Dale	77	C9	CLC	1967
Stocksfield	43	D3	NE	
Stocksmoor	37	E4	LY	
	79	H3		
Stockton — see [Teeside]				
Stockton Brook	31	B5	NS	1956
	73	D8		
Stockwith GDS	28	F10	GN/GE	
	34	G1		
Stogumber	6	E8	GW	1971
Stogumber R.O. PR. FR. CL. above	6	E8	SVR	
Stoke (Suffolk)	23	F10	GE	1967
Stoke Bruern	25	E2	EWJ/SMJ	1893
Stoke Canon 2nd, 1st — 1894	6	C3	GW	1960
	8	H10		
Stoke Climsland — see Luckett				
Stoke d'Abernon — see Cobham				
Stoke Edith	27	G1	GW	1965
Stoke Ferry (Norfolk)	22	G10	GE	1930
Stoke Golding	25	A8	AN JT	1931
Stoke Junction Halt	13	B3	SR	1961
Stoke Mandeville	15	D7	MET/GC	
Stoke Newington	65	B6	GE	
[Stoke-on-Trent]				
Bucknall and Northwood	31	B5	NS	1956
	73	C7		
Burslem	73	C8	NS	1964
Chatterley	31	A4	NS	1948
	73	D8		
Cobridge	73	C7	NS	1964
Etruria	31	A4	NS	
	73	C7		
Fenton	73	C6	NS	1961
Fenton Manor	73	C6	NS	1956
Ford Green and Smallthorpe	73	D8	NS	1927
Handford Road Halt	31	A4	NS	1913
Hanley 2nd, 1st — 1873	73	C7	NS	1964
Hartshill and Basford Halt	73	B6	NS	1926
Longport, Wolstanton	31	A5	NS	
	73	C7		
Longton	31	B4	NS	
	73	C6		
Meir	31	B4	NS	1966
Milton	31	B5	NS	1956
Mount Pleasant Halt	73	C6	NS	1918
Newchapel and Goldenhill	31	A5	NS	1964
	73	C9		
Normacot	31	B4	NS	1964
	73	C6		
Pitts Hill	73	C8	NS	1964
Sideway Halt	31	A4	NS	1923
Stoke-on-Trent 2nd, 1st — 1848	31	B4	NS	
Trentham	31	A4	NS	1964
Trentham Gardens	31	A3	NS	1939
Tunstall	31	A5	NS	1964
	73	C8		
Waterloo Road	73	C7	NS	1943
Wedgwood	31	A4	NS	
	73	C6		
Whieldon Road Halt	73	C6	NS	1918
Stoke Prior Halt	27	F3	GW	1952
Stokes Bay	5	A4	LSW	1915
Stokesley — see Craven Arms				
Stokesley	38	G5	NE	1954
Stoke Works	24	C4	GW	1966
Stoke Works	24	C4	MID	1855
Stone Junction	31	B3	NS	
Stonea	22	H7	GE	1966
Stonebridge Park	64	C4	LNW	
Stone Cross Halt	2	F1	LBSC	1935
Stone Crossing Halt	70	E9	SEC	
Stonegate Form. Ticehurst Road	2	G4	SEC	
Stonehall and Lydden Halt	3	F7	SEC	1954
Stonehaven	55	D7	CAL	
Stonehouse (Lanarks)	49	H5	CAL	1965

Station	Page	Block	Comp	Year of CL
Stonehouse, Bristol Road (Glos)	17	F6	MID	1965
Stonehouse, Burdett Road (Glos)	17	F6	GW	
Stoneleigh	68	C4	LBSC	
Stoneywood	55	A8	GNS	1937
Stony Hill	76	B2	PW JT	1872
Stony Stratford	25	F1	LNW	1926
Storeton for Barnston	77	D1	GC	1951
Stottesdon	27	G6	CMDP	1938
Stoulton	24	C2	GW	1966
Stourbridge Junction 2nd, 1st — 1901	80	F3	GW	
Stourbridge Town	80	F3	GW	
Stourpaine and Durweston Halt	7	G5	SD JT	1956
Stourport-on-Severn	24	B5	GW	1970
	80	G2		
Stourton	79	E7	EWYU	1904
Stow	47	A5	NB	1969
Stow Bardolph	22	F9	GE	1963
Stow Bedon	20	G3	GE	1964
Stowmarket	21	D4	GE	
Stow-on-the-Wold	14	C9	GW	1962
Stow Park for Marton	28	G8	GN/GE	1961
Stow St Mary Halt	13	B6	LNE	1939
Strathcathro Form. Inchbare	51	F10	CAL	1938
	55	G4		
Stradbroke	21	C6	MSL	1952
Strageath Halt	50	E4	BR	1964
Strand — see [Barrow]				
Strand Road — see Bideford				
Strand Road — see [Bootle] Marsh Lane				
Stranraer Harbour	44	B4	PPW JT	
Stranraer Town	44	B4	PPW JT	1966
Strap Lane Halt	7	E8	GW	1950
Strata Florida	26	C4	GW	1965
Stratford — see [London]				
Stratford Market — see [London]				
[Stratford-on-Avon]				
Evesham Road Crossing	24	G2	GW	1916
Hatton Branch Terminus	80	H7	GW	1863
Honeybourne Branch Terminus	80	H7	OWW	1863
Stratford and Moreton Terminus	80	H7	OWW	1859
Stratford-on-Avon	24	G3	EWJ/SMJ	1952
Stratford-upon-Avon	24	G3	GW	
	80	H7		
Strathbungo — see [Glasgow]				
[Strathaven]				
Central	49	G5	CAL	1965
North — Retained G. FR. 1904	49	G5	CAL	1945
Strathaven	49	G5	CAL	1904
Strathblane	49	F10	NB	1951
	74	G10		
Strathcarron	58	G4	HR	
Strathdon — see Gartley				
Strathmiglo	51	A4	NB	1950
Strathord	50	G6	CAL	1931
Strathpeffer	58	F10	HIGH	1946
Strathyre	50	A4	CAL	1965
	53	H4		
Stratton	14	C4	GW	1953
Stratton Halt — see Bradford Peverell				
Stratton Park Halt	14	C4	GW	1964
Stravithie	51	D4	NB	1930
Strawberry Hill	67	H8	LSW	
	68	A8		
Strensall	34	E9	NE	1930
Strensall Halt	34	E9	NE	1930
Streatham	68	G7	LBSC	
Streatham Common	68	G7	LBSC	
Streatham Hill	68	G7	LBSC	
Streatley — see Goring				
Street see Glastonbury				
Streetly — see [West Midlands]				
Stretford	77	B8	MSJA	
Stretford Bridge Junction	27	D6	BC	1935
Stretham	23	B7	GE	1931
Stretton (Derbys)	82	B4	ASH	1936
Stretton (Derbys)	31	D6	MID	1961
	82	B4		
Stretton (Staffs) and Clay Mills	31	F2	NS	1949
Stretton-on-Fosse	24	G1	GW	1929
Stretton-under-Fosse — see Brinklow				
Strichen	54	D8	GNS	1965
Strines	31	C9	GC/MID	
	77	C10		
Stromeferry	58	H3	HIGH	
Strood 2nd, 1st — 1856	2	H10	SE	
Stroud	17	F6	MID	1947
Stroud Central	17	F6	GW	
Stroud Green — see [London]				
Struan	50	D10	HIGH	1965

Station	Page	Block	Comp	Year of CL
Stubbins	76	D8	EL	1972
Studley and Astwood Bank	80	H5	MID	1962
Sturmer	23	F10	GE	1967
Sturminster Newton	7	F5	SD JT	1966
Sturry	3	E9	SEC	
Sturton	28	F9	GC	1959
Stutton	34	C7	NE	1905
	79	C9		
Styal	31	A9	LNW	
	77	D8		
Suckley	24	A3	GW	1964
Sudbury (Staffs)	31	E2	NS	1966
Sudbury (Suffolk)	21	F2	GE	
Sudbury — see [London]				
Sully	78	H6	TV	1968
Summer Lane — see [Barnsley]				
Summerston — see [Glasgow]				
Summers Town — see Earlsfield				
Summerseat	76	E8	EL	1972
Sun Bank Halt	33	G4	GW	1950
	72	C1		
Sunbury	67	F7	LSW	
[Sunderland]				
Fawcett Street	43	H2	NE	1879
Hendon	43	H2	NE	1879
Hendon Burn	43	H2	LOND	1868
Hylton	43	G2	NE	1964
Millfield	43	H2	NE	1955
Monkwearmouth	43	H2	NE	1967
Moor	43	H2	NE	1858
Pallion	43	G2	NE	1964
South Dock GDS	43	G2	NE	1965
Southwick	43	H2	NE	1965
Sunderland	43	H2	NE	
Wearmouth	43	H2	YNB	1848
Sundridge Park	69	E7	SEC	
Sunilaws	47	F4	NE	1955
Sunningdale and Windlesham	15	E2	LSW	
Sunninghill — see Ascot				
Sunnymeads	15	F3	LSW	
	67	A10		
Sunnyside — see Coatbridge				
Sunny Wood Halt	76	D8	LY	1952
Surbiton 2nd, 1st (Kingston) — 1845	68	B5	LSW	
Surfleet	22	D5	GN	1961
	29	E2		
Sutton (Cambs) 2nd Sta., 1st — 1878	23	B7	GE	1931
Sutton (Derbys) — see Palterton				
Sutton (Surrey)	68	F3	LBSC	
Sutton (Yorks) — see Barnby Moor				
Sutton-at-Hone — see Farningham Road				
Sutton Bingham	7	C5	LSW	1962
Sutton Bridge 2nd, 1st — 1867	22	E7	MGN	1959
	29	G1		
Sutton Coldfield — see [West Midlands]				
Sutton Common	68	F4	LSW	
[Sutton-in-Ashfield]				
Central	82	E5	GC	1956
Junction Station	82	E5	MID	1964
Sutton-in-Ashfield	82	E5	MID	1949
Town	82	E5	GN	1956
Sutton Oak — see [St Helens]				
Sutton-on-Hull — see [Hull]				
Sutton-on-Sea	29	H8	GN	1970
Sutton-on-Trent — see Crow Park				
Sutton Park — see [West Midlands]				
Sutton Scotney	4	H8	GW	1960
Sutton Weaver	77	E5	LNW	1931
Swadlincote 2nd, 1st — 1883	31	G1	MID	1947
Swaffham	20	F1	GE	1968
Swaffhamprior	23	D8	GE	1962
Swainsthorpe	20	G7	GE	1954
Swale Halt 2nd, 1st — 1960	3	B10	SEC	
Swalecliff — see Chestfield				
Swalwell for Whickham	43	E3	NE	1953
	81	G2		
Swanage	4	B1	LSW	1972
Swanbourne	15	C10	LNW	1968
Swanbridge Halt	78	H6	TV	1968
Swanley	2	E9	SEC	
	70	A6		
Swanley Junction	70	A6	SEC	1939
Swannington	25	B10	MID	1951
Swanscombe	70	F9	SEC	
[Swansea]				
Argyle Halt	19	F1	SIT	1960
Ashleigh Road	19	F1	SIT	1960
Baldwin's Halt	19	G2	GW	1933
Birchgrove	19	G2	MID	1875

Station	Page	Block	Comp	Year of CL
Blackpill	19	F1	SIT	1960
Brynmill	19	F1	SIT	1960
Cockett	19	G1	GW	1964
Copper Pit Platform	19	G2	GW	1956
Danygraig	19	G2	RSB	1933
Danygraig Halt	19	G2	GW	1936
Dunvant	19	F2	LNW	1964
East Dock (Fabians Bay)	19	G2	GW	1936
Felin Fran GDS	19	G2	GW	1965
Felin Fran Halt	19	G2	GW	1956
Glais 2nd, 1st — 1875	19	G2	MID	1950
Landore	19	G2	GW	1964
Landore Low Level	19	G2	GW	1954
Llansamlet North 2nd, 1st — 1875	19	G2	GW	1964
Llansamlet South	19	G2	MID	1875
Morriston East	19	G2	MID	1950
Morriston West	19	G2	GW	1956
Mumbles Pier	19	F1	SIT	1959
Mumbles Road	19	F1	LNW	1964
Oystermouth	19	F1	SIT	1960
Pentrefelin (Glam) Halt	19	G2	GW	1956
Plas Marl Halt	19	G2	GW	1956
Riverside	19	G2	RSB	1933
Rutland Street	19	G1	SIT	1960
St Gabriels	19	G1	SIT	1960
St Helens	19	G1	SIT	1960
St Thomas	19	G2	MID	1950
Southend	19	F1	SIT	1960
Swansea	19	G2	GW	
Swansea Bay 2nd, 1st — 1892	19	G1	LNW	1964
Upper Bank	19	G2	MID	1950
Victoria	19	G1	LNW	1964
West Cross	19	F1	SIT	1960
Wind Street, Burrows Lodge	19	F1	GW	1873
Swansea Bay — see [Swansea]				
Swan Village — see [West Midlands]				
Swanwick	4	H4	LSW	
Swarstoke — see Chellaston				
Swavesey	23	C6	GE	1970
Sway	4	E3	LSW	
Swaythling	4	G5	LSW	
Swimbridge	8	D7	GW	1966
Swinderby	28	H6	MID	
Swindon	14	C4	GW	
Swindon Town	14	C4	MSWJ	1961
Swine	35	C6	NE	1964
Swineshead	22	B4	GN	
	29	D4		
Swinton (Lancs)	76	G7	LY	
Swinton (Yorks) 2nd, 1st — 1899	82	D10	MID	1968
Swinton Central (Yorks)	82	D10	GC	1957
Swiss Cottage — see [London]				
Sydenham	69	A8	LBSC	
Sydenham Hill	69	B8	SEC	
Sykehouse GDS	34	E4	HB/GC	1958
Sylfaen Halt R.O. PR. FR. 1931 CL.	27	A9	W & L	
Symington 2nd, 1st — 1863	46	C3	CAL	1965
Symonds Yat	17	C8	GW	1959
Syon Lane	64	B1	LSW	
	68	A10		
Syston	25	D10	MID	1968
Tackley Halt	14	H7	GW	
Tadcaster	34	C7	NE	1964
	79	C9		
Tadworth and Walton-on-the-Hill	12	C1	SEC	
Taffs Well	78	F5	TV	
Tain	56	B4	HR	
Takeley	12	G9	GE	1952
Talacre	33	F9	LNW	1966
Talbot Road — see [Blackpool]				
Talerddig	26	F8	CAM	1965
Talgarth	15	E10	CAM	1962
Talley Road	19	G5	VT JT	1955
Tallington	22	F2	GN	1959
Talsarnau	32	G3	CAM	
Talsarn Halt	19	E9	GW	1951
	26	B2		
Talwrn Bach Halt	32	G1	GW	
Talybont Halt	32	G1	CAM	
Talybont-on-Usk	16	E9	BM	1962
Talybont (Pen Rhiw)	26	B7	H & T	1898
Tal-y-Cafn and Eglwysbach	33	A7	LNW	
Talyllyn	16	E9	MW	1878
Talyllyn (Brynderwen)	16	E9	BM	1869
Talyllyn Junction	16	E9	BM	1962
Talywain — see Abersychan				
Tamerton Foliot	9	D4	LSW	1962
Tamworth High Level — Combined with L.L.	24	G9	LNW	
	80	B9		

Station	Page	Block	Comp	Year of CL
Tamworth Low Level — Combined with H.L.	24	G9	LNW	
	80	B9		
Tanfield	38	D2	NE	1931
Tanfield Lea	43	E2	BJ	1844
Tanhouse Lane — see [West Midlands]				
Tankerton — see Whitstaple				
Tankerton Halt	3	D10	SEC	1931
	13	E2		
Tannadice	51	D9	CAL	1952
	55	H3		
Tanshelf — see [Pontefract]				
Tanworth — see Danzey				
Tan-y-Bwlch for Maentwrog	32	G3	FEST	1939
Tan-y-Bwlch R.O. PR. FR. CL. above	32	G3	FR	
Tan-y-Grisiau	32	H4	FEST	1939
Tan-y-Grisiau R.O. PR. FR. CL. above	32	H4	FR	
Tan-y-Manod	32	H4	FB/GW	1883
Taplow 2nd, 1st — 1872	15	E4	GW	
Tarbert — see Arrochar				
Tarbolton	49	D3	GSW	1943
Tarff	45	B4	GSW	1965
Tarleton Halt	36	D5	LY	1913
Tarleton — see also Hesketh Bank				
Tarporley — see Beeston Castle				
Tarset	42	H5	NB	1956
Tarvin — see Barrow (Cheshire)				
Tattenhall	30	E6	LNW	1966
	77	H4		
Tattenhall Road	30	D6	LNW	1957
	77	H4		
Tattenham Corner	68	D1	SEC	
Tattershall	29	D5	GN	1963
Taucher's Halt	54	D2	LMS	1964
Taunton	6	F7	GW	
Tavistock North	9	C4	LSW	1968
	11	H8		
Tavistock South	9	C4	GW	1962
	11	H8		
Tay Bridge — see [Dundee] Dundee				
Taynuilt	53	A5	CAL	
Tayport	51	D6	NB	1966
Tean	31	C3	NS	1953
Tebay	41	C5	LNW	1968
Teddington and Bushey Park	68	A7	LSW	
[Teeside]				
Allens West	38	F6	NE	
Belasis Lane	38	F7	LNE	1954
Billingham-on-Tees 2nd, 1st — 1966	38	F7	NE	
Eston — on site of South Bank	38	G7	NE	1885
Eston	38	G6	NE	1929
Haverton Hill	38	G7	NE	1954
Lazenby	38	G7	NE	1864
Newport	38	F6	NE	1915
Norton-on-Tees	38	F7	NE	1960
Port Clarence	38	G7	NE	1939
Stockton	38	F7	NE	
Stockton	38	F7	S & D	1848
Stockton North Shore GDS	38	F7	NE	1948
Teeside Airport	38	E6	BR	
Thornaby	38	F7	NE	
Tod Point	38	G7	NE	1960
Teigl Halt	33	H3	GW	1960
Teigngrace	9	C9	GW	1959
Teignmouth	9	C9	GW	
	11	C10		
Temple — see [London]				
Templecombe	7	E6	LSW	1966
Templecombe Lower 2nd, 1st — 1887	7	E6	SD JT	1966
Temple Hirst	34	E5	NE	1961
Temple Meads — see [Bristol]				
Temple Sowerby	41	C8	NE	1953
Templeton	18	H4	GW	1964
Tempsford	23	E4	GN	1956
Tenbury Wells	27	F4	TEN JT	1962
Tenby 2nd, 1st — 1866	18	H2	GW	
Tenterden St Michaels	3	A5	KES	1954
Tenterden Town	3	A5	KES	1954
Tenterden Town R.O. PR. FR. CL. above	3	A5	K & ES	
Tern Hill	30	F2	GW	1963
Terrington	22	E8	MGN	1959
	29	H1		
Teston Crossing Halt	2	G8	SEC	1959
Tetbury	17	G5	GW	1964
Tetbury Road	17	H6	GW	1882
Tettenhall — see [West Midlands]				
Tevershall	82	E5	MID	1930
Tewkesbury 2nd, 1st — 1864	17	G10	MID	1961
Teynham	3	B9	SEC	
Thackley	79	D3	GN	1931

Station	Page	Block	Comp	Year of CL
Thame	15	B6	GW	1963
Thames Ditton	68	A5	LSW	
Thames Haven	13	B4	LTS	1880
Thanet — see Minster				
Thankerton	46	C4	CAL	1965
Thatcham	14	H2	GW	
Thatto Heath	76	G3	LNW	
Thaxted	12	H10	GE	1952
	23	H9		
Thealby — see Winterton				
Theale	15	A2	GW	
The Avenue	43	G4	BT	1864
The Dell — see Falmouth				
Theddingworth	25	D7	LNW	1966
Theddlethorpe	29	G10	GN	1960
The Dyke	2	B2	LBSC	1939
The Hale Halt — see [London] Mill Hill				
The Lakes Halt	80	G7	GW	
The Lane	8	D4	BWA	1917
The Lodge Halt	72	C3	GW	1931
Thelwall	77	C6	LNW	1956
The Mound Junction	61	C1	HIGH	1960
The Oaks	76	D7	LY	1950
Theobalds Grove 2nd, 1st — 1919	12	D6	LNE	
	65	B10		
The Pilot Halt — see Pilot Halt				
Thetford	21	A2	GE	
Thetford Bridge	21	A2	GE	1953
The Warren Platform — see Dawlish Warren				
Theydon Bois	12	F6	GE	1966
Theydon Bois R.O. by LT	12	F6	LT	
Thirsk Junction Station	38	E2	NE	
Thirsk Town	38	E2	NE	1855
Thongs Bridge	79	H3	LY	1959
Thorganby	34	F7	DV	1926
Thorington	13	F9	GE	1957
Thornaby	38	F7	NE	
Thornbridge Halt	46	B9	CAL	1938
Thornbury	17	D4	MID	1944
Thorncliffe — see Chapeltown				
Thorndon — see Aspall				
Thorne North	34	F3	NE	
Thorne South 3rd, 1st — 1859, 2nd — 1866	34	F3	GC	
Thorneywood — see [Nottingham]				
Thornford Bridge Halt	7	D4	GW	
Thorner	34	B7	NE	1964
	79	C8		
Thorney	22	F4	MGN	1957
Thorney and Kingsbury Halt	7	B6	GW	1964
Thorneybank — see [Burnley]				
Thorneyburn	42	H5	NB	1956
Thornfalcon	6	H6	GW	1962
Thornhill (Dumfries)	45	D9	GSW	1965
Thornhill (Yorks) — see [Dewsbury]				
Thornhill (Yorks) — see also Ravensthorpe				
Thornielee	47	A4	NB	1950
Thornley	38	E9	NE	1952
Thornliebank	74	F2	CAL	
Thornton (Yorks)	79	E2	GN	1955
Thornton (Leics)	25	B9	LS	1842
Thornton Abbey	35	B4	GC	
Thornton for Cleveleys (Lancs)	36	C7	PW	1970
	76	A1		
Thornton Curtis	35	B4	MS & L	1848
Thornton Dale	39	C2	NE	1950
Thorntonhall	49	F6	CAL	
	74	G1		
Thornton Heath	68	H6	LBSC	
Thornton-in-Craven	37	B8	MID	1970
Thornton Junction Station	51	B2	NB	1969
Thornton Lane	25	B9	MID	1865
Thorp Arch (Boston Spa)	34	C8	NE	1964
	79	B8		
Thorpe	23	B2	LNW	1964
Thorpe Bay	13	C4	LTS	
Thorpe Cloud	31	E5	LNW	1954
Thorpe Culvert	29	G6	GN	
Thorpe-in-Balne GDS	34	E3	HB/GC	1958
Thorpe-le-Soken	13	G9	GE	
Thorpeness	29	D9	GE	1966
Thorpe-on-the-Hill	28	H6	MID	1955
Thorpe Thewles	38	E7	NE	1931
Thorp Gates GDS	34	D6	NE	1964
Thor's Cave and Wetton	31	D5	NS	1934
Thorverton	6	C4	GW	1963
	8	G10		
Thrapston, Bridge Street	23	B1	LNW	1964

Station	Page	Block	Comp	Year of CL
Thrapston, Midland Road	23	B1	MID	1959
Three Bridges	2	B5	LBSC	
Three Cocks Junction	16	F10	CAM	1962
Three Counties	23	G4	GN	1959
Three Oaks and Guestling Halt	3	A2	SEC	
Threkeld	40	G7	CKP	1972
Threshfield — see Grassington				
Threlwall	77	C6	LNW	1962
Thringstone Halt	28	B1	LNW	1931
Throsk Platform	50	D1	CAL	1966
Thrumster	62	G6	HIGH	1944
Thurgarton	28	E4	MID	
Thurgoland	37	F2	MS & L	1847
Thurlby	22	E2	GN	1951
Thurnby and Scraptoft	25	E9	GN	1957
Thurnham — see Bearsted				
Thurnscoe — see Goldthorpe				
Thurnscoe — see also Hickleton				
Thursford	20	C3	GE	1959
Thurso	61	H10	HR	
	62	D9		
Thurstaston	77	D1	B HEAD	1954
Thurston	21	D3	GE	
Thuxton	20	F6	GE	1969
Thwaites	79	C2	MID	1909
Tibbermuir Crossing	50	F5	CAL	1951
Tibshelf and Newton	82	C5	MID	1930
Tibshelf Town	82	C5	GC	1963
Ticehurst Road — see Stonegate				
Tickhill and Wadsworth	34	D1	SY JT	1929
	82	F9		
Tidal Basin — see [London]				
Tiddington	15	A7	GW	1963
Tidenham	17	B5	GW	1959
Tidworth	4	E9	MSWJ	1955
Tiffield	25	E3	NBJ	1871
[Tilbury]				
Marine	70	G9	LMS	1932
Riverside	12	H3	MID	
	70	G9		
Town	12	H3	LTS	
	70	G9		
Tile Hill	24	H5	LNW	
	80	E9		
Tilehurst	15	B3	GW	
Tillicoultry	50	E2	NB	1964
Tillietudlem	46	A5	CAL	1951
Tillyfourie	55	A5	GNS	1950
Tillynaught	54	C4	GNS	1968
Tilmanstone	3	G7	EK	1948
Tilton	25	F9	GN/LNW	1953
Timberland — see Scopwick				
Timperley	77	C8	MSJA	
Timsbury — see Radford				
Tingley	79	F5	GN	1954
Tinkers Green Halt	30	B2	GW	1965
	33	H2		
Tinsley — see [Sheffield]				
Tintern	17	B6	GW	1959
Tipton — see [West Midlands]				
Tipton St Johns	6	E2	LSW	1967
Tiptree	13	C8	GE	1951
Tir Phil and New Tredegar	78	B6	RHY	
Tirydail — see Ammanford				
Tisbury	4	A7	LSW	
	7	H6		
Tissington	31	E5	LNW	1954
Tisted	5	C6	LSW	1955
Titley	27	C3	GW	1955
Tittensor — see Barlaston				
Tiverton 2nd, 1st — 1885	6	D5	GW	1964
Tiverton Junction Station	6	E5	GW	
Tivetshall	21	A5	GE	1966
Tiviot Dale — see [Stockport]				
Tochieneal	54	B3	GNS	1951
Toddington	14	B10	GW	1960
Todd Lane Junction Form. Preston Junc.	76	B4	EL	1968
Todhills	38	C9	NE	1867
Todmorden	37	B5	LY	
	76	B10		
Tod Point — see [Teeside]				
Toft and Kingston GDS	23	E6	GE	1968
Tollcross — see [Glasgow]				
Tollcross — see also [Glasgow] Carntyne				
Toller	7	C3	GW	1975
Tollerton	34	C10	NE	1965
Tollesbury	13	D7	GE	1951
Tollesbury Pier	13	D7	GE	1921
Tolleshunt d'Arcy	13	D8	GE	1951

Station	Page	Block	Comp	Year of CL
Tolleshunt Knights	13	D8	GE	1951
Tolworth	68	C5	SR	
Tomatin	57	A4	HIGH	1965
Tonbridge 2nd, 1st — 1864	2	F7	SEC	
Tondu	78	E2	GW	1970
Tonfanau	26	B8	CAM	
Tong — see [Bradford] Birkenshaw				
Tonge and Breedon	28	B1	MID	1931
	31	H1		
Tongham	5	E10	LSW	1937
Tongwynlais	78	F6	CDFF	1931
Ton Llwyd Halt	78	C3	GW	1933
Tonmawr Junction	78	D2	SWM	1930
Tonteg Halt	78	E5	GW	1962
Tonteg Halt	78	E5	TV	1930
Tonypandy and Trelaw	78	D3	TV	
Tonyrefail	78	E3	GW	1958
Tooting 2nd, 1st (Tooting Jcn.) — 1894	68	F6	LSW/LBSC	
Topcliffe	38	E2	NE	1959
Topsham	6	D2	LSW	
[Torbay]				
Brixham	9	E10	GW	1963
Churston	9	E10	GW	
Churston R.O. PR. FR. CL. above	9	E10	T & D	
Goodrington Sands	9	E10	GW	
Goodrington Sands R.O. PR. FR. CL. above	9	E10	T & D	
Paignton	9	E10	GW	
Preston Platform	9	E10	GW	1914
Torre for Babbacombe	9	D10	GW	
Torquay	9	D10	GW	
Torksey	28	G8	GC	1959
Torpantau	16	D8	BM	1962
	78	A4		
Torphins	55	B5	GNS	1966
Torquay — see [Torbay]				
Torrance	74	H9	NB	1951
Torre — see [Torbay]				
Torrington	8	E4	LSW	1965
Torryburn	46	D10	NB	1930
Torver	40	F3	FUR	1958
Tothill — see [Plymouth] Mount Gould				
Totley — see Dore				
Totnes	9	D10	GW	
Totnes, Riverside	9	D10	DUR	
Toton	28	C3	MID	1863
Tottenham — see [London] Silver Street				
Tottenham Hale — see [London]				
Totteridge — see [London]				
Tottington	76	D8	LY	1952
Totton for Eling	4	F5	LSW	
Tovil	2	H8	SEC	1943
Towcester	25	E2	SMJ	1952
Tower Hill	9	A3	LSW	1966
	11	F10		
Tower [of London] — see [London]				
Towersey Halt	15	C6	GW	1963
Towiemore	54	E2	LNE	1968
Tow Law	38	B9	NE	1956
Towneley — see [Burnley]				
Town Green and Aughton	76	F2	LY	
Town Pier — see Gravesend Ferry Terminal				
Towyn — see Tywyn				
Trabboch	49	D2	GSW	1951
Trafford Park — see [Manchester]				
Tram Inn	17	A10	GW	1958
Tram Road — see [Pontypridd]				
Tranent — see Prestopans				
Tranmere — see [Birkenhead]				
Traveller's Rest (Abercynon Upper)	78	D5	TV	1932
Trawscoed	26	C5	GW	1964
Trawsfyndd	32	H3	GW	1960
Trawsfyndd Lake Halt	32	H3	GW	1960
Treamble GDS	10	F6	GW	1959
Treborth	32	F7	LNW	1960
Trecynon Halt — see [Aberdare]				
Tredegar	16	E7	LNW	1960
	78	A7		
Tredegar Junction	78	D7	LNW	1960
Treeton OP. 1884 on site of 1st	31	H10	MID	1951
	82	D8		
Treeton 1st Sta.	82	D8	NM	1843
Trefeglwys	26	G7	VAN/CAM	1879
Trefeinon	16	E9	CAM	1962
Treferig GDS	78	E4	TV	
Trefnant	33	D7	LNW	1955
[Treforest]				
Treforest	78	E4	TV	

Station	Page	Block	Comp	Year of CL
Treforest Estate	78	E4	TV	
Treforest High Level	78	E5	BARRY	1930
Treforest Low Level	78	E5	ANSW	1956
Trefriw — see Llanrwst				
Tregarron	19	G10	GW	1965
	26	C3		
Tregarth	32	G7	LNW	1951
Trehafod	78	E4	TV	
Treharris — see [Merthyr]				
Treherbert	78	D3	TV	
Trehowell Halt	30	B3	GW	1951
	33	H3		
Trelaw — see Tonypandy				
Trelewis Halt	78	C5	GW	1964
Trelewis Platform	78	C5	GW	1964
Trench Crossing	24	A10	LNW	1964
Trench Halt	30	C3	CAM	1962
Trenholme Bar	38	F5	NE	1954
Trent	28	C2	MID	1968
Trentham — see [Stoke-on-Trent]				
Trentham Gardens — see [Stoke-on-Trent]				
Trent Valley — see [Lichfield]				
Trent Valley — see Nuneaton				
Trent Valley — see Rugeley				
Trent Valley High Level — see [Lichfield]				
Trent Valley Junction — see [Lichfield]				
Treorchy	78	D3	TV	
Treowen Halt	78	D7	GW	1960
Trerhyngyll and Maendy Halt	78	G4	TV	1951
Tresavean GDS	10	F4	GW	
Tresmeer	9	A2	LSW	1966
	11	D10		
Trethomas	78	E7	BM	1962
Trevil Halt	78	A7	LNW	1958
Trevor	33	G4	GW	1965
	72	C1		
Trewerry and Trerice Halt	10	G6	GW	1963
Trewythan GDS	26	G7	CAM	1940
Triangle	79	G1	LY	1929
Trimdon	38	E9	NE	1952
Trimingham	20	B7	NS JT	1953
Trimley	21	G7	GE	
Trimsarn Road Halt	19	D3	BPGU	1953
Tring	15	E7	LNW	
Trinity — see [Edinburgh] Newhaven				
Trodigal Halt	48		CM	1931
Troedyrhiew Garth	78	E2	GW	1970
Troedyrhiw	78	B4	TV	
Troedyrhiw Platform — see [Merthyr]				
Troedyrhiwfuwch Halt	78	B6	RHY	1916
Troon 2nd, 1st — 1892	49	B3	GSW	
Troon	49	B3	K & T	1846
Trouble House Halt	17	G5	BR	1964
Troutbeck	40	H8	CKP	1972
Trowbridge	7	G10	GW	
Trowell	28	C3	MID	1967
	82	E1		
Trowse — see [Norwich]				
Troy — see Monmouth				
Trumper's Crossing Halt — see [London]				
[Truro]				
Newham	10	G4	WC	1863
Truro	10	G4	GW	
Truro Road	10	G4	WC	1855
Trusham	9	B9	GW	1958
Truthall Platform	10	D3	GW	1962
Tryfan Junction	32	E6	NWNG/WH	1936
Tubs Hill — see Sevenoaks				
Tue Brook — see [Liverpool]				
Tullibardine	50	E3	CAL	1964
Tullibody — see Cambus				
Tulloch	59	G9	NB	
Tulse Hill	68	H8	LBSC	
Tumble GDS	19	E4	GW	
Tumby Woodside	29	E6	GN	1970
[Tunbridge Wells]				
Tunbridge Junction	2	F5	SE	1864
Tunbridge Wells Central 2nd, 1st — 1846	2	F5	SE	
Tunbridge Wells West	2	F5	LBSC	
Tunnel Halt (Moelwyn)	32	H3	FEST	not known
Tunnel Junction	38	C8	NE	1863
Tunstall — see [Stoke-on-Trent]				
Turkey Street Form. Forty Hill	65	B10	GE	
Turnberry	44	D10	GSW	1942
Turnchapel — see [Plymouth]				
Turnham Green — see [Plymouth]				
Turnhouse — see [Edinburgh]				
Turriff	54	D6	GNS	1951
Turton and Edgeworth Form. Chapeltown	76	D6	LY	1961
Turvey	23	E1	MID	1962
	25	H3	MID	1962
Tutbury	31	E2	NS	1966
Tutshill Halt for Beachley	17	B5	GW	1959
Tuxford Central	28	F7	GC	1955
	82	H6		
Tuxford North	28	F7	GN	1955
	82	H6		
Twechar	75	C10	NB	1951
Tweedmouth	43	G10	NE	1964
	47	H6		
Twenty	22	G3	MGN	1959
	29	C1		
Twerton-on-Avon — see [Bath]				
Twickenham 2nd, 1st — 1954	68	A8	BR	
Twizell	47	F5	NE	1955
Twyford	15	C3	GW	
Twyford — see Shawford				
Twyford Abbey Halt — see [London]				
Twywell	23	B1	MID	1951
Ty Croes	32	D7	LNW	
Tydd	22	E7	MGN	1959
	29	G1		
Tyddyn Bridge Halt	33	B4	GW	1960
Tyddyn Gwyn	33	B4	GW	1883
Tygwyn Halt	32	G3	GW	
Tylacoch Halt	78	D3	TV	1912
Tyldesley	76	G6	LNW	1969
Tyllwyn Halt	78	B7	GW	1962
Tylorstown	78	D3	TV	1964
Tylwch	26	G6	CAM	1962
Tyndrum Lower 2nd, 1st — 1877	53	E6	CAL	
Tyndrum Upper	53	E6	CAL	
Tyne Dock — see [Tynemouth]				
Tynehead	46	H6	NB	1969
[Tynemouth]				
B.T. Station 2nd, 1st — 1864	81	E3	NE	1882
N.N.S. Station	81	E3	NE	1882
North Shields	81	E3	NE	
North Shields	81	E3	NE	1882
Tyne Commission Quay	81	E3	NE	1970
Tyne Dock	81	F2	NE	
Tynemouth	43	G4	NE	
	81	E4		
Tynycwm Halt	78	F9	GW	1962
Tynyllwynhen	26	B9	TAL	
Tyseley	80	E7	GW	
Tytherington	17	D4	MID	1944
[Tywyn] Form. Towyn				
Tywyn T.O. PR.	26	B8	CAM	
Tywyn Pendre T.O. PR.	26	B8	TAL	
Tywyn Wharf Form. Slate Wharf	26	B8	TAL	
Uckfield	2	D4	LBSC	
[Uddingston]				
Uddingston	75	D4	CAL	
Uddingston East	75	D4	NB	1955
Uddingston West	75	D4	NB	1955
Udny	54	G8	GNS	1965
Uffculme	6	E5	GW	1963
Uffington (Berks)	14	E4	GW	1964
Uffington and Barnack (Lincs)	22	F2	MID	1952
Ufford Bridge	22	F2	GN	1929
Ulbster	62	F6	HIGH	1944
Ulceby	35	C4	GC	
Ulleskelf	79	C10	NE	
Ullesthorpe and Lutterworth	25	C7	MID	1962
Ullock	40	D8	WCE JT	1931
Ulting — see Langford				
Ulverston	40	G2	FUR	
Ulverston Road Rep. by Lindal East	40	G2	FUR	1854
Umberleigh	8	D6	LSW	
Undy Halt	17	B4	GW	1964
Union Bank Farm	77	B5	LNW	1951
Unstone	82	B6	MID	1951
Up Exe Halt	6	C4	GW	1963
	8	G10		
Uphall	46	D7	NB	1956
Upholland 2nd, 1st — 1852 — Pimbo Lane	76	F3	LY	
Uplawmoor	49	D6	CAL	1962
	74	B1		
Uplawmoor	49	D6	CBK JT	1966
	74	B1		
Upminster	66	E5	MID	
Upney — see [London]				
Upper Bank — see [Swansea]				
Upper Batley	79	F5	GN	1952
Upper Birstall — see Birstall Town				

Station	Page	Block	Comp	Year of CL
Upper Boat	78	F5	CDFF	1931
Upper Boat Halt	78	F5	ANSW	1956
Upper Broughton	28	E2	MID	1948
Upper Greenhill	75	H10	NB	1870
Upper Greenock — see [Greenock]				
Upper Halliford	67	E7	LSW	
Upper Holloway	64	H6	LTS	
Upper Lydbrook	17	C8	SW JT	1929
Upper Mill	76	F10	LNW	1917
Upper Norwood — see [London] Crystal Palace				
Upper Pontnewydd	78	D10	GW	1962
Upper Soudley Halt	17	D7	GW	1958
Upper Sydenham — see [London]				
Upperthorpe and Killamarsh	82	E7	GC	1930
Upper Tooting — see [London] Balham				
Upper Warlingham	69	A1	CO JT	
Uppingham	25	G9	LNW	1960
Upstreet — see Grove Ferry				
Upton (Cheshire)	77	C1	GC	
Upton — see [London] Forest Gate				
Upton and Blewbury	14	H4	GW	1962
Upton and North Elmsall	34	C3	HB	1932
Upton-by-Chester Halt	77	F3	B HEAD	
Upton Magna	27	F10	S & WTN	1963
Upton-on-Severn	24	B1	MID	1961
Upton Park — see [London]				
Upwell	22	G8	GE	1928
[Upwey]				
Upwey 2nd, 1st — 1886	7	D2	GW	1952
Upwey and Broadway	7	D2	GW	
Upwey Wishing Well Halt	7	D2	GW	1957
Uralite Halt	12	A3	SEC	1961
Urmston	36	H1	CLC	
	77	B8		
Urquhart	56	E10	GNS	1968
Ushaw Moor	38	C10	NE	1951
Usk	16	H5	GW	1955
Usselby — see Claxby				
Usworth	43	F2	NE	1963
	81	D1		
Utterby Halt	29	E10	GN	1961
	35	E1		
Uttoxeter 2nd, 1st — 1881	31	D3	NS	
Uxbridge — see [London]				
Valley	32	C8	LNW	1966
Van Garth Road GDS	26	F6	CAM	1940
Varteg Halt	78	C9	LNW	1941
Vauxhall — see [London]				
Vauxhall — see [West Midlands]				
Vauxhall — see [Yarmouth]				
Vaynor — see Pontsarn				
Velvet Hall	47	G5	NE	1955
Venn Cross	6	E7	GW	1966
Ventnor	5	A10	IOW	1966
Ventnor West Form. Ventnor Town	5	A10	IWC	1952
Verney Junction Station	15	C9	LNW	1968
Verwood for Cranborne	4	C4	LSW	1964
Vicarage Crossing Halt	72	B3	GW	1931
Victoria	78	B7	GW	1962
Victoria — see [London]				
Victoria — see [Manchester]				
Victoria — see [Norwich]				
Victoria — see [Nottingham]				
Victoria — see [Sheffield]				
Victoria — see [Swansea]				
Victoria Dock — see [Hull]				
Victoria Dock — see [London] Custom House				
Victoria Park — see [London]				
Victoria Park (Whiteinch) — see [Glasgow]				
Victoria Road — see [Barnstaple]				
Vigo	43	F2	NE	1869
Vine Street — see [London] Uxbridge				
Virginia Water for Wentworth	67	A6	LSW	
Vowchurch	16	H10	GOLD V/GW	1941
Vulcan Halt	76	H4	LNW	1965
Wadborough	24	C2	MID	1965
Waddesdon Manor	15	C8	MET/GC	1936
Waddesdon Road	15	C8	MET/GC	1935
Waddington	29	A7	GN	1962
Waddon for Beddington and Bandon Hill	68	H4	LBSC	
Waddon Marsh	68	H4	LBSC	
Wadebridge 2nd, 1st — 1888	11	A8	LSW	1967
Wadhurst	2	F5	SEC	
Wadsley Bridge* — see [Sheffield]				
Waenavon	78	A9	LNW	1941
Waenfawr	32	F6	NWNG/WH	1936
Wainfleet	29	G6	GN	
Wainhill Halt	15	C6	GW	1957
Wainfelin Halt	78	C10	GW	1941
[Wakefield]				
Alverthorpe	79	G6	GN	1954
Kirkgate	34	A4	LY/GN	
	79	G6		
Sandal	79	H6	WRG JT	1952
Sandal and Walton	79	H6	MID	1957
Westgate 2nd, 1st — 1867	37	G5	GC/GN	
	79	G6		
Wakerley and Barrowden	22	G1	LNW	1966
Wakes Colne — see Chapel				
Walberswick	21	B10	S WOLD	1929
Walcot	27	F10	S & WTN	1964
Waldron and Horeham Road	2	F3	LBSC	1965
Waleswood	82	E8	GC	1955
Walford Halt	17	C9	GW	1959
Walham Green — see [London] Broadway				
Walkden High Level	76	F7	LY	
Walkden Low Level	76	F7	LNW	1954
Walker	81	D3	NE	1960
Walkerburn	46	H3	NB	1962
Walker Gate	81	D3	NE	
Walkeringham	34	G1	GN/GE	1959
	28	F9		
Wall	43	B3	NB	1955
Wallace Nick	47	E3	NB	1851
[Wallasey]				
Leasowe	77	B1	WIRRAL	
Leasowe Crossing	77	B1	HOY	1872
Liscard and Poulton	77	B1	WIRRAL	1960
Seacombe and Egremont	77	B1	WIRRAL	1960
Wallasey Grove Road	77	A1	WIRRAL	
Wallasey Village	77	A1	WIRRAL	
Wallgate — see [Wigan]				
Wall Grange and Longsdon	73	D8	NS	1956
Wallingfen	34	G5	HB	1955
Wallingford	15	A5	GW	1959
Wallington	68	G4	LBSC	
Wallsend	81	D3	NE	
Wallyford	83	H6	NB	1867
Walmer for Kingsdown	3	H7	SEC	
Walpole	22	E8	MGN	1959
	29	H1		
Walsall	80	A5	LNW	
Walsall Wood	80	A6	MID	1930
Walsden	76	C10	LY	1961
Walsingham	20	B3	GE	1964
Walsoken	22	F7	EC	1851
Waltham	35	E2	GN	1961
Waltham Cross and Abbey 2nd, 1st — 1885	12	E6	GE	
Waltham-on-the-Wold GDS	28	F2	GN	1964
[Walthamstow]				
Central	65	D7	GE	
Queens Road	65	D7	GE	
St James Street	65	D7	GE	
Wood Street	65	D7	GE	
Walton (Lancs) Junction Sta.	76	G1	LY	
Walton — see Barton				
Walton (Northants)	22	G3	MID	1953
Walton (Yorks) — see [Wakefield]				
Walton — see Hersham				
Walton and Anfield — see [Liverpool]				
Walton-in-Gordano	17	A3	WCP	1940
Walton Junction — see [Warrington]				
Walton-on-Naze	13	H9	GE	
Walton-on-Thames	67	F4	LSW	
Walton-on-the-Hill — see [Liverpool]				
Walton Park	17	A3	WCP	1940
Walworth Road — see [London]				
Wamphray	45	G9	CAL	1960
Wanborough for Normandy	5	F10	LSW	
[Wandsworth]				
Common 2nd, 1st — 1858	68	F8	LBSC	
Road	68	G9	SEC	
Town	68	E9	LSW	
Wangford — see Blythburgh				
Wanlockhead	46	B1	CAL	1939
Wansford	22	G2	LNW	1957
Wansford R.O. PR. FR. CL. above	22	G2	NVR	
Wansford Road	22	G2	GN	1929
Wanstead — see Snaresbrook				
Wanstead Park	65	E6	MID	
Wanstrow	7	E8	GW	1963
[Wantage]				
Wantage	14	F4	WT	1925

Station	Page	Block	Comp	Year of CL
Wantage Road	14	F4	GW	1964
Wantage Town	14	F4	WT	1925
Wappenham	25	D2	SMJ	1951
Wapping — see [London]				
Warblington Halt Form. Denville	5	D4	LBSC	
Warboys	23	B5	GN/GE	1930
Warburton — see Heatley				
Warcop	41	E7	NE	1962
Warden	43	A4	NC	1848
Wardhouse	54	G4	GNS	1961
Wardleworth — see [Rochdale]				
Wardley — see Moorside				
Ward Street — see [Dundee]				
Ware	12	D7	GE	
Wareham 2nd, 1st — 1887	4	A2	LSW	
	7	H2		
Wargrave	15	C3	GW	
Wark	43	A4	NB	1956
Warkworth	43	E8	NE	1958
Warley — see Brentwood				
Warlingham — see Upper Warlingham				
Warminster	7	G9	GW	
Warmley	17	D2	MID	1966
	72	F7		
Warmsworth	34	D2	MS & L/GC	1875
Warnham	2	A5	LBSC	
Warren	77	A1	WIRRAL	1915
Warren Halt* — see [Folkestone]				
[Warrington]				
Arpley	77	C5	LNW	1958
Bank Quay	36	F1	LNW	
	77	C6		
Bank Quay Low Level	77	C6	LNW	1963
Central	36	F1	LNW	
	77	C6		
Dallam Lane	77	C6	GJ	1837
Latchford 2nd, 1st — 1893	77	C6	LNW	1962
Walton Junction	77	C6	BLCJ	1857
White Cross on site of Litton Mill Crossing	77	C6	STH	1854
Wilderspool 2nd, 1st — 1854	77	C6	LNW	1871
Warsop	82	F6	GC	1955
Warthill	34	E9	SH LT	1930
Warthill	34	E9	NE	1959
Wartle	54	G6	GNS	1951
Warton (Lytham Dock)	76	C2	PW JT	1874
Warwick, Coventry Road	24	H4	GW	
	80	H10		
Warwick Road	25	A2	EWJ	1873
Warwick Road (Lancs) — see [Manchester]				
Washford	6	E8	GW	1971
Washford R.O. PR. FR. CL. above	6	E8	SVR	
Washford	6	E8	WSM	1898
Washingborough	29	B7	GN	1940
Washington (Durham)	43	G2	NE	1963
Washington (Tayside)	51	A7	SCMJ	1847
Waskerley	43	D1	NE	1859
Wassand	35	D7	NE	1953
Watchet	6	E9	GW	1971
Watchet R.O. PR. FR. CL. above	6	E9	SVR	
Watchet	6	E9	WSM	1898
Watchingwell Ht. (Isle of Wight)	4	G2	FYN	1953
Waterbeach	23	C8	GE	
Waterfall	32	G5	SMT	1924
Waterfoot for Newchurch	76	C8	EL	1966
Watergate Halt	8	F5	SR	1965
Waterhouses (Durham)	38	C10	NE	1951
Waterhouses (Staffs) 2nd, 1st — 1905	31	D5	NS	1935
Wateringbury	2	G7	SEC	
Waterloo (Lancs)	76	F1	LY	
Waterloo — see [London]				
Waterloo Junction — see [London]				
Waterloo Road — see [Blackpool] South				
Waterloo Road — see [Stoke-on-Trent]				
Waterloo Halt	78	E7	BM	1956
Watermoor — see Cirencester				
Water Orton	80	C8	MID	
Waterside	49	D1	GSW	1964
Water Stratford Halt	15	B10	BR	1961
Water Street — see Stamford East				
[Watford]				
High Street	15	B6	LNW	
	63	F10		
Junction 2nd, 1st — 1858	15	B6	LNW	
	63	F10		
North	15	B6	LNW	
West	15	B6	LNW	
	63	F10		
Wath	82	D4	HB	1929
Wath Central	82	D10	GC	1959
Wath-in-Nidderdale	38	C1	NIDD	1930
Wath North	82	D10	MID	1968
Watling Street — see Brownhills				
Watlington	15	B6	GW	1957
Watnall	82	E3	MID	1917
Watson's Crossing Halt	79	G1	LY	1929
Watten	62	E8	HIGH	1960
Watton — see [Brecon]				
Watton (Norfolk)	20	G6	GE	1964
Watton-at-Stone	12	D9	GN	1939
Wattstown Platform	78	D3	TV	1920
Wattsville GDS	78	E8	LNW	1929
Waverley — see [Edinburgh]				
Waverton 2nd, 1st — 1898	30	D6	LNW	1959
	77	G4		
Wavertree — see [Liverpool]				
Wealdstone — see [London] Harrow				
Wearhead	41	F10	NE	1953
Wearmouth — see [Sunderland]				
Wear Valley Junction	38	B8	NE	1935
Weaste — see [Manchester]				
Weaverthorpe	39	D2	NE	1930
Wedgwood — see [Stoke-on-Trent]				
Wednesbury — see [West Midlands]				
Wednesfield — see [West Midlands]				
Weedon 2nd, 1st — 1888	25	D3	LNW	1958
Weeley	13	F9	GE	
Weelsby Road Halt — see [Grimsby]				
Weeton (Yorks)	37	G8	NE	
	79	A5		
Weeton (Lancs)	76	B3	PW	1843
Welbeck — see Cresswell (Derbys)				
Welbury	38	F5	NE	1954
Weldon — see Corby				
Welford and Kilworth Form. Lutterworth	25	D6	LNW	1966
Welford Park	14	G2	GW	1960
Welford Road — see [Leicester]				
Well Hall, Eltham	69	E9	SEC	
Wellfield	38	E9	NE	1952
Welling	65	H1	SEC	
	69	G10		
Wellingborough	25	H5	MID	
Wellingborough, London Road	25	H5	LNW	1964
Wellington (Salop)	27	G9	LNW/GW	
Wellington (Somerset)	6	E6	GW	1964
Wellington College — see Crowthorne				
Wellington Road — see [Dewsbury] Dewsbury				
Wellow	17	E1	SD JT	1966
[Wells] (Somerset)				
East Somerset	7	C9	EAST SO/GW	1878
Priory Road	7	C9	SD JT	1951
Wells, Tucker Street	7	C9	GW	1963
Wells (Clwyd) — see Caergwrle				
Wells-next-the-Sea (Norfolk)	20	B3	GE	1963
Wellworthy Ampress Works Halt*	4	F3	LSW	
Welnetham	21	D3	GE	1961
Welshampton	16	D3	CAM	1965
Welsh Harp — see [London]				
Welsh Hook Halt	18	F6	GW	1964
[Welshpool]				
Raven Square	27	B9	CAM	1931
Seven Stars	27	B9	CAM	1931
Welshpool (W & L)	27	B9	CAM	1931
Welshpool	27	B9	CAM	
Welsh's Crossing Halt	62	G6	LMS	1944
Welton (Northants)	25	D5	LNW	1958
Welton (Somerset) — see Midsomer Norton				
[Welwyn]				
Garden City 2nd, 1st — 1926	12	C8	GN	
Junction	12	C8	GN	1860
North	12	C8	GN	
Wem	30	E2	LNW	
Wembley Central	64	B5	LNW	
Wembley Hill, Complex 1978	64	B5	BR	
Wembley North	64	B5	LNW	
Wembley Park	64	B5	LT	
Wembley GDS	64	B5	LNW	1965
Wemyss Bay	49	A8	CAL	
Wemyss Castle	51	B2	NB	1955
Wendlebury Halt	14	H8	LNW	1926
Wendling	20	E3	GE	1968
Wendover	15	D7	MET/GC	
Wenford Bridge GDS	11	B8	LSW	1967
Wenhaston	21	B9	S WOLD	1929
Wennington	41	C1	MID	

Station	Page	Block	Comp	Year of CL
Wensley	38	A3	NE	1954
Wentworth and Hoyland Common	82	C10	MID	1959
Wenvoe	78	H5	BARRY	1962
Werneth — see [Oldham]				
Wern Las	30	B1	SM	1933
Wesham — see Kirkham				
West Allerton — see [Liverpool]				
West Auckland Form. St Helens	38	C8	NE	1962
West Bay — see Bridport				
Westbourne Park	64	F3	GW	
West Bridge — see [Leicester]				
West Brompton — see [West Midlands]				
West Bromwich — see [West Midlands]				
Westbrook	27	B1	GOLD V/GW	1941
Westbury (Wilts)	7	G10	GW	
Westbury (Salop)	27	C9	S & WPL	1960
Westbury (Bucks) — see Fulwell				
Westbury-on-Severn Halt	17	D8	GW	1959
West Byfleet	15	F1	LSW	
	67	B2		
West Calder	46	D7	CAL	
West Cliff — see Whitby				
Westcliff-on-Sea	13	C4	LTS	
Westcombe Park	65	D2	SEC	
West Cornforth	38	D9	NE	1952
Westcott	15	B8	MET/GC	1935
Westcraigs for Harthill	46	B7	NB	1956
West Cross — see [Swansea]				
West Croydon	69	A5	LBSC	
West Cults	55	B7	GNS	1937
West Derby — see [Liverpool]				
West Dereham — see Abbey				
West Drayton and Yiewsley	12	A4	GW	
	15	F3		
West Dulwich	69	A8	LBSC	
West Ealing	64	B3	GW	
West End — see [Southampton]				
West End Lane — see [London]				
Westenhanger	3	D6	SEC	
Westerfield	21	F6	GE	
Westerham	2	D8	SEC	1961
Westerton	74	D8	NB	
West Exe Halt	6	D5	GW	1963
	8	F10		
West Felton — see Rednal				
West Fen Drove GDS	22	H5	GE	1964
West Ferry	51	D6	DA JT	1967
Westfield	46	C8	NB	1930
Westgate — see [Rotherham]				
Westgate — see [Wakefield]				
Westgate-in-Weardale	41	G9	NE	1953
Westgate-on-Sea	3	G10	SEC	
West Gosforth — see [Newcastle]				
West Green — see [London]				
West Grinstead	2	A4	LBSC	1966
West Hallam for Dale Abbey	31	H4	GN	1964
	82	C2		
West Halton	34	H4	GC	1925
West Ham — see [London]				
Westham — see Pevensey				
West Ham Halt — see [Weymouth]				
West Hampstead — see [London]				
West Harrow — see [London]				
West Hartlepool — see [Hartlepool]				
Westhead Halt	76	E3	LY	1951
West Helmsdale	61	F3	HIGH	1871
West Hill — see [London] East Putney				
West Hoathly	2	C5	LBSC	1958
West Horndon	12	H4	MID	
	66	H6		
West Horsham — see Christ's Hospital				
Westhaughton	76	E6	LY	
West House Rep. by Westhouses and Blackwell	82	C4	MID	1865
Westhouses and Blackwell	82	C4	MID	1967
Westhumble — see Box Hill				
West India Dock — see [London]				
West Jesmond	81	B3	NE	
West Kensington — see [London]				
West Kilbride	49	A6	GSW	
West Kirby 2nd, 1st — 1856	36	A1	WIRRAL	
	77	C1		
West Kirby	77	C1	B HEAD	1956
West Lancs — see [Preston]				
West Leigh	76	G6	LNW	1954
West Leigh and Bedford	76	G5	GC	1964
West Linton — see Broomlee				
West London — see [London]				
West Lynn	22	E9	EM	1886

Station	Page	Block	Comp	Year of CL
West Malling	2	G8	SEC	
West Meon	5	B7	LSW	1955
[West Midlands]				
Acocks Green and South Yardley	80	F7	GW	
Adderley Park	80	E7	LNW	
Albion	80	C3	LNW	1960
Aldridge	80	A5	MID	1965
Aston	80	C6	LNW	
Baptist End Halt	80	D3	GW	1964
Bentley	80	A3	MID	1898
Bescot	80	B5	LNW	
	24	E7		
Bescot Bridge	80	A4	LNW	1850
Bilbrook, Birches and	80	A1	GW	
Bilston Central	80	B2	GW	1972
Bilston West	80	B2	GW	1962
Birchills	24	D9	LNW	1916
[Birmingham]				
Curzon Street	80	D6	LNW	1854
Granville Street	80	D6	MID	1885
International	80	E8	BR	
	24	G6		
Lawley Street	80	D6	LNW	1869
Lawley Street	80	D6	MID	1851
Moor Street	80	E5	GW	
	24	F7		
New Street	80	E5	MID/LNW	
	24	F7		
Snow Hill	80	D6	GW	1972
Bloomsbury and Nechals	80	D6	LNW	1869
Blowers Green	80	D2	GW	1962
Bordersley 2nd, 1st — 1915	80	E6	GW	
Bournville Form. Stirchley Str.	80	F5	MID	
Bradley and Moxley	80	B3	GW	1917
Brettell Lane	80	E2	GW	1962
	24	C7		
Brierley Hill	80	E2	GW	1962
Brighton Road	80	E6	MID	1941
Brockmoor Halt	80	B1	GW	1932
Bromford Forge	80	D7	BDJ	1843
Bromley Halt	80	D1	GW	1932
Bushbury	80	A1	LNW	1912
Camp Hill 2nd, 1st — 1841	80	E6	MID	1941
Castle Bromwich	80	D7	MID	1968
Chester Road	80	C6	LNW	
Church Road	80	E5	MID	1925
Compton Halt	80	B1	GW	1932
Coombes Holloway Halt	80	E3	GW	1927
Coseley, Deepfields 2nd, 1st — 1902	80	B2	LNW	
Cradley	24	D6	GW	
	80	E3		
Daisy Bank and Bradley	80	B2	GW	1962
Darby End Halt	80	D3	GW	1964
Darlaston and James Bridge 2nd, 1st — 1887	80	A4	LNW	1965
Duddeston, Vauxhall and	80	D6	LNW	
Dudley 2nd, 1st — 1850	80	D3	GW/LNW	1964
Dudley Port High Level	24	D7	LNW	
	80	D4		
Dudley Port Low Level	80	C3	LNW	1964
Dunstall Park	80	B2	GW	1968
	80	A1		
Erdington	80	C6	LNW	
Ettingshall Road and Bilston	80	B2	LNW	1964
Five Ways 2nd, 1st — 1944	80	D5	MID	
Forge Mills	24	G7	MID	1960
	80	C8		
Frankley	80	F4	MID/GW	1927
Gornal Halt	80	C1	GW	1932
Gravelly Hill	80	C6	LNW	
Great Barr 1st, 2nd — see Hamstead	80	C5	LNW	1899
Great Bridge North	80	B3	LNW	1964
Great Bridge South	80	B3	GW	1964
Hagley Road	80	E4	LNW	1934
Halesowen	80	E4	GW/MID	1927
Hall Green	80	F6	GW	
Hampton-in-Arden	24	G6	LNW	
	80	E8		
Hampton-in-Arden 2nd, 1st — 1884	80	E8	MID	1966
Hamstead 2nd, 1st — Great Barr	80	C5	LNW	
Handsworth and Smethwick	80	D5	GW	1972
Handsworth Wood	80	C5	LNW	1941
Harborne	80	E4	LNW	1934
Hart's Hill and Woodside	80	D2	GW	1917
Hawthorns	80	D4	GW	1972
Hazelwell	80	F5	MID	1941
Heath Town	80	A2	MID	1910
Himley	80	C1	GW	1932
Hockley	80	D5	GW	1972

Station	Page	Block	Comp	Year of CL
Wharram	34	H10	NE	1950
Wharton — see Over				
Whatstandwell 2nd, 1st — 1894	31	G5	MID	
	82	B4		
Whauphill	44	G2	PPW JT	1950
Wheathampstead	12	B8	GN	1965
	15	H8		
Wheatley	15	A7	GW	1963
Wheelock and Sandbach	30	H6	NS	1930
	77	G8		
Wheldrake	34	F8	DV	1926
Whelley — see [Wigan]				
Wherwell	4	G9	LSW	1931
Whetstone (Leics)	25	D8	GC	1963
Whetstone — see [London] Totteridge				
Whieldon Road Halt — see [Stoke-on-Trent]				
[Whifflet]				
Lower	75	E5	CAL	1962
Station	75	E5	CAL	1886
Upper	75	E5	CAL	1964
Whifflet 2nd, 1st — 1895	75	E5	NB	1930
Whimple	6	E3	LSW	
Whimsey Halt	17	D8	GW	1930
Whippingham (Isle of Wight)	5	A2	IWC	1953
Whipton Bridge Halt — see [Exeter]				
Whissendine	25	G10	MID	1955
Whistlefield Halt	53	D1	NB	1964
Whitacre Junction 2nd, 1st — 1864	80	C8	MID	1968
Whitbeck Crossing	40	F2	WFJ	1857
Whitburn	46	C7	EG/NB	1930
Whitburn Colliery	81	F10	SSMWC	1953
Whitby 2nd, 1st — 1847	39	C6	NE	
Whitby, West Cliff	39	C6	NE	1958
Whitchurch — see Llandaff				
Whitchurch (Glam)	78	F6	CDFF	
Whitchurch Down Platform	9	C5	GW	1962
	11	G8		
Whitchurch Halt (Somerset	17	C2	GW	1959
	72	D6		
Whitchurch (Salop)	30	E3	LNW	
Whitchurch (Hants)	4	H9	GW	1960
Whitchurch North (Hants)	4	H9	LSW	
White Bear for Adlington	76	D5	LY/LU	1960
Whiteborough	82	D5	MID	1926
Whitebrook Halt	17	B7	GW	1959
Whitechapel — see [London]				
White City — see [London]				
White Colne	13	C10	CUM	1962
	21	H2		
Whitecraigs for Rouken Glen	74	E1	CAL	
Whitecroft	17	C7	SW JT	1929
White Cross — see [Warrington]				
Whitedale	35	D7	NE	1965
White Fen GDS	22	H5	GE	1964
Whitefield	76	E8	LY	
Whitegate	30	F7	CLC	1931
	77	G6		
Whitehall Halt	6	F5	GW	1963
White Hart Halt	78	E7	GW	1952
White Hart Lane	65	B8	GE	
[Whitehaven]				
Newtown	40	C7	WFJ	1852
Preston Street GDS	40	C7	FUR	1969
Whitehaven	40	C7	LNW	1874
Whitehaven, Bransty	40	C7	LNW/FUR	
Whitehouse	55	A4	GNS	1950
Whitehurst Halt	30	B3	GW	1960
	33	H3		
Whiteinch — see [Glasgow]				
Whitemill	19	D5	LLAN	1870
Whitemoor GDS	22	G6	GN/GE	1964
White Moss Level Crossing Halt	76	E3	LY	1951
White Notley	13	B9	GE	
Whiterigg	75	H7	NB	1930
White Sike Cottages	34	F9	SHLT	1930
White Sike Junction	34	F9	SHLT	1930
Whithorn	44	G2	PPW JT	1950
Whitland	19	A5	GW	
Whitland	19	A5	P & T	1869
Whitley	23	G10	CVH	1863
Whitley Bay 2nd, 1st — 1911	43	G6	NE	
	81	F4		
Whitley Bridge	34	D5	LY	
	79	F10		
Whitlingham	20	F6	GE	1955
Whitlocks End Halt	80	G6	GW	
Whitmore	30	H3	LNW	1952
Whitney-on-Wye	27	B2	MID	1962
Whitrigg	45	H4	CAL	1921
[Whitstable]				
C & W Terminus	3	D10	SE	1894
	13	E2		
Harbour	3	D10	SEC	1931
	13	E2		
Town 1st Sta.	3	D10	SEC	1915
	13	E2		
Whitstable and Tankerton 2nd	13	E2	SEC	
Whitstone and Bridgerule	8	G2	LSW	1966
Whittingham (Northumberland)	43	D9	NE	1930
Whittingham (Lancs) — see Grimsargh				
Whittingham Asylum Private Sta.	76	A4	PL JT	1957?
Whittington (Derbys) 2nd, 1st — 1873	82	C6	MID	1952
Whittington High Level (Salop)	30	B2	CAM	1960
	33	H2		
Whittington Low Level (Salop)	30	B2	GW	1960
	33	H2		
Whittington Moor — see Sheepbridge				
Whittlesea	22	G4	GE	
Whittlesford	23	F7	GE	
Whittlestone Head	76	D6	LY	1848
Whitton (Lincs)	34	H4	GC	1925
Whitton (London)	67	H8	LSW	
Whitton — see also Hounslow				
Whitwell (Derbys)	82	F7	MID	1964
Whitwell Halt (Isle of Wight)	4	H1	IWC	1952
Whitwell (Norfolk) and Reepham	20	E5	MGN	1959
Whitwick	25	B10	LNW	1931
Whitwood — see Altoft				
Whitworth	76	C9	LY	1947
Whyteleafe Form. Warblington	69	A1	SEC	
Whyteleafe South	69	A1	SEC	
Wichnor	24	G10	LNW	1877
Wick	62	G7	HR	
Wickenby	29	B9	GC	1965
Wicker — see [Sheffield]				
Wickford Junction Station	13	B6	GE	
Wickham	5	B5	LSW	1955
Wickham Bishops	13	B8	GE	1964
Wickham Market	21	E8	GE	
Wick Road — see Llandow				
Wick St Lawrence	16	H1	WCP	1940
Wickwar	17	E5	MID	1965
Widdrington	43	F7	NE	
Widford	12	E8	GE	1964
Widmerpool	27	E2	MID	1949
[Widnes]				
Central	77	C5	GC/MID	1964
Lugsdale Depot GDS	77	C5	LNW	1966
South 3rd, 1st — (Runcorn Gap) — 1852, 2nd — 1870	77	C5	LNW	1962
Tanhouse Lane	77	C5	GC/MID	1964
Widnes North Form. Farnworth	77	C5	CLC	
Widney Manor	80	F7	GW	
[Wigan]				
Central 2nd, 1st — 1892	76	F4	GC	1964
Wallgate 3rd, 1st — 1860, 2nd — 1896	76	F4	LY	
	36	F3		
Whelley	76	F4	LNW	1872
Wigan North Western 2nd, 1st — 1838	36	F3	LNW	
	76	F4		
Wighton Halt	20	A3	LNE	1964
[Wigston] (Leics)				
Glen Parva	25	D8	LNW	1968
Magna	25	D8	MID	1968
South	25	D8	MID	1962
Wigton (Cumbria)	42	A1	MC	
Wigtown	44	G3	PPW JT	1950
Wilbraham Road — see [Manchester]				
Wilburton	23	B7	GE	1931
Wilby	21	C6	MSL	1952
Wilderspool — see [Warrington]				
Willaston	30	G5	LNW	1954
Willenhall — see [West Midlands]				
Willerby and Kirk Ella	35	A6	HB	1955
	73	C3		
Willersey Halt	24	E10	GW	1960
Willesden Green — see [London]				
Willesden Junction — see [London]				
Williamstown	47	B9	NB	1850
Williamwood	74	E1	CAL	
Willington (Beds)	23	E3	LNW	1968
Willington (Derbys) — see Repton				
Willington (Durham)	38	C9	NE	1964
Willington Quay (Northumb)	81	D9	NE	1960
Williton	6	E9	GW	1971
Williton R.O. PR. FR. CL. above	6	E9	SVR	
Willoughby (Lincs) 2nd, 1st — 1886	29	G7	GN	1970

Station	Page	Block	Comp	Year of CL
Willoughby — see Braunston				
Wilmcote 2nd, 1st — 1907	80	H7	GW	
Wilmington — see [Hull]				
Wilmslow	31	A9	LNW	
	77	D9		
Wilnecote	80	B9	MID	
Wilpshire for Ribchester	76	B6	LY	1962
Wilsden	79	D2	GN	1955
Wilson	28	B1	MID	1871
Wilsontown	46	C6	CAL	1951
Wilsthorpe Crossing Halt	35	D10	LNE	1951
Wilstrop Siding	34	C8	NE	1931
Wilton North	4	C7	GW	1955
Wilton South	4	C7	LSW	1966
Wimbledon 2nd, 1st — 1881	68	E7	LSW	
Wimbledon Chase	68	E7	LSW	
Wimbledon Park	68	E7	LSW	
Wimblington	22	H6	GN/GE	1967
Wimborne	4	B3	LSW	1964
Wincanton	7	E7	SD JT	1966
Winchburgh	46	E8	NB	1930
Winchcombe	14	B10	GW	1960
Winchelsea	3	A3	SEC	
Winchester	4	H7	LSW	
Winchester, Chesil	4	H7	GW	1960
Winchfield for Hartley Wintney	5	D10	LSW	
Winchmore Hill	65	A9	GN	
Wincobank — see [Sheffield]				
Winder	40	D7	WCE JT	1931
Windermere	40	H5	LNW	
Windermere Lakeside	40	H3	FUR	1965
Windermere Lakeside R.O. PR. FR. CL. above	40	H3	L & H	
Windlesham — see Sunningdale				
Windhill — see Shipley				
Windmill End Halt — see [West Midlands]				
Windsor and Eton Central	15	F3	GW	
Windsor and Eton Riverside	15	F3	LSW	
Windsor Bridge — see [Manchester]				
Windsor Road — see [Southport]				
Wind Street — see [Swansea]				
Winestead	35	E5	NE	1904
Wingate	38	E9	NE	1952
Wingfield	31	H5	MID	1967
	82	B4		
Wingfield Villas Halt — see [Plymouth]				
[Wingham]				
Canterbury Road	3	F8	EK	1948
Colliery Halt	3	F8	EK	1948
Town	3	F8	EK	1948
Winkhill Halt	31	D5	NS	1935
Winnersh Form. Sindlesham and Hurst Ht.	15	C2	SEC	
Winnington GDS	77	F6	CLC	1969
Winscombe	7	B10	GW	1963
	17	A1		
Winsford	77	G6	LNW	
Winsford and Over	77	G6	CLC	1931
Winslow	15	C10	LNW	1968
Winslow Road	30	F6	MET/GC	1936
Winson Green — see [West Midlands]				
Winston for Staindrop	38	B7	NE	1964
Winterbourne	17	D3	GW	1961
Winteringham	35	A4	GC	1925
Wintersett and Ryhill	79	H7	GC	1930
Winterton and Thealby	34	H4	GC	1925
Winton	47	A8	NB	1925
Winwick	76	H5	GJ	1840
Wirksworth	82	A4	MID	1947
Wirksworth — see also Steeplehouse				
[Wisbech]				
East	22	E7	GE	1968
Harbour East	22	E7	GE	1966
Harbour North	22	E7	MGN	1965
North	22	F6	MGN	1959
St Mary	22	F6	MGN	1959
Wishaw Central	46	A6	CAL	
	75	H2	CAL	
Wishaw South	46	A6	CAL	1958
	75	H2		
Wishford	4	C8	GW	1955
Wistanstow Halt	27	D6	SH JT	1956
Wistow	34	E6	NE	1930
Witham (Essex)	13	B8	GE	
Witham (Somerset)	7	E8	GW	1966
Withcall	29	D9	GN	1951
Withernsea	35	F5	NE	1964
Withington (Hereford)	27	F1	GW	1961
Withington (Glos)	14	B8	MSWJ	1961

Station	Page	Block	Comp	Year of CL
Withington (Lancs) — see [Manchester]				
Within's Lane	76	E8	EL	1851
Withnel	76	C5	LY/LU	1960
Withyham	2	E5	LBSC	1967
Witley and Chiddingfold	5	F8	LSW	
Witney 2nd, 1st — 1873	14	F7	GW	1962
Wittersham Road	3	A5	KES	1954
Wittersham Road R.O. PR. FR. CL. above	3	A5	K & ES	
Witton	80	C6	LNW	
Witton Gilbert	38	C10	NE	1939
	43	E1		
Witton-le-Wear	38	B8	NE	1953
Wivelscombe	6	E7	GW	1966
Wivelsfield 2nd, 1st (Keymer Jcn.) — 1883	2	B4	LBSC	
Wivenhoe	13	E9	GE	
Wixford	24	E3	MID	1950
Wnion Halt	33	B1	GW	1965
Woburn Sands	15	E10	LNW	
Woking	15	F1	LSW	
	67	A2		
Wokingham	15	C2	LSW	
Woldingham	2	C8	CO JT	
Wolferton	21	C9	GE	1969
Wolf's Castle Halt	18	F5	GW	1964
Wollerton Halt	30	F2	GW	1963
Wolsingham	38	A9	NE	1953
Wolstalton — see [Stoke-on-Trent] Longport				
Wolston — see Brandon				
Wolvercot Halt — see [Oxford]				
Wolvercote — see [Oxford]				
Wolverhampton — see [West Midlands]				
Wolverton 3rd, 1st — 1863, 2nd — 1881	25	G1	LNW	
Wombourn — see [West Midlands]				
Wombwell Central	82	C10	GC	1959
Wombwell West	37	H2	MID	
	82	C10		
Womersley	34	C4	LY	1947
	79	F10		
Wonersh — see Bramley				
Woodborough	14	B1	GW	1966
Woodbridge	21	F7	GE	
Woodburn	43	B5	NB	1952
Woodburn Green	15	E5	GW	1970
Woodbury Road — see Exton				
Woodchester	17	F6	MID	1947
Woodend for Cleator & Bigrigg	40	C6	WCE JT	1947
Wood End Platform	80	G7	GW	
Woodfield — see [Huddersfield]				
Woodford	65	E8	GE	1966
Woodford R.O. by LT FR. CL. above	65	E8	LT	
Woodford and Hinton also known as Woodford Halse	25	C3	GC	1966
Woodford Halse — see entry above				
Woodgate or Bognor	5	F4	LBSC	1864
Woodgrange Park	65	F5	MID	
Wood Green, Alexandra Park	64	H8	GN	
Woodhall	49	C9	CAL	
Woodhall Junction Form. Kirksend	29	D6	GN	1970
Woodhall Spa	29	D6	GN	1954
Woodham — see Byfleet and New Haw				
Woodham Ferrers	13	B6	GE	
Woodhay	14	G1	GW	1960
Woodhead	37	D2	GC	1964
Woodhill Road Halt — see [Bury]				
Woodhouse Junction	28	B9	GC	
	82	D8		
Woodhouse Mill	31	H9	MID	1953
	82	D8		
Woodkirk	79	F5	GN	1939
Woodland	40	F3	FUR	1958
Woodland Park	33	E8	LNW	1930
Woodlands Road Halt	76	G9	LY	
Wood Lane — see [London]				
Woodlesford	79	E7	MID	
Woodley	77	B10	CLC	
Woodmansterne	68	G2	SEC	
Woodnesborough	3	G8	EK	1948
Woodnesborough — see also Roman Road				
Woodside — see [Aberdeen]				
Woodside — see [Birkenhead]				
Woodside — see [Leeds]				
Woodside — see [West Midlands] Harts Hill				
Woodside and Burrelton (Tayside)	51	A7	CAL	1967
Woodside and South Norwood (London)	69	B5	SEC	
Woodside, Halebank GDS	77	D3	LNW	1961
Woodside Park	64	F8	LT/GN	
Wood Siding	15	B8	MET/GC	1935

Station	Page	Block	Comp	Year of CL
York 3rd, 1st — 1841, 2nd — 1877	34	E8	NE	
Yorkhill — see [Glasgow]				
York Road — see [London]				
York Town — see Camberley				
York Town — see also Blackwater				
Yorton	30	E1	LNW	

Station	Page	Block	Comp	Year of CL
Ystalyfera	19	H4	MID	1951
	78	A1		
Ystradgynlais	78	A1	N & B	1932
Ystrad Mynach	78	D6	RHY	
Ystradowen	78	G4	TV	1951
Ystrad Rhondda	78	D3	TV	

List of Railway Companies (Mainland)

ABER	Aberdeen
AF	Arbroath and Forfar
AN JT	Ashby and Nuneaton Joint (LNW & MID)
ANSW	Alexandra (Newport and S. Wales) Docks & RLY
ASH	Ashover Light
AWC	Aberystwyth and Welsh Coast
AX JT	Axholme Joint (LY & NE)
BARRY	Barry
BC	Bishops Castle
BDJ	Birmingham and Derby Joint
BE	Bristol and Exeter
BG	Birmingham and Gloucester
B HEAD	Birkenhead Joint (GW & LNW)
BJ	Brandling Junction
BLACK	Blackwall
BLCJ	Birkenhead, Lancs and Cheshire Junction
BLUE	Bluebell
BM	Brecon and Merthyr Tydfil Junction
BP	Bolton and Preston
BPGV	Burry Port and Gwendraeth Valley
BR	British Railways
BRACK	Brackenhill Light
BSV	Birmingham, Wolverhampton and Stour Valley
BT	Blyth and Tyne
BWA	Bideford, Westward Ho! and Appledore
BWV	Brynmawr and Western Valleys Joint
CAL	Caledonian
CAM	Cambrian Railways
C & W	Canterbury and Whitstable
CB	Chester and Birkenhead
CC	Carmarthen and Cardigan
CDFF	Cardiff
CE	Clifton Extension Joint (GW & MID)
CGU	City of Glasgow Union (GSW & NB)
CKP	Cockermouth, Keswick and Penrith
CL	Central London
CLAR	Clarence
CLC	Cheshire Lines Committee (GN & GC & MID)
CL	Calstock Light, Bere Alston and (PDSW)
CM	Campbeltown and Machrihanish Light
CMDP	Cleobury Mortimer and Ditton Priors Light
CO JT	Croydon and Oxted Joint (LBSC & SEC)
CORR	Corringham Light
CORRIS	Corris
CS	Carlisle and Silloth
CSL	City and South London
CVH	Colne Valley and Halstead
CW	Cockermouth and Workington
C WALL	Cornwall
CWJC	Cleator and Workington Junction
DA	Dundee and Arbroath
DA JT	Dundee and Arbroath Joint (CAL & NB)
DART V	Dart Valley Light
DB JT	Dumbarton and Balloch Joint (CAL & NB)
DEARNE	Dearne Valley
DEE	Deeside
DIST	Metropolitan District
DJ	Dentonholme (Carlisle) Joint Committee (GSW & NB & MID)
DPA	Dundee, Perth and Aberdeen Junction
DRC	Denbigh, Ruthin and Corwen
DV	Derwent Valley Light
DVR	Dart Valley
EA	East Anglian Railways
EAS	Easingwold
EC	Eastern Counties
ECH	Easton and Church Hope (GW & LSW)
EG	Edinburgh and Glasgow
EK	East Kent Light
EL	East Lancashire (Including Blackburn — Preston)
ELB	Edenham and Little Bytham (Private)
E LOND	East London (DIST, GE, MET, LBSC, SEC)
EM	Eastern and Midlands
EN	Edinburgh and Northern (EPD after 1849)
EPD	Edinburgh, Perth and Dundee
ESK	Eskdale
EU	Eastern Union
EWJ	East and West Junction
EWYU	East and West Yorkshire Union
FB	Festiniog and Blaenau
FEST	Festiniog
FEST	Festiniog
FM JT	Furness and Midland Joint
FPWRJC	Fleetwood Preston and West Riding Junction
FUR	Furness
FYN	Freshwater, Yarmouth and Newport
GBK JT	Glasgow, Barrhead and Kilmarnock Joint
GBN	Glasgow, Barrhead and Neilston
GC	Great Central
GC (GI)	Great Central (Grimsby & Immingham Tramway)
GDC	Glasgow, Dumfries and Carlisle
G & G	Glasgow and Garnirk
GE	Great Eastern
GJ	Grand Junction
GKE	Garstang and Knott End
GN	Great Northern
GNS	Great North of Scotland
GO	Great Orme Tramway
GOLD V	Golden Valley
GP JT	Glasgow and Paisley Joint (CAL & GSW)
GPKA	Glasgow, Paisley, Kilmarnock and Ayr
GSW	Glasgow and South Western
GV	Gwendraeth Valley
GVT	Glyn Valley Tramway
GW	Great Western
HAL JT	Halesowen Joint (GW & MID)
HB	Hull and Barnsley
HC JT	Hammersmith and City (GW & MET)
HH	Hull and Holderness
HHL	Halifax High Level
HIGH } HR }	Highland
HO JT	Halifax and Ovenden Joint (GN & LY)
HOY	Hoylake
IAJ	Inverness and Aberdeen Joint
IOW	Isle of Wight
IOW (NJ)	Isle of Wight (Newport Junction)
IWC	Isle of Wight Central
KB	Kilsyth and Bonnybridge Joint
KE	Knott End
KES	Kent and East Sussex Light
K & ES	Kent and East Sussex
KIN	Kinross-shire
KT	Kilmarnock and Troon
KWV	Keighley and Worth Valley Light
KWVR	Keighley and Worth Valley Railway
L & B	London and Birmingham
LB	Lynton and Barnstaple
LBSC	London, Brighton and South Coast
LC	Lancaster and Carlisle
L & C	Liskeard and Caradon (GW)
LCD	London, Chatham and Dover
LCS	Liverpool, Crosby and Southport
LE	London Electric
LG	London and Greenwich
L & H	Lakeside and Haverthwaite
LL	Liskeard and Looe
LL	Llanberis Lake Railway
LLAN	Llanelly
LM	Liverpool and Manchester
LMM	Llanelly and Mynydd Mawr
LMS	London Midland and Scottish
LN	Leeds Northern
L & N	Llanidloes and Newtown
LNE	London and North Eastern

LNW	London and North Western
LO	Liverpool Overhead
L & OG	Llynvi and Ogmore
LONG	Longmoor Military
LP & B	Liverpool and Bury
LPJ	Lancaster and Preston Junction
LS	Leicester and Swannington
L & S	Leeds and Selby
LSW	London and South Western
LT	London Transport Authority
LTS	London, Tilbury and Southend
LY	Lancashire and Yorkshire
LU	Lancashire and Yorkshire Union
MAW	Mawddwy Light
MB	Manchester and Birmingham
MBB	Manchester, Bolton and Bury
MBM	Manchester, Buxton, Matlock & Midlands Jcn.
MDHB	Mersey Docks and Harbour Board
ME	Midlands and Eastern
MET	Metropolitan
METH	Methley Joint (GN & LY & NE)
MGN	Midland and Great Northern Joint
MID	Midland
MID C	Midland Counties
ML	Manchester and Leeds
MM	Manchester and Milford
MN JT	Mid Notts Joint (LMS & LNE)
MON	Monmouthshire Railway and Canal
MONK	Monklands
MS & L	Manchester, Sheffield and Lincolnshire (GC)
MSJA	Manchester South Jcn. and Altrincham
MSL	Mid-Suffolk Light
MSWJ	Midland and South Western Junction
MUM	Mumbles (see S.I.T.)
MW	Mid-Wales
NAH	Newport, Abergavenny and Hereford
NANT	Nantlle
N & B	Neath and Brecon
NB	North British
NBJ	Northampton and Banbury Joint
NC	Newcastle and Carlisle
NCA	Newtyle and Cupar Angus
NDJ	Newcastle and Darlington Junction
NE	North Eastern
N & E	Northern and Eastern
NIDD	Nidd Valley Light
NL	North London
NM	North Midland
NNS	Newcastle and North Shields
NOR	Norfolk
NR JT	Nantybwch and Rhymney Joint (LNW & RHY)
NRM	Narberth Road and Maenclochog
NS	North Staffordshire
NS JT	Norfolk and Suffolk Joint (GE & MGN)
N SUND	North Sunderland Light
NSWJ	North and South Western Jcn Joint (NL & LNW & MID)
NT	Newmarket
NU	North Union
NU JT	North Union Joint (LNW & LY)
NVR	Nene Valley Railway
NW	North Western
NWL	North Wales and Liverpool
NWNG	North Wales Narrow Gauge
NYM	North Yorkshire Moor Railway
OAGB	Oldham, Ashton & Guide Bridge Jcn. (LNW & GC)
OAT	Oxford and Aylesbury Tramroad (GC & MET)
O & I	Otley and Ilkley Joint (MID & NE)
OWW	Oxford, Worcester and Wolverhampton
PCB	Portmadoc, Croesor and Beddgelert
PDJ	Princes Dock Joint (GSW & NB & CAL)
PDSW	Plymouth, Devonport and South Western Junction
PEEB	Peebles
PEN	Pentewan
PLA	Port of London Authority
PL JT	Preston and Longridge Joint (LNW & LY)
PPW JT	Portpatrick and Wigtownshire Joint (MID & CAL & GSW & LNW)
PSNW	Potteries, Shrewsbury and North Wales
PSS	Pontop and South Shields
P & T	Penbroke and Tenby
PT	Port Talbot Railway and Docks
PW	Preston and Wyre Railway
PW JT	Preston and Wyre Joint
QYM	Quakers Yard and Merthyr Joint (GW & RHY)
R & C	Redruth and Chasewater
RCT	Rye and Camber Tramway
R & E	Ravenglass and Eskdale
RFK	Rowrah and Kelton Fell
RHD	Romney, Hythe and Dymchurch Light

RHY	Rhymney
RSB	Rhondda and Swansea Bay
RTA	River Tyne Authority
SAM	Sheffield, Ashton-under-Lyme and Manchester
SB	Shrewsbury and Birmingham
SBH	Snailbeach District Railways
SC	Shrewsbury and Chester
SCMJ	Scottish Midland Junction
SCNE	Scottish North Eastern
S & D	Stockton and Darlington
SD	South Devon
SD JT	Somerset and Dorset Joint (MID & LSW)
SDLU	South Durham and Lancashire Union
SE	South Eastern
SEC	South Eastern and Chatham
S & KD	Sittingbourne and Kemsley Down
SEV & W	Severn and Wye
SH	Shrewsbury and Hereford
SHD	Sheffield District Railway (MID & GC)
SH JT	Shrewsbury and Hereford Joint (LNW & GW)
SHLT	Sand Hutton Light
SIT	Swinton and Knottingley Joint (NE & MID)
SL	Selsey Light
SM	Shropshire and Montgomeryshire Light
SMJ	Stratford-upon-Avon and Midland Junction
SMT	Snowdon Mountain Tramroad and Hotel Co.
SMR	Snowdon Mountain Railway
SR	Southern
S & R	Sheffield and Rotherham
SS	South Staffordshire
SSMWC	South Shields, Marsden & Whitburn Colliery
ST H	St Helens
ST	Stanhope and Tyne
ST & D	Stirling and Dunfermline
SVR	Severn Valley Railway
SW	South Wales
SW JT	Severn and Wye Joint
SWTN	Shrewsbury and Wellington Joint (LNW & GW)
S WOLD	Southwold
SWPL	Shrewsbury and Welshpool Joint (LNW & GW)
SY	South Yorkshire and River Dunn Company
SY JT	South Yorkshire Joint (GN & GC & LY & MID & NE)
TAL	Talyllyn
TAN	Tanat Valley Light (CAM)
TB JT	Taff Bargoed Joint (RHY & GW)
T & D	Torbay and Dartmouth
TEN	Tenbury
TEN JT	Tenbury Joint (LNW & GW)
TFG	Tottenham and Forest Gate (MID & LTS)
THJC	Tottenham and Hampstead Junction (GE & MID)
TV	Taff Vale
VAN	Van Light
VN	Vale of Neath
VR	Vale of Rheidol (CAM)
VT	Vale of Towy Joint (GW & LNW)
W & C	Wishaw and Coltness
WB JT	Whitechapel and Bow Joint (MID & DIST)
WC	West Cornwall
WCE JT	Whitehaven, Cleator and Egremont Jcn. (FUR & LNW)
WCJ	Wath Curve Joint Committee (NE & MID & GC)
WCP	Weston, Clevedon and Portishead Light
WFJ	Whitehaven and Furness Junction
WH	West Highland
WIG	Wigtownshire
WIRRAL	Wirral
WL	West London (GW & LNW)
W & L	Welshpool and Llanfair Light
W LANCS	West Lancashire (LY)
WLE	West London Extension (GW & LNW & LSW & LBSC)
WM	West Midlands
WM JT	Wrexham and Minera Joint (LNW & GW)
WMC	Wilsontown, Morningside and Coltness
WMCQ	Wrexham, Mold and Connahs Quay
WOTTON	Wotton Tramway
WP JT	Weymouth and Portland Joint (LSW & GW)
WRG JT	West Riding and Grimsby Joint (MS & L, GC & GN)
W & S	Warrington and Stockport
WS	West Sussex Light
WS	West Somerset
WSC	Woodside and South Croydon (SEC & LBSC)
WSM	West Somerset Mineral
WT	Wantage Tramway
YNB	York, Newcastle and Berwick
YNM	York and North Midland

Appendix to Railway Companies (Mainland)

C & O	Callander and Oban (CAL)		MACC	Macclesfield Committee
CCSC	Carlisle Citadel Station Committee		MSC	Manchester Ship Canal
CGTC	Carlisle Goods Traffic Committee		M & E	Mellis and Eye (GE)
CHEADLE	Cheadle		NG & SL	Newport, Godshill and St Lawrence (IWC)
D & DJT	Dover and Deal Joint		NP & F	North Pembroke and Fishguard
CW & SL	Cawood, Wistow and Selby Light (NE)		PC & N	Pontypridd, Caerphilly and Newport (TV)
E & LJ	Epsom and Leatherhead Joint		R & SJT	Ramsey and Somersham Joint (GN & GE)
FDR	Felixstowe Dock and Railway		S & S	Seaham and Sunderland
F & R	Fishguard and Rosslare		SOLJC	Solway Junction (CAL)
FORTH	Forth Bridge (NB)		SHT	Swansea Harbour Trust
F & M	Furness and Midland Joint		TM & WJT	Tooting, Merton and Wimbledon Joint
K & B	Kilsyth and Bonnybridge (NB & CAL)		VG	Vale of Glamorgan (BARRY)
LAMV	Lambourn Valley		WJ	Wigan Junction (MS & L)
LDEC	Lancashire, Derbyshire and East Coast		W & CITY	Waterloo and City
LOS	Lee-on-the-Solent		LSPJC	Liverpool, Southport and Preston Junc. (LY)
L & IDC	London and India Docks Committee		TW	Tyne and Wear Metro

Alphabetical List of Stations (Ireland)

Station	Page	Block	Comp	Station	Page	Block	Comp
Abbeydorney	87	A2	W & L	Ballinasloe Form. Carrowduff	85	G5	MGW
Abbeyfeale	86	G3	W & L	Ballinasteenig	87	C1	T & D
Abbeyleix	86	D8	WCI	Ballincollig	87	F4	C & M
Achill	85	C1	MGW	Ballindangan	87	D5	GTS & W
Adare	86	G4	W & L	Ballinderry	84	F8	GN (I)
Adavoyle	85	C8	GN (I)	Ballindine	85	F3	GTS & W
Adelaide and Windsor	84	E9	GN (I)	Ballindrait	84	D4	CDJC
Adelaide Road — see Glenageary				Ballineen and Enniskean	87	G3	CB & SC
Adelphi Wharf — see Waterford				Ballinglen	86	E9	D & SE
Adoon	85	C5	C & L	Ballingrane	86	G4	GTS & W
Aghadowey	84	B6	BNC	Ballinhassig	87	G4	CB & SC
Albert Street — see [Cork]				Ballinlough	85	E4	MGW
Albert Quay — see [Cork]				Ballinosare	87	C1	T & D
Aldergrove	84	E6	GN (I)	Ballinrobe	85	F2	MGW
Amiens Street — see [Dublin]				Ballintogher	85	B3	SL & NC
Annadale	85	B5	C & L	Ballintra	84	E4	CDJC
Annaghmore	84	F8	GN (I)	Ballyards Halt	84	G8	GN (I)
Antrim	84	D8	BNC	Ballybay	85	B8	GN (I)
Antrim Junction	84	D8	BNC/GN (I)	Ballybeg	85	E7	GN (I)
Ardagh	86	G4	W & L	Ballybofey	84	D3	CDJC
Ardara Road	84	E2	CDJC	Ballyboley	84	C9	GTS & W
Ardee	85	D9	GN (I)	Ballybrack	87	C2	GTS & W
Ardfert	87	A2	W & L	Ballybrack — see also Killiney			
Ardglass	84	G10	B & CD	Ballybrophy	86	D7	GTS & W
Ardmayle	86	G6	GTS & W	Ballybunion	86	G2	BAL
Ardmore	84	B6	BNC	Ballycar and Newmarket	86	F4	GTS & W
Ardrahon	86	B3	W & L	Ballycarry	84	D10	M (NCI)
Ardsollus and Quin	86	E3	W & L	Ballycastle	84	A8	BAL
Arigna	85	A4	C & L	Ballyclare	84	D9	BNC
Arklow	86	F10	DWW	Ballyclare Junction	84	D9	M (NCI)
Armagh	84	G7	GN (I)	Ballycloughan	84	C8	M (NCI)
Armoy	84	B8	BAL	Ballyconnell	85	B6	C & L
Arva Road for Arva	85	D6	MGN	Ballycullane	87	G9	GTS & W
Ashtown	86	A9	MGW	Ballycumber	85	G5	GTS & W
Askeaton	86	G3	W & L	Ballydehob	87	G1	CBSC
Athboy	85	F7	MGW	Ballyduff (Leitrim)	85	C5	C & L
Athenry	86	A3	MGW/W & L	Ballyduff (Waterford)	87	F6	WDL
Athlone	85	G5	GTS & W	Ballyeaston Halt	84	D8	M (NCI)
Athlone	85	G5	GTS & W/MGW	Ballygarvey	84	C8	B (NCI)
Athy	86	B8	GTS & W	Ballygawley	84	G6	CV
Attanagh	86	E8	WCI	Ballyglunin	86	A3	W & L
Attymon Junction	86	A4	MGW	Ballygowan	84	F10	BCD
Aughacasla	87	C1	T & D	Ballyhaise Junction Station	85	B6	GN (I)
Aughaville	87	G1	CB & SC	Ballyhale	87	D8	WCI
Augher	84	G6	CV	Ballyhaunis	85	E3	MGW
Aughnacloy	84	G6	CV	Ballyheady	85	B6	C & L
Aughrim	86	E9	DWW	Ballyheather	84	C5	M (NCI)
Aunascaul	87	C1	T & D	Ballyhooley	87	E5	GTS & W
Aylwardstown — see Glenmore				Ballykelly	84	B6	BNC
Bagnalstown now Muine Bheag	86	F8	GTS & W	Ballyliffen	84	A5	L & LS
Balbriggan	85	F9	GN (I)	Ballymacarrett Halt	84	E9	BCD
Balla	85	E3	MGW	Ballymagan	84	A4	L & LS
Ballaghaderreen	85	C4	MGW	Ballymagorry	84	C5	M (NCI)
Ballina	85	B2	MGW	Ballymartle	87	G4	CB & SC
Ballinacurra — see Middleton				Ballymartle	84	C8	BNC
Ballinamallard	84	G5	GN (I)	Ballymena	84	C8	BNC
Ballinamore (Donegal)	84	C3	CDJC	Ballymena, Harryville	84	C8	BNC
Ballinamore (Leitrim)	85	B5	C & L	Ballymoe	85	F4	MGW
Ballinascarthy	87	G3	CB & SC	Ballymoney	84	B7	BAL/B (NCI)
				Ballymote	85	C4	MGW

Station	Page	Block	Comp
Ballymurray	85	F5	MGW
Ballynahinch (Down)	84	F10	BCD
Ballynahinch (Galway)	86	A1	BCD
Ballynahinch Junction	84	G10	BCD
Ballynashee	84	C9	BNC
Ballynoe	84	G10	BCD
Ballynure	84	D9	BNC
Ballyragget	86	E8	WCI
Ballyrobert Halt	84	D9	M (NCI)
Ballyroney	85	A9	GN (I)
Ballyshannon	84	F4	GN (I)
Ballyshannon	84	F4	CDJC
Ballysodare	85	A3	MGW
Ballyvary	85	C3	MGW
Ballyward	85	A9	GN (I)
Ballywilan Granard	85	E6	MGW
Ballywilliam	87	E9	DWW/GTS & W
Balmoral	84	E9	GN (I)
Baltimore	87	G2	CBSC
Baltinglass	86	C8	GTS & W
Banagher	86	A5	GTS & W
Banbridge	84	G8	GTN (I)
Bandon	87	G3	CB & SC
Bangor	84	E10	B & CD
Bangor West Halt	84	E10	B & CD
Bansha	87	B6	W & L
Banteer	87	D3	GTS & W
Bantry	87	G1	CB & SC
Barnagh	86	G3	W & L
Barnesmore	84	D3	DON
Barn Halt	84	D9	UTA
Basin	87	B2	T & D
Batterstown	85	G8	MGW
Bawnby Road and Templeport	85	B6	C & L
Beauparc	85	F8	GN (I)
Bective	85	F8	MGW
Bekan	85	E3	MGW
Belcoo	85	A4	SL & NC
[Belfast]			
Great Victoria Street R.N. Botanic	84	E9	GN (I)
Queens Quay R.N. Central	84	E9	B & CD
York Road	84	E9	B & NC
Bellarena	84	B6	BNC
Belleek	84	F4	GN (I)
Bellurgan	85	C9	DNG
Belmont and Cloghan	86	B5	GTS & W
Belturbet	85	B6	C & L
Belturbet	85	B6	GN (I)
Bennetsbridge	86	F8	WCI
Beragh	84	F5	GN (I)
Bessbrook	85	B8	GN (I)
Birdhill	86	F5	W & L/GTS & W
Birr	86	D6	GTS & W
Blackrock (Cork)	87	G5	CB & P
Blackrock (Dublin)	86	A9	DWW
Blackstaff Halt	85	C8	GN (I)
Blackweir	86	G1	WC
Blanchardstown	86	A9	MGW
Blarney	87	E4	GTS & W
Blarney	87	E4	C & MUS
Bleach Green Halt	84	D9	UTA
Blennerville	87	B2	T & D
Bloomfield	84	F9	BCD
Boher	86	G5	W & L
Booterstown	86	A9	DWW
Borris	87	B9	GTS & W
Boyle	85	C4	MGW
Bray	86	A9	DWW
Bridge End	84	C5	L & LS
Bridge Street — see [Newry]			
Bridgetown (Donegal)	84	E4	CDJC
Bridgetown (Wexford)	87	G10	GTS & W
Broadstone — see [Dublin]			
Broighter	84	B6	BNC
Brookeboro'	85	A6	CV
Brookhill Halt	84	G8	GN (I)
Brookmount	84	F8	GN (I)
Brosna Halt	86	D6	GTS & W
Bruckless	84	E2	DON
Bruree	87	B4	GTS & W
Buncrana	84	B4	L & LS
Bundoran	84	F3	GN (I)
Bundoran Junction	84	G4	GN (I)
Burnfoot	84	B4	L & LS
Burnt Mill	87	E3	C & MUS
Burtonpoint	84	D2	L & LS
Bush	85	C9	DNG
Bushmills	84	A7	GC & P
Buttevant and Doneraile	87	C4	GTS & W

Station	Page	Block	Comp
Cahir	87	C6	W & L
Cahirciveen for Waterville	87	E1	GTS & W
Caledon	84	G7	CV
Camolin	87	A9	DWW
Campile	87	G8	GTS & W
Capecastle	84	A8	BAL
Cappagh	87	F6	WDL
Cappoquin	87	F6	WDL
Capwell — see [Cork]			
Carragh Lake for Glencar	87	D1	GTS & W
Carbury	85	G7	MGW
Cargan	84	B9	BNC
Carlingford	85	C9	DNG
Carlow	86	D8	GTS & W
Carnalea	84	E10	BCD
Cardonagh	84	A5	L & LS
Carrickhue	84	B5	BNC
Carrickfergus	84	D9	BNC
Carrickmacross	85	C8	GN (I)
Carrickmines	86	A9	DWW
Carrickmore	84	E6	GN (I)
Carrick-on-Shannon	85	C4	MGW
Carrick-on-Suir	87	G5	CBP
Carrigaline	87	G5	CBP
Carrigaloe for Passage	87	G6	GTS & W
Carrigans	84	F4	C & MUS
Carrigtwohill	87	G6	GTS & W
Carrolls Cross	87	F7	WDL
Carrowen	84	C4	LET
Carrowmore	85	B3	W & L
Cashel	86	G6	GTS & W
Cashelnagore	84	C2	L & LS
Castlebar	85	D2	MGW
Castlebellingham	85	D9	GN (I)
Castleblayney	85	B8	GN (I)
Castlecaldwell	84	F4	GN (I)
Castlecomer Halt	86	E7	WCI
Castleconnel	86	F5	W & L
Castledawson	84	D7	BNC
Castlederg	84	D4	C & VB
Castlefinn	84	D4	DON
Castlegregory	87	B1	T & O
Castlegregory Junction	87	B2	T & D
Castlegrove	85	G3	W & L
Castleisland	87	C2	GTS & W
Castlemaine	87	D2	GTS & W
Castlerea	85	E4	MGW
Castlerock	84	B6	BNC
Castletown	85	G6	MGW
Castletownroche	87	D4	GTS & W
Castlewellan	85	A9	GN (I)
Cavan	85	C6	GTN (I)/MGW
Cavan Halt	84	D3	DON
Celbridge — see Hazelhatch			
Chapel	87	F9	DWW
Charlestown	85	C3	W & L
Charleville now Rathluirc	87	C4	GTS & W
Church Cross	87	G2	CB & SC
Churchill	84	C3	L & LS
Clady	84	D4	DON
Clara	86	A6	MGW
Clara	86	A6	GTS & W
Clar Bridge	84	E3	DON
Clare Castle	86	E3	W & L
Claremorris	85	E3	MGW
Claremorris	85	E3	W & L
Clifden	86	A1	MGW
Clipperstown Halt	84	D9	UTA
Cloghan	84	C3	DON
Clogher	84	G6	CV
Cloghroe	87	F3	C & MUS
Clonakilty	87	G3	CB & SC
Clonakilty Junction	87	G3	CB & SC
Clondalkin	86	A9	GTS & W
Clondulane	87	E5	WDL
Clones	85	B7	GN (I)
Clonhugh	85	G6	MGW
Clonmany	84	A5	L & LS
Clonmel	87	C6	W & L
Clonsilla	85	G8	MGW
Clontarf	86	A9	GN (I)
Cloughjordan	86	E5	GTS & W
Clough Road	84	C8	BNC
Cloyne — see Middleton			
Coachford	87	E2	C & MUS
Coachford Junction	87	F3	C & MUS
Coalisland	84	F7	GN (I)
Cobh — see Queenstown			
Cobh Junction — see Queenstown Junction			

Station	Page	Block	Comp	Station	Page	Block	Comp
Ferns Lock	85	G8	MGW	Holywood	84	E10	BCD
Fethard	87	C7	W & L	Horse and Jockey	86	G7	W & L
Fiddown	87	E7	W & L	Horseleap	85	G6	MGW
Finaghy Halt	84	F9	GN (I)	Howth	85	G10	GN (I)
Fintona	84	F5	GN (I)	Howth (Junction)	85	G9	GN (I)
Fintona Junction	84	F5	GN (I)	Inch	86	F9	DWW
Fintown	84	C3	DON	Inch Road	84	B4	L & LS
Firmount	87	E3	C & MUS	Inchicore	86	A9	GTS & W
Fivemiletown	85	A6	CV	Innishannon — see Upton			
Float	85	F5	MGW	Inniskeen	85	C8	GN (I)
Florencecourt	85	A5	SL & NC	Inny Junction now Mostrim	85	E5	MGW
Fota	87	G6	GTS & W	Inver	84	E3	DON
Foxford	85	B3	MGW	Irvinestown	84	G5	GN (I)
Foxhall	84	C3	L & LS	Islandeady Halt	85	D2	MGW
Foxrock for Leopardstown	86	A9	DWW	Island Road Halt	85	C4	MGW
Foxs Bridge	87	E3	C & MUS	Jordanstown	84	D10	BNC
Foyle Road — see [Londonderry]				Junction — see Howth			
Foynes	86	G3	W & L	Kanturk	87	D3	GTS & W
Fyfin	84	D4	C & VB	Kanturk	87	D3	K & N
Gallagh Road	84	B5	L & LS	Katesbridge	84	G9	GN (I)
Galway	86	A2	MGW	Keady	85	A8	GN (I)
Gaol Cross	87	F3	C & MUS	Kells (Antrim)	84	C8	BNC
Garradice	85	B5	C & Z	Kells (Kerry)	87	E1	GN (I)/MGW
Garrynadur	87	C1	T & D	Kells (Meath)	85	E7	GTS & W
Garvagh	84	C7	BNC	Kellswater	84	D8	BNC
Geashill	86	B7	GTS & W	Kellybridge Halt	85	D9	GN (I)
Georges Quay — see Tara Street				Kenmare for Parknasila	87	E2	GTS & W
Giants Causeway	84	A7	GC & P	Kesh	84	F5	GN (I)
Gibbstown	85	E8	MGW	Kilcock	85	G8	MGW
Gilford — see Tanderagee				Kilcoe	87	G1	CB & SC
Glanmire Road — see [Cork]				Kilcool	86	B10	DWW
Glanworth	87	E5	GTS & W	Kilcrae	87	F3	C & M
Glarryford	84	C8	BNC	Kildangan	86	B8	GTS & W
Glasnevin	86	A9	GTS & W	Kildare	86	B8	GTS & W
Glasslough	84	G6	GN (I)	Kilfenora	87	A2	W & L
Glasthule — see Sandycove				Kilfree Junction	85	C4	MGW
Glengeary, Adelaide Road	86	B10	DWW	Kilgarvan	87	E3	GTS & W
Glenavy	84	E8	GN (I)	Kilgobbin Halt	86	G4	W & L
Glenbeith	87	E1	GTS & W	Kilkee	86	F1	W & C
Glenbrook	87	G5	CBP	Kilkenny	86	F8	GTS & W/WCI
Glencar — see Carragh Lake				Kilagan	84	C8	BNC
Glenealy	86	D9	DWW	Killala	85	A2	MGW
Glenfarne	85	A4	SL & NC	Killaloe	86	E4	W & L
Glenmanus Halt	84	A6	UTA	Killarney	87	C2	GTS & W
Glenmaquin	84	C3	CDJC	Killeagh	87	G6	GTS & W
Glenmore (Donegal)	87	C1	DON	Killeshandra	85	C6	MGW
Glenmore (Kerry)	84	D3	CDJC	Killester Halt	86	A9	GN (I)
Glenmore and Aylwardstown	87	F8	D & SE	Killiney and Ballybrack	86	B9	DWW
Glenties	84	D3	DON	Killinick	87	G10	GTS & W
Glounagalt Bridge	87	C1	T & D	Killonon	86	G5	W & L
Glynn	84	C10	BNC	Killorglin	87	D2	GRS & W
Golf Links Halt — see Skerries				Killough	84	G10	BCD
Goolds Cross	86	G7	GTS & W	Killucan	85	G7	MGW
Goraghwood	85	B9	GN (I)	Killurin	87	F10	DWW
Goresbridge	86	F8	GTS & W	Killybegs	84	E2	DON
Gorey	86	G9	DWW	Killygordon	84	D3	DON
Gormanstown	85	E9	GN (I)	Killylea	84	G7	GN (I)
Gort	86	C3	W & L	Killymard	84	E3	DON
Gortaloughan Halt	84	H4	GN (I)	Killyran	85	B6	C & L
Gortatlea	87	B2	GTS & W	Kilmacow	87	F8	WCI
Gowran	86	F5	GTS & W	Kilmacrenan	84	C3	L & LS
Gracehill	84	B8	BAL	Kilmacthomas	87	F7	WDL
Granard — see Ballywillan				Kilmainham Wood	85	D8	MGW
Grange	87	F7	W & L	Kilmallock	87	B4	GTS & W
Grange Con	86	C9	GTS & W	Kilmeadan	87	G7	WDL
Great Victoria Street — see [Belfast]				Kilmessan	85	F8	MGW
Greencastle	84	E9	BNC	Kilmorna	86	G2	W & L
Greenisland	84	D9	BNC	Kilmurry (Clare)	86	F2	WC
Greenore	85	C9	DNG	Kilmurry (Cork)	87	F3	C & MUS
Greystones and Delgany	86	B10	DWW	Kilrane	87	G10	GTS & W
Groomsport Road	84	E10	BCD	Kilrae	84	C7	BNC
Gurteen	87	F3	C & MUS	Kilroot	84	D10	BNC
Gurth	87	F3	C & MUS	Kilrush	86	F2	WC
Gweendore	84	C2	L & LS	Kilsheelan	87	D6	W & L
Hamiltons Bawn	84	G8	GN (I)	Kiltimagh	85	E3	W & L
Harcourt Street — see [Dublin]				Kiltoom	85	G5	MGW
Harristown	86	B9	GTS & W	Kiltubrid	85	B5	C & L
Harryville — see Ballymena				Kilumney	87	F4	C & M
Hazelhatch and Celbridge	86	A9	GTS & W	Kilwaughter	84	C9	BNC
Headford Junction	87	C2	GTS & W	Kingsbridge	86	A9	GTS & W
Headwood Crossing	84	C9	BNC	Kingscourt	85	D8	MGW
Healys Bridge	87	F4	C & MUS	Kingstown now Dun Laoghaire	86	A9	DWW
Helens Bay	84	E10	BCD	Kingstown Pier now Dun Laoghaire Pier	86	A9	LNW
Heuston — see [Dublin]				Kinnegar Halt	84	E10	BCD
Hilden Halt	84	F9	GN (I)	Kinsale	87	G4	CB & SC
Hill of Down	85	G7	MGW	Kinsale Junction	87	G4	CB & SC
Hillsborough	84	F9	GN (I)	Knock	84	E9	BCD
Hollyhill	87	G1	CB & SC	Knockanally	84	C8	BNC
Hollymount	85	F3	MGW	Knockane	87	E3	C & MUS

Station	Page	Block	Comp
Knockcroghery	85	F5	MGW
Knocklong	87	B5	GTS & W
Knocklaughrim	84	D6	BNC
Knuckbue	87	G2	CB & SC
Laffans Bridge	86	G7	W & L
Laghey	84	E3	CDJC
Lambeg	84	F9	GN (I)
Lansdowne Road	86	A9	DWW
[Larne]			
Harbour	84	C10	BNC
Harbour (Narrow Gauge)	84	C10	BNC
Town	84	C10	BNC
Town (Narrow Gauge)	84	C10	BNC
Laurencetown	84	G8	GN (I)
Lawderdale	85	B5	C & L
Laytown	85	E9	GN (I)
Leemount	87	F4	C & MUS
Legatirriff Halt	84	E7	GN (I)
Lehinch	86	E2	WC
Leitrim	85	A9	GN (I)
Leixlip	85	G8	MGW
Leopardstown — see Foxrock			
Letterkenny	84	C3	LET
Letterkenny Junction	84	C3	LET/L & LS
Leyny	85	B3	W & L
Liffey Junction	86	A9	MGW
Lifford	84	D4	CDJC
Limavady	84	B6	BNC
Limavady Junction	84	B6	BNC
Limerick	86	G4	GTS & W/W & L
Limerick Junction	87	A6	W & L/GTS & W
Lisbellow	85	A5	GN (I)
Lisburn	84	F9	GN (I)
Liscooley	84	D4	DON
Lisduff	86	E6	GTS & W
Liselton	86	G2	W & L
Lismore	87	F6	WDL/GTS & W
Lisnagry	86	F5	W & L
Lisnakea	85	B6	GN (I)
Lisnalinchy	84	D9	M (NCI)
Lispole	87	C1	T & D
Listowel	86	G2	W & L
Little Island	87	F5	GTS & W
Lixnaw	87	A2	W & L
Lombardstown	87	D3	GTS & W
[Londonderry] *now* Derry			
Ballagh Road	84	B5	GN (I)
Foyle Road	84	B5	GN (I)
Graving Dock	84	B5	BCD
Victoria Road	84	B5	GN (I)
Waterside	84	B5	B & NC
Longford	85	E5	MGW
Long Pavement	86	F4	W & L
Loo Bridge	87	D3	GTS & W
Lorretto College Halt	85	C6	GTN (I)
Lough Eske	84	E3	DON
Loughgilly	85	B8	GN (I)
Loughrea	86	B4	MGW
Loughrea — see also Craughwell			
Lucan	85	G8	GTS & W
Lucan	85	G8	MGW
Lurgan	84	F8	GN (I)
Lusk — see Rush			
Maam Cross	86	A2	MGW
Macfin	84	B7	BNC
Macmine Junction	87	E10	DWW
Macroom	87	F3	C & M
Madore	87	G2	GB & SC
Mageney	86	C8	GTS & W
Maghera	84	D7	BNC
Magherafelt	84	D7	BNC
Magheramorne	84	C10	BNC
Magilligan	84	B6	BNC
Maguiresbridge	85	A6	CV
Maguiresbridge	85	A6	GN (I)
Malahide	85	G9	GN (I)
Mallaranny	85	C1	MGW
Mallow	87	D4	GTS & W
Manorcunningham	84	C4	LET
Manorhamilton	85	A4	SL & NC
Manulla Junction	85	D2	MGW
Marino	84	E10	BCD
Markethill	85	A8	GN (I)
Maryborough *now* Portlaoise	86	C7	WCI/GTS & W
Maynooth	85	G8	MGW
Maytown	85	B9	BNE
Maze	84	F9	GN (I)
Meen Glas	84	D4	DON
Meetinghouse Halt			

Station	Page	Block	Comp
Merrion	84	F8	DWW
Midleton	87	G6	GTS & W
Milford (Armagh)	84	G8	GN (I)
Milford (Carlow)	86	E8	GTS & W
Millstreet	87	D3	GTS & W
Milltown (Dublin)	86	A9	DWW
Milltown (Galway)	85	F3	W & L
Milltown (Kerry)	87	D2	GTS & W
Millvale	86	B9	BNE
Milltown Malbay (Clare)	86	E2	WC
Mitchelstown	87	D7	GTS & W
Moate	85	G6	MGW
Mogeely	87	G6	GTS & W
Mohill	85	C5	C & L
Moira	84	F9	GN (I)
Molahiffe	87	D2	GTS & W
Monaghan	85	A7	GN (I)
Monaghan Road	85	A7	GN (I)
Monasterevan	86	B7	GTS & W
Moneycarrie	84	B7	BNC
Moneymore	84	E7	BNC
Monkstown	87	G5	CBP
Monkstown Halt	84	D9	M (NCI)
Moorfields	84	C8	BNC
Morleys Bridge	87	D3	GTS & W
Mosney, Butlins	85	F10	UTA
Mossley	84	D9	M (NCI)
Mostrim — see Inny Junction			
Mount	84	D10	BNC
Mountain Stage	87	E1	GTS & W
Mountcharles	84	E3	DON
Mountmellick	86	C7	WCI
Mountrath and Castletown	86	D7	GTS & W
Mourne Abbey	87	D4	GTS & W
Moyasta Junction	86	F1	WC
Moycullen	86	A2	MGW
Moyvalley	85	G7	MGW
Muckamore Halt	84	D8	BNC
Muine Bheag — see Bagenalstown			
Mullafernaghan	84	G8	GN (I)
Mullaghlass	85	B9	BNE
Mullanboy Halt	85	G2	CDJC
Mullinavat	87	E8	WCI
Mullingar	85	G6	MGW
Multyfarnham	85	F6	MGW
Naas	86	A9	GTS & W
Narrow Water	85	B9	GN (I)
Navan	85	E8	GN (I)/MGW
Navan Junction	85	E8	GN (I)/MGW
Neills Hill	84	E9	BCD
Nenagh	86	E5	GTS & W
Newbliss	85	B7	GN (I)
Newbridge *now* Droichead Nua	86	B8	GTS & W
Newbridge — see Ovoca			
New Buildings	84	B5	M (NCI)
Newcastle (Down)	85	A10	BCD
Newcastle (Wicklow)	86	C10	DWW
Newcastle West	86	G3	W & L
Newcourt	87	G2	CB & SC
Newmarket	87	D3	GTS & W
Newmarket — see Ballycar			
New Mills	84	C3	L & LS
Newport	85	C1	MGW
Newrath Bridge — see Rathnew			
New Ross	87	F8	DWW
[Newry]			
Bridge Street	85	B9	DNG
Dublin Bridge	85	B9	GN (I)
Edward Street	85	B9	GN (I)
Newtowncunningham	84	C4	LET
Newtownforbes	85	E5	MGW
Newtonstewart	84	E5	GN (I)
Newtownards	84	F10	BCD
Newtownbutler	85	B6	GN (I)
Nobber	85	E8	MGW
North Wall — see [Dublin]			
Oldcastle	85	E6	GN (I)
Oldtown	84	C3	L & LS
Omagh	84	F5	GN (I)
Omeath	85	C9	DNG
Oola	87	A5	W & L
Oranmore	86	A3	MGW
Oughterard	86	A2	MGW
Ovoca for Newbridge	86	E6	DWW
Palace East	87	F9	DWW
Pallas	86	G5	W & L
Parkmore	84	B9	BNC
Parknasilla — see Kenmare			
Passage	87	G4	CBP

Station	Page	Block	Comp
Patrick's Well	86	G4	W & L/GTS & W
Peake	87	E2	C & MUS
Pearse — see [Dublin]			
Pettigo	84	F4	GN (I)
Pluck	84	C4	LET
Pomoroy	84	F6	GN (I)
Port	84	E3	DON
Portadown	84	F8	GN (I)
Portalaise — see Maryboro			
Portarlington	86	B7	GTS & W
Porthall	84	D4	GN (I)
Portmarnock	85	G9	GN (I)
Portrush	84	A6	BNC
Portrush	84	A6	GC & P
Portstewart, also known as Cromore Halt	84	B4	M (NCI)
Portstewart Town	84	B6	PT
Poyntzpass	85	A8	GN (I)
Puck Island	87	C1	T & D
Quay Road — see [Belfast]			
Queenstown now Cobh	87	G5	GTS & W
Queenstown Junc. now Cobh Junc.	87	F5	GTS & W
Quilty	86	F2	WC
Quin — see Ardsollos			
Raffeen	87	G5	CBP
Raheny	86	A9	GN (I)
Randalstown	84	D8	BNC
Ranelagh — see Rathmines			
Raphoe	84	D4	CDJC
Rashenny	84	A5	L & LS
Rathdrum	86	D9	DWW
Rathduff	87	E4	GTS & W
Rathgarogue	87	F8	DWW
Rathkeale	86	G3	W & L
Rathkenny	84	C9	BNC
Rathluirc — see Charleville			
Rathmines and Ranelagh	86	A9	D & SE
Rathmore	87	D3	GTS & W
Rathnew for Newrath Bridge	86	D10	DWW
Rathowen — see Street			
Rathvilly	86	D8	GTS & W
Recess	86	A2	MGN
Recess Hotel Platform	86	A2	MGN
Redhills	85	B7	GN (I)
Retreat	84	B9	BNC
Retreat Halt	84	G7	GN (I)
Richill	84	G8	GN (I)
Rochestown	87	G5	CBP
Rockcorry	85	B8	GN (I)
Roscommon	85	F5	MGW
Roscrea	86	D6	GTS & W
Rosharry	85	C5	C & L
Ross	86	A2	MGW
[Rosslare]			
Harbour	87	G10	F & R
Harbour (Mainland)	87	G10	GTS & W
Strand	87	G10	F & R
Rossnowlagh	84	F4	CDJC
Rosstemple	86	G4	GTS & W
Ruan	86	E3	WC
Rush and Lusk	85	G9	GN (I)
Rushbrooke	87	G5	GTS & W
St Anne's	87	E3	G & MUS
St Johnston	84	C4	GN (I)
St Patrick's Bridge — see [Cork]			
Sallins	86	A9	GTS & W
Saintfield	84	F10	BCD
Sallybrook	84	C4	LET
Salthill	86	A9	DWW
Sandycove for Glasthule	86	A9	DWW
Sandymount Halt	86	A10	DWW
Scarva	84	G8	GN (I)
Schull	87	G1	CB & SC
Seapoint	86	A9	DWW
Shallee	86	E5	GTS & W
Shallogans	84	D3	CDJC
Shankhill	86	A9	DWW
Shantona Junction	85	B7	GN (I)
Shillelagh	86	E9	DWW
Sidney Parade	86	A9	D & SE
Sion Mills	84	D4	GN (I)
Sixmilebridge	86	F4	W & L
Sixmilecross	84	F6	GN (I)
Skeaf	87	G3	CB & SC
Skerries	85	F9	GN (I)
Skerries Golf Links Halt	85	F9	GN (I)
Skibbereen	87	G2	CB & SC
Sligo	85	A3	MGW/SL & NC
Sligo	85	A3	W & L
Smithborough	85	B7	GN (I)
South Wexford — see Wexford (South)			
Spa	87	A2	W & L
Spamount	84	D4	C & VB
Staffordstown	84	D8	BNC
Stewartstown	84	E7	GN (I)
Stillorgan	86	A9	DWW
Strabane	84	D4	DON
Strabane	84	D4	GN (I)
Stradbally — see Durrow			
Straffan	86	A9	GTS & W
Stranocum	84	B7	BAL
Stranorlar	84	D3	DON
Streamstown	85	G6	MGW
Street and Rathowen	85	E5	MGW
Summer Hill — see [Cork]			
Sutton	85	G10	GN (I)
Swinford	85	D3	W & L
Sydenham	84	E9	BCD
Tallow Road	87	F6	WDL
Tamlagh Halt	84	C7	M (NCI)
Tandragee and Gilford	84	G8	GN (I)
Tara Street and Georges Quay	86	A9	DWW
Templemore	86	F6	GTS & W
Templepatrick	84	D9	BNC
Templeport — see Bawnby Road			
Thomastown	87	B8	WCI
Thurles	86	G7	W & L/GTS & W
Tillysburn	84	E10	BCD
Timoleague	87	G3	CB & SC
Tinahely	86	E9	DWW
Tipperary	87	B6	W & L
Tivoli	87	F5	GTS & W
Tomkin Road	85	B6	C & L
Tooban Junction	84	B4	L & LS
Toome Bridge	84	D7	BNC
Tower Bridge	87	E3	C & MUS
Town Bridge Halt	84	D4	DON
[Tralee]			
Tralee	87	B2	W & L
Tralee	87	B2	GTS & W
Tralee	87	B2	T & D
Tranmore	87	G8	W & T
Trew and Moy	84	F7	GN (I)
Trillick	84	G5	GN (I)
Trim	85	F7	MGW
Troopers Lane	84	D9	BNC
Tuam	85	G3	W & L
Tubber	86	D3	W & L
Tubbercurry	85	C3	W & L
Tullamore	86	A6	GTS & W
Tullow	86	D8	GTS & W
Tullymurry	84	G10	BCD
Tynan	84	G7	GN (I)
University Halt	84	A6	UTA
Upperlands	84	D7	BNC
Upton and Innishannon	87	G3	CB & SC
Valencia Harbour	87	E1	GTS & W
Vernersbridge	84	F7	GN (I)
Victoria	87	F4	C & MUS
Victoria Bridge	84	D4	C & VB
Victoria Bridge	84	D4	GN (I)
Victoria Park Halt	84	E9	BCD
Virginia Road	85	E7	GN (I)
Warrenpoint	85	B9	GN (I)
Waterfall	87	G4	CB & SC
[Waterford]			
Adelphi Wharf	87	G8	MGW
Manor	87	G8	W & T
Waterford	87	G8	WCI/W & L
Waterford	87	G8	WDL
Waterside — see [Londonderry]			
Waterville — see Cahirciveen			
Wellington Bridge	87	G9	GTS & W
Western Road — see [Cork]			
Westland Row	86	A9	DWW
Westport	85	D1	MGW
Westport Pier	85	D1	MGW
Wexford	87	F10	DWW
Wexford South	87	F10	F & R
Whiteabbey	84	E9	BNC
Whitehead	84	D10	BNC
Whitehouse	84	E9	BNC
Wicklow	86	E10	DWW
Wilkinstown	85	E8	MGW
Willbrook	86	E2	WC
Windsor — see Adelaide			
Woodenbridge Junction	86	E9	DWW
Woodlands	87	G1	CB & SC
Woodlawn	86	A5	MGW
York Road — see [Belfast]			
Youghal	87	G7	GTS & W

List of Railway Companies (Ireland)

BAL	Ballycastle		GTS & W	Great Southern and Western
B & CD	Belfast and County Down		GN (I)	Great Northern (Ireland)
BNC	Belfast and Northern Counties		K & N	Kanturk and Newmarket
BNE	Bessbrook and Newry Electric		LET	Letterkenny
CBP	Cork, Blackrock and Passage		L & LS	Londonderry and Lough Swilly
CBSC	Cork, Bandon and South Coast		LNW	London and North Western
CDJ	City of Dublin Junction		L & B	Listowel and Ballybunion
CDJC	County Donegal Joint Committee		MGW	Midland Great Western
C & L	Cavan and Leitrim		M (NCI)	Midland (Northern Counties of Ireland)
C & M	Cork and Macroom		PT	Portstewart Tramway
C & MUS	Cork and Muskerry		SL & NC	Sligo, Leitrim and Northern Counties
CV	Clogher Valley		T & D	Tralee and Dingle
C & VB	Castlederg and Victoria Bridge		UTA	Ulster Transport Authority
D & SE	Dublin and South Eastern		W & L	Waterford and Limerick
DNG	Dundalk, Newry and Greenore		WC	West Clare
DWW	Dublin, Wicklow and Wexford		WCI	Waterford & Central Ireland & Kilkenny Jcn.
F & R	Fishguard and Rosslare		WDL	Waterford, Dungarvan and Lismore
GC & P	Giants Causeway, Portrush and Bush Valley		W & T	Waterford and Tramore

Appendix to Stations (Mainland)

Station	Page	Block	Comp	Year of CL
Acrow Halt	23	G8	BR	1964
Adlam Junction	82	D10	SY	1856
Alfred Town — see Ashford (Kent)				
Altrincham — see also Hale				
Alveley Halt	80	E1	GW	never t/table
Ampleforth College — see Gilling				
Anderston — see [Glasgow]				
Argyle Street — see [Glasgow]				
Arnold — see [Nottingham] Daybrook				
Arnos Grove — see [London]				
Ashdown Forest — see Forest Row				
Ashton-in-Makerfield — see also Bryn (Lancs)				
Auchinlochan Halt	46	A3	CAL	1965
Aviemore (Speyside)	57	C5	SPEY RLY	
Bandon Hill — see Waddon				
Barnet — see High Barnet also New Barnet				
[Barnstaple] Quay	8	D5	LSW	1892
Barrowford — see Nelson (Lancs)				
[Barry] Pier	78	H5	BARRY	1971
Barwell — see Elmesthorpe				
Beachley — see Tutshill Halt				
Becontree — see also Chadwell Heath				
Beddington — see Waddon				
Bede	81	F3	TW	
Bessacarr	82	H9	GN/GE	1951
Bigrigg — see Woodend				
Birchwood	77	B6	BR	
Bilton — see Alnmouth				
Bisley Camp	15	E1	LSW	1952
Blackpole Halt	24	C3	GW	used war years
Blackwell Mill Halt	31	D7	MID	Private
Blaguegate — see Skelmersdale				
Blechynden — see [Southampton] West				
Blue Bell Halt	2	C5	LBSC	Temp
Bogside Racecourse	49	B5	GSW	1967
Bonhill — see Alexandria				
Boulevard Recreation Ground	35	D3	GC (GI)	1961
Bounds Green — see [London]				
Bowden — see also Hale				
Bowhill — see Cardenden				
Braco — see Greenloaning				
Bradwell — see Hope (Derbys)				
Brent Cross — see [London]				
Brentham Halt — see [London]				
[Bristol and Avonmouth]				
Avonmouth Platform	72	C7	GW	not t/table
East Pier Station	72	C7	GW	not t/table
Royal Albert Dock	72	C7	GW/MID	1964
Britannia Bridge Station	32	F7	C & H	1858

Station	Page	Block	Comp	Year of CL
Brookstown — see Ellenbrook				
Buenos Aires — see [Margate] West				
Burringham — see Althorpe				
Butler Street — see [Preston]				
Buttermere — see Cockermouth				
Byker	81	D3	TW	
Cannock Chase — see Hednesford				
Castleton (Derbys) — see Hope (Derbys)				
Cement Mills Halt	4	H3	IWC	1966
Cleveland Street	35	D3	GC (GI)	1961
Cellardyke — see Anstruther				
Chapeltown — see Entwistle				
Chenies — see Chorley Wood				
Cheriton Arch — see Folkstone Central				
Chichester	81	F3	TW	
Chiddingfold — see Witley				
Chillingham Road	81	D4	TW	
Chorley, Royal Ordnance Factory	76	C5	LY	Private
Church's Hill Halt	17	G5	BR	1964
Cleator — see also Bigrigg				
Colney Heath — see Smallford				
Cop End — see [Southport] Blowick				
Corringham — see Blyton				
Costessey — see Drayton				
Cowie — see Plean				
Coxlodge	81	C4	TW	
Craigendoran	49	B10	NB	1964
Cranborne — see Verwood				
Crawley Down — see Grange Road				
Crowland — see Postland				
Cwmdwyfram	19	D6	GWILI	
Cymmer General	78	D2	GW	1960
Dale Abbey — see West Hallam				
Dalmarnock — see [Glasgow]				
Deddington — see Aynho				
Denville — see Warblington Halt				
Ditcham Park Halt (Woodcroft Farm)	5	C5	LSW	1947
Dolrhyd Mill	26	H9	W & L	never in t/table
Donibristle Halt	46	E9	NB	1962
Dovenby Lodge	40	D9	MC	1921
Downside — see Chilcompton				
Droylsden — see also Fairfield				
Digby Halt — see Clyst St Mary				
Easingwold — see also Alne				
East Barnet — see Oakleigh Park				
Earl Shilton — see Elmesthorpe				
[Edinburgh]				
Bonnington	83	E8	CAL	
Easter Road Park Halt	83	E7	NB	1964
Elstow — see Kempston				
Elton — see Ince (Cheshire)				
Englefield Green — see Egham				
Eskdale — see also Ravenglass				
Ewhurst — see Cranleigh				

Station	Page	Block	Comp	Year of CL
Exmouth — see also Starcross				
Eastern Bournmouth — see Pokesdown				
Eling — see Totton				
Fawdon	81	C4	TW	
Ferndown — see West Moors				
Finnieston — see [Glasgow]				
Fossoway — see Crook of Devon				
Fotherby Gate House	29	E9	GN	1872
Four Lane Ends	81	D4	TW	
Garngaber Junction — see Lenzie				
[Gateshead]				
Gateshead	81	C3	TW	
[Glasgow]				
Bridgeton Cross	74	H5	NB	1917
Dalmarnock R.O. FR. 1964 CL.			BR	
Golf Club Halt	3	C3	R & C	1939
Gorton Platform	53	E8	BR	1964
Gunness — see Althorpe				
Hadrian Road	81	E4	TW	
Half Way	3	B3	R & C	1939
Hall Dene (Private Station)	43	H1	LOND	1925
Hampton Hill — see Fulwell				
Hanger Lane	64	C4	LT	
Hartley Wintney — see Winchfield				
Haslemere for Hindhead	5	E8	LSW	
Haymarket	81	B3	TW	
Heworth	81	D2	TW	
Hoe Farm Halt (Private)	5	E3	SLR	1935
Holywell Halt	2	C5	LBSC	1962–1963
[Hull]				
Cemetery Road Rep. by Botanic	73	D2	NE	1854
Newington*	73	D2	NE	1965
Neptune Street	73	D1	HB	1854
Ilford Road	81	C4	TW	
Ince (Lancashire)	76	D5	LY	
Jackson Street	35	D3	GC (GI)	1961
Jestmoor Flag Station (Private)	27	D1	MID	1962
Jordans — see Seer Green				
Keadby — see Althorpe				
Kenton Bank Foot	81	C4	TW	
Kidwelly Flats Halt	19	C3	GW	1964
Killearn Old — see Dumgoyne				
Killin Junction Station	53	H5	CAL	1965
Kingsbury (Middlesex)	64	C7	LT	
Kingsdown — see Walmer				
Kingston Hill — see Norbiton				
Kirkland (Cumbria)	40	D7	CWJC	1922
Knightswood — see Anniesland				
Lanark Racecourse Halt	46	B4	CAL	
Lando Platform	19	C3	GW	1964
Leamington Spa — see also Milverton				
Leeswood — see Penyffordd				
Lelant Saltings	10	C3	BR	
[Lewes] Friars Walk	2	C2	LBSC	1857
Lidget Green — see [Bradford] Great Horton				
Little Hereford — see Easton Court				
Little Ilford — see Manor Park				
Little Lever — see Bradley Fold				
[Liverpool]				
Walton Junction Station	76	G2	LY	
[London]				
Forty Hill	65	B10	GE	1919
Hackney Central — see Hackney				
Hackney Wick — see Homerton				
Northolt Park for Northolt Village	65	G5	GC	
West Ham — see Stratford Market				
Longfleet — see Poole				
Low Marishes	39	B2	YNM	1947
Lulworth Cove — see Wool				
Maentwrog — see Tan-y-Bwlch				
Malden — see New Malden				
Margaretting Halt (Private)	13	A6	GE	
Marton (Lincs) — see Stow Park				
Milford-on-Sea — see New Milton				
Milton Keynes	25	G1	BR	
Miteside	40	E4	R & E	unknown
Moelwyn Halt — see Tunnel Halt				
Monument	81	B3	TW	
Moredon Platform	14	C4	MSWJ	1924
Morden	68	E6	LT	
Moulsecoomb	2	B2	BR	
National Maritime Museum — see [London] Maze Hill				
Newington — see [Hull]				
Normandy — see Wanborough				
Old Ford	81	C2	TW	
Oxhey Golf Club — see Carpenders Park				

Station	Page	Block	Comp	Year of CL
Padarn Halt	32	G6	LNW	1930
Pans Lane Halt	14	A1	GW	1966
Park House Halt	42	C3	NB	1969
Parton (Cumbria)	40	C7	WCE	1914
Paulsgrove Halt* (Goodwood Racecourse)	5	B4	LSW	
Penn — see Beaconsfield				
Pimbo Lane — see Upholland				
[Plymouth]				
Stonehouse Pool, Ocean Quay	81	C7	LSW	1917
Portswood	4	H5	LSW	1866
Priory Halt (Private)	13	G10	GE	
Radnor Park — see Folkstone Central				
Redbridge (Middlesex)	65	F7	LT	
Regent Centre	81	C4	TW	
Riby Street Halt	35	E3	GC	never t/table
Rifle Range Halt	77	F2	GC	1955
Ripley (Derbys) — see Butterley				
Rye Hill and Burstwick	35	D5	NE	1964
St Abbs — see Reston				
St James	81	B3	TW	
Sandringham — see Hillington				
Shakespeare Cliff Halt	3	F6	SEC	never t/table
Shiremoor	81	F5	TW	
Silchester — see Bramley (Hants)				
Smiths Park	81	F4	TW	
Snape Junction Station	21	D8	GE	1863
[Southampton] Docks	4	E5	LSW	1966
Southbanks — see Parkstone				
Southbourne-on-Sea — see Christchurch				
Squirrels Heath — see Gidea Park				
Staindrop — see Winston				
Stanstead Abbots — see St Margarets (Herts)				
Stanwell Moor — see Poyle				
Stoke Climsland — see also Callington				
Stortford Street	35	D3	GC(GI)	1961
Sulgrave — see Helmdon				
Sulgrave — see also Morton Pinkney				
Sutterton — see Algakirk				
Swanwick — see Butterley				
The Green — see Eskdale Green				
Turners Hill — see Grange Road				
Ullswater Lake — see Penrith				
Uppingham — see Manston				
Vange — see Pitsea				
Villa Park — see [West Midlands] Witton				
Walmley — see [West Midlands] Penns				
Wansbeck Road	84	C4	TW	
Walton-on-the-Hill (Surrey) — see Tadworth				
Warthill Cottages Halt	34	E9	SH LT	1930
Welford-on-Avon — see Milcote				
Wentworth — see Virginia Water				
West Bromwich — see also [West Midlands] Spon Lane				
Westenhanger Race Station	3	D6	SEC	
West Hove — see Portslade				
[West Midlands]				
Bromford Bridge Racecourse Station	80	D7	MID	
Weston-on-Avon — see Milcot				
Wheatsheaf — see Gwersyllt				
Whickham — see Swalwell				
Whitrope	42	E7	NB	1969
Willingdon — see Hampden Park				
Wingham — see Adisham				
Winmarleigh — see Nateby				
Worsborough — see Dovecliffe				
Worstead — see Honing				
Wraysholme Crossing Halt	40	H1	FUR	1950
Wye Racecourse Station	3	C7	LCD	
Yarboro Street	35	D3	GC (GI)	1961
Yearsett	27	H2	GW	1877
Yoxford — see Darsham				

Appendix to Stations (Ireland)

Bibliography

History of the Whitby and Pickering (G.W.J. Potter)

The Prestatyn and Dyserth Railway (T. Thomas)

The Railways of Britain (Simmons)

The Impact of Railways on Victorian Cities (Kellett)

The Midland Railway (H. Ellis)

The Rise of the Midland Railway (E.G. Barnes)

The Great Western in the Nineteenth Century (O.S. Nock)

The History of the Great Western Vol. 1 (O.S. Nock)
                     Vol. 2 (O.S. Nock)

The Clogher Valley Railway (E.M. Patterson)

The Northern Counties Railway Vol. 1 (J.R.L. Currie)
                 Vol. 2 (J.R.L. Currie)

The Caledonian Railway (O.S. Nock)

The North British Railway Vol. 1 (J. Thomas)
               Vol. 2 (J. Thomas)

The Severn and Wye Railway (H.W. Parr)

The Great Western in Dean (H.W. Parr)

A Short History of the Midland and Great Northern Joint
     Railway (R.H. Clark)

Minor Railways of England and their Locomotives 1900–1939
     (G. Woodcock)

The Whitby and Pickering Railway (D. Joy)

The Lowgill Branch (R.G. Western)

The Railways of Consett and North West Durham (G. White)

The Isle of Man Railways (J.I.C. Boyd)

The Cambrian Railways (R. Christiansen and R.W. Miller)

The Story of the Cambrian Railways (C.P. Gasquoine)

Crewe–Carlisle (B. Reed)

The Barry Railway (D.S.M. Barrie)

The Chester and Holyhead Vol. 1 (P.E. Baughan)
                  Vol. 2 (P.E. Baughan)

Numerous Bradshaw Timetables

The Great North of Scotland Railway (H.A. Vallance)

The West Highland Railway (J. Thomas)

Britain's Railways (H. Pollins)

Regional History of the Railways of Great Britain
     Vol. 1 The West Country (D. St. John Thomas)
       Vol. 2 Southern England (H.P. White)

       Vol. 3 Greater London (H.P. White)

       Vol. 4 North East England (K. Hoole)

       Vol. 5 Eastern Counties (D.I. Gordon)

       Vol. 6

       Vol. 7 The West Midlands (R. Christiansen)

       Vol. 8 South and West Yorkshire (D. Joy)

       Vol. 9 The East Midlands

The Oxford, Worcester and Wolverhampton Railway
     (Jenkins and Quayle)

The Snowdon Mountain Railway (Turner)

On the Narrow Gauge (P.B. Whitehouse)

The Festiniog Railway Vol. 1 (J.I.C. Boyd)
               Vol. 2 (J.I.C. Boyd)

The Watlington Branch (J.S. Holden)

The Welshpool and Llanfair Light Railway (R. Cartwright and
     R.T. Russell)

The Ravenglass and Eskdale Railway (W.J.K. Davies)

The Ballycastle Railway (E.M. Patterson)

The County Donegal Railways (E.M. Patterson)

Victorian Stations (G. Biddle)

The History of the Lancashire and Yorkshire Railway
     Vols. 1, 2 and 3 (J. Marshall)

Numerous Railway Magazines (I. Allan)

Numerous Railway Worlds (I. Allan)

The Register of Closed Passenger and Goods Stations
     (C.R. Clinker)

The Handbook of Railway Stations – 1899
     (H. Oliver and J. Airey)

British Rail Pre-grouping Atlas and Gazetteer (W.P. Connolly)

Rail Atlas of Great Britain (S. Baker)

Shell Touring Atlas of Great Britain (G. Philip and Son)

The Holcombe Brook Branch (C.A. Cowan)

The Garstang and Knott End Railway (R.W. Rush and
     M.R.C. Price)

Railways in the Peak District (C.P. Nicholson and P. Barnes)

Railways in the Lake Counties (D. Joy)

The Great Northern Railway (J. Wrottesley)